COLLECTIVE ACTION AND EXCHANGE

D1716900

COLLECTIVE ACTION

AND EXCHANGE

*A Game-Theoretic Approach to
Contemporary Political Economy*

WILLIAM D. FERGUSON

STANFORD ECONOMICS AND FINANCE
An Imprint of Stanford University Press
Stanford, California

STANFORD UNIVERSITY PRESS
Stanford, California

Library of Congress Cataloging-in-Publication Data

Ferguson, William D., 1953– author.
    Collective action and exchange : a game-theoretic approach to contemporary political economy / William D. Ferguson.
        pages cm
    Includes bibliographical references and index.
    ISBN 978-0-8047-7003-3 (cloth : alk. paper)—ISBN 978-0-8047-7004-0 (pbk. : alk. paper)
    1. Game theory.   2. Economics—Mathematical models.   I. Title.
    HB144.F467 2013
    330.01′5193—dc23
                                                                                    2013007016

ISBN 978-0-8047-8556-3 (electronic)

Typeset by Newgen in 10/14 Minion

Dedicated to the memory of Elinor (Lin) Ostrom, political scientist, and my father Allen R. Ferguson, economist.

What is missing from the policy analyst's tool kit—and from the set of accepted, well-developed theories of human organization—is an adequately specified theory of collective action whereby a group of principals can organize themselves voluntarily to retain the residuals of their own efforts.

Elinor Ostrom

CONTENTS

ACKNOWLEDGMENTS

In 1995, while on sabbatical from Grinnell College, I attended Herbert Gintis' graduate course in game theory at the University of Massachusetts. Herb's enthusiasm for the power of game theory and its relationship to political economy has inspired me since. On returning to Grinnell, I started a faculty political economy reading group. Discussions with colleagues David Ellison, Wade Jacoby, Jack Mutti, Monty Roper, Pablo Silva, and Eliza Willis informed my perspective on political economy. In 1998, Wade Jacoby and I participated in a faculty–faculty tutorial on institutional political economy. Wade introduced me to the work of Elinor Ostrom. I began teaching my seminar in political economy at Grinnell College in the fall of 2001, and in the spring of 2005 I started teaching applied game theory as an upper-level economics class. This book draws upon both classes, and I thank my former students for their inquisitive enthusiasm. In June 2007, I wrote a memo to my economics department colleagues on incorporating new developments in economic theory into the undergraduate economics curriculum. Janet Seiz encouraged me to submit this memo as a paper. After revision and helpful encouragement from Lee Hansen and David Colander, "Curriculum for the Twenty-First Century: Recent Advances in Economic Theory and Undergraduate Economics" appeared in the *Journal of Economic Education*. While discussing a draft of this paper, my colleague Mark Montgomery suggested that I write a book. Fortunately, by that time, I had already met my future editor Margo Beth Fleming.

I offer my warm thanks to my editor Margo Beth Fleming for her advice, comments, and enthusiastic support. This project would not have been possible without her. I am deeply grateful to the late Elinor Ostrom for her wise advice and enthusiastic support for my book and for inviting me to Indiana University's Workshop in Political Theory and Policy Analysis for two visits while writing the manuscript. I benefitted greatly from sitting in on her graduate class on institutional analysis and from discussions with Workshop participants, including Stephen Bernard, Daniel Cole, Mike McGinnis, Eric Rasmusen, Armando Razo, Ceren Soylu, and James Walker. I am also grateful to the late Roy Gardner for his advice on this project.

I thank Steffen Huck for inviting me for a six-week visit to the Economics Department at the University College of London. While in Britain, I attended seminars at UCL and the London School of Economics and had useful discussions with many scholars, including V. Bhashkar, Richard Bronk, Wendy Carlin, Martin Cripps, Marina Della Giusta, Bob Hancke, Philippe Jehiel, Gilat Levy, Imran Rascul, Ronny Razin, David Soskice, Simon Weidenholzer, and Peyton Young. I also thank Robert Axtell for inviting me for a similar visit to the Center for Social Complexity at George Mason University, where I attended seminars and discussed ideas with Rob Axtell, Aaron Frank, Hilton Root, and Russell Thomas.

I offer my deep appreciation to my research assistants, former Grinnell College students (now alumni): Akshay Bajaj, Julia Reese, Catherine Scott, Ethan Struby, Katerina Suchor, Joshua Wassink, Yanwen Xu, and Jelal Younes. I thank Grinnell College and the Committee on Support of Faculty Scholarship for awarding me a faculty leave during which I wrote most of this manuscript and for their generous financial support. I am grateful for the support I received from grants to Grinnell College from the Andrew W. Mellon Foundation and the Howard Hughes Medical Institute; I thank associate dean and professor of biology Leslie Gregg-Jolly and associate professor of chemistry Mark Levandoski for their assistance in facilitating these grants and for their support of this project. I thank Dean Paula Smith her enthusiastic support. I would also like to thank the following scholars for their encouragement, advice, and comments: Kate Anderson, Sam Bowles, Keith Brouhle, Stephen Burks, Kathleen Carley, Poti Giannakouros, David Krackhardt, Mieke Meurs, Frank Page, Irene Powell, Gilbert Skillman, Eliza Willis, and two anonymous referees. I also thank Wade Jacoby, Mike McGinnis, Armando Razo, Janet Seiz, and Tim Werner for their detailed comments. I warmly thank Pat and Jeff Phelps—former owners of Saint's Rest Coffee House (in Grinnell), where much of this manuscript was revised—for their hospitality. I especially thank my wife, Claudia Beckwith, for putting up with me during the writing of this manuscript and for her loving support and encouragement.

COLLECTIVE ACTION AND EXCHANGE

I | PRELIMINARIES

INTRODUCTION: A FARMER'S MARKET

The Dane County Farmers' Market meets on Saturday mornings at Capitol Square in Madison, Wisconsin. Like many such markets, it is a place where small farmers can sell fresh produce to local customers. Local residents and visitors wander among clean, well-ordered stalls with displays of high-quality local produce and clearly marked prices. Farmers compete on the basis of price and readily observable quality. Exchanges are friendly, and most customers leave satisfied. The setting appears to fit an economist's conception of the benefits of unregulated free-market competition among many buyers and sellers (Basu 2000, 193–96).

Looking somewhat deeper, however, economist Kaushik Basu discovered a rule book. This book details how participating farmer-vendors must behave and stipulates the penalties for specific violations. In addition to rules that regulate fairly obvious concerns, such as how to set up and clean stalls, vendors must file an "Application For Permission to Sell." Basu (2000, 194) quotes from the rule book as follows:

> Raw fruits and vegetables must be grown from cuttings grown by the vendor or from seeds and transplants. . . . Purchased plant materials must be grown on the vendor's premises for at least 60 days before they can be offered for sale at the market. . . . Eggs must be produced by hens which have been raised by the vendor for 75 percent of their production weight. . . . Sellers must not bring pets into the Market for health and safety reasons. The sale or giving away of animals on the Capitol grounds is prohibited. . . . Vendors must discourage sales to people in vehicles or lengthy double parking by customers. . . . Vendors selling wild-gathered items must have an application to sell filed with the market prior to arrival at the market and either have proof of land ownership or show written permission from the land-owner to gather the product. . . . Vendors must have photocopies of all necessary licenses.

The rule book has 18 pages. Why are there so many detailed regulations for what appears to be a free market? What would happen if vendors failed to discourage double-parking or sold animals? What if vendors sold eggs from chickens they had not raised for 75% of production weight, or sold produce they had not grown on their premises for at least 60 days? What if they resold produce purchased from a supermarket or warehouse at a markup?

What if they failed to clean their stalls? Indeed, what would happen if there were no process for applying for permits to sell, no rules indicating who qualifies, or no way to enforce the rules? What if anyone could sell anything they wanted? How would stalls be allocated? Would disputes arise? Would consumers want to go to the market? Would producers of quality locally grown produce want to sell there?

This example of market governance illustrates why economics is really political economy. It raises the question as to whether there really is such a thing as a free market. It also raises the question of whether rules like these are coercive or voluntary. These rules are coercive in the sense that individuals who might profit by violating them (for instance, by reselling produce purchased at a warehouse) can be punished. Yet they also reflect largely voluntary efforts by vendors at self-organization: the vendors themselves made the rules and set up an enforcement mechanism. The boundary between voluntary action and coercion appears imprecise. The rule book, then, indicates that such governance is part of the political economy of the Dane County Farmers' Market.[1] More generally, governance and markets are not separable.

This interaction between rules and trade illustrates the thesis of this book: successful market exchange, and, more fundamentally, successful economic development, both require some resolution of underlying *collective-action problems*—that is, problems that arise when the individual pursuit of self-interest generates socially undesirable outcomes. It is easy to imagine that a vendor might profit from purchasing produce at a warehouse or supermarket and then reselling it at the Dane County Market at a markup. After all, such purchase and resale could be easier and cheaper than growing and marketing one's own produce. Indeed, violation of any of these rules—selling animals, chatting with double-parkers—could be in somebody's self-interest. Although it is not obvious that each rule is necessary or even well formulated (some may be silly, and some may reflect the interests of the committee that drafted them), absent some set of mutually understood and accepted rules for determining who is allowed to sell what kind of produce, the market would probably not function at all.

The farmers' elaborate set of trading rules thus exemplifies an apparently successful effort by a community to resolve a set of collective-action problems that would arise if potential market participants were to behave in any fashion that suited their individual interests—such as reselling produce from grocery stores. These rules also illustrate an exercise of self-governance that operates within a larger institutional context—the city of Madison, the state of Wisconsin, and so forth. According to the classical philosopher David Hume, some form of government emerges when some group would suffer in its absence (1739/1978, Bk. III, Sec. VII). Exchange, collective action, and governance are thus intricately linked. This book explores their connections.

1 COLLECTIVE-ACTION PROBLEMS AND INNOVATIVE THEORY

1.1. COLLECTIVE-ACTION PROBLEMS, POLITICAL ECONOMY, AND EXCHANGE

Collective-action problems (CAPs) arise from any deviation between unfettered pursuit of individual goals (typically, self-interest) and the perceived well-being of at least a portion of some group—be it a nation, region, community, firm, or sports club. Because CAPs represent the archetypal dilemma of strategic interaction among purposeful agents, and because exchange underlies economic and social development, the relationships between collective action and exchange serve as the unifying principle of this book. Collective-action problems reveal the logic behind multiple market failures, notably those associated with public goods, externalities, common-pool resources, and problems of coordination and enforcement. Furthermore, market success depends on resolving CAPs, especially those related to coordination and enforcement. Thus CAPs and the potential for their resolution lie at the foundations of political economy.

There are two basic types of collective-action problems: first- and second-order CAPs. *First-order* CAPs signify free-rider problems that are associated with providing public goods, reducing the production of negative externalities, increasing the production of positive externalities, and limiting the use of common-pool resources to sustainable levels. We define all of these terms broadly. For example, an institution is a public good, as is establishing a sense of trust that facilitates exchange within a community. *Second-order* CAPs are problems of orchestrating the coordination and/or enforcement needed to render agreements for resolving first-order CAPs credible. Indeed, coordination and enforcement are themselves types of public goods—namely, public goods that lend credibility to agreements.

Collective-action problems matter for political economy not only because they represent key linkages between politics and market exchange, but also because they indicate the core rationale for economic and social policy. Most policies seek to resolve or ameliorate CAPs (with varying degrees of success or failure). More fundamentally, the existence of first-order CAPs signifies market or group failure, and successful exchange requires some prior resolution of second-order CAPs. In fact, resolution of second-order CAPs precedes reliable definition and enforcement of the property rights that underlie market exchange. Furthermore, such resolution facilitates the formation of institutional environments, as well as the associated mutual understandings and trust that allow multiple forms of economic, political, and social exchange to occur at all. Resolution of collective-action problems thus underlies all substantive economic, political, and social development.

1.2. ANALYTICAL APPROACHES TO COLLECTIVE ACTION AND EXCHANGE

Much of the motivation for this book arises from relatively recent developments in game theory, economics, and policy theory. These developments both expand and refocus political-economic inquiry. They permit the formalization and modeling of principles that previously had been too complex or considered too indeterminate—and were thus relegated to the sidelines of analysis until recently. Our summary of these developments serves three purposes: it offers intellectual context, points to general methodology, and outlines important concepts that will appear in the remainder of this text.

Our discussion now proceeds to thumbnail sketches of eight critical realms of newly emerging theory: game theory, social network analysis, information economics, social preference theory, rationality theory, institutional and governance theory, policy theory, and spatial-location theory.[1] This section concludes by merging these ideas into a unified conception of game-theoretic political economy that summarizes the book's core assertions.

Game Theory

If CAPs represent the archetypal strategic dilemma for political economy, then game theory offers its methodological bedrock. Formally, game theory facilitates modeling strategic interaction among two or more agents. *Strategic interaction* occurs whenever agents share *strategic interdependence*—meaning that their actions affect outcomes for others and that agents typically understand such interdependence.[2] In an oligopoly, for instance, one firm's production can affect the quantities produced and prices set by other firms. Similarly, a decision by a contractor to hide mistakes can affect its client's profits. In political campaigns, one candidate's decision to advertise can alter prospects for opponents. Likewise, a decision by one student to invite another to a high-school prom may affect the happiness of would-be partners. These types of strategic interaction permeate this book's game-theoretic discussion of collective action and exchange.

By contrast, the constrained-maximization approach of traditional economics and rational choice theory often fails to address strategic interaction. Herein lies a core distinction between recent political-economy approaches to exchange and more conventional approaches based on pure competition and similar models. In pure competition, an agent's decisions focus only on self and environment. Firms and consumers individually choose their quantities produced or purchased—and respond to such external variables as market prices—without reference to actions of other participants. Others' actions merely become indistinguishable elements of an environment (a field) that constrains individual activity and affects outcomes. Although the sum of others' actions can (as part of the field) influence prices, no individual consumer or firm can have such impact. Given this lack of influence, agents can safely disregard others' strategies in their decision calculus.

Strategic interaction is more complicated and intricate than constrained maximization because other parties matter. For example, an oligopolistic firm considers the expected behavior of its (few) competitors before deciding on price or output—while understanding that its competitors share a similar strategic perspective. Such strategic interaction constitutes a *game*, not just an individual decision. Indeed, the constrained-maximization perspective of the traditional approach applies only to exceptional cases. Furthermore, even in competitive markets, game theory can represent transactions that involve any type of commitment, such as a contract, or any private information—such as knowing far more about one's qualities, motivation, or behavior than others do (Dixit, Skeath, and Reiley 2009, 19). Conditions of this sort are ubiquitous in complex economies. Even though market competition can undermine many possible strategies and force players to reveal information, economic choices remain profoundly strategic because outcomes depend on numerous interactions among participants.

This text draws upon four broad types of game theory: classical, evolutionary, behavioral, and epistemic. In classical game theory, agents share some level of mutual awareness of their interdependence. Chosen actions reflect best-response *strategies*—that is, action plans that specify responses to every conceivable contingency—most notably, envisioned combinations of others' actions. Game *outcomes* reflect the conditions (or states of the world) that follow from a game's enacted combinations of strategies. Examples of game outcomes include the price of an item, the distribution of resources, and the election of a candidate. Each possible outcome generates payoffs to each involved player, where *payoffs* capture the net utility gain (or subjective valuation) from that outcome. Utility returns may be either material (as in money) or social (as in status). Classical game theory thus mimics traditional economic reasoning by utilizing best-response maximization; yet it embeds such responses in strategic domains. Applications of these principles, moreover, extend beyond economics to any strategic interaction.

Evolutionary game theory offers an alternative perspective—one in which strategies consist of programmed or inherited "phenotypes."[3] In social scientific applications, inheritance reflects prior education and other forms of cultural (rather than genetic) transmission. Individuals—and, by extension, populations—inherit behavioral orientations, strategies, or established practices in various combinations.[4] Thus some individuals are naturally aggressive and others are shy; some speak Chinese, others English. As in classical game theory, specific combinations of strategies operating within particular contexts generate outcomes with payoffs, but evolutionary payoffs do not indicate players' utility, but instead show the fitness or reproductive viability of their employed strategies. Strategies that earn high fitness payoffs reproduce or transmit abundantly; low-payoff strategies (failed practices) fade away over time. Evolutionary game theory thus facilitates modeling of learning processes and other forms of selective social adaptation.[5]

Behavioral game theory uses experimentation in contexts guided by game-theoretic precepts (e.g., prisoners' dilemma scenarios) to explore relationships between context, perceptions, and agents' actual behavior. Experimental findings may then be incorporated into the other three types of game-theoretic modeling—for example, by informing representations of payoffs. Finally, epistemic game theory focuses on the cognitive dimensions of strategic interactions. Using classical reasoning with emphasis on the extent and limits of agents' prior knowledge and expectations, it illustrates how certain shared understandings can guide or correlate strategic decisions among multiple players. Epistemic game theory is especially useful for modeling the impact of institutions on strategic behavior.[6]

In short, game theory offers an extraordinarily flexible and widely applicable set of modeling techniques. Its use informs not only political science and economics but also biology, psychology, sociology, anthropology, business strategizing, and policymaking. In political economy, game theory enables us to model multiple intricate micro-level transactions within small groups, as well as macro-level patterns among nations or across populations. We may then specify the microfoundations of exchange as strategic social interactions that arise within or among groups of purposeful agents, rather than as a mere summation of independent acts of maximization. In so doing, game theory fosters a truly social scientific modeling framework for political economy. Agents' choices and even their preferences may depend on and respond to anticipated activity or reactions from other parties—all conditioned by social and institutional contexts. Even though game theory can incorporate such social influences, it also posits individuals (or unified organizations, such as firms) as critical decision-making or response units as it models goal-oriented and adaptive behavior. Game theory thus retains the core efficient rigor of economic or rational-choice logic—but vastly enhances its domain and profoundly alters its implications.[7] Modeling multiple facets of political economy becomes feasible.

Game-theoretic modeling permeates this book. As we shall see, the simple two-player prisoners' dilemma illustrates the core idea of a collective-action problem, and the analysis builds from there. Our approach to game theory mixes intuitive logic with relatively accessible mathematics. We use models to illustrate specific assertions or perspectives on political-economic interactions at multiple levels of analysis. Because it is never possible to model everything at once, the choice of modeling technique (e.g., the relevant type of game) will depend upon our analytical purpose and its accompanying questions. Much of the discussion in this text thus complements game-theoretic modeling with descriptions of problems, discussion of context, examples, intuitive arguments, relevant principles, and more general theory.

Social Network Analysis

Social network analysis offers a related modeling approach that focuses on connections among multiple agents. *Social networks* are configurations of relationships or communication pathways that, somehow, connect people. Virtually all economic, political, and social exchanges operate within social networks. Organizations are networks. A CEO, for instance, occupies a specific position within a complex corporate network. Political parties are networks, as are social clubs. Markets rely on, arise from, and sometimes embody networks of exchange among various buyers and sellers. Families and communities are networks. Network analysis encompasses all such entities. It allows specification and examination of the pathways that transmit information, ideas, influence, goods, services, and the like among specific groupings or vast populations of agents. Network analysis facilitates analyzing the origins and development of such pathways, the associated patterns of transmission among agents, possible micro- or macro-level impacts of such transmissions, and how the positioning of agents within networks affects the content or influence of their transmissions. Social network analysis thus provides another method for investigating how social context shapes the evolution, operation, and impact of social, political, and economic exchange.[8]

Information Economics

Information economics explicitly addresses implications of costly, incomplete, and asymmetric information on economic behavior. According to Joseph Stiglitz (2002), information economics alters the prevailing paradigm for economic theory. Not only does asymmetric information introduce a new set of strategic variables, it implies that contracts and other forms of agreement may not be fully enforceable. Second-order CAPs follow. The ensuing enforcement problems, in turn, indicate that labor and capital markets routinely fail to clear. Furthermore, such markets face unavoidable (though often manageable) efficiency losses—as well as exercises of power within exchange relationships. A political dimension of exchange thus emerges.

The game-theoretic distinction between imperfect and incomplete information speaks to the importance of information economics. *Imperfect information* connotes an equally distributed lack of knowledge regarding states of the environment or an equally shared inability to observe the actions of others. Such imperfect information underlies traditional risk analysis. Although agents may not know the exact values of certain variables, they do know the underlying probability distributions and can therefore maximize on the basis of expected values. *Incomplete information* poses more difficult problems. It connotes any information asymmetry among participants concerning conditions in their environment or any lack of knowledge among them concerning the characteristics, motivations (payoffs), or strategies available to other participants in their strategic interactions.

Information economics stresses that asymmetry permits strategic manipulation of information.[9] In this regard, the concept of *adverse selection* (Akerlof 1970) reflects the intuitive notion that, prior to signing a contract or conducting exchange, sellers usually know more about the quality of exchangeable goods or services than do buyers. Such asymmetry can lead to no exchange (a complete market failure) if buyers lack confidence in quality, sellers lack confidence in marketability, or both. Inefficient exchanges of lower-than-expected quality are also possible. More fundamentally, adverse selection implies imperfect definition or understanding of the de facto property rights to be exchanged because rights related to quality are unclear.

Similarly, principal-agent models indicate problems of post-contractual asymmetric information (moral hazard problems).[10] In these models, a *principal* contracts with an *agent* to perform certain services. Because providing service is costly to the agent, their interests differ. Additionally, the principal cannot fully observe or verify the agent's actions. The principal then faces an enforcement problem because the agent has an incentive to provide less effort, diligence, or information than specified by the contract. Resolution requires devoting resources to instituting an *internal enforcement* mechanism—that is, one that operates within the exchange process itself. For example, bosses may fire employees who appear to perform less diligently than expected when they were hired. The related literature on mechanism design addresses how social mechanisms that specify incentives may or may not elicit accurate information and rule-abiding behavior. When such mechanisms successfully align the incentives of principals and agents, they can mitigate underlying conflicts, enhancing prospects for resolving their information-based second-order CAPs.[11]

Principal-agent models yield four important implications for political economy. First, the need to devote resources to enforcement reduces the efficiency of exchange. Second, the need for internal enforcement leads to nonclearing markets, particularly labor and capital markets.[12] Third, nonclearing markets create power relations because some parties can credibly threaten to deny others access to valuable exchanges. Samuel Bowles (2004) calls this internal political dynamic *contested exchange*.[13] The enforcement mechanisms that address asymmetric information therefore influence the distribution of output. Fourth, costs of enforcement indicate sizable transaction costs. Inadequate enforcement may inhibit or even preclude profitable exchange and, by extension, development—market failure in the deepest sense.[14] Hence we cannot understand macro-level outcomes of economic development or growth without first understanding the informational and transaction-cost dimensions of enforcement problems (North 1990).

Social Preference

Like game theory and information economics, the concept of social preference extends the analytical domain of political economy. Social preference theory augments traditional concepts of motivation in a manner that suggests potential remedies to difficult second-order CAPs. It can also indicate how the manifestation or development of preferences responds to social context.

Traditional textbook theory presents a limited concept of preference—one based on the idea that self-interested individuals care only about their own material welfare and have no regard for the welfare of others—in either an absolute or relative sense. Likewise, these individuals do not care about key characteristics (e.g., fairness or equity) of the processes that generate material benefits. Textbook preferences are thus self-regarding and outcome-oriented (Bowles 2004, 96–97). Traditional theory also assumes that individual preferences are fixed or exogenous for the period of analysis. Although models based on these assumptions have generated many useful predictions, their applicability to the analysis of collective action is limited. For example, it is hard to explain many observed instances of cooperation and accompanying resolution of CAPs solely on the basis of self-oriented material preferences (Ostrom 2000a; Gächter 2007).

More recent approaches to motivation reflect the work of behavioral economists by incorporating the related concepts of social preference and social exchange.[15] Agents who possess *social preferences* care about their own outcomes, outcomes for others (either per se or relative to their own), and the processes that generate specific outcomes.[16] Evaluations of such processes may partially reflect the perceived intentions of involved parties. For example, one's utility gain from a given sum of money may partly depend on whether it is payment for time or effort, an award for accomplishment, a gift, a bribe, or proceeds from theft.

Two important forms of social preference receive significant attention in the literature: inequality aversion and intrinsic or strong reciprocity (Fehr and Fischbacher 2002; Bowles 2004; Sobel 2005). Inequality-averse players lose utility from an unequal distribution of benefits or costs within some comparison group (Fehr and Schmidt 1999; Bolton and Ockenfels 2000), but the origins of such inequality do not affect their utility. Reciprocity models extend this logic by allowing the perceived intent of others to influence utility (Rabin 1993). *Reciprocity* indicates a willingness to sacrifice material gain in order to reward seemingly kind or punish seemingly unfair or unkind behavior (Fehr, Gächter, and Kirchsteiger 1997, 839).[17] Because they willingly punish unfair activity, the presence of reciprocal players can help resolve second-order enforcement CAPs.

Reciprocity suggests potential for both social and material exchange. *Social exchange* involves trading approval or disapproval in response to various actions; it offers social incentives that may either reinforce or undermine material incentives.[18] Nonmaterial reciprocal punishment, such as "giving a dirty look," is a type of social exchange. In employment relationships, morale (or a lack thereof) reflects reciprocal social exchanges between workgroups and employers.[19] Furthermore, potential conflicts between social and material incentives may prevent the latter from providing adequate discipline in contexts ranging from work performance to international relations or criminal behavior.[20]

Finally, social preferences respond to social context (Falk, Fehr, and Fischbacher 2003).[21] Thomas Schelling (1978) offers an example: when choosing seats in an auditorium, most people prefer not to sit in front of most others. Individual seating preferences thus depend upon the actions of others; preferences are *interdependent*. Whenever preference responds to context, maximization problems transform conceptually from single first-order constrained-maximization events to n-person games ($n > 1$). Such interdependence generates utility externalities (such as conformity effects), along with path dependence, whereby initial actions influence subsequent actions.[22] Over longer time horizons, preference formation is endogenous to cultural and institutional context (Bowles 1998a). Collective-action problems may therefore emerge in unexpected places; social preference offers insight into both their nature and possible resolution—especially regarding coordination and enforcement.

At the Foundations: Rationality

Both information theory and social preference theory point to the most foundational issue of modeling in political economy: the nature of rationality itself. Yet traditional approaches to rational choice theory often lack explicit consideration of both social preference and limits to human cognition, and so overlook many possible implications on collective action. The concept of substantive rationality, as employed by classical game theory, can address the first omission. *Substantive rationality* connotes goal-oriented behavior with sufficient cognitive capacity to engage in best-response maximization. As game theory texts make clear, substantively rational goals can reflect both social and material preferences.[23]

By contrast, the concept of bounded rationality treats cognition as a scarce resource. Boundedly rational agents remain goal-oriented, but they have limited energy for costly cognitive effort and possess limited cognitive capacity (Conlisk 1996). In a *non-ergodic* environment—one that changes in ways that defy statistical regularity—agents do not know the underlying probability distributions for important social phenomena (North 2005). Accordingly, outside the confines of a narrow problem-complexity boundary—within which problems are simple—agents cannot maximize (Arthur 1992, 1994). They face a gap between their ability to understand and the complexity of problems they face (Heiner 1983). When confronted with such uncertainty, agents resort to heuristics that limit the number of options they consider to a manageable number (Conlisk 1996; Kahneman 2003; Bowles 2004). Daniel Kahneman and Amos Tversky (1979) link heuristics to social preferences and cognition via their concepts of framing effects and prospect theory.[24]

Arthur Denzau and Douglass North's (1994) concept of mental models illustrates boundedly rational reasoning and indicates how social influence and institutions can affect individual understanding. *Mental models* are conceptual representations that agents use for identifying and interpreting categories, patterns, and cause-and-effect relationships. Agents use mental models to produce conclusions or judgments concerning the consequences of various activities or interactions. Once established, however, mental models are difficult to alter. They exhibit properties of *punctuated equilibria*: long periods of stability interrupted by rapid episodes of significant change. Denzau and North proceed to assert that institutions constitute a type of *shared* mental model—that is, models whose key precepts are commonly held among members of various groups. Institutions reflect and embody shared understandings (shared models) of rules and consequences.

Institutional economists have long argued that bounded rationality offers a better description of human behavior than does self-oriented optimization (Rutherford 1994). But prior to recent developments in game theory, formal modeling of bounded rationality was virtually impossible, and the concept remained largely beyond the scope of economic analysis circa 1980. Nowadays, however, contributions from evolutionary and epistemic game theory render such modeling feasible. Evolutionary game theory can specify how boundedly rational agents select and discard strategies, ideas, traits, or even social norms, by adjusting individual and shared mental models.[25] Epistemic game theory can represent agents' cognitive limitations and shared understandings (Gintis 2009b). An epistemic approach allows conceptualizing the effects of institutional contexts on understandings that are shared (or commonly held) among boundedly rational agents, along with the impacts of such sharing on their strategic behavior. This approach also yields abundant implications related to exchange processes and CAPs.

Institutional Analysis and Governance

Recent institutional theory has addressed relationships between the contours of social context—as manifested in rules, norms, and organizations—and the foundations of boundedly rational behavior—as manifested in agents' cognition, information, and motivation. It relates micro-level strategic interaction to the inducements, constraints, and social coordination capacities of institutional systems. Institutional theory thus provides avenues for conceptualizing collective action and exchange at both micro and macro levels, ultimately illustrating relationships among CAPs, exchange, growth, and development.

The field of inquiry known as "the new institutional economics" (Williamson 2000, 2010) began with the 1937 publication of Ronald Coase's article "The Nature of the Firm." Coase proposed that firms exist because the transaction costs of conducting all exchanges on the basis of spot markets would be prohibitive. Instead, firms use hierarchical organization (governance) to coordinate internal transactions. Efforts to minimize the costs of conducting transactions in given conditions determine the extent of a firm's reliance on internal hierarchy, as opposed to external market exchange. Coase's (1960) article "The Problem of Social Cost" makes the related argument—later known as the *Coase theorem* (Stigler 1989)—that, in the absence of transaction costs, parties who face externalities can negotiate solutions that involve exchanging relative costs or benefits. Transaction costs thus become the foundation for understanding the role of markets, hierarchies, institutions, and even governance (Coase 1992).

The work of Oliver Williamson (1975, 1985, 2000) operationalizes relationships between transaction costs and firm governance. For Williamson, the simultaneous presence of bounded rationality, incomplete information, and self-interest generates "strategic opportunism." Such opportunism can arise when an agent's investment in a *specific asset* (i.e., one that cannot be deployed elsewhere) renders the agent dependent on the subsequent activity of others. Other agents could then strategically "hold up" the investor—that is, seize benefits after she has already invested sunk costs. For example, after a supplier has purchased expensive equipment, its client may offer it only a low price. Williamson's core assertion is that a firm's choice between market contracts and various forms of hierarchical governance reflects condition-specific and adaptive efforts to minimize transaction costs associated with holdup and related problems.

North (1990, 2005) focuses on relationships between institutions and development. Extending arguments from Coase and Williamson, he argues that transaction costs primarily arise from incomplete information and attendant problems of defining and enforcing property rights. For North, *institutions* are "the rules of the game in society or, more formally, are the humanly devised constraints that shape human interaction" (1990, 3).[26] By coordinating activity, institutions reduce the transaction costs of exchange, though often not optimally. More fundamentally, institutions reduce uncertainty in non-ergodic environments. Institutional rules not only structure incentives, but, as shared mental models, they also frame understandings and process information. Institutions render the nonergodic world at least somewhat predictable. Economic development would not be possible without them. Yet, unlike Williamson and Coase, North does not argue that efficiency is the goal of institutional construction. Instead, he argues that agents who possess political power shape the formation of institutions with their own interests in mind. Following on North's work, Avner Greif (2006a) stresses the importance of institutions in shaping cognition and transmitting information. Greif also asserts that organizations play a key role in shaping the understandings conveyed by institutional rules.

Institutions may be classified as either formal, such as written rules and laws, or informal, such as behavioral conventions and social norms (North 1990). Ernst Fehr and

Simon Gächter define a social norm as a behavioral regularity based on shared belief about appropriate behavior that is enforced by informal social sanction (2000, 166). Jon Elster (1989a, 1989b) asserts that norms have ethical content. A mix of social enforcement and internal obligation allows norms to rule out multiple antisocial behaviors, and so facilitate constructive collective action. From a game-theoretic perspective, norms shape incentives and expectations in a manner that focuses activity on one of several possible equilibria (correlating behavior); in this manner, norms render behavior in certain contexts predictable.[27] Formal institutions reinforce (or sometimes counteract) informal ones by establishing durable rules that can serve as foundations for external or third-party enforcement mechanisms. Complex exchange—that is, exchange among multiple parties who specialize and need not share repeated interactions or social contact—requires a mix of conventions, social norms, and formally established third-party enforcement (North 1990).

North (1990) also distinguishes between political and economic institutions. Political institutions shape political exchanges and allocate power, whereas economic institutions provide public goods and define and enforce property rights. Building upon this distinction, Daron Acemoglu, Simon Johnson, and James Robinson (2004a) make three assertions: economic institutions are the major source of long-term growth; parties with political power shape the formation of economic institutions; and long-term growth requires instituting a mechanism that credibly restrains politically powerful actors from using their power to seize the gains from investments made by others.

The related approach of polycentric governance appears in the work of Vincent and Elinor Ostrom. Using empirical analysis of metropolitan area government interactions, they developed the concept of *polycentric governance*: many overlapping centers of authority that compete for resources, negotiate agreements, and often utilize citizen input in their joint provision of public services (Ostrom, Tiebout, and Warren 1961; Ostrom and Ostrom 1977). Based upon extensive field and experimental research, scholars at Indiana University's Workshop in Political Theory and Policy Analysis (hereafter, IU Workshop) have developed the related concept of self-governance among users of localized common-pool resources for the purpose of resolving CAPs of overuse. As a mechanism that is neither market nor state, community governance involves crafting and implementing rules and enforcement procedures that incorporate local knowledge and respond to local norms. Because not all such efforts succeed in resolving relevant CAPs, much of the empirical research by IU Workshop scholars seeks to identify the distinguishing features of successful resource governance—including the precise nature of multiple rules and enforcement systems, as well as avenues for participation in their design.

Policy Analysis

Policies endeavor to resolve or ameliorate CAPs; yet sometimes policies create or exacerbate them—and would-be reformers face CAPs as they attempt to make or influence policy. The punctuated-equilibrium policy theory of Frank Baumgartner and Bryan Jones (1993) treats policymaking as an evolutionary process whose dynamics reflect information processing by boundedly rational agents. During relatively long periods of policy stasis, policy subsystems—networks of experts and interested parties affiliated with specific advocacy coalitions (Sabatier and Weible 2007)—process applicable policy information, and so dominate decision making within specific policy areas. Short periods of rapid change (or policy emergence; Kingdon 2003) occur when changing circumstances or oppositional coalitions attract enough attention to render significantly different approaches and decision structures conceivable, feasible, and desirable to parties who occupy policymaking positions. Collective-action problems accompany all such processes.

The Institutional Analysis and Development (IAD) framework developed at the IU Workshop offers a versatile and broad analytical foundation for examining policymaking and, more generally, operations of institutions, organizations, and governance at different levels.[28] The IAD framework envisions interactions among agents in specific action "situations" (or scenarios) that produce outcomes. For example, outcomes in fisheries might include numbers of fish harvested or rules that guide harvesting. A nested hierarchy of action situations may then indicate how outcomes of decisions made at one level (e.g., rules on fishing) provide context for interactions at the next level (e.g., fishing operations). The framework establishes a set of categories and possible relations that facilitate more detailed theoretical analysis of causal relationships. It also offers focused, game-theoretic modeling of specific interactions within designated social and/or physical environments.

Knowledge, the Spatial Location of Production, and Growth

Recent developments in growth and spatial-location theory can explain the strikingly uneven geographic clustering of productive activity. The neoclassical growth model (Solow 1956) and endogenous growth theory (Romer 1990) both point to technological knowledge as the proximate source of long-term growth. Endogenous growth theory emphasizes implications of the nonrival properties of knowledge on growth and distribution (Grossman and Helpman 1991). Because nonrivalry entails complementarity between new and existing knowledge, technological change generates increasing returns in production (Romer 1990). Furthermore, skills exhibit complementarities within productive units (Lucas 1988), and peer relationships within social groups generate complementarities in human capital acquisition (Durlauf 2006). Consequently, skills and knowledge tend to develop in clusters, and clustering leads to location-based uneven development (Krugman 1995). Because development requires assembling a critical mass of skills and knowledge, path-dependent poverty traps and growth circles emerge. Attempts to foster development and attenuate distributional inequity therefore encounter significant CAPs.

Game-Theoretic Political Economy

We may combine these ideas to formulate a comprehensive vision of political economy by developing ten related assertions. (1) Resolution of collective-action problems underlies economic development. (2) Boundedly rational agents operating in non-ergodic environments face multiple first-order CAPs related to public goods, externalities, and common-pool resources. (3) The near ubiquity of asymmetric information implies that negotiated agreements must have accompanying mechanisms of commitment: to attain credibility, agreements require prior resolution of second-order CAPs of coordination and enforcement. (4) Intrinsic reciprocity can resolve many such CAPs in small groups, but resolution in larger groups requires a mix of institutions and organizations. (5) Because they are shared mental models, informal institutions—especially social norms—shape the cognition, information, and motivation of agents within relevant communities. Hence norms may resolve second-order CAPs by invoking ethically based inclinations toward cooperative behavior, while implying the possibility of informal sanctions. (6) The complex configurations of exchange that underlie contemporary development, nevertheless, rely on established combinations of informal institutions and complementary formal institutions, along with accompanying mechanisms of external enforcement. (7) Because parties with political power seek their own gain, resolution of large-scale CAPs associated with development requires additional institutional provisions that restrain exercises of power. (8) Such provisions are often inefficient and seldom entirely successful. (9) In response, goal-oriented boundedly rational agents may attempt to design policies aimed at redressing institutional malfunction—and face a series of CAPs in the process. Such agents may also seek their own gain, introducing yet another set of CAPs for the rest of society. (10) Ultimately, establishing the sophisticated exchange mechanisms that underlie economic development requires suitable resolution of second-order CAPs in order to generate credible agreements that are capable of resolving first-order CAPs.

All of these statements lend themselves to classical, evolutionary, and/or epistemic game-theoretic modeling—with conceptual guidance from behavioral game theory. Modern game theory facilitates sophisticated modeling of first-order and second-order CAPs, incomplete information, material and social preferences, problems of incomplete contracting, various enforcement mechanisms, and the operation and development of informal and formal institutions. Classical game-theoretic models can employ substantive rationality, with either complete or incomplete information, to represent multiple strategic interactions related to collective action and exchange—along with possible impacts of institutional prescriptions and constraints. It can also represent potential resolutions of attendant CAPs. Evolutionary game theory can model adaptive learning processes of boundedly rational agents; their tendencies to acquire or modify heuristics, mental models, and behavioral dispositions; and the larger-scale evolution of conventions, norms, formal institutions, policies, and development (or lack thereof). Epistemic game theory can model the individual and shared understandings that frame and motivate strategic behavior. It can also represent institutions as *social choreographers*: social processes that coordinate understandings, information, and incentives. Such choreography plays a critical role in resolving CAPs, though it may also create them. The findings of behavioral game theory inform all of these applications. Finally, social network theory facilitates modeling many potential influences of agents' connections on their exchanges of information, ideas, goods, services, practices, beliefs, and power.

This book utilizes these game-theoretic tools in conjunction with less formal conceptual statements. Game-theoretic modeling illustrates strategic interactions in multiple action scenarios at various levels of analysis, ranging from micro-level operations within small groups to macro-level interactions within nations or among nations, regions, or large populations. Because no single methodology can simultaneously represent all relevant so-cial complexities, this text follows basic precepts of social scientific inquiry by employ-ing more than one approach. In particular, it complements relatively formal games with descriptions of problems, discussion of context, examples, intuitive arguments, relevant principles, general theory, and broad conceptual frameworks. The formality and tone of presentation vary accordingly.

1.3. PLAN OF THE BOOK

Part II of this text establishes foundations for analyzing exchange and collective-action problems by modeling strategic interactions among multiple agents. Chapter 2 explains the basic economics of CAPs and stresses their significance for economics, political economy, and policy analysis. Its game-theoretic presentation offers a unifying framework for under-standing traditional forms of market and group failure related to broadly defined public goods, externalities, and common resources. This chapter closes by asking how agreements to resolve CAPs can be enforced. Chapter 3 identifies prerequisites for market success or, more generally, for the success of any set of negotiated agreements. This chapter presents simple enforcement games along with adverse selection and principal-agent models. It as-serts that incomplete information generates second-order CAPs of coordination and en-forcement that underlie transaction costs—notably, problems of defining and enforcing the actual (or de facto) property rights that accompany exchange. Chapter 3 concludes by emphasizing that resolving these CAPs leads to nonclearing markets and to exercises of power within exchange processes. Chapter 4 opens on this last point. It uses the Nash bargaining model and the game-theoretic concept of strategic moves to discuss possible sources, instruments, dimensions, and implications of exercising power. By specifying re-lationships among exchange, contract enforcement, and power, this chapter offers concep-tual microfoundations of political economy.

Whereas Chapters 2–4 implicitly use a traditional conception of motivation—agents are self-regarding and outcome-oriented—Chapter 5 explicitly defines this motivational approach (agents are rational egoists) and contrasts it with intrinsic reciprocity. This chap-ter uses game-theoretic models to establish that reciprocity can resolve second-order CAPs that defy resolution when we presuppose rational egoist behavior. Yet, because intrinsic reciprocal response usually emerges from repeated social interaction, its ability to resolve CAPs applies mostly to small groups. Chapter 5 concludes by noting that social context influences reciprocal behavior.

Chapter 6 addresses the foundations of motivation. It opens by developing a broad con-cept of social preference that includes inequality aversion and concern for social welfare. It proceeds to discuss theories of substantive and bounded rationality in order to exam-ine how cognition relates to motivation. Substantive rationality underlies classical game-theoretic modeling of material and social preference, and bounded rationality arises from costs and limits to human cognition. This chapter discusses cognitive processes, heuris-tics, and mental models, arguing that the latter may be shared as mutually understood institutional rules or prescriptions. Chapter 6 closes with some evolutionary modeling of heuristics and mental models, setting the stage for Part III's discussion of institutions.

Part III develops the assertion that resolving large-scale CAPs—in particular, those related to the development of complex exchange—relies on combinations of informal and formal institutions, along with mechanisms of both second- and third-party enforcement that usually operate within organizations. Chapter 7 develops the conceptual foundations for this assertion. It first defines institutions and distinguishes them from organizations, arguing that both operate within institutional systems. Institutions shape the motivation, information, and (as shared mental models) cognition of agents. Chapter 7 then addresses institutional longevity. It closes by introducing the concepts of exit and voice (Hirschman 1970) as alternative mechanisms that agents employ to address organizational or institutional problems.

Chapter 8 discusses informal institutions. It opens by distinguishing between conventions and social norms and identifies three categories of norms based on ethical content, enforcement mechanisms, and the nature of their prescriptions. After summarizing concepts of epistemic game theory, this chapter asserts that institutions, and especially norms, coordinate (or choreograph) cognition, information, and motivation among multiple agents. Using both classical and evolutionary game-theoretic representations—with reference to social coordination—Chapter 8 models how social norms can help resolve otherwise intractable second-order CAPs. It concludes by discussing the powerful influence of norms on preference formation through concepts of identity.

Chapter 9 discusses self-organization, internal enforcement, and self-governance within groups or communities. It opens with a detailed discussion of social capital and trust. Citing examples of shared irrigation systems, this chapter discusses resolutions to common-pool resource problems among resource users. It uses classical game-theoretic reasoning to illustrate processes of negotiation and creating commitment. Chapter 9 closes by assessing the strengths and weaknesses of local self-organization and governance, noting relations to the motivation, information, and cognition of boundedly rational agents.

Chapter 10 then examines relationships between formal and informal institutions and accompanying relationships between third- and second-party enforcement. It asserts that formal institutions and third-party enforcement provide necessary foundations for the complex exchange that underlies modern economies, but such formal mechanisms work poorly when they are incompatible with social norms and second-party enforcement. To underscore this last point, Chapter 10 closes by describing the polycentric nature of functional governance. It asserts that successful governing employs multiple sources of coordination, enforcement, and provision of collective goods that operate simultaneously at various overlapping levels.

Most of the exchanges discussed in Chapters 2–10 implicitly rely on interactions in social networks. Chapter 11 introduces the basic concepts of social network analysis and proceeds to argue that network models can represent virtually any series of social, political, or economic exchanges among multiple agents. This chapter then develops simple network models to make three assertions about CAPs and institutional systems: (i) networks offer sources of power and influence; (ii) networks are searchable conduits of information; and (iii) network connections may occasionally generate the contagious imitation processes, called information cascades, that characterize such social phenomena as fads, financial crises, and revolutions.

Part IV of this book develops several macro, big-picture implications of the previous analysis concerning policy, long-term growth, and development. After discussing relationships between policy and institutions, Chapter 12 reiterates the argument that CAPs motivate the development of policy. Turning this argument on its head, it next asserts that policymaking processes themselves present a series of CAPs. With reference to information processing among boundedly rational agents, this chapter discusses several fundamental CAPs that confront policy reform. Here it uses a punctuated-equilibrium approach in which long periods of policy stasis (dominated by policy subsystems) may occasionally present opportunities for substantive change via coordinated opposition and/or unexpected events. Chapter 12 proceeds to address various CAPs of policy implementation. Echoing Chapter 10, it closes by asserting that successful policymaking requires attention to localized informal institutions and organizations.

Chapter 13 reiterates the core thesis of this text: development requires prior resolution of collective-action problems. This chapter opens with a discussion of technological knowledge as a proximate foundation for economic growth. It then discusses how the nonrival properties of knowledge generate increasing returns in production. This dynamic, combined with related complementarities among production teams and communities, leads to an extraordinarily uneven spatial location of production that, in turn, spawns both poverty traps and innovation clusters. The chapter proceeds to argue that sustained growth requires resolving CAPs related to establishing and maintaining institutional systems—in a manner that generates credible restraints on the ability of powerful parties to seize the benefits of growth. Such processes, moreover, inextricably link growth to distribution, yielding macro-level political economy. Chapter 13 applies these arguments to both democracies and dictatorships. It closes with reflections on various relationships among the location of production, power, and institutional development, along with CAPs that pertain to the equity and the sustainability of economic growth and democratic institutions.

Chapter 14 concludes. It links motivation, information, cognition, institutional contexts, policymaking, and governance to the resolution of second-order and then first-order CAPs, as foundations for creating the needed commitments for complex exchange and development: political economy.

II FOUNDATIONS OF COLLECTIVE ACTION AND EXCHANGE

2 THE BASIC ECONOMICS OF COLLECTIVE ACTION

> How can social interactions be structured so that people are free to choose their own actions while avoiding outcomes that none would have chosen? I call this the classical constitutional conundrum.
>
> Samuel Bowles (2004)

Two communities, Arruba (A) and Boratonia (B), share water from a common well that they use to maintain herds, which they sell competitively in a local market. If both communities use water extensively, they will gradually deplete their well; over time their animals will grow sick or die. Yet if both communities limit their use, the water will last, and each could maintain modest herds. Finally, if A uses extensively and B limits, then A could sell fat animals for enough revenue to import luxury goods, whereas B could not sell its lean animals and may lack funds for importing other foods as well as needed farm implements. The reverse occurs if A limits and B uses extensively. Given these incentives, both communities use water extensively.[1]

Readers may recognize this story as a collective-action problem (CAP) applied to limiting the use of a common-pool resource. The extensive-use outcome is known as the "tragedy of the commons" (Hardin 1968). From a slightly different perspective, we have a public-good story, since a state of joint limitation on resource use (i.e., achievement of sustainable use) is itself a public good. An externality story is also possible: the depletion of wells, an unintended consequence of using water, confers negative externalities on the other community and on future resource users. From any of these perspectives, the communities face a first-order CAP. Readers may also recognize that a classic two-player prisoners' dilemma game could illustrate this description. Our communities A and B face just such a dilemma.

The ability of different groups to resolve the social dilemmas posed by CAPs reflects their capacity to overcome various forms of market or group failure. Ultimately, such resolution underlies the social and economic development of communities and societies. This chapter offers a relatively simple overview of CAPs, stressing links to economics with policy implications. It focuses on first-order CAPs, or those that accompany various types of free-riding; notable examples include problems related to public goods, externalities, and common-pool resources. Second-order CAPs (discussed in Chapter 3) arise from a need to develop social mechanisms of coordination and enforcement. Resolution of second-order CAPs typically precedes resolution of first-order CAPs. For both types, game-theoretic modeling offers a unifying framework for conceptualizing core characteristics and potential avenues for resolution. Such modeling sheds light on the essence of market or group failure and on potential foundations of success.

Our discussion proceeds as follows. Section 2.1 presents a thumbnail sketch of the relevant history of thought on collective action. Section 2.2 develops two-player game representations of the core social dilemma that underlies political economy: conflicts between self-interest and group welfare. Section 2.3 presents *N*-player games in which both the problems of coordination and the potential for distributional strife are more prominent.

2.1. THE IMPORTANCE OF COLLECTIVE ACTION

Philosophers and economists have been contemplating collective-action problems in society for hundreds of years. The seventeenth-century philosopher David Hume's *Treatise of Human Nature* argues three relevant points: (1) society enables humans to overcome their natural disadvantages vis-à-vis animals, such as lack of protective fur; (2) social convention provides foundations for stable relationships of possession upon which society is founded; and (3) concern for reputation motivates individuals to adhere to convention. Hume proceeds to argue that inducements to act in a manner that can benefit strangers—in modern terminology, *prosocial behavior* or an inclination to contribute to public goods—can arise from reciprocal promises of trading favors over time. A sense of obligation, itself derived from convention, lends force to such promises (Hume 1739/1978, 524–25).[2] Thus Hume (somewhat optimistically) regards social convention, reputation, and reciprocity as what we might now call social mechanisms that can resolve CAPs.

Adam Smith's *Wealth of Nations* portrays an even more optimistic vision, one that is based on individuals rather than communities. For Smith, pursuit of individual self-interest in an environment of market competition leads to provision of the ultimate public good: economic growth and general prosperity over time. More precisely, he argues that the division of labor is the ultimate source of wealth, and that both the division of labor and economic growth arise from the propensity of humans to engage in trade based on self-interest. Smith (1776/1976, 13) states:

> But man has almost constant occasion for the help of his brethren, and it is in vain for him to expect it from their benevolence only. He will more likely prevail if he can interest their self-love in his favor, and shew [show] them that it is for their own advantage to do for him what he requires of them.

Smith asserts further that market competition disciplines the individual pursuit of self-interest (greed) toward broader social goals. In modern terminology, markets are social mechanisms that harness the pursuit of self-interest for the benefit of society. Accordingly, competition robs potential monopolists (exploiters) of their power.[3]

Coase (1960) presents a similar, yet more contingent, case for optimism. Relying primarily on localized two-player examples, he asserts that if transaction costs are zero, self-interested parties will bargain over how to share the (social) costs indicated by externalities—and so resolve associated problems. Stigler (1989) labeled this proposition the *Coase theorem*. Coase proceeds to assert that the presence of high transaction costs, a likely condition when there are many involved parties, hinders such resolution; hence the assignment of legal rights affects outcomes (e.g., the distribution of cost burdens). Coase argues against Arthur Pigou's suggested remedies of taxation or government regulation. Instead, he proposes using case-by-case cost-benefit analysis of feasible policy alternatives, including taxation and assignment of legal rights.[4] With adequate designation of rights, problems may be resolved.

By contrast, Garrett Hardin argues that, without external enforcement mechanisms, the rising demand for resources that accompanies population growth leads to depletion: the tragedy of the commons. Citing examples of common grazing grounds, ocean fisheries, pollution, and population growth (with a Malthusian argument on the latter), he argues that unrestricted use leads to unsustainable overuse. Furthermore, perhaps echoing Smith, he asserts that appeals to conscience will fail because those with little conscience will benefit at the expense of others. Hardin (1968, 1247) thus calls for "mutual coercion, mutually agreed upon"—such as taxation, presumably agreed upon in a democratic state.

Focusing specifically on collective action, Mancur Olson (1971) offers some limited room for optimism. Individuals contribute to collective goods only if their own marginal benefit exceeds their contribution cost. Thus, in the absence of selective incentives to induce contribution, minimal contribution follows. This proposition is known as Olson's *zero-contribution thesis* (Ostrom 2000a, 137). Small groups can, nonetheless, orchestrate contribution by applying selective social incentives. According to Olson (1982, 23), "those in a socially interactive group seeking a collective good can give special respect or honor to those who distinguish themselves by their sacrifices in the interests of the group and thereby offer them a positive selective incentive." Larger groups (e.g., business associations) face difficulties invoking social sanctions, but they may achieve the same effect by using other selective incentives, such as compulsory dues with exclusion of free-riders. Similarly, federations of groups may sometimes orchestrate selective incentives, though internal conflicts of interest may interfere.

Three relatively contemporary authors—Thomas Schelling, Elinor Ostrom, and Douglass North—more clearly address relationships among the foundations of market success, CAPs, collective organization, credible commitment, and mechanisms of enforcement.

Schelling, like Smith, marvels at the coordination capacities of markets, but he clearly delineates the complicated, difficult, and limited conditions that underlie their success. Success depends on establishing or facilitating the following: legal definitions of property rights, related enforcement procedures, techniques of product standardization, sufficient competition, protection from externalities, reliable information (particularly among buyers), and sufficient mechanisms for communication (1978, 29–30). With respect to CAPs, Schelling asserts that some sort of social contract must intervene to encourage socially beneficial behavior. He states: "A good part of social organization—of what we call society—consists of institutional arrangements to overcome these divergences between perceived individual interest and some larger collective bargain" (127).

Ostrom (1990, 2000a) investigates how users of small-scale common-pool resources (CPRs) can jointly organize to sustain them. She argues that both traditional market and government solutions rely too heavily on external authority, though in different fashions.

A Smithian or Coasian market solution would privatize: assign property rights over the resource and let owners determine use. For Ostrom, this solution works only if relevant conditions permit adequate external (as in government) definition and enforcement of pertinent property rights. Yet many CPR problems lend themselves to neither. Beyond coastal limits, for example, it is not obvious what property rights individuals or groups might exercise over ocean fisheries, who the relevant enforcement authorities would be, or how they would monitor infringement. Likewise, Hardin's solution of mandated limits works only if government has enough relevant information to monitor resource use and the ability to reliably sanction violators. These conditions may exist for problems like regulating automobile traffic, but monitoring ocean fishing poses more serious challenges.

Ostrom offers a third potential solution: self-organization among groups of resource users with mutual monitoring. Based on multiple observations by scholars at Indiana University's Workshop in Political Theory and Policy Analysis concerning the internal governance of CPRs, she identifies three core problems whose resolution usually distinguishes successful from unsuccessful attempts at collective organization. These are (1) supplying institutions—in this case, the rules of resource use; (2) achieving commitment to follow such rules; and (3) monitoring adherence with sanctions for violation (as in Olson's selective sanctions). All three processes present CAPs.[5] On the basis of similar research, she then develops several "design principles" that characterize successful resolution (Ostrom 1990, 2000b). For example, Ostrom (1990, 42–45) notes a successful case of a Turkish fishing cooperative. The co-op established rules that specified a random allocation of initial fishing locations to members, with daily movement to neighboring sites. Those awarded a good spot on a given day could observe intrusions and defend their rights. Knowing that violation would be detected and sanctioned, individuals found it in their interest to follow the rules. The co-op thus resolved its first-order CAP of overfishing by successfully addressing the second-order CAPs of negotiating mutually understood rules (institutions) and accompanying enforcement mechanisms. Both elements created credible commitments to abide by the agreed-upon rules.

Ostrom adds several final conditions that reflect the importance of internal relationships, external regulatory environments, and the scale of CPRs. Internally, local members must possess a capacity to communicate and develop trust—usually via reciprocal commitments enforced by social norms. Here she echoes Hume, though with more contingency. In terms of external relations, if co-ops were not legal in Turkey, then the described resolution mechanism would likely fail; not only could co-op members face external prosecution, cheaters could extort concessions by threatening to expose the co-op. More generally, there must be "access to rapid, low-cost, local arenas to resolve conflict among users or between users and officials" (2000a, 152). With regard to scale, Ostrom echoes Olson by focusing on solutions that apply to small-scale CPRs. When CPRs are somewhat larger, "the presence of governance activities organized in multiple layers of nested enterprises" (152) may achieve successful regulation. Ostrom notes that, at any level, these solutions are neither purely private nor purely public. Finally, she asserts that specifying the relevant conditions for successful self-organization is a key domain for policy analysis.

Schelling (1978) makes a useful distinction between strict and looser versions of CPR problems. In strict cases, depletion of a resource affects only users, and applicable social costs and benefits can be measured using the same "currency." Ostrom's Turkish fishing cooperative fits this description. Only co-op members suffer the costs of overfishing or limitation, and one may readily assess the associated benefits or costs by counting fish. A broader class of CPR problems includes instances where nonusers, too, suffer costs of depletion; hence externalities extend beyond the user group. Additionally, costs and benefits seldom lend themselves to evaluation by a single metric. For example, impacts of air pollution spread globally, and the costs and benefits of limitation (lost profits from low production, better health, more pleasant air, etc.) share no obvious common metric.[6] We refer to such cases as *complex* CPR problems. Not even the most successful organization of local resource users could resolve them—at least from the perspective of society at large. Nevertheless, Ostrom's principles of success and her concept of nested groups or enterprises point to likely elements of successful mechanisms that could resolve a large set of CPR and related problems.

Finally, North (1990) echoes and extends Ostrom's and Schelling's insights as he discusses the institutional foundations of economic development. Economic development requires establishing the credible commitments that underlie successful coordination and cooperation—in other words, resolution of second-order CAPs. Following Coase, North asserts that resolution requires sufficiently low transaction costs. Thus transaction costs are the chief barrier to economic development. North defines *transaction costs* as the "costs of measuring the valuable attributes of what is being exchanged and the costs of protecting rights and policing and enforcing agreements" (1990, 27). Because such activities operate in environments of asymmetric information, transaction costs reflect incomplete information. He estimates that transaction costs constitute 45% of US gross domestic product (28).

North asserts that enforcement problems have impeded development for most of human history (1990, 33). Yet institutions can sometimes foster sufficient coordination and enforcement to generate credible commitments; they structure incentives and often reduce uncertainty by effectively ruling out many forms of defection. Complex exchange may ensue. North points out, however, that institutional resolutions need not be socially optimal; constructing institutions presents (second-order) CAPs, and parties who possess bargaining power may steer institutional development to suit their own interests. Nevertheless, by orchestrating cooperation, institutions can sometimes reduce transaction costs to a level that permits complex exchange—and hence economic development.

Overall, this thumbnail sketch of ideas on collective action points to key themes of this book—most notably, relationships of CAPs to market and group failure. At a deeper level, these ideas imply pre-conditions for the success of markets and supporting institutions in the complex processes of economic development. Associated interactions lie at the foundations of political economy and policy analysis. The next section begins with game-theoretic models of first-order CAPs.

2.2. TWO-PLAYER GAME REPRESENTATIONS

A two-player prisoners' dilemma (PD) game succinctly illustrates the archetypal social dilemma that underlies political economy: divergence between individual and group interests. In other words, the PD game serves as a foundational model for representing

CAPs. More precisely, this game can illustrate problems related to public goods, negative or positive externalities, and common-pool resources—all broadly defined. We might, for example, regard establishing trust as a public good. Three other two-player games— assurance, chicken, and battle-of-the-sexes (hereafter, battle)—offer additional perspective on coordination, distributional conflict, and possible advantages to first movers. Because such dilemmas and possibilities are nearly universal in human interaction, these simple models—along with supply-demand models—belong at the foundations of economics and political economy.

Here is a literal rendition of a one-period PD game. The police interrogate prisoners Bonnie and Clyde in separate rooms. Each prisoner has two possible strategies: Mum (say nothing to the police) and Fink (report the other's nefarious deeds). The outcomes and payoffs are as follows. If both choose Mum (M), then the police, having scant evidence, can jail them for only two years (both receive a payoff of −2). If both choose Fink (F), then ample evidence lands both in jail for five years (both receive −5). If one chooses F and the other M, the former goes free (payoff = 0) while the latter faces ten years in jail (payoff = −10). Figure 2.1 shows the normal-form (or strategic-form) game matrix.[7]

It is easy to see that both players have a *dominant strategy* of choosing F: each does better playing F regardless of what the other does. Hence the *Nash equilibrium* occurs at (F, F), as neither would unilaterally deviate from this outcome.[8] Nevertheless, both would benefit if the other chose M. We call (M, M) the *social optimum*—the outcome that maximizes combined payoffs—for the two prisoners (though not for society). Yet self-interest militates against this cooperative solution: even if they could communicate, neither could trust the other to follow through on a verbal agreement to stay mum. Absent other influences (e.g., known death threats to finkers or "honor" codes among thieves), both will choose F and receive five-year sentences. Hence Bonnie and Clyde face a two-player first-order CAP: self-interest diverges from mutual interest.

This incentive structure applies to multiple first- (and second-) order CAPs. Figure 2.2 depicts a more general model. Players may either cooperate (strategy C) or defect (strategy D). Note that in Figure 2.2, the strategies C and D appear without italics, but payoff variables (C_A, C_B, D_A, D_B, etc.) appear in italics.[9] These two strategies may be defined in distinct manners that capture each of the major types of first-order CAPs. For provision of public goods, we define strategy C as contribute to provision and D as do not contribute. As an illustration, suppose that—prior to encountering the water-use problem discussed earlier in the chapter—Arruba and Boratonia needed to construct a mutually accessible well. Assume that the total cost of production, to be paid by either or both communities, is 10.

		Clyde	
		Mum	Fink
Bonnie	Mum	−2, −2	−10, 0
	Fink	0, −10	−5, −5

Figure 2.1   Literal PD game

	Player B	
	C	D
Player A C	C_A, C_B	L_A, H_B
Player A D	H_A, L_B	D_A, D_B

Figure 2.2   General PD game

NOTE: If $H > C > D > L$ and if subscripts A and B indicate equal payoffs for the same variable, then we have a symmetric PD game.

At the time of construction (before any depletion), access to the water is worth 9 to each. If both play C, then each receives $9 - 5 = 4$. If both play D, both receive 0. If one chooses C and the other D, the first pays all costs and so receives $9 - 10 = -1$, while the second receives 9. The dominant strategies, Nash equilibria (NE) and social optimum (SO), thus indicate a PD game structure similar to that in Figure 2.2. The communities face a CAP associated with provision of a public good—their well.

This simple PD model can also illustrate other basic forms of first-order CAPs. Turning to negative externalities, let strategy C = control pollution (at a cost) and D = do not. Players can be firms, communities, regions, or nations. Similarly, for positive externalities (e.g., research and development), we let C = produce the socially optimal quantity and D = produce the profit-maximizing quantity. For a CPR problem, such as the water-use story that opened this chapter, we may define C = limit the use of water and D = use water as desired.

Furthermore, various payoff structures specify distinct types of games that apply to distinct CAPs. In this regard, we may incorporate payoff functions that reflect different returns to scale on either the benefit or cost side, and we can introduce externality payoffs. Such alterations can generate two variants of PD, along with games of chicken (three variants), assurance, and battle.[10] The latter three games suggest CAPs related to coordination. Chicken and battle add complications from distributional conflict, and the presence of two NE implies advantages to a player who can move first.

To establish a general framework, consider a CAP associated with provision of a public good, as represented by Figure 2.2. Figure 2.3 illustrates such a game with payoff functions reflecting benefits and costs to contributions ($C_A = C_B = b(2) - c(2), \ldots$). Here $b(n)$ denotes each player's benefit (from provision of a public good) as a function of the total number of contributors (n), and $c(n)$ denotes an individual's cost of contribution as a function of n. In a two-player game, $n \in \{0, 1, 2\}$. For a public good, an individual payoff to strategy C is $C(n) = b(n) - c(n)$: contributors receive benefits and pay costs. The payoff to D is

	Player B	
	C	D
Player A C	$b(2) - c(2), b(2) - c(2)$	$b(1) - c(1), b(1)$
Player A D	$b(1), b(1) - c(1)$	$b(0), b(0)$

Figure 2.3   Public-good contribution game

$D(n) = b(n)$: defectors receive benefits without costs. For the remaining two-player games in this section (of whatever variant), assume that $b(2) \geq b(1)$, $b(0) = 0$, and $c(1) \geq c(2) > 0$.

If we now add the condition that $b(n) - c(n) < b(n-1)$, so that individually contributing always lowers one's payoff, we find a PD game with a suboptimal NE at (D, D). Even so, we cannot specify the location of the SO without first adding another condition. If returns to contribution are high enough that $2(b(2) - c(2)) > 2b(1) - c(1)$, then mutual contribution (C, C) generates higher total payoffs than either case of single contribution—that is, either (C, D) or (D, C). There is a unique SO at (C, C). This is the most common variant of PD; following Dixit, Skeath, and Reiley (2009), we call it prisoners' dilemma version I, or PDI. With somewhat lower net returns to joint contribution, the stated inequality reverses, and we have PDII. The NE remains at (D, D), but twin social optima emerge at (C, D) and (D, C).[11] Readers might consider whether a CAP that fits PDI is easier to resolve than one that fits PDII. Note that PDII adds the potential for distributional conflict over the choice between two social optima: Which player gets to free-ride?

Suppose now that contribution shows strongly increasing marginal net returns. A game of assurance follows. Players' interests are aligned, but achieving the best outcome requires some coordination. Assurance games can represent various complementarities in production processes related to workers' skills, areas of group expertise, combinations of technology, or even cooperative activities between nations. With reference to Figure 2.3, suppose that—as in PD—individual returns to a single contribution are negative ($b(1) - c(1) < 0$), but there are large gains to a second contribution ($b(2) - c(2) > b(1)$). Two Nash equilibria emerge. In each, players coordinate on the same strategy: either (C, C) or (D, D). The SO occurs at (C, C). Since both players prefer the SO, their interests are aligned. Given sufficient information and trust, two players can often resolve the (minimal) CAP associated with coordinating on C. Each player needs only some "assurance" that the other actually prefers (C, C) to (D, D). In fact, (C, C) may serve as an intuitive *focal point*: an NE upon which player expectations converge in cases of more than one NE. Sufficient information and trust allow resolution via *cheap talk* (statements made with no costs). Even so, Section 2.3 will demonstrate that multi-player assurance is more complicated.

If contribution instead generates diminishing marginal net returns, we have a game of chicken. Here distributional conflict may obstruct coordination. For chicken, contributing when the other defects increases one's payoff ($b(1) - c(1) > b(0)$), but contributing when the other contributes lowers one's payoff ($b(2) - c(2) < b(1)$). Two Nash equilibria emerge, (C, D) and (D, C). In the case of Figure 2.3's public good, community A now prefers (D, C) whereas B prefers (C, D); the presence of two NE indicates distributional conflict. If a player could manipulate the game's rules to stipulate that it moves first (with observation by the second player), the game would become a two-step sequential game. In sequential chicken, the first mover enjoys an advantage: by moving, it can effectively dictate its preferred NE, since the other player will do better by complying.[12] In subsequent chapters, we relate this first-mover advantage to strategic moves, power, and the political economy of institutional construction.

In the meantime, permutations on payoffs generate three variants. In chicken I, the SO occurs at (C, C): $2(b(2) - c(2)) > 2b(1) - c(1)$, as in PDI. In chicken II, this inequality is reversed so that, as in PDII, (C, D) and (D, C) emerge as twin social optima—but here they are also Nash equilibria. Note that chicken II shows a greater degree of diminishing marginal returns than does chicken I.[13] Again, returns to contribution influence the nature of the indicated CAP. For chicken I, achieving the SO requires that both parties avoid the NE. With only two players, transaction costs may be low enough that they achieve resolution through Coasian bargaining. For chicken II, by contrast, the previously discussed distributional conflict over the SO also emerges with respect to the Nash equilibria.

A third variant of chicken abandons the notion of a pure public good and clearly indicates how distributional goals may hinder coordination. Chicken III arises if we introduce negative externalities. For example, each community's contribution to construction of a well could flood the other's fields. For two or more players, define $e(n-1)$ as the externality imposed on a contributor by other players' choices of C; we have $e < 0$, indicating a negative externality. Now let $C(n) = b(n) + e(n-1) - c(n)$ and $D(n) = b(n) + e(n)$, where $e(0) = 0$. Figure 2.4 shows this game for two players.

To illustrate, let $b(2) = 8$, $b(1) = 6$, $c(2) = 3$, $c(1) = 4$, and $e(1) = -9$. We arrive at the traditional game of chicken that is analogous to a driving story.[14] Because it creates negative externalities, strategy C (construct) in Figure 2.5 is equivalent to "drive straight," and D (do not) is equivalent to "swerve." The SO now occurs at (D, D).[15] Resolution of the indicated CAP requires coordinated choices of D, avoiding both NE. Yet each player actually prefers the NE in which it constructs. Once again, a first mover would have an advantage. Furthermore, the (high-stakes) distributional conflict may sabotage coordinating on either NE, leading to the worst possible outcome (C, C). Bargaining tactics often exhibit such a chicken dynamic. For example, Steven Erlanger (2012) characterized the early 2012 negotiations between the EU and Greece over an austerity package and bailout as a game of chicken.

Table 2.1 summarizes the just-described relationships between game structure and returns to b and c.

		Player B	
		C	D
Player A	C	$b(2) + e(1) - c(2), b(2) + e(1) - c(2)$	$b(1) - c(1), b(1) + e(1)$
	D	$b(1) + e(1), b(1) - c(1)$	$b(0), b(0)$

Figure 2.4   Two-player chicken III (negative externalities)

		Player B	
		C	D
Player A	C	−4, −4	2, −3
	D	−3, 2	0, 0

Figure 2.5   Chicken III with numbers

TABLE 2.1
Game structure and cost-benefit relationships

Game/type	Benefit/cost conditions	SO condition	Externalities
A. General public-good (PG) games	$b(2) \geq b(1), b(0) = 0,$ $c(1) \geq c(2)$		
General PD	$b(n) - c(n) < b(n-1)$	Either	
PD I	Same	$2(b(2) - c(2))$ $> 2b(1) - c(1)$	
PD II	Same	$2(b(2) - c(2))$ $< 2b(1) - c(1)$	
General chicken	$b(2) - c(2) < b(1), b(1) - c(1) > 0$	Either	
Chicken I	Same	$2(b(2) - c(2))$ $> 2b(1) - c(1)$	
Chicken II	Same	$2(b(2) - c(2))$ $< 2b(1) - c(1)$	
Assurance	$b(2) - c(2) > b(1), c(1) > b(1)$	Follows	
B. Negative externality games	Can be same as PG		$e(n) < 0$ for $n > 0$
Chicken III	$C(n) = b(n) + e(n-1) - c(n),$ $D(n) = b(n) + e(n),$ $b(2) + e(1) - c(2) < b(1) + e(1),$ $b(1) - c(1) > 0$	Either	

		Player B	
		C(A)	C(B)
Player A	C(A)	4, 1	0, 0
	C(B)	0, 0	1, 4

Figure 2.6 Battle

Finally, introducing asymmetry in benefits, costs, or externalities generates a game of battle. As in chicken, distributional concerns may hinder coordination, and we find many applications to bargaining scenarios. Suppose that players A and B, who have complementary skills and capital, hope to cooperate on constructing a well, but each prefers its own plan. Plan A costs player A less, benefits it more, or imposes fewer negative externalities on it, and plan B confers similar advantages to player B. We could then construct values for the variables in Figure 2.3 that would generate the numerical payoffs shown in Figure 2.6. Here both Nash equilibria are also social optima, but the players prefer different wells. If each side insists on its preferred well, their distributional conflict will lead to a zero-payoff outcome. And, as in chicken, a player can claim the advantage of dictating its preferred NE by credibly seizing the ability to move first; the other will then find it best to acquiesce.[16] One could apply this game to the spring 2012 negotiations between Germany and France over how to resolve the Greek financial crisis: both parties desire a resolution but differ over how to achieve it.

Perfect External Enforcement

So far, we have ignored issues of enforcement. Although Chapter 3 will treat enforcement among involved parties as a second-order CAP, the rest of this section considers enforcement by external parties (e.g., police and courts) that are fully informed, motivated, and capable. In such cases, any of the previously described CAPs could be resolved—either through internal agreements whose terms are externally enforced or solely by external enforcement. Regarding the former, recall that the Coase theorem states that, in the absence of transaction costs, parties may resolve first-order CAPs by negotiating complete and binding agreements to share associated costs. But fully eliminating transaction costs would require engagement by an external agency that would sanction violation of any portion of such agreements—at no marginal cost to the involved parties. If taxes (or external enforcement fees) are sunk costs assessed independently of specific violations, and if external authorities are sufficiently informed, capable, and motivated, then such Coasian bargaining could resolve *first-order* CAPs.

From a game-theoretic perspective, Coasian bargaining—or any bargaining where enforcement of agreements can be taken for granted—lends itself to representation via a Nash *cooperative* bargaining game. Cooperative games assume the following: parties can gain by negotiating an agreement; agreements are both fully binding and complete in the sense of specifying all relevant contingencies; and these conditions are common knowledge. Given these assumptions, two parties (A and B) can bargain over sharing the mutual gains from cooperative agreement, and their relative bargaining power determines their shares of the net gains. Mathematically, the players agree on a payoff combination (x_A, x_B) that maximizes the product of their net gains: $(x_A - d_A)^\alpha(x_B - d_B)^\beta$. The terms d_A and d_B represent their respective payoffs in the event of breakdown (i.e., the players' exogenously determined *fallback positions*); exponents α and β, where $\alpha + \beta = 1$, indicate each party's bargaining strength.[17] Such negotiation over binding agreements can, in principle, resolve a first-order CAP between two parties.

A slightly more sophisticated bargaining model can account for the portion of transaction costs that is unrelated to enforcement. We now augment the prior equation with transaction costs to each party that stem from the bargaining process itself (e.g., travel to or time spent in bargaining sessions). Of course, transaction costs diminish net gains. Parties thus negotiate combination x_A and x_B so as to maximize

$$(2.1) \qquad (x_A - d_A - t_A)^\alpha(x_B - d_B - t_B)^\beta$$

for given fallbacks d_A and d_B and transaction costs t_A and t_B, where $t_A + t_B = TC_n$ (total non-enforcement transaction costs). Two complications arise. First, the distribution of TC_n (i.e., the ratio t_A/t_B) may itself be a subject of bargaining; and the potential for bargaining strength to affect ratio t_A/t_B may diminish prospects for achieving agreement by complicating negotiations.[18] Second, sufficiently high TC_n may eliminate any prospect for a bargained solution by depleting net gains ($x - d - t \leq 0$). This conclusion is consistent with Coase's (1960) propositions. Furthermore, Chapter 3 indicates how incomplete information—with ensuing enforcement costs—significantly augments transaction costs, thereby generating second-order CAPs.

Now consider a related and more general approach to exogenous enforcement. Assume that an external third-party enforcer (such as the state) can administer a punishment payoff

Player B

Player A		C	D
	C	$C_A + r, C_B + r$	$L_A + r, H_B - p$
	D	$H_A - p, L_B + r$	$D_A - p, D_B - p$

Figure 2.7   PD with enforcement

$(-p)$ to defectors and/or a reward payoff (r) to cooperators. Here cooperating may indicate either direct contribution to a collective good (as in Figures 2.2 and 2.3) or full adherence to a negotiated agreement—in which case external authorities enforce the cooperative agreements derived from equation (2.1). In either case, sufficiently high values of r and/or p can resolve PD-style CAPs. Figure 2.7 illustrates.[19] Again, the model is versatile. Variations among the rules for assigning r and p can reflect different exogenous enforcement regimes. For example, the US Internal Revenue Service (IRS) punishes infraction but does not reward compliance, whereas academic scholarships reward achievement. In various cases, a given p (or r) could apply either if only one player defects (cooperates) or if both do so. Additionally, the sizes of r or p could differ by player $(p_A \neq p_B)$. For example, sentences for drug law violations are sometimes allocated differently on the basis of race, often in violation of stated procedure (Mustard 2001).

Further complications suggest other likely impediments to resolving CAPs. If players observe either C or D imperfectly (with probabilities less than one), the expected values of r or p decline. The IRS, for instance, does not observe all tax cheating. To make matters worse, external authorities can make mistakes: they might sometimes confuse C with D and vice versa. Such mistakes undermine intended incentives and likely encourage defection. Furthermore, in situations of distributional conflict, external authorities may "take sides" or at least appear to do so. For these reasons, sufficient external enforcement cannot be taken for granted, and Section 2.3 drops the assumption of perfect enforcement.

2.3. MULTI-PLAYER CAPS

While two-player models capture many core incentive and coordination issues that underlie numerous CAPs, multi-player (N-player) games more clearly illustrate various difficulties of coordination and conflict that emerge in large groups or populations. Like their two-player counterparts, N-player games exist in PD, assurance, and chicken versions—each with its own implications.[20] Multi-player PD games can formally represent Olson's zero-contribution thesis; they indicate why large groups face considerable difficulties securing contributions to collective goods. Multi-player chicken games can illustrate negative externalities and CPR problems—with implied complications arising from distributional conflict. Multi-player assurance games point to difficulties of coordination associated with generating positive externalities; they often indicate properties of *path dependence*, whereby initial conditions influence future outcomes. Path dependence, in turn, creates a potential for *punctuated equilibria*: relatively long periods of stability interrupted by short periods of rapid change in response to relatively large external shocks (Gould and Eldredge 1977). Many political, economic, and social arrangements, ranging from negotiated outcomes to social norms and formal institutions, exhibit properties of punctuated equilibria.

Provision of Public Goods as a Multi-Player PD Game

By specifying how group size influences the resolution of CAPs, multi-player PD games illustrate Olson's zero-contribution thesis. More precisely, these games suggest that, as group size increases: individual incentives for contributing to collective goods diminish; the potential for negotiating a workable sharing of contribution recedes; and enforcing negotiated agreements becomes correspondingly more difficult.[21] We now illustrate.

Suppose that a group of N agents could achieve higher levels of individual income (y_i) if they cooperate in providing certain mutually beneficial public goods (G), such as safe and navigable seaways or airways, epidemic control, clean air, and a stable common currency. Each agent has endowment $q_i \geq 0$, which represents returns on private production in the absence of G. Each agent decides its level of contribution toward the provision of G ($c_i \geq 0$). Each unit of c_i adds amount α to quantity G: α is the marginal product of c_i.[22] In equation form, we have

(2.2)
$$y_i = q_i - c_i + G$$
$$= q_i - c_i + \alpha \sum_{j=1}^{N} c_j.$$

Assume there are no fixed costs. Note that i is a member (any member) of the group j, where $j = 1, \ldots, N$. Total production $G = \alpha \sum_{j=1}^{N} c_j$.

Equation (2.2) indicates several principles of public-good CAPs. Suppose that providing G to a group of size N would require a minimum average contribution of $c_i = c_m$ from each agent in N, so that $G = N\alpha c_m$. As group size N increases, the marginal product of each individual contribution to G (αc_m) offers a steadily declining portion of G. Thus, as N increases, the public-good contribution game is more likely to take on a PD structure, indicating an incentive to free-ride. Formally, whenever $\alpha < 1 < \alpha N$, the game has a PD structure.[23] Given these payoffs (and no enforcement mechanism), the NE occurs at $c_i = 0$ for all $i \in \{j = 1, \ldots, N\}$. This is a formal statement of Olson's zero-contribution thesis. If constructing a well requires the participation of a thousand individuals, none may contribute.

Figure 2.8 shows an N-player PD game from the perspective of a marginal contributor. Payoffs to strategies D and C are linear functions of the number of contributors (n or $n + 1$), where n is the number of other players who contribute.[24] The marginal contributor chooses D or C, taking the actions of all others as given. The $D(n)$ line always lies above $C(n + 1)$, indicating an incentive to free-ride by avoiding contribution c_i. The NE occurs at $D(0)$: none contribute.

With regard to negotiation and the Coase theorem, both Figure 2.8 and equation (2.2) imply that a larger N creates a greater bargaining problem for participants. Coase himself says as much (1960, 18). This difficulty reflects transaction costs arising from a greater potential for internal conflict, problems of coordination, and the like. In fact, a bargaining

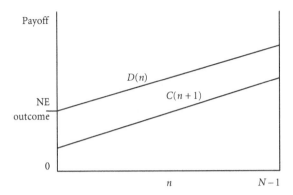

Figure 2.8   Multi-player PD

solution itself constitutes a type of public good; individuals may hesitate to invest resources in designing a resolution from which all could benefit—especially when resolution entails conceding resources or reputation.

Negative Externalities and Common-Pool Resources

Because pure public goods confer equal positive benefits to all irrespective of contribution levels, we may represent a public-good CAP with only one equation (2.2). Externalities, on the other hand, imply that the impacts of contribution (or production) extend beyond private costs and benefits and so may affect various parties differently.[25] Often the magnitude of such impacts depends on how many others contribute to (or participate in) specific activities.

Consider the following framework. There are $N = 1,000$ players (agents). Each agent chooses between activities C and D, where C connotes participation in any activity that creates externalities, and D connotes either nonparticipation or participation in an alternative activity. We call those who choose C *contributors* and those who choose D *noncontributors*. We shall explore the following three cases:

  (i) Activity C generates (positive or negative) externalities, which are proportionate to n, for the n contributors, but generates no externalities for noncontributors; D generates no externalities for anyone.

 (ii) Externalities from C also spill over to noncontributors, but D generates no externalities.

(iii) Both C and D generate externalities that may affect anyone.

There are many possibilities, but here we focus on a few illustrative cases.

Versions of Chicken: Common-Pool Resources, Fish, and Auto Emissions

We consider classic and complex CPR problems. A *classic* CPR problem fits case (i): only CPR users experience the negative externalities from use that may lead to depletion. *Complex*

CPRs exhibit more widespread externalities—as in cases (ii) and (iii).[26] For either type of CPR, an N-player chicken game offers a useful modeling tool.

Suppose that salmon fishing in the Pacific Northwest presents a classic CPR problem, but cod fishing poses no such problem. Fishing salmon generates high payoffs when there are few participants (n), but net benefits decline as n increases. By contrast, cod are so plentiful, that fishing does not deplete the resource (or returns to fishers), and cod fishing generates no externalities. We represent the strategic choice of a marginal agent who considers expected payoffs from salmon and cod fishing as functions of the number of others who are expected to fish salmon (n). The function $C(n + 1)$ describes the agent's expected payoff from fishing salmon, and $D(n)$ describes the corresponding payoff from fishing cod (which is independent of n in this case). Define h as the payoff from fishing salmon if $n = 0$, and let α represent the (constant) marginal effect of each salmon fisher on the payoffs to other salmon fishers; q shows the payoff from fishing cod.[27] We have payoff functions

(2.3)
$$C(n + 1) = h - \alpha n,$$

(2.4)
$$D(n) = q.$$

At low levels of n, salmon fishing has higher payoffs than cod fishing: $h > q$. Figure 2.9 illustrates this game where $n \in \{0, N - 1\}$. At the NE (n^*), the expected payoffs to strategies C and D are equal. Solving for n^*, we have

(2.5)
$$n^* = (h - q)/\alpha.$$

Whenever $0 < n^* < N$, we have an N-player game of chicken. At n^*, no player wants to unilaterally switch activities. This equilibrium is stable because small deviations in one direction create incentives to move in the opposite direction: whenever $n < n^*$, $C(n + 1) > D(n)$, leading to an increase in n; the converse statement also holds.[28] Unlike two-person chicken (in pure strategies), at n^* there is no distributional inequality at the margin (if we assume continuous payoff functions).[29]

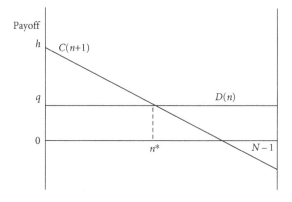

Figure 2.9   Salmon CPR problem

Yet, comparing n^* with n_{so}, the socially optimal level of n, we find a potential for distributional conflict that would complicate CAPs associated with attempts to reach n_{so}. Here is the logic. Equation (2.6) shows the total social payoff (T) as a function of n:[30]

$$(2.6) \qquad\qquad T(n) = n(h - \alpha n) + (N - n)q.$$

Using the relevant first-order condition for maximizing T with respect to n, it can be shown that

$$(2.7) \qquad\qquad n_{so} = (h - q)/2\alpha.$$

Thus the socially optimal number of salmon fishers is half of that at the NE. At n_{so}, moreover, fishing salmon earns higher returns: $C(n_{so}) > D(n_{so})$. This distributional inequity implies that a fishing community may face substantial difficulties in deciding which of its members should abandon salmon for cod. Even with an agreement, the community may face a second-order CAP of enforcing it.

As with the two-player PD game, a well-informed external authority could resolve this CAP. A sufficient tax on salmon could equate the expected returns to C and D at n_{so}, so that $n^* = n_{so}$. As an alternative, authorities could assign property rights over salmon to a single agent who may then manage the resource in a sustainable fashion—assuming the agent does not discount future payoffs excessively.[31] But as Ostrom (1990) points out, both remedies may face unresolvable problems. For the first, authorities may not know enough to assign an optimal tax rate or may face difficulties collecting taxes. For the second, authorities may be unable to adequately define, much less enforce, property rights over entities like international ocean fisheries.

Complex CPRs typically present larger CAPs. Consider pollution: automobile emissions pollute the air not only for auto users, they pollute the air for everyone—indicating a standard negative-externality problem. To see pollution as a CPR problem, think of clean air as a rival, non-exclusive resource that pollution depletes. In terms of modeling, this problem fits case (ii): activity C (driving a car) confers negative externalities on both those who engage in C (motorists) and those who engage in D (bike riders). With equivalent background assumptions and terms, the $C(n + 1)$ function remains as shown by equation (2.3), but $D(n)$ becomes

$$(2.8) \qquad\qquad D(n) = q - \gamma n,$$

where q denotes the payoff to $D(0)$, and γ shows the per-driver external costs imposed on bike riders; again, $h > q$. Solving for n^* and n_{so} reveals that, for given levels of h, q, and α, both n^* and n_{so} indicate lower levels of n than for a classic CPR case. This result is not surprising since activity C now creates additional externalities. Furthermore, the discrepancy between n^* and n_{so} is greater for complex CPRs.[32]

The size and distributional elements of complex CPRs may likewise complicate the resolution of CAPs. For a classic CPR, we treat N as a subset of society that is limited to users of a resource, whereas, for a complex CPR, N can represent society at large. With a (much) larger N, transaction costs of negotiation may be higher by orders of magnitude. Note also that the larger difference $n^* - n_{so}$ indicates greater potential for distributional strife related to negotiating or enforcing any resolution. Therefore, complex CPRs may not respond to organizational or policy solutions that could, in principle, resolve the CAPs related to classic CPRs.

Network Externalities: Assurance, Path Dependence, and Punctuated Equilibria

A third important category of multi-agent CAPs relates to positive *network externalities*—that is, external benefits to activities that increase with the number of agents pursuing the same activity. Such activities fit case (iii) under "Negative Externalities" and, more importantly, lead to path-dependent punctuated equilibria. For example, the benefits to users of an operating system, such as Windows, increase with the number of others who use the same system. So once Windows became well established, potential users had an incentive to use it. The same principle applies to other technologies and activities—such as skill acquisition—for which individual benefits depend on learning economies and interactions with others.

In order to model network externalities, we suppose that the payoffs from both activities C and D increase in the number of people choosing the same activity. For example, let C represent choosing Unix as one's operating system, and let D represent choosing Windows.[33] Defining n as the number of other users who choose Unix, we have

$$(2.9) \qquad\qquad C(n + 1) = h + \alpha n,$$

$$(2.10) \qquad\qquad D(n) = q + \gamma(N - n) = (q + \gamma N) - \gamma n,$$

where $\alpha > 0$ and $\gamma > 0$.[34] The presence of network externalities implies that $h < q$: with few users of Unix, Windows yields higher benefits. But when $n = N - 1$, Unix offers the higher benefits. Thus we have an N-player game of assurance with three Nash equilibria: $n_L = 0$, $n_H = N - 1$, and $n^* = (q + \gamma N - h)/(\alpha + \gamma)$. The internal equilibrium (n^*) is unstable; for any $n < n^*$, payoffs from strategy D exceed those from C; hence the NE moves to $n = 0$, while the converse holds for all $n > n^*$.[35] The internal NE thus becomes a *tipping point*: a critical mass of some activity beyond which momentum builds toward an equilibrium in which all (or most) agents pursue that activity (as in Schelling 1978).

This game's property of path dependence implies a possible CAP of coordination. Suppose that the highest total payoff occurs at n_H (so that $n_{so} = N - 1$) and that society starts in a situation with $n < n^*$. In this case, the NE will move to n_L, where all players choose strategy D. Shifting activity to n_{so} would constitute a large coordination CAP, one of inducing more than n^* players to switch—simultaneously—from strategy D to C. Now suppose that some authority hopes to persuade the minimal number (i.e., $n^* + 1$) to switch to C but that switching cannot be perfectly simultaneous. Those who do not volunteer, or those who volunteer last, will receive higher payoffs than those who switch early. A distributional issue thus complicates achieving coordination: some unlucky members must switch first. This late-mover advantage complicates resolution, as sufficient assurance may not be forthcoming. Numerous political-economy problems exhibit such a wait-and-see property. In political conflicts, many hesitate before switching sides. Such hesitancy, combined with some potential for large-scale shift, generates punctuated equilibria. For example, the political regime in Eastern Europe survived until a critical mass of opposition arose in 1989.

William Easterly (2002) identifies a similar path-dependent relationship between complementary skills and economic development.[36] An individual's payoff to investing time and energy into acquiring such skills depends on how many others do the same. We may call activity C investing in skill acquisition (e.g., staying in school) and activity D not investing (e.g., working instead of school). Below some critical mass of accumulated human capital within a society, individual payoffs from such investment are negative. Accordingly, societies with low average levels of human capital may become trapped in a path-dependent punctuated equilibrium of low development. Achieving significant growth would then require a large and coordinated shift of activity toward skill acquisition. Using similar logic, Easterly states that "poverty is a failure of coordination" (168). Chapter 13 will expand on this point.

2.4. CONCLUSION: CLIMATE CHANGE AS A MULTI-DIMENSIONAL CAP

Consider the myriad collective-action problems associated with climate change.[37] The models presented in this book offer considerable insight into these CAPs. One might consider an amenable (sustainable, desirable) climate as a global public good. Initially, we can represent the core CAP as a two-player game in which players North and South (respectively developed and developing countries) decide between limiting carbon emissions (C) and not limiting (D). Because strategy C is costly to each player, yet mutually beneficial if jointly adopted, the game has a PD structure with an NE at (D, D). Even so, if the players could act as either individuals or unified organizations, it may be possible to strike a bargain.

More realistically, each of these "players" represents an only semi-coherent amalgam of countries whose interests differ. Their global interactions may resemble a multi-player PD game with low prospects for resolution. Furthermore, within each country, a collection of interests (e.g., firms, organizations, or agencies) influences decisions.[38] N-player games of assurance or chicken may then represent the associated difficulties of internal coordination and possible distributional conflict over assigning limitation costs. What is more, countries may encounter difficulties even as they seek to establish a workable bargaining position, and stated promises to abide by international agreements may lack credibility. Absent national and international mechanisms for coordination and enforcement, something close to zero-contribution emerges. This was arguably the outcome of the United Nations Copenhagen Climate Change Conference of December 2009.

From another perspective, the climate itself is a (huge) complex CPR that fits case (iii) from Section 2.3. Production activity emits carbon and other greenhouse gases, depleting the climate resource. Suppose there are two types of production: clean, non-carbon-intensive (C) and dirty, carbon-intensive (D). In terms of an N-player chicken game, the current NE may reflect predominant use of D, whereas the SO may require much greater use of C. Attempts to shift toward more reliance on C would encounter significant distributional conflict. In the current climate debate, we observe sharp differences among countries and various constituencies concerning the problem's existence, nature, and severity, along with how to assign responsibility and share costs.

From a third angle, the process of creating a low-carbon economy resembles a path-dependent multi-player game of assurance. Suppose there are two possible technology regimes: clean (C) and dirty (D). Each generates its own network externalities because R&D, skill sets, and needed infrastructure are complementary within each regime. Establishing either regime involves enormous fixed costs associated with the technical design and construction of infrastructure, such as a system of highways with accessible gas stations. Once established, a technology regime becomes a path-dependent punctuated equilibrium. From this perspective, the current situation resembles a multi-player game of assurance with its current NE at $n = 0$ (all choose D). Switching to a C regime would require orchestrating a massive shift from D to C—enough to pass a distant n^*. Distributional conflict abounds: the coal industry, for example, may oppose any reallocation. Other, less interested players may adopt a wait-and-see strategy.

Global climate change thus generates multiple problems of free-riding, distributional conflict, and coordination that lend themselves to representation via this chapter's models. Many other political-economy problems invite similar representation. The sovereign debt crisis in Europe (as of October 2012) indicates a similar series of multi-national, national, and internal CAPs related to distribution, coordination, and enforcement among a smaller but still huge set of individuals, interests, coalitions, and governments.

Overall, for problems that involve few players, transparent activities, and access to low-cost enforcement, Coasian bargaining could yield agreements that resolve relevant first-order CAPs. Yet, absent such conditions, our models tend to reiterate Hardin's tragedy of the commons and Olson's zero-contribution thesis. Furthermore, given the ubiquity of divergent distributional interests and incomplete information about others' intentions—along with multiple problems of coordination—stated agreements often lack credibility. Multiple second-order CAPs thus emerge.

In pursuit of this theme, Chapter 3 discusses the substantial second-order CAPs that accompany efforts to orchestrate coordination and implement mechanisms of enforcement. But first, we offer the following transitional reflection. The potential for productive exchange—and, indeed, prospects for economic development—depend upon implicit and explicit contracts: promises to deliver on a specified set of commitments. Stated promises, however, often invite temptations to cheat or seek self-advantage at the expense of other parties—variations on free-riding. Otherwise, contracts would not be necessary. Consider Figure 2.2, the basic PD game; strategy C can represent the faithful execution of a contract, while D can represent cutting corners or pilfering. Likewise, before signing a contract, C can represent truthful revelation of one's situation or abilities, including limitations, while D may represent partial concealment or outright deception. Like the more traditional free-riding CAPs in this chapter, resolution of contracting CAPs requires establishing reliable commitments that, in turn, depend on achieving sufficient coordination, enforcement, and/or trust. On this basis, we now turn to problems of orchestrating coordination and enforcement—that is, to second-order collective-action problems.

EXERCISES

2.1. Draw a sequential game of chicken in extensive (game tree) form and use it to explain the presence of first-mover advantage.

2.2. Draw a sequential game of battle in extensive form and use it to explain the presence of first-mover advantage.

2.3. Prove the assertion that if G is fixed, as N increases, a game represented by equation (2.2) becomes more likely to have a PD structure.

2.4. Derive equation (2.7) by taking the relevant derivative of equation (2.6).

2.5. Prove that the NE (n^*) in a complex CPR game occurs at a higher level of n than that for a classic CPR game, like the one in Figure 2.9.

2.6. Solve for the SO in the complex CPR game shown in equations (2.3) and (2.8). Is it at a higher or lower level of n than the SO for the classic CPR game, shown in equations (2.3) and (2.4)?

2.7. Prove that the difference $n^* - n_{so}$ is greater for the complex CPR case than for the classic CPR case.

2.8. Draw a diagram that illustrates the model expressed by equations (2.9) and (2.10).

3 COORDINATION, ENFORCEMENT, AND SECOND-ORDER COLLECTIVE-ACTION PROBLEMS

> A credible threat of collective, multilateral punishment supported the beliefs that the short-run gain from cheating today was less than the long-run benefit of being honest.
>
> Avner Greif (2006a)

Suppose that communities Arruba and Boratonia notice their common interest in maintaining their resource and agree to set aside immediate self-interest in order to limit each community's withdrawals from their shared well. Given the stakes involved, why should either trust the other to abide by the agreement? Perhaps their community councils genuinely intend to abide, but council and community are not the same entity. What will deter individuals within each community from using extensively for their own gain? If a few defect, others may do the same until the agreement collapses into rounds of hostile accusations. If both communities are "small" in Olson's sense, each might invoke selective social sanctions—perhaps praise for honorable cooperators and scorn for greedy defectors. We postpone discussion of social sanctions until after Chapter 5's discussion of social preference. In the meantime, we ask: Is there some purely material mechanism that might restrain potential defectors from pursuing their self-interest?

The fundamental exchanges that underlie micro- and macro-level economic development depend upon the ability of involved parties to create and implement credible commitments. Establishing credibility is thus a core problem in political economy. Such commitment, in turn, requires resolution of second-order collective-action problems (CAPs) of orchestrating reliable coordination, enforcement, and even trust. The associated difficulties suggest that material incentives alone offer only partial and costly remedies. Chapter 2 addressed first-order CAPs of free-riding: divergences between individual and group interests that emerge from interactions that generate or depend upon some form of (broadly defined) public good, externality, and/or common-pool resource. Although involved parties could, in principle, resolve these CAPs by agreeing to restrain self-interest for the common good, Olson (1971) suggests that, in the absence of some form of selective social or material incentive (or *sanctions;* here defined as either punishment or reward), such commitments typically lack credibility. Thus resolution of second-order CAPs precedes resolution of first-order CAPs by fostering credible commitments.

We define a *credible commitment* as one that involved parties would find in their interest to honor in any contingency (likely or not) for which adherence could be called for. Credible commitment, in turn, depends upon social mechanisms that can somehow orchestrate coordination, enforcement, and trust. Either the involved groups or society at large must somehow institute measures that encourage individuals to set aside some individual interests for some mutual benefit. Reliable contracts, for example, depend on procedures that induce parties to honestly reveal pertinent capabilities or qualities (of relevant people, services, or products) before entering agreements—and also to faithfully execute stated commitments. Yet such procedures or mechanisms constitute public goods: contributing to their design and provision is costly, and benefits can ensue without contribution. The attendant processes of mechanism design and implementation involve *second-order* CAPs, CAPs whose raison d'être arises from first-order CAPs.[1]

Thus, given the nearly universal presence of incomplete information and ensuing transaction costs, resolving first-order CAPs requires more than just agreements to address primary (or explicit) divergences between individual and group interests. Involved parties must also confront secondary divergences of interests with respect to designing, organizing, and implementing social mechanisms that can coordinate and enforce agreed-upon behavior—so that primary agreements become credible. Note, however, that the analytical relevance of second-order CAPs—like that of most other modeling tools—depends on the focus of inquiry. Modeling enforcement might not, for example, significantly improve our understanding of price and quantity outcomes for transparent exchanges that operate in environments with well-established procedures for enforcing applicable property rights. On the other hand, analyzing second-order CAPs yields considerable insight into the following macro and micro issues: the political economy of development; achieving financial stability; business cycles; short- and long-term growth; operating a currency union or free-trade area; the distribution of income or wealth; reliable contracting; technical change; motivating employees or managers; and discrimination by race or gender—along with many other public-good, externality, and common-pool resource problems. Establishing credible commitments in any of these areas requires constructing and implementing reliable social mechanisms of coordination and enforcement.

Our discussion proceeds as follows. Section 3.1 relates problems of coordination and enforcement to transaction costs, stressing the role of asymmetric information. Section 3.2 addresses coordination and enforcement under conditions of complete information. It finds some potential for external enforcement in one-time encounters and for internal enforcement in repeated encounters. Section 3.3 introduces incomplete, asymmetric information. This section asserts that information asymmetry compromises both of Section 3.2's solutions; yet the analysis also points to possible internal enforcement mechanisms—at the expense of added transaction costs. Section 3.4 concludes somewhat pessimistically: absent functioning organizations or agencies that possess enough will and information to administer selective sanctions, we nearly replicate Mancur Olson's zero-contribution thesis. Even so, analyzing second-order CAPs clarifies the dynamics of coordination and enforcement and suggests some potential for resolution via internal efforts to structure incentives.

3.1. THE ECONOMICS OF TRANSACTION COSTS

As discussed in Chapter 2, transaction costs play a central role in the theories of Coase and North. Only in the absence of transaction costs does Coase expect negotiation to fully resolve problems of social costs. North focuses on specifying the nature of transaction costs—in particular, their origins in incomplete information and their relationship to institutions.[2]

Transaction costs reflect the expenses of attaining the coordination and commitment that allow exchange to occur. One category of transaction costs reflects the need for spatial and temporal coordination of exchange (Milgrom and Roberts 1992). The New York Stock Exchange (NYSE), for instance, opens at 9:30 a.m. and closes at 4:00 p.m. (Eastern Time); it is located at 11 Wall Street; and it lists offerings at http://www.nyse.com. All three of these specifications serve as simple, but necessary, coordination mechanisms.

More complex elements of transaction costs arise from asymmetric information. Following North (1990, 27–28), we identify three information-based sources of transaction costs:

(i)   measuring the precise attributes to be exchanged;

(ii) specifying rights that could be transferred; and

(iii) enforcing related commitments (agreements) concerning attributes, rights, and activities.[3]

Items (i) and (ii) matter because coordinating exchange requires shared understandings of the qualities, services, and rights that could be exchanged. For example, exchanging even simple items like pieces of fruit requires measuring what is transferred (e.g., number of pieces, volume, or weight)—along with some buyer inspection prior to purchase—all at some cost. At a more complex level, health insurance and mortgage contracts delineate multiple contingencies that are difficult to foresee and specify. Exchange nonetheless requires some shared, though often incomplete, perception of relevant attributes (e.g., costs of insurance policies; possible values of claims) as well as conditions under which rights will be transferred (when certain types of claims can be filed). These shared understandings coordinate exchange processes by allowing buyers and sellers to assess whether and when they want to engage in exchange. Without such assessment, exchange is unlikely to occur or develop.

At a more foundational level, processes of specifying rights of transfer and ownership become methods of defining applicable property rights. Such definition involves a complex set of political decisions regarding the conditions under which specific parties—whose interests likely differ—attain rights of transfer or control over products, services, income flows, and various assets, including the means of production. For many analytical questions, the outcome of the relevant political/historical processes may be taken for granted; when estimating next month's price of corn in Iowa, we need not analyze the state's political origins. We thus postpone examining this essential (and contested) side of defining property rights until Part III's discussion of institutions.

Item (iii), the enforcement side of transaction costs, reflects a need for monitoring adherence to agreements and also for implementing mechanisms that can provide selective sanctions—be they positive (rewards) or negative (punishments). For example, homeowners who hire plumbers often lack confidence that the work performed will meet desired standards. Owners may then spend time observing or inspecting, and might refuse payment if the final outcome appears unsatisfactory. In principle, either second or third parties may administer such enforcement. Here *second parties* are the exchange parties themselves or relevant social groups or communities to which they belong, while *third parties* are external enforcers who neither participate in such exchanges nor belong to the relevant groups. Third-party enforcement typically arises from an agency of the state, although for some problems, non-state agencies (such as professional review boards) serve as third parties. The American Medical Association (AMA), for example, enforces rules associated with a wide variety of medical practices. Whether one regards the AMA as a second or a third party depends on the question or level of analysis. For a localized group of physicians, the AMA serves as a third party; for the medical profession as a whole, it constitutes a second party.

Transaction costs therefore belong at the center of economic analysis, along with production costs. Exchange occurs when perceived benefits exceed the expected sum of both types of costs. For North, transaction costs—particularly those associated with enforcement—are the chief impediment to extending the division of labor, the chief reason for the existence of institutions, and, ultimately, the chief obstacle to economic development:

> But one cannot take enforcement for granted. It is (and always has been) the critical obstacle of increasing specialization and the division of labor. Enforcement poses no problem when it is in the interests of the other party to live up to the agreements. But without institutional constraints, self-interested behavior will foreclose complex exchange, because of the uncertainty that the other party will find it in his or her interest to live up to the agreement. The transaction cost will reflect the uncertainty by including a risk premium, the magnitude of which will turn on the likelihood of defection by the other party and the consequent costs to the first party. Throughout history the size of this premium has largely foreclosed complex exchange and therefore limited the possibilities of economic growth. (1990, 33)

In order to relate transaction costs to second-order CAPs, we now turn to modeling coordination and enforcement.

3.2. COORDINATION AND ENFORCEMENT WITH COMPLETE INFORMATION

This section opens by using game-theoretic logic to address second-order CAPs that pertain to spatial and temporal coordination, noting the importance of their resolution. It proceeds to model enforcement under conditions of complete information, finding that resolution of second-order CAPs follows if enforcement procedures generate sufficiently high expected costs to defection.

Problems of spatiotemporal coordination arise whether or not the involved parties' interests are aligned. For aligned interests, assurance games can represent CAPs of choosing mutually beneficial locations, whereas nonaligned interests suggest games of battle that illustrate conflict over how to coordinate. In the former case, coordination among multiple parties with multiple strategies involves focusing expectations on a single set of strategies. For example, participants in the NYSE could, in principle, meet at 33rd and 3rd (or any other New York address); the exchange could open at 7:30 a.m. and close at 11:04 p.m.; it could use a different website. Coordinating on times and places thus resembles multi-player games of assurance, where any mutual choice of specific locational or temporal strategies (e.g., meeting at 11 Wall Street) creates substantial network externalities.

Second-order CAPs in such instances involve allocating the transaction costs of constructing mechanisms that can focus the activities of multiple agents on specific times and places. These mechanisms are public goods: they are costly to provide, and, once in place, potential "consumers" can benefit without contributing. Either second or third parties can provide the needed mechanisms. For example, for individual stockbrokers, the NYSE is a third party that coordinates activity to facilitate trading stock. Membership fees cover the costs of provision.[4]

In cases of nonaligned interests, various parties who benefit from possible coordination prefer different arrangements. To illustrate, suppose that stock trader 1 lives in Manhattan and trader 2 lives in Queens. Both would gain from a single stock exchange, but each prefers a location in her own neighborhood. Their CAP of coordinating location resembles the battle game shown in Figure 3.1. Distributional strife may even preclude coordination: if each insists on her preferred location, they could end up at outcome (M, Q), where both earn zero payoffs. Adding players and multiple locations would, as Olson's logic suggests, further complicate resolution.

Greater challenges arise from the tendency of nonaligned interests to generate CAPs of enforcement. As noted, credible commitments to abide by agreements that might conflict with parties' interests require prior creation of enforcement mechanisms. Like coordination mechanisms, enforcement mechanisms typically possess public-good attributes, and the related expenses indicate an important type of transaction cost. Enforcement, however, tends to conflict more directly with individual interests and invites more conflict among involved parties. The ensuing second-order CAPs may prevent resolution of first-order CAPs. Hence their presence further justifies Olson's zero-contribution hypothesis.

In order to illustrate enforcement CAPs, we begin with a few counterexamples. In situations where parties can take well-informed external enforcement for granted, second-order CAPs do not arise because potential violators of cooperative agreements can expect to be observed, reported, and sanctioned. Sufficient transparency combined with reliable external enforcement thereby lends credibility to agreements to avoid free-riding. Figure 2.7 offered a two-player example. With sufficiently high values for p and/or r, an agreement to play C would be credible, and the first-order CAP would be resolved. Figure 3.2 presents a related sequential reporting game. A shopper and owner have agreed to exchange goods

		Trader 2	
		M	Q
Trader 1	M	2, 1	0, 0
	Q	0, 0	1, 2

Figure 3.1   Battle over location

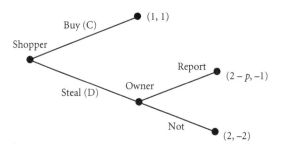

Figure 3.2   Reporting game

for money with no stealing. The shopper moves first, choosing between Buy (C; honor the contract) and Steal (D; violate it). The owner may then either Report a theft to an authority or Not report. In the case of a report, authorities automatically administer punishment p. As long as $p > 1$, the outcome is (Buy, Not report). A slightly more complicated example might combine Figures 2.7 and 3.2 into a two-stage game.[5] Note, however, that we assume the following: the owner observes the shopper's actions perfectly at no cost; reporting costs nothing; external agents (e.g., police) always punish reported violators; and the owner would never want to report a paying shopper. Any of these assumptions could be violated.

We now turn to a multi-player game with perfect observation and external enforcement. Recall that equation (2.2) represents a basic multi-player public-good CAP. Suppose now that each player has agreed to contribute an amount $c_i = c$, and that observation, reporting, and external enforcement are costless. Any contributor could report a violator, in which case authorities would administer p. The ensuing potential for sanctioning violators transforms the game so that

$$(3.1) \qquad y_i = q_i - c_i + \alpha \sum_{j=1}^{N} c_j - p;$$

here, if $c_i \geq c$, $p = 0$; otherwise, $p > 0$. Recall that y_i denotes individual income, q_i is initial endowment, and α is the marginal benefit from contribution; there are no fixed costs, and i belongs to group $j = 1, \ldots, N$.

Whenever $p > c - \alpha$, each player has an incentive to adhere to the stated agreement. Having resolved the second-order CAP, negotiations over levels c_i can then resolve the first-order CAP. Note that the underlying assumptions of perfect costless observation, reporting, and external enforcement (combined with zero costs to spatiotemporal coordination) meet the information conditions of the Coase theorem.[6] This set of assumptions can apply when well-established institutions of third-party coordination and enforcement render cooperative agreements credible.

To proceed, we drop the assumptions of costless reporting and third-party enforcement but retain complete information. Administering enforcement must now depend, at least in part, on costly activities conducted among relevant second parties. Any group that faces a free-rider problem might still resolve a first-order CAP with an agreement to cooperate backed up by a second agreement that each member will report or punish violations. But if the costs to an individual of reporting or administering punishment exceed his gains from doing so, the second agreement will lack credibility, undermining the first. Free-riding ensues.

Returning to Figure 3.2, suppose we add a cost of reporting (or punishing) that exceeds an owner's benefit from doing so (a cost greater than 3). The backwards-induction outcome then becomes (S, N), or (Steal, Not report). A community of such owners now confronts a second-order CAP. They need to design and implement a social mechanism that will credibly enforce their initial agreement to cooperate. Without reliable enforcement, owners will not stock their stores.

More generally, under many payoff configurations, parties that might agree to cooperate on resolving first-order CAPs encounter multi-player second-order CAPs of enforcement. We can represent such second-order CAPs with a variant of equation (2.2). Defining g as contribution to an enforcement mechanism and β as each player's marginal gain from contribution (via induced cooperation with primary agreement at the margin), we have

$$(3.2) \qquad y_i = q_i - g_i + \beta \sum_{j=1}^{N} g_j.$$

Mimicking (2.2), if $\beta < 1$ and $N\beta > g$, the parties face an N-player prisoners' dilemma CAP—now of second order.

We may illustrate relationships between first- and second-order CAPs with a two-stage process involving equations (3.1) and (3.2). Players first decide their individual contribution levels $c_i \geq 0$ (in (3.1)); next, the cooperators among them decide whether to administer punishment $p_{ij} \geq 0$ (from (3.2)) to defectors. Combining these decisions into one equation yields

$$(3.3) \qquad y_i = q_i - c_i + \alpha \sum_{j=1}^{N} c_j - n p_{ji} - \gamma(N - n) p_{ij}.$$

The first three terms on the right-hand side duplicate terms in (3.1). As in Chapter 2, N denotes group size, and n is the number of cooperators. The fourth term indicates the total punishment that player i can expect to receive from n cooperating j players, if it decides to defect. The final term shows the total cost to player i of administering punishment p_{ij} (not p_{ji}) to $N - n$ defectors if i cooperates. Here $\gamma > 0$ is the marginal cost of administering a unit of punishment to a single defector. Note that if $c_i > c_{min}$ (the minimum acceptable contribution), then $p_{ji} = 0$: nobody punishes cooperators.[7]

Backwards induction in this model works as follows. In the second stage, if $\gamma > 0$, cooperators will not punish defectors, meaning that nobody contributes to the second-order public good of administering punishment. Thus, whenever $\alpha < 1$, the equilibrium outcome is $c_i = p_i = 0$ for all i.[8] Failure to resolve the second-order CAP undermines the credibility of possible agreements to cooperate on the first-order CAP. We can thus restate Olson's thesis as follows: an unwillingness to contribute to creating a mechanism for selective sanctions results in zero contribution to collective goods.

A two-player game replicates this problem and suggests alternative enforcement regimes. Ignoring endowments q_i, Figure 3.3 translates equation (3.3) into a symmetrical

First stage

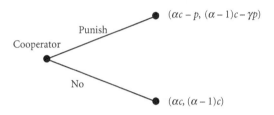

Second stage

Cooperator — Punish → $(\alpha c - p, (\alpha - 1)c - \gamma p)$

Cooperator — No → $(\alpha c, (\alpha - 1)c)$

Figure 3.3   Two-stage public-good game

two-player, two-stage game. In the first stage, players choose C or D. Given that $N = 2$, the payoffs to strategy combinations (C, C) and (D, D) follow. If one player chooses C and the other D, the game moves to the second stage, where the C-player decides whether or not to punish the D-player (in Figure 3.3's second stage, the D-player's payoff is listed first). Whenever $\gamma > 0$, the second-stage outcome is No. To solve the entire game, we redraw the first stage and replace "*next stage*" with the second-stage payoffs to No. Once again, with $\alpha < 1$, the players face a public-good PD game: because no cooperator will punish a defector, we find zero contribution.[9]

By varying basic relationships (or rules) within games of this nature, we can represent different kinds of sanctioning arrangements (or regimes) that could influence agents' incentives to cooperate or defect:

1. Who punishes whom: (i) Cs punish Ds as in prior examples; (ii) all punish Ds; (iii) Ds punish Cs; (iv) Cs punish Ds and Ds punish Cs.

2. External punishment (p_e): (i) $p_e = 0$ (as assumed in Figure 3.3); (ii) $0 < p_e < 1 - \alpha$, indicating that resolution still requires internal punishment, but less than in Figure 3.3; (iii) $p_e > 1 - \alpha$; indicating no need for internal punishment (given sufficient observation); (iv) external and internal punishment mechanisms conflict (e.g., external punishes D but internal punishes C).

3. Rewards for cooperators (r): Introducing costs of administering rewards yields implications similar to those of γ in equation (3.3) and Figure 3.3. Variations analogous to items 1 and 2 above are possible.

4. Imperfect observation: Probability ε of observing either C or D ($\varepsilon < 1$) alters expected payoffs to p or r.

5. Number of players: $N \geq 2$.

6. Spillover effects: For example, γ could increase or decrease in the number or proportion of Cs or Ds or in the proportion of N taking the same action. Games of assurance or chicken may follow.[10]

These variations highlight the versatility of game-theoretic modeling. Many social arrangements fit one or more of these possible cases, and all of the listed contingencies affect the credibility of agreements to resolve first-order CAPs. The reader is encouraged to reflect upon and model these possibilities.

An important variant of a second-order CAP, a "race to the bottom" phenomenon, can arise among external enforcers. Consider a group of agents that act as third-party enforcers for transactions among others—perhaps a group of local governments hopes to enforce local pollution regulations. A two-stage sequence of two-player games (four total players) can illustrate. In the first stage, firms A and B play the PD game of Figure 2.2, now associated with limiting pollution. In the second stage, local governments E and F play a similar game with respect to administering punishment (fines to polluters). Because pollution crosses borders, E and F hope to cooperate in administering fines. If fining polluters is costly to governments (e.g., firms may relocate, decreasing tax revenue), $\gamma > 0$ and E and F face a PD game in which C means "fine polluters" and D means "do not fine." Consequently, an agreement between E and F to cooperate on enforcement would lack credibility. Anticipating a (D, D) outcome in the second stage, firms A and B also defect; they pollute.[11] This race-to-the-bottom outcome may help explain why potential polluters sometimes prefer state to national regulation. It may also apply to international location of firms or banks with respect to taxes and environmental, labor, or financial regulations.

By focusing on nonrepetitive interactions, the preceding examples indicate that—even with complete information—the transaction costs of administering enforcement create second-order CAPs that can undermine resolution of first-order CAPs. Introducing repeated interactions, however, generates new dynamics that permit some limited potential for internal enforcement.

Contingent Strategies, Tit-for-Tat, and Second-Party Enforcement

There is one important qualification to our prior pessimistic assertions. Repeated interaction among a stable group of agents frequently creates transparent gains from sustained cooperation: the sum of payoffs from successive cooperative outcomes exceeds that from defection. With sufficient net gains to such cooperation, low enough discount rates, adequate observation, and high enough probabilities of continued relationships, specific strategies may offer interacting pairs (or other very small groups) low-cost avenues for internal enforcement. In such cases, coordination on strategic choices can resolve second-order CAPs and, by extension, first-order CAPs. But success depends on meeting specific conditions. We begin by discussing the most common contingent strategy, tit-for-tat, before moving to the second-order question of coordinating joint enactment.

A *tit-for-tat* (t-f-t) strategy involves playing C on the first move of a repeated game; for all subsequent moves, each player copies the other's previous move. Suppose two parties use a t-f-t strategy in repeated engagements. To evaluate its viability as an enforcement

		Player B	
		C	D
Player A	C	C, C	L, H
	D	H, L	D, D

Figure 3.4 Symmetric PD

mechanism, consider whether a player can profit from a unilateral one-time defection from t-f-t (i.e., by playing D once and then returning to t-f-t). Figure 3.4 redraws Figure 2.2 with symmetric payoffs. In an infinitely repeated game, unilateral one-time defection does not pay whenever the immediate gain from defection is less than the discounted cost of receiving the other player's retaliation in the next period—that is, whenever $(H - C) < \delta(C - D)$, where $\delta = 1/(1 + r)$; here δ is the discount factor and r is the discount rate.[12]

Repeated interactions among people, however, do not last forever. One can show that for finite two-player PD games of known duration, the Nash equilibrium is for both players to always defect.[13] Nevertheless, for finite games of uncertain duration, resolution via t-f-t is possible since neither player knows when the game will end. Assume now that the game in Figure 3.4 continues to the next period with probability $\rho < 1$. For example, there may be a small chance that an individual will die or a firm will go out of business. With $\rho < 1$, one-time defection against t-f-t does not pay whenever

$$(3.4) \qquad\qquad H - C < \rho\delta(C - D).$$

Four propositions immediately follow: tit-for-tat more easily sustains cooperation the

(i) lower the gains from defection $(H - C)$;

(ii) higher the post-defection punishment $(C - D)$;

(iii) higher the probability of continuation (ρ); and

(iv) greater the players' patience (meaning a higher δ or lower r).

One may relate each of these points to various internal or external influences. For example, the stage of the business cycle can affect the longevity of cooperation among firms. Likewise, the level of patience implied by δ (or impatience implied by r) may reflect internal utility, market interest rates, and/or perceptions of risk.

Imperfect observation may further compromise the effectiveness of t-f-t as a resolution mechanism. Let $\varepsilon \leq 1$ represent the probability that one player correctly observes defection by the other. One-time defection does not pay whenever

$$(3.5) \qquad\qquad (H - C) < \rho\delta[\varepsilon(C - D) + (1 - \varepsilon)C].$$

The lower ε is, the more difficult cooperative resolution becomes.

Imperfect observation of strategy C creates an even larger problem. Suppose that at some point player B chooses C, but A mistakenly observes D. Then A will retaliate by playing D on the next move. If B observes D correctly, then B will retaliate with D on the subsequent move and the players will enter a C → D → C → D cycle until one mistakes D for C. If we allow any incorrect observation of C or D, the expected long-run (infinite) outcome of t-f-t is that each player chooses C 50% of the time and D 50% of the time (Dixit and Nalebuff 1991, 111). That said, a less reactive contingent strategy—one that allows for possible mistakes by evaluating an observed D in light of a previous history of Cs—could avoid this potentially fatal pitfall.[14]

Now consider a choice between two related contingent strategies. In *suspicious* t-f-t (hereafter, st-f-t; Dawkins 2006, Chap. 12), a player opens with strategy D and then copies the other's previous move. If player A moves first using st-f-t and B follows using t-f-t, both would then play D for the duration of the game. Now suppose that, prior to a similar game, both players simultaneously choose between t-f-t and st-f-t. Figure 3.5 illustrates such a game. Here C^* and D^* denote (respectively) the expected discounted C and D payoffs for the game's duration and $(CD)^*$ and $(DC)^*$ indicate the same for alternating C-D sequences that start, respectively, with payoffs C and D. If equation (3.4) holds, we have a game of assurance. With only two players, t-f-t can emerge as a focal point, thereby resolving the second-order CAP of coordinating on strategies. Resolution of first-order CAPs may then follow.

Increasing the number of contingent strategies can magnify such coordination problems. Indeed, repeated games entail multiple contingent strategies, yielding huge numbers of Nash equilibria; the folk theorem of Fudenberg and Maskin (1986) formalizes this statement. Although this theorem also indicates that sufficient patience may enable many potential resolutions of second-order CAPs (t-f-t is one), coordinating on a single such strategy, by itself, presents a substantial second-order CAP. Achieving coordination may involve transaction costs, and conflicts of interest regarding preferred alternatives may arise (as in battle). Prospects for resolution may decline further with low probabilities of continuation and low probabilities of observation (low values of ρ and ε, respectively). Large group size exacerbates these difficulties, probably at exponential rates. Thus, even in repeated games with contingent strategies, second-order CAPs frequently undermine resolution of first-order CAPs; we remain approximately at Olson's zero-contribution outcome.

The foregoing discussion clearly implies a need for additional coordination and enforcement mechanisms. But first, we more fully address yet another layer of complication: incomplete information. This factor, perhaps surprisingly, can lead to additional enforcement strategies.

		Player B	
		t-f-t	st-f-t
Player A	t-f-t	C^*, C^*	$L + \rho\delta(DC)^*, H + \rho\delta(CD)^*$
	st-f-t	$H + \rho\delta(CD)^*, L + \rho\delta(DC)^*$	D^*, D^*

Figure 3.5   t-f-t and st-f-t

3.3. ASYMMETRIC INFORMATION, CONTRACTING, ENFORCEMENT, AND EXCHANGE

Asymmetric access to costly and incomplete information may further obstruct processes of creating credible agreements. The ensuing second-order CAPs may then undercut prospects for exchange, contracting, cooperation, and, ultimately, economic development. Yet, not surprisingly, participants often attempt to redress these problems. This section's models of asymmetric information not only deepen our understanding of the causes and nature of second-order CAPs, they also point to second-party (internal) resolution mechanisms—with their own set of implications: such mechanisms may fail to develop; they consume resources, indicating transaction costs; and they affect the distribution of gains in a manner that opens the door for exercises of power.

Before proceeding, note the game-theoretic distinction between *imperfect* and *incomplete* information. The former indicates a symmetrically distributed lack of knowledge regarding states of the relevant environment (external uncertainty) or an inability to observe contemporaneous or previous moves of other players (strategic uncertainty). The simultaneous games described in Section 3.2 are games of imperfect information. Incomplete information is more profound. It indicates asymmetric knowledge of the environment (asymmetric external uncertainty) or any lack of information related to the strategies available to others and the attributes of goods or services that could be exchanged, along with the characteristics, motivations, number, or even identity of other players.

Incomplete information facilitates opportunities for its manipulation, including withholding or distorting information and outright lying.[15] Second-order CAPs of coordination and enforcement follow. Broadly speaking, these CAPs may arise either before or after parties negotiate an agreement or conduct an exchange. We model the former by using the concept of adverse selection and the latter with the concept of moral hazard. Resolving either or both problems involves establishing social mechanisms, such as selection processes or contracts that achieve *incentive compatibility*: specifications whereby incentives induce agents to report honestly and/or abide by the terms of a contract (Hurwicz 1972).

Adverse selection arises from a tendency of parties to withhold or misrepresent private information concerning attributes of items, services, or persons (including themselves) that affect the nature or value of a subsequent exchange or agreement. Potential exchange participants may then lack some information related to appraising the desirability of possible agreements or exchanges. Adverse selection thus implies incomplete understandings of the de facto property rights subject to exchange. Collective-action problems of coordinating exchange follow. For example, sellers of used cars usually know more about the quality of their vehicles than do potential buyers; job seekers know more about their qualifications than do potential employers, while employers know more about announced jobs; and borrowers know more about their credit histories than do lenders. Such asymmetry can lead to undesirable or inefficient exchanges (or agreements) or even preclude desirable exchanges. Employers may hire poorly qualified workers, overlook qualified ones, or not even bother searching.

By contrast, the concept of moral hazard refers to problematic behavior that occurs only after agreements are made or contracts signed. *Moral hazard* (a term coined by the insurance industry to describe tendencies to engage in risky behavior after purchasing insurance) reflects "post-contractual opportunism" in situations where parties' interests are not fully aligned and where "actions that have efficiency consequences are not freely observable and so the person taking them may choose to pursue his or her private interests at others' expense" (Milgrom and Roberts 1992, 167). Stated commitments within various agreements may then lack credibility, and second-order CAPs emerge.

An Adverse Selection Model

George Akerlof's famous lemons model offers an intuitive example of how adverse selection undermines exchange. We represent his basic argument as a sequential game. Nature chooses the quality of each specific used car (q_i) with a uniform distribution (i.e., all values have the same probability of occurrence) such that $0 \leq q_i \leq 1$. Potential sellers observe nature's move but potential buyers do not. The following items are common knowledge: Sellers will accept any price (p_s) that is greater than the value of their specific car, $p_s > q_i$. Buyers will pay any price up to, say, 3/2 of a car's expected value ($p_b \leq (3/2)q^e$). Knowing only the uniform quality distribution, buyers estimate that $q^e = 1/2$. Thus buyers would offer only $p_b \leq (3/2)(q/2)$—that is, $p_b \leq (3/4)q$. Knowing this, any seller of a car with $q_i > 3/4$ would not place it on the market. Now the maximum q_i becomes 3/4, and so q^e falls to 3/8; hence all sellers of cars with $q_i > 3/8$ withhold their cars from the market. This (conceptual) backwards-induction process continues, leaving no cars with $q_i > 0$ on the market—the Nash equilibrium outcome. Potentially beneficial sales do not occur. Thus adverse selection has undermined the market: a strong form of market failure.[16]

Even so, individuals often attempt to circumvent adverse selection. Parties with superior goods or desirable abilities strive to credibly signal their quality, and potential buyers may screen for quality. Contracting devices (e.g., warranties) can signal quality by promising to reimburse buyers for low quality, potentially aligning incentives of sellers and buyers. Job interviews can screen for qualified applicants. These mechanisms, however, consume resources, indicating transaction costs. Game-theoretic signaling and screening models can represent such devices, and mechanism design theory can shed light on their effectiveness and efficiency (or lack thereof).[17]

Overall, the information asymmetries of adverse selection may render credible signaling or reliable screening so costly that sellers, buyers, and other participants will avoid conducting potentially beneficial exchanges or entering cooperative agreements. The long quotation from North near the end of Section 3.1, therefore, applies equally to problems of adverse selection: when the transaction costs of adverse selection are sufficiently high, parties will not commit to profitable exchanges or agreements. Under these conditions, markets fail to coordinate exchange, development, and growth. We have market failure writ large.

Incomplete Contracts, Principals, and Agents

Moral hazard generates second-order CAPs related to enforcing commitments made in contracts or agreements. Our analysis of these problems generates four basic assertions: first, exchange parties themselves must engage in enforcement activities; second, enforcement creates transaction costs, reducing efficiency; third, relevant markets often do not clear; and fourth, enforcement implies exercises of power.

We begin this discussion with an important labor market example. Suppose an employer hires a worker to make goods or perform services. While both parties want the firm to survive, the employer hopes to minimize costs, and the worker desires high pay and comfortable levels of effort. Worker effort matters economically because the quality and intensity of the effort exerted within each labor hour influences the value of output: diligent attention improves quality. Diligent effort is thus valuable to employers and costly for workers to provide. Asymmetric information enters because workers know their actual effort, whereas employers observe it only imperfectly and at a cost. Thus employers face problems motivating and enforcing high-quality effort among their workers.

Readers may recognize the preceding paragraph as a verbal summary of an effort model, a labor market variant of a principal-agent problem. Principal-agent problems portray the "canonical form of a moral hazard problem" (Bowles 2004, 250).[18] A *principal* signs a contract with an *agent* who agrees to perform services for (or provide information to) the principal. Moral hazard arises because their interests are not fully aligned and because the agent's actions or reports are not fully observable. The agent, following her own interests, may take action or withhold or distort information in a manner that compromises the principal's stated goals. The effort story offers a case in point: given incomplete and costly observation of worker activity, workers may not provide high-quality effort and/or fully share relevant information. Employees may, for example, spend work time answering private e-mail or fail to report problems with co-workers or machinery.[19]

In addition to labor contracts, similar principal-agent problems accompany such exchanges as home contracting, supplier relationships, loan agreements, and governance. For example, a homeowner and a plumber are, respectively, principal and agent. Analogously, some firms (principals) hire others (agents) to deliver quality inputs or perform services, such as legal advice. In financial markets, banks are principals and borrowers are agents. After securing loans, borrowers may undertake risky activities that increase default probabilities. The recent financial collapse testifies to the importance of principal-agent problems in finance. In democracies, governments are agents and citizens are principals.

The asymmetric information that underlies principal-agent (P-A) problems thus undermines commitments by agents to uphold certain goals of their respective principals, creating second-order enforcement CAPs. Because this information asymmetry resides within the process of exchange, external agencies frequently cannot provide adequate enforcement. Judicial officials, for example, know even less than employers do concerning the on-the-job effort exerted by specific employees. Moreover, relevant information that does exist is seldom verifiable.[20] In order to circumvent P-A problems, the involved parties must strive to design costly internal enforcement mechanisms—typically with the principal taking the lead, a first-mover advantage. We now turn to such mechanisms.

Arguably the most important internal enforcement mechanism for P-A problems is *contingent renewal*: a promise to continue a repeated relationship as long as certain conditions are met. In labor relations, an effort model (a type of efficiency wage model) illustrates how contingent renewal—when combined with monitoring of worker effort—can deliver internal, second-party enforcement. In addition to illustrating enforcement dynamics in labor relations, these models can explain patterns of interindustry wage differentials and the presence of involuntary unemployment (nonclearing labor markets).

Here is a summary of an effort model. Employers (principals) desire to elicit diligent effort or reliable information from workers (agents), who exercise discretion over both the quality and intensity of an hour's effort and over the information they share with employers.[21] Because competitive firms strive to minimize costs, they need to design (or negotiate) a mechanism that can elicit motivated effort and reliable information from their workers. Consequently, employers utilize a contingent renewal contract: they monitor workers and retain only those whose effort performance appears satisfactory. Workers who might contemplate on-the-job shirking face possible dismissal—a costly outcome that offers an incentive for motivated effort. Since the cost of dismissal depends on the wage, a profit-maximizing wage exceeds a hypothetical wage that would clear the labor market in the absence of this effort dynamic. Effort models thus offer microfoundations for the presence of involuntary unemployment. Their precise logic unfolds as follows.

We begin with three core assumptions that reflect stylized facts of the labor process:

1. The amount of work actually performed within the space of an hour cannot be fully specified in advance by contract; there are too many unforeseeable contingencies. For example, my contract with Grinnell College does not specify how I should answer specific questions in my game theory class.[22]

2. Left to themselves, workers prefer to work at levels of effort that will not maximize employer profits. Workers need not dislike work per se; there need only be activities—such as chatting with co-workers or answering private e-mail—that attract worker attention in a way that does not maximize employer profits.

3. Monitoring worker performance is both costly and imperfect. Supervisors require pay, cannot observe all activity, may not themselves be fully motivated, and may have their own agendas.

Firms therefore face an effort-enforcement problem that resides within the labor exchange itself.

Here is a basic effort model.[23] Workers choose their effort level in order to maximize the expected utility of income and work effort:

$$(3.6) \qquad\qquad u = u(y, e),$$

where y denotes income and e is hourly effort; the partial derivatives $u_y > 0$ and $u_e < 0$. Workers caught offering less than suitable effort (shirking) can be fired; they face a potential cost of job loss defined as

$$(3.7) \qquad\qquad c = v(w, e, d) - z(b, U, \zeta).$$

Here c is the present value of the cost of job loss over the relevant time horizon; v is the present value of the future income stream from employment ($v_e < 0 < v_w$); d is the probability of dismissal; z is the present value of future income in the event of dismissal (a fallback position); b is the expected value of non-employment earnings (e.g., unemployment benefits); U signifies aggregate, industry, occupational, and regional unemployment or other relevant market conditions, such as hiring rates; and ζ signifies worker characteristics, such as skill level, job tenure, gender, or race.

All else equal, a higher real wage (w) increases the cost of job loss ($c_w > 0$). The fallback position (z) depends on an implicit probability of reemployment, which, in turn, depends on U and ζ. These last points appear more readily in a simpler expression that shows the hourly cost of job loss (ς):

$$(3.8) \qquad \varsigma = w - j(U, \zeta)w + [1 - j(U, \zeta)]b,$$

where j (itself a function of both U and ζ) denotes the probability of finding a new job in the relevant period. Note that since w appears in the first two terms on the right-hand side, a reemployed worker would earn the same wage at a new firm that faces the same effort-enforcement problem. Thus, whenever $j < 1$ and $b < w$, the worker faces a cost of job loss. The utility-maximizing level of effort chosen by workers (e) is a function of both the cost of job loss and the firm's level of monitoring (m).[24] We have

$$(3.9) \qquad e = e(c, m),$$

where the partial derivatives e_c and e_m are positive. We refer to equation (3.9) as the *effort function*.

Firms maximize profits subject to the effort function. To do so, they minimize costs of labor per unit of effort, $(w + p_m m)/e$, where p_m is the hourly cost of a unit of monitoring. The product $p_m m$ is the hourly cost of monitoring using m units. Assuming (for simplicity) that $p_m m$ is constant, the firm minimizes the ratio w/e (or maximizes e/w). Figure 3.6 graphs this relationship. At the worker's reservation wage (w_r), there is no cost of job loss. With no cost to being dismissed, workers exert their comfortable level of effort ($\bar{e}$). To elicit more effort, firms can increase w; doing so leads to $c > 0$, and the implicit threat of costly dismissal induces more effort. In Figure 3.6, the positive slope of the effort function indicates this relationship between e and c (for a given m); its concave shape reflects an assumption that effort exhibits diminishing returns to increases in the cost of job loss.[25] Firms thus increase the wage up to level w^*, the point at which the ray from the origin is tangent to the effort function $e(c, m)$. This tangency shows the maximum attainable ratio e/w, indicating the firm's minimum cost per unit effort (w/e).[26] Because e depends on w (via c), this tangency also determines the worker's equilibrium effort e^*.

This model yields three key results related to efficiency, distribution, and market clearing. First, the simultaneous presence of $w > w_r$ and a need for costly monitoring ($p_m m > 0$) indicates how the asymmetric information regarding effort (the P-A problem) generates transaction costs that reduce efficiency and compromise potential gains from trade. Absent asymmetric information, higher levels of both w and e would be attainable; both parties could be better off (Bowles 1985). Second, because the employer has a first-mover advantage—the

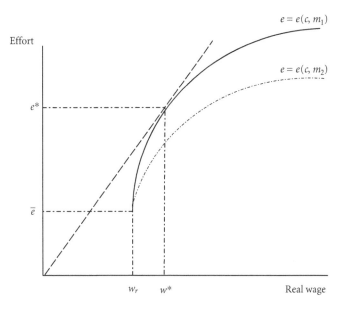

Figure 3.6 Effort model

N O T E : $\bar{e}$ = voluntary level of effort; w = real wage; w_r = reservation wage; m = hourly level of monitoring ($m_2 < m_1$); c = cost of job loss.

ability to give a take-it-or-leave-it offer—the equilibrium (w^*, e^*) is the most advantageous for the employer of all possible outcomes that could resolve the effort CAP.[27]

Third, this model can explain the existence of involuntary unemployment. Conventional labor market theory argues that firms pay the reservation wage ($w = w_r$) at which the labor market would clear. At the macroeconomic level, unemployment would then be at its "natural" rate with only frictional unemployment and no involuntary unemployment. In contrast, the effort-enforcement problem induces firms to set $w^* > w_r$ in order to motivate effort via a positive cost of job loss. This model thus provides a microeconomic foundation for macro-level involuntary unemployment.[28]

Comparative statics generate additional results. External developments that influence determinants of the cost of job loss (j, or b) or the hourly monitoring cost ($p_m m$) can also affect the equilibrium values w^* and e^*. For example, a reduction in national unemployment (U), on account of monetary or fiscal expansion, would increase the reemployment probability (j), reducing c for any given w. The effort function shifts to the right, increasing w^*. Similarly, an increase in monitoring cost (p_m) would induce employers to substitute wages for monitoring, pivoting the effort function down and to the right. We find a lower e at each w (see the dashed curve in Figure 3.6), and w^* again increases.[29] This logic also indicates a possible cause of persistent interindustry wage differentials among equally skilled workers. Because industries face unique monitoring costs related to observing effort in distinct production environments, the slope and position of their effort functions may differ. Similarly, the impact of effort on profits may vary by industry, yielding correspondingly different effort functions. Consequently, equivalent workers may earn different wages according to their industry of employment.[30]

Overall, the effort model illustrates how the asymmetric information that accompanies labor effort creates internal enforcement problems—second-order CAPs. By depicting the dynamics of a contingent renewal enforcement mechanism, the model illustrates how second-party enforcement creates transaction costs, affects distribution, and generates involuntary unemployment. We now present a more general discussion of internal resolutions for market enforcement problems.

Related Enforcement Problems and Mechanisms

Similar P-A problems appear in other major categories of market exchanges. Resolution involves contingent renewal, sometimes in combination with mechanisms that more directly align agents' interests with those of principals.

To model contingent renewal for a broader class of P-A problems, we relabel and reinterpret Figure 3.6. In P-A problems, agents receive payment for hard-to-observe action related to contracted quality. We may thus label the vertical axis as "Quality" and the horizontal axis as "Price" (Bowles 2004, 255). For example, in many supplier relationships, a principal firm contracts with an agent firm to provide quality parts. Because their interests differ and the principal cannot observe the agent's production processes, the contract alone cannot assure quality. Even so, contingent renewal with a price that exceeds the supplier's next-best alternative can ameliorate the principal's contract-enforcement problem. Similarly, Figure 3.6 can represent a contingent renewal solution to a P-A problem between shareholders and managers regarding managerial effort or dedication to shareholder goals. Price here might signify salary. In financial markets, lenders are principals and borrowers are agents.[31] To discourage risky borrower behavior, lenders can charge low rates of interest that (across the market) generate an excess demand for loans in the financial market. They may then refuse to extend loans to (or renew loans with) agents who have bad credit histories (Stiglitz 1987).[32]

All of these cases involve transaction costs to enforcement that lead to nonclearing markets. We thus achieve the important but counterintuitive result that in market equilibrium, where price and quantity adjustment processes have come to an end, there is either excess supply (labor or supplier markets) or excess demand (credit markets).[33] As Chapter 4 will make clear, this result introduces power into exchange processes.

Alternative mechanisms, which may either complement or replace contingent renewal, can partially align the interests of agents and principals. One such mechanism is gain sharing. Managerial contracts, for example, often include some form of incentive pay or profit sharing. Suppose that a manager works on a problem for which success generates value V in profits and failure generates nothing. High managerial effort generates a probability of success ρ_H and low effort generates ρ_L, where $0 < \rho_L < \rho_H < 1$. Managers require at least salary s_H to compensate high effort, whereas low effort only requires $s_L < s_H$.[34] If shareholders were to pay s_H unconditionally, managers would exert low effort. One can show, however, that if shareholders offer managers a bonus (profit share) B for success, managers will exert high effort provided that

(3.10) $$B \geq (s_H - s_L)/(\rho_H - \rho_L).$$

If this inequality holds, the expected value gain from high managerial effort exceeds its cost of exertion. The bonus induces managers to adhere to contractual commitments, effectively aligning the (pertinent) interests of agent and principal (an example of incentive compatibility). This managerial P-A problem is thereby resolved, but at a transaction cost: with $p_H - p_L < 1$, $B > s_H - s_L$.

Similarly, in financial markets, collateral requirements can partially align the interests of lenders and borrowers in a manner that complements contingent renewal. In order to discourage risky borrower behavior, lenders demand a down payment before extending credit. In the event of default, the borrower loses the collateral. The borrower's stake in the loan's success discourages undue risk. Yet the difficulties of raising collateral, and the opportunity costs of posting it, constitute informational transaction costs of finance.

Summarizing the related arguments, Table 3.1 indicates that P-A problems arise in virtually all sectors of the economy. Second-party enforcement mechanisms can resolve the problems shown in Table 3.1, but only by imposing transaction costs. Sufficiently high transaction costs may preclude exchanges that would be profitable in the absence of asymmetric information. Moreover, the relevant markets usually fail to clear, and, because enforcement may involve conflict, power enters exchange.

3.4. CONCLUSION

This chapter has focused on second-order CAPs—problems that reflect divergences between individual and group interests with respect to processes of designing, organizing, and implementing social mechanisms of coordination and enforcement. Resolution of second-order CAPs is a necessary—though not always sufficient—condition for resolving first-order CAPs, notably those related to conducting reliable exchanges. Without sufficient coordination and enforcement, stated commitments made in agreements or contracts lack credibility and so exchange processes collapse (or fail to develop) under the weight of mistrust. Second-order resolution mechanisms thus establish pre-conditions for growth and development.

In principle, either second or third parties can provide or administer enforcement. The effectiveness of third-party enforcement of agreements depends on (a) the ability of third parties to reliably observe second-party actions and (b) the magnitude of third-party sanctions relative to potential gains from defecting. Recall that sanctions can be either positive (rewards) or negative (punishments). Effective third-party enforcement can resolve second-order CAPs that might otherwise compromise the credibility of second-party agreements. Nevertheless, third-party enforcement is itself costly to administer, pointing to second-order CAPs at a broader level of analysis—for example, problems within a community of establishing government. The relevance of second-order CAPs to specific questions of analysis, therefore, depends on whether or not the parties subject to analysis can take third-party enforcement for granted. In transparent economic exchanges, third-party enforcement may often be taken for granted, but many important exchanges in all sectors of the economy lack such transparency.

Absent reliable third-party enforcement, small numbers of actors who engage in repeated interactions may be able to resolve second-order CAPs at a quite low cost by coordinating

TABLE 3.1

Principal-agent problems and types of exchange

Exchange (good or service)	Observation problem (noncontractible aspect)	Principal/agent	Enforcement mechanism(s)	Transaction costs and party that bears them (P or A)	Market outcome
Labor	Quality of effort; information sharing	Employer/worker	Contingent renewal with monitoring and above-market-clearing wage	$w > w_r$ (P); Monitoring effort (P)	Excess supply of labor (unemployment)
Managerial services	Quality of effort; information sharing; attention to profits	Shareholders/managers	Contingent renewal and gain sharing	Pay > NBA (P); Monitoring effort (P); Contract writing (P)	Excess supply of managers
Business supply	Quality of good or service	Purchasing firm/supplier	Contingent renewal	Pay > NBA (P); Monitoring quality (P); Contract writing (P)	Excess supply of contractors
Finance (loans)	Borrowers actions: risk of default	Lender/borrower	Contingent renewal; collateral payment	Interest < market (P); Screening (P); Contract writing (P); Raising collateral (A)	Excess demand for loans (credit rationing)
Residential tenancy	Renter's care of property	Landlord/tenant	Contingent renewal; collateral (deposit)	Contract writing (P); Monitoring (P); Maintenance (P); Raising collateral (A)	Unclear
Sharecropping in agriculture	Quality of effort; care of land	Landlord/sharecropper	Gain sharing (% of crop)	Contract writing (P); Monitoring crop (P); Raising collateral (A)	Excess supply of tenants
Nontransparent consumer goods or services	Quality of good or service	Consumer/firm	Contingent renewal	Monitoring quality (P)	Excess supply of goods (demand deficiency)
Government	Quality; restraint on use of power	Public/officials	Contingent renewal in democracies	Monitoring (P); Election costs (P)	n/a

SOURCE: The first four columns of this table borrow heavily from Table 7.1 in Bowles (2004).

NOTE: w_r = wage that would clear the market; NBA = next best alternative; P = principal; A = agent.

on a contingent strategy, such as tit-for-tat. Joint enactment of t-f-t can induce cooperation if actions are sufficiently observable and if there are large enough gains to cooperation, low enough discount rates, and a high enough probability of continued exchange. Even so, the presence of many alternative contingent strategies can impede coordination, and larger group cooperation remains problematic.

More typically, incomplete, asymmetric information engenders transaction costs related to both defining and enforcing the de facto property rights that accompany exchanges. Prospects for development depend upon restraining such costs. Adverse selection models illustrate pre-agreement failure to credibly communicate important attributes of items or services that are subject to exchange—that is, the de facto property rights that might be transferred. Because coordinating exchange requires shared understandings of both attributes and rights, adverse selection compromises exchange efficiency and may even lead to market collapse or failure to develop. Resolution mechanisms, such as warranties, can mitigate these CAPs but at the expense of transaction costs that reduce or eliminate the gains from exchange.

Principal-agent models of moral hazard address post-contractual problems of attaining adherence to commitments when subsequent actions cannot be fully observed. Enforcement problems—related to quality, effort, or information sharing—affect critical arenas of exchange, including labor, supplier, rental, credit, and consumer markets, along with government. Exchanging parties must then develop enforcement mechanisms, such as contingent renewal.[35] These efforts may resolve attendant second-order CAPs, but again with transaction costs. Finally, internal enforcement mechanisms affect the distribution of returns and frequently yield nonclearing markets that confer a potential for the exercise of power within exchange processes.

Overall, we encounter partial success at a cost. Partial resolution of second-order CAPs of coordination and enforcement permits partial resolution of first-order CAPs of free-riding. Ensuing transaction costs may still inhibit mutually beneficial exchange and, ultimately, development. Our analysis thus translates North's assertion that transaction costs impede development into a restatement of Olson's zero-contribution thesis: absent a selective sanctioning mechanism, parties may not only fail to directly contribute to collective goods, they may also fail to contribute to developing needed coordination and enforcement mechanisms that could lend credibility to the cooperative agreements that underlie multiple exchanges.

Before turning to additional resolution mechanisms that involve reciprocity, norms, and institutions (Chapters 5–13), Chapter 4 discusses exercises of power—many of which emerge from second-party enforcement mechanisms.

EXERCISES

3.1. Draw a two-stage game with Figure 2.7 as the first stage and Figure 3.2 as the second stage.

3.2. Prove that, when $\gamma > 0$ in equation (3.3), the Nash equilibrium will occur at $c_i = p_i = 0$ for all i. *Hint:* Agents can decide whether or not to punish others after observing their action.

3.3. Referring to Figure 3.3 and the related discussion and to item 1 on page 50, prove that if $\alpha c > (2\alpha - 1)c$, and if $\gamma > 0$, neither (ii), (iii), nor (iv) change the outcome of Figure 3.3. *Hint:* For (iii) and (iv), calculate the payoff earned by a defector.

3.4. Think of several real-world examples of situations where internal and external punishments conflict (as in item 2(iv) on page 50). Draw a simple game model for one of them. Explain your payoffs and possible solutions to the model.

3.5. Suppose that cooperators are willing to punish defectors as long as the cost of administering punishment $\gamma \le \gamma_x$. Now, referring to item 6 on page 51, assume that $\gamma = \gamma(n)$ in equation (3.3), where $\gamma(0) > \gamma_x > 0$, $\partial\gamma/\partial n < 0$, and $\gamma(N) < \gamma_x$. Furthermore, assume that the cost of being punished by $n*$ others exceeds the gain from defecting, where $0 < n* < N$. This is a multi-player game. What kind of game is it? Explain in words.

3.6. Draw the "race to the bottom" game described in Section 3.2.

3.7. Looking at equation (3.5), recall that ε is the probability that A correctly observes B's defection on the previous move. Now define $\omega < 1$ as the probability that one party correctly observes cooperation by the other in the previous move. How would this change affect prospects for attaining cooperation? Make an argument referring to appropriately adjusted equations.

3.8. Prove that if $(H - C) < \delta(C - D)$, where $\delta = 1/(1 + r)$, then defecting once from t-f-t does not pay.

3.9. Considering the potential problems with t-f-t that arise from possible mistakes in observation (discussed in Section 3.2), design a superior strategy that accounts for previous history of cooperation before choosing D as a punishment. Justify your strategy.

3.10. Construct a model that illustrates Section 3.3's description of Akerlof's lemons game applied to an adverse selection problem for market exchange of health insurance contracts. Consider the buyer's point of view.

3.11. Draw a diagram (roughly analogous to Figure 3.6) that illustrates a relationship between a borrower and a lender. Explain your model. *Hint:* Think about how to label the axes to fit this problem.

4 SEIZING ADVANTAGE: STRATEGIC MOVES AND POWER IN EXCHANGE

> The efforts of men are utilized in two different ways: they are directed to the production or transformation of economic goods, or else to the appropriation of goods produced by others.
>
> Vilfredo Pareto (1905)[1]

Suppose that, after signing a limitation agreement with Boratonia, authorities in Arruba hope to induce their own farmers to limit water use, but the farmers would rather not. Alternatively, the farmers as a group may hope to restrain the water use of individual members who also would rather not. In either case, compliance requires an exercise of power—likely some mix of explicit or implicit rewards and punishments. For example, authorities might impose fines for overuse.

Chapter 3's closing has set the stage for this chapter. Because asymmetric information creates second-order CAPs of enforcement associated with moral hazard, parties to exchanges need to create or negotiate internal mechanisms of enforcement. And because enforcement involves exercising power, power resides within exchange processes. Power infuses political economy from the ground up. There are many ways to conceptualize power. This chapter focuses on concepts that inform our game-theoretic approach to CAPs and exchange.

Webster's dictionary defines power as the "capacity or ability to direct or influence the behavior of others or the course of events." Physicists define power as the "time rate at which work is done by a force" (Halliday, Resnick, and Walker 2008, 131). A force performing work can move an object from a state of rest to motion or alter the speed or trajectory of an object already in motion. Applying these definitions to political economy, we may regard economic or political processes as courses of events or behavior with states of rest (equilibria) or motion trajectories; power may alter either. Economist Kaushik Basu (2000) defines power in a manner that he says spans concepts from such diverse thinkers as Max Weber, Bertrand Russell, Friedrich Hayek, John Kenneth Galbraith, and Steven Lukes. "All agree that power is, broadly speaking, the ability of one person to get another person to do something that is of advantage to the former but not in the latter's interest" (134).

A related conception of power appears in Bowles and Gintis (2008). They identify four characteristics: (i) power involves relationships between or among people (and so is not a property of an individual); (ii) power involves the use or threat of sanctions; (iii) power "should be *normatively indeterminate*, allowing for Pareto-improving outcomes . . . but also susceptible to abuse in ways that harm others in violation of ethical principles"; and

(iv) to be enduring, power must be "sustainable as a Nash equilibrium of an appropriately defined game" (Vol. 6, 566). Comparing concepts, note that Basu's definition implicitly incorporates Bowles/Gintis characteristic (i) and is consistent with (iv). On the other hand, Basu's "not in the other's interest" disallows possible Pareto improvement from (iii). Because (iii) could also allow forms of influence that do not fit power—such as benevolent persuasion—Bowles and Gintis include sanctions (ii).[2] The two conceptions, then, are overlapping sets.

An inclusive concept of power should allow for both Pareto improvements and use of nonsanctioning forms of influence that are intended to harm another's interests. We will call harmful forms of influence *manipulations* (defined more fully below). Exercises of power are also deliberate strategies, and those who exercise power can, like everybody else, make mistakes and thereby generate unintended consequences. Accordingly, we define *power* as

> the ability of an individual or group to deliberately employ sanctions or manipulation in order to induce other individuals or groups to take, alter, or avoid specific actions in a manner that the former (perhaps mistakenly) believes is in its own interest and that the latter would not otherwise pursue.

Several elements of this definition merit further comment. Note the implied asymmetry between at least two parties; power is asymmetric. The reference to belief implies an equilibrium in a strategic encounter. The term *manipulation* means an action taken by an individual or group (hereafter, agent) that induces one or more other agents to take, alter, or avoid specific actions in a manner that the former believes is in its own interest but against the long-term interests of the latter. We subsequently designate manipulative communication as an instrument of power. Note that many manipulations involve actual or threatened sanctions, but some do not. Moreover, some used or implied sanctions are nonmanipulative because they can generate Pareto improvements. Even so, asymmetric allocations of power affect the distribution of benefits along a Pareto frontier or along an interior realized frontier representing possible outcomes of relevant engagements.[3]

Power relationships permeate political economy. Obviously, at a macro level, states exercise power, and markets and states interact. The use of power by the state as an external contract enforcer, often taken for granted in economic models, is nonetheless relatively straightforward in the sense of basic enforcement actions. In contexts with established legal systems, authorities may sue, fine, or jail violators of contracts—clearly exercises of power. Yet, when one considers average citizens in average transactions, the implicit and often subtle nature of these sanctions often obscures the role of external enforcement mechanisms. In states with strong legal systems, most people do not contemplate breaking most laws. Consider the alternative.

Power relationships operate at the foundations of micro-level political economy. Chapters 2 and 3 asserted that partial resolution of CAPs underlies economic development and that second-order CAPs can undermine potential agreements to resolve first-order CAPs. Chapter 3 stressed that asymmetric information can undermine the credibility of contractual commitments, rendering comprehensive (or full) enforcement by external agents— who lack detailed on-site information—impossible. In order to circumvent post-contractual moral hazard problems, exchange parties must apply internal enforcement mechanisms such as contingent renewal. Contract enforcement then typically involves a mix of external and internal enforcement. At either level, enforcement connotes an exercise of power: it alters the behavior of agents away from action trajectories they might otherwise take, at the behest of some other individual or group. Thus the near-universal presence of second-order CAPs requires that power enter all but the simplest exchanges. Yet, in resolving second-order CAPs, exercises of power can focus expectations in ways that rule out multiple forms of defection; we expect little shoplifting and few bank collapses. Such Pareto-improving roles of power are often overlooked.

Another frequently overlooked implication of incomplete contracting is that second-order CAPs link economic growth to distributional conflict. Growth requires exchange, and exchange requires contracts. Owing to the pervasive presence of asymmetric information, workable contracts necessarily rely, at least partially, on internal (as opposed to external) enforcement mechanisms. Exercises of power between or among exchanging parties necessarily follow. Naturally, we expect self-interested parties who exercise power in exchange to steer distribution in their direction. Economics becomes political even at the micro level. Hence the macro-level growth that emerges from exchange processes cannot be separated from the distributional goals that accompany the exercise of power in exchange. Processes that resolve second-order CAPs of contracting thus bind growth to distribution.[4]

Why, then, is power so rarely discussed in traditional economics? Basu provides a simple historical answer. Until recently, economists simply lacked the conceptual tools to formally address power: "given the importance attached to formalization in economics, the only effective option has been to ignore them [power and coercion]" (2000, 132).[5] Fortunately, game theory with information economics now offers formal methodologies for analyzing power. To establish context for modeling power, we begin by discussing its absence in pure competition.

Competition, Markets, and Power

The assumptions of pure competition imply that neither individuals nor firms can affect market outcomes, leaving no role for power in exchange. The basic assumptions are as follows:

1. Consumers maximize utility and firms maximize profits. Both are rational in the sense that they care only about individual material gains and also possess the cognitive capacity to maximize.[6]

2. Every market has many buyers and sellers—enough so that no single agent can influence the market price.

3. All relevant goods and services are identical (homogeneous).

4. Every agent has full, equal, and free access to information that affects market decisions; thus information is a non-economic good rather than a scarce resource.

5. There are no barriers to entry or exit to any market (free entry and exit).

Assumption 1 guarantees that agents cannot manipulate the goals (preferences) of other agents. Given assumption 1, assumptions 2–5 imply that no single agent can influence any market outcome for another. More precisely, assumptions 2, 3, and 5 indicate that numerous potential competitors would undercut possible exercises of market power, and assumption 4 insures that all parties know enough to engage in such competition. Because market participants cannot affect outcomes for others, individual participants cannot exert power in the market.

In conventional price theory, where contract enforcement is largely taken for granted, power enters only as the market power that accompanies imperfect competition.[7] *Market power* is the ability of a firm, group, or individual to influence prices. Monopolies, oligopolies, and monopolistic competitors may affect prices because product heterogeneity or entry barriers (violations of assumptions 3 and 5, respectively) limit the market access of potential competitors. In fact, for Adam Smith, a core virtue of competition is its ability to undermine such influence. Accordingly, Abba Lerner states: "An economic transaction is a solved political problem" (1972, 259).[8] Recent theoretical developments, however, have rendered this opinion—and its underlying assumptions—obsolete.

Assumptions 4 and 5 are particularly important and problematic. Perfect information (assumption 4) requires that all relevant characteristics of potentially exchanged goods and services be fully transparent to all involved parties. The attributes of a fruit market approximate these stringent conditions. Yet, as prior discussion indicates, exchanges of labor services or complex commodities like health insurance or mortgage contracts are far less transparent. Hence the analytical problem with the assumption of perfect information is not its blatant unrealism—but rather its erroneous implications on market clearing and power. The internal enforcement mechanisms that respond to second-order CAPs of contract enforcement engender unsolved political problems—namely, nonclearing markets and exercises of power within exchange.

Correspondingly, assumption 5 implies that entry and exit have no consequence: that the value of the option chosen equals that of the next-best alternative. Absent consequence, exertion of power becomes meaningless. If free exit applied to the Nash bargaining model (see equation (2.2) and Section 4.1), bargained outcomes would generate values equal to next-best alternatives (fallback positions). Because neither party could affect such outcomes, neither could exert power.[9] Lerner's political problem would be, as it were, "solved." The presence of costly entry or exit—virtually ubiquitous in contract relationships—however, drives a wedge between negotiated outcomes and fallback alternatives. Thus power enters. Indeed, we expect self-interested agents to seize relevant opportunities for their own gain. For example, in most employment relationships, losing one's job is costly (else unemployment would not be a persistent topic of political debate). Employers may then exert power in the sense of inducing workers to do what they might not otherwise do—augment their effort, thereby altering the trajectories of employee activity (see Figure 3.6). As Table 3.1 indicates, similar dynamics arise in other markets; power permeates exchange.

Our discussion proceeds as follows. Section 4.1 establishes context for subsequent analysis by discussing the sources, instruments, and domains of power. For the latter, we use Steven Lukes' (1974) three-dimensional (or three-face) conception of power to distinguish between its direct impacts on behavior (power1), the strategic altering of rules and expectations (power2), and the manipulation of preferences or beliefs (power3). These concepts will inform Part III's discussion of second- and third-party enforcement, institutions, policy, and development. Section 4.2 uses a Nash cooperative bargaining model with given fallback positions to model sources and impacts of power1. Section 4.3 uses the concept of strategic moves in two-player games to represent power2, stressing the importance of credibility. Section 4.4 illustrates power asymmetry and more closely relates power to exchange by developing Basu's (2000) concept of triadic power relationships. It closes with a multi-player version of triadic power focused on manipulations of community expectations, moving in the direction of power3. Using Basu's concept of a diffused dictatorship, Section 4.5 outlines power3's ability to influence beliefs—implying more deep-seated manipulation. Section 4.6 concludes by linking the three faces of power back to CAPs that, in turn, bind growth to distribution. Thus we show how power permeates political economy.

4.1. SOURCES, INSTRUMENTS, DOMAINS, AND THE THREE FACES OF POWER

Robert Dahl (1957) identifies three fundamental elements of power relations: sources, instruments, and domains of power. The base or *source of power* indicates where an agent's power originates. Fundamentally, power arises from three related sources: position (social, political, or economic), access to resources, and an ability to resolve CAPs associated with mobilizing support. For example, a US senator occupies a legislative position, has access to campaign funds, and can mobilize support by turning out voters. These three sources can reinforce each other: positions may grant access to resources that facilitate resolving organizational CAPs. Likewise, resolving CAPs or having resources may facilitate attaining various positions.

The means or *instruments of power* indicate the manner through which one party can exercise power over another.[10] There are two basic types of power instruments:

(i) actual, threatened, or promised sanctions; recall that we use the general term *sanction* to include both punishment and reward (respectively, negative and positive sanctions); and

(ii) the use of communication as a means of manipulation independent of sanctions.[11]

Instrument types (i) and (ii) may be used separately or in combination.

Dahl's third element of power, the *domain of influence*, refers to its scope—the broad spheres of activity that power affects. Here we incorporate Lukes' three faces or dimensions of power. Roughly speaking, power has three fundamental domains of influence (faces): (i) behavior, (ii) conditions of engagement or rules of access, and (iii) players' inclinations. For example, one senator (Ann) might try to directly induce another (Ben) to pursue actions he would not otherwise undertake by pressuring him to vote a certain way, blocking his appointment to a committee, or influencing his overall desire to challenge her. Specifically, she could exert power in one of these three domains:

1. Ann could directly affect Ben's behavior within a given context or arena.

2. Ann could bias procedures against Ben by altering any of the following: rules of access to or participation in relevant arenas; other parties' perceptions of the legitimacy of Ben's participation; or Ben's expectations concerning possible reactions of others.

3. Ann could influence Ben's own preferences concerning the desirability of undertaking certain actions, his beliefs regarding the feasibility of such actions, or his understanding of her role in relevant decisions.

This triad of influence—(i) behaviors, (ii) rules/expectations, and (iii) preferences/beliefs—constitutes the core of Lukes' three-dimensional approach.[12]

Table 4.1 summarizes the elements of power. Note that all three domains (faces) emerge from the same three sources and all share use of instrument (i), though with differences in its precise manifestations. We now turn to more precise discussion of the three faces of power.

The first face (power1) has the narrowest and most easily observed domain of influence. *Power1* reflects a party's ability to directly affect others' behavior related to observable decisions that are made within established arenas, with given and understood rules. It takes the institutional foundations that shape each party's access to and participation within decision arenas as given and known. Exercises of power1 can be observed by examining which parties prevail in contested decisions. Concerning sources, Lukes (1974) states that possession of power1 depends on the ability of parties to mobilize support using traditional political means such as assembling coalitions, lobbying, and garnering votes—an ability to solve organizational CAPs. A party's position and its access to resources may facilitate such mobilization. In terms of instruments, power1 utilizes well-understood and observable rewards and punishments (instrument (i)) that are already implicit in the established context. For example, in a traditional labor negotiation, both parties know that a union has some ability to call a strike and likewise a company has some ability to operate during a strike. Such transparency implies that power1 does not use manipulative communication (instrument (ii)).

Lukes (1974) links power1 to the pluralist tradition of Dahl (1961) and Nelson Polsby (1963). For pluralists, excessive influence from one party energizes actual or potential opponents, ultimately limiting its impact. Summarizing Lukes' argument, John Gaventa (1980) identifies two assumptions that underlie a pluralist conception of power1: (1) concerned parties can participate in decision forums (arenas), and (2) parties know and

TABLE 4.1
Elements of power relations

Sources	Instruments	Domain (face)
(i) Position	(i) Direct or threatened	1. Behavior
(ii) Access to resources	sanctions	2. Rules/expectations
(iii) Resolution of CAPs	(ii) Manipulative	3. Preferences/beliefs
	communication	

can articulate their interests. Accordingly, leaders speak for constituents, and nonparticipation among constituents reflects voluntary choice, signifying contentment with the status quo. Open access to forums makes power competitive; latent groups can mobilize when their interests are threatened—counteracting disproportionate influence. There is, in effect, a negative-feedback mechanism that counteracts excessive use of power.[13]

Our discussion, however, does not bind exercises of power1 to pluralist assumptions of open access. A nonpluralist conception of power1 recognizes that institutionally determined or influenced positions in governing bodies, markets, or social groups affect the ability of various parties to exercise power. A senior senator, for example, possesses means of shaping legislation (e.g., connections, seats on influential committees) that are not available to new members, much less average citizens. An employer has more access to productive resources and decision arenas regarding employment than does a typical employee. Lenders have more access to finance than borrowers. We take such positions, equal or not, as given, and then proceed to examine how exercises of power1 influence outcomes within fixed and well-understood contexts.

The second dimension of power, *power2*, treats the following parameters of strategic engagement as manipulatable: rules of interaction, the corresponding positions from which agents operate, their access to arenas, and their expectations concerning possible reactions of others to their activity (or lack thereof). Hence manipulative communication (instrument (ii)) often plays a role. Power2 violates Gaventa's (1980) assumption (1): parties may use power2 in order to impede others' ability to effectively participate in decision-making arenas. Such exercise of power reflects a "mobilization of bias" (Bachrach and Baratz 1962, 1970).[14] One party (Ann) could act directly or indirectly to limit or preclude another's (Ben's) participation. Directly, Ann (or some group) may immediately apply force, as in political assassination or military invasion.[15] Alternatively, she could threaten to punish Ben's participation or promise to reward his nonparticipation. Such reward may be considered "buying off" a potential opponent. Indirectly, she may design or influence rules of access or participation with bias against Ben. The framers of the US Constitution, for example, limited voting to nonslave male property holders.

Ann could also marginalize Ben by influencing certain beliefs of other parties (e.g., Chris) concerning the credibility or legitimacy of Ben's statements or actions. She might use the media or other forms of communication to appeal to cultural values, symbols, or labels. Such manipulations, moreover, could influence Ben's own expectations concerning possible reactions from others (Ann and Chris). For example, in the early 1950s, Senator Joseph McCarthy effectively silenced potential opponents by labeling them as communists or sympathizers and by implicitly threatening many others with similar treatment. Anticipating ostracism or job loss, many potential challengers to the senator remained silent.

While, broadly speaking, the foundational sources of power do not distinguish power2 from power1, their actual manifestations typically differ. Both types of power may arise from institutional positions, but certain positions, such as membership in legislatures, confer an ability to alter rules (power2). Similarly, both types of power use instrument (i); both employ direct or implied sanctions, but the accompanying ends and contexts differ. Power1 involves already available and understood direct sanctions—such as military or physical force, or the political "force" of organized support—directed toward behavior within understood, observable, and established contexts. For power2, direct sanctions may impede or prevent access to arenas (alter rules). Use of power2 may also involve threatened sanctions that are not already understood from the existing context. Indeed, manipulative promises and threats constitute critical exercises of power2. It is important to note that the presence of asymmetric information—a largely inescapable condition in social, political, and economic encounters—invites opportunities for exercising power2. Furthermore, various parties often employ combinations of power1 and power2. Agents may directly engage within existing arenas as they strive, perhaps over longer time horizons, to manipulate rules and expectations to their advantage.

Finally, note that because the exercise of power2 biases access, incidents of nonparticipation by certain agents or groups may not reflect voluntary choice, but rather prior exercises of power2. For example, before the enactment and enforcement of the 1965 Voting Rights Act, the near-universal absence of voting on the part of African Americans in the US South did not reflect voluntary choice. Biased access, moreover, can prevent decision-making bodies from even considering the aspirations or grievances of some concerned parties. In such cases, exercises of power do not reflect pluralist voluntarism and political competition. Nonetheless, parties who are subject to manipulation via power2 still know that others hold power and may still desire to challenge them, as the emergence of the civil rights movement in the 1950s clearly indicates. Conflict is still observable (at least in principle), as are various interests of relevant parties (Lukes 1974, 23–24).[16]

The third and even more obscure face of power, *power3*, extends its domain beyond observable conflict to manipulation of preferences and beliefs, violating Gaventa's assumption (2). Ann exerts power over Ben by "shaping or determining his very wants" (Lukes 1974, 27), in order to diminish or eliminate Ben's will to challenge Ann.[17] Exercises of power3 always involve manipulative communication (instrument (ii)).

Within power3 we may identify four relevant subdomains of influence (Gaventa 1980, 15–20):

(i) Immediate preferences: Ben believes he does not desire change or participation in decisions.

(ii) Conceptions of appropriateness of action: Ben desires participation but believes he should not act on this desire.

(iii) Deep-seated beliefs concerning one's own ability to influence: Ben may desire change and want to act but suffers from an internalized sense of powerlessness.

(iv) Beliefs concerning how to effect change: Ben believes he could influence outcomes but does not know what to do or holds mistaken ideas about strategy— as in failing to understand Ann's role so that he goes after the wrong target.[18]

The following example illustrates: Suppose that Ann abuses Ben in some kind of relationship. In case (i), Ben believes that he "deserves it." He does not even want recourse. He has fully acquiesced to her power. For (ii), Ben does not think that he deserves abuse but believes that a person in his position should not challenge someone in Ann's position. His acquiescence reflects a sense of propriety. For (iii), Ben would like recourse but believes it is completely hopeless; he feels trapped. Acquiescence reflects his own beliefs about his ability to influence his environment. For (iv), Ben wants recourse and is willing to act but does not know what action to take, believes that an ineffective action will help, or takes action on someone other than Ann. Ben is not acquiescent per se, but he still cannot challenge Ann's power because of his beliefs. To the extent that Ann (or some coalition of agents) induces any of beliefs (i) to (iv), she exerts power3 over Ben.[19]

Combining these ideas, Gaventa argues that the three faces of power interact and reinforce each other and that power grows cumulatively as its exercise moves up the numbers. If Ben consistently loses to Ann in successive exercises of power1, she may find opportunity for exercising power2; she may devote resources to biasing rules or expectations against his participation, and so diminish his access. Persistent bias against Ben's participation may then allow Ann to exercise power3, manipulating his conceptions of the feasibility, appropriateness, or desirability of participation. Here Ann may invoke cultural symbols and notions of legitimacy to influence Ben's beliefs in her favor. Subsequently, Ben may not even try to enter arenas, much less exercise power1 within them; the conflict disappears.

Ann's power over Ben thus grows cumulatively and exhibits properties of path dependence. Once Ann can exercise power2, her power attains some inertia. Exercising power3 increases such inertia. "The most effective and insidious use of power is to prevent such conflict from arising in the first place" (Lukes 1974, 27). On the other hand, challenges to Ann's power can reverse this process and work cumulatively in the opposite direction. If Ben can undo Ann's power3 by changing his beliefs, specifically if he "develops consciousness of the needs, possibilities, and strategies of challenge" (Gaventa 1980, 24), he may then demand access to arenas. If Ben gains access, undoing Ann's power2, he can then participate in power1 bargaining.

Two additional points deserve mention. First, even though power1 may appear to be the weakest of the three faces, its exercise critically influences the outcomes of multiple contests among relevant participants within established decision arenas. In particular, relative possession of power1 directly influences distribution. Second, note the informational aspects of the three dimensions of power. In power1, the parameters of conflict are understood or observable by both (or all) parties. Power2 introduces information asymmetry and, correspondingly, use of instrument (ii). Ben may not understand Ann's motives or observe her actions; he may not know how she biases, impedes, or blocks his access or his participation. Even so, he is cognizant of his conflict with Ann, understands that she holds power, and has some conception of how change could come about. Power3 extends the realms of asymmetric information, always using instrument (ii). Ben is either not aware that Ann holds power, not aware of how to initiate change, or not even aware that a conflict of interest exists.[20] Table 4.2 summarizes key elements of power in terms of the three faces. Subsequent discussion will illustrate game-theoretic modeling of these concepts.

4.2. POWER1 AND THE NASH COOPERATIVE BARGAINING MODEL

The Nash cooperative bargaining model, with fixed rules, offers a succinct representation of power1.[21] It can illustrate the impacts of various sources of power on two-party bargaining within given contexts—notably effects on their relative bargaining strength and, by

TABLE 4.2
Characteristics of power

	Domain	*Fixed*	*B knows*	*A influences*	*Instruments*	*Ultimate sources*
P1	Behavior	Rules and beliefs	Context, rules, own pref., A's pref. and available strategies, conflict with A	Bargaining outcome	(i) Understood sanctions: force and known pre-existing threats	Position; access to resources; ability to resolve mobilization CAPs
P2	Rules and expectations	Beliefs	Some context, own pref., conflict with A	As above plus B's access and expectations, Cs' beliefs and expectations	(i) Sanctions understood (as above) and threatened (ii) Manipulative promises and other manipulative communication	Position; access to resources; ability to resolve mobilization CAPs
P3	Beliefs and preferences	Neither	Possibly none of the above	As above plus B's own beliefs and his will to challenge (possibly via Cs' beliefs)	(i) As above (ii) Always	Position; access to resources; ability to resolve mobilization CAPs

NOTE: A = Ann; B = Ben; P1 = power1; P2 = power2; P3 = power3; pref. = preferences.

extension, negotiated outcomes. This model applies to numerous circumstances in which agents can benefit from credible negotiated agreements to share gains from some form of cooperation. For example, two politicians may know that they both would benefit from agreeing on legislation, but the precise terms of agreement influence their relative gains, such as who gets more credit for success, whose district gets more jobs, and the like. Similar descriptions could apply to negotiations between nations, firms, coalitions, leaders, entrepreneurs, and so forth. A need for such negotiated agreement permeates economic, political, and social relationships.

In order to model power1, we take the rules of the Nash bargaining game—notably, the determination of each party's fallback position—as given.[22] We also assume that negotiated agreements are fully enforceable and that there are no transaction costs to bargaining. As in Chapter 2, bargaining parties A and B agree on a payoff distribution (x_A, x_B) that maximizes the product of their net gains:

(4.1) $$(x_A - d_A)^\alpha (x_B - d_B)^\beta,$$

where d_A and d_B denote each party's fallback position (payoff with no agreement), and the exponents α and β indicate their respective *bargaining strengths*; $\alpha + \beta = 1$. The two parties' relative share of the net gains (the surplus ratio) is a function of the ratio α/β. Maximization is subject to the constraint that $x_A + x_B = v$, where v (the maximum value of the jointly bargained outcome) is assumed to be constant.[23]

Figure 4.1 illustrates. We note several properties of this diagram. The segment vv, known as the efficiency (or Pareto) frontier, represents all efficient combinations of (nonnegative) payoffs, given the constraint $x_A + x_B = v$. Point P maps the fallback values d_A and d_B. If we assume that neither party would accept an outcome below its fallback position, the range of all possible bargaining outcomes (the contract zone) occurs within triangle *PRS*. Any point within *PRS* to the right of or above P indicates some improvement for at least one party. Efficient bargaining occurs along the segment *RS*. Point Q, at values (x_A, x_B), indicates the ensuing negotiated payoffs, given d_A, d_B, α, and β. Note that the slope of segment *PQ* represents shares of the surplus $(x_A - d_A)/(x_B - d_B)$, as determined by the bargaining power ratio α/β.

There are two ways to evaluate relative bargaining success: shares of total value (x_A/x_B), and shares of the surplus $(x_A - d_A)/(x_B - d_B)$. Here fallbacks d_A and d_B determine the position of segment *PQ*. A lower d_A would shift *PQ* to the right, reducing x_A/x_B but not altering $(x_A - d_A)/(x_B - d_B)$. In analyzing power1, we take d_A and d_B to be exogenous; hence P is fixed. Given P, the power1 ratio α/β determines both x_A/x_B and $(x_A - d_A)/(x_B - d_B)$. If α were to decrease, *PQ* would pivot to the right (on P). Both x_A/x_B and $(x_A - d_A)/(x_B - d_B)$ would fall. Relative bargaining strength thus determines the distribution of both output and surplus.

We now examine specific (proximate) sources of power1 that can be derived from its basic sources (a party's position, its access to resources, and its ability to resolve organizational CAPs). Gaventa (1980), for example, cites an ability to offer jobs as a source of power1. More generally, Samuel Bacharach and Edward Lawler (1981) assert that the bargaining power of one party (A) arises from party B's dependence on A. Such dependence reflects a mix of position and access to resources. In Figure 4.1, if party A has a better position or

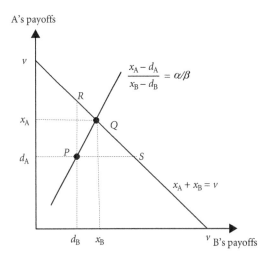

Figure 4.1   Nash cooperative bargaining model

more access to pre-existing resources than B, we expect $d_A > d_B$. For example, suppose that communities Arruba (A) and Boratonia (B) seek to negotiate a binding agreement concerning their respective contributions to a joint well. If A has more surface water within its boundaries, it would fare better than B without an agreement. Moreover, because B needs cooperation more than A does, it follows that $\alpha > \beta$ (A has more power1). Hence distribution ratios x_A/x_B and $(x_A - d_A)/(x_B - d_B)$ should both favor A.

With respect to collective action, Lukes (1974) argues that power1 arises from the ability of agents to mobilize support. Mobilized support, an outcome of resolving CAPs, can enhance one party's ability to pressure another. In union-management bargaining, for instance, the level of unity (or solidarity) among unionized workers may influence the costs to management of not meeting at least some union demands. If we designate the union as party A, mobilization leads to a relatively high α, generating a similarly high union share of the bargained surplus $(x_A - d_A)/(x_B - d_B)$.

Note further that this concept of collective action allows us to incorporate outcomes of multi-player interactions into our two-player Nash model. Suppose that group A is unified. If group B cannot resolve internal organizational CAPs, A might exercise power over each member of B individually: divide and conquer. For example, a regime could rule over a large population by implicitly threatening each person with imprisonment for disobedience. By contrast, if group B resolves its CAPs, A faces a coalition that may possess considerable bargaining strength (a high β).[24] Intermediate cases are possible.

We may also consider the possession of first-mover advantage and patience as derived sources of bargaining power. Either condition may emerge from greater access to resources or from a better position in decision arenas (Ann chairs a meeting) or exchange processes (Ann extends offers). We first illustrate with a noncooperative bargaining game and then apply outcomes to the Nash bargaining model.

Here is a summary of Dixit, Skeath, and Reiley's (2009, 703–14) intuitive description of Rubenstein's (1986) alternating-offers model. A fan arrives at a football game with no ticket, but a scalper is there ready to sell one. Each quarter of the game is worth $25 to the fan; this is common knowledge. Before the game, the scalper offers a price. If the fan rejects the offer, she waits out the first quarter and then makes a counteroffer. If the scalper rejects that offer, the fan waits out the second quarter. The scalper then makes another offer before the third quarter. If the fan refuses again, she waits and makes a final offer before the fourth quarter. With no discounting, the backwards-induction solution is straightforward. The fan knows the ticket is worthless at the end of the fourth quarter, so (before the fourth quarter) she offers the scalper one cent. Knowing this, as well as the fan's $25 valuation of each quarter, the scalper offers to sell a ticket at the beginning of the third quarter for $25. Before the second quarter, the fan offers the scalper $25 (and one cent). Before the first quarter, the scalper offers to sell a ticket for $50, and the fan accepts.

More generally, consider an alternating-offers game that lasts n periods. Ann makes the first, third, fifth, . . . offers, and Ben makes the second, fourth, sixth, . . . offers. If the total number of periods (n) is an even number, Ben makes the last offer (right before period n). He gives Ann essentially nothing and keeps that period's value x_n. In the next-to-last period, Ann offers Ben x_n and keeps value x_{n-1} for herself.[25] Offers proceed in this fashion back to the first offer. In the end, Ann receives values $(x_1, x_3, x_5, \ldots, x_{n-1})$ and Ben receives $(x_2, x_4, x_6, \ldots, x_n)$. If all periods are equally valuable to both, they end up with a 50/50 split.[26]

If we add impatience to this model, it shows that bargaining strength emerges from both first-mover advantage and greater patience. To simplify, suppose that Ann and Ben split $1 and that both have fallbacks of zero. The first mover can offer $1 - x$ to the other, keeping x. If that offer is refused, the second mover can offer the same. Now assume that Ann moves first and that both players discount the future at rate $r = 0.05$. The present value of payment x received one period in the future is thus $0.952x$. Ann knows that if Ben refuses her offer, he can make an identical offer in the next period. Ann therefore offers Ben $0.952x$ and keeps $1 - 0.952x$. Thus $x = 1 - 0.952x = 0.512 > 0.50$. Ann has a first-mover advantage (Dixit, Skeath, and Reiley 2009, 709–14). Furthermore, if Ann is more patient than Ben, her bargaining advantage increases. Ann's greater patience indicates that she discounts future values at a lower rate ($r_A = 0.05$ and $r_B = 0.10$). Because Ben values future payoffs less than Ann, at any move she can offer him a smaller amount than he would need to offer her at the same point in time. Thus, in terms of Figure 4.1, the ratio of bargaining strength, α/β, increases if either Ann is the first mover or if she is more patient.[27]

Overall, as a representation of power1, the Nash bargaining model can illustrate how the basic sources of power—position, access to resources, and ability to resolve organizational CAPs—influence more specific manifestations, such as dependency, mobilized support, first-mover advantage, and patience. These more proximate sources of power affect each party's (given but still relevant) fallback position as well as their relative power1 bargaining strengths. Thus, in established and understood arenas, the distribution of negotiated gains to economic, political, and social cooperation depends upon the relative possession of power1 among involved parties.

While power1 influences outcomes in fixed and well-understood arenas, the near ubiquity of asymmetric information suggests that such conditions arise infrequently in economic, political, and social transactions. Pure exercises of power1 may thus be quite rare. Exercises of power2 can emerge whenever the rules and expectations that condition participation in decision arenas are malleable. To secure subsequent power1 advantages, parties may consciously manipulate the "rules of the game." We now address that topic.

4.3. POWER2 AND STRATEGIC MOVES WITH TWO PARTIES

Owing to the near-universal presence of asymmetric information, along with the opportunities it offers for manipulating expectations and otherwise altering effective rules of engagement, power2 infuses economic, political, and social exchanges. Peter Bachrach and Morton Baratz argue that exerting power2 involves deliberate attempts to thwart "manifest challenges to the values or interests of the decision maker" (1970, 44). Such exercise may utilize "a set of predominant values, beliefs, rituals, and institutional procedures ('rules of the game') that operate systematically and consistently to the benefit of certain persons and groups at the expense of others" (1970, 43).

The game-theoretic notion of strategic moves fits this description. A *strategic move* is an attempt—either prior to or during the execution of a game—to alter its rules in one's favor. Normally, we envision strategic moves arising in a pre-game that alters the rules of a subsequent game.[28] The *rules of a game* indicate the following: who plays and who does not; the strategies available to each player; the order (timing) of moves; all possible outcomes; payoffs to each player at each outcome; and what each player knows (or does not know) at every point where it can move. For example, if Ann prefers playing against Ben to playing against Chris or Don, she may try to manipulate rules of engagement accordingly. Alternatively, Ann may do well against Ben as long as he cannot employ certain strategies or lacks access to certain information. Along these lines, in June 2010 the United Nations (UN) Security Council announced sanctions on Iran in an effort to deny it nuclear weapons technology (United Nations 2010) and thereby shift future global power games.

Broadly speaking, there are two categories of strategic moves. *Unconditional strategic moves* involve binding commitments to follow a strategy, such as driving straight in a game of chicken. *Conditional strategic moves* are if-then statements (e.g., if you do *x*, then I will do *y*) that take the form of either threats or promises. The June 2010 UN resolution on Iran (SC/9948) issued the following promise: "The Council affirmed that it would suspend the sanctions if, and so long as, Iran suspended all enrichment-related and reprocessing activities" (United Nations 2010).

Unless executed in secret (as in an example below), strategic moves involve attempts to alter the expectations of other players regarding conduct in a subsequent move or game. A successful strategic move by Ann should alter Ben's expectations concerning either Ann's ensuing behavior or possible reactions from other parties (i.e., Chris).[29] Ann must credibly signal that her (or Chris') future actions will deviate from what otherwise would have been expected. A *credible* move or statement by Ann is one that others expect her to adhere to at every point where she may be called upon to do so—even if the indicated action appears to undermine her interest at that point. Technically, a credible move or statement must be a *subgame perfect equilibrium* (SPE), a combination of strategies in which all players use best responses for every possible contingency within the appropriate (now altered) game.[30] Put differently, a strategic move effectively ties one's own hands or arranges to have them tied (Schelling 1960); else, one would just play the game as it would otherwise have been played. One's present self (with a long-run view) constrains the possibly unreliable actions of the future self, who might be tempted to take an easy way out. In such cases, credibility is not guaranteed; it is not cheap talk.[31] One must devote resources to tying one's hands and shifting expectations. UN Resolution SC/9948 states: "the Council also requested the Secretary-General to create a panel of experts to monitor implementation of the sanctions." Panels cost money and consume resources. Along similar lines, a large firm may deliberately generate excess capacity in order to deter entry by potential competitors. In so doing, it effectively issues a credible threat to lower its prices should any of them enter the market.

Two additional points deserve mention. First, strategic moves arise in environments of asymmetric information. Iran does not fully understand the motives of Security Council members. By creating a panel with monitoring powers, the council tried to shape Iran's expectations regarding its intent to execute sanctions. Second, the fundamental sources of power2, like those of power1, reflect attained position (membership on the Security Council), access to resources (UN funds), and an ability to resolve CAPs of mobilization (the Security Council vote). The latter can assist in tying hands: if the council fails to carry out these sanctions, it will lose face.[32]

Unconditional Moves and Conditional Threats or Promises

Either unconditional or conditional strategic moves can bias game outcomes. Opportunities for profitable unconditional moves arise in games that confer advantages to first or second movers. Unconditional first moves include actions like setting an agenda to one's advantage, a military invasion to seize a strategic resource, a firm's investment in research and development (R&D) on new techniques or products, and a patent on a new technology. Unconditional second moves—potentially beneficial when observing the activity of adversaries can improve one's strategic response—include intelligence gathering by countries, firms, or political organizations.

In a two-player game, Ann may effectively seize the first move by credibly committing to a strategy. If so, she alters rules that might otherwise have allowed simultaneous play or a first move by Ben. For games with multiple Nash equilibria, such as chicken or battle, a credible first mover can pick her desired Nash equilibrium—and so bias the game against an opponent. In the classic high-school driving game of chicken, if Ann can credibly commit to driving straight—that is, if she can manipulate Ben's expectations so that he expects her to drive straight no matter what—Ben's best response is to swerve.

There are two requirements for success here. First, Ann must signal her strategy to Ben; he must actually observe her signal. Indeed, Ben could move strategically by demonstrating that he does not see Ann's move, perhaps by wearing a blindfold. Second, as indicated, Ann's strategic move must be credible: it must convince Ben that she will drive straight even if he does.[33] She might devote time and energy (resources) to establishing a reputation for unyielding toughness, perhaps by fighting other students for months before the race. If so, a statement such as "I'm driving straight; deal with it" may actually alter Ben's expectations. Note that Ben's manipulated expectations also become a source of Ann's power1: she can drive so as to win the now-altered game.

After landing in Mexico, Spanish conquistador Hernán Cortés burned all but one of his ships, allowing the Aztecs to see the smoke. This act credibly informed not only the Aztecs but also Cortés' own troops that the Spanish would fight to the death (Dixit and Nalebuff 1991, 152–53). By demonstrating that his troops' hands were tied (no retreat), Cortés altered available strategies and expectations so as to bias the subsequent power1 war game against the Aztec fighters, who still could retreat. Figure 4.2 illustrates this game under the assumption that, without any strategic move, Cortés and the Aztecs would have played a game of chicken. In that case, both players expect to receive the average of the two Nash equilibria in the left-hand game, giving each an expected payoff of −0.5 (payoff to Leave ships on the right). The strategic move (Burn ships) awards the Spanish a payoff of 2. History indicates that this move succeeded.

Similarly, for games of battle, in which alternative forms of coordination distribute benefits differently, a player could use an unconditional first move to establish its preferred type of coordination. Suppose that two firms can benefit from collaborating on R&D but that method A awards firm A higher profits and method B awards firm B higher profits. Firm A could seize a first-mover advantage by hiring experts in method A and communicating that it has done so. Firm B may then realize that if it wants cooperation, it must adopt method A. A similar logic can apply to cooperation between nations, political coalitions, and social groups.[34]

In simultaneous games, orchestrating a second move can sometimes confer advantage by eliminating strategic uncertainty.[35] Opportunities for such moves arise in games that lack Nash equilibria and in other encounters where predicting another's move is both difficult and advantageous. In sports, a team can profit from reading an opponent's signals. Nations hire spies, as do business firms and political operatives. When intelligence gathering is secret, credibility is not an issue, but the strategic move still requires resources; informants must be paid.

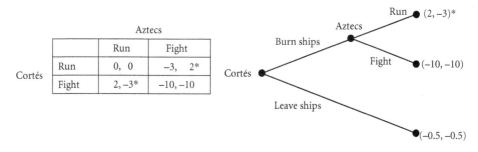

Figure 4.2   Cortés' strategic move

Conditional strategic moves are more complicated. They take the form of two-part if-then statements: if you do x, then I will do y; if you do not do x, then I will not do y. There are two basic types of conditional strategic moves: (i) threats (e.g., if you misbehave (x), then I will punish you (y)) and (ii) promises (e.g., if you behave (x), then I will reward you (y)). Furthermore, each threat contains an implied promise: if you do behave, then I will not punish you: $\sim x \to \sim y$. Likewise, each promise contains an implied threat: if you behave badly ($\sim x$), then no reward ($\sim y$).

Both parts of each statement (i.e., both $x \to y$ and $\sim x \to \sim y$) require credibility to be effective. *Primary credibility* concerns the first part—the direct threat or promise ($x \to y$). Because executing threats or honoring promises is costly to the parties who issue them, recipients may not believe such statements. For example, a threat by the United States to bomb Pyongyang if North Korea does not dismantle its nuclear weapons would not be credible. Thus establishing primary credibility requires some commitment of resources. By contrast, *secondary credibility* (that pertaining to the second part—the implied statement $\sim x \to \sim y$) is usually automatic for the same reason: if Iran stops enriching uranium, it is easier for the UN to drop sanctions than to maintain them. In some cases, however, a party must devote resources to establishing both primary and secondary credibility.[36] In all cases, conditional strategic moves, like unconditional ones, amount to tying player A's hands in order to alter player B's expectations regarding A's conduct in a subsequent move or game. Again, the shift in expectations should bias the game in A's favor.

Arguably, threats are the most important type of strategic move. One party may preclude or reduce another's ability to participate in various arenas by credibly threatening some form of punishment. For example, the Iranian government has threatened domestic opponents with arrest in order to reduce their participation in power1 arenas, such as street demonstrations. Likewise, a large firm may threaten to lower prices to deter entry by others. Threats may also limit opponents' strategies in power1 arenas, as when authorities threaten to arrest demonstrators for marching in certain public places. To establish credibility, the government may hire police and construct prisons. Similarly, a large firm may stockpile inventory in order to signal its ability to flood the market should a competitor enter.

An analogous logic applies to strategic (manipulative) promises.[37] Ann may say to Ben: "If you stay quiet, I will pay you." Figure 4.3 offers a simple example of a (so far unsuccessful) attempt by the United States (US) to induce North Korea (NK) to quit the nuclear club. The normal-form game on the left involves no strategic move. The Nash equilibrium (No aid, Keep) is bad for the US. As a strategic move, the US could promise to reward NK with aid should it dismantle its nuclear weapons. A credible promise (the US may have invested reputation) with enough aid (if $x > 8$) could improve the outcome for the US. Figure 4.3 also illustrates secondary credibility. Because No aid is the US's best response to Keep (since aid is costly), the implicit threat (Keep $\to$ No aid) is automatically credible. Similar logic applies to most implicit promises that accompany threats. Overall, establishing credibility is the key barrier to successful execution of any strategic move, but credible strategic moves indicate exercises of power2 that can bias subsequent interactions in favor of those who use them.

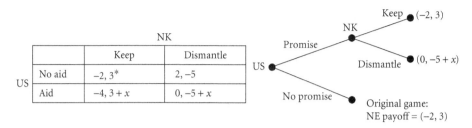

Figure 4.3   A strategic promise

Strategic Moves and the Nash Bargaining Model

We now use the Nash cooperative bargaining model (Figure 4.1) to compare strategic moves (power2) to exercises of power1. As an unconditional move, Ann could seize a first-mover advantage by credibly signaling that she will accept nothing less than a 90/10 split of the surplus. If Ben refuses, he runs the risk of receiving only his fallback. Ann's move, then, could bias the game in her favor in cases where the initial power1 game would indicate a more equitable split, such as 50/50 ($\alpha/\beta = 1$). Alternatively, prior to a power1 bargaining game, Ann could move strategically to alter one or both fallback positions. In Figure 4.1, Ann (as player A) could reduce d_B, increase d_A, do both, or lower d_B more than d_A. In all such cases, segment PQ shifts upward, granting Ann a larger share of x_A/x_B.

An example of union-company bargaining illustrates how exercises of both power1 and power2 apply to Figure 4.1. For power1, the bargaining arena is clear; the timing and key issues for negotiation are understood, as are the capabilities of both parties. Relative bargaining strengths (α/β) depend on each side's position in production, access to resources such as strike funds and profits, ability to mobilize support, potential for moving first, and patience. Prior to any strategic move, fallbacks d_A and d_B signify the payoffs to each side of facing a strike—the expected outcome of failing to negotiate an agreement.[38] Power1 bargaining yields outcome Q. Either side could, however, exercise power2 by manipulating the other's expectations about the consequences of a strike. The company (A here) might visibly stockpile production to bolster the union's perception of company fallback d_A. It might also threaten to shut down during a strike in order to reduce the union's expected fallback (d_B). For its part, the union might threaten a longer-than-expected strike in order to reduce d_A, and rally its members to achieve credibility. If either side succeeds in such efforts, segment PQ shifts in its favor. Furthermore, exercises of power2 may influence subsequent power1 bargaining. A credible threat to shut down may tilt the ratio α/β in management's favor.

Appropriately, this kind of manipulation in a Nash bargaining game is called "variable-threat bargaining" (Dixit, Skeath, and Reiley 2009, 701). Formally, in the first stage of an applicable game (or pre-game), one or both parties use a strategic move to manipulate fallbacks. In the second stage, they play the ensuing power1 bargaining game of Figure 4.1 with altered parameters d_A, d_B, α, and/or β.

In sum, two-player representations of power2 indicate that participants in negotiations or disputes may alter the effective rules of interaction in subsequent moves or games, along with associated expectations, by devoting resources to establishing unconditional moves, threats, or promises. When credible, such endeavors become strategic moves—exercises of power2 that diminish or eliminate an opponent's ability to utilize power1—by barring its access to or limiting its participation within relevant decision arenas.

The power2 idea of "mobilizing bias," however, goes further. It includes one party's (A's) use of cultural symbols and other forms of communication in order to influence other parties' (Cs') perceptions of A's opponent (B). Section 4.4 introduces this issue using a triadic concept of power.

4.4. EXTENSIONS OF POWER2: TRIADIC POWER RELATIONS AND POWER IN EXCHANGE

A more expansive concept of power2 includes attempts to manipulate perceptions or actions of various parties who have connection with one or more adversaries. This broader notion applies to power within exchange processes and moves us in the direction of power3. For modeling these relations, we present Basu's triadic model of power (2000, 132–65). Triadic power relationships indicate how coercion can enter voluntary exchange, affect distribution, and also contribute to resolving second-order CAPs of contract enforcement.

Basu asserts that triadic models often illustrate power asymmetry more clearly than dyadic models. *Dyadic models of power* examine relations between agents matched in pairs (A and B) such that their exercises of power have no impact on either's relations with other agents (various Cs) and vice versa. By contrast, in *triadic models of power*, at least one party may influence the other's interactions with one or more Cs, or the presence of Cs may affect interactions between A and B. If Ann can alter Ben's relationship with Chris or Claire while Ben lacks such ability (or has less of it), then power is fundamentally asymmetric. For dyadic models, on the other hand, power asymmetry is sometimes hard to identify.[39] Moreover, power relationships that accompany market exchange typically involve triads of some sort.

To illustrate triadic power, Basu uses an example of a landlord, laborer, and merchant who engage in labor and product exchanges. Suppose that landlady Ann hires laborer Ben to till her land, offering wage w, and that Ben has some non-employment next-best alternative (his fallback, d_B). In a competitive model, the equilibrium wage would equal the fallback ($w_r = d_B$). With voluntary exchange, Ben is no worse (or better) off working for Ann. Now suppose that both Ann and Ben have trade relations with merchant Chris; trading generates values V_A, V_B, V_{CA}, and V_{CB}. If Ann can credibly threaten to cut off Ben's trade relationship with Chris, Ann can pay any wage (w) that meets the condition $d_B - V_B \leq w < w_r$. For Ann's threat to be credible, however, Chris must value his relationship with Ann more than his relationship with Ben ($V_{CA} > V_{CB}$).[40]

The important point for the present discussion is that Ann has exercised power2 in order to shift the distribution of income in her favor. Her threat has altered the game's rules (expected payoffs) so that the competitive outcome no longer applies. Ann can now *exploit* Ben in the sense of paying him less than his fallback ($w < d_B$). Because he fears losing his relationship with Chris, Ben voluntarily accepts the offer. Basu proceeds to assert that the presence of voluntary choice in exchange does not itself guarantee (i.e., is not a sufficient condition for) the absence of coercion. Thus, in environments where triadic relationships accompany voluntary market exchanges, exercises of power2 can influence distributional outcomes. In such cases, contra Lerner's prior statement, a market transaction is actually an unsolved political problem.

A more expansive concept of triadic relationships—one that incorporates many Cs—can illustrate more fundamental applications of power2 to market exchange. In fact, contracting relationships (foundations of exchange) engender such exercises of power. Recall from Chapter 3 that, in principal-agent relationships, asymmetric information about an agent's post-contractual actions creates a need for an internal enforcement mechanism. The effort model (Figure 3.6) illustrates such enforcement via contingent renewal. The firm (Acme) enjoys a first-mover advantage because it can make a take-it-or-leave-it offer.[41] Acme offers a worker (Beth) a wage w that is better than her next-best alternative ($w > d_B$) and stipulates that it will renew her contract only if she provides sufficient effort (e). Acme's implicit threat of termination is credible because, in this nonclearing market, there are unemployed workers (Charlies) who would gladly replace Beth. Beth takes the threat seriously because termination would impose a cost of job loss ($w > d_B$). As indicated in Chapter 3, this credible threat motivates Beth to exert greater effort than she otherwise would. Acme has thus exercised power2 over Beth in order to alter her effort trajectory. The triadic element here is the presence of Charlies. Without them, Acme would not be able to exert power2.

A few additional points merit discussion. First, Acme's ability to make credible threats (and thus exercise power) arises from its position in the exchange process. Employers occupy what Bowles and Gintis call the *short side* of the labor market—the side that desires fewer transactions in a nonclearing market (1992, 339). By contrast, workers occupy the *long side*—the side with an excess supply.[42] The ensuing relative scarcity of employment opportunity renders threatened job loss credible. Second, the effort model's triadic relationship differs from that in the landlord-laborer-merchant case. Acme does not directly influence Beth's relationship with any particular Charlie. Rather, the presence of Charlies conditions interactions between Acme and Beth—again, lending credibility to Acme's threatened sanction of job loss.

Third, Beth is not exploited in the sense described previously. In fact, $w > d_B$; she earns an employment rent. This impact of power on distribution may seem counterintuitive, but recall that Beth increases e and Acme maximizes profits (minimizing w/e in Figure 3.6). The consequent employment rent is the cost Acme bears because of Beth's discretion over effort in an environment of asymmetric information (Bowles and Gintis 1992). Accordingly, Table 3.1 indicates that, in labor relationships, the principal (the employer) bears the transaction costs associated with enforcement.[43] Acme's credible threat costs it resources. Similar rents arise in other principal-agent models, such as credit markets (Stiglitz 1987; Bowles 2004). Fourth, note that we do not know whether the final w is greater or less than the hypothetical market-clearing wage (w_c) of an imaginary competitive market with perfect and complete information. There is an employment rent, $w > d_B$; yet with unemployed Charlies, d_B is less than it would be under pure competition. In any case, as noted in Section 3.3, the firm's first-mover advantage allows it to choose its most favored combination (w^*, e^* in Figure 3.6).

Finally, Bowles and Gintis (1992) assert that the exercise of power in this case facilitates a Pareto improvement over a similar situation without power (even so, the final outcome is not Pareto optimal).[44] Given asymmetric information and B's discretion over e, a failure to exert power would yield a lower w, lower e, and lower profits ($w = w_r$, $e = \bar{e}$, and $\bar{e}/w_r <$ $(e/w)^*$, as shown in Figure 3.6). Acme's exercise of power thus serves as a coordination device (Bowles and Gintis 2008). This outcome fits perfectly with the analysis in Chapter 3: the contingent renewal enforcement mechanism helps to resolve the second-order CAP associated with providing effort in contractual labor relationships. The attendant exercise of power ameliorates some of the market failure that arises from asymmetric information.

Lest we become too optimistic about the use of authority within firms, however, Bowles and Gintis add that employers may also use their position to exert somewhat arbitrary managerial authority over the workplace environment. They point to employer influence over working conditions and various managerial practices, including forms of harassment and discrimination. The credible threat of job loss allows management discretion that would not appear in a hypothetical world of pure competition. Along similar lines, William Ferguson (2005) argues that the implicit bargaining power embedded within employment relationships can lead to systematic and persistent workplace discrimination. Thus exercises of power in exchange generate both socially beneficial and undesirable outcomes.

Finally, it is important to emphasize that the exercise of power2 in market exchange is confined neither to employment relationships nor to the exercise of authority within firms. In credit markets, similar models indicate that lenders offer below-market-clearing interest rates in order to discipline subsequent borrower behavior, yet lenders and borrowers do not share positions within the same firm. The ability to exercise this form of exchange-related power2 arises from the positions of exchanging parties in their relevant markets. In credit markets, lenders occupy the short side (supply). Such use of power2 can again lead to Pareto improvement. Indeed, one could argue that the financial crisis of 2007–2010 occurred in part because lenders (notably investment banks)—seizing short-term profit opportunities with vastly unrealistic expectations—failed to exert normal discipline over extensions of loans—and thereby contributed to making most of the world worse off.[45]

Table 3.1 lists additional types of markets that use contingent renewal as a contracting enforcement strategy, including markets for managerial services, business supply, and residential tenancy. All of these contractual relationships utilize power2 to ameliorate the second-order CAPs that accompany contractual information asymmetry—and all have distributional implications. Thus our principal-agent models of contracting relationships imply that triadic exercises of power2 reside within critical types of market exchange. Because of CAPs, power permeates micro-level political economy.

Before proceeding to Section 4.5, we briefly consider a third variation on triadic power in which agent A influences B's relationship with many Cs. Expanding on Basu's landlord-laborer-merchant model, suppose that Ann can threaten Ben as follows: "If you do not accept my offer of w, I will cut off your exchanges with the town's merchants, mechanics, and medics (Cs)." For this threat to be credible, most Cs would need to value their exchanges with Ann more than those with Ben. Backed by such a credible threat, Ann could offer Ben a wage below that from the prior single-C example, and Ben would still accept. Ann's ability to influence many Cs amplifies her impact on distribution because it enhances her exercise of power2.

A person who employs this type of power2 needs to occupy a particular type of niche within a structure of exchange. Examples include an employer in a one-company town, the leader of a religious cult, a particularly well-placed middleman in an exchange network, and a corrupt political operator with multiple connections.[46] Discussing the early twentieth-century New York municipal planning/construction machine of Robert Moses, Akerlof states:

> But it was clear to all concerned that disobedience to the boss's dictates regarding construction would lead to outcasting from the machine. For the politician, this meant loss of campaign funds and of the construction pork barrel . . . for engineers, it meant loss of a job. Furthermore . . . persons who failed to respect the outcast status of those in Moses' disfavor, were in turn threatened. (1976, 616)

As suggested at the beginning of this chapter, exercises of power2 may also involve manipulative communication—including the use of various cultural symbols—in order to undermine the legitimacy of a potential adversary, his beliefs, or his actions. In this sense, Ann literally mobilizes bias against Ben. We have seen the example of Senator Joseph McCarthy's use of labels. McCarthy's use of power2 may be understood as an example of Basu's triadic power relations with multiple Cs who had political, social, or economic relationships with his targets. McCarthy silenced his adversaries by credibly threatening to end many such relationships.

A triadic concept of power relations, then, informs our understanding of the possibly counterintuitive yet nearly ubiquitous use of power2 within market exchanges—with implications on coercion in voluntary exchange, the distribution of output, and the resolution of second-order CAPs. Furthermore, this concept can illustrate the mobilization of bias via political manipulation of cultural symbols. We have now set the stage for a discussion of conditioned power—an idea that suggests an initial approach to conceptualizing power3.

4.5. THE INFLUENCE OF MANY CS: CONDITIONED POWER AS AN ILLUSTRATION OF POWER3

A full modeling of power3 lies beyond the scope of this text.[47] Basu, however, provides an insightful model that illustrates the core intuition by drawing on John K. Galbraith's (1983) related concept of conditioned power. *Conditioned power* arises when "the oppressed are so habituated to their situation that they are unaware of being oppressed" (Basu 2000, 134). One party's beliefs concerning others' behavior generates a habitual response. An example appears in Akerlof's (1976) discussion of caste relationships. By custom, any inappropriate interaction with members of other castes leads to social ostracism, and everyone follows the caste rules because they expect others to do so. To the extent that agents can affect such conditioning, they exert power3.

Basu approaches modeling conditioned power by using Vaclav Havel's (1986) idea of a post-totalitarian system or diffused dictatorship. We first consider a classical dictatorship model. Ruler Ann demands tribute t from all subjects (Bs) and threatens punishment for withholding. Because Ann has an army, her threat is credible. Bs who fail to cooperate keep value t (pay no tribute) but face punishment $-k$. As long as $t - k < 0$, each B has an incentive to pay the tribute. Subjects would rather not pay, but they face a first-order CAP with respect to organizing resistance; no one wants to risk jail time.[48] Note that power relations here are dyadic: Ann interacts separately with each B without affecting their interactions with others. Nevertheless, her greater access to resources (the army) indicates asymmetric power.

To model a post-totalitarian or *diffused dictatorship*, we create multiple triadic relationships that reflect Ann's ability to influence relations among the Bs. Suppose that anyone who does not pay tribute suffers social ostracism, indicating utility loss $-f$. Basu then defines disloyalty from the ruler's point of view. A *disloyal* subject either (i) does not pay tribute or (ii) interacts with someone who does not pay. If we add the assumption that each B expects all others to be loyal, any who refuse to pay tribute should expect payoff $t - k - f < 0$. Hence we no longer need the condition $k > t$. Furthermore, if $f > t$, all will pay even if $k = 0$. At this threshold, we transition into a diffused dictatorship: conditioned power. Subjects are so conditioned to expect ostracism from disloyalty that the ruler need not actually administer any real punishment. Basu (2000, 136–37) goes so far as to say that we do not even need a ruler! We have thus moved from power2 to power3 in the sense that it is only the Bs' own beliefs that hold them subject. If Ann (or some coalition) has contributed to influencing such beliefs, she has exercised power3.[49]

To pursue a game-theoretic interpretation, note that a person need only be "loyal" in the following sense: as long as each B expects others to be loyal, he will refuse interaction with any disloyal B. We could illustrate this dynamic with a multi-player game of assurance in which payoffs depend on the number of agents who expect certain behaviors. If all expect loyalty, then an equilibrium of full loyalty can emerge as a focal point. Should they hope to dismantle such conditioned power, the Bs would face an *expectational* CAP—that is, one founded in belief. They must somehow achieve a coordinated shift in the expectations of a critical mass of previously loyal Bs.[50] Echoing our discussion of Gaventa's challenges to accumulated power, such a change in shared expectations (an unraveling of power3) is a pre-condition for any coordinated behavioral change.

Basu draws analogies with Havel's (1986) discussion of the post-totalitarian state in Eastern Europe. The power of the communist governments in the 1970s and 1980s resided primarily in a society-wide expectation of nearly unanimous loyalty to the state in the sense defined here. The enforcers (police and army) did not actually believe in the system any more than the people did, but all shared the same expectations. Basu also draws a parallel to the phenomenon of McCarthyism in the United States in the early 1950s. As mentioned previously, McCarthy strategically manipulated cultural symbols of loyalty. But he exerted even greater power because he contributed to creating a society-wide expectation of pervasive anticommunist "loyalty," as he defined it—much like Basu's ruler.[51] In this manner, McCarthy's power extended beyond power2 into conditioned power3. Basu (2000, 147) cites Eric Posner (1997, 782): "one of the most striking aspects of McCarthyism, was that this campaign resulted from McCarthy's entrepreneurial modification of focal points, not from changes in the law."[52]

Overall, agents who occupy specific political, social, and economic positions can sometimes exercise power3 by manipulating beliefs about acceptable behavior or about the
possible reactions of others to one's own behavior in multi-player triadic relationships.
Subsequent chapters will relate such influence—along with that of power1 and power2—
to the concepts of social preference, social norms, formal institutions, and policy.

4.6. POWER AND POLITICAL ECONOMY

That power enters political relationships is obvious. That political power influences economic outcomes is also obvious, as is its relevance to bargaining processes. It is far less obvious, however, that resolution of CAPs requires the entry of power relationships into the
foundation of economic exchanges, even competitive ones. Whenever there is asymmetric
information or costs to entry or exit, as implied by contracting, the resolution of attendant
second-order CAPs both generates and requires opportunities for exercising power. Thus
power infuses political economy from its elemental micro levels to its overarching macro
levels.

Analyzing power involves identifying its three basic sources (position, access to resources, and an ability to resolve organizational CAPs), its two instruments (sanctions and
manipulative communication), and its three domains or faces. Power1 directly affects behavior, power2 affects underlying rules and expectations, and power3 affects deeper-level
preferences and beliefs. Power1 manifests itself in contests—such as union bargaining, assembling voting coalitions, or expected exercises of force—that arise in given, mutually
understood contexts or arenas. A Nash bargaining model with fixed fallback positions can
represent how power1 bargaining strength (the ratio α/β) affects the distribution of gains
from cooperation. This ratio depends, in turn, on parties' relative access to the three basic
sources of power and the corresponding derivative sources of relative dependency, mobilized support, first-mover advantage, and relative patience.

Given the prevalence of asymmetric information in economic and political exchanges,
exercises of power2 often precede or accompany uses of power1. Asymmetric information
affords opportunities to bias subsequent interactions by manipulating adversaries' expectations concerning subsequent interactions and by altering rules of participation. In such
cases, the concept of strategic moves facilitates modeling power2. Agents may bias subsequent strategic interactions by devoting resources to signaling credible alterations of expected game procedures or payoffs. To do so, they may credibly seize first or second moves
and/or issue credible threats or promises. Agents may thereby limit or preclude others'
access to power1 arenas that affect decisions and material payoffs.

A triadic conception of power2, in which one agent may credibly threaten to interfere
with another's relations with external parties, indicates a fundamental power asymmetry
and offers numerous applications to exchange. Basu models a case in which a landlord
exploits a laborer (wage below fallback) by credibly threatening to terminate the latter's
exchange relationship with a merchant. Extending this logic, the example of Robert Moses
suggests that the presence of multiple vulnerable outside exchanges enhances the impacts
of triadic exercises of power2. Alternatively, the presence of multiple outsiders frequently

conditions power dynamics between (or among) specific exchange participants. Notably, in the effort model, the presence of unemployed workers in labor markets allows employers to exert power2 by credibly threatening workers with costly job loss. Yet, by resolving the second-order CAP of a principal-agent problem, such exercise of power generates Pareto improvement. Unfortunately, it also introduces some potential for abuse, in particular various forms of discrimination. Many other fundamental exchanges, such as credit markets, allow for analogous exercises of power2. By affecting distributional outcomes, such micro-level power dynamics link growth to distribution.

The more elusive concept of power3 implies the use of manipulative communication to alter preferences and beliefs—so as to diminish the willingness of potential opponents to enter relevant arenas. Basu's diffused dictatorship, in which subjects obey because they otherwise expect ostracism, offers a rough modeling approach. Power3 emerges from and reflects an ability to manipulate such conditioned behavior, as Senator McCarthy's appeals to anticommunist loyalty did so effectively. Opponents to such moves, then, face a multi-player expectational CAP of mobilizing a sufficient shift in belief before they can even attempt to alter behavior.

Moving forward, power3 will inform our subsequent discussion of the foundations of preference as well as the role of informal and formal institutions in framing and altering collective beliefs. Power3's ability to alter beliefs both facilitates resolution of CAPs and offers ways for parties to manipulate existing institutions or affect institutional development in their favor. A fuller exploration of such influence on belief, however, requires a broader conceptual framework. Up to this point, we have assumed traditional, self-interested rational actors. Chapter 3 argued that internal enforcement mechanisms among such actors can only partially resolve second-order CAPs of contract enforcement and cannot adequately explain the observed resolution of many seemingly intractable CAPs. Analogously, our present discussion of power2 and power3 points to a need for more comprehensive concepts of motivation and even cognition. Chapter 5 will introduce reciprocity as a key alternative source of motivation, and Chapter 6 will more fully address motivation and introduce the more complicated topic of cognition. Part III will then apply these ideas to institutional formation and development.

EXERCISES

4.1. Design a two-stage bargaining game between ruler A and subject group B. In the first stage, group B faces a CAP of mobilizing solidarity. Model this stage and indicate possible outcomes. For each outcome, draw and label a Nash cooperative bargaining model that represents the second-stage negotiations between A and B.

4.2. Describe and show equations for an alternating-offers bargaining game with an odd number of offers. Solve for the outcomes (bargained payoffs) to players Ann and Ben. Briefly explain.

4.3. In an alternating-offers game, prove that if one player (Ann) has a higher discount rate than the other player (Ben), Ann's payoff, as either a first or second mover, is lower than it would be if the discount rates were equal.

4.4. Find an example of a political-economy problem (one with gains to exchange or cooperation and costs to enforcement) that may be modeled as a game of chicken in which one player may seize a first-mover advantage. Construct a simple model and explain how this relates to exercising of power2.

4.5. Repeat Exercise 4.4 for a game of battle.

4.6. Construct a game of battle that resembles the description on pages 80–81 and supply an example.

4.7. Using the discussion of threats and promises as a foundation, construct an example of a two-player game that illustrates a case in which one party (row) can improve her outcome only by devoting resources to achieving both primary and secondary credibility for a strategic threat or promise (choose the one that best fits your example).

4.8. Prove that, as claimed in Section 4.4, A's threat will not be credible unless C values his relationship with A more than his relationship with B ($V_{CA} > V_{CB}$). *Hint:* What would happen if $V_{CA} < V_{CB}$?

4.9. In Section 4.5, the Bs (who hope to oppose As) face an expectational CAP. Design a model, consisting of equations and graphs, that represents such a situation. Explain your model. *Hint:* Recall that a change in shared expectations of a critical mass of the Bs is a pre-condition for any coordinated behavioral change.

5 BASIC MOTIVATION: RATIONAL EGOISTS AND RECIPROCAL PLAYERS

> Allegiance, after all, has to work two ways; and one can grow weary of an allegiance which is not reciprocal.
>
> James Baldwin (1961/1991)

The farmers in Arruba and Boratonia intermingle with varying degrees of frequency and closeness of association. Friends, neighbors, or regular colleagues may know each other well. Acquaintances know each other slightly, and some are known only by reputation. In their social lives, farmers may trade favors or reprimands, particularly with others whom they know well. Suppose that the governing body of Arruba has agreed to limit water use and stipulated punishments for overuse but that officials cannot observe night activity. Farmers agree in principle, but everyone knows that an individual could make more money by drawing off extra water at night. Thus those who adhere to the agreement end up sacrificing their own profit for the common good. Farmers who make this sacrifice may expect others to reciprocate with similar restraint. Indeed, abiding farmers may consider adherents to be fair or giving and regard violators as unfair or greedy. They may then reward the former with praise or kind actions and punish the latter with scorn or hurtful actions. If the presence of these inclinations among a large portion of the community is common knowledge, these reciprocal exchanges can help resolve the water-limitation CAP.

Chapters 2–4 have, following standard convention in economics, implicitly assumed that all agents are rational in the traditional sense of striving to maximize their own material payoffs. We now refer to such players as *rational egoists*. Chapter 3 left us with two main implications. First, because asymmetric information generates second-order CAPs of enforcement within exchange processes, power relations enter exchange; Chapter 4 developed the implications of this statement. Second, the near-universal presence of second-order coordination and enforcement CAPs limits society's potential for resolving first-order CAPs of free-riding. In fact, models based solely upon rational egoists cannot adequately explain observed cooperation within many groups in many circumstances (Ostrom 2000a; Gächter 2007).

The present chapter's discussion of reciprocity begins to address this disjuncture by augmenting our models with reciprocal actors. Unlike rational egoists, reciprocal actors possess an intrinsic desire to reward kind, friendly, or fair behavior and to punish unkind, hostile, or unfair behavior. Within groups, reciprocal actors alter the dynamics of second-order CAPs because they may willingly bestow selective positive or negative sanctions on friends, colleagues, or acquaintances—even with no expectation of subsequent material gain. Reciprocity can thereby indicate credible enforcement of cooperative agreements and so resolve second-order CAPs that would otherwise inhibit agreement or exchange among rational egoists.

By helping to resolve second-order CAPs, notably in small groups, reciprocity facilitates the enforcement of contracts and other agreements—and so enhances prospects for multiple forms of social, political, and economic exchange. Reciprocity may help address all of the principal-agent problems listed in Table 3.1, and thereby elicit diligent effort at work, quality output from suppliers, sensible behavior from borrowers, and so forth. Reciprocity thus extends the domain of feasible contracting or agreement, lending credibility to arrangements that might otherwise fail. Parties who understand the dynamics of reciprocity may even attempt to design provisions in contracts that signal good intentions or trust, perhaps by allowing others considerable discretion. By facilitating contract enforcement as it simultaneously influences the content of contracts, reciprocity helps establish foundations for economic exchange and multiple forms of cooperation in political and social realms. Reciprocal relationships thus underlie development and growth, though their influence is strongest within small groups.[1]

Our discussion proceeds as follows. Section 5.1 develops the key concepts of rational egoists and reciprocal players. Section 5.2 models interactions among these two types of players, noting the impact of reciprocal actions and reciprocal material sanctions on resolving CAPs. Section 5.3 introduces reciprocal social rewards and punishments and asserts that such social exchanges engender flexible, low-cost enforcement mechanisms that can enhance a group's ability to resolve second-order CAPs. Section 5.4 applies reciprocity to workplace morale, holdup problems, and reciprocity-based conflicts. Section 5.5 concludes by addressing the implications of reciprocal second-party enforcement on the development of trust and mistrust, with brief commentary on social capital and limitations related to group size.

5.1. UNDERLYING CONCEPTS

Both neoclassical economic theory and rational choice models in political science begin with an assumption of rational actors. We proceed with a general definition: a *rational* actor exhibits consistent, goal-oriented behavior. *Consistency* here encompasses both logical and temporal dimensions. Logically, it means transitivity of preference orderings: if I prefer apples to oranges and oranges to lemons, I must also prefer apples to lemons. The temporal dimension, the *stability of preferences*, means that preference orderings do not change during the period of analysis. The general modifier *goal-oriented* allows for any goal, including helping or harming others. The pursuit of such goals need only be consistent to count as rational behavior. Rational actors, then, consistently pursue their goals—whether selfish, reciprocal, or even altruistic. Assumptions of rationality may thus represent many forms of economic, political, and social behavior.

Generally speaking, neoclassical economic theory need not restrict this versatile approach to rationality. Nevertheless in practice, particularly at the undergraduate level, economists often employ a far narrower definition of rational behavior—what Bowles calls the *self-interest axiom* (2004, 97).[2] Here economic agents pursue only self-interested goals, and such pursuit is common knowledge. *Self-interest* means something quite specific: preferences are both self-regarding and outcome-oriented (Bowles 2004, 96).[3] *Self-regarding* stipulates that preferences relate only to possible conditions for oneself, independent of anyone else. In other words, agents do not care about outcomes experienced by others or about comparisons between their own outcomes and those for others. Self-regarding employees, for example, do not care about their colleagues' earnings either per se or compared to their own earnings. The term *outcome-oriented* indicates concern only for actual material outcomes, independent of any procedures that generate them. If I receive $100, once I have it in hand, I gain the same utility from it regardless of whether it is pay for work performed, a merit award, a gift from my mother, a bribe, or an outcome of theft.[4]

Borrowing from Ostrom (2000a), we use the term *rational egoist* to refer to an agent who follows outcome-oriented material self-interest in precisely this sense. Prior analysis has suggested that the strategic calculus of rational egoists (hereafter, e-types) offers, at best, a limited conceptual foundation for understanding the resolution of CAPs. In particular, rational-egoist models provide insufficient insight into the role of coordination and cooperation in economic development.[5] Indeed, the self-interest axiom cannot even explain the resolution of relatively small-scale CAPs envisioned by Olson and observed by Ostrom (1990, 2000a). Olson's concept of selective social incentives (1971, 60–64) operates outside of the preference domain of e-types. Likewise, individuals who work to resolve small-scale common-pool resource CAPs express concern not only about outcomes for others but also about the actual processes or procedures that generate outcomes for themselves and others (Ostrom 2000a). Involved individuals may, for example, care about their input into decisions or about the intentions of others with whom they interact. Note here that intentions are part of the process that generates outcomes: if you give me $20, I may enjoy it less if I suspect your motives. Overall, agents who care sufficiently about either procedures or outcomes for others may conditionally cooperate with or willingly punish others (Ostrom 2000a).[6]

While this chapter incorporates e-types as one category of agent, it departs sharply from the self-interest axiom (but not rationality) by introducing a second type of agent: *reciprocal actors*.[7] Such agents (hereafter, r-types) observe *intrinsic reciprocity*: they possess an intrinsic desire to reward behavior that appears to be kind or fair and likewise punish seemingly unkind or unfair behavior (Sobel 2005). These agents willingly sacrifice limited material gain in order to offer either material or social rewards or punishments in response to certain behaviors.[8] For example, an r-type may undertake the effort of a dirty look or risk expressing a complaint to someone who cuts in line, litters, or smokes inside a public place, but probably not much more. Greater violations of one's sense of fairness may prompt more serious reprisals, including violence. Moreover, the strength of reciprocal sentiment tends to grow with frequency of interaction.

Before proceeding, it is important to distinguish intrinsic reciprocity from instrumental reciprocity. *Instrumental reciprocity* involves calculated use of reciprocal behavior to achieve other (usually material) ends (Sobel 2005). Instrumental reciprocity, in fact, accompanies any standard economic transaction. If I offer my labor time, my employer reciprocates by paying me. If I offer a few dollars, a store owner reciprocates by giving me fruit. A more interesting form of instrumental reciprocity, sometimes called "reciprocal altruism" (Gintis 2000), appears in the tit-for-tat resolution of a PD game (see Section 3.2). Recall that a player using t-f-t starts out by cooperating and then duplicates the other's last move. Obviously, this is a form of reciprocity; furthermore, the implied reciprocity underlies the intuitive appeal of the model. But the motivation for t-f-t emerges from expected material gain, rather than from an intrinsic desire to either reward fair or punish unfair behavior. As Chapter 3 indicates, if the discount rate is too high, the probability of continuation too low, or the gains from cooperation too low relative to gains from defection, the t-f-t strategy fails to resolve a repeated PD game—precisely because material gain would not follow. Another variant of instrumental reciprocity, sometimes called "indirect reciprocity" (Fehr and Henrich 2003), involves trading favors (or punishments) in order to gain a good reputation. Various types of agents, including e-types, may utilize these variants of instrumental reciprocity. Such behaviors often operate in conjunction with intrinsic reciprocity, frequently as complements, sometimes as substitutes.

Intrinsic reciprocity, on the other hand, implies that a desire to reward or punish can sometimes overcome one's desire for immediate or expected material gain. Fehr and Gächter capture this core intuition nicely:

> Reciprocity means that in response to friendly actions, people are frequently much nicer and much more cooperative than predicted by the self-interest model; conversely, in response to hostile actions, they are much more nasty and even brutal. (2000, 159)

Subsequent sections will show that this intrinsically motivated willingness to reward or punish—even at a cost to oneself—introduces new dynamics to models of consistent goal-oriented behavior that can facilitate resolution of CAPs within small groups.

5.2. INTRINSIC RECIPROCITY, UTILITY, AND TWO-PLAYER MODELS

Adding r-types to our models moves us in the direction of explaining previously inexplicable cooperative behavior, particularly within relatively small groups—though reciprocal punishment sometimes intensifies conflict. In either case, r-types can, within limits, credibly promise or threaten sanctions: positive for fair or cooperative behavior and/or negative for defection. Within a given community, some might praise contributors to public goods, such as public gardens, for "doing their fair share." They may also condemn selfish slackers. On the other hand, when relevant parties lack consensus on the value or legitimacy of certain collective goods or activities, reciprocity may interfere with resolving CAPs.[9] In some circles, cooperation with others induces scorn. For example, some high-school students might mock other students who study hard or show too much school spirit. Note further that we may sometimes interpret unified groups or even nations as reciprocal agents. International relations offer many examples of reward and punishment between nations that appear to reflect more than sheer material self-interest.

To model reciprocity, we first address the basic utility responses that motivate reciprocal agents. The core intuition of intrinsic reciprocity resides in how r-types respond to both the intentions and payoffs of other players, compared to their own (Sobel 2005).[10] Unlike e-types, r-types possess *other-regarding* preferences; they care about the payoffs received by others. They also possess a type of *process-regarding* preference—concern about the procedures used to generate outcomes.[11] R-types care about the intentions of others, and intentions affect procedures.

More precisely, r-types distinguish kind or fair intentions from unkind or unfair intentions. They gain utility from either increasing payoffs to apparently kind players or decreasing payoffs to apparently unkind players. Conversely, rewarding unkind or punishing kind behavior would reduce an r-type's utility. We further stipulate that the strength of reciprocal sentiment increases with the frequency of interaction. For a two-player game between players i and j, we have

$$(5.1) \qquad u_i(s) = \pi_i(s) + \phi_i(s) + \kappa_j(a_j; t) \times \Delta_i(\pi_j + \phi_j(s)),$$

where s denotes the strategies of both players; π_i and π_j represent material payoffs to players i and j; here π can represent outcomes of supply-demand interactions or a game with material payoffs; and $\phi_i(s)$ and $\phi_j(s)$ represent net social payoff received from others—net praise and scorn—as functions of s. The third term, $\kappa_j(a_j; t) \times \Delta_i(\pi_j + \phi_j(s))$, represents the reciprocity payoff to i. It is the product of two elements: player i's perception of j's kindness $\kappa_j(a_j; t)$ and the change in player j's payoffs that i attributes to their interaction $\Delta_i(\pi_j + \phi_j(s))$. These terms require some explanation.

The kindness function $\kappa_j(a_j; t)$ shows i's intrinsic response to her perception of j's kindness. If i regards j as kind, $\kappa_j > 0$ and vice versa. Whether κ is positive or negative depends on i's observation or expectation concerning j's actions (attitudes, attributes; a_j).[12] The absolute value of κ depends on t, the number of times i and j have interacted; $|\partial\kappa/\partial t| > 0$, indicating that the strength of a reciprocal response depends on the degree of familiarity between players. Now, to represent the impact of reciprocity on i's utility, we must multiply $\kappa_j(a_j; t)$ by $\Delta_i(\pi_j + \phi_j(s))$, the change in j's material and social payoffs that i attributes to their interaction.[13] Thus, if $\kappa > 0$ and $\Delta_i(\pi_j + \phi_j(s)) > 0$ or if $\kappa < 0$ and $\Delta_i(\pi_j + \phi_j(s)) < 0$, i gains reciprocity utility from their interaction (perhaps pride from repaying a favor or satisfaction from scolding an infraction). Alternatively, if these two terms have opposite signs, i loses utility (as in feeling anger that a cheater did well or guilt from harming a friend).

For example, suppose that i and j are roommates. If j contributes (C) to a joint public good such as cleanliness, say, by taking out the trash, i may infer kind intentions ($\kappa > 0$) and may then gain utility by doing something nice for j, perhaps washing the dishes. On the other hand, if j persistently fails to clean (D)—indicating $\kappa < 0$—i may want to punish j, perhaps by failing to mention a party. The magnitude of i's feelings in either case increases over time with repeated interaction ($|\partial\kappa/\partial t| > 0$).

Generally speaking, there are three types of actions player i could take to alter j's payoff $(\pi_j + \phi_j(s))$ in the desired direction; i could offer:

(i) a strategic response, as in following C with C or D with D;

(ii) a direct material reward or punishment, such as a gift or damaging j's property; or

(iii) a direct social reward or punishment, such as praise or scorn.

We address these possible responses in the context of public-good contribution games.

All players belong to social group G of size N whose members interact frequently enough to support reciprocal relationships; $N \in [2, N^s]$, where N^s indicates the maximum (small) group size that allows repeated reciprocal interaction. In terms of equation (5.1), when $N \leq N^s$, t is large enough so that $|\kappa_j(a; t)| \geq |\kappa(a_j)_{min}|$, where $|\kappa(a_j)_{min}|$ has sufficient value to affect outcomes. Each member of G chooses whether to contribute (C), which induces $\kappa > 0$ for other players, or to defect (D), which induces $\kappa < 0$. Thus, if player j plays C, player i has an intrinsic desire to increase j's payoff; the reverse happens if j plays D. In either case, i wants to respond "in kind" via strategy, reward, or punishment.

To construct a general model, we first restrict attention to strategic reciprocity. If player i either observes or expects j to play C or D, i has an intrinsic desire to do the same. If j plays C, i receives positive reciprocity utility β if i increases j's payoff by also playing C. Player i would also receive β if, in response to an observed (or expected) D, she lowers j's payoff by also playing D—getting even. If, on the other hand, j plays C and i plays D, i loses utility ψ (guilt); she also loses utility ψ (as in anger without recompense) if she plays C and j plays D.[14] Using a modified version of public-good equation (2.2), we have[15]

$$(5.2) \qquad u_i = -c_i + \alpha \sum_{j=1}^{N} c_j + z_s \beta - z_o \psi.$$

As in (2.2), c is the cost of contribution, $\alpha < 1$ is the marginal return from contribution, and $1/N < \alpha < 1$. Here z_s is the proportion of other players in G who take the same action as i (C or D), where $z_s \in [0, (N-1)/N]$. Similarly, z_o denotes the proportion of other players in G who choose the opposite action. Note the conformity (or solidarity) element of this model. Agents gain utility from using the same strategy as others and lose utility (discomfort) from using different strategies. To generate additional results, we now turn to simpler models.

Two-Player Models

Our two-player models offer two main results. First, the potential for strategic reciprocity to foster cooperation depends on the types of players involved and on whether a game is sequential or simultaneous. In particular, cooperation is more likely with r-types and in sequential games. Second, and not surprisingly, adding direct sanctions enhances enforcement. Intrinsic reciprocity facilitates sanctioning because it motivates r-types to undertake the costs of rewarding or punishing others. Direct material sanctions can discipline e-types away from free-riding, but they can be costly to administer and may not be appropriate or even feasible. We postpone discussion of social sanctions until Section 5.3.

We begin with strategic reciprocity. Consider a two-person, two-move sequential game in which player types are common knowledge and j moves first, inducing i's reciprocal response. Figure 5.1 illustrates, using payoffs from equation (5.2). If both players are r-types, (C, C) is the backwards-induction outcome whenever

$$(5.3) \qquad \beta + \psi > c(1 - \alpha).$$

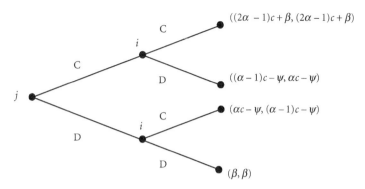

Figure 5.1   Two-player strategic reciprocity

The sum of reciprocity utility gained from taking the same action plus that lost from taking the other action $(\beta + \psi)$ must exceed the material gain from free-riding $(c(1 - \alpha))$.[16] If so, reciprocity utilities β and ψ effectively provide a mutually understood, internalized enforcement mechanism that induces joint cooperation. We say that β and ψ are *potent*: inclusion of one or both alters the game outcome from (D, D) to (C, C). Note, however, that potency requires a sufficiently low cost of contribution c, for any given values of β and ψ. Thus reciprocity-induced contribution follows a "law of demand" whereby an increase in the cost of contributing to a public good lowers the level of reciprocity-induced contribution.[17]

Now assume that one player is an e-type and the other is an r-type. With potent reciprocity payoffs, if the second mover (i) is an r-type, a (C, C) outcome follows. But if the e-type moves second, (D, D) follows.[18]

Simultaneous games offer a less intuitive framework for modeling reciprocity, but they more clearly illustrate the role of trust in fostering cooperation. Consider the game between two r-types in Figure 5.2. Each player responds reciprocally to expected, rather than observed, behavior of the other.[19] If equation (5.3) holds, we have an assurance game with Nash equilibria at (C, C) and (D, D). We may regard this game as an *emotional coordination game*, meaning that the players can coordinate their reciprocal responses so as to create a focal point at (C, C)—provided they each trust the other to prefer cooperation. With only two players, they might simply discuss their emotional responses (β and ψ) and so coordinate via cheap talk (Camerer and Thaler 2003).[20] More generally, let ρ represent the probability that the players generate sufficient trust (through either intuition or communication) to play (C, C). With probability $1 - \rho$, they play (D, D).[21] Figure 5.2's expected payoff then becomes $\rho(2\alpha - 1)c + \beta$.[22] The greater ρ (the more they trust each other), the more likely a (C, C) outcome becomes and the higher its expected payoff. On the other hand, if (5.3) does not hold, or if one or both players are e-types, the Nash equilibrium becomes (D, D). Thus, even when one cannot observe the other's prior action, sufficient trust can facilitate resolution of CAPs.

Player B

		C	D
Player A	C	$(2\alpha - 1)c + \beta, (2\alpha - 1)c + \beta$	$(\alpha - 1)c + \psi, \alpha c - \psi$
	D	$\alpha c - \psi, (\alpha - 1)c - \psi$	β, β

Figure 5.2   Two-player simultaneous strategic reciprocity (emotional coordination)

Two Players with Reciprocal Punishment

The potential to administer punishment, not surprisingly, strengthens reciprocal enforcement. Sanctions may be either material or social; for now, think of them as material. Because intrinsic reciprocity can motivate r-types to accept the costs of administering sanctions, it enhances the credibility of either threats to punish or promises to reward. Accordingly, prospects for resolving second-order enforcement CAPs improve—particularly when r-types discipline e-types. Small social groups may then achieve more or less spontaneously motivated selective incentives for cooperation or against defection. Ostrom's Turkish fishery offers an example: fishers assigned to specific areas would willingly punish any observed intruder.

Continuing with two-player models, we augment Figure 5.1 with a third move that allows an r-type first mover (i) to sanction an e-type second mover (j).[23] Should j choose to play D after i plays C, the ψ in equation (5.1) indicates that i would gain utility from lowering j's payoff—motivation for reciprocal punishment. Player i may then punish j by amount p at a per unit administration cost of c_p; hence the total cost (to i) of punishing (j) is $c_p p$.[24] We assume that administering punishment relieves anger, so that i's net utility loss from a (C, D) outcome is $\psi - c_p p$.[25] Figure 5.3 illustrates this scenario. Player i chooses between C and D, followed by j facing the same choice; i then observes j's move and decides between punish (P) or not (N).[26] Player i is willing to bestow sanction $p \geq 0$ on j under two

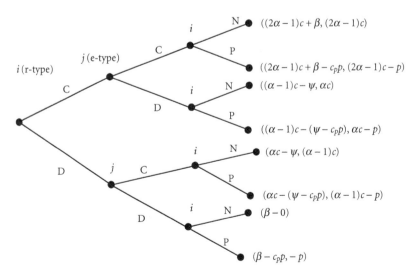

Figure 5.3   Public-good game with i as an r-type and j as an e-type

	Simultaneous	Sequential	Sequential and sanction
r vs. r	$\rho(C, C) + (1 - \rho)(D, D)$	(C, C)	(C, C)
r vs. e	(D, D)	0.5(D, D) + 0.5(C, C)	(C, C)
e vs. e	(D, D)	(D, D)	n/a

Figure 5.4   Expected SPE/NE outcomes by player and game type

conditions: (i) if, as before, $\kappa_j < 0$ following (C, D) or (D, C) (both are possible, though the first is more likely); and (ii) if the total cost of administering punishment does not exceed the anger disutility: $c_p p \leq \psi$. Assume that both conditions hold and (for simplicity) that i administers the same p at cost c_p for either a (C, D) or a (D, C) combination. If the cost of being punished exceeds the gain from defecting ($p > \alpha(1 - c)$), j prefers C to D; hence we attain a cooperative outcome (C, C, N). Thus intrinsic reciprocity has successfully resolved the CAP by motivating punishment.

Under the assumption that equation (5.3) holds and that $c_p p \leq \psi$, Figure 5.4 summarizes our two-player game outcomes. Intrinsic reciprocity engenders a greater likelihood of resolution in sequential games than in simultaneous games, and an ability to sanction after observing the other's move enhances this effect. Hence, not surprisingly, rules of the game influence prospects for success. We now turn to multi-player games, beginning with strategic reciprocity and then incorporating social sanctions.

5.3. MULTI-PLAYER RECIPROCITY AND SOCIAL EXCHANGE

Multi-player games reinforce the results of two-player games. They also point to the effects of group size on resolution, introduce relationships of conformity or solidarity, illustrate path dependence, and establish that trust affects the stability of cooperation. We begin with a description of multi-player strategic reciprocity. After pausing to compare social and material sanctions, we proceed to generate a multi-player model with negative sanctions.

Consider a multi-player strategic reciprocity game (no direct sanctions) among r-types, based on equation (5.2). Without intrinsic reciprocity, we would have a PD game, like that shown in equation (2.2) and Figure 2.8. Instead, we find a multi-player game of assurance. Unlike the two-player assurance game in Section 5.2, however, communication among many players is not likely to be cheap or fully reliable.[27] To illustrate, we adopt modified versions of public-good contribution equations (2.9) and (2.10). As in those equations, the functions $C(n + 1)$ and $D(n)$ show the payoffs to strategies C and D as a function of the number of other players (members of G) who contribute (n). We incorporate equation (5.2)'s β and ψ, now with subscripts c and d to distinguish (C, D) from (D, C) responses. We also replace z_s and z_o from (5.2) with n/N or $(N - 1 - n)/N$ as appropriate (where $N \leq N^s$). Recall, that when agent i cooperates, we have $n + 1$ cooperators. Thus:

(5.4) $C(n + 1) = [(n + 1)\alpha - 1]c + n(\beta_c/N) - (N - 1 - n)\psi_c/N;$

(5.5) $$D(n) = n\alpha c + (N - 1 - n)(\beta_d/N) - n\psi_d/N.$$

Figure 5.5 presents this multi-agent assurance game from the perspective of a marginal agent. Stable Nash equilibria (NE) occur at (D, $n = 0$; nobody contributes) and (C, $n = N - 1$; all contribute). The unstable internal NE at n^* indicates a critical-mass tipping point. If the number of others who cooperate (n) exceeds n^*, the marginal agent will prefer to contribute, creating momentum toward the cooperative NE. We encounter a *positive-feedback mechanism*—that is, a dynamic process in which motion in one direction induces further motion in the same direction. The opposite response (again with positive feedback) occurs when $n < n^*$; hence n^* is a tipping point.

The presence of a tipping point in Figure 5.5 (as in other multiplayer games of assurance) suggests the property of path dependence over time. Starting from a stable equilibrium at (D, $n = 0$), moving to (C, $n = N - 1$), or vice versa, requires crossing the n^* threshold; the initial equilibrium (starting point) thus influences future development. To assess the difficulty of such crossing, we solve for n^*. Setting $\psi_c = \psi_d$ and $\beta_c = \beta_d$, for simplicity, and setting $C(n + 1) = D(n)$, we have

(5.6) $$n^* = \frac{N[(1-\alpha)c + \beta + \psi] - \beta - \psi}{2(\beta + \psi)}.$$

Equation (5.6) indicates that an increase in contribution costs (c) or group size (N) moves the tipping point n^* farther from the origin. Consequently, when starting from a zero-contribution equilibrium, coordinating full cooperation becomes more difficult—as $n^* + 1$ agents would have to simultaneously shift their strategy from D to C. Increases in reciprocity utilities β and ψ, however, have the opposite effect. Moreover, if a cooperative outcome can be established, β and ψ generate stability.[28] Recall that the absolute values of β and ψ increase with repeated interaction; thus stability can increase over time with repetition. We may now interpret a common perception of relatively high values for β and ψ as reflecting mutual trust that agents will act reciprocally. Such common trust fosters resolution of CAPs and generates stability, reinforcing relevant (punctuated) social equilibria.

With similar reasoning, this model can represent conformity or solidarity effects. Suppose that a group of students plan a party and that everyone is asked to bring a treat. Treats

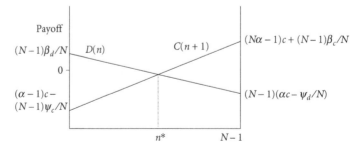

Figure 5.5   Multi-player strategic reciprocity

cost money and anyone can partake regardless of contribution. Because they are friends, the students have an intrinsic desire to bring treats if they expect others to do so (β), but they would resent bringing treats if others do not (ψ). If each expects enough others to bring treats ($n > n^*$), each student will want to do so and vice versa. An analogous logic can apply to the creation of either political or economic public goods among groups, such as daring to oppose a dictator, joining a union, interfirm cooperation on R&D, collusion among oligopolists, and adherence to international conventions. We could model each of these problems as a large-scale or high-stakes conformity, solidarity, or trust game.

Before augmenting this model with sanctions, we pause to compare material and social variants. Direct material sanctions can discipline all types of players, but their applicability is limited, particularly within small groups. Many forms of noncontractual material punishment or reward, though potentially flexible and effective, are either not legal or not appropriate—or both. It is illegal to shoot shoplifters or offer bribes. Accordingly, third parties, such as the state, often administer material punishments (and sometimes rewards). Furthermore, even legal material rewards or punishments may violate applicable norms. Few of us pay friends, neighbors, or helpful colleagues for favors; actually, paying them would usually be considered an insult.

Thus, in many informal situations, the direct rewards and punishments that accompany reciprocal exchange have a social dimension: various forms of approval or disapproval. Gächter and Fehr (1999) refer to such interactions as social exchanges. More precisely, a *social exchange* is a noncontractual expression of approval or disapproval (respect or disrespect) made in response to specific actions of others. We regard social exchange as a component of reciprocal behavior that involves direct social rewards and punishments. People often praise actions or attitudes that they regard as kind, fair, or good and condemn those they regard as unkind, unfair, or bad.[29]

Social exchanges avoid many problems that confront informal material sanctions. Social sanctions are typically less costly to administer—often much less so. Their informal, noncontractual nature allows more spontaneity and flexibility; social exchange can respond precisely to subtle changes in actions or context. Social sanctions are rarely illegal and often possess far more legitimacy than material sanctions. Most people would not punish a bothersome neighbor by damaging property—even with no chance of being caught—but they might avoid eye contact, frown, sneer, complain, or even scold. Likewise, many smile at, thank, or praise a helpful neighbor. The importance of social exchanges is stressed by Olson (1971), who cites selective social incentives as the key factor that makes providing collective goods (resolving CAPs) easier for small groups than for large groups. Social exchanges foster informal second-party enforcement that can help small groups resolve second-order CAPs and so discourage free-riding.

Social exchanges may have either purely social or both social and material consequences. In cases with material consequences, social exchange can provide low-cost, informal (and legal) methods for applying or credibly threatening adverse—though not necessarily precise—material consequences. Social ostracism is a particularly important type of materially consequential social punishment (Bowles and Gintis 2004a). For example, a workgroup may ostracize a member who does not carry his own weight or who cozies up to the boss. He may subsequently experience reduced access to information, or less cooperation from workmates, and thus become less productive. When social sanctions have material consequences, e-types should respond. In terms of modeling, the material consequences of social punishment can be included in Figure 5.3's term p, once we note that the costs of social sanctioning are typically lower than those for pure material punishment ($c_{ps} < c_{pm}$, where $c_p = c_{ps} + c_{pm}$). Relatively low levels of the reciprocity utilities β and ψ (signifying a low intensity of reciprocal sentiment) might then still motivate (low cost) social disciplining of e-types.

We note three more points on the effectiveness of social exchange. First, *pure social exchange*—that with only social consequences—offers selective social incentives to those that care about social opinion (r-types). Thus adding a pure social punishment term (p_s) to Figure 5.3 would influence an r-type second mover without affecting an e-type. Likewise, adding social rewards would enhance the effect on r-types. Second, the influence of a given social exchange (with or without material consequences) decreases with greater social distance between or among relevant parties. And greater distance reduces the probability of repeated interaction. We thus find another factor that tends to limit the size of effective reciprocal groups, pointing to another advantage of small groups in resolving CAPs.[30] Third, although social exchange may more easily facilitate resolution of CAPs than equally consequential material rewards or punishments, the consequences of pure social punishments can be low compared to material alternatives—such as murder, to cite an extreme example.

Our final model adds direct social or material sanctions to the multi-player public-good game shown in equations (5.4) and (5.5). Not surprisingly, this addition enhances prospects for cooperation. We assume that only cooperators sanction defectors and, for simplicity, that all sanctions are punishments.[31] As before, agents administer punishment at a cost to themselves. The motivation to do so depends on the strategic intrinsic reciprocity term ψ_c in two manners. First, applying punishment p reduces the utility loss that cooperators experience from defection by others (from ψ_c). Second, the utility gain from punishing malfeasance can offset the cost of punishing (c_p). We assume a cost-of-punishment function $c_p(p) = p^2/\psi_c$. Note that c_p increases (nonlinearly) in p and is inversely proportional to ψ_c. We also assume that if there is at least one defector, each cooperator sanctions (on average) one defector. Incorporating these ideas into equation (5.4) yields

$$(5.7) \quad C(n+1) = [(n+1)\alpha - 1]c + n(\beta_c/N) - [(N-1-n)/N](\psi_c - p) - p^2/\psi_c.$$

The first two terms on the right-hand side, as well as the ratio that precedes the third term, are identical to those in (5.4) and retain the same interpretations. The second parenthetical element of the third term indicates that sanctioning reduces utility loss ψ_c by amount p. Because each cooperator sanctions one defector, the ratio $[(N-1-n)/N]$ applies to p the same as it does to ψ_c. The final term specifies the net cost of punishing described in the previous paragraph. It can be shown that an agent maximizes its utility from sanctioning a defector by choosing $p = \psi_c/2$.[32] Substituting $\psi_c/2$ for p in the third and fourth terms of (5.7) and writing separate payoff equations for C and D (adjusting (5.5)), we have

$$(5.8) \quad C(n+1) = [(n+1)\alpha - 1]c + n(\beta_c/N) - (N-1-n)\psi_c/2N - \xi\psi_c/2;$$

(5.9) $D(n) = n\alpha c + (N - n - 1)(\beta_d/N) - n\psi_d/N - [n/(N - n)]p,$

where $\xi = 1$ if $N - n \geq 2$ (at least one defector) and 0 otherwise (no defectors). In equation (5.9), the first three terms are identical to those in (5.5) and carry the same interpretations. The final term shows the expected punishment p received from the $n/(N - n)$ cooperators, given that each cooperator sanctions (on average) one defector. Combining implications, equation (5.7) shows that reciprocal anger at defectors (ψ_c) not only motivates sanctioning but also determines its precise amount, accounting for its costs, while (5.9) indicates the amount of sanctioning that defectors should expect to receive.

Figure 5.6 illustrates these equations. As in Figure 5.5, there are three Nash equilibria: two stable NE at (D, $n = 0$) and (C, $n = N - 1$) and an unstable tipping point at $n = n^*$. In Figure 5.6, however, the intercept of $C(n + 1)$ is closer to zero than in Figure 5.5, and the endpoint of $D(n)$ is lower. Both effects push the tipping point n^* closer to the origin.[33] Again we have path dependence, but now with a lower n^* threshold. Thus, adding reciprocal sanctions to a multi-player model of intrinsic reciprocity makes an initial full-defection NE (D, $n = 0$) somewhat easier to reverse—and correspondingly makes a cooperative NE (C, $n = N - 1$) more resistant to external shocks, indicating a more stable punctuated equilibrium.

We conclude this section with a few additional comments on models, sanctions, and players. Multi-player games like that of Figure 5.6 address only r-types, since e-types would not administer sanctions.[34] For two-player games, a variant on Figure 5.3 that includes terms for both material and pure social sanctions could show that the larger the material share of sanctions, the greater the likelihood of e-type response. If players are drawn randomly from a population of both types, the higher the proportion of r-types, the greater the likelihood that social sanctions with little material consequence (i.e., predominantly pure social sanctions) would induce cooperation. Moreover, considering the cost and normative limitations to material sanctions, social exchange may offer the most efficient method for inducing cooperation in groups with high proportions of r-types. Once again, however, group size constrains the effectiveness of intrinsic reciprocity. For example, social exchange likely enhances prospects for cooperation among groups of friends more than it does among populations who hope to oppose dictatorships.

Overall, intrinsic reciprocity can facilitate resolution of second-order CAPs: more so in sequential games than in simultaneous games; more so with high proportions of r-types in

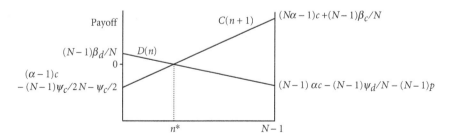

Figure 5.6   Multi-player reciprocity with sanctions

relevant groups; and more so in small groups with close connections that foster stronger reciprocal responses. Within groups, intrinsic reciprocity can generate path-dependent tendencies toward either cooperation or defection. In multi-player games, whose participants expect either general cooperation or general defection, the NE outcome will ratify their expectations. In such cases, intrinsic reciprocity can reinforce a cooperative NE or impede resolution of CAPs associated with dislodging a full-defection equilibrium. The next section's three applications will more fully illustrate the breadth of these models.

5.4. APPLICATIONS AND EXTENSIONS

Reciprocity may either facilitate or impede resolution of the full range of CAPs discussed in Chapters 2 and 3: provision of public goods, limiting use of common-pool resources (CPRs), problems of externalities, and the myriad coordination and enforcement problems that accompany asymmetric information—notably, problems of contract enforcement. Equations (5.2)–(5.9) and their associated game diagrams have indicated how intrinsic reciprocity can facilitate provision of public goods by offering flexible, context-sensitive, and often relatively low-cost mechanisms of coordination and enforcement. Variants of these models could illustrate a corresponding potential for addressing externality and CPR problems.[35] In all cases, intrinsic reciprocity helps explain empirical findings of significant self-organization among relatively small groups. We proceed by applying intrinsic reciprocity to three basic domains of interaction: workplace morale, the holdup problem, and reciprocal conflict.

Workplace Morale

Reciprocal employment relationships can increase efficiency in relatively complex jobs. Employers care deeply about worker morale because it decisively influences workplace productivity. This concern explains why employers rarely cut nominal wages during recessions (Bewley 1999). Workplace morale (or lack thereof) reflects social exchanges with material consequences that arise within workgroups and between workgroups and employers.

Fair-wage models illustrate such reciprocal processes. Workgroups and employers exchange "gifts" as follows: employers offer a wage above the minimum amount that they could get away with—the market-clearing wage. Workgroups regard such a wage as a *fair wage* (w_F), a signal of kind intentions from their employer. They reciprocate by establishing a group effort standard (an effort norm) that exceeds the minimum they could get away with—an indication of high morale. Labor productivity increases. Employers understand this reciprocal, noncontractual exchange (Akerlof 1982; Akerlof and Yellen 1990).[36] As in Chapter 3's effort model, increasing the wage (within some range) increases profits by augmenting labor productivity.

More precisely, higher effort per hour (e) reduces *unit labor costs*: labor costs per unit output. Formally, we may express labor productivity as

(5.10) $$Q/H = q(\tau)e(w),$$

where Q is output; H is labor hours; q is output per unit effort (technical productivity), a function of technology τ; and e indicates the quality of effort per hour, a function of w, as in Chapter 3. Unit labor costs (ULC) are

$$(5.11) \qquad\qquad \text{ULC} = \frac{wH}{Q} = \frac{w}{Q/H} = \frac{w}{q(\tau)e(w)}.$$

In the function $e(w)$, as in Figure 3.6, the first derivative is positive ($e' > 0$), and the second derivative is negative ($e'' < 0$). The latter condition reflects diminishing returns of effort to increases in the wage (as shown by the curvature of Figure 3.6's effort function). Before diminishing returns set in too much, an increase in w reduces ULC by increasing e, which lowers unit production costs. In fact, the effort function graph of Figure 3.6 could be applied to a fair-wage model by replacing $e(c, m)$ with $e(w_F)$: effort as a function of the workgroup's estimation of the fairness (or kindness) of the wage. In terms of reciprocity equation (5.1), we could say that $\kappa(w_F) > 0$, indicating that workers could increase their utility by undertaking a reciprocal action that increases their employer's payoff (π_j). Accordingly, they establish a norm of motivated effort.

Both the effort model and the fair-wage model point to social mechanisms—contingent renewal and reciprocal gift exchange—that help resolve the principal-agent problem of assuring quality effort in employment relationships. These mechanisms partially compensate for incomplete contracting with respect to worker effort. In the effort model, the credible threat of costly dismissal, which arises from paying an above-market-clearing wage while monitoring workers, gives workers an incentive to increase e. As in Chapter 4, this threat signifies employer power within triadic exchange relationships. In a fair-wage model, on the other hand, the "gift" of a higher-than-necessary wage motivates the reciprocal gift of a high group effort norm; the firm trusts that workers will reciprocate, and such trust fosters sharing information and providing diligent effort.

As the complexity of work increases (over time and across occupations), associated labor contracts become less complete owing to vast increases in the details and contingencies that surround the provision of quality effort and information sharing. The importance of reciprocity and trust correspondingly increases. Accordingly, the reciprocal exchanges of the fair-wage model more readily apply to a primary or "good jobs" sector of the labor market—a sector characterized by complex tasks and labor that is often costly to replace—whereas the effort model applies more readily to a secondary or "bad jobs" sector that typically lacks these characteristics (Ferguson 2005). For example, doctors, lawyers, computer programmers, and engineers usually encounter more amenable and reciprocal employment relations than do fast-food workers, janitors, nurse's aides, and migrant farm workers. Furthermore, both survey and experimental evidence indicate that disciplinary dismissal can backfire by crowding out worker goodwill, thus lowering morale (Campbell and Kamlani 1997; Bewley 1999; Howitt 2002). Where feasible, the reciprocal gift-exchange mechanism of the fair-wage model can increase efficiency more than a threat-of-job-loss mechanism can. We thus expect a greater positive response of effort to wages (a larger e') in a fair-wage model than in an effort model, indicating a steeper effort function in Figure 3.6 and correspondingly lower ULC.[37]

These implications extend to other forms of complex exchange. As Table 3.1 indicates, incomplete contracting generates principal-agent problems in the major categories of economic exchange (finance, etc.), indicating second-order CAPs that require some internal resolution. Within each category, reciprocal relationships can augment internal coordination or enforcement mechanisms, such as contingent renewal or gain sharing, and thereby facilitate levels of cooperation between principals and agents that would not otherwise be feasible. Thus reciprocity expands the set of enforceable contracts beyond those that would exist among purely selfish agents (Fehr, Gächter, and Kirchsteiger 1997, 833). Likewise, political relationships, such as those among legislators or between legislators and vocal constituents, may involve implicit agreements that emerge from reciprocal relationships. Reciprocal exchanges, then, not only enhance within-group efficiency, they also engender the levels of trust needed for complex economic and political exchanges.

The Holdup Problem

Our second example, the holdup problem, offers a related and widely applicable category of post-contractual moral hazard problems that arise from asymmetric information.[38] Once again, intrinsic reciprocity facilitates resolution. This example also suggests limits to the application of explicit incentives, echoing the just-mentioned potential for dismissal threats to reduce morale.

A *holdup problem* has the following two features:

(i) One or more parties engage in a *relationship-specific investment*: an investment that possesses more value within a particular relationship than outside of it. Firm-specific human capital is an example.

(ii) The subsequent activities of one or more parties within the relationship cannot be fully designated by prior contract. Thus, after one party invests in a relationship-specific asset, the other party may attempt to renegotiate arrangements to its own advantage. For example, a trained employee could bargain up her wage by threatening to quit.

Here is a more detailed example. A firm that supplies aircraft parts to, say, Boeing may invest in specialized equipment that would have little value to anyone else. If the supplier makes the investment, Boeing would be in a position to negotiate the price of those parts down to the supplier's ex post reservation price, leading to a loss on its investment. Anticipating this outcome, and absent external enforcement or a credible commitment on prices, the supplier would not invest. Figure 5.7 illustrates this problem as a sequential holdup game. The supplier moves first, choosing between Invest (I) and Not invest (N). If it chooses I, Boeing chooses either Low price (LP) or Good price (GP). The backwards-induction outcome is N. If this figure were to show a move for Boeing at the node following N, we would see a PD game with dominant strategies of N and LP. Thus we interpret actions I and GP as cooperating and N and LP as defecting.

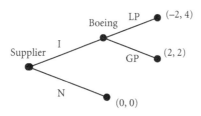

Figure 5.7   Simple holdup game
N O T E : I = invest; N = not invest; LP = low price; GP = good price.

More generally, after one party makes a relationship-specific investment, another party may take actions that reduce its value. For example, after two business partners have invested time and human capital into building a joint enterprise, either could reduce the value of the other's investment by working inefficiently or taking undesirable actions that damage their firm's reputation. In analogous circumstances, some parties may exert power by threatening to damage another's relationship-specific investment. Extortion can take this form. In terms of a simultaneous game, we could represent a post-investment holdup problem as a two-player PD game like that depicted in Figure 2.2. Here we interpret C as "cooperate with partner to enhance the value of their investment" and D as "act selfishly in a manner that demeans the value of the partner's investment."

The literature makes clear that—in a hypothetical world of complete contracting, where all contingencies are fully specified and enforcement is costless and perfect—the holdup problem would not arise. Unfortunately, many elements of post-investment behavior by one or more parties cannot be fully contracted (Grossman and Hart 1986; Milgrom and Roberts 1992).[39] We could interpret workplace morale as a holdup problem: low-quality effort can reduce the value of an employer's prior investment in equipment or training. Even so, the conventional literature argues that holdup problems can be resolved by firm integration (Williamson 1985; Grossman and Hart 1986) or sophisticated, incentive-compatible contracting (Edlin and Reichelstein 1996).

Our discussion of workplace morale suggests that reciprocity theory offers additional mechanisms for remedy, but also indicates the possibility of conflicting material and reciprocal incentives, as when threats of dismissal for insufficient effort compromise worker morale. In this regard, Joel Sobel (2005) argues that the traditional approach fails to consider that chosen strategies may signal intentions. For example, a strategy (such as designing a contract) that allows another player considerable discretion may create benefits by signaling trust, whereas excessive reliance on explicit rewards and penalties can backfire by signaling mistrust: "explicit rewards may have the adverse consequence of crowding out the agent's intrinsic motivation for performing the task" (416).[40]

The implications of these statements go further. Not only can reciprocity influence the tendencies of parties to abide faithfully by given agreements, the mere anticipation of reciprocity can affect how agents stipulate contractual provisions—because such specifications could, perhaps inadvertently, signal intentions or attitudes. Citing Truman Bewley (1999) and George Homans (1953, 1954), Sobel contends that—in order to signal good intentions (or trust) to their workforce—firms seek investments or relationships that are actually vulnerable to holdup, often without even adding feasible contractual safeguards (2005, 414–16). For example, an employer may put workers in charge of expensive machinery with less than the maximum feasible contractual protections against low effort or negligence, in order to signal that it trusts workers to perform responsibly. Indeed, many employers eschew certain contractual safeguards, such as explicit incentive pay, for fear of compromising morale or crowding out good intentions within their workforce.

To model this idea, using Figure 5.1, let player *j* be the employer and let player *i* be the worker. For employer *j*, we interpret C as "give the worker responsibility without explicit rewards and punishments" and D as "offer explicit rewards and punishments for specific actions." For worker *i*, we interpret C as "provide diligent, careful effort" and D as "work carefully only if it pays." With potent reciprocity payoffs, employer *j* should be able to anticipate that a less explicit contract is more likely to elicit motivated effort. Along these lines, experiments show that, when given a choice, "firms" deliberately avoid explicit contracts and instead cultivate reciprocal relationships via implicit exchanges of noncontracted favors (Fehr and Gächter 2000; Fehr, Klein, and Schmidt 2007).

Attempts to offer detailed incentives in (necessarily incomplete) contracts may then backfire by compromising needed reciprocity. Yet cultivating reciprocal relationships can extend the domain of feasible contracting by generating trust that the other party will not defect, thereby resolving attendant second-order CAPs. This crucial function of reciprocity applies to the principal-agent problems that inhabit critical economic exchanges, such as employment relationships, credit relationships, supplier relationships, and landlord-tenant relationships (see Table 3.1). Reciprocal exchange thus provides foundation for economic exchange, but its influence is not always constructive.

Reciprocal Conflict

Our third application illustrates an instructive but negative manifestation of intrinsic reciprocity. Reciprocal exchange inspires a broad range of seemingly irrational conflicts, including the failure of potentially profitable mergers, as well as labor strikes and wars. A two-player game between r-types can illustrate. If each player holds mistrustful expectations concerning actions or attitudes of the other, a unique Nash equilibrium at a point of conflict emerges.[41] Suppose that players A and B each have their own plans for some joint cooperative venture, such as a business partnership or political collaboration. Either plan would create benefits for both players, but A's plan favors A and B's plan favors B—in other words, there is a distributional conflict. For any outcome in which they both choose the same plan, the favored player gains a material payoff of 2 while the other gains only 1. Any failure to cooperate on a single plan generates material payoffs of 0 for both. So far, we have described a game of battle.

Now suppose that A and B each expect the other to insist upon its own plan and that each player regards such insistence as an unkind, unfair act ($\kappa < 0$ in equation (5.1)). Each would then face a strategic reciprocity utility loss ψ if it chooses the other's plan (cooperating with an unfair person). Thus, in Figure 5.8, we see at least one $-\psi$ payoff in the three

Player B

		A's plan	B's plan
Player A	A's plan	$2, 1-\psi$	$0, 0$
	B's plan	$-\psi, -\psi$	$1-\psi, 2$

Figure 5.8   Battle augmented with reciprocity and distrustful expectations

cells where at least one player chooses the other's plan. Now, by insisting on its own plan, each avoids the loss $-\psi$ (as when A moves from B's plan to A's plan).[42] As long as $\psi > 1$, the game generates a unique conflict Nash equilibrium at (A's plan, B's plan): both insist upon their own plan and so gain (and lose) nothing. In addition, each party's negative expectation about the other becomes a self-fulfilling prophecy: I insist on my way because I believe you will insist on yours, which makes me angry, and then we both insist. Various mutually destructive conflicts—including ethnic or territorial conflicts, strikes, crime as a form of revenge, and wars—possess this kind of reciprocal dynamic. Thus understanding the role of reciprocity contributes to policy analysis.

5.5. CONCLUDING REMARKS

As we saw in Chapter 3, models of CAPs that rely solely on rational egoists tend to replicate Olson's relatively pessimistic outlook on free-riding. Various social mechanisms based upon material incentives, such as contingent renewal, can alleviate principal-agent problems, but these mechanisms are costly and imperfect. Intrinsic reciprocity offers some potential for improved outcomes. It introduces the prospect of a credible willingness to behave reciprocally: to match cooperation with cooperation and defection with defection, or to administer direct material or social sanctions, as in rewards for kind acts and punishments for unkind acts. As such, reciprocity offers an informal social mechanism that can foster coordination, enforcement, and trust, especially within small groups.

As Section 5.2 indicates, intrinsic strategic reciprocity can induce mutual cooperation, but its ability to do so depends on game structures, types of players, and numbers of players. Achieving reciprocal cooperation is typically more difficult in simultaneous games, in groups with many e-types, and in large groups. Because intrinsic reciprocity can motivate a desire to sanction, it can sometimes resolve the second-order CAPs that accompany administering material sanctions. The prospect of sanctions, willingly administered by r-types, can deter e-type free-riding.

As Section 5.3 indicates, however, there are numerous legal and social limitations to the application of material sanctions. Social exchange offers a less costly and more flexible alternative that may or may not have subsequent material consequences. When social exchange confers material consequences—as is often the case with social ostracism—it can provide a low-cost method for disciplining e-type behavior. Indeed, social exchange underlies the core advantage that Olson (1971) cites for small groups: the ability to credibly employ selective social incentives. If we incorporate both material and social sanctions into multi-player games among r-types, we find games of assurance with conformity effects and path-dependent (punctuated) equilibria at either full cooperation or full defection. Reciprocal inclinations reinforce both types of equilibria. Unraveling a defection equilibrium thus presents a considerable CAP.

Section 5.4's examples of fair-wage models and the holdup problem speak to the generality and importance of reciprocity in promoting trustworthy exchanges or agreements. Informal reciprocal enforcement plays a key role in complex exchanges—that is, exchanges for which contracting is fundamentally incomplete. Reciprocity not only expands the domain of enforceable contracts, it also influences contract design. In this regard, potential conflicts between material incentives and reciprocal inclinations can affect contract provisions, sometimes discouraging overuse of explicit individual incentives that may signal mistrust and crowd out reciprocal cooperation.

Ultimately, the core importance of intrinsic reciprocity resides in its ability to foster and reinforce either trust or mistrust. Reciprocal trust accompanies the economic, political, and social exchanges and agreements that characterize contemporary complex economies; it underlies development and growth. Unfortunately, reciprocal mistrust may also enter such arrangements, creating new CAPs and impeding resolution of others. Reciprocal mistrust accompanies many conflicts, ranging from office or family disputes to full-scale war. The positive-feedback nature of reciprocal interaction tends to reinforce either trust or mistrust. Hence understanding the dynamics of reciprocity informs policy analysis.

Even so, the concept of intrinsic reciprocity as an attribute of some individuals does not fully explain the observed resolution of certain CAPs contrasted against multiple cases of incomplete or failed resolution. Moreover, people who act reciprocally in certain social settings or contexts may choose not to do so in other contexts; hence our notion of (pure) r-types and e-types oversimplifies motivation in strategic encounters. Social context not only influences the expression of reciprocity in particular circumstances, it influences individual inclinations toward either r-type or e-type behavior as well as the proportion of such types in a given population.

Chapters 7–10 will discuss how social norms and formal institutions affect agents' understandings and motivations—including their preferences—and how these influences condition the conduct of exchange and the resolution of CAPs. To solidify the foundations for subsequent analysis, Chapter 6 extends this chapter's discussion of reciprocity into the more general concept of social preference; it then develops the concept of bounded rationality, and relates both bounded rationality and reciprocity to evolutionary social processes.

EXERCISES

5.1. Referring to equation (5.1) and Figure 5.1, construct relations among the variables α, c, κ, and ψ (incorporating relevant numbers as well) to attain each of the following games:

a. a PD game;

b. a game of assurance; and

c. a game with a unique Nash equilibrium at (C, C).

5.2. Suppose that a game like that shown in Figure 5.1 includes one r-type and one e-type.

    a. With potent reciprocity payoffs, if the second mover (i) is an r-type, a (C, C) outcome follows. Show this.

    b. If the e-type moves second, (D, D) follows. Show this.

    c. If we assume that the order of moves is assigned randomly, the expected subgame perfect equilibrium payoffs are $(2\alpha - 1)c/2 + \beta$ for the r-type and $(2\alpha - 1)c/2$ for the e-type. Show this.

5.3. In the reciprocal PD game of Section 5.2, suppose that external enforcers accurately observe defection and assign punishment p to any player observed defecting.

    a. Modify Figure 5.1 to incorporate external punishment. Discuss the implications.

    b. Modify equation (5.1) to incorporate external punishment. Discuss the implications.

    c. Now suppose that a sense of intrinsic reciprocity exists between internal players and external enforcers (where such reciprocity may be exercised by representatives of either or both sides). Modify Figure 5.1 to incorporate the appropriate reciprocity payoffs. Discuss the implications.

    d. Modify equation (5.1) along these same lines and discuss the implications.

    e. Modify Figure 5.2 to incorporate external punishment; discuss the implications.

5.4. Modify Figure 5.3 by substituting reciprocal reward for reciprocal punishment. Discuss the implications.

5.5. Develop a model like that shown in equation (5.7) that incorporates positive sanctions (i.e., rewards) for cooperators.

5.6. Variants of equations (5.2), (5.4), and (5.5) can be used to address standard externality and common-pool resource problems such as those discussed in Chapter 2.

    a. Equations (2.3) and (2.4) represent a simple CPR problem (where use of the resource confers negative externalities only on users and where the size of the resource is not specified). Using these equations as expressions of the material payoff component, alter equations (5.4) and (5.5)—and the corresponding definitions of $C(n)$ and $D(n)$—to address a CPR problem in which reciprocity influences payoffs. (Equivalently, alter equations (2.3) and (2.4) to include the reciprocity utilities ψ and β. Think about where these terms belong in your new definitions of $C(n)$ and $D(n)$.)

    b. Make an assumption about the relative size of ψ so that you have a game of assurance. Specify your assumption and draw the model.

    c. Now revise your equations from part a so that they incorporate a general negative externality, arising from $C(n)$, that affects both C-players and D-players.

    d. Repeat part b for the equations derived in part c.

    e. Positive network externalities: Equations (2.9) and (2.10) indicate $C(n)$ and $D(n)$ functions for activities that generate positive network externalities. Suppose instead that only activity C generates a positive externality and that activity D is a pure private good. To make the problem interesting, let D have a higher private payoff. Modify equations (2.9) and (2.10) to reflect this condition, and draw the corresponding diagram.

f. Now add reciprocity utilities ψ and β and stipulate the conditions under which this turns into a game of assurance.

5.7. Draw a variant of Figure 5.8 for a case where each player believes that the other has good intentions.

5.8. Develop a variant of Figure 5.8 in which each player believes the other has good intentions.

6 FOUNDATIONS OF MOTIVATION: RATIONALITY AND SOCIAL PREFERENCE

> But to improve the human prospect we must understand the sources of human decision making. That is a necessary condition for human survival.
>
> Douglass North (2005)

Suppose that authorities in Boratonia hope to design policies that would ameliorate their CAP of limiting water use. They base policy choices on their understandings of local farmers' motivations. For example, if authorities believe that farmers care mostly about material benefits such as income, they might apply taxes on water use or subsidies for limitation. If farmers care only about their own material returns, authorities would not need to consider possible evaluations of ensuing distributional impacts or the processes used in making decisions. But authorities could be mistaken. Farmers might also care about the relative impacts of the policy on neighbors or about the procedures used, such as levels of public input. Farmers who find procedures or outcomes unfair might conceal or distort information on their use patterns—impeding resolution of the water-use CAP. In any case, neither farmers nor authorities may really know much about others' motivations, but they have impressions and may try to learn more. Authorities might experiment with a few different policies and attempt to assess their impact. Farmers may explore avenues for influencing policy decisions. If occasionally outcomes differ dramatically from prior expectations, various parties may reformulate their basic understandings of procedures or the motivations of others.

As noted in Chapter 5, Chapters 2–4 utilize a traditional concept of economic preference that implies rational egoist (or e-type) behavior based upon the self-interest axiom. Chapter 5 then augmented our concept of preference by introducing intrinsic reciprocity as the core motivation for r-type behavior. The present chapter makes two critical contributions. First, it informs our understanding of motivation by developing the concept of social preference. We not only find additional mechanisms that can facilitate or impede resolution of CAPs, we also establish foundations for modeling the influence of social context on motivation—the basis for modeling interdependent and endogenous preferences. Second, we develop a conception of bounded rationality that treats cognition as a scarce resource. Here we employ evolutionary game theory to model social learning processes, noting implications on the evolution of behavioral predispositions, social norms, and formal institutions. Ultimately, bounded rationality implies that institutions shape human cognition. Subsequent chapters will elaborate, but first we offer some background.

Economic theory—and more generally rational choice theory—utilizes what Thomas
Schelling calls "vicarious problem solving" (1978, 18). By modeling agents' motivation and
decision calculus, a theorist can anticipate their responses to specific situations. Preference
theory conceptualizes motivation—the impetus for goal-oriented behavior. Rationality
theory characterizes the cognitive procedures (e.g., estimates or inferences) that translate
perceived goals into specific choices or actions. In traditional economics, as indicated by
the self-interest axiom, exogenously determined preferences focus on self-regarding and
outcome-oriented material utility (or profit) payoffs. In that framework, rationality connotes maximizing one's attainment of such goals based upon assumed full cognition—
that is, complete awareness of relevant context and all possible contingencies at least in a
probabilistic sense. The method of vicarious problem solving, however, allows considerably broader conceptions of both preference and rationality. A more detailed discussion of
preference and rationality theory is thus in order.

We define *preferences* as reasons for behaviors that are independent of capacities—that
is, "pro and con attitudes" (Nowell-Smith 1954, cited in Bowles 2004, 99). In introductory
economics, preferences rank alternative goods and services or allocations of time. If I prefer
candy to peanuts, I will pay more for candy than for peanuts; for enough money, I will work
overtime. We now develop a more inclusive concept. As already suggested by the concept
of intrinsic reciprocity, preferences also reflect ethical values, respond to our conceptions
or framing of specific situations, and incorporate psychological predispositions. The latter
may include habits or addictions (Bowles 1998a, 79). For ethical reasons, one might prefer
earning $100 from work to stealing $100. One may regard taking a dollar off someone's
desk as an act of theft, but consider picking up a dollar from a sidewalk as a token of good
luck—and thus prefer the latter. Alternatively, an addiction to nicotine influences preferences toward smoking.

There are two basic types of preference. *Material preference*, as the name suggests, ranks
purely material outcomes (e.g., goods, services, income). As we saw, Chapter 5's rational
egoists (e-types) exhibit self-regarding, outcome-oriented material preference: they care
only about material outcomes for themselves, regardless of possible impacts on others or
the processes that generate such outcomes. *Social preference* augments material preference
with concern over one's relative position (economic, political, or social), concern over outcomes for others, and/or concern over the processes that generate outcomes (Fehr and
Fischbacher 2002; Bowles 2004, 96–126). Chapter 5's reciprocal players (r-types), for example, have an intrinsic desire to respond in kind to perceived intentions (e.g., fairness) of
others, accounting for their apparent role in generating comparative outcomes. R-type utility evaluations of "kindness" thus consider a mix of relative outcomes (e.g., distributional
shares) and perceived intention (a type of process). As indicated, intrinsic reciprocity can
motivate r-types to bear some cost in order to sanction defectors, even in the absence of
expected material gain. Section 6.1 elaborates on the concept of social preference.

Recall that Chapter 5 closed by suggesting that social context influences agents' propensities to exhibit reciprocal behavior. The concept of social preference takes us farther.
It allows us to conceptualize and model possible impacts of social, political, and economic
context on the short-term expression of preference and on its long-term development.

Regarding the former, social preference implies *context-dependent preferences*: the manifestation of preferences responds to the immediate strategic context in which interactions occur. Perhaps my desire to punish you for treating me badly depends on whether I think you had any choice; perhaps my choice of a seat depends on where others sit. Likewise, prospects for receiving social approval or disapproval can influence an agent's desire to free-ride. At a deeper level, preference formation over time responds to (is endogenous to) its social context: the cultural transmission of basic understandings—such as social categories or cause-and-effect relationships—affects the development of agents' preferences (Bowles 2004; Bowles and Polanía-Reyes 2012). Understandings lead us to cognition and rationality.

In Chapter 5 we defined a *rational* actor as someone who exhibits consistent, goal-oriented behavior. This broad definition facilitates two distinct approaches to modeling goal-oriented decision making: substantive rationality and bounded rationality. *Substantive rationality* has the following characteristics:

- Both logical and temporal consistency of goal orientation, as discussed in Section 5.1.
- Sufficient cognitive capacity, motivation, and information to undertake best-response analysis. Even with incomplete information, agents can maximize expected utility or profits or (equivalently) choose their expected best responses to specific strategic situations.
- Broadly defined goals which include both maximization of material payoffs and various social goals such as reciprocity, concerns for equity, and concerns about appropriateness of procedure.

Despite their multiple applications (as illustrated in preceding chapters), substantive rationality models do not address the cognitive limitations of agents, the costs of cognitive effort, learning processes, or basic misinterpretations of the environment: "We do not need to distinguish between the real world and the decision maker's perception of it" (Simon 1987, 27).[1]

By contrast, for *boundedly rational* agents, cognition is a scarce resource. These agents remain goal-oriented, using the same broad definition of goals, but they possess only limited cognitive energy and capacity with which to address complex environments, compromising their ability to offer strictly "best" responses. Rational response here involves both process (how one thinks) and choice. Rather than maximize at a point in time, agents adjust to changing environments with limited cognition and memory. Thus perceptions may not only differ from reality, they may also respond to context and framing—that is, to the way information is presented. Even so, decisions reflect current goals and understandings, and chosen actions appear to be better than known feasible alternatives. But these responses are not maximal in a formal sense, and they may lack consistency over time as perceptions change and preferences develop. Overall, agents pursue evolving goals using adaptive trial-and-error learning. Examples include learning to walk, to read, to perform a new job, to work with colleagues, to "get along," to manage a firm, and to negotiate myriad informal and formal agreements.

Just as the best-response calculus of classical game theory supplies an extremely powerful and versatile framework for modeling substantively rational interactions, the dynamic adaptive logic of evolutionary game theory facilitates the modeling of learning processes. Evolutionary game theory can represent procedural adjustment of individual or group strategies (learning) as well as dynamic economic, political, and social processes—including the evolution of conventions, social norms, formal institutions, and, ultimately, political-economic development. We postpone further discussion of these more complex topics until Chapters 7–13, and now proceed with foundational concepts.

Our discussion proceeds as follows. Section 6.1 develops the concept of social preference and distinguishes among several varieties. Social preference suggests additional mechanisms for resolving CAPs and provides groundwork for further analysis. Section 6.2, which may be skipped by those less interested in technical aspects, develops a hybrid model that merges a sophisticated representation of intrinsic reciprocity with possible concern over the distribution of material payoffs that does not depend on intention. This model informs relationships between strategic context and preference, establishing preliminaries for analyzing short-term responses of preferences to social context. Section 6.3 introduces bounded rationality. By relating costs and limits of cognition to cognitive processes, this section develops the concepts of heuristics and mental models. Both concepts underlie our subsequent approach to institutions. Section 6.4 uses evolutionary logic to explain why agents facing true uncertainty employ heuristics that focus on certain options and ignore others. It proceeds to address specific implications of heuristics on individual and shared understandings, along with further implications on norms and formal institutions. After briefly comparing classical with evolutionary game theory, Section 6.5 develops evolutionary models of cooperation within team production and then models the emergence of a disposition toward reciprocity. These final three sections identify important cognitive functions and properties—notably, path dependence and punctuated equilibria—that Part III will then apply to norms, formal institutions, networks, policymaking, growth, and development.

6.1. SOCIAL PREFERENCE WITH SUBSTANTIVE RATIONALITY

Chapter 5's concept of intrinsic reciprocity has augmented our understanding of possible resolutions to second-order CAPs: in small groups, reciprocal agents may willingly punish defectors or reward contributors, and, over time, reciprocal relationships can generate trust. Yet Chapter 5 did not fully consider how context influences reciprocity. The broader concept of social preference enables us to model the impact of context on exercises of reciprocity and other types of preferences. It also points to additional motivation for resolving CAPs along with potential avenues for exercising power. We now turn to developing a substantively rational concept of social preference.

Agents with social preferences augment self-regarding material preferences with two additional domains for concern: other-regarding preferences and process-regarding preferences (Bowles 2004). *Other-regarding preferences* respond to either the relative or absolute outcomes received by some set of reference agents. *Reference agents* are those whom one cares about per se and/or to whom one compares oneself. For example, some people may gain utility if a friend or disadvantaged person receives some absolute gain, such as winning a lottery, a pay raise, or government aid. Others may experience resentment if they receive lower pay for performing the same work as someone else, especially if they feel more deserving. Still others may feel guilty after receiving higher rewards than equally worthy candidates.

Process-regarding preferences reflect subjective evaluations of the processes that generate specific outcomes, independent of the outcomes themselves. One might, for example, gain different satisfaction from the same income depending on whether one earned, stole, or chanced upon it. More precisely, process-related sentiments reflect perceptually based evaluations in three possible areas: the intentions of those with whom one interacts; the fairness of the specific procedures that generate outcomes; and/or the adherence of agents or procedures to relevant social norms. For example, a lower-paid employee's satisfaction with her wages may reflect how she perceives her employer's intentions: does an observed pay differential reflect an honest evaluation of merit, a mistake, or deliberate discrimination? Likewise, some workers may regard seniority or merit-based pay procedures as fair (or unfair) or may take offense if their employer violates workplace norms pertaining to merit or equity. In political contexts, agents may evaluate the procedural fairness of decisions: Were the actual decision makers elected? Whom do they represent? Was there adequate citizen input?

We can illustrate the implications of other- and process-regarding social preferences with models of substantively rational best responses to social and material goals. In this regard, the general concept of social preference allows us to envision several basic types of agents, each having different implications on tendencies for collective action. More specifically, Fehr and Fischbacher (2002, C2–C4) indicate five basic categories of preference: the pure material preference of selfish players (our e-types), along with four varieties of social preference: reciprocal preference, inequality aversion, pure altruism, and pure spite. Chapter 5 has developed reciprocal preference. We now address the remaining three types of social preference, noting comparisons to reciprocity.

Inequality aversion represents a particular type of other-regarding preference: agents lose utility when faced with unequal outcomes between themselves and members of a reference group. They may feel anger for earning less money than certain colleagues or guilt for making more. Like reciprocity, inequality aversion can help to resolve CAPs by motivating punishment of defectors, but inequality-averse agents do not care about intention (or any procedure). Thus its impacts may extend beyond small reciprocal groups. Moreover, the magnitude of inequality aversion responds to context: concern for equity manifests itself far more strongly in bargaining contexts (e.g., labor relations) where individual actions influence outcomes, than in competitive contexts (e.g., product markets) where individual actions cannot influence outcomes such as product prices or levels of income.

Fehr and Schmidt (1999) develop a model of "self-centered inequality aversion" (819) in which agents lose utility from observed inequality between themselves and others but do not care about inequality among others. Their two-player equation is[2]

(6.1) $$u_i = \pi_i - \lambda_i \max\{\pi_j - \pi_i, 0\} - \gamma_i \max\{\pi_i - \pi_j, 0\},$$

where u denotes utility, and π signifies the material payoffs received from the underlying game or exchange by an agent (i or j). The second and third terms represent player i's concern over disadvantageous and advantageous inequality, respectively, when $\pi_j - \pi_i > 0$ and $\pi_i - \pi_j > 0$; parameters λ_i and γ_i indicate the strength of such effects. Here $\gamma_i \leq \lambda_i$, meaning that guilt over advantageous inequality never causes more utility loss than anger over disadvantageous inequality. Furthermore, $\gamma_i < 1$: agent i will never give up more than a dollar to reduce its advantage over j by one dollar.[3] By contrast, λ is not strictly limited. If disadvantageous inequality causes enough anger, i may sacrifice more than a dollar to reduce j's advantage by one dollar.[4]

Using equation (6.1), we elaborate on distinctions between inequality-averse agents and r-types. Both types willingly punish defectors. Because free-riding generates disadvantageous inequality for contributors to public goods, a sufficient λ in (6.1) motivates a willingness to sacrifice material gain in order to punish noncontributors. A large enough proportion of inequality-averse players may then discipline e-types away from free-riding, facilitating resolution of second-order CAPs—as r-types can. Unlike r-types, however, inequality-averse players do not respond to perceived intentions of others (or any procedure); thus equation (6.1) does not include equation (5.2)'s kindness term (κ). Agents do not care whether inequality arises from ill intent, a failed attempt at goodwill, or an act of nature. Consequently, models of inequality aversion are typically simpler than models of reciprocity. Furthermore, because inequality aversion does not require knowledge of intention, its ability to motivate punishment need not depend on familiar small-group interaction. For example, members of large workgroups or organizations may reprimand slackers whom they hardly know. Social enforcement may then extend beyond small reciprocal groups.

Finally, with a mixed population of inequality-averse players and e-types, this model can explain experimental observations that many players sacrifice payoffs in order to reduce inequality in bargaining games, but virtually none do so in fully competitive games (Fehr and Schmidt 1999). In bargaining games, individuals influence outcomes, whereas in competitive situations, as conventional theory argues, no single individual has impact. Individuals are far more likely to sacrifice resources to reduce inequality in situations that they can actually affect. For example, because effort cannot be fully contracted in labor markets, effort decisions influence profits (as explained in Chapter 3). Hence a form of implicit bargaining arises, even in nonunion environments (Ferguson 2005), and managers worry about relationships between fairness and morale (Bewley 1999). Institutional context conditions the impact of social preferences on economic (and other) outcomes.

Pure altruism represents a third type of social preference. *Purely altruistic* players want to help others unconditionally. By contrast, reciprocal rewards depend upon perceived good intentions. Unlike inequality aversion, pure altruism includes a desire to help those who are better off. Pure altruism (like pure competition) is interesting theoretically as an extreme case but quite unusual. Approximately altruistic behavior, however, may exist within families and other close social groups—even large ones, such as alumni from the same university, members of ethnic groups, military units, or even nations. A fourth type of social preference, pure spite, is essentially the opposite of pure altruism: *spiteful* players want to lower the utility of others unconditionally.

Charness and Rabin (2002) develop a hybrid model that merges reciprocity with concern for *social welfare*: a desire to help all players with particular concern for the least well off. Note that a general desire to help others includes concern for group or aggregate efficiency, a particular type of process-regarding preference.[5] Production, exchange, and other processes that avoid wasting resources can, in principle, benefit all. Likewise, a desire to help the least well off indicates a particular type of outcome-oriented concern over distribution. Charness and Rabin's experimental findings provide support for both intrinsic reciprocity and a social welfare variant of preference theory.

6.2. CONTEXT-DEPENDENT RECIPROCITY AND
SOCIAL PREFERENCE OVER DISTRIBUTION

Building on Section 6.1's discussion of social preference, this section argues that social context—in particular the known or perceived strategic options available to various players—influences reciprocal responses. Cognizance of such influence, moreover, can facilitate exercises of power. Recall from Chapter 4 that resolution of second-order CAPs involves exercising power. We thus expect enforcement, power, and social preference to interact. Furthermore, purely distributional concerns may complement reciprocal response. With these ideas in mind, this section develops a hybrid model that mixes context-dependent reciprocity with distributional concern that could be interpreted either as inequality aversion or an aspiration for social welfare. We begin with experimental evidence on strategic context.

Falk, Fehr, and Fischbacher (2003) report two relevant experimental findings. First, the nature of the feasible alternatives available to specific actors (a type of strategic context) influences others' interpretations of their intentions, and so affects reciprocal responses. Second, some agents show concern for distributional outcomes that are partially independent of intention. These findings reflect outcomes from an *ultimatum game*. In ultimatum, a proposer divides an initial endowment (10) by offering some portion of it ($\mu \geq 0$) to a receiver—and keeping the rest. If the receiver accepts, the players receive amounts $10 - \mu$ and μ; if the receiver rejects the offer, both end up with nothing.[6] Note that an e-type proposer would offer the smallest possible amount (say, 0.1), and an e-type receiver would accept.

Falk, Fehr, and Fischbacher (2003) set up their ultimatum experiment so as to focus on how strategic context—specifically the proposer's available strategic options—influences the receiver's reciprocal response. They investigate four pairs of strategic options. In all cases, the proposer can either offer 2 (and keep 8) or offer one of four specific alternatives as follows: in case (i), the alternative is to offer 5 (split evenly); in case (ii), the alternative is to offer 8 (disadvantageous to the proposer); in case (iii), effectively there is no choice (both options are to offer 2); and in case (iv), the alternative to offering 2 is to offer 0 (the most unfair possible).

Figure 6.1 illustrates the ultimatum game with these four alternative offers. Note that in each case, the proposer's actual choice conveys information about both intentions and distribution. In case (i), an offer of 2 may appear selfish and unequal. In case (ii), offering 2 may seem more excusable, since the alternative would require a large sacrifice by the

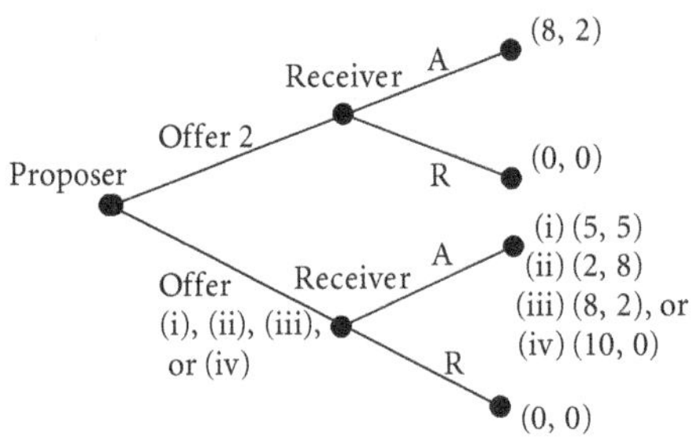

Figure 6.1 Ultimatum with four strategic contexts
NOTE: A = accept; R = reject.

proposer. In case (iii), the distributional inequality is not intended because the proposer has no choice. In case (iv), an offer of 2 (instead of 0) could actually signal fair intentions.

The authors' experimental findings suggest that agents do indeed consider the available strategic alternatives when judging intentions of others. The degree to which a proposer can offer a fairer distribution influences reciprocal assessments. More specifically, the authors find that responders rejected (punished) the same (unequal) offer of 2: most often in case (i), where a fair alternative (5) was available; followed by case (ii) (large proposer sacrifice); then (iii) (no alternative); and least often in case (iv), where the alternative of 0 is even less fair. Perhaps surprisingly, they find some rejections in cases (iii) and (iv), suggesting that at least a few agents care about distribution independent of intention—independent of an intrinsic reciprocity response.[7]

Falk, Fehr, and Fischbacher (2003) present two broad conclusions concerning strategic context and distribution. First, because the presence of strategic alternatives can signal an agent's intentions, players who hope to gain material advantage without angering others might strategically limit their own options, or attempt to conceal their true alternatives from others.[8] For example, an official might justify unpopular actions by saying "my hands are tied; I had no choice." When feasible alternatives do exist, deliberately concealing one's alternatives constitutes a strategic move (power2). Powerful players who can alter or conceal their true alternatives may not only bias games against potential opponents but also deceive potential opponents into believing that opposition is fruitless (power3). Thus agents' understandings of the reciprocal motives of potential opponents can inform how they exercise power.

Second, reflecting their experimental findings that both intentions and distribution matter, the authors propose designing hybrid models that mix intrinsic reciprocity with distributional concern that is independent of intention. Falk and Fischbacher (2006) develop such a model. We present a simpler version that expands on equation (5.1)—in order to offer a context-dependent representation of reciprocity along with (independent) concern over distribution.

Recall, equation (5.1) indicated that, for r-types, player i's utility depends on her material payoffs plus the product of a kindness function ($\kappa_j(a_j; t)$) and the change in player j's material and social payoffs that i attributes to their interaction ($\Delta_i(\pi_j + \phi_j(s))$). Recall that $\kappa_j(a_j; t)$

represents i's perception of j's intentions as a function of j's actions (a_j) and the frequency of their interaction (t). Kind or fair actions correspond to $\kappa_j > 0$, signifying a desire to reciprocate by increasing π_j (and vice versa). We now adjust equation (5.1) by omitting the ϕ and t terms (for simplicity) and by altering the third term in order to offer a more sophisticated concept that merges reciprocity with independent concern over distribution:

$$(6.2) \qquad u_i(s, s^*) = \pi_i(s) + \kappa_j(\lambda\kappa_{je}(s^*) + (1 - \lambda)\pi_D) \times (\Delta_i\pi_j(r_i(s^*, \pi_D))).$$

As in equation (5.1), s denotes strategies chosen by both players, and π_i represents player i's material payoff, as a function of s.[9] As in (5.1), the function $\kappa_j(\cdot)$ reflects i's perception of j's kindness (or fairness); $\kappa_j(\cdot)$ can take either positive (kind, fair) or negative (unkind, unfair) values. In (6.2), however, $\kappa_j(\cdot)$ responds to two arguments: i's evaluation of j's intentions $(\kappa_{je}(s^*))$, which depends on i's beliefs about j's strategic choices (s^*; more on this below); and the actual (or expected) distribution of material payoffs (π_D). This second argument is independent of intentions and thus reflects i's perception of the fairness of the outcome (material distribution π_D) independent of j's intent. Parameter λ shows the relative importance of intentions in this new κ_j function.

The entire second term, the product $\kappa_j(\cdot) \times (\Delta_i\pi_j(r_i(\cdot)))$, specifies the interaction between κ_j and the impact (positive or negative) of i's response (r_i) on j's payoffs $(\Delta\pi_j)$. For example, if i believes that j is kind $(\kappa_j > 0)$ and also responds (r_i) in a manner that increases j's payoff $(\Delta\pi_j > 0)$, then i's utility increases; i could also increase her own utility by punishing unkind behavior. On the other hand, if the signs of these two terms differ (as when reward follows unkindness), i loses utility. As in Chapter 5, responses r_i may be strategic (following C with C), or r_i may indicate positive or negative material or social sanctions. Finally, (6.2)'s last term shows that i's response $r_i(\cdot)$ depends on both s^* and π_D.

Now the term s^* introduces context into the model. It reflects three elements of i's beliefs about strategy:

(i) *Action beliefs:* i's beliefs regarding j's actual or expected actions.

(ii) *Context beliefs:* i's beliefs regarding j's available strategies, indicating i's perception of the strategic context in which j exercises his choices.

(iii) *Second-order strategy beliefs:* i's beliefs concerning j's expectations about i's strategic choices.

All three levels of beliefs about j inform i's evaluation of j's intentions, and each carries implications on resolving CAPs. For (i), as in Chapter 5, an observed or expected unkind action from j (such as defection) can motivate i to willingly punish j. If j anticipates this possibility, j may cooperate to avoid punishment. For (ii), if i believes that j had no other option, j's defection may reflect neutral rather than unkind intentions, and so may not merit reciprocal punishment. The just-discussed experiment by Falk, Fehr, and Fischbacher (2003) points to the importance of such contextual beliefs. Concerning (iii), suppose that, in a simultaneous game, player i believes that j expects i to defect. If so, a defection by j could indicate an attempt to avoid exploitation rather than unkind intentions. On the other hand, if i thinks that j expects i to cooperate, then the same defection could reflect a blatant attempt to exploit i—unkind intentions. Thus i's second-order beliefs about j's strategy become part of the context that influences i's judgment of j's actions. One's reciprocal willingness to contribute to a public good could depend in part on what one thinks other players expect one to do.

Finally, the term π_D in equation (6.2) incorporates a quite general notion that agent i could care about the distribution of material benefits irrespective of i's evaluation of j's intentions. There are a variety of ways in which we could further specify the influence of π_D. For example, for inequality aversion, we could equate π_D with the last two terms of (6.1). Falk and Fischbacher (2006), like Falk, Fehr, and Fischbacher (2003), observe concern for both pure outcome equality and perceived intentions in a variety of experimental settings. Alternatively, π_D could represent Charness and Rabin's (2002) concept of concern for social welfare.[10] Overall, equation (6.2) indicates that social preferences related to reciprocity, inequality aversion, and social welfare not only respond to context but also permit exercises of power; consequently, such preferences may facilitate resolution of CAPs.

6.3. INFORMATION, COGNITION, AND BOUNDED RATIONALITY

As the previous discussion indicates, substantive rationality offers a strong foundation for modeling social interactions. When substantive rationality models include social preference, such as intrinsic reciprocity or inequality aversion, they can explain observed resolutions to various difficult CAPs, and simultaneously address possible influences of context on strategic decisions. Nevertheless, a bounded rationality approach more adequately addresses the informational, cognitive, and dynamic properties of exchange relations and CAPs. In so doing, this approach offers principles for modeling the development of behavioral predispositions, social norms, and even formal institutions.

The Case for Using Bounded Rationality

A substantive rationality (SR) approach assumes that agents possess enough information, will, and cognitive ability to calculate best responses to strategic contexts—all without encountering any cost of cognitive effort. SR-based models perform well under three conditions: (i) when the complexity of the task or decision is not too great relative to agents' prior understandings; (ii) when the environment provides sufficient informational response to activity (*information feedback*) for correction of misunderstandings; and (iii) when agents are sufficiently motivated to expend the effort required to make reasoned decisions (Denzau and North 1994). Consequently, substantively rational calculation applies only within the confines of a rather narrow *problem-complexity boundary*: a conceptual delineation within which problems are sufficiently simple for substantive rationality to operate successfully, but outside of which bounded rationality applies (Arthur 1992, 1994).

Competitive markets for relatively transparent private goods without externalities basically meet these criteria, indicating problems that, by and large, lie within the problem-complexity boundary. Because competition diminishes or eliminates the ability of single agents to affect market outcomes, participants need not know much about the motivation of others.[11] Strategic calculation becomes manageable (condition (i)). Moreover, prices provide accessible information feedback by signaling scarcity and opportunity (condition (ii)); they also offer clear incentives that motivate predictable responses ((i) and (ii)). Given such motivation, agents are willing to undertake the effort to make reasoned decisions (condition (iii)). Unfortunately, these conditions are restrictive. In particular, CAPs typically reflect complicated situations with limited information feedback and conflicting incentives. Problematic enforcement compounds these problems. At the expense of adding detail, bounded rationality models can more adequately address these complexities.

We proceed with a brief review of empirical and theoretical arguments for a bounded rationality approach. John Conlisk (1996) asserts that bounded rationality is far more consistent with experimental observations than is substantive rationality. Contributing to a large and growing literature, he reviews consistent experimental findings of cognitive failures, such as not understanding statistical independence, false inferences about causality, and failure to discount the future. Many studies noted by Conlisk report inconsistencies with important precepts of economic rationality. Contrary to the permanent-income hypothesis, for example, consumption data indicate that consumers pay considerable attention to short-run fluctuations in income, often failing to adequately consider expected future changes in income.[12] Likewise, money illusion abounds, and inefficient purchases of insurance point to flawed calculations of expected future values. Similarly, it is extremely difficult to square observed asset price bubbles with theories of rational maximization.[13] Daniel Kahneman (2003) reinforces these concerns by discussing another large and disappointing list of experimental reports of systematic biases. For example, people have been shown to value the same group of items differently depending on whether the items are presented separately or together.[14] Kahneman notes, however, that the presence of systematic biases actually presents opportunities for predictability. Indeed, the predictability of behavior that violates substantive rationality creates opening or opportunity for theories of bounded rationality.

Theoretical arguments for bounded rationality arise from two related problems: lack of information and limited cognition. A bounded rationality approach to information problems includes and extends Chapter 3's concept of incomplete, asymmetric information. There are three related information problems: cost, asymmetry, and true uncertainty. Although substantively rational principal-agent models incorporate effects of costly and asymmetric information on calculated decisions and strategic outcomes, these models do not address how incomplete information alters agents' capacities for problem solving—in other words, their ability to engage in meaningful strategic calculus. Inadequate information imposes three basic limits on problem solving. First, costly information can interfere with agents' motivation and/or ability to acquire enough information to adequately solve optimization problems. I may end up paying more than needed for an insurance policy because I did not investigate alternatives. Related limitations arise from the free-riding CAPs associated with the public-good qualities of information (let somebody else do the research). Optimal information processing may then fail for both individual and collective reasons.

Second, information asymmetry implies that agents often enter strategic environments without understanding the motivations of others—especially when some agents misrepresent or withhold information. For example, students may not know enough about their professors' grading criteria to optimize their allocation of time spent studying. Instead, they employ heuristics such as study reasonably hard, consult with classmates, and write clearly. More ominously, in multi-national or multi-ethnic environments, agents may resort to stereotypes when inferring motives of those with different backgrounds.

Third, instability in social environments generates deeper uncertainty. The rational calculus of conventional economics (rational expectations in particular) assumes that economic interactions follow *ergodic stochastic processes*: processes in which statistical averages derived from large numbers of past observations apply to the future (Davidson 1991, 132). A stable, ergodic economy is "one in which the fundamental underlying structure of the economy is constant and therefore timeless" (North 2005, 16). Agents with imperfect information can still employ probabilistic risk calculus to maximize expected utility or profits.[15] By contrast, true uncertainty (hereafter, uncertainty) arises in non-ergodic environments that lack such structural and statistical stability. Thus *uncertainty* (or Knightian uncertainty) implies that agents simply do not know the probability distributions of important variables, rendering traditional risk calculus impossible.[16] If so, they cannot rank expected outcomes in terms of their own valuations (Denzau and North 1994). For example, college students may face agonizing choices because they lack meaningful probabilistic knowledge of outcomes associated with alternatives such as whether an internship will lead to better long-run career prospects than a research assistantship. Entrepreneurs rely on intuition for similar reasons. Like other boundedly rational agents, they address true uncertainty with a mix of intuition and deliberation.

Limitations on cognition strengthen the case for a bounded rationality approach. Cognition involves costly effort to process information, and cognition is a scarce resource (Conlisk 1996). The assumption of full cognizance overlooks the associated economic tradeoffs. Moreover, among groups, cognitive costs generate yet another CAP. Agents not only free-ride on information gathering, they also free-ride on cognitive effort (Denzau and North 1994). Why bother figuring out answers to complex problems if someone else will do the work? A full modeling of goal-oriented behavior should then reflect both costs and limits to cognition in uncertain environments.

Ronald Heiner specifically links uncertainty to limited cognition. He defines a *competence-difficulty gap* (CD gap) as the gap "between an agent's competence and the difficulty of the decision problem to be solved" (1983, 562). The CD gap represents uncertainty, accounting for cognition. Agents face uncertainty concerning multilevel relationships among actions, environments, and outcomes. In many strategic situations, the same action may generate either good or bad outcomes depending on what others do. Even simple two-player games of chicken, assurance, and battle illustrate this principle: a specific move can either increase or decrease one's payoffs (relative to alternatives) depending on the other's move. With multiple players, multiple strategies, and strategic withholding of information, complexity expands exponentially, but cognition does not. Consequently, agents' understandings of relationships between mixes of action, circumstance, and relative success diminish. With limited cognition, agents may encounter uncertainty—a CD gap whereby they do not know the probabilities related to achieving success; they operate outside of a pertinent problem-complexity boundary. For example, most startup businesses fail.

To sum up, a substantive rationality approach offers important insight into relatively stable strategic interactions in relatively predictable (ergodic) environments, but it cannot adequately explain dynamic phenomena in uncertain environments, such as entrepreneurship. In this regard, bounded rationality theory facilitates formal representation of behavioral responses to complex problems that arise in non-ergodic social environments.

Cognition and Bounded Rationality

We now turn to modeling bounded rationality. Our purpose is to develop what Ostrom calls a minimalist conception of rationality—one that utilizes the principle of vicarious problem solving in a manner that incorporates both potential influences of social context on understandings and the cognitive limits that accompany uncertainty in non-ergodic environments. Our approach to boundedly rational behavior is consistent with that of Heiner (1983), Denzau and North (1994), Conlisk (1996), Ostrom (1998a), Kahneman (2003), and Gintis (2009b). We maintain the notion of consistent goal-oriented behavior but discard the SR requirement of optimization or best response:

> Consistent with all models of rational choice is a general theory of human behavior that views all humans as complex, fallible learners who seek to do as well as they can given the constraints that they face and who are able to learn heuristics, norms, rules, and how to craft rules to improve achieved outcomes. (Ostrom 1998a, 9)

Similarly, Gintis (2009b) defines rationality as consistent goal-oriented behavior, with two important caveats that distinguish his approach from an SR approach. First, individual preferences respond to social context. Consideration of such response can resolve problems of internal inconsistency in SR models associated with apparent preference reversals. For example, some people may choose steak when eating alone, but order tofu when dining with vegetarian friends. By allowing context to influence preference, we can account for such reversals and thus retain consistent goal orientation—the cornerstone of rationality. Second, for Gintis, there is no presupposition that such (boundedly) rational behavior maximizes well-being (often an implicit, though not necessary, assumption of SR models).[17] For example, student drinking at parties is goal-oriented, but may not maximize student welfare even within a relatively short time horizon.

Daniel Kahneman's conception of mental systems establishes a basis for bounded rationality theory. It indicates how individuals address cognitive limitations and how context influences both preference and cognition. Kahneman (2003) asserts that people use two mental systems to process information: a reactive, habitual, impressionable, doubt-suppressing, and essentially effortless intuitive system (S1); and a slow, deliberate, reflective, and effortful reasoning system (S2). Despite its grounding in intuition, S1 employs previously stored knowledge, responds to language (with association, or quick approval or disapproval), and incorporates learning with repetition over time.[18] With practice, physical motions (learning to ride a bicycle) or mental processes (simple addition) can become intuitive. The outcomes of S1 processes are impressions. By contrast, S2 outcomes are reasoned deductions, such as solutions to differential equations. Furthermore, S2 can

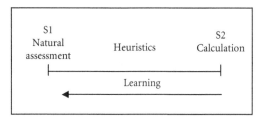

Figure 6.2   Accessibility spectrum

sometimes monitor S1 processes and make corrections. *Judgments*, as outcomes of mental processes, typically mix S1 and S2 processing.

The notion of accessibility, or the "ease with which mental contents come to mind" (Kahneman 2003, 1452), distinguishes S1 from S2 processes. We may regard accessibility as a spectrum with S1 "natural assessments" at one end and S2 conscious deliberation at the other (see Figure 6.2).[19] On one hand, people can easily access physical properties like size or loudness as well as abstractions like similarity or mood (1453). On the other hand, solving differential equations requires deliberate effort. As the examples of bike riding and addition suggest, however, learning can increase the accessibility of difficult processes, moving them toward the S1 end of Figure 6.2's spectrum. Furthermore, such learning generally improves the accuracy of S1 procedures (a key role of education). Changes in the non-ergodic environment can, however, render prior lessons inappropriate to current circumstances.

In addition to ready accessibility, S1 processes possess two other important properties: reference dependence and framing effects. Both indicate how context can influence preference. *Reference dependence* means that intuitive evaluations respond to changes from some reference point, such as the status quo.[20] For example, people show markedly different preferences toward risk depending on whether the same probabilistic outcome is described in terms of losses from a high reference point or gains from a low one (Kahneman and Tversky 1979; Tversky and Kahneman 1992). One might ask: Who should be happier, a person whose wealth declined from $4 million to $3 million or one whose wealth increased from $1 million to $1.2 million? With no status quo bias, the first person should be happier, but perhaps not if that person is loss averse (a form of status quo bias). Likewise, employers hear many more complaints after reducing pay than praise after increasing it (Bewley 1999).[21]

Framing effects, another S1 property, are conceptual responses to the manner in which ideas or events are presented. Initial descriptions or impressions often influence subsequent judgments. Evaluations of two plans for reducing disease, for example, differ according to whether mathematically equivalent probable impacts are framed in terms of lives saved or deaths avoided (Kahneman 2003). Likewise, pollsters find that the wording of questions about specific policies influences rates of policy approval (Schuman and Presser 1981). Political, religious, or ethnic labels can elicit immediate associations or judgments.

Using these ideas, we define *heuristics* as mental procedures that readily combine various inputs from current and prior experience to produce impressionistic judgments. Specifically, heuristics incorporate accessible cognitive inputs, which arise from observation and/

or memory—typically in a reference-dependent or framed fashion—to generate intuitive (primarily S1) impressions. For example, an *attribute substitution* heuristic involves judging people, objects, or events on the basis of their most accessible (salient) attributes, such as a person's looks.[22] Attribute substitution tends to lower the threshold number of observations needed to form a judgment—and so lowers the required cognitive effort. For example, knowing that John is a lawyer makes it easy to associate his actions with aggressiveness, but if one did not know his occupation (or assumed erroneously that he is a first-grade teacher), this impression might require more observations or may never even arise. Although heuristics economize on cognitive costs, they can introduce systematic bias and so yield inaccurate judgments.

Judgments mix S1 intuition and heuristics with S2 deliberation to generate conclusions. For Kahneman, "Judgments are always explicit and intentional, whether or not they are overtly expressed" (2003, 1452). The relative importance of the S1 and S2 processes here depends on the effort required to reach judgment, which, in turn, for any given problem, depends on the accessibility of applicable deliberation processes. With limited cognitive resources, agents strive to economize on such processing.[23]

Using ideas from Conlisk (1996), we outline a simple model that demonstrates why agents who encounter problems outside of a problem-complexity boundary will mix S1 heuristics with S2 deduction. For simplicity, assume complete information—that is, no informational constraint on optimization. With respect to cognitive processes, S1 heuristics operate at zero cognitive cost, whereas S2 optimization requires expending cognition cost ($c_c > 0$) per unit cognitive effort (e_c). Assume that c_c increases linearly in cognitive effort; $c_c(e_c) = \lambda e_c$. The product $c_c(e_c)e_c = \lambda e_c^2$ then indicates the total cost of cognitive effort per unit time.[24] Note further that the cognitive effort needed to solve an optimization problem (e_{cs}) depends on the difficulty of the problem at hand, which, in turn, depends on the complexity of the strategic environment ($e_{cs} = e_{cs}(\xi)$). Previous discussion suggests that e_{cs} increases exponentially in elements of environmental complexity, such as numbers of players and their available strategies.[25] Now suppose that the expected marginal benefit from using heuristics and cognitive effort are respectively β_0 and β_c, where $\beta_0 < \beta_c$. It is relatively straightforward to show that any problem for which optimization requires more effort than some minimal level ($e_c(\xi) > e_{csL}$) will necessitate mixing S1 and S2 processes. We may call this procedure boundedly rational suboptimizing.[26]

Mental Models and Learning Processes

Having justified the need to combine S1 and S2 processes on economic grounds, we now develop the concept of mental models. This concept allows us to elaborate on the nature and dynamics of cognitive processes, learning, and the responses of both to social influence. *Mental models* are "the internal representations that individual cognitive systems created to interpret the environment" (Denzau and North 1994, 4). Mental models combine S1 and S2 evaluations of prior experience into understandings of key categories, patterns, and cause-and-effect relationships. More specifically, outside of a problem-complexity boundary, people use a partly intuitive, partly inductive, and partly deductive mix of S1 and S2 processes for developing categories that store and organize observations (e.g., tall, short;

liberal, conservative). With reflection, they also perceive patterns (US Republicans tend to be conservative) and cause-and-effect relationships (if I extend my right hand to a stranger, we will shake hands).[27] These categories, patterns, and relationships congeal into internal mental representations, internalized frameworks for interpreting input from observations and memory: mental models.

Mental models not only reflect previous learning, they also inform future learning. Such learning occurs at two levels: internal hypothesis testing and reevaluative learning. Both levels embody evolutionary, adaptive processes. *Internal hypothesis testing* employs existing mental models to run thought experiments. People evaluate plausible hypotheses that arise from their mental models as they strive to predict outcomes of strategic interactions and other processes. Before making an investment decision, for example, an entrepreneur imagines possible contingencies, responses, and outcomes on the basis of her current conceptions of the enterprise, its environment, and related causal relationships. Information feedback from the environment (e.g., revenue earned), filtered through her existing mental model, tends to confirm or refute specific hypotheses. For example, she might think: "OK, the first idea was not so great, but I hadn't really expected to make a profit the first year. If I keep trying, I will succeed." Hypotheses that survive this internal (evolutionary) selection process tend to solidify into expectations or judgments. In Brian Arthur's terminology, people develop "temporarily fulfilled expectations" (1992, 12).

Within given mental models, information feedback on relationships between inputs (strategies) and outputs (outcomes and associated payoffs) allows agents to adjust their expectations and strategies; they develop new hypotheses. Our entrepreneur decides the first strategy was not sufficient and so tries a second, still believing in her basic business model. In stable environments, repeated testing of related hypotheses tends to lower the cognitive costs of specific mental tasks, moving them toward the S1 end of Figure 6.2's accessibility spectrum. Such repetition typically improves both cognition and information. But environments can change in non-ergodic manners that undermine the accuracy of previously developed mental models, indicating a need for more profound learning.[28]

The considerably less frequent *reevaluative learning* adjusts mental models themselves in response to significant adverse feedback. Because mental models economize on cognitive effort and adjusting them is costly, agents have an incentive to retain their models. The circumstances that prompt internal hypothesis testing change far more quickly than the mental models that frame such hypothesis testing. The durability of mental models and their reliance on accumulated prior assessments thus jointly generate properties of path dependence that can lock in misperceptions and lead to inferior choices. More precisely, the evolutionary dynamics of reevaluative learning create punctuated equilibria. Mental models persist with small adjustment until a sufficient volume of salient information feedback (e.g., a dramatic surprise) demonstrates large enough inconsistencies to undermine them (Denzau and North 1994).[29] After the fifth successive year of losses, our entrepreneur needs to revise her entire conception of business prospects. Such reassessment of cognitive frameworks constitutes reevaluative learning. Kahneman notes, however, that correction processes are often incomplete.[30]

Both types of learning are context dependent in that they reflect specific social, political, economic, or physical circumstances or outcomes. Learning is a social process that responds to observed or communicated behavior, ideas, and mental models of others (Young 2009).[31] Thus cultural transmission shapes much of the learning that informs the creation, use, and adjustment of mental models. Learning reflects an "ecology" of interactive evolution (coevolution; Arthur 1992). Influence from others leads to gradual alteration of judgments within mental models and occasionally generates (punctuated) reassessments. Professors often hope to induce such reevaluative learning among their students.

Some mental models are shared. While different individuals do not possess identical sets of mental models, sharing models greatly facilitates communication. Sharing generates common vocabulary, categories, perceptions of patterns, and expectations. Indeed, in the absence of communication or cultural transmission, individual models tend to diverge, increasing the costs or difficulties of communication.[32] Not surprisingly, the cultural learning that accompanies shared models reduces costs of cognition. Cultural transmission of impressions and judgments creates and shapes heuristics, lowering cognitive costs for individuals. Nevertheless, free-rider problems accompany the social learning processes that complement the development and transmission of mental models (Denzau and North 1994). Thus leaders tend to play disproportionate roles in shaping shared models (Bikhchandani, Hirshleifer, and Welch 1992). For example, during the 1960s and beyond, Martin Luther King exerted profound influence on conceptions of race relations and social protest. More broadly, an ability to influence shared mental models is a key source of power3.

Denzau and North show particular interest in two broad categories of shared mental models: ideologies and institutions. Communication within and across groups, particularly those that share culture, fosters the creation of ideologies and institutions in a coevolutionary process (1994, 20). *Ideologies* are shared mental models that interpret the environment, incorporate understandings of cause-and-effect relationships, and indicate a normative vision of how aspects of the social environment should be structured or changed (a type of judgment). For example a libertarian ideology might interpret government activity as largely interfering with tendencies of people to produce and exchange, and so might prescribe cutting taxes in order to reduce the size of government. Two people who share an ideology can often readily communicate about problems, causes, or potential solutions.

A simple definition of *institutions* appears in North (1990, 3): "institutions are the rules of the game in society."[33] The idea that institutions are shared mental models may seem counterintuitive, but institutions reflect shared understandings of possible actions and consequences. Institutions embody shared models of cause-effect relationships that emerge from commonly understood behavioral rules. For example, many members of contemporary society share the following understanding: if a store manager observes somebody shoplifting, the manager may tell the police and the shoplifter may go to jail.

By coordinating activity, institutions reduce uncertainty (North 1990). In the absence of mutually understood rules, the possibility of myriad technically feasible actions among multiple agents in complex society would render deductive prediction impossible. The CD gap would be impenetrable.[34] Thus, by limiting actions among multiple agents, the shared expectations embodied in institutions dramatically enhance the predictability of human interaction, rendering certain predictions possible (Heiner 1983). Most shoppers do not consider shoplifting, and most owners know that. Absent that shared understanding, running a store would be far more complicated (if not impossible). Furthermore, institutions, as path-dependent shared mental models, preserve common expectations and understandings of causal relationships along with related accumulated collective knowledge—as suggested by the term "institutional memory."

We thus expect both ideologies and institutions to possess the punctuated-equilibrium properties of individual mental models, but with greater durability. Changing shared models involves social reevaluative learning. The strong path dependency of ideologies and institutions emerges from free-rider problems (first-order CAPs), coordination and enforcement problems (second-order CAPs), differing perceptions, conflicting interests, and power relationships. Agents who benefit from existing institutional structures may use their available power to oppose change. Dislodging ideologies or institutions thus typically requires dramatic surprises that spread rapidly across groups, as in Tunisia's revolution of January 2011.

More precisely, collective reassessment of shared ideologies or institutions depends on attaining the following related conditions:

(i) sufficiently salient perceptions of inconsistencies or problems among individuals (the condition for individual reevaluation);

(ii) a large enough number of appropriately positioned individuals who experience such perceptions;

(iii) sufficient communication of perceived problems by concerned individuals to reach sufficiently large (or well-positioned) groups; and

(iv) an imitative social learning process of collective reassessment.

For example, after the financial debacle of 2007–2010, a sizable number of economists and analysts have begun to reconceptualize financial behavior, in effect redesigning partially shared models. We have yet to see whether a fundamental shift in economic modeling of finance will follow, as the critical-mass levels for conditions (ii), (iii), and (iv) have, so far, not been reached.

Furthermore, leadership and power interact within collective reassessments in a manner that increases the path dependence of shared mental models. Leaders and other power holders who benefit from existing ideologies and institutions may take action to prevent reassessment; and leadership itself is usually path dependent. Having established that both individual and shared mental models emerge from path-dependent evolutionary processes, we now turn to an evolutionary conception of cognition.

6.4. THE EVOLUTIONARY LOGIC BEHIND BOUNDEDLY RATIONAL PROCESSES

As background for Section 6.5's evolutionary approach to boundedly rational behavior, this section models boundedly rational strategic decision making in two related steps.

First, we review Herbert Simon's (1955) model of bounded rationality to illustrate heuristics. Second, we present a modified version of Heiner's (1983) model of a "reliability condition" for the evolutionary screening of various strategies and habits. This model posits a reliability threshold (a selection criterion) that strategies must cross before they become elements of heuristics. The model demonstrates why boundedly rational actors ignore potentially beneficial but unreliable strategies and why heuristics tend to arise from repeated interaction. This same logic applies to information gathering, to hypothesis testing within mental models pertaining to their inclusion of specific heuristics, and to the reevaluative learning that accompanies displacing mental models. Implications extend to social norms and formal institutions. It is important to note, however, that reliability does not imply optimality.

Simon (1955) models decision making for a boundedly rational agent using three elements: a set of alternatives (A), a set of possible future states of the world or outcomes (S) that follow from combinations of actions, and payoff functions $V(s)$. Set A includes all possible actions or strategies that an agent and its interactive partners could employ in a specific situation. We could represent A as all of the strategic choices that emerge from a single node or information set in an extensive-form game. With limited cognition, however, the agent perceives (and hence considers) only subset $A° \in A$. Set S includes all possible outcomes that could arise from a specific strategic situation or, equivalently, all outcomes that could follow a node or information set in an extensive-form game. The contingencies within S depend on the social, political, economic, and natural environment, on the prior actions of all players, and on all possible future actions for all players. In other words, S indicates all potential outcomes embodied in the context (or environment) within which all relevant players make strategic decisions. The function $V(s)$ specifies the utility payoffs to players that arise from a specific future state $s \in S$.

In substantively rational classical games, agents consider all actions (so $A° = A$), and they understand function $V(s)$, at least as it applies to themselves, for all game states $s \in S$. Agents know the payoff structure of the game in terms of their own payoffs, though in cases of asymmetric information they may not know payoffs to other players. They also know how all possible combinations of specific actions affect future states: they know all relations $A \rightarrow S$ or the associated probabilities. On the basis of this knowledge, they choose best responses to expected actions of others.

By contrast, boundedly rational agents operate within the confines of a CD gap. They need not know $A \rightarrow S$ or related probabilities, but they can observe outcomes of their own behavior as well as some outcomes from others' behavior, within limited proximities. More precisely, agents begin with prior conceptions (inherited from past experience) that allow a coarse mapping of relations between A and S. These priors isolate a subset of considered actions $A_g^o \in A$ that they expect to generate good future states $S_g^s \in S$. *Good states* S_g^s are expected to generate $V(s) = 1$ in the simplified value set $V(s) \in \{1, 0, -1\}$, whose numbers respectively correspond to an improvement, no change, and a decline.[35] We may regard $A_{1g}^o \rightarrow S_{1g}^s$ mappings as inherited heuristics, where subscript 1 indicates an initial time period ($t = 1$). For example, an agent entering a bargaining context may believe that, if her opponent bargains hard, compromising up to 20% will be OK.

Boundedly rational agents learn adaptively. They follow one or more of their heuristics for some time (following temporarily fulfilled expectations). They observe outcomes and then occasionally use S2 monitoring to reevaluate. In a subsequent period, an agent may adopt a new heuristic that employs a new mapping between actions and states: $A^o_{2g} \to S^s_{2g}$. Having done poorly a few times with 20% compromises, the agent decides that limiting compromises to 10% makes more sense. Evolutionary game-theoretic models can represent this sequential adaptive learning.

We now construct a model, based largely on Heiner (1983), that uses evolutionary logic to show why heuristics improve outcomes for boundedly rational agents facing uncertainty. We use Simon's concepts of A, S, and V—noting that S includes current states of the world (outcomes of prior actions) as conditions under which strategies are chosen (i.e., $A(S_0) \to S_1$). The core idea of this model is that heuristics improve average performance by eliminating consideration of certain feasible actions when the likelihood of identifying appropriate circumstances for use of such actions is too low. Applications of this model are vast; they include acquisition of information, selection of heuristics within mental models, and reevaluative learning as a method for altering or replacing individual or shared mental models. Implications extend to social norms and formal institutions.

We begin with the CD gap. The extent of the CD gap encountered by boundedly rational agents depends on relationships between environmental complexity and agents' cognitive abilities. We represent such complexity by the set of all possible states that exist within or could arise from the current environment, the set S. Cognitive abilities (Θ) indicate an agent's "competence in deciphering relationships between its behavior and the environment" (Heiner 1983, 564). Thus we have

$$(6.3) \qquad\qquad\qquad \text{CD gap} = \upsilon(S, \Theta),$$

where υ indicates the extent of uncertainty. An increase in the number of possible states increases uncertainty ($\partial\upsilon/\partial S > 0$), whereas increasing cognition reduces uncertainty ($\partial\upsilon/\partial\Theta < 0$). Note that an increase in either the number of agents or the set of feasible alternatives (A) increases the size of S exponentially. For example, in a one-time, two-player, two-strategy simultaneous game, there are 2^2 elements in S—the four cells of the game matrix. In an otherwise similar three-player, three-strategy game, there are $3^3 = 27$ cells; $4^4 = 256$ and so on. Population growth and technical change exponentially increase environmental complexity—and hence the CD gap—because these trends increase both the number of interacting agents and the size of set A.[36] Even though some technologies, such as binoculars or computers, counteract this effect by increasing perception and/or cognition, economic development necessarily engenders rising complexity (North 1990).

Now consider a bargaining encounter between a boundedly rational worker and a firm. The firm offers the worker wage w. The worker has a prior set of reasonably understood actions $A^o_1 \in A$. Suppose A^o_1 includes two strategies: bargain hard (ask for 5% above the offer; a) and bargain easy (accept the offer; a'). Consider a new (mutant) action: bargain really hard (ask for 10% above the offer; a''). Suppose there is some set of good states (circumstances) $S_g(a'') \in S$ under which asking for 10% would improve outcomes:

$V(a''; S_g) = 1$. For example, a type-E (easy) firm might not want to risk losing the worker, but other firms would rather hire a replacement. Define probability ρ_g as the probability that a good situation (state) for using a'' actually exists at an appropriate time. Defining $S_g(a'')$ as the set of all possible states that are "good" for using a'' (so that $V(a''; S_g(a'')) = 1$), we have $\rho_g(a'', S) = S_g(a'')/S$.

Because they face a CD gap, however, agents do not necessarily know when circumstances $S_g(a'')$ will occur or even the value of ρ_g. Still, there exists a probability—which is conditional on the level of uncertainty $(\rho_r(a''; v))$—that the agent will, even with limited information and cognition, choose a'' under the "right" circumstances. In the bargaining example, ρ_r indicates the probability that the agent correctly identifies a situation (employer is type E) when asking for 10% (a'') would actually improve her outcomes. Note that uncertainty lowers ρ_r $(\partial\rho_r/\partial v < 0)$. Identifying an opponent's type may be difficult, especially when opponents try to hide their intentions. We now define $\rho_w(a''; v)$ as the conditional probability that the agent picks the "wrong" situation for using strategy a'' (employer is not type E).[37] Again, the boundedly rational agent does not know either $\rho_r(a''; v)$ or $\rho_w(a''; v)$. Note further that $\rho_r(v)$ and $\rho_w(v)$ need not sum to 1.[38]

On this basis, we address conditions under which it makes sense to consider using a''. Define $g(a'', S)$ as the average gain from using a'' at the "right" time (i.e., in a good state $S_g(a'')$). Likewise, $l(a'', S)$ indicates the average loss from choosing the "wrong" circumstance for using a''. Equation (6.4) specifies the condition under which adding action a'' to the list of considered actions (A^o) improves an agent's likely outcomes:

(6.4) $g(a'', S) \times \rho_r(a''; v) \times \rho_g(a'', S) > l(a'', S) \times \rho_w(a''; v) \times (1 - \rho_g(a'', S)).$

The left-hand side of (6.4) shows the expected gain from a "right" decision on a'': the gain from making a right decision, multiplied by the probability that the agent will make such a decision, multiplied by the probability that a good state will actually arise (or exist) at the right moment. Analogously, the right-hand side shows the expected loss from a "wrong" decision.

Rearranging, we find the *reliability condition*:

(6.5) $$\frac{p_r(a''; v)}{p_w(a''; v)} > \frac{l(a'', S)}{g(a'', S)} \times \frac{1 - \rho_g(a'', S)}{\rho_g(a'', S)}.$$

The left-hand side of (6.5) is the *reliability ratio*. It indicates the reliability of an agent's decision making with regard to a'' when faced with a CD gap: it specifies the probability that the agent makes a "right" decision to use a'' relative to that of making a "wrong" decision. The right-hand side of (6.5) indicates the threshold that ratio ρ_r/ρ_w must exceed in order for a'' to be a *reliable* action—an action that should, on average, improve outcomes (Heiner 1983, 564–67). To simplify notation for the right-hand side, let $T(a''; S, v) = (l/g)(1 - \rho_g)/\rho_g$. Given S and v, the threshold ratio $(\rho_r/\rho_w)^* = T^*$ distinguishes reliable from unreliable use of a''. If the existing CD gap $(v(S, \Theta))$ allows $\rho_r/\rho_w > T^*$, then a'' is reliable: $V(a''; S) = 1$.

If $\rho_r/\rho_w < T^*$, then $V(a''; S) = -1$, and a'' is not reliable. Note that rising uncertainty (v) reduces ρ_r and increases ρ_w; consequently, reliability (ρ_r/ρ_w) falls.

We may now use the selection criteria implied by the reliability condition, together with Simon's value function, to explain the emergence and operation of heuristics. If new action a'' satisfies condition (6.5), $V(a'') = 1$; if it fails to do so, $V(a'') = -1$. From an evolutionary perspective, then, agents tend to earn higher payoffs (in terms of criteria from value function V) if they consider an action a'' (i.e., add it to their set of contemplated actions A^o) only when they know enough about the environment to facilitate reliable use of that action. When an action a'' fails to meet the reliability condition, agents actually do better on average by using heuristics that exclude a'' from their choice set.[39] For example, there are some agents who could profit from shoplifting under the "right" circumstances, yet they do not even consider doing so because they do not trust their ability to correctly identify such circumstances.

Equation (6.5) also indicates that heuristics tend to include only actions that fit recurrent or otherwise likely circumstances.[40] Mathematically, for given values of g and l, a lower ρ_g (lower S_g/S) increases the threshold T^* that ρ_r/ρ_w must cross for satisfying (6.5). Equivalently, a low prevalence of good situations for using a'' makes it relatively unlikely that an agent will know, observe, or hear about such occasions. Conversely, if good circumstances for a'' are prevalent, agents may well know when to use it. Thus heuristics tend to include strategies that arise repeatedly in agents' prior experience, ones that they often hear about, or strategies for which good circumstances are otherwise relatively noticeable.

On this basis, we specify heuristic (h) as a set of considered actions ($a_h \in A_h^o$) that satisfies (6.5)—in other words, a set of actions or strategies that fit likely or recurrent contingencies (S_h). Set A_h^o then includes actions for which amenable conditions arise frequently enough to generate a sufficiently high probability of good use ($\rho_g = S_g(a_h)/S$) for crossing the reliability threshold ($\rho_r(a_h)/\rho_w(a_h) > T^*$). For example, if the worker in the previous example had no prior experience with type-E employers, her heuristic would likely exclude asking for 10% above her employer's offer. Even though her current employer could be of type E, the worker's previous experience would not adequately inform (or enable) reliable use of hard bargaining.[41]

We now develop three extensions. First, the reliability condition (6.5) applies to the acquisition of information related to strategic decisions. If an action a'' fails to meet the reliability condition, agents who devote resources to investigating a'' will, on average, do worse than those who do not (unless such acquisition facilitates crossing T^*). If asking for 10% above an offer is seldom a viable strategy, agents may not benefit from devoting scarce resources to discovering the rare circumstances under which it could work. This fits common sense: we do not waste energy investigating the consequences of activities that we have no intention of pursuing (even though such activities might be useful). This outcome reinforces the idea that heuristics, norms, and rules are path dependent.

Second, equation (6.5) illustrates the selection of heuristics for inclusion in mental models. Mental models incorporate heuristics as part of their S1/S2 processing related to categories, patterns, and causal relationships. Selection among heuristics can reflect outcomes of hypothesis testing within a given mental model. Heuristics that meet a pertinent reliability condition, by standards of the applicable mental model, tend to persist as behavioral regularities. To apply equation (6.5) to sets of heuristics, replace A^o and a'' (and related terms) with H^o and h'', respectively, in the preceding text and in both (6.4) and (6.5); then repeat the logic of the previous discussion.

Third, reliability influences the long-term selection of mental models via processes of reevaluative learning. We may now replace A^o and a'' (and related terms) in (6.4) and (6.5) with M^o and m'' (for mental models), respectively. Models that tend to satisfy (6.5) in relevant social contexts tend to persist. Reevaluative learning arises when altered circumstances sufficiently undermine the prior reliability of a mental model (it no longer satisfies (6.5)). We can extend this logic to shared mental models. Social norms are shared mental models that combine group heuristics that, then, typically meet some reliability condition in their relevant social environments—given the attendant perceptions, conflicts, and distributions of power. Likewise, formal institutions emerge from analogous selection procedures that rely on collective decision making in pertinent social contexts.

Finally, it is important to realize that reliability does not imply optimality.[42] For all of these applications, the performance criteria that underlie the reliability condition can reflect different types of payoffs (social or material) in value functions, for different kinds of players (individuals, firms, etc.) in different contexts. Performance criteria may track profits, sociality, accountability, leadership, loyalty, obedience, popularity, and so on. More generally, fitness may reflect different biological, economic, social, and/or political reproductive capabilities exhibited by information, strategies, individual mental models, norms, formal institutions, and relevant organizations.[43] Different selection pressures—such as pursuing short-term profits versus developing cooperative relationships with employees, or short- versus long-term viability—may push in distinct and conflicting directions.[44] Because multiple potentially conflicting selective pressures operate in a non-ergodic world, evolutionary selection need not generate optimality. As Heiner notes, "Such a world will be a continual mixture of appropriately and inappropriately structured behavior" (1983, 569).

Overall, the reliability condition facilitates conceptualizing the selection pressures that underlie the evolution of strategies, heuristics, individual mental models, social norms, and formal institutions. We now turn to evolutionary game-theoretic modeling.

6.5. EVOLUTIONARY GAME THEORY, PROPERTY, TEAM COOPERATION, AND RECIPROCAL DISPOSITION

A bounded rationality approach to evolutionary and classical game-theoretic reasoning elucidates the complex foundations of exchange and development. In particular, such an approach offers insight into the emergence of institutions. Building on the implications of Section 6.4's reliability condition concerning the existence and development of heuristics and mental models, we proceed to employ evolutionary game theory to model adaptive learning processes. After a brief comparison of evolutionary game theory with classical game theory, we develop a simple Hawk/Dove evolutionary model. Extending that model yields some insight into the origins of property rights. We proceed with a simple evolutionary model of team production that illustrates some potential for both efficient and inefficient outcomes. We next discuss indirect evolutionary modeling, a method that adds classical game-theoretic interactions to an evolutionary framework. We close this section with a model that illustrates how an innate reciprocal disposition could emerge from adaptive responses in a public-good game—a logic that represents endogenous preference formation and also relates to institutional formation.

Evolutionary and Classical Game Theory

Evolutionary game theory was initially developed by biologists to illustrate processes of natural selection.[45] From a social scientific perspective, evolutionary selection focuses on the reproductive or transmission capacities of learned strategies or behaviors, rather than the biological reproductive capacities of genes or organisms. We interpret "strategies" broadly to include plans of action (typical game-theoretic strategies), specific heuristics, individual mental models, and shared mental models (institutions in particular).

There are five fundamental differences between classical game theory (CGT) and evolutionary game theory (EGT). These differences reflect various approaches to cognition, choice/response, payoffs, analytical focus, and equilibrium:

1. Cognition: CGT agents employ substantive rationality. Even though they may possess social preferences and respond to incomplete information, they do so without cognitive limits or costs. By contrast, boundedly rational EGT agents face a CD gap in which the complexity of encountered problems exceeds their cognitive capabilities. Consequently, they resort to heuristics and mental models that are inherited from previous learning.

2. Choice/response: CGT agents choose among a set of available strategies on the basis of calculated best responses that are derived from their utility functions and their expectations concerning others' moves in specific strategic contexts. EGT agents do not choose per se; rather, they inherit strategies as elements of heuristics or mental models, where such inheritance reflects accumulated judgments derived from prior experience, cultural transmission, and education.[46] Language and styles of greeting offer examples.

3. Payoffs: CGT payoffs represent utility values derived from material and social preferences. EGT payoffs represent evolutionary *fitness*: the average expected ability of specific strategies to reproduce (transmit) among groups of agents (across populations) over time. A relatively high fitness payoff to a strategy signifies high rates of adoption relative to feasible alternatives. Strategies with low fitness (failed practices, unsuccessful ideas or models) tend to die out over time. As in any strategic encounter, received payoffs depend upon the player/strategy combinations actually encountered within the relevant contexts (society, group, firm)—hence, a game.

4. Analytical focus: CGT analyzes relationships between strategic best-response choices of agents, game outcomes from various combinations of choices, and ensuing utility payoffs. In EGT, strategies, not individuals, are the "*dramatis personae* of the social dynamic" (Bowles 2004, 60). Because selection operates on strategies, EGT analysis

TABLE 6.1
Basic approach and concepts: CGT versus EGT

	Cognition	Choice/response	Payoffs	Analytical focus	Equilibrium
CGT	Substantive rationality	Agents choose best response strategies	Utility of agents in current period or at end of game	Interaction of agents' choices	NE, SPE
EGT	Bounded rationality	Strategies are inherited and reflect past learning	Reproductive fitness of strategies	Emergent mix of strategies	ESS; stable polymorphic mix

focuses on mixes of strategies—held among a population of agents—that emerge from dynamic adaptive selection processes. Over time, such selection reflects adaptive learning.

5. Concept of equilibrium: CGT equilibria, in particular Nash equilibria and subgame perfect equilibria, reflect a mutually consistent best-response calculus based upon given (or predictably adjusting) mutually consistent expectations. By contrast, EGT (as its name suggests) is inherently dynamic. Equilibria signify stable trajectories over time rather than conjunctions of responses and expectations at moments in time. One type of EGT equilibrium is an *evolutionary stable strategy* (ESS): a strategy that, when predominant in a population (or group), can resist invasion by feasible mutant (new) strategies. A second type of equilibrium is a stable polymorphic mix of strategies.[47]

Table 6.1 summarizes these distinctions.

Subsequent arguments in this book employ both CGT and EGT modeling. For strategic interactions in which agents use given mental models within understood institutional environments, we tend to employ CGT—reflecting the idea that stable contexts facilitate S2 reasoning. On the other hand, we employ EGT to illustrate the relative reproductive potential of alternative practices, ranging from heuristics to institutions. Evolutionary game-theoretic models can represent the processes and outcomes of reevaluative learning among groups of boundedly rational agents, where learning reflects evolutionary selection among socially inherited traits.[48] Finally, an *indirect evolutionary model* employs CGT reasoning for on-the-spot decision making, but uses evolutionary fitness to evaluate longer-term selection among various individual predispositions or shared mental models—notably, social norms and formal institutions.

Simple EGT Models

A simple EGT model can illustrate reevaluative learning outcomes embodied in heuristics, individual mental models, and institutions. Figure 6.3 illustrates a two-player Hawk/Dove game. This is a *stage game* for an evolutionary model; it captures a basic interaction between two agents, both of whom employ one of two inherited strategies (or heuristics), either Hawk or Dove. Figure 6.3 shows the "stage" on which they play. As in any normal-form game, the cells of Figure 6.3 indicate the payoffs received from each possible combination of

		Player B	
		Hawk	Dove
Player A	Hawk	$(V-c)/2, (V-c)/2$	$V, 0$
	Dove	$0, V$	$V/2, V/2$

Figure 6.3   Hawk/dove game

strategies, in this case Hawk and Dove. Here V denotes the reproductive value of a resource (e.g., food) and c denotes the total cost of fighting over that resource. Strategy Hawk (H) is aggressive. If two H-players (hawks) meet, they fight over V, and each receives $(V - c)/2$: half of the difference between the value of food and the (total) cost of fighting over it. Strategy Dove (Dv) is passive: Dv-players share with other doves and yield to hawks.

To convert this stage game into an evolutionary game, we assume random matching of players from a large population of agents that includes both types. Such matching generates the four possible combinations of H and Dv shown on the diagram—in various proportions. Let h be the proportion of strategy H in the population at a point in time. The average fitness payoffs (W) to the Hawk and Dove strategies are, respectively:

$$(6.6) \qquad W(\text{H}) = h(V - c)/2 + (1 - h)V;$$

$$(6.7) \qquad W(\text{Dv}) = (1 - h)V/2.$$

The nature of the ensuing game depends on the relative sizes of V and c. If $V > c$, we have an evolutionary multi-player PD game. If $V < c$, we have evolutionary chicken.[49]

The concept of an evolutionary stable strategy (ESS) offers one tool for evaluating the relative fitness of inherited strategies Dv and H. We begin by assuming one predominant type in the population (in this case, H) and consider whether a few mutants of the other type (Dv) could invade it. Evaluation here reflects two criteria. The *primary criterion* for evolutionary stability compares how each type performs when matched against a member of predominant type H. It compares how well an H does when matched with another H to how well a mutant Dv does when also matched with an H. If an H does better in an H-H match than a Dv does in a Dv-H match, then H is an ESS. If H does worse, then H is not an ESS. If both matches generate equal payoffs, we consider the secondary criterion. The *secondary criterion* evaluates how each strategy performs when matched with a mutant. In this case, how does an H fare in an H-Dv match compared to how a Dv fares in a Dv-Dv match? If H does better, it is still an ESS; if it does worse, it is not an ESS. If these outcomes are equal, we say that H is an *evolutionary neutral strategy*.

More generally, we may write fitness equations for the predominant type (P) matched against a mutant (M) as follows:

$$(6.8) \qquad W(\text{P}) = mE(\text{P, M}) + (1 - m)E(\text{P, P}),$$

$$(6.9) \qquad W(\text{M}) = mE(\text{M, M}) + (1 - m)E(\text{M, P}),$$

where $W(\cdot)$ indicates the overall fitness payoff to types P and M; m is the proportion of mutants in the population; and $E(\cdot)$ indicates the expected (evolutionary) fitness of type P in (6.8) and type M in (6.9) that emerges from a match between the types indicated (in parentheses). Combining equations (6.8) and (6.9) then yields the fitness difference:[50]

$$(6.10) \qquad W(P) - W(M) = m[E(P, M) - E(M, M)] + (1 - m)[E(P, P) - E(M, P)].$$

If we assume that the proportion of mutants in the population (m) is quite small, the first term on the right-hand side represents the primary criterion, and the second term represents the secondary criterion. With a small m, the ESS standard provides an accurate assessment of the potential for mutant strategies to invade a dominant population of (currently used) strategies.[51]

Applying the Hawk/Dove strategies to equation (6.10) reveals that, when $c < V$, the primary criterion designates H (but not Dv) as an ESS. But when $c > V$, neither H nor Dv is an ESS; instead we have a stable polymorphic equilibrium in which the proportion of hawks is $h^* = V/C$; analogously, for doves, $d^* = (1 - h^*) = (1 - V/C)$.[52] If the proportion of hawks in the population exceeds h^*, conciliatory doves can enter because hawks tend to destroy each other. Too great a proportion of doves, however, makes invasion (exploitation) by hawks easy. We can readily translate this model into a bargaining story among mixed populations of bargainers, where H represents an orientation (heuristic) that favors bargaining hard and Dv represents a concessionary orientation. The model predicts a mix of both types—as we frequently observe in society.

Now consider a slightly more complicated model where each agent owns a piece of property. We introduce a third strategy, called "bourgeois" (B). Strategy B means play H on your own property (familiar territory) but play Dv on someone else's (Bowles 2004). Assume that, for each match, each agent has a 50% chance of bargaining from its own property. Of the strategies H, Dv, and B, only B is an ESS. Furthermore, relating evolutionary stability to Section 6.4's reliability condition (equation (6.5)), an ESS as defined by equation (6.10) also satisfies equation (6.5).[53] Intuitively, it is easy to see why strategy B could possess the familiarity that often accompanies achieving reliability. After all, people frequently observe or experience interactions in which one party owns property and another does not. Note further that, at an individual level, strategy B is a heuristic: it rules out many other sequences of actions. For example, strategy B does not address factors—such as socioeconomic background or observable preparedness for negotiation—that could affect a party's bargaining strength.[54] Among groups, a shared conception of strategy B could be a social norm—as it appears to be in many contexts.

Evolutionary Assurance Based on Team Production

Assurance versions of EGT models offer insight into the punctuated-equilibrium characteristics of reevaluative learning, with direct applications to mental models. There are many possible illustrations. Any simple two-player game of assurance can serve as a stage game for a multi-player EGT assurance model. We might consider the need for a supply firm and

	Player 1	
	Strategy X	Strategy Y
Strategy X	G, G	L, L
Strategy Y	L, L	R, R

Player 2 (labels row headers for Strategy X / Strategy Y)

Figure 6.4   Team production stage game

a purchasing firm to coordinate on relevant technology, where any coordination is better than none, but one technology is better for both firms than another. Alternatively, the two firms might coordinate on location, sales networks, publicity, and so forth. A variety of political phenomena (e.g., a need for compatible fundraising strategies) and social phenomena (e.g., choosing one's associates) also fit this framework.

Figure 6.4 portrays a symmetric two-player game of assurance that represents a production process. Players 1 and 2 may use either strategy X or strategy Y. If they coordinate on using the better method X, both receive a good payoff (G). Coordinating on Y yields reasonable payoff (R), and using different methods yields a low payoff (L). Here $G > R > L$; $G > 0$; $R > 0$. In many such games, $L = 0$. This formulation is more general, indicating that failure to coordinate might also generate either positive returns lower than R or negative values. Figure 6.4 can also represent the corresponding stage game for an evolutionary version. Applying the primary criterion for evolutionary stability, we find that X and Y are both evolutionary stable strategies.

To illustrate a punctuated equilibrium, consider the applicable fitness equations

(6.11) $$W(X) = \lambda G + (1 - \lambda)L;$$

(6.12) $$W(Y) = \lambda L + (1 - \lambda)R.$$

Here λ is the proportion of players who have inherited strategy X.[55] As in a CGT multi-player assurance game, there is an unstable (here, polymorphic) population equilibrium at $\lambda^* = (R - L)/(H + R - 2L)$ for $0 < \lambda^* < 1$, where λ^* denotes a critical-mass tipping point. Moving from an inefficient ESS where $\lambda = 0$ to an efficient ESS where $\lambda = 1$, or vice versa, requires crossing the λ^* threshold. Recall that we interpret "inheritance" in an EGT model to reflect social learning. Thus, to move out of an inefficient ESS, proportion λ^* agents would have to simultaneously reevaluate their heuristics in response to accumulated learning so as to adopt the other strategy. Although such a shift is not impossible, it is typically extremely difficult to coordinate. Hence our EGT model generates punctuated equilibria at both $\lambda = 0$ (all Y) and $\lambda = 1$ (all X). In this regard, we may interpret each ESS as a shared mental model—perhaps a convention, norm, or formal institution. Shifting to the other ESS (more likely from inefficient "all Y" to efficient "all X") requires simultaneous discovery and communication of problems or inconsistencies; more precisely, it requires meeting conditions (i)–(iv) listed at the end of Section 6.3: a substantial CAP of social coordination.

A more sophisticated and accurate model of evolutionary learning (based on Young 1996) introduces the possibility that agents make strategic "mistakes" with some random probability $\varepsilon > 0$. This model specifies another mechanism that could lead to a shift between punctuated equilibria: a large enough coincidence of mistakes. Here ε denotes the probability that an X-player actually uses Y and vice versa.[56] To illustrate, we rewrite fitness equations (6.11) and (6.12) as follows:

$$(6.13) \qquad W(X) = \lambda[(1-\varepsilon)^2 G + 2(\varepsilon - \varepsilon^2)L + \varepsilon^2 R] + (1-\lambda)[(1-\varepsilon)^2 L \\ + \varepsilon(1-\varepsilon)R + \varepsilon(1-\varepsilon)G + \varepsilon^2 L];$$

$$(6.14) \qquad W(Y) = \lambda[(1-\varepsilon)^2 L + \varepsilon(1-\varepsilon)R + \varepsilon(1-\varepsilon)G + \varepsilon^2 L] \\ + (1-\lambda)[(1-\varepsilon)^2 R + 2(\varepsilon - \varepsilon^2)L + \varepsilon^2 G].$$

In (6.13), the first term shows that, with probability λ, an X-player encounters another X-player. Each plays its correct strategy X with probability $1 - \varepsilon$, and thereby generates an expected payoff of $(1-\varepsilon)^2 G$. If one plays X correctly (probability $(1-\varepsilon)$) and the other mistakenly plays Y (probability ε), the expected payoff accounting for either's making a mistake is $2(\varepsilon - \varepsilon^2)L$. The remaining terms in these equations reflect a similar logic.[57] In this model, a sufficiently large concurrence of mistakes among members of a population can move the outcome from one ESS to the other (Young 1996), shifting the punctuated equilibrium. In terms of Sections 6.3 and 6.4, we can interpret such coincidence either as simultaneous (or rapidly transmitted) discovery of inconsistencies across much of a population, or as similarly transmitted misperceptions. Transmission of either can fundamentally alter shared mental models. The 2011 revolutions in Tunisia and Egypt offer examples of such rapid collective reassessment.

Overall, standard EGT models can represent the adaptive learning dynamics of heuristics and mental models as well as behavioral patterns or strategies that emerge from them, such as approaches to bargaining. In so doing, EGT models can reflect the impact of strategic context on relative fitness by, for example, illustrating how different ratios of strategy types in a population can affect the rates of adoption of various strategies. Closely related phenomena that are also amenable to evolutionary modeling include the development of general preference orientations (dispositions) such as intrinsic reciprocity. Cultural processes may transmit dispositions among individuals and across generations.

An Indirect Evolutionary Model of a Reciprocal Predisposition

Established preferences in stable environments can influence behavior in a calculated S2 manner (as argued by utility theory), yet preference orientations evolve over time. We may employ indirect evolutionary modeling to illustrate interactions between immediate choices and the longer-term evolution of preference orientations. *Indirect evolutionary game theory* (IEGT) combines principles from classical and evolutionary game theory. It mixes CGT evaluation of utility payoffs in given strategic contexts on the basis of existing preference orientations with EGT modeling of the adaptive processes that generate or alter such orientations over time.

We now return to examining the impact of context on preferences, focusing on the evolution of preference orientations or dispositions (e.g., an intrinsic inclination toward reciprocal behavior): endogenous preference formation.[58] To do so, we incorporate an indirect evolutionary model (Güth 1995; Berninghaus, Güth, and Kliemt 2003). Here EGT fitness principles represent the generation and persistence of preference dispositions, and CGT best responses reflect decisions made on the basis of given preference dispositions. Such models capture both the "shadow of the past" via evolutionary development of preference predispositions and the "shadow of the future" via strategic decision making based on given preference orientations (Berninghaus, Korth, and Napel 2007, 583). We could apply equivalent logic to origins of heuristics and mental models.

In this IEGT context, we distinguish between utility and fitness payoffs. We assume that the utility values experienced by agents of various dispositions can incorporate both social and material payoffs, whereas the reproductive fitness of their preference orientations depends only on material payoffs. Preference orientations that generate strategic decisions that, in turn, lead to relatively high average material payoffs in actual encounters tend to reproduce more rapidly than those that do not.[59] This fitness assumption reflects the prevalence of physical competition over scarce material resources (Güth and Napel 2006) and also the notion that relative material success of strategies is likely to be readily observed and communicated among agents. Güth and Yaari (1992) construct an IEGT model of a public-good PD game that demonstrates how a reciprocal disposition toward punishing defection can be evolutionary stable. Reciprocal dispositions reproduce at a higher rate than purely selfish dispositions (or possible mixed strategies) because reciprocal players make decisions that lead to relatively high average material payoffs.

We now apply a straightforward version of indirect evolutionary logic to the origins of a simple form of intrinsic reciprocity.[60] We borrow Güth and Yaari's (1992) basic framework. Consider the two-player PD game represented in Figure 6.5, where $H > C > D > L$. This game could represent a problem of cooperating to create any joint surplus, such as a public good. Now consider a two-stage game. In the first stage, the players simultaneously choose either C or D. Both observe the outcome. In the second stage, a player who has cooperated may choose to punish (P) or not punish (N) the other player if she has chosen D. We assume that punishment results in payoff D for both players; perhaps upon seeing that the other player has not contributed, the contributor destroys the surplus. A contributor who decides to punish earns net punishment utility u_p (reciprocity utility from punishing a defector minus the costs of administering punishment); u_p may be either positive or negative.[61] Figure 6.6 shows this game in extensive form. Note that, on the third move (should it occur), the cooperator i (or j) decides whether or not to punish the defector j (or i).

Both players have the following strategies: D, CP, or CN. In the latter two terms, the first letter (C) indicates the player's first move (if it cooperates); the second term indicates what it does if the other should defect (either P or N). In this IEGT model, the net utility

		Player B	
		C	D
Player A	C	C, C	L, H
	D	H, L	D, D

Figure 6.5   Simple PD game

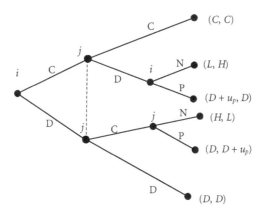

Figure 6.6   Public-good game with reciprocal punishment

N O T E : The dashed line shows an information set: player *j* does not observe player *i*'s move (e.g., the first-stage move for both players is simultaneous).

gain from punishing (u_p) is subject to evolutionary selection. For e-types or for players with weak intrinsic reciprocity, a positive cost of administering punishment leads to $u_p < 0$, whereas for r-types (players with strong intrinsic reciprocity), reciprocal utility gain offsets that cost; hence $u_p > 0$. Incorporating their inherited values of u_p, players engage in Figure 6.6's game, using CGT principles. Their strategic choices then determine their earned material payoffs (H, C, D, or L) and, over time, the fitness of their behavioral type.

It is straightforward to see that, whenever $u_p < 0$ (as it is for e-types), the subgame perfect equilibrium (SPE) indicates that both players choose strategy D. On the other hand, if $u_p > 0$ for both players (i.e., if both are r-types), they each choose strategy CP at the SPE. As in standard EGT games, players match randomly in pairs to play the stage game in Figure 6.6. Assuming that the proportion of r-types in the population is λ, we construct the following fitness equations for r-types ($u_p > 0$) and e-types ($u_p < 0$):

(6.15) $$W(r) = \lambda C + (1 - \lambda)D;$$

(6.16) $$W(e) = D.$$

Since $C > D$, the primary criterion shows that r-types are evolutionary stable.

This simple model demonstrates how a behavioral predisposition that induces a willingness to punish defectors (or unkind behavior) can spread across populations: when r-types match to produce a surplus, they generate higher material payoffs than matches either between e-types or r-e matches.[62] Thus, if material payoffs determine the average long-run fitness of behavioral dispositions via relative rates of sociocultural transmission of such dispositions, this model offers a selection-based logic for expecting r-type behavior in human populations.[63] Thus the emergence of reciprocal behavior is endogenous to social context.

Furthermore, we may extend the logic of this model to the development of shared mental models, such as social norms of reciprocity (see Chapter 8), and other institutions. Groups that develop relatively cooperative norms may achieve higher material fitness than those that fail to do so because the former are more likely to resolve CAPs that typically impede development.

6.6. CONCLUSION

The concept of social preference, discussed at the beginning of this chapter, augments that of material preference. Using classical game-theoretic models with substantively rational agents, we show that social preferences can motivate agents to resolve otherwise difficult CAPs—noting that inequality aversion tends to extend such influence across somewhat larger groups than intrinsic reciprocity does. Furthermore, such modeling can illustrate how social context—such as the perceived strategies available to other players or the degree to which they even have a choice—affects interpretations of fairness or "kindness" that, in turn, influence context-specific manifestations of intrinsic reciprocity. Indeed, potential manipulation of such perceptions introduces opportunities for exercising power. Analogous impacts of social context also apply to inequality aversion or a preference for social welfare. The expression of social preference in specific contexts thus responds to (is endogenous to or depends on) the economic, social, and political processes that we seek to investigate.

At a deeper level, preference orientations (or dispositions) themselves are endogenous to the social transmission of understandings. More precisely, preference orientations—characterized in our argument by types of players, such as r-types—emerge from understandings of social categories, interpretations of context, and cause-and-effect relationships that are socially transmitted. Moreover, rates of transmission of these understandings respond to the relative success or failure that various dispositions tend to generate across experienced strategic encounters. These developments affect not only the mix of preference orientations within a population of agents, but perhaps more significantly, a general willingness to conduct exchange as well as the inclination and potential within or among various groups to resolve CAPs. A bounded rationality approach to cognition, when combined with evolutionary game-theoretic modeling, can represent relevant dynamics and outcomes.

In moderately complex situations, boundedly rational agents face a CD gap that arises from the costs and limitations of cognition. Agents adapt by mixing minimal-effort S1 intuition with high-effort S2 deliberation—in order to produce impressions and judgments that pertain to activities, relationships, other people, social context, and so forth. Over time, impressions congeal into heuristics that rule out consideration of multiple strategies—those that fail to meet a reliability criterion based on their potential for successful use, given a CD gap. At a deeper level, mental models are cognitive frameworks that combine S1 intuition, associated heuristics, and S2 reasoning to establish categories, patterns, and conceptions of cause-and-effect relationships. Like heuristics, mental models tend to emerge from context-dependent selection based upon perceived reliability in uncertain environments. Because they are costly to establish, mental models exhibit the related properties of path dependency and punctuated equilibria. The social transmission of commonly held ideas and understandings then leads to the emergence of shared mental models, such as ideologies and institutions. Institutions are commonly held understandings of rules that facilitate transmission of relevant categories, patterns, and cause-effect relationships across social groups. As shared mental models, institutions are path-dependent, punctuated social equilibria that shape common understandings of categories and cause-and-effect relationships, with some longevity.

Evolutionary game theory facilitates modeling the dynamics and outcomes of learning processes associated with adoption of strategies, heuristics, and mental models, as well as behavioral predispositions. Relatively simple EGT models can, for example, represent the emergence of property rights over territory or the benefits of team cooperation—in either case, accounting for influences of behavioral dispositions or social norms. Indirect evolutionary game theory allows for combined modeling of substantively rational CGT responses within established stable contexts, based on material and social preference, along with evolutionary development of basic predispositions, such as intrinsic reciprocity. Indirect evolutionary game theory models can thus explain the emergence of such predispositions—that is, the development of socially endogenous preferences over time. On a larger scale, both EGT and IEGT models offer insight into the evolution and longevity of norms and formal institutions.

Overall, Part II of this book has used a classical game-theoretic framework to establish the foundational concepts of first- and second-order CAPs, power, intrinsic reciprocity, and social preference. This chapter has added bounded rationality and mental models—noting relations to punctuated equilibria—along with direct and indirect evolutionary game-theoretic representations of social learning via adaptive adjustment to social contexts. All of these elements provide conceptual foundations for Part III's discussion of the potential role of informal and formal institutions in fostering complex exchange, resolving (or sometimes exacerbating) CAPs, and ultimately facilitating (or impeding) development.

EXERCISES

6.1. Graph the inequality aversion model of equation (6.1) in (u_i, π_i) space, with π_i on the horizontal axis.

6.2. Write a definition (in equation form) for the term π_D in (6.2) that fits the Charness-Rabin concept of social welfare.

6.3. Use the equations representing cognition costs, outlined on page 127, to show that any problem for which optimization requires more cognitive effort than some minimal level $(e_s(\xi) > e_{sL})$ will necessitate mixing S1 and S2 processes.

6.4. Explain why a boundedly rational player does not know the probabilities $\rho_r(v)$ or $\rho_w(v)$ in the reliability condition equation (6.5).

6.5. Diagram equations (6.6) and (6.7) with h on the horizontal axis and the associated fitness payoffs on the vertical axis. Compare this drawing to Figures 2.8 and 2.9.

6.6. Using equations (6.6), (6.7), and (6.10), show that the following statements hold:
   a. When $c < V$, the primary criterion indicates that H is an ESS and that Dv is not.
   b. When $c > V$, there is a stable polymorphic equilibrium in which the proportion of hawks is $h^* = V/C$ and the proportion of doves $d^* = (1 - h^*) = (1 - V/C)$.

6.7. Draw the Hawk / Dove / Bourgeois game discussed on page 139. Show that strategy Bourgeois is the only evolutionary stable strategy.

6.8. Show that an ESS from equation (6.10) also meets the reliability condition (6.5). *Hint:* Review Section 6.5's discussion of the Hawk / Dove / Bourgeois game.

6.9. Show that both strategies X and Y in Figure 6.4 are each an ESS.

6.10. Use equations (6.11) and (6.12) to reaffirm that X and Y are both evolutionary stable strategies. Graph these two equations in (payoff, λ) space.

6.11. Explain the terms in equation (6.14).

III INSTITUTIONS, INSTITUTIONAL SYSTEMS, AND NETWORKS

7 INSTITUTIONS, ORGANIZATIONS, AND INSTITUTIONAL SYSTEMS

> A good part of social organization—of what we call society—consists of institutional arrangements to overcome these divergences between perceived individual interest and some larger collective bargain.
>
> Thomas Schelling (1978)

Creating the foundations for complex exchange requires resolving collective-action problems. In addition to negotiating legitimate agreements for allocating contributions to collective goods, societies must orchestrate social coordination and foster credible commitments to abide by myriad informal and formal agreements. Establishing credible commitment, in turn, requires trust, expectations of enforcement, and related organizational infrastructure. Institutions provide the motivational, informational, and cognitive social foundations for establishing both social coordination and credible commitment; they also emerge as outcomes of the involved social processes. The resolution of CAPs that underlie the potential for complex exchange thus depends on the creation and operation of institutions, and the associated processes influence institutional and organizational development.

Part III of this book develops these assertions utilizing Part II's core concepts: first- and second-order CAPs, power, reciprocity, social preference, and bounded rationality. The present chapter establishes additional foundations. Section 7.1 defines institutions, organizations, and institutional systems, and discusses their critical influences on motivation, information, and cognition among multiple agents. Section 7.2 addresses response or adaptation to organizational or institutional problems via either escaping from them (exit) or attempting to change them (voice). The latter constitutes a major source of institutional development. On this foundation, Chapters 8–10 address relationships between CAPs, different levels of governance, and exchange. These chapters consider the following: the role of informal institutions, especially social norms; the potential for community self-governance; and various interactions between informal and formal institutions, along with similar interactions between second- and third-party enforcement, both of which depend on supporting organizations. Chapter 11 provides a brief sketch of social network analysis. It asserts that networks reflect and also indicate relationships between institutionally created positions, power, and the dynamics of information flows.

To frame this chapter's discussion, we present Douglass North's critique of traditional rational actor models that are based on the self-interest axiom. This account serves two purposes. First, it identifies conceptual problems with traditional models that institutional theory can address. Second, by echoing concerns over first- and second-order CAPs, it links institutional theory to core arguments of this text.

North identifies five, often implicit, assumptions of conventional economic theory that generate conceptual obstacles to understanding economic processes and development (1990, Chap. 3):

(i) Existing economic institutions provide sufficient competition for efficient exchange via arbitrage. This assumption overlooks virtually all first- and second-order CAPs, with attendant information problems.

(ii) Individual preferences concern only material outcomes for oneself, and such preferences are stable and exogenous to economic activity. This assumption over-looks social preferences and the influence of social context on the formation and expression of preference.

(iii) Economic actors possess sufficient information and cognitive capacity to under-stand the properties and future implications of the transactions they consider entering—and then perform the relevant maximizations. This assumption over-looks strategic manipulation of incomplete information as well as the costs of and limitations to human cognition.

(iv) Institutions provide sufficient information feedback so that actors may, on aver-age, correct errors; summing adjustments across individuals generates a similar correction for society.[1] In fact, combined with an implicit assumption of collective coordination, such correction processes can apply to institutional design.[2] North argues that economic history simply does not bear out these notions.

(v) Actors encounter stable environments; they "repeatedly face the same choice situations or a sequence of very similar choices" (19). This assumption ignores the inherent dynamism and non-ergodic tendencies of social and economic environ-ments. Neither physical nor social environments sit still while agents endeavor to figure them out. Many choices arise in novel circumstances.

A game-theoretic approach to institutional theory provides a framework for addressing all of these conceptual weaknesses.[3] It permits sophisticated conceptualization and mod-eling of multi-leveled economic, political, and social interactions—notably those related to ever-present CAPs and processes of development. In so doing, this approach incorpo-rates asymmetric information, social preference, and limited cognition in both static and dynamic frameworks. It thus facilitates understanding critical impacts of institutional con-texts on agents' motivation, expectations, and cognition, along with feedback influences of individual and organizational strategic behavior on the formation, development, and durability of institutions. Ultimately, a game-theoretic approach enables systematic repre-sentation of complex exchange and collective action.

Part II of this book has already established foundations for institutional theory, partially addressing these issues. Chapter 2's first-order CAPs of free-riding and Chapter 3's second-order CAPs of coordination and enforcement constitute critical and pervasive exceptions to assumption (i)'s notion of sufficient arbitrage. Chapter 4's discussion of power provides context for institutional responses to CAPs. Concerning assumption (ii), the concepts of intrinsic reciprocity and social preference, from Chapters 5 and 6, fill important gaps in motivational theory. Chapters 8–11 will extend these ideas by examining impacts of social context—especially applicable norms—on the development and expression of preferences.

Chapters 3 and 6 address the information and cognitive elements of assumption (iii). In Chapter 3, we saw that informational problems of adverse selection and moral hazard underlie second-order CAPs, particularly those related to establishing credible contracts or agreements. Chapter 6's discussion of bounded rationality, uncertainty, the competence-difficulty (CD) gap, and evolutionary game theory addressed limited cognition and adaptive learning. On this foundation, Chapters 7–10 will assert that institutions not only provide the motivational, informational, and cognitive foundations for coherent strategic decision making, they also facilitate coordination and enforcement among multiple agents.

Finally, concerning assumptions (iv) and (v), Chapter 6 indicates that evolutionary game theory—sometimes joined with classical game theory—facilitates modeling dynamic processes of strategic and cognitive adaptation, including individual and social learning. Such adaptation underlies individual or group responses to inadequate or partial information feedback in continually changing environments. In Part III, we consider institutional evolution as an adaptive property of communities that both contributes to and resolves multiple CAPs and, ultimately, permits complex exchange to occur. We now discuss the concept of institutions in more detail.

7.1. CONCEPTS OF INSTITUTIONS, ORGANIZATIONS, AND INSTITUTIONAL SYSTEMS

Institutions are social mechanisms that facilitate development by resolving many (but not all) CAPs. The concept of institutions, however, is complicated and multi-faceted. We thus draw upon related discussions of institutions that appear in North (1990, 2005), Knight (1992), Denzau and North (1994), Bowles (2004), Ostrom (2005), and Greif (2006a). For North: "Institutions are the rules of the game in a society or, more formally, are the humanly devised constraints that shape human interaction" (1990, 1). For Bowles, they are "the laws, informal rules, and conventions that give a durable structure to social interactions among the members of a population" (2004, 47–48). He adds: "a combination of centrally deployed coercion (laws), social sanction (informal rules), and mutual expectations (conventions) . . . make conformity a best response for virtually all members of the relevant group" (2004, 48). Thus established institutions indicate equilibria in large social games.

According to Ostrom (2005), institutional rules "determine who is eligible to make decisions in some arena, what actions are allowed or constrained, what aggregation rules will be used, what procedures must be followed, what information must or must not be provided, and what payoffs will be assigned to individuals dependent on their actions." Knight (1992, 2–3) contends that, "for a set of rules to be an institution, knowledge of these rules must be shared by the members of the relevant community or society."[4] Denzau and North's (1994) assertion that institutions are shared mental models (see Section 6.3) points to a cognitive role. As shared mental models, institutions embody common understandings of social (and other) categories, patterns, and cause-and-effect relationships.[5] Institutions thus shape the perceptions and understandings of multiple individuals. Finally, Greif (2006a) incorporates all of these elements, stressing the importance of shared beliefs and normative elements as factors that motivate adherence to institutional rules. Like Bowles, he interprets institutions as self-enforcing social equilibria in the sense that beliefs and actions support each other. Unlike the other cited authors, however, Greif includes organizations: "An institution is a system of rules, beliefs, norms, and organizations that together generate a regularity of (social) behavior" (30).[6]

We modify Greif's inclusive approach by distinguishing between institutions (rules, etc.) and institutional systems. Only the latter includes organizations (a type of player). Institutions prescribe or indicate behavioral regularities associated with social equilibria. By also incorporating organizations as actors that operate within institutional contexts, institutional systems actually generate such regularities. We now proceed by defining institutions, discussing specific elements of this definition, and then distinguishing basic categories of institutions. We then define an institutional system, and elaborate on the definition of organizations, how they differ from institutions, and the roles of organizations within institutional systems. The remainder of this section returns to the more foundational concept of institutions, beginning with a discussion of what they do—with implications on exchange and CAPs—followed by additional implications for socially desirable outcomes and institutional longevity. All subsequent chapters build on these foundations.

An *institution* is a combination of mutually understood and self-enforcing beliefs, conventions, social norms, social rules, or formal rules that jointly indicate or prescribe behavioral regularities in specific or varied social contexts. We may interpret this definition as a precise specification of "the rules of the game in society." Institutions establish the core motivational, informational, and cognitive structure upon which agents condition their strategic decisions.[7] Turning to elements of this definition, the term *self-enforcing* indicates that institutions specify social equilibria: institutionally prescribed behaviors and beliefs jointly support and sustain each other—as strategic choices and expectations do in Nash equilibria.[8] The term *social* means created by humans and beyond the control of a single actor. Institutions are human artifacts (V. Ostrom 1980), though clearly subject to many unintended consequences. *Beliefs* have two components: (i) expectations concerning the behavior of others, as in classical game-theoretic expectations;[9] and (ii) mental models—cognitive frameworks that indicate categories, patterns, and cause-and-effect relationships. Greif asserts: "Together these components motivate, enable, and guide individuals to follow one behavior among the many that are technologically feasible in social situations" (2006a, 30).

Several additional distinctions inform our understanding of institutions. The key difference between formal and informal institutions depends on the processes that generate prescriptions or rules. Rules that accompany *formal institutions* arise from specified collective decision-making processes. Such rules are typically, though not always, written. Examples include constitutions, virtually all legislation, and formally decided corporate rules, such as personnel policies. By contrast, *informal institutions* constitute conventions, norms, or social rules that emerge either more or less spontaneously from repeated social interactions

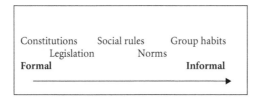

Figure 7.1   Formal and informal institutions

(in cases of conventions or norms) or from somewhat informal decision procedures (in the case of social rules). *Social norms* are expected behavioral prescriptions with ethical content and unspecified but generally understood social enforcement. Examples include norms against cutting in line or shouting during solemn moments. *Social rules* are expected behavioral prescriptions with informally designated enforcers that arise from group self-organization. Examples of social rules include farmer-designed regulations on use of common irrigation facilities in rural communities in Nepal (Lam 1998).

We may consider the formal-informal distinction as either a dichotomy or a spectrum. Figure 7.1 shows a spectrum with national constitutions at the most formal end and small-group habits at the other. Chapters 8 and 9 address informal institutions, including social rules; Chapter 10 considers formal institutions and their interactions with informal institutions.

Institutional Systems and Organizations

The encompassing concept of an institutional system adds organizations to our concept of institutions; these systems generate (rather than prescribe) social equilibria. More precisely, an *institutional system* is a combination of mutually understood and self-enforcing beliefs, conventions, social norms, social rules, and formal rules that incorporates organizations in order to generate behavioral regularities in specific or varied social contexts. *Organizations* are somewhat fluid coalitions of boundedly rational individuals with differing interests who more or less jointly pursue sets of negotiated goals and use evolving decision rules to understand and coordinate key operations (Cyert and March 1963). As coalitions, organizations operate as actors (agents) within institutional contexts. The combination of mutually understood institutional prescriptions and organizational actors generates social equilibria. For example, a social equilibrium outcome with little or no shoplifting depends on the existence of police departments and courts, along with laws and social norms.

We elaborate on the often misunderstood distinction between institutions and organizations. As "rules of the game," institutions provide contexts within which both individuals and organizations operate as agents. Institutions establish who makes certain kinds of choices (who plays), available strategies, timing, relationships between strategies and outcomes (outcome functions), available information, and common beliefs—specifically, mutual expectations and shared mental models.[10] Organizations (as agents) choose, develop, or inherit strategies, but they do so within institutional contexts and constraints. Whereas institutions are outcomes of complex historical processes, organizations participate in such processes. In so doing, organizations create, alter, and destroy institutions, sometimes un-intentionally.

The institution-organization distinction offers different perspectives on the same en-tity. Consider General Motors Corporation (GM). As an organization, GM produces and sells automobiles, contributes to political campaigns, and lobbies Congress. As an institu-tion, we take GM as a set of understood rules and procedures that prescribe when certain types of people can be hired or fired, levels of pay for various tasks, promotion procedures, how to price automobiles, when or how to advertise, and so forth. From either perspec-tive, GM embodies outcomes of intricate historical processes. It emerged from complex interactions among myriad agents—founding entrepreneurs, stockholders, managers, union negotiators, production workers, secretaries, and many others. Whether one re-gards GM as an institution or as an organization, depends on the focus of analysis. A standard economic approach to the oligopoly market for automobiles, for example, would treat GM as one of several organizations (firms) that set prices or quantities strategically in order to maximize profits. On the other hand, an investigation into potential career paths for new employees might consider institutional attributes, such as GM's rules concerning promotion and pensions.

With this distinction in mind, we elaborate on the role of organizations in institutional systems. Organizations participate in generating specific social outcomes and equilibria. Following Greif (2006a, Chap. 2), we delineate three specific roles of organizations as they interact with institutions. Organizations:

(i)   Provide arenas within which various combinations of agents create, alter, and disseminate rules. For example, GM uses committees to develop its personnel policies.

(ii) Reinforce or perpetuate certain existing beliefs and norms. GM's operations up-hold beliefs of employees and citizens concerning things like appropriate behavior at work and the role of corporations in the economy.

(iii) Affect agents' beliefs concerning relationships between feasible actions and con-sequences—often pertaining to mechanisms of enforcement. For example, the existence of a police department influences expectations concerning the conse-quences of shoplifting.[11]

In combining these roles, organizations—as entities with more or less defined interests and generally coherent strategies—participate in creating, modifying, and undermining both institutions and institutional systems. We now address the more complicated topic of the role of institutions in social interactions.

What Institutions Do

Institutions create predictability in social interactions by signaling mutually understood be-havioral patterns (Heiner 1983; North 2005). Institutions both limit and—more subtly and fundamentally—define the choice sets of agents. Extending this logic, Greif states that in-stitutions "provide individuals with cognitive, coordinative, normative, and informational microfoundations of behavior as they enable, guide, and motivate them to follow specific behavior" (2006a, 14).

To address these complexities, we list three domains of institutional influence on social interaction. Broadly speaking, institutions affect motivation, provide information, and shape both beliefs and cognition. Within each of these three domains, institutions provide two specific kinds of influence:

1. Institutions motivate adherence to their indicated behavioral prescriptions in two basic manners:
   a. They influence motivation directly by affecting outcomes of strategic interactions, most notably by establishing material and social incentives along with constraints—a direct contribution of norms and rules to social coordination.
   b. Less directly, but more fundamentally, institutions shape (endogenous) preferences by indicating social and normative prescriptions, with accompanying informational and cognitive guidance.

2. Institutions affect available information in two basic manners:
   a. They provide contextual information—most importantly, common understandings of coordination and enforcement patterns—and thereby render the behavior of other agents far more predictable than it would otherwise be.
   b. They generate and channel *informational feedback*: observable elements of outcomes or signals that inform agents' hypothesis testing of relationships between actions and outcomes, within the conceptual frameworks of given mental models.

3. Institutions shape agents' beliefs and overall cognitive frameworks in two basic manners:
   a. Behavioral prescriptions influence agents' expectations in various strategic contexts.
   b. More fundamentally, as shared mental models, institutions structure agents' understandings of social categories, contexts, and causal relationships.

All three domains of influence (hereafter, influences) guide strategic decision making among multiple agents in complex social contexts with multiple participants and available strategies.

We elaborate by relating each of these basic institutional influences to ideas in this text, starting with the most straightforward. Conceptually, influence 1a involves traditional economic logic with the caveat that incentives can be social as well as material. For example, a tax on gasoline creates a material incentive to reduce consumption; a bike-to-work week may establish a social incentive. Many analytical statements consider incentives while taking other institutional impacts for granted. For short-run analysis within stable institutional contexts, this approach can be extremely useful.[12] Moving further, game-theoretic logic may represent influences 2a and 3a. For substantively rational agents who encounter manageable asymmetric or imperfect information, institutional rules specify what agents do and do not know and how expectations are formed. For example, Chapter 3's effort model indicates how the rules associated with contingent renewal can motivate worker effort in contexts where employers cannot fully observe their actions. Influences 1a, 2a, and 3a operate simultaneously.[13]

The combined impact of influences 1a, 2a, and 3a guides and facilitates decision making among either substantively or boundedly rational agents by rendering the behavior of others sufficiently predictable. More precisely, institutions point out prescribed equilibria from many possibilities; they establish focal points by effectively ruling out multiple defection options.[14] For example, in the United States it is illegal for managers to hit uncooperative employees (1a). This rule effectively removes various strategies from employers' choice sets. By channeling behavior, such rules enhance the predictability of others' behavior (2a). Potential employees can reasonably expect (3a) that employers will not hit them, allowing them to make employment decisions. Consider employment decisions without this expectation. Commonly understood institutional rules thus offer context for making strategic decisions. With this in mind, we consider the more foundational influences 1b, 2b, and 3b, starting with 2b (informational feedback).

Institutions facilitate both individual and social learning by specifying channels and procedures for information feedback (e.g., who receives reports). Agents use such feedback to test hypotheses about causal relationships related to their activity. For example, entrepreneurs use reports on revenue and profits to judge the success of prior investment strategies. Similarly, politicians may adjust stated positions to reflect feedback from opinion polls. In a classical game-theoretic framework, we may represent such processes as Bayesian adjustment of conditional probabilities. Evolutionary game-theoretic modeling can represent associated social learning processes of boundedly rational agents, where fitness payoffs could reflect information feedback.

More fundamentally, influences 1b (shaping preferences) and 3b (shaping mental models) jointly indicate how institutions can provide motivational and cognitive foundations for decision making. Indeed, without understanding these two core institutional roles, we cannot fully analyze economic, political, or social choice. Institutions establish the microfoundations of behavioral responses (Greif 2006a). Here 1b indicates how we may conceptualize endogenous preference formation. Individual preference orderings respond to social contexts and shared understandings provided by institutions, with social norms playing a key role.[15] For example, a person who adheres to a norm that treats littering as unethical will likely prefer not to litter, regardless of possible sanctions (i.e., independent of direct incentives). More dramatically, one may be willing to die for a just cause.

Influence 3b explicitly links institutions to Chapter 6's discussion of boundedly rational strategic decision making. As shared mental models, institutions frame boundedly rational agents' interpretations of activity and environment. For example, in order to establish businesses, entrepreneurs need to predict with reasonable confidence that suppliers will honor contracts. An institutional context that indicates shared understandings of general contract enforcement (cause-effect relationships) thus facilitates entrepreneurial decisions. More generally, such shared mental models permit exchange to extend beyond boundaries of personal and reciprocal contact to more impersonal and complex transactions.[16] Furthermore, influences 3b and 1b interact: shared models affect preferences and vice versa.

A shared understanding that few will attempt cheating can influence preferences so that most people would not even desire to do so. Conversely, one's normative preferences may influence how one categorizes others or how one expects them to behave. One might, for example, consider someone who cheats on a contract to be unethical.

Combining these influences, we see that by effectively eliminating many defection strategies, institutions create the motivational, informational, and cognitive focus that makes choice possible. Institutions thus define and shape understandings of the relevant choice sets (North 1990). They create informational, cognitive, coordinative, and normative guidance that frames and motivates individual decision making, and so facilitate associated behavioral responses in pertinent social contexts (Greif 2006a). To understand economic, political, and social choice, therefore, we must consider such institutionally conditioned framing and motivation. Game-theoretic modeling offers a methodological foundation for such inquiry.

Finally, returning to the core thesis of this book, these three institutional influences facilitate coordination and enforcement among multiple individuals (who have different interests) as they encounter uncertain, non-ergodic environments. Institutions thus offer context in which agents can resolve multiple second-order CAPs. They render possible the development of legitimate and credible cooperative or exchange agreements, such as contracts—in turn, potentially resolving first-order CAPs. Such institutional resolution of fundamental CAPs is a pre-condition for economic, political, and social development in complex societies.

Collective Action, Power, and Optimality

It is important to stress that, despite their essential role in fostering complex exchange and other manifestations of development, institutions, institutional systems, and the behaviors they generate need not resolve CAPs optimally or even well. Likewise, they need not generate or reflect socially optimal or necessarily good outcomes.[17] Previous chapters have pointed to considerable motivational, informational, and cognitive barriers to creating and implementing social mechanisms of coordination and enforcement. Accordingly, institutional creation and development presents societies with multiple first- and second-order CAPs.

Four specific impediments to generating beneficial outcomes merit discussion. First, processes of institutional creation and reform are shaped by the mental models of cognitively limited agents—models that developed under the influence of extant institutions. Second, these processes operate with incomplete, asymmetric underlying information and similarly incomplete information feedback that is shaped by existing institutions. Such feedback, moreover, need not foster sufficient convergence of individual perceptions for relevant agents to jointly envision, create, or reform institutions in optimal or even good fashions (North 1990). Indeed, divergent perceptions typically compound CAPs. Third, the quest of self-interested agents for strategic and distributional advantage shapes institutional construction, modification, and demise.[18] As Chapter 4 indicated, enforcement involves exercises of power, and social positions are sources of power. Because institutions establish such positions, indicating various forms of hierarchy, institutions enable and condition

exercises of power (Greif 2006a). Self-interested agents in relevant positions can thus manipulate existing institutional rules for their own benefit. Anticipating future benefits, they
may also manipulate processes of institutional creation and reform, or use their power to
oppose reforming or dismantling institutional arrangements from which they benefit. For
example, in 2011, several state legislatures charged with redrawing Congressional districts
redrew them so as to benefit the party in power (Helderman and Kumar 2011).

Fourth, social and environmental processes are non-ergodic: the world changes in ways
that need not mimic stable and knowable probability distributions. Thus existing institutions, which may have supported exchange or addressed CAPs successfully when they
were created, may not function well in contemporary environments. Furthermore, by
creating fundamental uncertainty, non-ergodic change exacerbates information problems
and imposes limits on conceptual capacities; non-ergodic change increases the CD gap of
boundedly rational agents. Again, strategically placed individuals may exercise power—in
this case, to resist institutional adjustments to environmental change. As an example, the
regime in North Korea has survived for several generations. In sum, there is little reason
to expect socially optimal outcomes from institutional construction. Even so, institutions
foster exchange, resolve CAPs, and often survive for long periods. We now turn to the question of their ability to reproduce their prescribed behaviors and associated beliefs over time.

Dynamic Considerations: Institutional Sustainability or Demise

Recall that institutions indicate self-enforcing equilibria. When agents act according to institutional prescriptions—for example, by not stealing because they either find it unethical
or fear sanction—they reinforce shared beliefs regarding the viability of such prescriptions.
Institutions that persist are self-reproducing in this fashion (Greif 2006a). But an institution's ability to self-reproduce may increase or decrease over time. The possible strength-
ening or weakening of beliefs and behavioral patterns as time passes introduces dynamic
considerations of institutional stability.

We define a *self-reinforcing* institution or institutional system as one that can sustain its
self-enforcing equilibrium properties under increasingly larger sets of circumstances—in
other words, more possible states of a world subject to non-ergodic change (Greif 2006a;
Young 1996). For example, when first established, a company might go bankrupt during a
minor recession. If, after several years, however, its ability to withstand a similar recession
increases, we say that, as an institution, the company is self-reinforcing. A self-reinforcing
institution thus generates an increasingly durable path-dependent equilibrium via *negative-
feedback processes*: processes in which movement in one direction engenders response in the
opposite direction.[19] Thus, within limits, disruptions actually tend to enhance durability.
In contrast, a *self-undermining* institution can maintain its social equilibrium only in successively narrower sets of circumstances: it becomes increasingly vulnerable to internal or
external changes that could upset its balance of beliefs and behaviors. A company with significant internal conflict, for example, may become more susceptible to bankruptcy during
a cyclical downturn or disruption in its revenues.

To model these concepts, we introduce the idea of a quasi-parameter. In classical game
theory, a *parameter* is an externally determined and relatively constant term or condition

that influences game interactions in a predictable fashion. For example, we may regard a medium-term rate of economic growth as a parameter that conditions economic transactions in specific contractual relationships. Expecting a growth rate of, say, 3%, a company may decide to invest in new equipment. Similarly, elements of the US Constitution are parameters that condition political transactions within Congress. The First Amendment, for example, states that "Congress shall make no law respecting an establishment of religion or prohibiting the free exercise thereof; . . ." As a consequence, Congress has, for the most part, refrained from either supporting or prohibiting religion in the United States. By contrast, a *quasi-parameter* behaves like a parameter in the short run but, over longer time horizons, responds to one or more outcome variables—altering its (parametric) influence on game interactions.

An *institutional quasi-parameter* exerts a stable influence on relevant transactions within a given institutional setting (institution or system) in the short run. Yet as time passes, certain transactions alter its value in a manner that affects patterns of behavior or belief within relevant institutional systems in latter periods. Hence quasi-parameters act as exogenous environmental conditions for specific short-run interactions. Over time, however, they respond to institutional outcomes and longer-term feedbacks in a manner that alters institutional processes (Greif 2006a). In fact, tipping points in adjustments of quasi-parameters may induce the unraveling of institutional punctuated equilibria.

Accumulated changes in quasi-parameters can undermine institutions in two fashions. First, these changes may undercut internal patterns of behavior that support self-enforced institutional equilibria. For example, the British Atlantic trade that operated under the protection of the English monarchy between the fifteenth and seventeenth centuries gradually increased the wealth of the merchant class—a quasi-parameter. This slow augmentation had no large effects on the monarchy before the English Civil War, beginning in 1642. By that time, however, the merchants had amassed sufficient resources to fund an army to fight the king (Brenner 1993). The monarchy had not anticipated this spillover effect of its trade promotion policy. When Parliament, with merchant support, raised an army that attacked the king, beliefs in the strength of the monarchy rapidly eroded. Second, long-term alterations in institutional quasi-parameters can render an institution more vulnerable to changes in external conditions (shocks). Such internal and external impacts may interact. Decay within the Roman Empire increased its vulnerability to external attacks from the Visigoths.

Over time, institutions and institutional systems possess the properties of path dependence, with associated punctuated equilibria. Recall that the difficulties of reevaluative learning and the accumulated impact of prior judgments confer properties of path-dependent punctuated equilibria on individual mental models. Institutions are shared mental models. Hence the difficulties of coordinating mutual change in belief and behavior—along with resistance to change from current beneficiaries, some of whom may occupy positions of power—typically generate far more enduring punctuated equilibria for institutions.

Furthermore, the path-dependent influence of institutions can extend beyond their own point of survival (Greif 2006a). An institution that has recently ceased to be a self-enforcing equilibrium can still exert three basic influences on how agents design new institutions:

(i) Environmental (or parametric) effects: new rules of the game are created while the old rules are still at least partially operating.

(ii) Coordination effects: instituting new, mutually understood rules and beliefs requires considerable coordination. Because altering social arrangements is difficult, mechanisms established by prior institutions may persist beyond the longevity of associated institutions, especially in the case of formal institutions.[20]

(iii) Internalization effects: because internalization of social norms shapes identities of agents (see Chapter 8), the influence of norms may extend well beyond the lifetime of formal rules and enforcement mechanisms of prior institutions.

The American Revolution illustrates these forward impacts of prior institutional arrangements. After successfully abolishing British rule, the former colonies founded their new legal system on British common law. Moreover, the Founders based their understandings of legal institutions largely on British models and internalized British norms and precedents.

Overall, self-reinforcing institutions tend to accumulate path dependence, indicating increasingly durable equilibria. By contrast, self-undermining institutions exhibit successively weaker equilibria. Even so, they may still influence the path of future institutional development. Path-dependent institutional systems in a non-ergodic world need not coincide with, or generate, socially optimal procedures or outcomes; yet without path-dependent institutions, CAPs would remain unresolved and complex development would not occur. Whether functional or not, the creation, operation, maintenance, and replacement of institutional systems requires exercises of influence, leading to our next topic.

7.2. METHODS OF INFLUENCE AND REDRESS: EXIT, VOICE, AND LOYALTY

Broadly speaking, individuals or coherent groups who confront problems related to the design, functioning, or maintenance of elements of institutional systems—or the myriad exchanges that operate within them—may either try to escape such problems or endeavor to address them. Albert Hirschman's (1970) concepts of exit, voice, and loyalty inform our subsequent discussion of responses to CAPs, institutional systems, levels of governance, and exchange. In this regard, salient deterioration in the functioning or quality of a system, organization, institution, specific relationship, or exchange can induce two types of response: exit and voice. Loyalty affects their relative use. More generally, either instrument (especially voice) may accompany efforts to improve or reform a given social, economic, or political structure, situation or relationship. Agents may use either exit or voice as they strive to avoid, ameliorate, or resolve CAPs; conversely, excessive use of either may create CAPs.

Exit is precisely what it sounds like: a decision to leave an economic, political, or social relationship. Exit is the prototypical mechanism of economics, though it may also affect political and social relations. In the economic sphere, consumers may stop buying products, firms may terminate contracts with suppliers or employees, workers may quit, or banks may refuse to refinance loans. In politics or social life, one may quit an organization or leave a group of friends. Exit involves a clear yes-no decision: one either exits a relationship, or one does not. Exit is typically impersonal; it avoids or minimizes face-to-face contact and is often completely anonymous. When customers switch products, they rarely inform management, and management rarely knows their identity. Exit tends to affect organizations indirectly via indicators such as declines in revenue, profits, or membership. Concern over downward trends in such statistics can motivate improvement. In the economic sphere, agents exit in response to changing prices or quality. As suggested by the free-entry/exit assumption, exit is a core mechanism of market competition.[21] Costly exit, on the other hand, indicates potential for exercising power, as illustrated by the cost of job loss in the effort model (see Section 3.3).[22] Moreover, a credible threat of exit sometimes signals bargaining power—a source of voice. A valued employee may attain a raise by mentioning an alternative job offer.

Hirschman defines *voice* as "any attempt at all to change, rather than to escape from, an objectionable state of affairs" (1970, 30). Voice is the archetypical mechanism of politics; it emerges within myriad efforts to reform institutions or alter organizational behavior. Voice is rarely anonymous and can be quite personal. It has many gradations, ranging from mild complaints to revolution. Expressions of voice may operate either horizontally (among colleagues) or vertically (up or down levels of organizational or social hierarchy). Within workgroups, for example, effort norms may reflect an outcome of horizontal collective voice within workgroups. Vertical exercises of voice tend to reflect actual or attempted exercises of power. Supervising employees, for example, constitutes a downward vertical exercise of voice by management. Examples of upward vertical voice include workgroup or union pressure on management as well as voting and citizen protest.

Agents may regard exit and voice as alternatives.[23] An individual or group decision on which of these strategies to employ depends on the relative costs and benefits. Costs of exit reflect the availability and quality of substitutes for the relevant product, relationship, or organization, in addition to the transaction costs of shifting to an alternative. For example, if a senator wants to change political parties, she might consider whether the other party will accept her and meet her political or ideological criteria. For voice, costs and benefits depend on both the prospects for success and its relative value. Prospects for successful voice, in turn, depend on the nature of the relevant problem and on agents' ability to mobilize bargaining power. As in Chapter 4, power arises from economic, political, social, or physical positions, access to resources, and an ability to resolve CAPs of assembling workable coalitions. If the relevant parties appear to have enough power to generate reasonable prospects for sufficiently valuable success—relative to the net benefits of exit or tolerating the status quo—then voice becomes desirable.[24]

Loyalty affects interactions between exit and voice. *Loyalty* signifies a propensity to delay exit beyond a point where nonloyal members or customers would do so. Loyalty is not equivalent to obeying orders; in fact, it may occasionally involve violating them. Instead, loyalty reflects a positive sentiment for or attachment to the relevant organization, relationship, or product. It is a form of social preference that frequently accompanies reciprocity. An employee may hesitate to quit an undesirable job because her employer has treated her well. Furthermore, loyalty may arise from norms of reciprocity, norms that discourage leaving commitments, or even from a tendency to identify oneself with a relevant organization—perhaps by internalizing its norms. By contrast, nonloyal customers or members lack such identity, norm internalization, or sense of reciprocity toward relevant organizations or relationships. Within organizations or communities, loyalty can be a form of local social capital.

Loyalty thus affects utility tradeoffs between exit and voice. Not only are loyal customers or members less likely to exit than others, they are also more inclined to exercise voice. Figure 7.2, reprinted from Hirschman (1970), illustrates relationships between levels of disagreement and the ensuing amount of voice, accounting for the influence of loyalty. The right-hand end of the diagram shows full agreement and, consequently, no voice. Moving leftward and focusing on the "normal loyalist behavior" function, unconscious loyalist behavior begins to emerge at point ULB and lasts until the beginning of the upward-sloping (straight) line.[25] Over this distance, loyalists experience cognitive dissonance regarding disagreement: even though their goals differ slightly from practices of the relevant organization, they are not conscious of the discrepancy. This level of disagreement is not salient. With greater disagreement, however, loyalists begin to exercise voice; hence the upward slope. Point XAL (exit without loyalty) indicates a threshold level of disagreement at which nonloyal members (or customers) would exit: having analyzed the relative costs and benefits of voice versus exit, they quit. Loyalty thus starts exerting its unique influence on voice after this point. Hence the steepness of the line increases: loyalists start exercising more voice per unit of disagreement. At point TX (threat of exit), the loyalist informs management that—unless something is done—she will leave. Assuming that management values

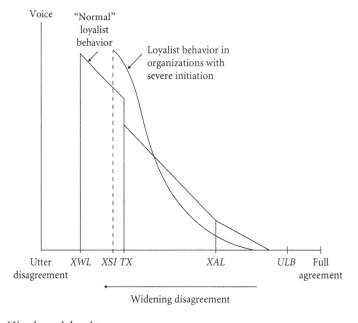

Figure 7.2   Hirschman's loyalty

SOURCE: Reprinted by permission of the publisher from EXIT, VOICE, AND LOYALTY: RESPONSES TO DECLINE IN FIRMS, ORGANIZATIONS, and STATES by Albert O. Hirschman, p. 87, Cambridge, Mass.: Harvard University Press, Copyright © 1970 by the President and Fellows of Harvard College.

her, the volume of voice increases abruptly at this point, as indicated by the upward shift of the function. Moving farther to the left, disagreement and volume of voice again steadily increase until disagreement is so extreme that the loyalist quits, at point XWL (exit with loyalty). Thus, by delaying exit, loyalty facilitates voice. Loyal members are often the most useful to organizations, but if things go wrong, they can also be the most troublesome.[26]

So far we have analyzed exit, voice, and loyalty from the point of view of substantively rational agents. For Hirschman, however, exercising voice is an art, a set of techniques that individuals and groups improvise and usually improve with practice. Boundedly rational agents learn to apply voice by trial and error. We may then use Heiner's reliability condition (equation (6.5)) to indicate when certain methods of exercising voice merit consideration. Agents tend to contemplate forms of voice that fit their prior experience.[27] Individual and organizational heuristics therefore include certain forms of voice and exclude others. Social norms may favor specific types of voice and discourage others; formal institutions may do the same. Consequently, individual and especially organizational use of voice tends to be path dependent and potentially self-reinforcing. Indeed, among various groups, organizations, and communities, an ability to exercise forms of voice becomes a form of social capital that facilitates the crafting and emergence of adaptive institutional systems.

In subsequent chapters, the concepts of exit, voice, and loyalty will inform our discussion of relationships between internal self-governance and external governance along with related interactions between second- and third-party enforcement. Efforts to engineer coordination and enforcement—often important elements of organizational dynamics—constitute exercises of voice that can translate institutional prescriptions into actual effects on outcomes. All such interactions operate within institutional systems that are based upon formal and informal institutions, along with attendant organizations.

7.3. CONCLUSION

Institutions—as mutually understood and self-enforcing combinations of beliefs, conventions, social norms, social rules, and formal rules that designate context-specific behavioral prescriptions—shape the motivational, informational, and cognitive foundations of individual decision making. Institutions motivate specific behaviors by credibly signaling incentives and by influencing preferences via normative and cognitive guidance. Institutions reduce uncertainty by facilitating flows of information and by rendering the behavior of others relatively predictable. They influence beliefs because predictability affects expectations. More fundamentally, as shared mental models, institutions affect understandings of social classifications and causal relationships. Institutions thus render strategic decision making possible in complex, non-ergodic social environments.

Organizations are coalitions of individuals who share goals based upon mutually held understandings, values, and/or material interests—though often with less-than-perfect alignment. They act as agents that operate within contexts of institutional rules. Yet, like individuals, organizations participate in the collective construction, alteration, and destruction of institutions. Jointly, organizations and institutions constitute institutional systems. Organizations provide arenas in which individuals interact, and their operation reinforces norms and beliefs. As vehicles for enforcement, organizations influence individual beliefs concerning the consequences of specific actions, such as defecting. As the dual components of institutional systems, organizations and institutions together generate the social coherence that makes complex economic, political, and social exchange possible. To borrow a phrase from Jon Elster (1989a), institutions and organizations are the "cement of society."

Yet institutional and organizational outcomes often fail to achieve social optimality (or generally desirable outcomes) indicating CAPs. Agents may then endeavor to escape, alter, or sometimes destroy various apparently responsible organizations or institutions. Significant exit may induce organizational reform via its impacts on revenue or membership. Horizontal and/or vertical exercises of voice constitute not only attempts to affect the operations of organizations but also attempts to alter, create, or abolish various institutions, especially formal institutions and their attendant prescriptions (e.g., legislation). Loyalty can enhance the incidence and effectiveness of voice. Overall, the deliberate creation and reform of institutions, with specific goals in mind, reflects efforts to design or craft social mechanisms for resolving collective-action problems—also known as policymaking.

Before addressing policy (in Chapter 12), we first (in Chapters 8–10) examine multiple relationships between informal institutions, second-party enforcement, self-governance, formal institutions, third-party enforcement, and external governance.

EXERCISES

7.1. Summarize the distinctions between an institution, an organization, and an institutional system.

7.2. Discuss the three core domains of institutional influence and relate them to resolution of CAPs.

7.3. Describe how influences 1a, 2a, and 3a (in Section 7.1) operate in the effort model of Section 3.3.

7.4. Explain the difference between a self-enforcing behavioral equilibrium—as prescribed by an institution—and a self-reinforcing institution.

7.5. Relate the concept of a punctuated equilibrium to the concepts of a quasi-parameter and a self-reinforcing institution.

7.6. Develop an equation that represents a decision to engage in voice (instead of exiting) as a function of pertinent variables.

7.7. Create several two- or multi-player games that illustrate exit-voice tradeoffs.

7.8. Relate the potential for successful exercise of voice to Heiner's reliability condition (equation (6.5)).

7.9. Give an example of a CAP associated with exercising voice. Draw a game theory model based on utility payoffs to nonloyal players. Now consider the same game with loyal players.

7.10. Discuss how exit, voice, and loyalty relate to institutional formation, institutional reform, power, and path dependence.

8 INFORMAL INSTITUTIONS

> On a wider scale, the history of civilization can be organized around a theme of groping for social-rule mechanisms.
>
> Ronald Heiner (1983)

Now suppose that the farmers of Arruba had established a norm of limiting their water use. Believing that neighbors will both limit their use and expect the same from others, individual farmers also limit. In fact, a failure to limit might invoke a social penalty, such as scorn from others, or perhaps internal feelings of guilt. As long as the cost of limiting is less than the utility loss from violating the norm, farmers will limit their use. The second-order CAP of enforcing an internal limitation agreement is, barring complications, resolved. Moreover, if Boratonia follows the same norm, the two communities may readily negotiate a mutual limitation agreement at a low transaction cost. Even if Boratonia's norm prescribes a different limit, negotiation may still permit resolution, as long as at least one side is not too insistent. On the other hand, if Boratonia has no such norm, farmers in Arruba may feel cheated by the other community and so may use extensively without guilt. Worse yet, Boratonia could have a custom that allows free use regardless of community impacts. Differing community norms might then complicate bargaining and enforcement prospects.

Recall that agreements to resolve Chapter 2's first-order CAPs of free-riding are not credible unless Chapter 3's second-order CAPs of coordination and enforcement have also been resolved. Although Chapter 3 discussed several internal enforcement mechanisms, such as contingent renewal, it did not address more comprehensive approaches that augment material incentives with social incentives. Chapter 4 then asserted that enforcement involves exercises of power and that social, political, and economic positions are sources of power. That chapter, however, did not explain how such positions confer power. Next, Chapter 5 argued that, by establishing credible motivation for sanctioning, intrinsic reciprocity facilitates resolution of enforcement CAPs among small, frequently interacting groups. That chapter, however, left unanswered the question of how context influences reciprocal motivation. Chapter 6 asserted that social preferences, such as reciprocity and inequality aversion, respond to social context. It also established that boundedly rational agents use mental models to navigate uncertain, complex social environments, noting that institutions are shared mental models. It did not, however, address the major types of institutions or how specific types operate. Chapter 7 began to address these questions by distinguishing among the basic concepts of institutions, organizations, and institutional systems.

Chapter 8 continues to address all of these questions. Building on Chapter 7, it asserts that informal institutions produce complex signals: bundles of institutional statements or prescriptions. Such prescriptions can coordinate, or choreograph, beliefs and behavior of multiple agents in specific social contexts, often facilitating trust among them. Informal institutions contribute decisively to resolving otherwise intractable second-order coordination and enforcement CAPs, and so facilitate resolution of first-order CAPs. On the other hand, informal institutions—especially norms—also generate rigidities, impediments, and conflict.

Our discussion proceeds as follows. Section 8.1 develops a typology of institutions based upon the content or syntax of institutional prescriptions. It proceeds to identify core attributes of the principal informal institutions—conventions, social norms, and social rules—with some variants. Section 8.2 develops underlying concepts of correlated equilibria and social choreography, using ideas from *epistemic game theory*: an approach to game theory that models agents' cognitive frameworks as foundations for their strategic decisions. On this basis, Section 8.3 discusses how conventions and social norms can respectively foster resolution of second-order CAPs. Section 8.4 then discusses a specific type of norm that limits consideration of alternatives—a rationality-limiting norm. It proceeds to develop an evolutionary approach to the emergence of such norms and their potential influences on CAPs. Section 8.5 argues that social norms establish conceptual and motivational foundations of identity, another important avenue for social choreography. Section 8.6 concludes.

8.1. INFORMAL INSTITUTIONS AND INSTITUTIONAL TYPOLOGY

Recall that informal institutions are expected, mutually understood, and context-dependent behavioral prescriptions that emerge from repeated social interactions, rather than from formally designated deliberation. These prescriptions, in turn, apply to specific types of people or groups and respond to pertinent social and economic contexts. In relevant circumstances, agents tend to follow an indicated prescription for three main reasons: (i) because they benefit from doing so when others do the same; (ii) because they could face social sanctions for violating a prescription; and/or (iii) because they value the prescription itself. Informal institutions can then foster the coordination and enforcement needed for resolving multiple second-order CAPs.

We now distinguish among types of informal institutions. There is some debate concerning whether categorization of informal institutions—specifically, distinguishing between conventions and social norms—is a worthwhile exercise. Acknowledging a problem analogous to that of partitioning a spectrum, we nonetheless distinguish among conventions, norms, and social rules in order to delineate characteristics and influences of informal institutions that pertain to their impact on CAPs. Generally speaking, conventions tend to resolve second-order CAPs of pure coordination, whereas social norms and social rules also address problems of enforcement. As background, we briefly discuss relevant literature.

Mary Burke and Peyton Young (2009) assert that distinctions between conventions and social norms are too imprecise to be worth making. Instead, they define norms inclusively as "a standard, customary, or ideal form of behavior to which individuals in a social group try to conform" (3). Young (2007) does, however, indicate three distinct norm-enforcement mechanisms:

(i) Shared expectations that resolve coordination problems: In the United States, people drive on the right-hand side of the road because they expect others to do so. Driving on the left would be dangerous. This shared expectation is sufficient to enforce the behavioral prescription.[1]

(ii) Social sanction, negative or positive: If someone smokes inside a public space, others may offer dirty looks or complain. By contrast, someone who rescues a drowning person may become a local hero.

(iii) Internalization: If I believe in a norm, such as not littering, I follow it even when I know nobody will notice. An internalized sense of impropriety for violation thus "enforces" the prescription.

Other authors distinguish between coordinating conventions (hereafter, conventions) and norms; some also differentiate types of norms based upon enforcement mechanisms. Many regard ethical prescription as the distinguishing characteristic of norms (e.g., Elster 1989a, 1989b; Bowles 2004; Mengel 2008; Dequech 2009). Because conventions lack ethical content, they rely only on mechanism (i) for enforcement. Norms, on the other hand, signal obligation, indicating enforcement via both (ii) and (iii), and often by (i) as well. Pushing further, Friederike Mengel distinguishes between norms that are enforced by mechanisms (ii) and those enforced by (iii) (2008, 610).

Kaushik Basu (2000) presents three categories of norms. First, equilibrium-selection norms rely on mechanisms (i) and (ii). Such norms create focal points among members of groups by guiding their expectations to converge upon one of many possible equilibria in complex games.[2] Expecting social sanction from violation, agents usually abide by the indicated prescriptions. Moreover, an expectation of general adherence to the norm's prescribed equilibrium significantly reduces uncertainty in social encounters. Second, a preference-changing norm becomes internalized—mechanism (iii). Because internalization connotes accepted ethical propriety, individuals usually prefer to follow internalized norms, even with no expectation of sanctions. Note that Basu's term, "preference-changing," directly implies that such norms influence preference orderings. Indeed, norms are the key mechanism through which social processes shape endogenous preference formation.

Basu's third type of norm operates at a deeper level. A *rationality-limiting norm* (RLN) is a behavioral regularity within a group that is so strong that alternatives to its prescription are not even considered; such options are effectively removed from agents' choice sets. There is no contemplation of benefits, sanctions, guilt, or any consequences. Basu (2000, 94) states, "A rural woman in India may choose to wear a red sari, but she does not choose to wear a sari. Non-sari clothes lie beyond the set she would even consider."[3] Lack of considered alternatives guarantees enforcement. Rationality-limiting norms thus reduce uncertainty because there is no need to worry about actions that others will not even contemplate. Furthermore, distinct RLN can influence encounters between different cultures.[4]

People in one culture may simply not anticipate actions that are typical, or at least considered, in another. For example, the Incas never imagined that the Spanish, after receiving a huge ransom of gold, would then murder their chief and massacre thousands (Diamond 1997). For the Incas, contemplation of such action was precluded by an RLN—though clearly not for the Spanish (Basu 2000).

In order to distinguish more precisely among institutional prescriptions, Sue Crawford and Elinor Ostrom (2005) develop a "syntax" of institutions that identifies key elements of institutional statements. The presence or absence of one or more of these elements indicates three basic types of institutions: shared strategies, norms, and rules. More precisely, their typology, called the *ADICO* framework, identifies five types of statements that appear in institutional prescriptions: attributes (*A*), deontic (*D*), aims (*I*), condition (*C*), and or-else (*O*). *A*-statements indicate to whom a particular institutional statement applies. *D*-statements specify a type of obligation: must, must not, or is permitted to do.[5] *I*-statements identify specific goals: the intended actions or non-actions for the parties indicated by *A* or sometimes desired outcomes from their actions. *C*-statements describe when and where an institutional prescription applies—the conditions or contexts in which they are applicable. *O*-statements are outcomes of collective decisions that specify consequences of violating institutional prescriptions and also indicate specific enforcers to apply designated sanctions. Examples of all of these statements follow.

Crawford and Ostrom apply the *ADICO* elements to three types of institutions. First, they define *shared strategies* as mutually expected strategic responses, operating within a group, that members find in their interest to follow—given that others are expected to do so. Shared strategies make only *AIC* statements. For example, everyone expects all drivers (*A*) to drive on the left-hand side of the road (*I*) if they are in India (*C*). Second, norms add a deontic: anyone over the age of 5 (*A*) should not (*D*) litter (*I*) outside or inside (*C*). Third, rules add an or-else clause with one or more designated enforcers. Designated enforcement readily accompanies formal rules. If you do not pay taxes, legislation indicates that the IRS can investigate and apply specific sanctions (*O*). *O*-statements may also apply to informal rules. The informal rule that everybody (*A*) should (*D*) dress appropriately (*I*) for church, synagogue, or mosque (*C*) or they will be denied entry (*O*) could be enforced by the person who hands out programs at the door on a specific day. Such an arrangement could arise from informal meetings.

Our approach to informal institutions merges several concepts from this literature. We maintain the ethical-content distinction between conventions and norms, noting that conventions are equivalent to Crawford and Ostrom's shared strategies (*AIC* statements). More precisely, we define a *coordinating convention* (*CC*) as a shared, expected, and ethically neutral behavioral regularity observed among the members of some group that, once established, is self-enforcing without recourse to sanctions or internalized sentiments. Ever since the practice of driving on the right-hand side of the road was established in Mexico and the United States, it has been in everyone's self-interest to follow it. By contrast, a *social norm* is a mutually understood and expected behavioral regularity that serves as an ethical prescription within some group.[6] Norms add a deontic (*D*) to *AIC* statements. Normative prescriptions can be quite specific. If you have a seat at the front of a crowded bus and an elderly person enters (C) and if you are in good health, not a child, not elderly, and not tending to children (A), then you should (D) offer your seat (I).

As mentioned previously, norms utilize enforcement mechanisms (ii), (iii), and often (i). Moreover, mechanisms (ii) and (iii) complement each other, though both need not apply to every agent; social sanction and internalization are common to norms—but not necessarily to all individuals. Those who do not really accept a norm may still follow it to avoid social sanction. Some do not smoke inside public places for this reason. Others, whose preferences have been influenced by norms they believe in, internalize them. In fact, those who internalize norms have reason to sanction violators. People who believe that no one should smoke inside (perhaps asthmatics or ex-smokers) may comment or stare at those who do. Accordingly, we define a *typical social norm* (TSN) as a norm that relies on both internalization and social enforcement. These twin mechanisms facilitate resolution to second-order CAPs among potentially large groups of individuals who generally subscribe to relevant TSN.

As a second type of norm, more potent but less common than TSN, we utilize Basu's concept of an RLN. The ethical messages of RLN are so deeply internalized that adherents do not consider alternatives to their prescriptions. Thus, while social sanction could well follow violation of RLN, RLN adherents need no such incentive.

We now draw two further distinctions. First, occasionally shared behavioral prescriptions are not internalized by anyone but are still socially enforced, as in Basu's equilibrium-selection norm. We use the term *socially enforced convention* (SEC): a mutually expected behavioral regularity that is both ethically neutral and socially enforced. Social enforcement distinguishes SEC from *CC*, and lack of internalization distinguishes SEC from norms. Basu describes the strict behavioral prescriptions that applied to his widowed aunt as an example of social enforcement without ethical belief—one that fits our SEC concept. Basu's aunt married in India in the 1930s, and her husband died shortly thereafter. At the time, widows in India were expected to wear only white saris with black trim and to abide by strict restrictions on socializing. Moreover, people who associated with widows were expected to reprimand them in cases of violation. Neither she, her family, her friends, nor her family's friends actually believed that these restrictions were appropriate or fair. Yet she abided for the remainder of her life at enormous personal sacrifice because she believed that violation would induce social reprimand. Basu (2000) notes that, before her husband's death, his aunt loved to wear colors.

Why did family and friends abide in the sense of not giving her permission to violate? They believed that deviation from their prescribed role as enforcers would also invoke sanction. Basu (2000, 88) contends that these mutual expectations created "a web of self-reinforcing sanctions." Enforcement required only a shared belief of sanction for violation; internalization was not necessary.[7] Chapter 4's discussion of Havel's (1986) post-totalitarian system offers another example. SEC may thus reflect exercises or outcomes of power2 and power3. Indeed, Havel's point is that nobody—including police and soldiers—really believed in the system.

Before proceeding to social rules, we compare the enforcement dimensions of our two types of conventions and our two types of norms by placing them along a spectrum that

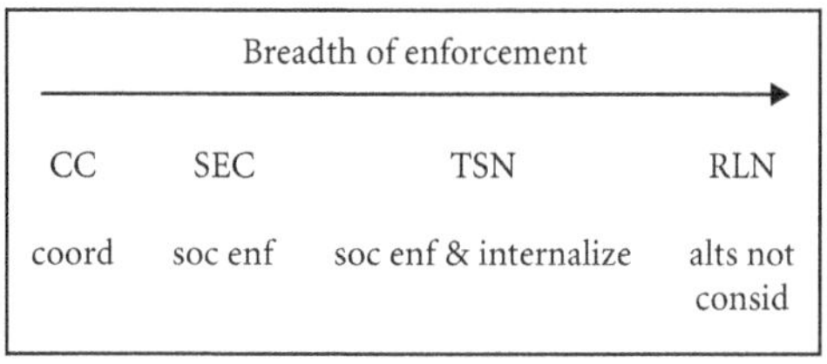

Figure 8.1   Breadth of informal enforcement mechanisms

illustrates the breadth of potential enforcement. As we move to the right in Figure 8.1, the corresponding coordination or enforcement mechanisms for given behavioral prescriptions apply to broader sets of circumstances. To reiterate, *CC* apply only to circumstances where coordination alone can align interests. Few people avoid littering on the basis of coordination. For SEC, fear of sanctions alone can generate adherence. On the other hand, TSN combine such social enforcement with internalization. Internalizers adhere even in the absence of possible observation. Note, however, that compliance is not guaranteed for any of these first three mechanisms. Agents weigh the material and social costs or benefits from adherence against those for violation. While being chased by a thief, even a devoted nonlitterer would not pick up a dropped tissue. By contrast, for RLN, a failure to consider alternatives to prescriptions guarantees enforcement. Basu's rural Indian woman simply does not consider the social or material costs of sari versus non-sari clothing.

Following this logic, other things equal (and often they are not), enduring informal institutions tend to acquire broader compliance mechanisms—sometimes moving them to the right in Figure 8.1. If a *CC* such as showing up to class on time has been in place for a while, violation may invoke social sanction, perhaps indicating an SEC among affected students. An SEC that persists can gain legitimacy and so become a TSN. Many students have internalized a norm of arriving for class on time. Finally, if a TSN remains in place long enough and if it also gains enough legitimacy that agents simply do not consider violation (a rare occurrence), it becomes an RLN.[8]

To complete our typology of informal institutions, we define *social rules*: prescribed and mutually understood behavioral regularities that are enforced by sanctions administered by informally designated agents or groups. Social rules necessarily involve syntax elements *ADICO*, but their *D*-statements may or may not be internalized—that is, they may or may not have salient ethical content. Social rules are informal in the sense that they emerge from informal decision processes, such as orally communicated arrangements at meetings. By contrast, formal rules arise from designated formal collective decision-making processes. As in Figure 7.1, social rules occupy a slightly informal position on the spectrum from least to most formal institutions.

Overall, we designate two types of conventions, coordinating conventions (*CC*) and socially enforced conventions (SEC); two types of norms, typical social norms (TSN) and rationality-limiting norms (RLN); and two types of rules, social rules and formal rules.[9] Table 8.1 summarizes these distinctions. Columns 2–6 indicate classifications based upon reasons for adherence; column 7 reports on the presence or absence of a conscious

TABLE 8.1
Types of institutions

Type	Syntax	Coord.	Internalized	Social sctn.	Material sctn.	Consc. D	Formal CD
CC	*AIC*	Y	N	N	N	Y	N
SEC	*ADIC*	M	N	Y	N	Y	N
TSN	*ADIC*	M	Y	Y	N	Y	N
RLN	*ADIC*	M	Y[a]	Y	N	N	N
Social rules	*ADICO*	M	M	M	M	Y	N
Formal rules	*ADICO*	M	M	M	Y	Y	Y

N O T E : Coord. = mutual benefit to coordination (as a motive for adherence); sctn. = sanction; Consc. D = conscious decision; CD = outcome of a formal collective decision (i.e., one that adheres to written rules in use); Y = yes; N = no; M = maybe.

[a]Not consciously considered—extremely deep.

decision; and column 8 indicates the formality of the procedures used to create or modify an institution.

Having established core categories of institutions, we proceed to conceptual background concerning how institutions coordinate both belief and behavior via their influence on cognition, information, and motivation. To do so, we introduce the concepts of correlated equilibria, epistemic game theory, and social choreography.

8.2. CORRELATED EQUILIBRIA, EPISTEMIC GAME THEORY, AND SOCIAL CHOREOGRAPHY

Section 8.1 established that we may use the syntax of context-specific institutional prescriptions to categorize institutions. We now consider how institutional statements of any type coordinate or choreograph beliefs and behaviors among multiple agents. Such social choreography both conditions and enables strategic decision making among boundedly rational agents in a non-ergodic world. It is the foundation of complex society.

Recall that a Nash equilibrium specifies a mutually consistent and self-enforcing set of beliefs and strategic choices among relevant agents. More precisely, a *Nash equilibrium (NE)* is a set or list of strategies that includes one strategy for each player in a game, where (i) each player holds correct beliefs (estimates) concerning the strategies that have been or will be chosen by all others, and (ii) each player's indicated strategy offers a best response to such beliefs (Dixit, Skeath, and Reiley 2009). Unfortunately, classical game theory (CGT) offers no rationale concerning why or how such expectations actually come into existence (Aumann 1987).[10] More generally, CGT by itself suffers from "its lack of a theory of when and how rational agents share mental constructs" (Gintis 2009b, xiv). In other words, CGT fails to address how multiple individuals come to hold the shared beliefs (expectations and mental models) that accompany Nash equilibria or, more generally, social equilibria.[11] On the other hand, an NE makes sense if we assume that agents somehow expect others to use their specified strategies. One way to generate such a shared expectation among multiple players is for some commonly observed and similarly interpreted signal to identify the relevant strategic responses.

The concept of a focal point (Schelling 1960) moves us decisively in the direction of re-solving this problem. Recall that, in a game with two or more Nash equilibria, a *focal point* specifies a single equilibrium—a single set of mutually consistent strategies—upon which players' expectations converge. Traffic signals offer an intuitive example: everybody knows to stop at a red light. Schelling offers a more complicated example (1960, 55n1): when asked where and when they would meet someone in New York City without prior communica-tion, many people chose the information booth at Grand Central Station at noon. This focal point selects among millions of alternatives (33rd and 3rd at 1:03 a.m., etc.).[12] A sufficient condition for the emergence of a focal point is a salient, mutually understood, and similarly interpreted signal (a red light). In a sequential game of perfect information with a small number of (mostly) reciprocal players, a cooperative first move might offer such a signal. But in cases with greater numbers, some degree of simultaneity, imperfect observation, asymmetric information, or fundamental uncertainty, a more substantive signal is usually required.

A related and more general concept is that of a correlated equilibrium (Aumann 1987). Consider a game G that has multiple equilibria. Suppose that, before playing G, each player observes some event or signal (γ) that "suggests" a specific action (pure strategy) to each player ($a_i = a_i(\gamma)$).[13] A *correlated equilibrium* exists if each player follows her own suggestion $a_i(\gamma)$, each player expects the others to follow their own suggestions ($a_j(\gamma)$), and no player can do better by unilaterally deviating from its $a_i(\gamma)$. Note that players do not necessarily know the contents of others' signals ($a_j(\gamma)$). Even so, γ induces a shared expectation among players, prior to playing G, that all will follow some suggestion from γ.[14] We call event γ a *correlating device*; it generates a shared expectation that directs behavioral outcomes. Note further that we may interpret signal γ as a first move, made by nature or another player, in a larger game $G+$, which includes G subsequently.

For example, Figure 8.2 illustrates a game of battle in which two pure-strategy NE ex-ist, (U, L) and (D, R), along with a mixed strategy NE in which Ann plays U and Ben plays L with probability 0.5 for expected payoff (2.5, 2.5). A simple correlated equilibrium arises as follows: with probability 0.5, event γ simultaneously signals U to Ann and L to Ben; also with probability 0.5, it signals D to Ann and R to Ben. Both players execute their indicated strategy. Expected payoffs are (3, 3). In this simple example, both players know the sugges-tions for the other player.[15]

Extending this logic, the concept of an epistemic game allows us to represent informal institutions as correlating devices for complex social interactions. In an *epistemic game*, as in any game, all players have a strategy set (S_i) and there is a set Ω of all possible states of the world. Each specific state ω (in Ω) indicates a specific strategy for each player ($s_i = s_i(\omega)$).

	Ben	
	L	R
Ann U	5, 1	0, 0
Ann D	4, 4	1, 5

Figure 8.2   Two-player game of battle

In Figure 8.2, Ann plays U and Ben plays L in one such state. For multi-player games, the set Ω is enormous. Furthermore, in epistemic games the following statements hold:

- Each agent i has a *knowledge partition* $(\mathbf{P}_i)$ that represents the degree to which she can distinguish among the different possible states of the world. Agents distinguish among cells (C_j) within partition $(\mathbf{P}_i)$, but within each cell, they do not know which specific state ω applies. For example, in Figure 8.2 (without γ), Ann's partition consists of two cells: $\mathbf{P}_A = \{(U, L; U, R); (D, L; D, R)\}$. She distinguishes the first cell (where she plays U) from the second (where she plays D), but within each cell, she does not know whether Ben plays L or R.[16]

- Thus the actual current state of the world ω_c may not be discernible from other possibilities. If ω_c is that Ann plays D and Ben plays L, Ann cannot distinguish ω_c from alternate state ω_a in which she plays D but Ben plays R.

- We represent an agent's conception of the world for a given actual state ω_c with her possibility operator. Ann's *possibility operator* $P_A\omega_c$ = cell (D, L; D, R) shows the states that she considers possible when the actual state of the world is ω_c (where Ann plays D and Ben plays L). In this circumstance, Ann knows she plays D and considers it possible that Ben plays either L or R.

- For any state ω, each agent i forms a *subjective prior* $\rho_i(\omega)$ that specifies her conjectures about the strategies used by others in ω. Technically, $\rho_i(\omega)$ indicates positive probabilities for all strategies of other agents that are considered possible in state ω. Having played D, Ann might conjecture that Bob plays L with probability 25% and R with probability 75%.

We say that the *knowledge structure* of an epistemic game includes these three elements: knowledge partitions $(\mathbf{P}_i)$, possibility operators $(P_i\omega)$, and conjectures about others' strategies for specific states $(\rho_i(\omega))$.

Combining concepts, an epistemic game proceeds as follows: Nature or an event sends a signal γ. On this basis, agents share an initial conjecture, with greater or lesser detail. They share a common element of their subjective priors $\rho_i(\omega; \gamma)$. In a minimally informed case, agents know only that everyone follows some suggestion from γ. By contrast, in a fully correlated case—equivalent to a focal point—agents know (or accurately expect) γ's strategy suggestions for the others.[17] Intermediate cases with various degrees of correlation are possible. Agents then act upon their conjectures: they play G on the basis of priors $\rho_i(\omega; \gamma)$.

The concept of *social epistemology* addresses how institutions (notably, conventions and norms) provide motivation, information, and cognitive frameworks for agents within epistemic games (Gintis 2009b). Recall Chapter 7's assertion that, as shared mental models, institutions exert precisely these influences: they offer motivational, informational, and cognitive context within which individual agents understand and make strategic decisions. In other words, institutions operate as correlating devices. Institutional prescriptions (*ADICO* statements) provide signals (γ) to agents, indicating correlated equilibria and focal points. Thus institutions are *social choreographers*; they act as social correlating devices.[18] More specifically, we relate institutions to epistemic game theory in three basic fashions.

First, commonly understood institutional prescriptions shape agents' motivation via signaled social and material incentives. Second, and at a deeper level, normative prescriptions affect preference orderings, creating internalized values (ethical deontics) that promote adherence. Third, institutional signals convey information that influences conjectures about others' behavior ($\rho_i(\omega_c)$) in specific social contexts. Such common priors render others' behavior more predictable. Before meeting a stranger, I expect to shake hands. Before entering a classroom for the first time, students expect others to sit down at desks, as opposed to, say, dancing.

More fundamentally, as shared mental models, institutions indicate social categories—important elements of knowledge partitions ($\mathbf{P}_i$)—and causal relationships that enter possibility operators ($P_i\omega$). A norm that prescribes precisely who (young people) should offer bus seats to elderly passengers partitions the social world of the bus into specific age-based categories. Likewise, the convention of driving on the right-hand side of the road (in the US) creates expectations concerning the actions of other drivers.

Overall, institutions perform *social choreography*: they orchestrate or correlate beliefs and behaviors across multiple individuals. Institutional signals—as specific, context-dependent *ADICO* prescriptions—facilitate strategic decision making by influencing and indeed shaping agents' motivation, information, and cognitive frameworks. Institutions thus provide and constitute shared mental models that guide social coordination; institutions indicate correlated equilibria and focal points. Such social choreography allows boundedly rational agents in non-ergodic environments to conceptualize alternatives, envision possible outcomes, and make strategic decisions. On such institutional foundations, agents navigate situations that would otherwise defy comprehension, on account of a multiplicity of possible actions, strategies, and equilibria. Institutions reduce the competence-difficulty (CD) gap enough so that agents can sometimes effectively offer best responses to the behavior of others in specific social contexts. Institutions thus enable boundedly rational agents to behave as substantively rational actors within certain contexts: as social choreographers, institutions create the potential for relatively predictable and consistent goal-oriented behavior among multiple agents—in certain contexts.

On this basis, we now turn to informal institutions and second-order CAPs.

8.3. INFORMAL SOCIAL COORDINATION AND ENFORCEMENT

We now elaborate on the coordination and enforcement functions of the most important informal institutions, coordinating conventions (*CC*) and typical social norms (TSN). We first address *CC* with a game-theoretic illustration and examples. Coordinating conventions can resolve a limited but important set of second-order CAPs—namely, those that solely address coordination among multiple agents. We proceed with more detailed discussion of TSN, beginning with a review of their core influences. We then present a general model of norm internalization, followed by specific game-theoretic illustrations that distinguish among types of players by their respective levels of adherence to norms. Classical game-theoretic models indicate that strong internalization with no accompanying sanctions can induce cooperation in homogeneous groups, but tends to encourage defection by self-interested players in mixed groups. Models based on indirect evolutionary game theory (IEGT) lead to an analogous conclusion regarding the relative fitness of different types of players. IEGT models also generate implications for the evolution of preferences and the potential impacts of such evolution on the viability of norms. This last result indicates a coevolution (interrelated development) between preferences and norms.[19]

We next develop a conformity model in which one agent's adherence depends on that of others. We find a multi-player assurance game, with its associated path dependence and punctuated equilibria arising at either full adherence or at no adherence. Dislodging either outcome would present a substantial CAP. We then add social enforcement by introducing reciprocal players. Norm internalization motivates r-types to sanction violators, possibly facilitating resolution of otherwise troublesome second-order CAPs. We close by considering reciprocity itself as a type of TSN. The ethical content of reciprocity norms extends reciprocal relationships beyond small groups. These norms can resolve second-order CAPs and build trust within large groups and across different groups, but norms of reciprocity may also motivate reciprocal conflict.

Coordinating Conventions

As we saw in Section 8.1, coordinating conventions (*CC*) lack the ethical content of norms; they specify *AIC* (attributes, aims, conditions) statements but not *D* (deontic) statements. In terms of Section 8.2, *CC* are able to choreograph beliefs and behaviors among multiple agents in contexts where pure coordination is needed. They establish focal points that specify particular mutually understood strategic responses in situations where multiple social equilibria are possible. Agents follow *CC* prescriptions in such contexts because failure to coordinate with others is costly.

Figure 8.3 illustrates a *CC* for a driving game. There are two Nash equilibria (NE): (L, L) and (R, R). Players are indifferent between them but must coordinate on one. A *CC* of either (L, L) or (R, R) choreographs drivers' behavior toward a focal point. Accordingly, people drive on the right in Chad, Mexico, the United States, and Germany but drive on the left in Japan, India, the United Kingdom, and Botswana. While driving on the wrong side of the road is illegal and would likely invoke social sanction, coordination offers the key enforcement mechanism: fear of accidents plays a far greater role than fear of tickets—unlike for other offenses, such as running stop signs, where legal (or social) sanctions are typically needed. Moreover, the distinction between driving on the right and driving on the left lacks ethical content. For less dramatic coordination problems, such as scheduling meetings, individuals still avoid costly noncoordination by adhering to shared expectations. In all such

		Driver B	
		Left	Right
Driver A	Left	1, 1	−10, −10
	Right	−10, −10	1, 1

Figure 8.3   Coordinating convention game

cases, established *CC* can induce the prescribed coordination among various types of players, including rational egoists (e-types) and reciprocal actors (r-types)—absent strong incentives to do otherwise.

More generally, conventions can focus behavior in various encounters or exchanges, avoiding multiple undesirable combinations of activity. The calendar is a *CC*, as is the 24-hour clock, a train schedule, and the metric system. In principle, the day could be divided into 100 or more units rather than 24 hours. Trains could arrive or leave at any time. Class could start at 9:00 or 9:57 or 3:23. In each case, the relevant *CC* motivates behavior, provides information, and influences cognition.[20] For example, if the course schedule indicates that my game theory class starts at 11:00 a.m. every Monday, Wednesday, and Friday in Alumni Recitation Hall room 120, my students and I have a strong incentive to be in that room at that time. Moreover, the schedule informs us about others' behavior: students know when and where the professor and classmates will show up. The schedule also allows us to infer the consequences of showing up at, say, 10:45 or 11:15. Similar logic applies to systems of measurement: coordination on units is self-enforcing. Prior to purchasing milk, both the consumer and store owner need to know how much will be sold, or exchange may not occur. We think in terms of 24-hour days, seven-day weeks, miles or kilometers, liters or gallons, pounds or kilograms, and so forth. Absent such *CC*, orchestrating multiple social activities and economic exchanges would simply not be possible.[21] Even so, there is a limited range of second-order CAPs that *CC* may resolve because most CAPs do not lend themselves to self-enforcement solely via coordination.

Social Norms and Core Institutional Influences

The ethical properties of typical social norms exert particularly strong influence on agents' motivation, information, and cognition. Recall that TSN add ethical deontic (*D-*) statements to *AIC* statements. They also combine social enforcement with internalization, both of which rely on ethical content, indicating unique potential for resolving second-order CAPs.

With respect to motivation, the ethical content of TSN influences both incentives and preferences. Even though TSN do not designate specific enforcers, their mutually understood ethical prescriptions motivate norm internalizers to sanction violators and, simultaneously, signal possible sanctions to potential violators. For example, a person who might wish to smoke inside a public space may refrain from doing so for fear of receiving dirty looks from someone who would consider it inappropriate. Typical social norms also influence preferred activity by identifying social conditions under which certain actions appear to be appropriate (or not). By and large, smoking outside does not violate norms. At a deeper level, norms affect the endogenous preferences of both adherents and enforcers. People internalize norms when they value (or believe in) their ethical prescriptions. By 2012, not smoking inside public places has become a social norm in many parts of the United States—unlike 40 years earlier. Preferences of both smokers and nonsmokers have adjusted in a manner that has motivated both social and internalized enforcement.[22]

The informational and cognitive functions of TSN overlap and reinforce each other. Regarding the former, normative *ADIC* statements inform boundedly rational agents about the social contexts in which they make strategic decisions. Referring to the previous bus example, a TSN statement indicates who (young people) should take specific actions (offer their seats) in which circumstances (when an elderly person enters). The prospect of unassigned social enforcement offers additional strategic information. Such information allows agents to interpret specific situations: they have some idea of what to do or not do, how others might behave, and possible consequences. Normative prescriptions thereby reduce uncertainty in relevant social contexts (those indicated by their C-statements). Furthermore, ethical content lends salience to such information. Interpretation and salience lead us to cognition.

As shared mental models, TSN indicate social categories along with cause-and-effect relationships. The ethical content of norms influences social categorization. Many people, particularly norm internalizers, would classify violators as somewhat unethical. People may even use gradations of norm adherence to designate ethically based categories of behavior. Furthermore, $ADIC$ statements serve as inputs into the predictive elements of individual and shared mental models. Thus, as an elderly man enters a bus, a rider predicts that one of the young people sitting in front will offer a seat. Furthermore, the ethical content of norms can lend urgency or importance to indicated causal relationships; it can enhance the salience of certain predictions. Such predictions, however, need not be entirely accurate. Sometimes norm internalizers may overestimate the likelihood of adherence by others. Ensuing misunderstandings can generate conflict.

Overall, the ethical content of TSN exerts strong influence over boundedly rational agents' motivation, their received information (notably its salience), and their cognitive understandings of pertinent complex social interactions. Ethical content thus generates powerful social choreography that can resolve second-order CAPs in large or small groups as long as mutual adherence is generally understood and accepted. The potential for such TSN-induced resolution depends on the strength of internalization and anticipated social enforcement, weighed against any expected gains from nonadherence. These factors may, in turn, depend on the mix of player types, group size, and other group characteristics such as cohesion and frequency of interaction. With this foundation, we turn to modeling the impact of TSN on behavior.

Models of Norm Internalization

We begin by addressing how different levels of norm internalization affect potential resolutions of CAPs—independent of social enforcement. Broadly speaking, we find that in sufficiently homogeneous groups, strong internalization of norms fosters resolution of second-order CAPs, while in mixed groups, strong internalization by some tends to encourage free-riding by others. This analysis utilizes both CGT and IEGT models. The former illustrate distributional impacts of these statements. Probing deeper, IEGT models offer implications on the relative fitness of distinct levels of norm internalization, with further implications on the long-run viability of norms—indicating two-directional causality, or coevolution.

Consider the provision of public goods within a social group G of size N. With no norm and with only rational egoist (e-type) players, we encounter the free-riding problems of

Chapter 2 exacerbated by the second-order enforcement problems of Chapter 3. Norms, however, may choreograph cooperation. Using Section 8.1's institutional syntax, suppose that a TSN (Ψ_C) stipulates the following: Under reasonable circumstances (C), all members of $G(A)$ should (D) contribute to the provision of a public good (I), such as a community well.[23]

To analyze such normative influence, we follow López-Pérez (2006) (with modified notation) to specify a TSN as a correspondence (rule) Ψ. We write

$$(8.1) \qquad \Psi: h(A, C) \to D(I \mid A, C).$$

Here h (an information set in a game) indicates the applicable attributes and context: the social categories of agents to whom Ψ applies (A) and the situational/environmental conditions within which Ψ operates (C). If one arrives at situation h, one "should" ($\to D$) follow prescribed (or avoid prohibited) actions or strategies (I), given A and C.[24] This prescription ($\to D$ ($I \mid A, C$)) identifies a focal point. In this manner, TSN Ψ shapes motivation, information, and cognition; it is a shared mental model. In terms of epistemic game theory, Ψ influences knowledge partitions (P_i), possibility operators ($P_i(\omega)$), and priors ($\rho_i(\omega)$), indicating a specific form of social choreography. A mutually understood and accepted norm Ψ_C may then similarly correlate beliefs and behavior toward cooperation.

We proceed with a general modeling framework that addresses how Ψ_C can influence the behavior of various types of agents. Assume that all agents receive material payoff (π), a function of the specific strategies ($s_i \in S_i$) chosen by each member ($1, 2, \ldots, N$) of group G. Agents who have internalized Ψ_C and then violate it experience guilt (g) regardless of how others behave. Such violators may also feel shame (ς), where the magnitude or intensity of ς depends on the proportion of members who adhere to Ψ_C.[25] We write $\varsigma = \varsigma(\eta(s))$, where η is the proportion of N who follow Ψ_C, and η depends on agents' chosen strategies $s = s_1$, $s_2, \ldots, s_N$. Here function $\varsigma(\cdot)$ represents the conformity element of internalization; $\varsigma(\cdot)$ can be associated with group solidarity. Furthermore, some agents who follow Ψ_C experience anger (ψ) toward violators; ψ increases in proportion $1 - \eta(s)$.[26] For an individual agent, we have

$$(8.2) \qquad \begin{aligned} u_i &= \pi_i(s_i, s_{-i}) - \psi(1 - \eta(s_{-i}) \mid s_i = \text{C}) \\ &= \pi_i(s_i, s_{-i}) - g - \varsigma(\eta(s_{-i}) \mid s_i = \text{D}). \end{aligned}$$

Here $g, \varsigma, \psi \geq 0$; $s = (s_i, s_{-i})$, where s_{-i} denotes strategies of the $N-1$ other players, and C and D (as before) represent strategies "contribute" and "defect." In the first line, i's utility equals material payoffs minus anger at the portion of G who violate Ψ_C, given that i adheres. The second line shows that violation induces guilt and shame, where the latter depends on the portion that adhere.

We may now use the parameters of (8.2) to delineate four types of agents. Rational egoists (e-types, indicated by subscript e) do not internalize norms. For them, $g_e = \varsigma_e = \psi_e = 0$. For the remaining three types (norm-using agents), internalization influences preferences. First, *principled-types* (p-types, subscript p) internalize a norm Ψ without considering adherence by others. They experience guilt for violating Ψ regardless of how others behave: $g_p > 0$; $\varsigma_p = \psi_p = 0$. Second, *conditional cooperators* (c-types, subscript c) feel guilt plus shame for violation in proportion to relative adherence, but they do not feel angry when others violate. Thus $g_c > 0$; $\varsigma_c(\eta) > 0$ if $\eta > 0$; and $\psi_c = 0$. Third, reciprocal players (r-types, subscript r) conditionally cooperate and experience anger when they adhere and others violate. For r-types, $g_r > 0$; $\varsigma_r(\eta) > 0$ if $\eta > 0$; and $\psi_r(1 - \eta) > 0$ if they abide and $1 - \eta > 0$. As in Chapter 5, r-type anger motivates reciprocal punishment—here because perceived violation of Ψ_C constitutes an unkind act. Thus Ψ_C influences r-type understandings of kind and unkind behavior. This cognitive influence of norms can motivate r-type punishment among groups that are much larger than the small reciprocal groups discussed in Chapter 5.

With this background, we discuss two-player CGT games—played between various combinations of e-types and p-types—in which the latter internalize Ψ_C with different levels (or degrees) of strength. We then develop a multi-player indirect evolutionary model that represents the impact of different levels of internalization on the relative fitness of e-types vis-à-vis p-types. Both models indicate that, within homogeneous populations of p-types, stronger norm internalization improves prospects for resolution of CAPs, but in mixed populations, stronger internalization fosters e-type free-riding. In a CGT framework, such free-riding obstructs resolution of CAPs; in an IEGT framework, free-riding reduces the fitness of strongly internalizing p-types. These findings motivate our subsequent exploration of c- and r-types.

Two-Person Classical Models

Figure 8.4 presents a variation of Figure 2.2's two-player public-good game with simplified symmetrical payoffs.[27] As in Chapter 2, both players are e-types, payoffs are material, strategy C represents "contribute," and strategy D represents "do not contribute." With a PD structure, the payoffs have the following relations: $1 > C > D > 0$. The game's NE is (D, D).

We now add norm Ψ_C and consider both e- and p-type players. Figures 8.5a and 8.5b respectively show a game between two p-types and a game between one p-type and one e-type. The p-types experience guilt ($-g$) whenever they play D, since not contributing violates Ψ_C; e-types receive the indicated material payoffs. Following Mengel (2008, 610–11), and referring to Figure 8.5a, we delineate four specific levels of internalization on the basis of specific threshold magnitudes of g that affect the game's structure.[28]

Referring to Figure 8.5a, we define our levels of norm internalization as follows:

- *Weak internalization* of Ψ_C: $g < \min\{1 - C, D\}$. The PD structure is not altered, and the NE remains at (D, D).

<table>
<tr><td></td><td></td><td colspan="2">Player B</td></tr>
<tr><td></td><td></td><td>C</td><td>D</td></tr>
<tr><td rowspan="2">Player A</td><td>C</td><td>C, C</td><td>0, 1</td></tr>
<tr><td>D</td><td>1, 0</td><td>D, D</td></tr>
</table>

Figure 8.4   PD for two e-types

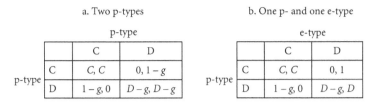

Figure 8.5   Contribution game

- *Intermediate case (i):* $1 - C < g < D$. Figure 8.5a now represents a game of assurance: players cooperate if they expect or trust the other to do so. Mutual knowledge of internalization could choreograph such trust so that a focal point at (C, C) emerges.[29]
- *Intermediate case (ii):* $D < g < 1 - C$. In Figure 8.5a, each player cooperates if it expects the other to defect (reverse conditional cooperation), generating a game of chicken. Distributional conflict may emerge over who "gets to" defect, and neither NE—that is, (C, D) or (D, C)—need be socially optimal.
- *Strong internalization* occurs when $g > \max\{1 - C, D\}$, generating unconditional cooperation in Figure 8.5a, with an NE at (C, C). This is the only case where full resolution is guaranteed.

Applying these internalization levels to Figure 8.5b's p-e matches, we see that increasing internalization shifts the outcome from total defection, in cases of weak internalization and intermediate (i), to partial resolution with an NE at (C, D) for both intermediate (ii) and strong internalization. Note, however, that stronger internalization allows e-types to exploit the unconditional willingness of p-types to cooperate. In terms of distribution, stronger internalization by p-types favors e-types.

Table 8.2 summarizes these results. The first column shows the four levels of internalization. The second shows the payoff conditions for each. The third reports p-type responses at each level. The next four columns indicate various outcomes for matches between two p-types. Finally, the last two columns report the NE and CAP resolution for matches between one p- and one e-type.

The contrasting outcomes of p-p as opposed to p-e matches suggest that norm enforcement that relies solely on internalization is most functional in cohesive social groups. Resolution in the strong internalization p-p model may represent interactions within groups who share long-term cohesion in the sense of adherence to shared norms. For example, one could argue that—in terms of generating accessible economic prosperity—the Scandinavian welfare states have functioned well for decades because relatively homogeneous populations have strongly internalized norms that discourage various forms of abuse, such as calling in sick in order to take a day off work. On the other hand, such internalization may undermine CAP resolution when strong internalizers interact with others who do not share local norms. Some fear this prospect for Scandinavia, given contemporary levels of immigration from other parts of the European Union and elsewhere (Lindbeck 1995; Nannestad 2004).

TABLE 8.2
Strength of TSN internalization and impacts

| Internalization | Condition | p-type response | P-P MATCHES | | | | P-E MATCHES | |
			NE	Game	Res.?	Other	NE	Res.?
Weak	$G < \min\{1 - C, D\}$	Always D	(D, D)	PD	No	—	(D, D)	No
Int. case (i)	$1 - C < g < D$	C if exp.	(C, C) or (D, D)	Assurance	If (C, C) is a focal point	Path dep.	(D, D)	No
Int. case (ii)	$D < g < 1 - C$	RCC	(D, C) or (C, D)	Chicken	Possible	Conflict	(C, D)	Partial
Strong	$G > \max\{1 - C, D\}$	Always C	(C, C)	NE at SO	Yes	—	(C, D)	Partial

NOTE: Res. = resolution of CAP; Int. = intermediate; exp. = expect other to cooperate; dep. = dependent; RCC = reverse conditional cooperation; SO = social optimum.

An Indirect Evolutionary Model of Norm Internalization

An IEGT model that interacts p-types with e-types applies a potential for e-type exploitation of p-types to the relative fitness of the just-described levels of internalization—generating further implications for the viability of underlying norms. In this model, player types signify preference orientations that agents inherit from past experience and learning. Recall from Chapter 6 that an *indirect evolutionary model* determines the fitness of particular orientations (or, more generally, strategies) on the basis of the average material payoffs that bearers of specific orientations earn from their encountered matches. Agents, however, base their on-the-spot strategic decisions on both material and social payoffs. And, as indicated in the previous section, a player's orientation (or type) designates the applicable categories of social payoffs. Over time, players abandon unfit orientations—those that generate relatively low average material payoffs in encountered matches. The mix of types in the population evolves accordingly. These dynamics may then represent the evolution of preference orientations—at the same time implying that the evolution of preference orientations can influence the viability of certain norms. Thus preferences and norms coevolve (Bowles 2004).[30] In the present case, levels of p-type internalization affect that type's fitness vis-à-vis e-types.

We assume an initial population with both p- and e-types within which agents match randomly in pairs. The probability of a specific match (p-p, p-e, or e-e) depends upon the proportions of player types in the population.[31] Figure 8.4's material payoff PD game stipulates the fitness payoffs to all players arising from the indicated combinations of C and D strategies. E-type players base their strategic decisions solely on these payoffs. By contrast, p-types also consider the social payoffs in Figures 8.5a (for a p-p match) and 8.5b (for a p-e match).[32] In other words, internalized guilt (*g*) influences p-type strategic decisions, but once all players have chosen their strategies, material payoffs from the applicable cells of Figure 8.4 indicate the ensuing fitness of their orientations.

Ultimately, this model shows that CAP resolution and relative fitness depend on the mix of types, the availability of information, and the pertinent levels of p-type internalization. Here we consider only the three levels of internalization that affect game outcomes, and we initially assume full information: all players know others' types. In terms of internalization levels, we find the following:

- Intermediate internalization (i): In Figures 8.4, 8.5a, and 8.5b, a p-p match yields a cooperative NE, whereas all other combinations yield full defection. These results indicate that both p- and e-types are evolutionary stable strategies (ESS). Outcomes are thus path dependent: initial predominance of either type fosters continued predominance. This result is consistent with observed social homogeneity in many contexts.[33]

- Intermediate (ii) and strong internalization: A p-e match generates a (C, D) outcome in which the e-type free-rides. The e-type is the only ESS.[34]

Once again, stronger internalization among p-types facilitates e-type free-riding. Hence the relative fitness of p-types decreases with stronger internalization. On the other hand, moderate levels of norm internalization may lead to socially desirable outcomes.[35]

Introducing private information into our model replicates most of the above results, and also creates the possibility of a polymorphic equilibrium for intermediate case (i). We now assume that each player's type is private information, but the proportion of p-types in the population (ρ) is common knowledge. All agents thus expect to encounter a p-type with probability ρ and an e-type with probability $1 - \rho$. We now illustrate the case of intermediate (i), discuss case (ii), and mention results for strong internalization.

Recall that, for intermediate case (i) with full information, Figure 8.5a portrays a p-p match as a game of assurance. Assume that p-types have a response threshold at $\rho = 0.5$, so that if $\rho > 0.5$, they decide that the chances of encountering another p-type warrant playing C, but if $\rho < 0.5$, they cautiously play D. Note that e-types always play D. The following functions show the fitness of each type as a function of the share of p-types (ρ):

$$(8.3) \qquad W(p) = D \qquad\qquad \text{for } \rho < 0.5, \text{ and}$$
$$= \rho C + (1 - \rho)0 = \rho C \quad \text{for } \rho \geq 0.5;$$

$$(8.4) \qquad W(e) = D \qquad\qquad \text{for } \rho < 0.5, \text{ and}$$
$$= \rho + (1 - \rho)D \qquad \text{for } \rho \geq 0.5.$$

This model generates the curious result that, when $\rho < 0.5$, both types are *evolutionary neutral strategies*: all mixes have equal fitness. On the other hand, if $\rho > 0.5$, e-types are more fit because they can often free-ride on p-types. Greater e-type fitness reduces the proportion ρ over time, pushing it down to 0.5 or lower: a polymorphic equilibrium where both types may coexist for long periods. Figure 8.6 illustrates this game.[36]

For intermediate case (ii), recall that $D < g < 1 - C$, and that a p-p match in Figure 8.5a indicates a game of chicken. If p-types expect to encounter one of their own, they play C and D with equal probability, for an expected payoff of $(C + D)/2$. If they expect to meet an e-type, they play C. As before, e-types always play D. We thus arrive at the following fitness functions:

$$(8.5) \qquad W(p) = \rho(C + D)/2 + (1 - \rho)0 = \rho(C + D)/2;$$

$$(8.6) \qquad W(e) = \rho + (1 - \rho)D.$$

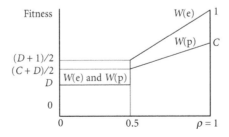

Figure 8.6 Evolutionary internalization of norms

In this case, one can show that the e-type is the unique ESS. Likewise, if internalization is strong, e-types free-ride; again an e-type orientation is the only ESS.

Overall, strong norm internalization enhances the potential for e-type free-riding. Even for intermediate case (i), coexistence arises only if the proportion of p-types is not too high. Because relative material payoffs determine relative fitness in IEGT models, stronger internalization reduces the evolutionary fitness of p-types in mixed encounters; thus excessive internalization of subgroup norms may be dysfunctional. This result may help explain why cooperative norms that function well in isolated groups may unravel over time in mixed encounters. The evolution of norms, then, may respond to the evolution of preferences—reflecting a process of coevolution.

If internalization were the sole manifestation of norm adherence, we would expect only limited impacts of norms on resolving CAPs. The present model, however, does not incorporate c-type conformity or potential sanctions from r-types.[37]

Conditional Cooperators

Returning to equation (8.2), we now focus on c-types. A multi-player model based on c-types reaffirms the prior result that strong internalization within homogeneous groups fosters resolution of CAPs. It also illustrates two additional principles that often apply to TSN: a law-of-demand tradeoff between values and material payoffs, and a conformity effect. The conformity effect, moreover, generates multi-player games of assurance with path dependence—the strength of which depends on the magnitude of these two effects.

To proceed, recall that c-types experience shame that increases in the proportion of adherents ($\varsigma\eta(s) > 0$), though without anger. For simplicity, we assume no guilt ($g_c = \psi_c = 0$).[38] We also assume constant per-person costs of contribution (c) and a linear shame function so that $\varsigma(\eta(s)) = \varsigma\eta(s)$. Recall that s indicates strategies for all players. Equations for contribution and defection (which resemble equation pairs (2.3) & (2.4) and (5.4) & (5.5)) are, respectively,[39]

$$(8.7) \qquad\qquad C(n) = c(\alpha n - 1),$$

$$(8.8) \qquad\qquad D(n) = \alpha n c - \varsigma\eta.$$

In (8.8), note the distinction between the number (n) and proportion (η) of cooperators. We can see that, whenever

$$(8.9) \qquad\qquad c < \varsigma\eta(s),$$

the contribution cost is less than the shame from defecting. Hence a c-type finds it worthwhile to follow Ψ_C.

Equation (8.9) offers three notable results. First, in a homogeneous group of c-types, stronger internalization (a larger ς) facilitates cooperation. Second, we find a law-of-demand relationship regarding norm adherence (López-Pérez 2006, 2009): an increase in cost (c) reduces compliance with Ψ_C, ceteris paribus. This result mirrors North's observation of a tradeoff between wealth and values. The higher the cost of following a conviction, the less impact it has on actual decisions (1990, 22). For example, many would contribute to a community improvement project that demands a few hours but not to one that requires weeks of effort. In the latter case, a contribution norm may not affect decisions. Third, we see a *conformity effect*, also called a solidarity effect: for a given c, the greater the proportion of adherents (η), the more desirable adherence becomes. Many social phenomena, ranging from fads to participation in revolution, reflect norm-induced solidarity effects.

Not surprisingly, interactions with conformity generate a multi-player game of assurance. We may then solve (8.7) and (8.8) for the tipping point (unstable NE) in terms of η: $\eta^* = c/\varsigma$. As in other such games, we find path dependence. Adherence can become a self-reinforcing punctuated equilibrium in which generalized adherence reinforces normative prescriptions. Furthermore, starting from an NE of zero contribution ($\eta = 0$), the greater c or the lower ς, the more difficult the CAP of orchestrating a behavioral shift across threshold η^* becomes.[40] Thus the law-of-demand and conformity effects of norm internalization jointly influence the strength of path dependency for relevant social practices.[41]

Note, however, that, as in the case of p-types, adding e-types to a group of c-types eliminates prospects for cooperation. Replacing Figure 8.5b's p-type with a c-type indicates either a noncooperative (D, D) outcome (if $\varsigma < 1$) or exploitation of the c-type by the e-type (if $\varsigma > 1$). In either case, the unwillingness of c-types to sacrifice material gain to punish e-type defection precludes disciplining the latter.[42] Hence the social enforcement properties of norms do not fully emerge unless some portion of the population is willing to punish nonadherents. Reciprocal players introduce this element.

Reciprocal Players and Social Enforcement of TSN

Adding reciprocal players (r-types) to the model generates potential sanctions for norm violators. Of the players discussed in this section, only r-types fully utilize deontic (D) normative statements. Typical social norms translate specific behaviors (offer bus seat or not; I) by specific individuals who possess specific attributes (young, healthy; A) in specific social contexts (on a bus; C) into the key r-type behavioral categories (partitions) of kind and unkind. These inputs generate r-type judgments that, in turn, motivate reciprocal response: r-types want to reward norm adherence with reciprocal adherence, even at some personal sacrifice.[43] Likewise, a sense of impropriety at violation of internalized norms generates r-type anger ($\psi_r > 0$), motivating a willingness to sacrifice material gain in order to sanction violators.[44]

In this sense, TSN function as social choreographers that signal kind and unkind behavior, invoking reciprocal response. Typical social norms thus answer Chapter 5's closing question about how context influences reciprocity. Furthermore, p-, c-, and e-types who understand TSN statements may anticipate the possibility of an r-type response. In relevant contexts, these players can infer possible sanctions for violation, and so find motivation to adhere to normative prescriptions. The presence of r-types thus enhances the social choreography of TSN in a manner that enhances prospects for resolving second-order CAPs.[45]

Chapter 5's CGT models indicated how r-types can discipline e-types into cooperating. Indeed, r-types apply such discipline to promote adherence to TSN that they have internalized. Here internalization motivates reciprocal response. In terms of IEGT models, adjusted versions of equations (8.3)–(8.6) can indicate fitness outcomes for various pairings of e-, c-, and r-types. For e- and c-type matches, e-types are ESS and c-types are not. For r- and c-type matches, both are evolutionarily neutral strategies. For r- and e-type matches, e-types will cooperate if ψ_r is large enough to motivate r-types to punish nonadherents and sanctions are large enough to induce e-type compliance. More complicated models that incorporate three types of players can generate polymorphic mixes of r-types, c-types, and e-types.[46]

Finally, TSN can motivate social enforcement over large groups. Because norms convey information and cognitive frameworks that do not rely on small-group familiarity, adherents of norms can apply *ADIC* statements and associated reciprocal responses to complete strangers. Citizens of a specific country, say, Sri Lanka, can often quickly identify other nationals among strangers—and thereby interpret certain behaviors in light of relevant norms. Likewise, the motivational, informational, and cognitive content of social norms exhibits longevity that small-group reciprocal relationships simply lack. Norms can outlive both individuals and social groupings and persist across generations—as in the case of greeting by shaking hands.

For all of these reasons, the social choreography of norms can resolve CAPs that lie well beyond the capacities of small reciprocal groups. Even so, TSN enforcement faces limits imposed by requirements of social coherence within relevant groups. For a final perspective on norms and reciprocity, we consider reciprocity itself as an important type of norm.

Reciprocity as a Social Norm

Reciprocal behavior is ubiquitous in social life. It involves exchanges ranging from greetings to transfers of goods and services, along with myriad forms of trading favors or reprisal. Such exchanges occur among friends, colleagues, acquaintances, and even strangers. Chapter 5 treated reciprocity as an intrinsic quality that gains strength with repeated contact. The present chapter has discussed reciprocal responses to norm adherence and violation. Extending both lines of logic, and accounting for the prevalence, endurance, and universality of reciprocal responses, we now treat a basic reciprocal prescription to reward kind and punish unkind behavior as a common type of social norm (Ψ_R). Norms of reciprocity appear in most societies (Ostrom 1998a). They offer broadly applicable *ADIC* statements that facilitate the creation of trust among parties to various social, political, and economic exchanges. Norms of reciprocity thus choreograph resolution of CAPs within small or large social groups and even between or among them.

To represent Ψ_R game-theoretically, we can utilize Chapter 5's models of intrinsic reciprocity, with the caveat that ethical obligations of reciprocity may even apply to complete strangers. Furthermore, as TSN, reciprocity norms provide conceptual frameworks for distinguishing ostensibly kind from unkind behavior in specific social contexts—and thereby motivate reciprocal response. In terms of the *ADIC* statements, a Ψ_R specifies the following:

- Attributes (*A*): relevant agents are identifiable participants in some type of exchange. Criteria for inclusion may be broad (almost everyone exchanges smiles or waves) or quite narrow (as with secret cult handshakes).

- Deontic (D): as for any TSN, abiding by Ψ_R is a social obligation.
- Aim or prescribed action (I): behave in a reciprocal fashion.
- Condition (C): reciprocal exchanges are expected in some contexts but not in others. Applicable contexts may be quite restrictive and may interact with A-statements. Sorority sisters, for example, may be expected to trade invitations to social engagements that involve sorority members but not invitations to other engagements.

Relating these statements to types of actors, a reciprocity norm Ψ_R instructs relevant agents to act like r-types who—in relevant circumstances—conditionally cooperate, reward kind acts through mutual cooperation, and willingly punish unkind acts with similar acts and/or social or material punishments. Note that, within abiding groups, reciprocity norms may instruct adherents to punish violators of other norms, say, Ψ_C, because not contributing to a public good may violate Ψ_R.[47] Reciprocity norms can likewise inform agents that reciprocal behavior from others is likely.

More specifically, Ostrom (1998a, 10) identifies five basic strategies that adherents use to apply Ψ_R to specific interactions:

(i) Identify participants in relevant exchanges.

(ii) Assess the likelihood that others will conditionally cooperate (act like c- or r-types).

(iii) Decide to cooperate initially if others can be trusted to do so.

(iv) Refuse to cooperate with those who do not reciprocate cooperation.

(v) Be willing to punish those who betray one's trust in cooperative behavior.

A shared understanding that others will likely employ these strategies facilitates cooperation.[48]

Reciprocity norms are a particularly important mechanism for resolving CAPs, though they may also be a source of conflict. Because repeated interaction over time is not a prerequisite for normative reciprocal response, Ψ_R can apply to very large groups and can even transcend group boundaries. Individual strangers from different social groups may act reciprocally regarding exchanges of greetings or small favors. Different groups, even nations, may also act reciprocally by trading favors. On the other hand, a perceived failure by some person or group to reciprocate kindness or shared sacrifice may become a source of conflict. If one party punishes another for failing to adhere to a Ψ_R, increasing mutual hostility may accompany successive rounds of reciprocal punishment. International relations offers many examples of both positive and negative reciprocity among nations, some of which reflect either adherence to or violation of understood norms of international behavior (Keohane 1984).

Finally, norms of reciprocity frame and motivate many forms of social learning. Agents perform tentative experiments with initial small acts of reciprocity as a means for identifying conditional cooperators and reciprocal players: small tests that can identify Ψ_R adherents in relevant social contexts. Reciprocal norms create cognitive frameworks for classifying various behaviors and, by extension, individuals. Identifiably reciprocal players often appear trustworthy: other players expect them to cooperate in relevant circumstances. Sorority members, for example, may trust their sisters to help with class assignments even when grades are competitive. Alternatively, reciprocal hostility may offer lessons in mutual distrust. Norms of reciprocity, then, serve as a critical social mechanism or correlating device for resolving CAPs within and between multiple social groups of various types and sizes, but they also generate conflict.

8.4. RATIONALITY-LIMITING NORMS

By ruling out certain extreme forms of defection, rationality-limiting norms (RLN) contribute to resolving second-order CAPs and so enhance prospects for beneficial exchange and economic development within adherent groups. Even so, RLN also create "normative loopholes" (Basu 2000) that may render adherents vulnerable to exploitation by nonadherents.

Recall that adherents to an RLN have internalized its prescriptions so completely that they do not even consider actions that would violate it. They will always abide in relevant contexts; enforcement is automatic. Basu's rural Indian woman always wears sari clothing. Lest the reader doubt the prevalence of RLN, consider the following. In principle, people could lie, cheat, steal, bribe, extort, destroy property, yell, spit, hit, shoot, or murder on many occasions—yet they do not even consider such strategies. Basu observes:

> So economics, which is based so much on optimization over sets of alternatives, would have very little foundation if we really tried to start from *all* the things a person can do. In reality, the "set" from which a person chooses is, in the end, quite a restricted set for a variety of reasons but one of the most important is norms. (2000, 94)

We may use an evolutionary framework based on Basu (2000, 93–101) to explain the emergence and persistence of RLN. Consider a set S of all feasible strategies relevant to a particular encounter among agents in group G. An RLN $\Psi_{\sim T}$ effectively removes some feasible strategies (T; such as Western attire) from the set (S; clothing) that is considered by specific agents (Basu's rural Indian woman). Relevant agents end up choosing from the smaller set $S - T$ (various colors and styles of saris). At a given point in time, a population has inherited such RLN through various processes of cultural transmission, such as child rearing and education. Alternative norms (mutations) may enter via the cumulative impacts of nonconformity, experimentation, misinterpretation, or in-migration of outsiders.

To model RLN selection, suppose that agents in population G possess a set of technically feasible strategies S, but RLN $\Psi_{\sim Q}$ limits the effective choice set to the (nonempty) subset $S - Q$. Consider a mutant RLN, $\Psi_{\sim Z}$, that limits the considered alternatives to subset $S - Z$. Suppose that most members of G adhere to $\Psi_{\sim Q}$ and only a few adhere to $\Psi_{\sim Z}$. Agents of either persuasion encounter each other randomly. Such agents play game $\Gamma(Q, Z)$, where this notation specifies players' strategy sets in terms of their respective adherence to $\Psi_{\sim Q}$ or $\Psi_{\sim Z}$. Perhaps they engage in trade using different prescriptions. For example, adherents of $\Psi_{\sim Q}$, unlike adherents of $\Psi_{\sim Z}$, may never consider stealing. We say that $\Psi_{\sim Q}$ is an *evolutionary stable norm* (ESN) if it is immune to invasion from all feasible alternative RLN that could arise in its environment. Relative to $\Psi_{\sim Z}$, norm $\Psi_{\sim Q}$ is an ESN if

$$(8.10) \qquad\qquad N(\Psi_{\sim Q}, \Psi_{\sim Q}) > N(\Psi_{\sim Q}, \Psi_{\sim Z}) \text{ or}$$

$$(8.11) \qquad N(\Psi_{\sim Q}, \Psi_{\sim Q}) = N(\Psi_{\sim Q}, \Psi_{\sim Z}) \text{ and } N(\Psi_{\sim Q}, \Psi_{\sim Z}) \geq N(\Psi_{\sim Z}, \Psi_{\sim Z}).$$

Here $N(\Psi_{\sim Q}, \Psi_{\sim Z})$ signifies the Nash equilibrium payoff from game $\Gamma(Q, Z)$ awarded to an adherent of $\Psi_{\sim Q}$ who encounters an adherent of $\Psi_{\sim Z}$.[49] Other terms have analogous interpretations. Note, however, that an evolutionary stable RLN is not immutable; like other norms, it is a punctuated equilibrium. Changing circumstances can induce contemplation of previously inconceivable alternatives: previously nonexistent or nonviable alternatives could invade. Urban Indian women often wear non-sari clothing.

To more precisely model the emergence of an RLN, consider a *sophisticated* PD game (SPD game). This game augments a typical PD game with a third strategy: A = abstain. Figure 8.7 illustrates. If either player chooses A, both earn zero. For example, a business person who does not trust a potential trading partner might abstain; no trade occurs. Accordingly, in Figure 8.7, the NE occur at strategy combinations (A, A), (D, A), and (A, D), signifying no trade and no development in all three cases. Furthermore, one can show that none of the three listed strategies is an ESS.[50]

Nevertheless, there is an ESN for Figure 8.7. Consider RLN $\Psi_{\sim D}$, which restricts the choice set to {A, C}. If group G follows $\Psi_{\sim D}$, each of its members will earn a payoff of 1 for every encounter; whereas allowing consideration of D generates NE payoffs of 0 to all. Counterintuitively, then, an RLN that restricts the choice set of agents can enhance their payoffs.

Figure 8.8 (based on Basu 2000, Fig. 4.4) lists all possible RLN that could apply to this game. Adherents of $\Psi_{\sim C}$ consider only set {A, D}; adherents of $\Psi_{\sim A}$ consider only {C, D}; adherents of $\Psi_{\sim CD}$ consider only {A}, and so forth. Agents match randomly in pairs. Suppose that the pertinent RLN for all players are common knowledge. All know that adherents of $\Psi_{\sim D}$ ($\Psi_{\sim D}$-types) do not consider defecting, et cetera. A $\Psi_{\sim D}$-type would then expect $\Psi_{\sim C}$-, $\Psi_{\sim A}$-, $\Psi_{\sim AC}$-, and Ψ-types to defect, and so would choose A in matches with them.[51] Applying this logic, the cells in Figure 8.8 denote the NE payoffs to agent Ellen for the associated matches with Fred, accounting for all possible RLN for each player. For example, if Ellen adheres to $\Psi_{\sim A}$ and Fred adheres to $\Psi_{\sim D}$, they play a variant of the game in Figure 8.7

		Fred		
		A	C	D
Ellen	A	0, 0	0, 0	0, 0
	C	0, 0	1, 1	−2, 2
	D	0, 0	2, −2	−1, −1

Figure 8.7   Two-player sophisticated PD

Fred

	$\Psi_{\sim CD}$	$\Psi_{\sim AC}$	$\Psi_{\sim AD}$	$\Psi_{\sim C}$	$\Psi_{\sim D}$	$\Psi_{\sim A}$	Ψ
$\Psi_{\sim CD}$	0	0	0	0	0	0	0
$\Psi_{\sim AC}$	0	−1	2	0	0	−1	0
$\Psi_{\sim AD}$	0	−2	1	−2	1	−2	−2
$\Psi_{\sim C}$	0	0	2	0	0	0	0
$\Psi_{\sim D}$	0	0	1	0	1	0	0
$\Psi_{\sim A}$	0	−1	2	0	0	−1	0
Ψ	0	0	2	0	0	0	0

Ellen (label to the left of the rows)

Figure 8.8 Alternative RLN
SOURCE: K. Basu (2000), *Prelude to Political Economy: A Study of the Social and Political Foundations of Economics*, Oxford: Oxford University Press. Reprinted with permission.
NOTE: Cells show payoffs to Ellen.

in which she rules out A and he rules out D. Knowing that Ellen will defect, Fred abstains and both earn 0.[52]

By incorporating Figure 8.8's payoffs into equation (8.10), we see that $\Psi_{\sim D}$ is immune to invasion from all other RLN except for $\Psi_{\sim AD}$ (look down the column headed by $\Psi_{\sim D}$). That result in itself is interesting: only an RLN that rules out contemplation of both D and A does equally well. By substituting the relevant payoffs into equation (8.11), we see that a $\Psi_{\sim D}$ matched with $\Psi_{\sim AD}$ does as well as $\Psi_{\sim AD}$ matched with itself (all earn 1). Thus $\Psi_{\sim D}$ is immune to invasion by any of the listed alternative RLN: the RLN that rules out contemplating defection is an ESN.

Relating this argument to CAPs, social groups that effectively preclude consideration of various forms of defection (e.g., murder) can more readily resolve CAPs and may thus exhibit greater fitness than other groups. This is an example of group selection.[53] Rationality-limiting norms that resolve CAPs can exhibit adaptive fitness by generating relatively high average material payoffs for their boundedly rational adherents. Indeed, the fact that economists so rarely model extreme forms of defection—such as murdering business partners—testifies to the strength of various RLN and their role in addressing CAPs whose resolution is essential for economic development.

On the other hand, the example of the Incas' encounter with Spanish conquistador Pizarro indicates that RLN may confer enormous disadvantages in certain intercultural encounters. Moreover, changes in condition or context can undermine RLN functionality. Rationality-limiting norms sometimes create "normative loopholes" (Basu 2000, 95)— failures to consider potentially relevant strategies. Along these lines, Basu argues that European colonialists exploited the normative loopholes of various indigenous populations in Latin America, India, and elsewhere.

8.5. SOCIAL NORMS AND IDENTITY

So far, this chapter has established that social norms can profoundly influence individual and group behavior—including various approaches to exchange and resolving CAPs—by signaling prescriptions that choreograph cognition, information, and motivation. An important element of such choreography is the tendency for individuals to internalize ethical normative prescriptions. Such internalization reflects the impact of norms on endogenous preferences. At a deep level, people who internalize social norms often identify with their prescriptions; they tend to adopt such prescriptions as behavioral standards by which they judge their own performance. Identity theory then links internalized norms to endogenous preference formation and, more profoundly, to the cognition of self. Notably, identity theory sheds light on how self-concepts related to gender, ethnic, racial, national, religious, and other cultural attributes can affect interactions within or between communities and organizations. Not surprisingly, identity concepts can both facilitate and impede resolution of CAPs.

Akerlof and Kranton (2005, 2010) relate their concept of *identity* to a person's self-image, which largely reflects pertinent social categories and norms to which that person subscribes. People use their concepts of identity to differentiate themselves from others (Akerlof and Kranton 2000). Self-image, in turn, influences preferences; usually people prefer activity that affirms their perceptions of who they are. Identity, moreover, is a fundamentally social concept; the responses of others to one's actions and attributes strongly influence one's self-image. Accordingly, identities are somewhat chosen and somewhat conditioned or externally imposed. For example, many students may begin to identify with their chosen major or field of study. On the other hand, society conditions and sometimes imposes identities associated with fundamental social categories such as ethnicity, race, and gender.[54] Akerlof and Kranton argue that choices of identity (like other decisions) need not imply conscious deliberation: "People may just try and fit in; they may simply feel more or less comfortable in different situations" (2010, 23).

Identity is a type of mental model that shapes preferences. It addresses individual conceptions of self in relation to others, and then applies such conceptions to desired behavior. Internalized social norms link such self-concept to motivation. These norms indicate how individuals believe they should behave, establishing internalized standards of behavior. In other words, people tend to identify with behavior prescribed by norms they believe in. When individuals follow such prescriptions, they abide by their own conceptions of appropriate behavior—and so affirm their self-concept, their identity. Violating internalized norms has the reverse effect. Furthermore, in relevant contexts, individuals often apply the same behavioral standards to others who share certain characteristics, such as age, religion, gender, ethnicity, occupation, or political affiliation. Unfortunately, violation of pertinent standards by others, particularly close associates, may compromise one's identity concept.[55]

Citing four years of research by Lipsky (2003, 145–54), Akerlof and Kranton (2005, 9) illustrate their identity concept with the following example. New recruits arriving at the US Military Academy at West Point undergo a process of identity transformation. On the first day (called R-day), recruits (plebes) have their heads shaved. They are stripped to their underwear and then put into uniform. They must stand straight and salute over and over until they master every detail perfectly, in the process suffering criticism for every miniscule mistake. According to Lipsky: "On R-day you surrender your old self in stages." The first day initiates a process of "re-engineering . . . so that West Point graduates emerge four years later as loyal officers in the U.S. Army" (Akerlof and Kranton 2005, 9).

Following Akerlof and Kranton, we model the effects of identity by incorporating identity payoffs into agents' utility functions. The associated payoffs respond to actions, context, social categories, and social norms. This approach augments our prior analysis in the following ways:

- Identity terms specify how social norms influence endogenous preferences.
- Over long-term time horizons, identity can shape the evolution of preference orientation—for example, proclivities toward reciprocity.
- Identity indicates a specific type of externality whereby actions of one person affect another's identity payoffs. Some, for example, may be offended by openly gay behavior; others may find it self-affirming.
- Identity externalities can explain certain forms of cooperation and conflict: complementary identities within groups may facilitate resolution of otherwise intractable CAPs, yet disjoint identities within or between groups can initiate or intensify conflict.
- Identity informs our understanding of organizational loyalty; identification with organizational goals plays an important role in resolving organizational CAPs.

To model identity, we begin with a utility function. Broadly speaking, utility depends upon chosen actions and returns to identity:

$$(8.12) \qquad u_i = u_i(a_i, a_{-i}, I_i) = u_i(a_i(\pi, I_i), a_{-i}(\pi, I_{-i}); I_i).$$

Here a_i and a_{-i} denote the actions chosen respectively by agent i and all (relevant) others, and I_i signifies agent i's identity. Actions (undertaken elements of strategies) influence utility payoffs in the manners discussed previously; we could fit them into relevant games. Note, however, that decisions on actions (or, more broadly, strategies) now reflect consideration of identity payoffs, in addition to material payoffs (π). Identity payoffs (I_i) depend on the extent to which one's actions are consistent with one's identity concept.[56]

More precisely, identity payoffs respond to one's own actions, actions of others, relevant social categories, and prescriptions from internalized social norms. Accordingly, we specify an identity function as

$$(8.13) \qquad I_i = I_i(a_i, a_{-i}, C_i, \varepsilon_i, \Psi),$$

where C_i denotes individual i's conception of social categories to which she and others belong. In terms of Section 8.2's discussion, "social categories" are knowledge partitions that serve as classification operators in mental models. These categories can be socially assigned (as for ethnicity) or chosen (as for identifying with a fraternity), or a mix of both. Because social categories often confer degrees of status or lack thereof, individuals may either gain or lose identity utility by simply belonging to specific categories. The next term, ε_i, indicates one's own characteristics: physical, such as tall or short, and dispositional, such as shy or aggressive. The term Ψ indicates applicable internalized norms (TSN) with accompanying

ADIC statements—indicating context- and attribute-specific deontic prescriptions. Note that the attribute (A) statements can refer to both social categories C_i and individual characteristics ε_i. Thus a TSN Ψ utilizes (or invokes) equation (8.13)'s C_i and ε_i terms as elements of prescriptions that influence identity.

Overall, identity payoffs from (8.13) reflect the following: interactions between one's own activity and that of others; applicable social categories; one's own characteristics; and attribute- and context-specific deontic normative prescriptions for oneself and for others. Individuals gain utility when they follow internalized normative prescriptions, thus affirming their identity. Likewise, violating internalized normative prescriptions diminishes identity utility via a sense of impropriety. As in Section 8.1, violating a TSN can prompt feelings of guilt; here, however, guilt accompanies one's violation of behavioral standards that underlie one's own self-concept. A person who has internalized norms against theft, but nonetheless shoplifts some particularly tempting item, may not only feel guilty but also quite out-of-place. On this foundation, we turn to examining external identity effects.

Identity Externalities and Conflicts

The activities of one person may either support or challenge (reaffirm or diminish) the identity concepts of those with whom she or he interacts. These effects are *identity externalities*. Unfortunately, negative identity externalities often create individual or group discomfort or conflict. Interactions between gender and occupation at the workplace offer many examples. Such discomfort may help explain a few (admittedly extreme) examples of gender-occupation correlation. In 2011, 91.1% of registered nurses and 95.9% of secretaries and administrative assistants were women, whereas 95.6% of machinists and 97.5% of highway maintenance workers were men (US Bureau of Labor Statistics 2011). Akerlof and Kranton observe: "Women lose utility from working in a man's job. And men lose utility from working in a woman's job. Men also lose utility when a woman works in a man's job" (2010, 87).

Sociologist Irene Padavic worked as a coal handler. After a short time on the job, her male co-workers "picked her up bodily, tossed her back and forth, and attempted to push her onto the coal conveyor belt. The men said it was just a joke" (Akerlof and Kranton 2010, 86).[57] One might conclude that a woman's presence on the job threatened her colleagues' male identity. Akerlof and Kranton also report that *Male Nursing Magazine* advocates for men in a female-dominated occupation (2010, 83).

To illustrate how identity-based interactions can generate externalities, we borrow an identity model from Akerlof and Kranton (2000). We apply this two-player, two-identity, two-activity model to workers Burt and Mary. Assume two jobs: job 1 is construction work and job 2 is secretarial work. Identity M (man) incorporates norm Ψ_M, which prescribes that men and only men should work in job 1. Identity W (woman) incorporates norm Ψ_W, which prescribes that women should work in job 2. Burt identifies as M and prefers job 1. Mary identifies as W, but she also prefers job 1. Referring to Section 8.3's levels of internalization, Burt strongly internalizes Ψ_M, whereas Mary's internalization of Ψ_W is weak or intermediate. Mary has a lingering, but not necessarily strong, feeling that, as a woman, she should do "woman's work," but construction would be more interesting or fun.

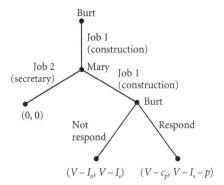

Figure 8.9 Gender/occupational identity game

SOURCE: G. Akerlof and R. Kranton (2000), "Economics and Identity," *Quarterly Journal of Economics* 115(3), 715–52.

Figure 8.9 illustrates the game. Burt moves first, choosing job 1. Mary then chooses 1 or 2, and Burt either responds or does not. As shown, payoffs to job 2 are 0 for both players, and both receive utility V from job 1. The term I_s denotes Mary's identity loss from not following Ψ_W if she chooses job 1, and I_o shows Burt's loss of identity if Mary violates Ψ_M by working in a "man's job." Because Burt has strongly internalized Ψ_M, Mary would compromise his manhood if she, too, works in construction. Burt could respond by administering punishment (p) to Mary, at cost c_p. This act would restore his identity loss ($I_o = 0$). Mary would then experience being punished and lose $-p$.

This game generates four possible equilibrium outcomes. Which of these applies depends on the relative strengths of identity payoffs, traditional utility payoffs, the cost of being sanctioned, and the cost of sanctioning. We find:

(i) If $c_p < I_o$ and $I_s < V < I_s + p$, Burt would respond and Mary chooses secretarial work.

(ii) If $c_p < I_o$ and $I_s + p < V$, Burt would respond but not deter Mary from choosing construction.

(iii) If $c_p > I_o$ and $I_s < V$, Burt does not respond and Mary chooses construction.

(iv) If $I_s > V$, Mary chooses secretarial work regardless of Burt's response. In this case, she has strongly internalized Ψ_W.[58]

Notice that identity payoffs alter the outcome of the game in cases (i), (ii), and (iv)—but not (iii). In cases (i) and (ii), the identity externalities experienced by Burt influence his behavior, but in (iii) these externalities influence his net utility without affecting his behavior.

This model could apply to a wide variety of situations where violating norms threatens or compromises identity. Men or women could be offended by "non-male" or "non-female" behavior from other men or women; members of various ethnic or cultural groups may be offended by those who do not adhere to certain customs; members of political or ideological groups may be offended by others who are more willing to compromise with adversaries; and so forth.

This model also indicates a policy dilemma regarding intervention in identity conflicts: it is extremely difficult for policymakers to intervene on behalf of one side of identity conflicts without harming the other. Authorities could try to protect Mary from Burt by penalizing him for responding, but such action would always hurt Burt: if he reprimands Mary, he faces the cost of external sanction; if he does not, he faces identity loss I_o. At a community level, third-party enforcers who could intervene on behalf of disadvantaged minorities or subgroups within self-governing groups face the same problem: if identity externalities are involved, one cannot protect the disadvantaged without harming the advantaged—at least initially. Moreover, such intervention may challenge firmly held identities that could emerge from norms of autonomy. Amartya Sen (1970) refers to essentially the same dilemma as the "impossibility of a Paretian liberal": in circumstances where individual preference orderings respond differently to externalities, social value and individual liberty conflict.[59]

More broadly, the concept of identity can inform our understanding of intercultural interactions. Members of a dominant culture with one set of normative prescriptions may expect adherence from members of subcultures who subscribe to alternative prescriptions. Alternatively, members of dominant groups may try to exclude subgroup members from certain activities. Race relations in the United States offer many examples of both phenomena. In either case, members of minority or disadvantaged groups are likely to feel identity conflict concerning which set of prescriptions to follow. Journalist Jill Nelson reports:

> I've also been doing the standard Negro balancing act when it comes to dealing with white folks, which involves sufficiently blurring the edges of my being so that they don't feel intimidated, while simultaneously holding on to my integrity. There is a thin line between Uncle-Tomming and Mau-Mauing. To fall off that line can mean disaster. On one side lies employment and self-hatred; on the other, the equally dubious honor of unemployment with integrity. (1993, 10)[60]

We now use identity concepts to outline a simplified model, based on Akerlof and Kranton (2000, 2010), that can illustrate social exclusion. Consider an insider group with identity (I) and norm Ψ_I and an outsider group with identity (O) and norm Ψ_O. Group distinctions may arise from nationality, ethnicity, race, religion, gender, and so forth. Suppose that norm Ψ_I specifies mainstream work—with dominant cultural attitudes and appearance—but norm Ψ_O specifies a distinct and possibly oppositional cultural identity. Now assume two activities: mainstream employment (E) generates relatively high income; alternative activity (A)—such as informal-sector work, crime, or unemployment—generates relatively low income and perhaps poverty.[61] Members of outsider communities face the following set of choices:

- Choose identity I, follow Ψ_I, and earn high income—but face rejection from some insiders for not fitting idealized appearance and/or cultural attitudes of Ψ_I.[62]

- Choose identity O and pursue activity E. Earn high income—but face identity loss from violating Ψ_O.

- Choose identity O, pursue activity A, and earn low income or face unemployment—but without identity loss.

The model's identity payoffs can explain apparently irrational behavior by members of disadvantaged groups, such as confining oneself to poverty by eschewing mainstream training or work.[63] Along these lines, identity theory can explain observations made by William Julius Wilson of a shift away from market employment in US inner-city neighborhoods as manufacturing employment and real wages for low-skilled workers have declined over several decades. Wilson notes that, in the 1950s, inner-city ghettos were poor, but employment rates were high (1996, esp. 52–55). Thus the lower real wages of the recent period may not sufficiently compensate for identity conflicts that accompany mainstream employment.

On a larger scale, identity externalities can generate conflicts between communities or internal subgroups either who follow different norms or who interpret similar norms and prescriptions differently. For example, in sixteenth-century Europe, followers of Martin Luther, John Calvin, Huldrych Zwingli, and the Catholic Church identified with differing interpretations of Christian norms so intensely that multiple religious wars ensued (Dunn 1970).

Overall, negative identity externalities indicate a deep source of potential conflict, one that resides in individual conceptions of self. Positive identity externalities, on the other hand, can help resolve CAPs by fostering unity. We now turn to that topic.

Identity, Loyalty, and Resolving Organizational CAPs

Norm internalization can help resolve otherwise intractable CAPs. The tendency of internalizers to identify with normative prescriptions facilitates resolution because identification can shift preferences toward prosocial behavior. Organizations provide important arenas within which such dynamics operate. Self-identification with normative prescriptions that embody or complement organizational goals can engender loyalty—in this case, a sentiment of attachment to the relevant organization. Ensuing identity payoffs may then reduce the costs or increase the benefits of achieving cooperation among an organization's members or constituents.

Many organizational CAPs take the form of principal-agent problems: managers, employees, or members are expected to undertake difficult-to-monitor tasks that may conflict with their interests. Akerlof and Kranton (2005) develop a model that incorporates identity payoffs into the principal-agent problem of eliciting quality worker effort. Recall from Chapter 3 that, whenever effort is costly to provide and hard to observe, employers face an effort-enforcement problem. Now consider a work environment in which groups of workers may subscribe to two possible identities: insiders (I) share the goals of the firm and outsiders (O) do not. We have the following worker's utility function:

(8.14) $$U(y, e; \Psi_e, I_c) = \ln y - e + uI_c - t_c |\Psi_e(I_c) - e|.$$

The first two terms on the right-hand side indicate that workers gain utility from income (y) and lose utility from effort (e). In the third term, $I_c \in \{I, O\}$ indicates the worker's identity category, and uI_c denotes the utility gained or lost from belonging to category I_c. The fourth term shows the impact of normative prescriptions on utility. It multiplies parameter t_c by the absolute value of the difference between the effort norm prescribed for category $I_c(\Psi_e(I_c))$ and the individual's actual effort e. When $I_c = $ I, workers share the firm's goals, leading to a high norm $\Psi_e(I_c) = \Psi_{eH}$. Conversely, when $I_c = $ O, $\Psi_e(I_c) = \Psi_{eL}$ (low effort). Workers whose own effort (e) differs (in either direction) from that prescribed suffer the indicated utility loss.

This model implies that firms may enhance worker productivity by devoting resources to creating or enhancing identity I among workgroups. Firms might, for example, provide good working conditions and allow workers to participate in decisions that affect their work.[64] Ensuing loyalty could increase effort norms and reduce monitoring costs. Such loyalty-induced norms may also allow firms to pay lower wages than would otherwise be required. In contrast, the alternative mechanism of explicit incentive pay may even crowd out employee loyalty, as workers may identify strict incentive pay with employer mistrust.[65] Similarly, employers may find loose supervision to be more efficient than strict supervision because the latter can foster outsider identity and reciprocal resentment.[66] Firms may then face a tradeoff between more predictable results from close supervision weighed against greater loyalty from less restrictive supervision. Generally speaking, creating worker loyalty is most important for complex tasks, such as surgery, where monitoring is difficult and modest lapses in diligence are costly. Nevertheless, most US employees appear to identify at least somewhat with the goals of their employer (Akerlof and Kranton 2010, 51).

More generally, organizations can improve their operations by encouraging managers, employees, and members to identify with organizational goals. As suggested by the West Point example, the military invests considerable resources into creating loyal identification with its goals and personnel, particularly within units.[67] Likewise, in civilian endeavors, gain sharing and participation in decision making can foster cooperation and organizational loyalty.

Overall, identity theory informs resolution of CAPs in two key manners. First, negative identity externalities can create or exacerbate myriad potential conflicts within or between communities, groups, and organizations. Understanding the origins of such conflicts may help to resolve them. Second, the close relationship between developing loyalty to an organization or community and identifying with its goals implies that organizational (or community) investments in creating identity can harness the power of norm internalization toward the resolution of otherwise difficult internal CAPs.

8.6. CONCLUSION

Informal institutions choreograph social activity via their influence on cognition, information, and motivation. In terms of epistemic game theory, they transmit shared information and cognitive frameworks that shape agents' knowledge partitions, possibility operators, and subjective priors. By correlating understandings across individuals or groups, informal institutions similarly influence motivation, often in prosocial directions—social choreography.

Coordinating conventions, such as class schedules or the practice of driving on one side of the road, shape individual expectations concerning others' behavior in situations where desirable outcomes rely on coordination among participants. By conveying mutually understood AIC statements, conventions select among multiple potentially self-enforcing combinations of actions to focus attention on a single equilibrium set: everyone shows up at 9:00, not 9:35. Individuals follow established conventions because failing to do so would be costly. Although modern society would not exist without such conventions, most social interactions do not lend themselves to choreography via coordination alone.

Social norms cast a wider net. Unlike conventions, typical social norms constitute behavioral prescriptions with ethical content: $ADIC$ statements of social obligation. By invoking ethically motivated internalization along with social enforcement, TSN choreograph interactions that lie beyond the reach of conventions and that extend across large groups. More precisely, game-theoretic modeling of norm internalization offers three basic results. First, cohesive communities with strongly internalized norms can achieve mutual cooperation, but they may be vulnerable to free-riding by nonadherents. Moreover, such free-riding may compromise the long-run fitness of strong internalization (as a type of preference orientation), and may even undermine associated norms. Second, models that incorporate conformity or solidarity effects generate path-dependent punctuated equilibria of either full adherence or nonadherence. Third, introducing reciprocal actors creates avenues for social enforcement that can discipline nonadherents. Indeed, we may illustrate relationships between norms and reciprocity in two fashions: (i) adherence to or violation of specific norms, such as cooperative norms (Ψ_C), may arouse reciprocal response or sanction; and (ii) reciprocity is itself a widely applicable norm (Ψ_R) that transcends specific groups. By signaling $ADIC$ prescriptions that shape understandings and influence preferences, TSN may thus achieve large- and sometimes inter-group social choreography for resolving CAPs. Yet disagreements over norm adherence may generate conflict.

Two related conceptions address how norms often convey deeper cognitive influences. First, rationality-limiting norms are so ingrained that adherents do not even consider alternatives to their prescriptions. Within sufficiently cohesive communities, RLN may resolve CAPs by simply eliminating contemplation of specific defection strategies. On the other hand, RLN may leave groups vulnerable to exploitation by others—as the Incas discovered in their encounters with Spanish conquistadors.

Second, internalized norms shape both cognition and preference by influencing conceptions of identity. Indeed, identity theory suggests cognitive and motivational foundations of endogenous preference formation. Over time, normative prescriptions shape the self-concepts of faithful adherents: their identities. Identities, in turn, serve as mental models that relate self to others by interpreting relationships between actions and idealized behavioral categories—using degrees of adherence to internalized norms as a key criterion for evaluation. Because agents gain or lose utility according to the correspondence between behavior and identity concepts, identity offers a fundamental channel through which norms choreograph social interaction. Thus a sense of loyalty that arises from identification with organizations or communities can facilitate resolution of internal CAPs. Yet conflicting identities or expectations regarding adherence to identity-related prescriptions may engender divisive conflict.

Overall, informal institutions—and especially norms—operate at the core of the social fabric that underlies multiple social, political, and economic exchanges. Informal institutions shape individual and group motivation, provide critical information, and establish cognitive frameworks that tend to correlate understandings and behavior. As social choreographers, conventions and especially norms facilitate resolution of otherwise intractable CAPs, and yet also sow the seeds of social conflict.

In the next chapter, we turn to the operation of community self-governance: internal (or second-party) regulation that relies critically on informal conventions, norms, and social rules.

EXERCISES

8.1. Describe the institutional syntax of coordinating conventions, typical social norms, and rationality-limiting norms.

8.2. Show that the expected payoffs for the correlated equilibrium outcome (as described) for the game in Figure 8.2 are the combination $(3, 3)$.

8.3. Develop an epistemic assurance game representation of the emotional coordination game shown in Figure 5.2.

8.4. Show why weak internalization does not alter the PD structure that the game in Figure 8.5a would have using only its material payoffs.

8.5. Design a multi-player game model that reflects intermediate internalization case (i) (see page 180) among all p-types. Explain the logic of the basic equations, and relate your model to the concept of path dependence.

8.6. (Advanced) Demonstrate the point about errors and punctuated evolutionary equilibria made in note 33.

8.7. Demonstrate the points made in the first bullet on page 182.

8.8. Show that in a p-type versus e-type match where the p-type has either intermediate (ii) or strong internalization, the e-type is the only ESS.

8.9. (Advanced) Design an IEGT model with two (or three) variants of p-types mixing with e-types.

8.10. In Figure 8.5b, replace the p-type with a c-type (adjusting payoffs accordingly) and show the two results for c-type encounters with e-types discussed on page 185.

8.11. (Advanced) Use an IEGT model—like that of equations (8.3) and (8.4) and Figure 8.6—to illustrate results similar to those in Exercise 8.10.

8.12. Rewrite each line of equation (8.2) as $C(n)$ and $D(n)$ functions, where the former shows the payoff to r-types from adherence, and the latter shows their payoff from violation. Discuss the implications of your equations on reciprocity and norm enforcement.

8.13. (Advanced) Develop one or more IEGT models that can incorporate three player types (r-, c-, and e-types) as discussed in Section 8.3.

8.14. (Advanced) Model the adherence to and violation of Ψ_R by using equations and figures from Chapter 5, along with elements from your answer to Exercise 8.12.

8.15. Prove that none of the three strategies shown in Figure 8.7 is an ESS.

8.16. In Figure 8.8, explain the payoffs in four of the cells that are not explained in the text (choose any four).

8.17. Demonstrate the relations shown in cases (i)–(iv) on page 194.

8.18. (Advanced) Using the logic of Section 8.5's discussion of social exclusion as a guide, develop a game-theoretic model.

9 INTERNAL RESOLUTION VIA GROUP SELF-ORGANIZATION

> On occasion there are attempts to make rural communities minirepublics in certain spheres of life.
>
> Partha Dasgupta (2000)

Suppose that the farmers of Boratonia understand their water-use CAP. They know that if all farmers use as much water as they would like, they will jointly deplete their wells. They recognize that because water is a rival good, one person's use diminishes that available to others. They also understand that short-term individual material incentives unambiguously push farmers in the direction of overuse. In fact, the rivalry over the resource may encourage greater overuse, in fear that others will get the water first.[1] Perhaps while traveling, farmers have observed some communities successfully create sustainable resource regimes, others try and fail, and still others live with the consequences of dysfunctional overuse. What would it take for Boratonian farmers to design, implement, and enforce a credible and sustainable mutual limitation agreement without recourse to external enforcers? Can their sentiments toward each other, their patterns of repeated interaction, their propensities to reciprocate, their social norms, and their ability to agree on and enforce limitation rules generate sufficient social cohesion to overcome individual temptations to cheat?

Nepali farmers who work and live near the Lothar and Rapti rivers have constructed an irrigation system that draws from both rivers. The system requires considerable maintenance, such as removing silt from a canal that crosses the floodplain. To ensure adequate labor, farmers created a system of rules. Each of about 300 farm owners must contribute one laborer to maintenance, regardless of the size of their land holdings. But 300 laborers are not enough. So they also recruit labor from landless tenant farmers, using additional rules to order exchanges. Before the dry season, a general assembly decides what percentage of the total land can be irrigated. All farmers must limit their irrigation to this percentage, with one exception: large landholders who rent land to landless farmers in exchange for maintenance labor may exceed the irrigation limit. Thus, using their knowledge of local environmental and social conditions, the famers have designed and enforced these rules (Laitos 1986; Lam 1998).

Sometimes groups like the Nepali farmers self-organize and successfully resolve CAPs internally; other times they fail. Extensive field research has documented both outcomes.[2] Because successful resolution does not arise automatically, social scientific and policy analysis should endeavor to distinguish conditions that facilitate resolution from those that do not. Current research indicates straightforward, though quite general, ingredients for success: establishing sufficient mutual trust to facilitate cooperative behavior based upon credible agreements, along with mutually understood and reliable mechanisms for coordination and enforcement. But the social dynamics that facilitate or impede such resolution are complicated.

Recall that Chapter 3 closed on a pessimistic note: asymmetric information hampers resolution of second-order CAPs because it diminishes or eliminates prospects for negotiating and implementing credible agreements to resolve first-order CAPs. Chapter 4 asserted that enforcing agreements involves exercises of power. Chapters 5–8 successively offered possible resolution mechanisms—including intrinsic reciprocity and other forms of social preference—along with conventions, social norms, and social rules as forms of shared mental models that coordinate (choreograph) beliefs and behavior among boundedly rational agents. Recall the distinction between second- and third-party enforcement. In the former, groups self-organize; they design and implement social mechanisms of coordination and enforcement. They engage in what we call *community self-governance.* For the latter, external parties, such as the police and legal system, provide enforcement and coordination. Furthermore, recall that the distinction between second and third parties depends on the level of analysis: for a local medical practice, the American Medical Association (AMA) is a third party, whereas for the medical profession as a whole, the AMA is a second-party enforcer.

We now focus on self-organization among groups—such as trade associations, farmers' cooperatives, workgroups, social organizations, and residential communities—that operate without recourse to third parties. Admittedly, such focus is an abstraction: in complex societies, all groups are embedded within a larger society that employs third-party enforcement, yielding implications on prospects for success or failure of second-party groups. Even so, separate analysis of self-governance informs our understanding of local CAPs, along with the context in which third-party enforcement operates.

Within any community or group, sufficient *prosocial behavior*—mutually beneficial cooperation or avoidance of potentially attractive defection opportunities—can resolve CAPs. Dasgupta (2011) attributes prosocial behavior to three sources: (i) mutual affection among members, which is often an outcome of close repeated interaction, such as that within families or tightly knit social groups; (ii) individual prosocial disposition, a possible outcome of reciprocal interactions and informal institutions that generate shared understandings that group members are, for the most part, trustworthy; and (iii) credible enforcement of various agreements and commitments.

This chapter asserts that successful self-organization fosters prosocial orientation among group members in specific contexts. With respect to resolving local CAPs, self-organization possesses substantial motivational, informational, and cognitive advantages over both market mechanisms and external regulation. Even so, the outcomes of self-organization are not always beneficial to all group members—or to larger society.

Our discussion proceeds as follows. Section 9.1 identifies social capital as a foundation for group self-organization. Social capital tends to promote relationships of trust, facilitating resolution of multiple CAPs. Section 9.2 develops two models of social capital formation. The first focuses on negotiating agreements that possess enough legitimacy to create some potential for resolving pertinent first-order CAPs. The second focuses on how conditional cooperation can lead to resolution of second-order CAPs. Section 9.3 then models a critical source of motivation for undertaking the effort of negotiation and coordinating enforcement: the claims participants have over the fruits of cooperative agreement. Section 9.4 expands upon the concept of community self-governance, discusses its advantages, and then identifies a set of conditions (or principles) that appear to influence the likelihood of successful self-organization. Section 9.5 addresses the—often quite substantial— internal and external problems that arise from isolated self-organization—the "dark side" of social capital and self-governance.[3] Section 9.6 concludes by asserting that a core dilemma for the political economy of development concerns balancing the enormous advantages and disadvantages of group self-governance.

9.1. GROUP SELF-ORGANIZATION, SECOND-PARTY ENFORCEMENT, AND SOCIAL CAPITAL

Elinor Ostrom (1990) poses the following question: Under what conditions can groups organize internally to overcome CAPs associated with limiting use of common-pool resources (CPRs) or, more generally, any CAP?[4] Doing so requires two steps: (1) negotiating agreements for resolving first-order CAPs that have enough legitimacy to offer a credible foundation for subsequent implementation, and (2) addressing second-order CAPs by establishing mutually understood and credible mechanisms of coordination and enforcement. For both steps, a group's success largely depends on its ability to develop a shared sense of trust that its members will usually negotiate responsibly and, subsequently, both honor and enforce ensuing commitments to their agreements. To do so, a group needs to develop shared understandings of the likely behavior of its members in relevant contexts vis-à-vis the costs and benefits of cooperation versus defection. They must incorporate such understandings into the negotiation of agreements and into the design and operation of social mechanisms of coordination and enforcement. Equivalently, the group needs to develop sufficient social capital to create mutual trust, and thus render cooperative commitments credible. We now discuss the concept of social capital.

For Robert Putnam, social capital consists of the "features of social organization such as trust, norms, and networks that can improve the efficiency of a society by facilitating coordinated actions" (1993, 167). For Ostrom (2000b, 176), social capital "is the shared knowledge, understandings, norms, rules, and expectations about patterns of interactions that groups of individuals bring to a recurrent activity." Dasgupta (2000) relates social capital to trust and mutual enforcement of commitments and, in a later work (2011), focuses on networks as the core community asset that creates trust and mutual enforcement.[5] Ostrom and Ahn (2009) emphasize three specific forms of social capital: trustworthiness, networks, and formal and informal institutions.

Relying primarily on Ostrom and Ahn (2009), with input from the others, we define *social capital* as the shared understandings and social mechanisms that foster mutual trust regarding commitments by individuals and groups to abide by cooperative agreements, with accompanying shared expectations of mutual coordination and enforcement. Each component of this definition requires explanation. *Shared understandings* include conceptions of the trustworthiness of relevant parties as well as shared perceptions that accompany relevant social mechanisms. *Social mechanisms* include reciprocal relationships, conventions, social norms, social rules, formal rules, and social networks. *Networks* are relationship links through which individuals communicate or interact, such as family, friendship, and collegiality.[6]

The concept of trustworthiness, and its distinction from the closely related concept of trust, requires further elaboration. As a rule, we trust people whom we regard as trustworthy—that is, worthy of our trust. *Trust* indicates an individual's own belief concerning the reliability of others' dispositions or motivations, while taking their possible actions into account. *Trustworthiness*, on the other hand, concerns a person's reputation: a shared understanding held among others concerning the degree to which she is disposed to honor commitments. For example, if Ann is trustworthy, Ben and Chris believe she is inclined to cooperate even when it may not be in her short-term self-interest to do so. In Chapter 6's terminology, Ann's trustworthiness is an element of Ben's and Chris' mental models that indicates their perceptions of Ann's social preferences (e.g., selfish versus other-regarding).

By contrast, *trust* reflects an individual's own beliefs concerning the dispositions and motivations of other people—specifically beliefs pertaining to others' unobservable current or future actions (or strategies) that could influence her own well-being or that of others she cares about. Ann *trusts* Ben when:

- Ben occupies a position from which he may undertake unobservable contemporaneous or future actions that could benefit or harm Ann or other people she cares about (Chris), possibly including Ben's future self; and
- Ann believes that Ben will undertake (or is undertaking) actions that, relative to his feasible alternatives, are beneficial to her or those she cares about.[7]

For example, I trust that my plumber will diligently fix the pipes under my sink, that my son and daughter will not drink too much at parties, that my students will do their homework, that my employer will pay me more or less fairly, that pharmaceutical firms will produce medicines that usually enhance my family's health, that the courts will, by and large, enforce the law, and so forth. I could be wrong about any of these beliefs. Trust involves more than consideration of possible actions; it frequently involves assessment of disposition, motives, and incentives (Dasgupta 2000). Accordingly, when I trust my plumber and the other parties listed, I believe that they possess the requisite disposition and sufficient motivation to undertake the indicated actions.[8] Indeed, I believe that they are trustworthy in the relevant contexts.

Trustworthiness is an element of social capital, whereas trust is a product of social capital. One agent's trustworthy reputation serves as an informational input into other parties' evaluations regarding the desirability of cooperating with that agent (Ostrom and Ahn 2009, 27). Ann cooperates with Ben if she finds him to be trustworthy; that is, if *she* trusts him. Trust follows trustworthiness. Trustworthiness is an informational asset: it reflects prior effort, and it signals potentially beneficial opportunities. In this regard, repeated interactions, along with accompanying social norms and social rules, generate incentives for parties to develop trustworthy (prosocial) reputations—that is, reputations for keeping promises and sacrificing short-term gains—in order to signal opportunities for mutually beneficial cooperation or exchange (Ostrom 1998a). Investments in trustworthiness reduce transaction costs by generating predictability.

Yet, because it resides in the perceptions of others, trustworthiness is a fundamentally social asset: it is a form of social capital that typically produces prosocial behavior. In a group or community, mutual reputations for trustworthiness produce mutual trust—beliefs that cooperation will be rewarded. Trust, then, is a product of—rather than an element of—social capital.[9] Arguably, trust is the most immediate and most important product of social capital.[10] Trust links social capital to CAPs: social capital generates trust, and trust facilitates resolution of CAPs (Ostrom and Ahn 2009).

To summarize, there are three basic elements or dimensions of social capital: (i) shared understandings of trustworthiness; (ii) mutually understood social mechanisms of coordination and enforcement (such as social norms); and (iii) accompanying social networks. All three elements are, as Putnam (1993) says, "features of social organizations." Social capital facilitates cooperation within and sometimes between or among organizations.[11] Social capital renders agreements to resolve first-order CAPs credible because it fosters development of generally acceptable agreements and establishes foundations for coordination and credible enforcement.

As a concept, social capital offers a unified approach to understanding community (or group) self-organization (Ostrom and Ahn 2009). In terms of this book, social capital bridges and extends concepts from Chapters 4–8. Because social capital facilitates enforcement, its existence implies power relationships (Chapter 4). Repeated reciprocal exchanges tend to generate mutual understandings of trustworthiness among small groups (Chapter 5). Heuristics and mental models of boundedly rational agents follow cues from social context and provide cognitive foundations for shared understandings (Chapter 6). Social norms motivate willing punishment of defectors among groups that extend well beyond reciprocal familiarity. Moreover, as shared mental models, norms coordinate or correlate preferences and understandings, facilitating predictable cooperative behavior among boundedly rational agents (Chapter 8). Finally, more or less deliberately constructed social rules enhance prospects for applying material sanctions to potential defectors—an arrangement that is often necessary to discipline selfish community members and to assure others that sufficient cooperation will, in fact, be forthcoming. For example, Nepali farmers who exceed their irrigation quotas face sanctions. Knowing this, farmers who limit their own use do not fear that others will squander the benefits of their efforts. Social capital encompasses all of these influences, and so unifies our approach to understanding the complex mechanisms through which groups or communities create the trust that facilitates resolving specific internal CAPs. Social capital underlies group self-organization. Before turning directly to self-organization, we elaborate on the properties of social capital.

Social capital (SK) resembles its physical and human capital counterparts in six respects, but differs in a seventh:

(i) Creating any form of capital involves some investment of money, material, or effort for some anticipated future benefit. Firms invest in plant and equipment, hoping for future profit. Individuals invest in acquiring skills, hoping to enhance future earnings or quality of life. Members of communities invest effort into constructing networks, shared understandings, and rules, hoping to bear the fruits of cooperation.

(ii) Investment in all three kinds of capital reflects deliberate decisions.[12]

(iii) Like the other two types of capital, SK takes on different forms or manifestations (rules, norms, networks). Similarly, physical capital may exist as infrastructure, buildings, or machines.

(iv) Like its physical and human counterparts, social capital usually enhances efficiency. It allows groups to more effectively utilize effort, physical capital, and human capital in cooperative endeavors. It enhances total factor productivity in creating collective goods.

(v) Like other forms of capital, SK creates some opportunities by foreclosing others (Ostrom 2000b). A machine for making airplane engines cannot make candy. A surgeon cannot practice law. Social norms and rules create opportunities for cooperation by limiting opportunities for defection.

(vi) Investment in any kind of capital involves risks of bad outcomes. Products may not sell. Educated individuals may not find work. Community relationships may generate internal or external conflicts.

(vii) In one important sense, however, social capital is unlike other forms of capital: it cannot be individually owned. It is a property of communities, social relationships, and networks (Bowles and Gintis 2002).[13]

Five additional properties of social capital merit discussion. First, SK is tacit knowledge, a "set of cognitive aptitudes and predispositions" that facilitates production (Stiglitz 2000, 60). Students, for example, may easily communicate using heuristics related to cell phones or the Internet. Second, SK may help community members interpret reputations, allowing them to distinguish reliable reputations from unreliable ones (Stiglitz 2000). Third, the network properties of SK can coordinate expectations across social groups. Agents often know how to behave in specific small groups, even though they typically belong to many different groups. Social capital serves as a "meta-organizing device" that orders the differing expectations of distinct groups (Stiglitz 2000). For example, students may know that wearing jeans is fine in class but not at work. Social capital thus provides social choreography that can resolve CAPs within or across small or large groups.

Fourth, unlike physical capital, but like human capital, social capital does not wear out with use; rather, it erodes with disuse. If social capital is not employed regularly, shared understandings fade. As group memberships evolve through attrition and in-migration, somebody needs to inform new members about shared understandings. Such understandings might be referred to as "institutional memory." For example, retiring officers of student organizations may post accounts of organizational histories and procedures on websites or wikis as a way of informing new members and officers. Such efforts are attempts to preserve and transmit organizational social capital. Furthermore, maintenance of social capital and associated enforcement and coordination mechanisms could be regarded as a third-order CAP.[14]

Finally, the construction and maintenance of social capital reflect both deliberate effort and more or less spontaneous outcomes of unplanned social interactions. Communities that successfully resolve CAPs rely on deliberate effort for creating and maintaining social mechanisms of cooperation, but many of the properties of these mechanisms emerge from informal social interaction (Ostrom 2000b).[15] Thus deliberate processes interact with unplanned responses, and so unavoidably create unintended consequences, even in small groups.

Overall, a group's possession of social capital reflects shared understandings that a sufficient, and usually sustainable, number of its members will cooperate in specific endeavors: they will behave in a prosocial manner. By promoting mutual trust, SK at least partially resolves second-order CAPs, facilitating resolution of accompanying first-order CAPs. Accordingly, social capital is "a social means of coping with moral hazard and incentive problems" (Stiglitz 2000, 59). For example, repeated relationships and common community membership with one's mechanic can assure that only legitimate problems receive attention.

Three caveats apply: First, as indicated, there is nothing automatic about generating sufficient SK to actually resolve CAPs. Second, nothing guarantees that the kind of social capital developed within a particular group will, in fact, resolve all relevant second- and first-order CAPs. As even a sporadic reading of the news indicates, partially dysfunctional groups and social arrangements survive in abundance. Third, even when it successfully resolves CAPs, social capital is not always beneficial to all group members or to larger society. Organized crime, for example, uses its own internal social capital to generate mutual trust that its members will not confess to the police—usually to the detriment of the rest of society, and sometimes of even the members themselves (particularly those who are sanctioned for confessing).

With this foundation, we now turn to modeling how the creation of social capital can lead to cooperative outcomes.

9.2. MODELS OF ATTAINING COOPERATION

Broadly speaking, creating functional social capital involves two steps: (i) designing legitimate agreements on how to share the costs and benefits of resolving first-order CAPs (or "pre-commitments"; Ostrom 2000b; see also Ostrom and Gardner 1993); and (ii) establishing credible mechanisms of coordination and enforcement—that is, resolving associated second-order CAPs. This section models these two processes in order. The first model combines elements of public-good and common-pool resource problems. The second focuses on public goods, but it could readily be applied to CPRs as well.

Recall Chapter 2's discussion of public goods. The two-player PD game in Figure 2.1 and the multi-player game of equation (2.2) both depict core divergences between self-interest and group benefit—with Nash equilibria at full defection. Note, however, that while all players have incentives to avoid contributing to public goods, distributional conflicts do not affect the (nonrival) use of already existing (pure) public goods. For CPRs, on the other hand, rivalry can lead to distributional conflict.[16]

We now offer a general model of a CPR problem. Consider a community of N individuals (say, farmers), each with an endowment q_i. Each farmer may invest q_i in one or both of two activities as follows: (1) devote amount $0 \leq x_i \leq q_i$ to a CPR-using activity, such as growing crops that require irrigation water; and (2) devote the remaining amount, $q_i - x_i$, to alternative production—growing crops with rainfall. Because x_i is rival, its return depends on total community use $(\sum x_i)$ according to production function $F(\sum x_i)$. Here $F'(0) > 0$, indicating that, starting from no use, small amounts of use generate positive marginal returns. But $F'(Nx_i) < 0$, indicating that the total (desired) resource use by all community members generates negative returns at the margin. By contrast, sole reliance on rainfall always earns per unit return w. A farmer's return to combined activities then is

$$(9.1) \qquad \pi_i = \frac{x_i}{\sum x_i}\left(F\left(\sum x_i\right)\right) + (q_i - x_i)w.$$

The first term denotes the return to use of the resource (activity 1)—each agent's share of total production, summed over $i = 1, \ldots, N$ farmers. The second term shows the return to activity 2. Here total resource use at the Nash equilibrium exceeds the social optimum.[17] Thus each individual has an incentive to overuse the resource system at a cost to the group as a whole, indicating a first-order CAP that includes distributional conflict.

Here are a few categories of problems that this model could represent:

- For rural areas: problems associated with grazing, soil or land conservation, or those arising from use of inland or coastal fisheries, rivers, and forests.
- For urban areas: crime, local pollution, use of transportation systems, use of public facilities such as parks, and use of public services such as courts.
- Within firms or organizations: use of internal administrative or technical support services (Dur and Roelfsema 2010) or managerial time (Penrose 1959).
- For larger areas, such as nations: the above problems plus air and water pollution, and perhaps macroeconomic stability in times of speculation or deep recession.
- For groups of nations: limited resources for enforcing treaties or discouraging conflict (e.g., UN resources).
- Globally: depletion of stratospheric ozone, reduction of biodiversity, climate change.

We now develop two models that illustrate complementary aspects of creating the social capital and ensuing trust that fosters cooperative behavior in social dilemmas. The first model, from Ostrom (2000b), represents bargaining over the distribution of costs and benefits that accompany producing, maintaining, and limiting use of an at least partially manufactured resource, such as a common irrigation system. She calls such an agreement a *pre-commitment*, a first step. Actual implementation requires that any such agreement be generally acceptable to relevant parties; it needs to be legitimate.[18] Subsequently, farmers must resolve second-order CAPs of creating mechanisms for coordination and enforcement; else pre-commitments will lack credibility. Accordingly, the second model—based on Isaac, Walker, and Williams (1994)—offers a dynamic representation of generating credible commitment by establishing conditional cooperation, with possible sanction. Each model reflects different aspects of creating social capital.

Ostrom's Model of a Bargaining Agreement

Ostrom's (2000b) pre-commitment model reflects field research, reported in Ostrom (1992) and Lam (1998), concerning self-governance of common irrigation systems in many parts of the world. Some of these systems have survived for hundreds of years, an astonishing success for efforts at self-organization. In particular, Ostrom and Lam each report on how Nepali farmers have addressed CAPs related to constructing and maintaining sustainable irrigation systems. These farmers have confronted three types of first-order CAPs:

(i) Constructing their irrigation system: a first-order CAP of providing a public good.

(ii) Maintaining existing irrigation systems: another first-order public-good CAP, though one that arises only after the preceding problem has been addressed.

(iii) Limiting use: Because unregulated water use would compromise group productivity, communities need to limit water removal by farmers, particularly those situated at the upstream end of the system; this is a CPR-specific CAP with location-based distributional elements.

Ostrom's model represents the process of negotiating agreements to overcome these kinds of first-order CAPs. More specifically, she models bargaining over the content of rules that allocate the various costs and benefits of construction, maintenance, and limiting use. Participants, whose interests differ, face multiple options; yet they must agree on specific courses of action. In order to establish enough legitimacy to succeed, negotiations must include relevant parties, and agreements must somehow reflect environmental conditions—along with the social, economic, and political positions of relevant agents, and some of their objectives. Legitimate agreements then constitute a form of social capital that facilitates resolving CAPs.

To proceed with the model, assume that farmers have sufficiently stable land tenure to foresee long-term net benefits from investment in irrigation, and that they engage in repeated, reciprocal, face-to-face relationships. To facilitate cooperation on a possible irrigation project, such relationships must lead to a set of shared understandings (shared mental models) concerning the following factors:

• farmers' incentives related to both cooperation and defection, including incentives generated by pertinent enforcement mechanisms;

• the types of individuals with whom they will interact—specifically, as regards a willingness to abide by stated commitments;

- alternative ways of structuring their relationship; and
- an at least partial focus on rulemaking, as opposed to a sole focus on day-to-day operations (Ostrom 2000b).

Mutual understandings that meet these conditions can motivate efforts to design, and then implement, a set of requisite rules. Upon this possibly fragile basis, farmers might construct a set of rules that could generate shared expectations of mutual cooperation. By agreeing on such a set of rules, farmers then signal a pre-commitment to abide by them.[19] Subsequent actions that accord with these rules usually ratify and reinforce such pre-commitments, whereas nonabiding behavior tends to undermine them.

Now suppose that sufficient access to an established irrigation system would allow farmers to grow three crops, whereas sole reliance on rainfall allows only one. There are two teams of farmers: team A farms along branch X of a possible irrigation project, and team B farms along branch Y. Each team acts as a unit; internal reciprocity has resolved each team's in-house CAPs. Specific irrigation rules govern the between-team allocation of either total costs (C-rules) or total benefits (B-rules). Each team can propose one rule of each type from various possibilities. An agreement on both types of rules indicates a pre-commitment to the project.

Suppose further that contribution costs depend only on how many laborers a team supplies to the project. Team A can offer up to 10 laborers to the project and team B can offer up to 5. Consider the following possible rules:

RB1: Irrigation water is split evenly.

RB2: Irrigation water is split on the basis of labor contribution.

RC1: Each team contributes five laborers to the project.

RC2: Each team contributes all available laborers to the project.

If both teams follow material self-interest, team B will propose combination RB1 & RC2. Team A's rule preference, however, depends on the marginal returns to labor contribution. If such returns are diminishing, it will propose RB1 & RC1; but if they are increasing, it will propose RB2 & RC2. Note that the impact of each B-rule depends on the C-rule with which it is combined.[20]

For a (standard) case of diminishing returns, Figure 9.1 illustrates the strategic interaction between the two teams as a game of battle. Both teams gain from agreement, but each prefers one type of agreement. We could then use a Nash bargaining model—reflecting the distribution of power1 between the two parties (see Figure 4.1)—to indicate a compromise

		Team B	
		RB1 & RC1	RB1 & RC2
Team A	RB1 & RC1	2, 1	0, 0
	RB1 & RC2	0, 0	1, 2

Figure 9.1 Pre-commitment game

outcome. We could complicate these models by adding social payoffs or strategic moves (power2; see Section 4.2) or by adding more possible rules.

If the teams have unequal access to irrigation water, their terms of the agreement will usually reflect such asymmetry. Assume that team A occupies a position upstream of team B. If A uses its desired amount of water, it can grow four crops, leaving B with only enough water to grow two crops. Asymmetric rivalry intensifies the conflict over allocation rules: team A has a greater incentive to overuse and B prefers greater limits.[21] Team A prefers rules that allow it to take all the water it wants—which A might refer to as "liberty"—whereas team B prefers rules that restrict A's use—which B might call "justice."[22] Moreover, location confers a power1 bargaining advantage to A.

Team A's advantage diminishes, however, to the extent that it depends on team B's labor to construct or maintain the project.[23] Now suppose that construction costs depend on the distance of A's farms from an initial water source (e.g., a spring) and that there are three possible distances: close, intermediate, and far. We call the associated costs of constructing an irrigation system that brings water to A (respectively) low, medium, and high. Now assume two possible rule packages:

RBC3: Team A takes as much water as it wants, and both teams' labor contributions are voluntary.

RBC4: Team A can only take half of the water, leaving half for team B, and each team contributes five laborers.

Let the benefit of irrigation = 100; and let low cost = 25, medium cost = 50, and high cost = 75. In a case of low costs, team A prefers RBC3 and team B prefers RBC4; thus we have a battle game like that shown in Figure 9.1. Since team A has a power1 bargaining advantage, something close to RBC3 is the likely outcome. With medium costs, however, team A needs B's labor and the teams reverse preferences: now A prefers RBC4 and B prefers RBC3. Team A's power1 advantage diminishes, as team B can "credibly assert that the extra water is not worth the contribution" (Ostrom 2000b, 191). So the teams agree to terms that are closer to B's preference than in the prior case. Finally, in the high-cost case, team A depends even more on B's labor and does not even consider RBC3 (a worse outcome than its fall-back). Hence RB4 is the unique equilibrium outcome, indicating that enlisting team B's labor will require team A to give B half of the water. Table 9.1 summarizes these outcomes. Note that if we were to allow additional rules in the last case, team B might use its power1 advantage to bargain for more than half of the water or less than half of the labor.[24]

TABLE 9.1
Irrigation construction costs and bargaining outcomes

Cost	Team A prefers	Team B prefers	A's need for B's labor	Bargaining advantage	Outcome
Low	RBC3	RBC4	Low	A	RBC3 (approx.)
Medium	RBC4	RBC3	Medium	Unclear	Intermediate
High	RBC4	RBC4	High	B	RBC4

More generally, community members—whose interests typically differ somewhat—could, in principle, construct many different rules to address their CPR problems. Unfortunately, there is no guarantee that negotiation over allocating costs and benefits will succeed in generating any agreement, much less a credible pre-commitment. To achieve enough legitimacy for credibility, such agreements must reflect two principles: (1) a procedural principle whereby affected parties must participate in the negotiation process; and (2) an outcome-based principle whereby the emergent agreement must somehow reflect pertinent desires and positional asymmetries (locational, social, etc.) among negotiating parties, as well as pertinent environmental conditions (e.g., annual rainfall).

When resource users succeed in negotiating credible pre-commitments, they create a type of social capital. They have devoted effort to producing a common understanding of future group interactions that, if honored, can enhance the productivity of physical and human capital. Citing Lam (1998), Ostrom (2000b) states that the actual rules used in 150 Nepali irrigation systems follow this model's predictions concerning the impact of locational advantages on the distribution of costs and benefits. Furthermore, Lam argues that externally managed (as opposed to farmer-managed) irrigation systems in Nepal often fail because they tend to undermine such locally developed social capital. We will return to this point in Chapter 10.

Even a legitimate pre-commitment to resolve a first-order CAP cannot, however, stand alone. To succeed, it needs social mechanisms of coordination and enforcement, a second type of social capital that focuses on resolution of second-order CAPs.[25] Our next model addresses how sequential conditional cooperation can foster such resolution.

A Model of Adaptive, Conditional Cooperation

Repeated reciprocal interactions can set in motion a virtuous social feedback mechanism—one in which reciprocity fosters trustworthy reputations that, in turn, engender mutual trust, as well as a willingness to sanction defectors: prosocial behavior. In such processes, trustworthy agents seek others with similar reputations in order to conduct beneficial reciprocal exchanges. Successful exchanges then encourage repetition, thus building reciprocal relationships with involved parties that tend to confer trustworthy reputations. Such investments in establishing trustworthy reputations thereby generate mutual trust that others will abide by norms of reciprocity (Ostrom 1998a). In this manner, boundedly rational agents learn patterns of reciprocity (heuristics). Over time, these patterns find group expression as norms of reciprocity that prescribe mutual reciprocal cooperation with social sanction for defectors. Isaac, Walker, and Williams (1994) present a model that illustrates this kind of prosocial learning process, along with accompanying mechanisms for mutual enforcement.

As background, recall that, in a sequential classical game-theoretic (CGT) model, agents use *backwards induction*. In other words, they envision likely responses in the final stage of a multi-stage game. Using that projection, agents make a similar projection for the next-to-last stage and repeat this process back to the initial (or present) stage. These projections inform each agent's first-stage best response. It is well known that, in a finite sequential prisoners' dilemma game of complete information—one that could represent a standard public-good contribution problem—the backwards-induction Nash equilibrium is for all players to defect. Nevertheless, volumes of experimental and field studies indicate substantial degrees of cooperation.[26]

Unlike CGT models, a bounded rationality framework suggests trial-and-error learning. Using their mental models, agents engage in forward-looking experimentation (hypothesis testing) rather than CGT backwards induction. The model developed by Isaac, Walker, and Williams (1994) illustrates how agents may engage in adaptive, forward-looking conditional cooperation. By anticipating short-term responses from others, agents develop expectations concerning the gains from their own contributions to cooperative endeavors.[27] The following discussion adapts the Isaac, Walker, and Williams model to the present context and notation.

We assume a repeated multi-player public-good contribution game of finite duration. This game may apply to a wide variety of local public goods, ranging from recreational opportunities in urban neighborhoods to constructing (but not using) irrigation facilities. It can also apply to "goods" of a less concrete nature, such as inducing cooperation in designing social mechanisms (constructing institutions) that could, for example, foster sustainable use of resources, such as fisheries. This model might even offer insight into the difficulties of arranging international cooperation on such issues as disarmament, currency unions, trade negotiations, and climate change.

Recall that equation (2.2) models a one-shot, multi-player, public-good contribution game. Adding a time subscript to represent the impact of current contributions, we have

$$(9.2) \qquad y_{it+1} = q_{it} - c_{it} + \alpha \sum_{j=1}^{N} c_{jt},$$

where i denotes any member of the group N, $j = 1, \ldots, N$ (including i); t signifies the current time period; y is income; q is endowment; α is the marginal product from each unit contributed; and $\alpha < 1 < \alpha N$, indicating that the game has a PD structure. With backwards induction, we would find the Nash equilibrium for the final time period (T) at $c_{iT} = 0$, for all i. In the next-to-last stage, players would draw the same conclusion (no contribution). Continuing logically backwards to period t, they contribute nothing.

Instead, we assume that some portion m of players ($m \in (0, 1]$) are *adaptive conditional cooperators* (ACCs) who use the following logic:

1. An ACC believes that a contribution $c_{it} \in [0, q_{it}]$ will signal conditional cooperation (or lack thereof) to other players.

2. Each ACC uses a benchmark earnings level of subsequent contributions by others (described below) for measuring the success of its own contribution signal c_{it}.

3. At every stage of the game, each ACC develops a subjective probability function (a subjective prior) for evaluating the likely success of its signal.

For simplicity, we assume no discounting and apply the success criterion to only one period in the future (the next period). Thus, in period t, ACC player i evaluates the likely success in period $t + 1$ of currently allocating amount c_{it} to the public good.[28] Following Isaac, Walker, and Williams (1994), we now specify a simple (and admittedly ad hoc) success criterion that illustrates the core logic of adaptive conditional cooperation. Assume that ACC player i's period-t contribution (c_{it}) conveys a signal that generates a (possibly reciprocal) response from others in period $t + 1$. This signal is *successful* if i's next-period earnings (y_{it+1}) indicate that free-riding by others has not reduced his income. More precisely, for c_{it} to be a success, y_{it+1} must be at least as large as i's initial endowment: $y_{it+1}(c_{it}) \geq q_{it}$.[29]

To show the ACC logic more precisely, let $C^*_{jt+1}(c_{it})$ represent the exact sum of contributions from the $N - 1$ other players ($\Sigma c_{jt+1}; j \neq i$), in response to i's contribution c_{it}, that would indicate no loss from free-riding by others: $C^*_{jt+1}(c_{it}) \rightarrow y_{it+1}(c_{it}) = q_{it}$. Level C^*_{jt+1} thus specifies the threshold amount of induced contribution (from the $N - 1$ other players) that i's contribution signal c_{it} must cross in order to be successful.[30] Substituting this threshold into equation (9.2) yields

$$(9.3) \qquad y_{it+1} = (q_{it} - c_{it}) + \alpha[c_{it} + C^*_{jt+1}(c_{it})] = q_{it}.$$

Solving for $C^*_{jt+1}(c_{it})$, we find that

$$(9.4) \qquad C^*_{jt+1}(c_{it}) = \frac{c_{it}(1-\alpha)}{\alpha}.$$

Equation (9.4) has several implications. First, note that an increase in the marginal product to contribution (α) lowers threshold C^*, increasing the likelihood that player i's signal will succeed. Assuming a sufficient number of more or less similarly inclined ACCs, overall contribution $C_t = \Sigma_{i=1}^{N} c_{it}$ increases in α. Although this outcome appears intuitively sensible, it violates backwards-induction reasoning, under which the zero-contribution outcome is independent of α (except in the extreme case where $\alpha > 1$). Isaac and Walker (1988) and Isaac, Walker, and Williams (1994) report experimental evidence of precisely this effect of α on aggregate contribution.

Second, this model suggests a possible exception to Mancur Olson's (1971) principle concerning advantages of small groups in generating cooperation. To see this, consider the average size of contribution among the $N - 1$ other players at threshold C^*:

$$(9.5) \qquad \frac{C^*_{jt+1}(c_{it})}{N-1} = \frac{c_{it}(1-\alpha)}{\alpha(N-1)}.$$

Examining the right-hand side, we see (perhaps surprisingly) that, for a constant α, an increase in group size reduces the average contribution (from each of the $N - 1$ other players) needed to achieve the C^* threshold. Thus, with a constant marginal product to contribution (i.e., a linear production function) and a sufficient proportion of ACC players ($m > m_{min}$), the likelihood of contribution increases in group size (N). The experimental evidence presented by Isaac, Walker, and Williams (1994) suggests that these conditions can be met in relatively straightforward public-good contribution games.[31]

Additional specification of equation (9.5), however, allows for a more general model. The marginal return to contribution α need not be constant; we could instead write a function $\alpha = \alpha(nc)$. In particular, suppose that after some total contribution level nc_h, the public-good production function exhibits diminishing marginal returns (for $nc > nc_h$, $\alpha''(nc) < 0$). After this point, given that $\alpha < 1$, $\partial y/\partial n < 1$ and $\partial y/\partial c < 1$, the average contribution threshold $C^*/(N-1)$ increases in N, rendering cooperation more difficult. The intuition goes as follows: if there are diminishing returns to additional contributions, a larger group needs higher average contributions to generate success; thus threshold $C^*/(N-1)$ increases in group size N.[32] Now assume a public-good production function for which diminishing returns start to set in above some large group size N_L. As long as $m > m_{min}$, increasing group size up to N_L correspondingly increases the probability of resolution; but for $N > N_L$, this probability decreases in group size. Accordingly, we may say that, for small and medium-sized groups (with sufficient proportions of ACC agents), adding members makes resolution easier; but the reverse holds for large groups.[33]

We complete the model by discussing the subjective probability functions of ACCs in order to indicate how context-specific variables influence probabilities of success (point 3 on page 213). Adaptive conditional cooperators evaluate the subjective probability of successful contribution at each stage of the game. Let $\rho_s = \rho_s(c_{it} \mid \Omega_{it})$ indicate player i's subjective estimation of the conditional probability that its contribution (signal) c_{it} will cross the C^* threshold (an example of a subjective prior). Here Ω_{it} represents a vector of contextual (or state) variables as perceived by player i at time t. More precisely, Ω_{it} represents the following elements: variables α, n, and N; the relevant environmental and institutional context, including social norms; observed prior moves of other players (known history of the game); and player i's perception of others' characteristics and dispositions. For example, a social norm of reciprocity (Ψ_R) could promote ACC behavior by generating a shared expectation of mutual adherence. Success probabilities ρ_s would then increase. The norm Ψ_R thus offers a signal that tends to correlate behavior toward contribution (social choreography).

On the surface, it may appear that the ACC model has addressed enforcement only in the sense of conditional cooperation, a type of strategic reciprocity (see Section 5.2). Chapters 5 and 8, however, indicated that intrinsic reciprocity and norms of reciprocity can generate more stringent internal enforcement, arising from the willingness of reciprocal players to sanction unfair behavior or violation of norms. To model reciprocal punishment, we could incorporate the sanctioning terms from equations (5.8) and (5.9) into Ω, augmented with a probability of observing defection. Equation (9.5) could then reflect mutual understandings of both a group's willingness to sanction defectors and the sanctions themselves.[34] This equation would then represent how forward-looking reciprocal behavior can generate a social mechanism for resolving second-order CAPs associated with the provision of public goods.

To summarize, both the Ostrom model and that of Isaac, Walker, and Williams illustrate complementary approaches to conceptualizing the development of social capital. Ostrom's model stresses how bargaining processes among participants or teams can lead to mutual agreements that serve as legitimate pre-commitments to resolve first-order CAPs. The Isaac, Walker, and Williams model offers a forward-looking approach to developing reciprocal trust among boundedly rational agents that can then serve as a foundation for resolving second-order CAPs of coordination and enforcement. Effective group self-organization requires success in both of these endeavors: pre-commitments must be legitimate, and enforcement mechanisms must be credible. The motivation that underlies efforts to resolve these problems, in turn, usually depends on the extent to which group members share the gains of cooperation or, equivalently, the degree to which they have claim to such benefits. We now turn to that topic.

9.3. RESIDUAL CLAIMANCY, TEAM PRODUCTION, AND THE MOTIVATION FOR EFFECTIVE SELF-GOVERNANCE

Having discussed the idea of self-governance, and noting that not all groups successfully resolve CAPs, we now address an important method for motivating contributions to resolution. Our core assertion is that individuals typically need to receive at least some material gain from their efforts to produce substantive collective goods—in addition to whatever social tradeoffs they face. Residual claimancy offers a key (typically formal) mechanism for transferring net material gains from joint production to individuals. A *residual claimant*, as its name suggests, is an agent who possesses a claim over the net value (the residual) of some joint production process. Thus, in a traditional capitalist enterprise, residual claimants are a firm's owners or shareholders: once all costs are paid, they claim the (positive or negative) profit—the residual. In employee-owned firms or profit-sharing firms, employees claim some portion of the residual.

Most production of goods and services involves teams. *Team production* signifies any productive activity in which the marginal product of one agent depends on that of others (Alchian and Demsetz 1972). If we assume that effort induces some kind of reward, each team member's effort creates positive externalities for others. As with any positive externality, inducing a socially optimal amount presents a first-order CAP—in this case, free-riding on others' effort. To compound the problem, because output is produced jointly, it may be difficult or impossible to detect actual levels of individual contribution or shirking. Functional teams, then, need to create a mechanism that will motivate individual members to exert effort.[35]

Jeffrey Carpenter and coauthors (2009) develop a model of team production in which the ability to claim a portion of the jointly created residual motivates team members to address CAPs related to individual shirking. Residual claimancy, moreover, can foster cooperation in teams that are larger than Chapter 5's reciprocal groups. Note that these principles apply not only to the production of private goods and services by most firms, but also to the provision of most public goods. Coase (1937), Williamson (1985), and others discuss how capitalist firms design hierarchical command structures (social mechanisms) that reduce transaction costs by resolving organizational CAPs—usually designating owners or shareholders as residual claimants.[36] In terms of Chapters 3 and 4, owners or managers exert power1 and power2 over employees in order to induce needed effort and cooperation, and such coordination reduces transaction costs. An analogous mechanism for provision of public goods could involve similarly hierarchical government production or a government mandate to coordinate private-sector activities.[37]

As Ostrom (1998a), Bowles and Gintis (2002), and others argue, community (group) governance offers an alternative to either market or government mechanisms. Applications of the Carpenter et al. (2009) model include the following types of relationships: community governance, team production activities within enterprises (work teams, management teams, or worker management), and group production of multiple public goods. Any of these activities—especially the latter—may involve negotiation of pre-commitments and the design of enforcement mechanisms for resolving second-order CAPs related to CPRs or public goods.

With this background, we turn to the model. Our initial assumptions are as follows:

- Coordinated production activity among team members generates a surplus.
- Team size is moderate: between 100 and 10,000 members.[38]
- Information on individual effort is not fully observable or verifiable; thus contracts are incomplete.
- A large portion of team members are reciprocal players (r-types) who conditionally cooperate and willingly punish defectors.
- Team members are the residual claimants of any surplus from team effort.

On this basis, we develop an equation that specifies the material return to a team member's contribution of productive effort. Such effort (like other positive externalities) has attributes of a public good: it is costly to provide, and each individual benefits from the efforts of others. With equal sharing of output, each member's material payoff to providing effort in team production (π_i) can be represented as

$$(9.6) \qquad \pi_i = q(1 - \bar{\sigma}) - \frac{(1 - \sigma_i)^2}{2}.$$

Here q is technical productivity (output per unit effort); σ is the portion of production time spent shirking; $0 \leq \sigma \leq 1$; and $\bar{\sigma}$ is average team shirking (hence $(1 - \bar{\sigma})$ is average effort).[39] The first term on the right-hand side indicates the average output each team member would receive by free-riding—namely, the product of others' effort.[40] The second term reflects the steadily increasing individual cost of exerting effort (the cost of not shirking). With pure material payoffs and no reciprocity, the Nash equilibrium for this multi-player game would be $\sigma = 1$ (full shirking), yielding $\pi_i = 0$: another first-order CAP of free-riding. Yet team production occurs.

In this model, a combination of residual claimancy, intrinsic (or strong) reciprocity, concern for one's standing in the team, and group norms of reciprocal contribution jointly resolve the second-order CAP of making cooperative agreements credible. Because team members share the residual, shirking by any individual inflicts costs on all other team members. Specifically, each member's loss from another's shirking is $\beta = q/N$, where N is the number of team members. In this context, any r-type who contributes at least the group's average effort $(1 - \bar{\sigma})$ resents any greater-than-average shirking by another team member (j) because shirking reduces the shared residual in a manner that indicates free-riding. Correspondingly, team members develop a social norm of acceptable contribution (Ψ_C), which prescribes that "responsible" team members should contribute at least the average team effort $(1 - \overline{\sigma})$.

As in Chapter 8, r-types resent violation of Ψ_C and willingly punish violators—even at some cost to themselves. Now assume that each team member i who adheres to Ψ_C can punish violator j by imposing a social or material punishment p_{ij} at personal cost $c_p(p_{ij})$. We assume that punishment levels p_{ij} cannot be specified by contract because, like effort, p_{ij} is nonverifiable.[41] Furthermore, the cost of punishment increases in the amount offered and is strictly convex $(c_p'(p_{ij}) > 0$ and $c_p''(p_{ij}) > 0)$.[42] Finally, assume that group member j's reputation (b_j) depends on the (net) cost that his shirking imposes on the team, in terms of lost residual. Specifically,

$$(9.7) \qquad\qquad b_j = \beta(1 - 2\sigma_j).$$

This specification indicates that full shirking $(\delta = 1)$ yields $b_j = -\beta$, so that the loss to j's reputation equals the cost his shirking imposes on one other team member. Conversely, with full effort $(\sigma = 0)$, (9.7) yields $b_j = \beta$; in this case, j gains reputation by an equivalent magnitude.

Now, allowing that each player's utility (u_i) depends on material payoffs (π_i), a reciprocal response to another's reputation (b_j), the cost of sanctioning others $(c_p(p_{ij}))$, and sanction received from others (p_{ji}), we have

$$(9.8) \qquad u_i = \pi_i(\sigma_i; \overline{\sigma}) + \sum_{j \neq i}^{N} \Big[\lambda_i b_j (\pi_j - p_{ij}) - c_p(p_{ij}) - p_{ji}(\sigma_i) \Big],$$

where π_i is i's material payoff from (9.6). The first term inside the brackets indicates i's intrinsic reciprocity payoff, the utility i gains or loses from the degree to which others contribute acceptable effort. Parameter $\lambda \geq 0$ shows the importance of reciprocity (or strength of reciprocal sentiment) to player i. The reputation term b_j, from (9.7), reflects i's perception of j's kindness.[43] The difference $(\pi_j - p_{ij})$ captures j's material payoff. If j has a "good" reputation $(b_j > 0)$, the product $\lambda b_j (\pi_j - p_{ij})$ indicates that, since j is acting responsibly, i gains utility if j does well. The reverse holds when $b_j < 0$. In this latter case, i can at least partially offset her utility loss by applying sanction $p_{ij} \leq \pi_j$. The next term $(-c_p(p_{ij}))$ indicates the cost to i of punishing j by amount p_{ij}. Comparing these two terms shows that, when j has a bad reputation $(b_j < 0)$, i can gain utility by sanctioning j, provided that the marginal cost of administering punishment is no higher than the marginal utility gain from punishing (taking derivatives: $c_p'(p_{ij}) \leq \lambda b_i = \lambda\beta(2\sigma_j - 1))$.[44] Finally, the third term in the brackets $(-p_{ji}(\sigma_i))$ represents i's loss from possible sanctions received from j; this term applies only if i has a bad reputation. Finally, the summation term before the brackets indicates that i experiences the same reaction to the effort/shirking of all other team members.

It can be shown that, under quite general conditions, the amount of sanction imposed on j (p_{ij}) increases in the strength of reciprocal sentiment (λ), j's shirking (σ_j), and the loss to others from shirking (β). Furthermore, the amount of sanction (p_{ij}) decreases in group size (N) (Carpenter et al. 2009, 4). From here, one can solve for i's optimal level of shirking, where the marginal benefit from shirking (lower effort) equals its marginal cost in terms of i's expected utility gain or loss from imposing costs on others, plus the impact of i's own shirking on the sanctions it receives from others (Carpenter et al. 2009, 235). At the Nash equilibrium,

$$(9.9) \qquad \sigma_i^* = 1 - \beta - \beta \sum_{j \neq i} \lambda_i b_j - p_i'(\sigma_i).$$

Thus one's level of shirking decreases in the harm it causes others $(-\beta)$, in the strength of interaction between reciprocity and reputation $(\lambda_i b_j)$, and in the marginal punishment induced by shirking $(p_i'(\sigma_i))$. Together, equations (9.8) and (9.9) show how a shared understanding of a general willingness to punish free-riders can contribute to resolving the team's second-order CAP of enforcing agreements to reduce shirking. Such understanding provides individuals an incentive to reduce shirking to a level that does not damage their reputations, and thereby facilitates resolving the team's first-order CAP of generating sufficient effort.

With this foundation, we can explain how residual claimancy motivates self-governance among teams, groups, and communities. Note that, in equation (9.7), reputation depends on the relationship between one's shirking (σ_i) and the cost it imposes on others or, equivalently, the benefit that effort confers on others (i.e., the positive externality from contributing to the shared residual)—reflected in the term β. We have seen that a bad reputation from too much shirking motivates reciprocal sanction. Note, however, that if the team had no claim to the residual of its joint effort (i.e., if $\beta = 0$), reputation would drop out of (9.8); b_j would equal 0. Hence the first term in brackets would vanish, as would the motivation for punishing shirkers. Because administering punishment is costly, nobody would sanction (i.e., $p_{ji}(\delta_j) = 0$ for all team members). Equation (9.9) would then yield $\sigma^* = 1$: full shirking. The group's claim to the residual of their joint effort therefore motivates the exercise of reciprocal sanction. Furthermore, this claim establishes the context in which the contribution norm Ψ_C operates: in its absence, everyone shirks, and it is OK to shirk. Resolution of second-order enforcement CAPs from team production thus relies on residual claimancy and, by extension, so does resolution of the associated first-order effort CAP.[45]

Again, this model can represent any scenario involving team production—a necessary condition for virtually all private and public production of goods and services, and even for the creation and maintenance of institutions. Furthermore, the ability of residual claimancy to motivate internal enforcement has implications for the operation of self-governance (this chapter), for relationships between second- and third-party enforcement (Chapter 10), for policy (Chapter 12), and for economic growth (Chapter 13). We now turn to a more complete discussion of the nature and advantages of group self-organization.

9.4. SECOND-PARTY ENFORCEMENT, COMMUNITY SELF-ORGANIZATION, AND SELF-GOVERNANCE

The primary advantage of community self-organization or self-governance is that it fosters the development and use of localized social capital. In so doing, it develops mechanisms for resolving localized CAPs that are largely inaccessible to other social arrangements—notably, market exchange based on individual ownership, and external governance (Ostrom 1998a; Bowles and Gintis 2002). Recall the three core elements of social capital: (i) mutual understanding of trustworthiness; (ii) social mechanisms, including conventions, social norms, and social rules; and (iii) social networks. Groups that possess sufficient social capital can harness trustworthy reputations, norms, and social rules for generating sufficient trust to permit or even encourage cooperation among parties whose interests differ. Such efforts may be interpreted as exercises in collective voice. Sometimes such self-governance operates (largely) independently of external authorities, at other times with their blessings, and still other times in opposition. This section discusses characteristics and advantages of community governance; Section 9.5 discusses disadvantages.

To the extent that communities at various levels (residential, work-related, etc.) can produce sufficient social capital to resolve internal CAPs, they engage in self-organization or self-governance. For example, Japanese Toyama Bay fishermen established a cooperative that addressed problems related to managing large variation in shrimp catches, maintenance costs, and technologically induced shifts in skill requirements. The co-op has pooled repair costs to boats and nets, trained new members, and shared information concerning the changing quality of shrimp fishing areas (Platteau and Seki 2001). The co-op's reciprocal relationships, internal negotiating procedures, rules, and enforcement mechanisms have generated confidence among its members that commitments to abide by agreements are usually honored—a form of self-governance. Similarly, plywood cooperatives in the Pacific Northwest utilize peer monitoring along with residual claimancy to resolve CAPs associated with operating efficient, self-governing, worker-managed firms (Pencavel 1992). At a less formal level, residents of specific Chicago neighborhoods monitor their own schoolchildren and verbally reprimand them for actions such as skipping school (Sampson, Raudenbush, and Earls 1997). Similarly, neighborhood groups in Seattle, Washington, have—via community organization and asset-based development, with assistance from the city government—successfully achieved a vast array of improvements (resolved CAPs related to providing collective goods), ranging from community "P-patches" and traffic improvements, like replacing a dilapidated bridge, to revitalizing entire neighborhoods and business districts (Diers 2004). This implicit conditional cooperation of residents constitutes another form of social capital offering an informal governance mechanism that resolves second-order CAPs regarding specific forms of local misbehavior.[46]

Community governance, like other forms of governance, involves designing, altering, and implementing three basic levels of rules: operational rules, collective-choice rules, and constitutional rules. *Operational rules*, as the name suggests, regulate day-to-day operations. For example, operational rules for irrigation projects might indicate how much water specific farmers may withdraw at specific times or who contributes how much labor to maintenance on what days. *Collective-choice rules* designate the mechanisms and procedures that create and alter operational rules, including how decision makers are chosen, the methods they use to make decisions (e.g., voting), as well as processes for resolving operation-related disputes. *Constitutional rules* designate the criteria that establish community membership (who does and does not belong), with corresponding rights and responsibilities; they also establish procedures that assign decision makers for collective-choice rules, procedures that formulate or alter collective-choice rules, and procedures for resolving disputes over collective-choice rules (Ostrom 1990, 2005).

In any governance system, a major function of economic institutions is to define and enforce property rights—usually by establishing rules. Self-governance of CPRs typically involves common property ownership—as distinct from either individual property ownership or complete nonownership (e.g., over the high seas or upper atmosphere; McKean 1992). Indeed, a simple dichotomy between individually based property rights and no property rights obscures the complexities of successful resource management.[47] In particular, it fails to address the central role of self-organization and social capital. Summarizing and interpreting extensive comparative field research, Poteete, Janssen, and Ostrom (2010, 95–96; citing Schlager and Ostrom 1992) indicate five basic types (or dimensions) of *property rights* relevant to CPRs:

1. *Access rights* concern rights to enter delineated (physical) resource boundaries. Because such rights define the community of users, these are constitutional rules.

2. *Withdrawal rights* concern the degree to which various parties who have access may use or withdraw from the resource—a type of operational rule.

The remaining three rights are types of collective-choice rules:

3. *Management rights* concern who has rights to manage withdrawal and conduct other resource activities such as extensions or improvements.

4. *Exclusion rights* concern determining access to nonmembers and whether or not such access can be transferred.

5. *Alienation rights* concern the ability of individuals or groups to sell or lease any of the above rights to other parties.

These rights are nested and lend themselves to categorization. Withdrawal requires access. Agents who possess rights 1 and 2 and no more are *authorized users. Claimants* may also manage (3), and *proprietors* may manage and exclude (4). Finally, *individual owners* have all five rights: they may sell or lease rights 1–4 to others.[48] Self-governance of common-pool resources, however, rarely involves individual ownership. *Community property rights* (forms of social or formal rules) assign various combinations of rights 1–4 to individual users, but not alienation rights (5).

As stated, self-governance employs elements of social capital: rules—including those that define and enforce property rights—social norms, other shared understandings that influence myriad interactions within communities, and supporting networks. Of these elements, rules are most subject to deliberate creation and revision. Rules are human artifacts, objects of design (usually by teams) that are intended to serve specific purposes (V. Ostrom 1980). Rules interact with social norms and shared expectations—elements of social capital that are far less subject to design. For this and other reasons, the outcomes of rule design often deviate from designers' intentions. Generally speaking, the effectiveness of given institutional configurations for resolving CAPs, such as those associated with CPRs, depends on their ability to accomplish the following goals:

- Generate shared understandings of the benefits to cooperation and how to achieve it.
- Generate trust that cooperative agreements will be honored and that defections will (usually) be detected and punished.
- Possess enough flexibility to respond to changes in the environment—technological, social, and physical.

Local self-governance can sometimes achieve these goals.[49] When it does, it often possesses significant advantages over either market or external enforcement mechanisms with respect to resolving local CAPs. We now address these advantages more specifically.

Advantages of Community Self-Governance

The models described in Section 9.2 indicate that community participation in negotiation procedures can generate legitimate pre-commitments. Furthermore, repeated reciprocal interactions that are coordinated and reinforced by local norms can lead to mutual expectations of successful conditional cooperation, with sanctioning of defectors. The chief advantage of community governance concerns its ability to develop, employ, and reinforce such localized social capital. As we saw in Chapters 2 and 3, these context-specific social mechanisms are largely unavailable to markets and, as we will see in Chapter 10, to external enforcers as well.

Drawing on the work of Ostrom (1990, 1998a, 2000a, 2000b), Bowles and Gintis (2002), Dasgupta (2000, 2011), Ostrom and Ahn (2009), and Lam's (1998) analysis of extensive fieldwork in Nepal, we discuss basic advantages of community governance as it pertains to public goods and common-pool resources. In this regard, Nepali farmers have encountered CAPs of constructing, maintaining, and regulating use of local irrigation systems, and have responded with intricate systems of localized rules. Many other types of localized governance—such as neighborhood watches, workgroups, producers' cooperatives, political parties, consumer organizations, and charities—face somewhat related public-good or CPR problems. In all such cases, community governance systems that incorporate participation from affected parties exhibit the following five basic advantages over external governance:

(i) opportunities for context-specific learning;

(ii) utilization of localized information;

(iii) cognitive benefits to participation;

(iv) construction of context-specific incentives; and

(v) restraints on the full use of bargaining power by advantaged parties.

We address these advantages in order.

First, community governance facilitates individual and group learning via repeated interactions that involve processes of negotiating, designing, and implementing rules—often with face-to-face contact. Successive interaction with one's environment and colleagues allows individuals to reevaluate prior conceptions. Individuals observe and respond to the following: the operation of their resource; local environmental phenomena (e.g., floods); the histories, habits, and motivations of colleagues; patterns of reciprocity and other modes of interaction within or among various groups; accompanying networks; local social norms and social rules; enforcement activities; and degrees of adherence among various participants. Face-to-face communication enhances such learning by offering cues from facial expressions and mannerisms. Furthermore, personal encounters can create or reinforce group identity and loyalty, improving prospects for cooperation (Ostrom 1998a).[50] Anticipation of such repeated encounters motivates agents to invest effort into context-specific learning. Over time, participants develop heuristics whose effectiveness (in relatively stable environments) tends to improve in repeated encounters.

Furthermore, participation in the crafting of operational rules (e.g., limits on resource use) facilitates trial-and-error experimentation. As Lam (1998) notes, locally managed irrigation systems allow participating farmers to design and alter rules in response to community experiences with events like floods or technical innovation. Farmers may then learn from the successes and failures of specific rules. Accompanying processes of negotiation create similar learning opportunities. Participation in these processes deepens common understandings of rules, leading to their institutionalization: rules thus become shared mental models rather than mere statements.

Local learning both reflects and generates localized information. Accordingly, the second advantage of community governance concerns its ability to utilize and transmit "dispersed private information" that is often unavailable to external entities such as states and banks (Bowles and Gintis 2002, 424). Localized observation is particularly important for effective enforcement. As an outcome of the learning processes just mentioned, community residents typically possess unique insider information concerning their resource, local environment, patterns of social interaction, histories, motivations, norms, rules, local networks, and so on. Consequently, community members often know far more than outsiders do about potentially beneficial exchanges, such as appropriate days for trading maintenance labor, opportunities for pooling risk, manners of detecting overuse, and the like. They can thus design rules and enforcement mechanisms that reflect and respond to such local information. This chapter's opening summary of Nepali irrigation rules offers an example.

The third advantage of community governance operates at a cognitive level. Joint participation in the design and enforcement of social rules, such as those for use of irrigation resources, constitutes an exercise of voice. And mutual exercise of voice is a developmental learning process.[51] More specifically, sharing in rule design enhances farmers' conceptions of possible courses of action, such as ways to coordinate maintenance (Lam 1998). Active engagement in designing and implementing rules thus improves cognition. It augments participants' mental models, enhancing their ability to conceptualize solutions. A governance system that requires farmers to craft their own rules, moreover, forces them to directly confront the problems of organizing cooperation. Consequently, they develop more expansive, flexible, and sophisticated concepts of things like possible labor exchanges or methods of observation and sanctioning—along with greater awareness of their mutual interdependence. Such awareness tends to encourage cooperation.

Fourth, all of these arguments point to an ability of community governance to generate context-specific, prosocial incentives. Shared knowledge of repeated interactions that involve communication and mutual observation creates incentives for cooperation via exercises of reciprocity and accompanying social exchanges. By trading information on solutions, favors, and commitments, participants develop mutual trust.[52] The accompanying emergence or reinforcement of norms of reciprocity—when combined with the (often significant) ability of participants to observe defection—alters payoff structures in a manner that encourages cooperation. Indeed, within communities, an important part of the incentive provided by punishing defection originates in the shame it generates (Bowles and Gintis 2002). All of these social mechanisms increase the predictability of agents' actions; and when prosocial behavior becomes predictable, agents face larger and more salient incentives to cooperate. The often attendant development of loyalty-enhancing group identity can reinforce these tendencies by augmenting other-regarding preferences and the internalization of relevant (location-specific) norms.

Thus participation by community members in the design of local rules tends to improve their quality and viability. Enhanced opportunities for (community) learning—along with context-specific information, enhanced cognition of local problems or solutions, and community participation in rule design—jointly foster the incorporation of context-appropriate incentive structures into operational rules (Lam 1998). Furthermore, participation in rule crafting creates incentives to implement them, adhere to them, and amend them in response to salient problems. Farmers who contribute to rule design have incentives to invest time and energy in order to maintain their resource system, encourage cooperation, and abide by the rules they helped craft.

The fifth basic advantage of relatively broad community participation in governance is that it sometimes diminishes tendencies of certain parties to fully exploit bargaining advantages. Lam (1998) finds that broad participation in governance of irrigation systems increases the likelihood that upstream farmers will depend on downstream farmers for various inputs (labor, making, etc.). As indicated in Section 9.2, such dependency reduces upstream farmers' ability to use their positional advantage for their own material gain. Furthermore, if downstream farmers participate in the crafting of constitutional rules, they can create channels for their own input into the design of collective-choice and operational rules. Opportunities for upstream exploitation of positional advantages would diminish further.[53]

We conclude this section by listing attributes—design features—of successful long-term self-governance of CPRs discovered by Ostrom (1990, 2005) and colleagues at the Workshop in Political Theory and Policy Analysis. This list reflects years of field research along with a substantive review of hundreds of related studies. Successful self-organized CPR management includes the following components:

1. Clearly defined physical boundaries of the resource and social boundaries concerning who has rights to use it.

2. Rules for allocating benefits of resource use that generally reflect the distribution of provision costs among community members, and that respond to local environmental conditions.

3. Collective-choice arrangements that involve local users in designing rules.

4. Monitors who are accountable to users.

5. Graduated sanctions for rule violations that permit some forgiveness for mistakes and encourage small violators to return to cooperation.

6. Low-cost mechanisms that can rapidly resolve internal conflicts.

7. At least minimal recognition of local rights by external authorities—important so that free-riders cannot avoid sanction by threatening to report local activity to authorities.

8. For larger systems, nesting of organizations so that small units monitor local activities and larger units coordinate among smaller ones.[54]

Note that items 1–6 and 8 explicitly incorporate elements of local self-governance and that item 7 indicates some tolerance of self-governance by external authorities. As item 8 suggests, self-organization can sometimes span different groups.

Multi-Group Organization

Individuals from different locally organized groups often engage in exchanges with each other. Avner Greif (2006a, 2006b) argues that the development of cross-community reputation facilitated the creation of trade networks across the Mediterranean in the late medieval period, roughly 1050–1350. Each community (e.g., Florence) valued exchanges with another community (e.g., London) enough to willingly devote some of its enforcement resources to protecting the rights of outsiders who had signed contracts with insiders. Local laws, for example, punished debtors for defaulting on contracts with individuals or firms from other communities. Communities as a whole could then develop reputations for supporting honest trade. Individuals and firms could then use community reputations as a foundation for extending trade beyond community boundaries. Consequently, merchants and bankers from various parts of the region willingly traded with distant strangers, about whom they knew virtually nothing beyond their membership in a certain community. Greif calls this mix of intra- and intercommunity institutional arrangements the "community responsibility system."

Independent communities in Germany, Italy, France, Flanders, Poland, and England thus jointly created reputational social capital through reciprocal promises of honest enforcement. Community reputations, as social assets, conveyed trustworthy reputations across community boundaries, acting as coordinating devices that signaled opportunities for reliable trade. In the absence of overarching external authorities, this social mechanism resolved second-order CAPs associated with various kinds of cheating and thereby rendered contractual commitments credible. Similar arrangements between nations underlie much contemporary international trade. Unfortunately, rising competition among merchants gradually undermined the rents upon which enforcement depended, and the community responsibility system collapsed after 1350 (Greif 2006a, 2006b).[55]

Overall, the ability of self-organization to create, reinforce, and utilize localized social capital is not confined to specific communities. Reputational social capital can span community boundaries. More deliberate efforts to craft coordinated intercommunity enforcement, however, tend to involve formal institutions and external third-party enforcement—topics for Chapter 10. First, we discuss the often considerable problems associated with local self-governance.

9.5. PROBLEMS WITH SELF-GOVERNANCE: FAILURES, INEQUITIES, EXPLOITATION, AND INSULARITY

Despite the enormous advantages of local self-governance, we do not intend to offer a rosy, quasi-utopian image of it. Like other social arrangements, self-governance generates substantial problems. As already suggested, attempts to establish and maintain functional self-governance often fail. Successful endeavors, moreover, may create problems of internal inequities and exploitation, as well as insularity regarding outside people, communities, and environments. We discuss these problems in order.

A naïve reading of the Coase theorem might suggest that self-organization is automatic and inherently successful: groups can readily identify advantages of negotiating cooperative agreements and will therefore do so. By now it should be obvious that such a perspective reflects a complete failure to understand collective-action problems. In fact, there is nothing automatic about successful self-organization (Ostrom 1998a).[56] Many local efforts to regulate use of CPRs have failed outright or not survived subsequent motivational failures, internal conflicts, technical change, environmental change, or pressures from external groups.

In this regard, some elements of common resources are more difficult to regulate than others. Only 10% of self-organized Japanese fisheries have instituted successful arrangements to pool risks among their members, and percentages are much lower elsewhere in the world. This organizational failure has led to a substantial welfare loss for those concerned (Platteau and Seki 2001).[57] As a general rule, relatively mobile and perishable resource units (fish rather than grains) pose greater difficulties for self-organized regulation (Poteete, Janssen, and Ostrom 2010). Moreover, in-house political difficulties—such as a low tolerance for internal differences—can complicate organization. For example, despite their proximity to the successfully self-managed Turkish Alanya fishery, users of the Izmir fishery never successfully organized effective use limitations. Competition among rival cooperatives with loyalties to different subgroups precluded successful negotiation of limitation rules (Ostrom 1990). Broadly speaking, potentially destructive tensions often arise from unequal sharing among individuals who depend on each other's cooperation—despite economic reasons for rewarding high performers.[58]

More generally, Bloch, Genicot, and Ray (2007) argue that the *fragility* of self-enforcement mechanisms reflects their susceptibility to disturbances, such as technical or environmental change. Virtually any social mechanism can survive small shocks (else it would not exist), but many lose their effectiveness or collapse entirely after experiencing larger shocks. For example, Sri Lankan irrigation systems that had lasted for a millennium unraveled under the pressure of out-migration during the twelfth century (Ostrom 1990). Likewise, social norms may successfully motivate enforcement in some conditions—but not in others.[59] Furthermore, subgroups within larger groups may discover profitable deviations from group norms. On occasion, dissident factions can enhance their influence by openly violating larger-group procedures or norms. In the case of the Izmir fishery, perhaps differing interpretations of norms and rules exacerbated organizational problems among users. Thus the ability of norms and other forms of social capital to successfully resolve CAPs is (not surprisingly) context-dependent. External shocks or internal divisions may erode the enforcement mechanisms that underlie functional self-governance. Consequently, local institutional systems may become self-undermining rather than self-reinforcing.

Even successful self-governance creates its own internal and external problems. Internal problems involve inequities in the distribution of burdens or benefits and unequal access to participation arenas, along with an attendant potential for exploitation. Negotiated distributional outcomes often reflect inequities of bargaining power among participants—as embodied, for example, in the upstream versus downstream positions of farmers in Section 9.2. More generally, we may interpret the terms "upstream" and "downstream" as indicators of any positional bargaining advantage or disadvantage—political, social, economic, or locational. Thus, in many locally managed CPRs, the net benefits of resource management are distributed in a manner that reflects prior inequality in private land holdings (McKean 1992; Dasgupta 2000). As in Sections 9.2 and 9.4, participation by the less advantaged in rule design can mitigate (though seldom eliminate) various inequities of participation and distribution. Furthermore, participation by less advantaged members is not at all guaranteed. Women are often excluded, as are ethnic minorities and the poor (Dasgupta 2000).[60]

Recall that shared mental models, including social norms and social rules, possess the path-dependent properties of punctuated equilibria. Once established, they become self-enforcing and even self-reinforcing, and thus difficult to dislodge. The economic, political, and social inequities of local self-management possess such tendencies. Relatively disadvantaged community members often lack access to economic, political, and social resources that would facilitate more equal participation and distributional shares. In short, they lack power. Furthermore, those who occupy positional advantages with respect to designing rules often use their power to bolster their various positions and to hinder or preclude participation by others (power2).

Unequal distributions of power can lead to exploitation. Dasgupta (2000) asserts that exploitative arrangements often arise in community-managed CPRs. Using game-theoretic terminology, he defines an *exploitative* relationship as one within which the value of the minimax position for one party is pushed below the value of that party's fallback position. The *minimax* for a player is the "lowest payoff others can push the person to" via their choice of strategies, "provided the person foresees this and chooses his best response to it" (Dasgupta 2000, 344). For example, in Basu's (2000) triadic model of power (summarized in Section 4.4), a landlord pushes a laborer's wage below the reservation wage by credibly threatening to end the laborer's trade relationship with a local merchant. More generally, when an agent's best response to strategic interactions within its community confers a payoff lower than its fallback payoff, exploitation occurs. Why then does the agent not just exit—move to the outside option? Punishment would follow. Dasgupta argues that conformists (followers of local social norms) cooperate with other conformists. Motivated by internalized local social norms, they willingly punish nonconformists and bestow social approval on other conformists and on punishers (informal norm enforcers). In many local communities, women and other disadvantaged parties face this kind of punishment for asserting themselves or for attempting to exit established social arrangements.[61] Indeed, social exclusion may become a norm or a socially enforced convention (SEC).

A final source of internal conflict involves differing levels of adherence to—or different interpretations of—social norms held among subgroups, notably groups formed around political, religious, national, or ethnic identity. Different groups may subscribe to unique interpretations concerning when specific norms do or do not apply to specific circumstances (Bloch, Genicot, and Ray 2007), or they may adhere to altogether different norms. Definitions of cooperation and defection may then vary, as may contexts for applying social sanctions. Localities that manifest such conflict often lack social cohesion; exchange and development likely suffer.[62]

Turning now to external relationships, note first that networks are, by definition, exclusive; hence local social capital and self-organization always involve some degree of exclusivity or insularity. Such insularity may reinforce internal inequities of distribution and participation by impeding interactions with groups who follow different prescriptions. Furthermore, local organization can generate or reinforce ignorance of (or insensitivity to) external environments, problems, individuals, and communities. There is, for example, no inherent reason for local governance systems to consider, much less address, externalities that extend beyond their realms of interaction. Like market participants, local groups have material incentives to ignore them: addressing externalities is costly. Recall Chapter 2's discussion of Schelling's (1978) distinction between strict and looser (classic and complex) CPR problems. For classic CPR problems, resource depletion affects only users (community members) and both costs and benefits can be measured in the same "currency" (e.g., numbers of fish). For complex CPR problems, on the other hand, use externalities extend beyond community boundaries, yielding diverse impacts that are not unambiguously convertible to a single metric.[63] Thus even successfully self-regulated CPRs may overuse resources from the perspective of neighbors or larger society—at times imposing substantial negative externalities on others. Disputes between organized American and Canadian fishers in the Pacific Northwest testify to this problem.

Community insularity regarding other individuals or groups, sometimes manifested as parochialism, tends to reinforce externality problems and leads to additional problems ranging from missed opportunities to outright conflicts. Many self-organized groups form around similarities in salient ascriptive characteristics of their members, such as age, shared cultural perspectives, race, ethnicity, ideology, or religion.[64] Communities may not know about, may not bother to learn about, or may actively avoid potentially beneficial relationships with outsiders. If they rely solely on the productive activity of insiders, communities may lose substantive benefits from productive, organizational, or informational economies of scale. Communities that fail to exchange with outsiders may likewise lose various economic, political, or social gains from trade. Why, then, would communities desire isolation? Because their internal social capital resolves CAPs that would otherwise be difficult or irresolvable, and because local power holders often benefit from insularity. Furthermore, as punctuated equilibria, local institutional systems could be vulnerable to external shocks.

Community members or power holders may then fear (perhaps realistically) that too much in-migration, or any interaction with outsiders, would undermine locally shared understandings, local arrangements for provision of public goods or limitations on CPRs, and/or local social, economic, or political positions. Stiglitz (2000, 67) observes: "We do not want to forget that when associations are organized around provincial economic interests, they rarely contribute to overall economic efficiency or equity."

Furthermore, interactions with outsiders can generate problems enforcing internal CPR rules. Outsiders may free-ride on internally enforced use limitations that effectively end up leaving more of the resource available to them. Additionally, with costly and limited observation, internal overusers may undermine enforcement and escape sanction by blaming their own overuse on outsiders. Knowing that such problems could arise, communities may avoid trying to regulate resource use entirely, may settle for ineffective regulation, or may give up over time. Similar problems may apply to the provision of many public goods.[65]

Finally, as is all too obvious, interacting groups that possess different social norms or that compete over access to resources may engage in various forms of destructive conflict. Unfortunately, myriad national, ethnic, and religious conflicts testify to this statement. The recent civil war in Sudan is only one of many examples.

9.6. CONCLUSION

We find that the core elements of social capital—shared understandings of trustworthiness; mutually understood social mechanisms of coordination and enforcement, including social norms and social rules; and accompanying social networks—tend to generate mutual sentiments of trust among local community members. Such mutual trust facilitates resolution of CAPs (especially second-order CAPs) that often defy resolution via market exchange or external enforcement.

Broadly speaking, community self-organization for the purpose of resolving CAPs involves two steps, each of which can be modeled game-theoretically. First, members must design and negotiate agreements concerning the distribution of costs and benefits of resolution. Such agreements must possess enough legitimacy to permit credible future coordination and enforcement of their terms. Legitimate agreements tend to follow from participation of the most affected or well-positioned parties, and so at least partially reflect their goals as well as their economic, political, social, and locational bargaining positions—though not exclusively: successful agreements also tend to address at least some concerns of other parties (e.g., those located downstream). Moreover, such agreements must respond to pertinent environmental conditions. Second, self-organization must establish credible mechanisms of coordination and enforcement that reflect and incorporate existing patterns of reciprocal interaction, local social norms, and locally designed rules. As indicated in our discussion of the model from Isaac, Walker, and Williams (1994), conditional cooperation among reciprocal agents provides a foundation for such arrangements.

Community self-governance generates and utilizes local social capital in ways that are largely inaccessible to individually based market exchange or to external enforcers. The advantages of self-governance via self-organization stem from its ability to incorporate, respond to, and promote localized, context-specific learning, along with context-specific information. Moreover, by activating joint exercises of voice among participants, self-organization enhances their cognitive capacities with respect to addressing local problems and creating avenues for cooperation. Self-organization thereby encourages development, implementation, and adherence to context-specific incentive structures. Furthermore, inclusive participation in rule design tends to attenuate the use of bargaining advantages by well-positioned parties. All of these advantages can facilitate resolving otherwise intractable localized second-order coordination and enforcement CAPs—and thereby permit resolution of pertinent first-order CAPs.

Unfortunately, community self-governance can fail outright or can create and perpetuate inequities of distribution and participation among community members—along with insularity to external environments, problems, individuals, and communities. Consequently, for Dasgupta, a "central dilemma in the political economy of rural development" (2000, 358) concerns weighing the enormous informational and participatory advantages of local self-governance against the tendencies of local power holders to usurp benefits for themselves and deny access to others. These same tensions exist in many nonrural settings as well. For example, in some urban neighborhoods, the most sophisticated self-organization occurs within gangs. Indeed, Dasgupta's statement holds true for political economy generally, not just for rural settings. Thus a central dilemma of political economy concerns balancing the considerable informational, adaptive-learning, cognitive, and motivational advantages of local self-governance against local insularity and the tendencies of local power holders to exploit others, usurp benefits, and deny participatory access to disadvantaged groups or individuals.

Formal institutions and third-party enforcement mechanisms can mitigate some of these problems, but at the cost of undermining local social capital and introducing yet another set of CAPs. Chapter 10 addresses formal institutions and third-party enforcement.

EXERCISES

9.1. Referring to equation (9.1), show that, at the Nash equilibrium, each agent's use of the resource (x_i) exceeds the socially optimal level of use.

9.2. (Creative) Design a signaling model of pre-commitment (see the discussion on pages 208–9).

9.3. Justify the statements on page 210 concerning the rule combinations (e.g., RB1 & RC1) that teams A and B would propose.

9.4. Demonstrate the relationships, summarized in Table 9.1, among construction costs, team preferences, and bargaining advantages.

9.5. Design a third rule combination (RBC5) that allows team B more than half of the water.

9.6. (Creative) Referring to possible agreements between teams A and B discussed in Section 9.2, describe three possible enforcement mechanisms for an irrigation agreement, and model one of them.

9.7. Demonstrate the assertion that C^* increases in group size N (made on page 215).

9.8. (Advanced) Augment equation (9.5) to incorporate intrinsic reciprocity terms from equation (5.1) and the punishment terms from (5.8) and (5.9) into the term Ω (and the associated probability ρ_s) as discussed on page 215. Discuss the implications of this change.

9.9. Show that equation (9.6) is a variant of equation (2.2).

9.10. Referring to the discussion following equation (9.8), demonstrate that when player j has a bad reputation $(b_j < 0)$, i can gain utility by sanctioning j, as long as $c_p'(p_{ij}) \le \lambda b_i = \lambda \beta (2\sigma_j - 1)$.

9.11. Demonstrate that equation (9.8) is a version of equation (5.2).

9.12. (Advanced) Construct an indirect evolutionary model that illustrates why a reciprocity norm like Ψ_R could be successful.

THIRD-PARTY ENFORCEMENT, FORMAL INSTITUTIONS, AND INTERACTIONS WITH SELF-GOVERNANCE

> Evidence has mounted that the simple policy prescriptions that are so often recommended as panaceas—privatize, turn over to the government, or create communal rights—can also fail.
>
> Poteete, Janssen, and Ostrom (2010)

Suppose that communities Arruba and Boratonia (A and B) have solved their internal water-use CAPs and have even implemented an acceptable agreement on joint limitation. Unfortunately, their wells occupy an upstream position on an aquifer system that also serves communities Creatonia, Doslovia, and Eggratia (C, D, and E). Hence every gallon used by A or B reduces the water available to C, D, and E. Moreover, C, D, and E find this two-party agreement to be unfair: it leaves them insufficient water, and they resent the disparity. Perhaps the five communities could negotiate an agreement; perhaps not. Even if they could, enforcement poses a problem. Credible enforcement based upon intercommunity reputation might emerge from repeated interaction and negotiation over larger-scale CAPs. On the other hand, different interpretations of "fairness"; various religious, ethnic, or ideological differences; or even repeated incidents of negative reciprocity could inhibit or preclude either reaching agreement or enforcing its terms. If so, the communities might request some form of external arbitration or enforcement.

Alternatively, external third parties might intervene with or without being asked. Perhaps only one or two of the communities request intervention, or perhaps only a few influential residents or interest groups do so. Suppose now that the water source is the Rio Grande and that communities A, B, and C are (respectively) Colorado, New Mexico, and Texas, while D and E are the Mexican states of Chihuahua and Coahuila. As external third-party enforcement agencies, the US and Mexican governments can, in principle, resolve water disputes among or between their own states. In so doing, they may favor particular states or particular interests. Disputes between Mexican and US states, however, cannot rely on arbitration and enforcement by either government; instead, cross-border agreements or treaties are required.[1]

This chapter argues that the complex exchange that underlies modern economic development requires creating and maintaining institutional systems that, in turn, establish and utilize mechanisms of third-party coordination and enforcement that are capable of spanning many exchanges and communities. Third-party enforcement, in turn, rests on relatively formal institutional foundations. Mutually understood formal rules establish

positions from which third-party enforcers operate, along with key functions and procedures. The success of such arrangements, however, depends critically on interactions with
the second-party enforcement (and other governance mechanisms) of constituent groups
and communities. These, in turn, rely on less formal localized rules, social norms, and
conventions.[2] Disjuncture at either level of enforcement tends to undermine prospects for
macro-level group success.

Before proceeding, we expand briefly on four topics: types of rules; categories of institutions; interactions between institutions and organizations within institutional systems; and
the concept of group failure.

Regarding types of rules, Chapter 9's distinction between operational, collective-choice,
and constitutional rules indicated nested categories or hierarchies in rulemaking that apply
to both formal and informal rules. At the foundation, constitutional rules establish contexts
within which collective-choice rules operate, including designation of positions for making collective-choice rules. For example, the US Constitution specifies that tax legislation
should originate in the House of Representatives. Collective-choice rules then frame the
design of operational rules. The US Congress designates certain powers to the Environmental Protection Agency for regulating pollution by designating applicable operational rules.[3]

For all three levels, *working rules* (or rules in use) point to interpretations that actually
apply in practice: "Working rules are the set of rules to which participants would make
reference if asked to explain and justify their actions to fellow participants" (Ostrom 2005,
19). For example, a neighborhood organization may, via informal precedent, implement
a practice that the chair of a meeting sets its agenda—an informal, working, collective-
choice rule. Many working rules combine prescriptions from formal and informal rules,
demonstrating that social and formal rules operate in tandem. Legislation may establish a
committee chair and informal rules may establish the chair's actual powers.

Regarding categories of institutions, it is often useful to distinguish between economic
and political variants. Both variants can be formal or informal, and distinctions may not be
clear-cut. *Economic institutions* are sets of informal and formal rules related to economic
transactions. Economic institutions define property rights and prescribe enforcement procedures related to them and (more generally) to market exchange; they also specify procedures related to key market failures, such as providing public goods. In so doing, economic
institutions designate relevant material incentives and also establish positions within exchange processes (e.g., employer). As discussed in Chapter 4, positions in exchange may
confer power—implying a political dynamic within economic institutions. For their part,
political institutions structure the allocation of power within or across governance units,
including firms—where at least the latter implies an economic component to political institutions. Formal political institutions include rules that prescribe who gets to make what
decisions, when, and how:[4] they establish *de jure* power. When institutionalized, these rules
structure governance mechanisms in four basic manners. They:

   (i) establish specific positions of authority;
   (ii) designate specific powers, responsibilities, and limitations to such positions;

(iii) establish collective-choice procedures for assigning individuals or organizations to such positions; and

(iv) delineate hierarchical relationships among such positions.[5]

Naturally, economic and political institutions interact. Resolving CAPs, such as enforcing property rights or providing public goods, involves both.

At first blush, one might think that economic institutions involve operational rules whereas political institutions involve collective-choice and constitutional rules. Both statements are true, but economic institutions also incorporate collective-choice rules and political institutions include operational rules. Concerning the former, recall that within Section 9.4's list of property rights, management, exclusion, and alienation rights are collective-choice rules that apply to economic interactions—indicating a political dynamic that necessarily accompanies property rights.[6] Likewise, political rules may establish day-to-day procedures, such as who convenes meetings. Such arrangements often have collective-choice implications; conveners may set meeting agendas.

Recall from Chapter 7 that institutional systems include organizations, and the combination of institutions and organizations actually generates prescribed behaviors. Regarding interactions between institutions and organizations, we use Greif's (2006a) distinction between core and auxiliary transactions. A *core transaction*, such as a purchase of clothing, involves an economic, political, or social exchange between two or more individuals. An *auxiliary transaction* is a potential (or latent) transaction that operates only if certain conditions regarding the core transaction are either met or violated. Auxiliary transactions underlie the resolution of many second-order CAPs and arise in conjunction with institutional rules: violating a rule can prompt an auxiliary transaction. Anticipated auxiliary transactions coordinate activities across multiple agents (or agencies), by influencing expectations concerning consequences of possible actions in core transactions. For example, the potential for police departments to arrest shoplifters—an occasionally necessary auxiliary transaction—influences expectations of both buyers and sellers in a manner that vastly enhances the predictability of shopping behavior. Within institutional systems, organizations permit and condition auxiliary transactions; they serve as "arenas in which actions in auxiliary transactions take place" (Greif 2006a, 48). Formal (or sometimes informal) institutions then specify which organizations—often as third-party enforcers—should carry out specific auxiliary transactions in response to specific violations of rules.

Finally, the notion of group failure was implicit in Section 9.5's discussion of problems with self-governance. *Group failure* occurs when either internal interactions or internal governance generates outcomes that are undesirable for a group, for subgroups within a group, for other groups, or for society at large. Group failure may apply to small groups, communities, or governments. It arises from any of the following sources: insufficient resources or political will to address localized CAPs; internal conflicts; lost opportunities for creating economies of scale via larger-scale coordination; insularity in the form of disregard for externalities and other CAPs that affect outsiders, other groups, or larger society; hostility to external groups; and persistence of localized inequities—particularly regarding access to power.

Group success and failure are somewhat analogous to market success and failure, particularly in the policy-relevant sense that external authorities should try to minimize interference with success but, on some occasions, intervene to reduce or ameliorate failure.[7] While market failure tends to indicate problems with economic organizations and institutions, group failure applies to communities and governments at various levels. Both may operate simultaneously and reinforce each other.

Returning to our discussion of levels of governance, we note that larger-scale, transcommunity or macro-level governance may eliminate, ameliorate, exacerbate, or even create group failures among constituent self-organized groups. Macro-level governance arises from institutional systems that incorporate formal (largely political) institutions, which then designate the positions and functions of third-party enforcers, often organizations. The corresponding enforcement responsibilities span multiple exchanges and communities. Macro-level systems thus establish external or trans-community governance with respect to specific within- or between-group interactions. Effective trans-community governance, however, needs to incorporate information gathered from diverse experiences of different groups as it crafts intergroup incentives. Ideally, such governance combines motivational, informational, and cognitive elements derived from diverse sources of local social capital, interactions among various groups, and broader-scale experiences of intergroup coordination. Reasonably well-functioning larger systems are thus *polycentric* in the sense that governance operates at many different levels of localization and interaction, ranging from minimally local to systemwide.[8]

Effective large-scale governance thus requires adequate flow of information among different authority levels in polycentric systems. Information flows, in turn, depend on perceptions of *legitimacy*—in particular, the degree to which agents at specific levels within the system perceive both rules and agents at other levels to be appropriate, or largely compatible with their values.[9] Such legitimacy, in turn, depends on more or less complementary relationships between large-scale formal institutions and less formal local institutions—norms in particular—along with similar compatibility between (and within) second- and third-party enforcement organizations. It requires macro-level compatibility across groups and communities, or (equivalently) social cohesion (Easterly 2006). Such compatibilities are by no means guaranteed. Indeed, establishing them often constitutes a formidable CAP.

Trans-community governance is thus subject to the same problems as self-governance, but on a grander (though perhaps less detailed) scale. Attendant inequities of distributional gain and access to power can affect entire communities, in addition to subgroups and individuals within them. External governance, moreover, can undermine or destroy many advantages of localized social capital. Self-interested individuals and organizations will, naturally, attempt to alter macro-level institutions, including enforcement mechanisms, to their advantage. Thus, like self-governance, systemic governance is both essential and subject to tremendous failure. Political economy is difficult.

Our discussion proceeds as follows. Section 10.1 considers how formal institutions and third-party enforcement establish foundations for complex exchange. Section 10.2 addresses interactions between second- and third-party enforcers and related interactions between informal and formal institutions. Section 10.3 discusses polycentric governance, and Section 10.4 concludes.

10.1. FORMAL INSTITUTIONS, THIRD-PARTY ENFORCEMENT, AND COMPLEX EXCHANGE

Over the course of economic history, the growth of productive knowledge has facilitated a rising division of labor along with increasingly complex levels of exchange. Such augmented exchange has relied on increasingly sophisticated social choreography provided by progressively more developed institutions.[10] We thus modify Adam Smith's (1776/1976) dictum, "the division of labor is limited by the extent of the market," to say: the division of labor is limited by the ability of institutions to support complex exchange. Other things equal, as exchange complexity increases, the predictability of individual behavior declines. Maintaining credible trade relations thus requires corresponding augmentation of coordination and enforcement. And resolving these second-order CAPs depends on more intricate and extensive social choreography that, in turn, relies on more comprehensive and formal institutional foundations. Complex exchange also requires third-party enforcement that extends across groups, communities, and exchanges. The effectiveness of such larger institutional systems, however, depends on achieving rough complementarity between formal and informal institutions, with similar compatibility between third- and second-party enforcers. In particular, external enforcement should not destroy local social capital, and institutional structures need to restrain possible exploitation of bargaining power by the most well-positioned agents (including organizations). All of these conditions are problematic; none of them are guaranteed.

This section addresses these arguments with historical examples that point to relationships between types of exchange, productive knowledge, the division of labor, the complexity of economic environments, and the need for extensive social choreography.

The Complexity of Exchange and Social Choreography

Following North (1990), we identify three broad levels of exchange: personal exchange, impersonal exchange, and complex exchange.[11] *Personal exchange* relies on repeated reciprocal relationships, face-to-face contact, and localized social norms as mechanisms that create trust, coordination, and enforcement; in short, it relies on small-group social capital. Personal exchange emerged in the hunter-gatherer societies of the Neolithic era, reflecting human adaptations to the physical environment by developing small coherent teams that created internal loyalty (group identity).[12] Although personal exchange remains important to this day, the development of external memory storage—notably, writing—has dramatically increased opportunities for specialization. The ensuing extension of the division of labor depended upon developing the larger and more rule-driven exchange networks of impersonal exchange (North 1990).

Impersonal exchange reaches beyond small social networks to incorporate non-repeated (or not necessarily repeated) exchange among many, possibly distant strangers.

Historically, the move from personal exchange to impersonal exchange entailed develop-ing three shared conceptual foundations: (i) mutual trust that trading partners would avoid defection strategies, such as cheating on contracts; (ii) shared conceptions (or mental mod-els) of potential gains from trading beyond immediate social circles; and (iii) expectations of reliable coordination and enforcement. These developments emerged from community social networks that were capable of using social norms and social rules whose influence extended across relatively large communities (North 2005, 116–22).

Greif's (2006a) discussion of the Maghribi traders on the Mediterranean between the tenth and twelfth centuries illustrates a transition from personal to impersonal exchange that facilitated credible trade relations across long distances. The Maghribi were Jewish traders who emigrated from Baghdad to Tunisia during the tenth century and then spread to Egypt and other locations on the Mediterranean. During the eleventh century, they es-tablished an extensive kin-based system of multilateral enforcement founded upon indi-vidual reputation, based on mutual observation and reporting. These informal institutional arrangements allowed them to extend merchant trade across the Mediterranean.

The Maghribi institutional system resolved a classic principal-agent problem. Mer-chants needed agents in distant ports to undertake multiple tasks, such as insuring suit-able delivery of products to customers or dealing with local officials. They hired Maghribi agents, but, across such distances, monitoring was both imperfect and expensive. Drawing upon the social capital of common heritage, they established a kin-based informal coali-tion and a corresponding set of social rules that—combined with social norms—specified and enforced proper trading practices: a set of largely informal economic institutions. The merchants defined the complicated notion of "cheating" on contracts, given the near-universal presence of many hard-to-observe contingencies. On this basis, they established a joint sanctioning mechanism that relied on information concerning agents' prior behavior, which they subsequently exchanged across their kin network. Maghribi merchants would refuse to trade with any agent who was reported cheating. Defecting agents (also Maghribi) were economically and socially ostracized.[13]

This nexus of kin network, social rules, social norms, beliefs, and mutual observation es-tablished a viable institutional system. It choreographed trading activity by transmitting in-stitutional influences on agents' cognition (understanding of cheating), information (past histories of agents), and motivation to cooperate (expected sanction for defection). As both merchants and their agents found reason to make and keep agreements, such agreements became credible. The Maghribi institutional system was thus self-enforcing, but the extent of trade was limited to the kin network.

The Mediterranean community responsibility system (CRS), which operated between 1050 and 1350, relied on more sophisticated institutional foundations that enabled exten-sive trade between cities (Grief 2006a, 2006b). Because communities did not share common heritage, they faced a more complex set of principal-agent problems than did the Maghribi. The CRS merchants could not rely on kin-based social norms and loyalties to motivate information exchange. Instead, their system established community-based reputations for honoring property rights of distant, nonmember traders. Each participating city devoted resources to protecting property rights of outsiders through its nexus of laws, courts, and policing. Residents caught cheating outside traders were punished. From a trader's perspective, these arrangements involved substantial third-party enforcement: court officials and police are not merchants. Compared to the Maghribi system, CRS institutions were more formal and more political, using a greater proportion of constitutional and collective-choice rules and greater designation of direct authority.

Absent such community-based application of resources to resolving fundamental second-order CAPs, trade agreements would have lacked credibility—because outsiders could not have expected reliable protection of their rights. Merchants, then, would not have committed to such distant exchanges. In a similar vein, Basu (2000), citing Strayer (1970), argues that the modern nation-state had its origins in the twelfth and thirteenth centuries. Increases in literacy and associated extensions of the division of labor generated a need for shared understandings that appointed third-party (nonmerchant) agents would, in fact, devote resources to enforcing contracts. Nation-states provided such enforcement and, more importantly, credibly signaled that they would do so.[14]

The CRS system illustrates an early stage of complex exchange. *Complex exchange* combines personal and impersonal exchange with substantial third-party enforcement based upon formal economic and political institutions (North 1990). For example, agreements between Grinnell College and Microsoft Corporation regarding the purchase and distribution of software rely on a large set of laws that specify intellectual property rights with attendant third-party enforcement procedures. Such enforcement depends on shared understandings that certain violations can lead to adjudication by the formally established legal system. Adjudication, moreover, operates on foundations of complex sets of legislation and judicial precedent. More generally, in the contemporary world, all developed and developing economies engage in complex exchange.

Complexity accompanies development. During the aforementioned historical transitions, the combination of technological advance and a rising division of labor engendered four potentially unsettling (complicating) developments that affected exchange environments:

(i) Technological advance and increasing specialization have jointly augmented the efficiency of production and thereby facilitated population growth—increasing the numbers of agents who interact in given environments.[15]

(ii) Larger populations and a greater diversity of tasks (via specialization) have created more opportunities for economic, political, and social interaction. For example, accountants interact with lawyers, surgeons, and sales clerks.

(iii) Technical change has vastly increased the set of possible strategies for agents. Recent developments in computer technology, for example, enable countless information exchanges that were inconceivable 40 years ago.

(iv) The steadily rising division of labor has created fundamentally different opportunities for learning among disparate agents. Knowledge has become increasingly balkanized.

These developments have steadily created a growing need for extensive social choreography.

Developments (i)–(iii) have dramatically increased both the number of agents who can affect a person's well-being, and their possible actions. For example, in contemporary society, the following kinds of people might affect a college student's utility: family, friends, classmates, college personnel; anyone with whom she engages in either economic or social exchange; local, state, and federal authorities; lobbyists, foreign governments, and so forth. Nobody can predict the consequences of the myriad actions available to such diverse actors. Without some kind of institutional response, the competence-difficulty (CD) gap would increase exponentially.[16]

Some communities have adapted to rising social complexity by developing increasingly sophisticated institutions. Recall that Heiner's (1983) reliability condition (equation (6.5)) implies that uncertainty renders many strategies unreliable because agents cannot distinguish between good and bad circumstances for using them.[17] Agents thus develop heuristics that rule out contemplation of strategies that seem unfamiliar, arise infrequently, or otherwise do not fit within causal relationships of their (socially influenced) mental models. At a community level, shared heuristics become conventions, social norms, social rules, or formal rules. Rising complexity, therefore, creates greater need for institutional choreography. Accordingly, the Mediterranean CRS rendered exchange relationships with non-kin strangers sufficiently predictable to support substantial cross-Mediterranean trade, precisely because it ruled out many potentially profitable opportunities for defection among thousands of competing merchants.

Development (iv), the tendency of a rising division of labor to balkanize knowledge and experience among agents, compromises their ability to communicate—another impetus for a rising CD gap. For instance, performing sophisticated and specialized tasks, such as heart surgery, requires extremely focused and accurate information. Typical accountants (or lawyers, economists, etc.) know little about surgery and vice versa.[18] Successful complex exchange, however, requires credible and coordinated transmission of disparate, asymmetrically held information. Before entering surgery, a typical patient, who knows virtually nothing about it, needs assurance that her surgeon is both competent and honest. Moreover, as explained in Chapter 3, agents may have strong material incentives to conceal or misrepresent information. Again, institutional adaptation is called for.

Overall, the increases in productive knowledge that facilitated extending the division of labor have relied on increasingly sophisticated institutional choreography to restrain (or perhaps tame) the potential for dramatically rising uncertainty that has accompanied historical transitions from personal, to impersonal, and then complex exchange. The emergent combination of more agents, more avenues for interaction, more technically feasible strategies, and greater balkanization of knowledge has, unfortunately, created vast potential for defection. Consequently, these developments have increased transaction costs, thereby creating a need for increasingly extensive and formal institutions (North 2005, 99–101). Thus, for personal exchange, localized social norms and reciprocal interaction generated sufficient predictability and trust for exchange within small groups during the Neolithic era (and since). The greater division of labor that accompanied Maghribi trading relied on more sophisticated, but still largely informal, institutions that fostered credible exchange agreements via kin-based reputational enforcement. The Mediterranean CRS used more extensive third-party enforcement, based on formal institutions, to establish city reputations for protecting outsider rights that, in turn, facilitated trade among distant, non-kin strangers. The far more complex exchanges of contemporary society depend upon far denser institutional systems.

These developments, however, were not automatic: the mere presence of a need for them did not dictate either their occurrence or their apparent success. Complex exchange and its institutional foundations are both outcomes of intricate historical processes. Furthermore, the complex social choreography that emerges from both formal institutions and third-party enforcement has depended (and still depends) critically on elaborate interactions with continuously evolving, less formal institutions—especially social norms—along with second-party enforcement mechanisms. We now address such interactions.

10.2. FORMAL AND INFORMAL INSTITUTIONS; SECOND- AND THIRD-PARTY ENFORCEMENT

Section 10.1 asserted that complex exchange requires sophisticated social choreography to resolve the second-order CAPs of establishing credible agreements among unrelated strangers. It has not, however, fully explained why such macro-level choreography depends upon formal institutions and third-party enforcement. The answer is simple and economic: institutional systems that augment informal institutions and second-party enforcement with complementary formal institutions and third-party enforcement offer economies of design and application related to social coordination and enforcement. As such, they can be the most efficient, and often the only effective, large-scale social choreographers. Section 10.1 also did not address the many weaknesses of large-scale institutional systems—the most important of which is their tendency to undermine locally developed social capital. We now discuss both of these topics.

To proceed, we discuss two fundamental levels of compatibility that critically influence the functionality of institutional systems: compatibility between formal and informal institutions—especially that between laws and social norms—and compatibility between third- and second-party enforcers. Functional large-scale institutional systems require general compatibility in both respects. Macro-level institutional systems, which necessarily rely on formal institutions and third-party enforcement, operate in social environments conditioned by less formal institutions and smaller-scale mechanisms of second-party enforcement, and vice versa.[19] Indeed, these social mechanisms interact to produce myriad social, political, and economic outcomes—including exchange—at various levels of complexity. Larger- and smaller-scale components of institutional systems may interact functionally, dysfunctionally, or more typically somewhere in between. Ultimately, the governance created by these systems is polycentric: it combines influences of largely independent sources of coordination and enforcement (Ostrom 2010). To illustrate these interactions, we first discuss relationships between laws and social norms, proceed to relations between levels of enforcement, and then evaluate advantages and disadvantages of external governance.

Laws, Social Norms, and Self-Enforcing Equilibria

Recall that credible laws occupy the formal end of Figure 7.1's institutional spectrum, whereas social norms lie on the informal end.[20] Both are shared mental models. Thus laws and norms interact at cognitive, informational, and motivational levels. Laws that conflict substantially with locally pertinent social norms cannot effectively alter behaviors that respond more readily to norms; such laws tend to lack sufficient legitimacy and/or credible means of enforcement to be effective. For example, the 1957 Civil Rights Act, which nominally protected the voting rights of African Americans, was ignored in the South. The law specified local trial by jury as an enforcement mechanism. At the time, relevant parties understood that all-white, norm-abiding southern juries would not convict violators. Summarizing the law's impact, Patterson (1996, 413) states: "By 1959 the law had not added a single black voter to the rolls in the South."

More generally, laws cannot effectively implement actions that are inconsistent with operating social equilibria; and social norms constitute important elements of such equilibria. For a law to be effective, citizens must normally find it in their interest (or otherwise desire) to follow its legal prescriptions. Likewise, enforcers, as agents with their own motivations, must find it in their interest to sanction violators. Furthermore, all concerned must understand these relationships and expect others to do so as well. In other words, to be effective, laws must be institutionalized. Indeed, taken as just a set of words, a law merely designates "legal" and "illegal" activity in some context. Such definitions do not, by themselves, alter payoffs or available strategies of players in broadly conceived games—that is, games that include all technically feasible actions and enforcement strategies (Basu 2000).

The following simple model, borrowed from Basu (2000, 124–26), illustrates relationships between legal definitions, strategies, and payoffs. Consider an expanded game with two stages: first, a one-period action stage, and then a multi-period punishment stage. More precisely, the following features apply:

- Action stage: in period $t = 0$, player 1 produces pollution level $x \in [0, 1]$ with payoff x.

- Punishment stage: in period $t = 1$ and all subsequent odd-numbered periods, agent 2 decides whether to punish agent 1 (P) or not (N); in period $t = 2$ and all subsequent even-numbered periods, agent 1 decides whether or not to punish agent 2.

- There is a per-period discount factor $\delta \in [0, 1)$.

- Any player who receives punishment experiences loss $-p$. For simplicity, we assume that administering punishment is costless.[21]

Note that we may regard agent 2 as a third-party enforcer and agent 1's ability to punish 2 as some form of retaliation.[22] Figure 10.1 illustrates the first three moves of this game.

Now suppose there are two laws: an anterior law (a collective-choice rule) that defines legal punishment and an operational law that defines legal activity. The anterior law states that, for any period $t \geq 1$, an agent's action is "illegal" if he does one of two things: (i) chooses P when the other player's action in period $t - 1$ was not illegal or (ii) chooses N

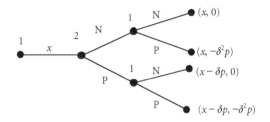

Figure 10.1 Law and pollution game

SOURCE: A text description of this model appears in K. Basu (2000), *Prelude to Political Economy: A Study of the Social and Political Foundations of Economics*, Oxford: Oxford University Press.

when the other player's action in $t - 1$ was illegal. In other words, it is illegal to either punish legal activity or not punish illegal activity. The operational law states that any amount of pollution that exceeds a specified level $\alpha \in [0, 1)$ is illegal. These laws, however, are just definitions. They do not alter the strategies or payoffs of either player in Figure 10.1.[23]

To actually influence outcomes, laws must alter understandings: they must generate expectations of consequences that could follow specific actions—consequences that follow from expected auxiliary transactions. When they do so effectively, laws specify focal points for expectations and for activity, which correlate understandings; laws can create (or alter) shared mental models. More precisely, an effective law can shift outcomes toward its stated (behavioral) prescriptions. It does so by (conceptually) pointing to a specific attainable social equilibrium among many possibilities—where possible equilibria include varying configurations of enforcement and punishment, or lack thereof.

To illustrate a law-induced social equilibrium, assume that in Figure 10.1's game, player 1 wants to maximize profits and that both players are law-abiding. Player 1 plays α in period 0, and both players act legally regarding punishment. As long as $\alpha \geq 1 - \delta p$, it does not pay either player to deviate unilaterally.[24] The system is self-enforcing. Given the law-abiding character of the players, both laws coordinate expectations, and thus create a focal point at the self-enforcing equilibrium of mutual legal action. Moreover, if we take the anterior law as given, the pollution law focuses expectations on amount $x = \alpha$.

What does this model tell us about laws and social norms? Note that the assumed law-abiding orientation of both agents could reflect adherence to a social norm. Suppose instead that norm Ψ_N prescribes the opposite: disregard pollution laws. The focal-point equilibrium now collapses. A more sophisticated third-party enforcement mechanism might address this problem, but it could do so only at a cost. Two contemporary examples illustrate similar conflicts between laws and norms. College students often violate laws on underage drinking; in some circles, such violation is a social norm. Likewise, police often do not ticket drivers on highways who exceed speed limits by 5 miles per hour (mph) but will do so for those exceeding the limit by 15 mph. Here social norms interact with speed limit laws to designate the actually enforced limit on highways—the applicable working rule—as somewhere between 5 and 10 mph above the posted speed limit.

More generally, Basu (2000) asserts that anything that law accomplishes could, in principle, be accomplished by social norms.[25] In principle, norms could prescribe acceptable drinking behavior, as they often do. In principle, norms could prescribe acceptable speed limits, though one might doubt their effectiveness. In principle, norms could prescribe acceptable levels of pollution, though generalized compliance might require degrees of cultural conditioning that are rarely observed in large societies. For normative prescriptions alone to provide sufficient choreography in large societies—that is, for social equilibria to emerge only from norms—some complex constellation of norms would have to suitably coordinate beliefs and behavior across multiple agents for multiple changing contingencies. Norms would need to exert readily adaptable mixes of specific and general transcommunity influence on cognition, information, and motivation. Expecting as much from informal ethical prescriptions that do not designate specific enforcers and that, for the most part, arise spontaneously from complex and poorly understood sociohistorical processes would be utopian: hence the need for formal institutions.

Indeed, despite their reliance on basic compatibility with social norms, institutionalized formal rules possess five basic advantages over norms and other less formal institutions as macro-level social choreographers.[26] First, as outcomes of deliberate collective decisions, formal rules are designed or negotiated with specific social goals in mind.[27] Although they may fail to achieve such goals, rules are far more easily created and modified than norms. Procedures for changing laws or regulations usually appear in anterior legislation (collective-choice rules) or constitutions. Agents who occupy appropriate positions (e.g., members of Congress) can initiate, revoke, or alter laws over relatively short time spans; of course, political obstacles may inhibit adjustment. Because social norms usually emerge slowly from complex evolutionary processes, they are impossible to design and difficult to alter—at least predictably over short time horizons.

Second, by designating specific positions with specific responsibilities, often within complex organizations, accepted formal rules can achieve relatively predictable coordination across many contexts. For example, companies in the United States that face environmental regulation can find out which agencies regulate relevant pollutants and the likely penalties for violation. Likewise, formally designated positions, when institutionalized, foster predictable enforcement—predictable auxiliary transactions. By contrast, norms tend to be more subject to the vagaries of collective memory; disputes over interpretation by parties with differing interests often arise. Though formal rules obviously generate contested interpretations, the presence of a written prescription—especially when accompanied by recorded prior interpretation in the form of legal precedent—substantially limits the range of interpretation.

Third, recorded formal rules provide foundations for multiple informal working rules that accompany (and point to) on-site interpretation and implementation of applicable prescriptions. For example, written company procedure may specify that the CEO chairs the board meeting and sets the agenda. On that basis, the CEO and other key players may then establish informal working rules that indicate which types of agenda items usually appear first, how long proponents of new ideas usually speak, and so forth.

Fourth, as outcomes of designated collective-choice decisions, formal rules can stipulate levels of material sanction—such as life imprisonment or fines for pollution—that are largely unavailable to less formal institutions. Often society will not accept less-than-formal decision processes regarding the specification and administration of such sanctions. Democracies usually do not tolerate vigilante "justice."[28]

Finally, institutionalized laws and formal regulations possess considerable economies of scale, design, and application because, as a group, they are self-referencing. Current laws make systematic reference to prescriptions that appear in foundational or anterior laws. For example, when a legislature passes a law to increase a highway speed limit from 65 to 70 mph, the new law need not repeat that state police enforce speed limits and courts arbitrate traffic disputes. Anterior legislation has already done so. Prior legislation has conditioned citizens to expect such enforcement and arbitration. The new law builds upon such pre-established mutual expectations. This ability of laws to reference anterior laws vastly enhances their potential for efficient design and modification.

Thus, when perceived as legitimate, self-referencing sets of laws exhibit substantive economies of scale, design, and application with respect to the production and modification of behavioral prescriptions. By also assigning positions that facilitate coordination and enforcement, relatively formal institutions create predictability by designating adjustable focal points. In so doing they can attain macro-level, trans-community social choreography that largely escapes their less formal counterparts. When laws possess sufficient legitimacy to influence expectations in the prescribed directions, their power to coordinate activity and enforcement is enormous. Power, however, leads to additional CAPs and to potential failure.

Again, effective implementation of legal prescriptions requires that laws be consistent with attainable social equilibria that depend on conventions, norms, and social rules—and also on the motivations of potential third- and second-party enforcers. Such complementarity can be difficult to achieve.

Relations between Third- and Second-Party Enforcers

Successful implementation of formal and informal institutional prescriptions requires compatibility between external (third-party) and internal (second-party) enforcement mechanisms. As noted in Chapter 9, effective second-party governance harnesses local problem-solving capacities and information to develop context-specific rules, related incentives, and enforcement procedures—all for addressing local CAPs. Effective third-party or macro-level governance addresses broader CAPs; it functions best when it complements local second-party mechanisms. Often it does not.[29]

Research by Wai Fung Lam (1998) on the governance of irrigation systems in Nepal illustrates problems of compatibility between external and internal governance—CAPs that largely reflect the motivations and information available (or not available) to external enforcers. He also offers a counterexample. More specifically, Lam's research compares the performance of self-governing, farmer-managed irrigation systems (FMIS) and agency-managed irrigation systems (AMIS). He finds that FMIS perform well because they utilize and develop local social capital, whereas AMIS suffer from poor adaptation to local contexts and conflicts with farmers. Hence they underperform, despite having greater access to technology and resources. More precisely, agency-managed irrigation systems face six related problems (Lam 1998, 26–49):

1. Officials have few incentives to manage systems efficiently. Hiring depends on civil service exams, promotion is often unrelated to irrigation performance, and low salaries encourage outside employment or corrupt practices. Operating budgets and personnel are often inadequate, and important decisions are made further up the hierarchy.

2. Officials have few incentives to engage productively with local farmers. As engineers, they have little training for such engagement. When they convene user groups, they typically focus on powerful farmers, sometimes exacerbating local bargaining advantages or conflicts. They often attempt to recruit farmers to implement management policies, rather than actively participate in problem solving.

3. As a result of problems 1 and 2, officials tend to favor rigid, easy-to-implement rules, such as assigning specific time slots for irrigation. Such rules are unresponsive to local information and changing local circumstances, such as floods.

4. Low motivation and limited access to information often lead to poor enforcement of AMIS rules.

5. Weak enforcement of agency rules signals to farmers that officials are unreliable partners for cooperative efforts.

6. Overall, agency-farmer interactions undermine local social capital. Agency management tends to discourage the learning properties of local self-governance. When farmers regard officials as the responsible parties for solving irrigation problems, they may develop a "dependent mind-set" that discourages local innovation and erodes common understandings: "what was a close community can easily be turned into a group of strangers who do not care for one another" (47).

Empirically, Lam finds statistically significant evidence that FMIS outperform AMIS in terms of providing and maintaining sustainable irrigation resources—despite having fewer resources, inferior technology, and less training.

Lam does, however, report one exception that suggests some potential for more constructive relationships. In Nepal's Chitwan District, the local AMIS and FMIS operate jointly. External managers focus on major problems that farmers cannot address by themselves. For example, the AMIS offers technical assistance for repair of irrigation intake structures before each year's monsoon, but it leaves basic system operation to farmer management on the basis of localized social capital. This pattern offers a useful general prescription for such relationships: third parties should perform tasks that are difficult or inaccessible to second parties, including coordination across communities and addressing excessive internal inequities; second parties should manage local affairs, provided they can do so without creating external harm or internal exploitation. Applicable definitions of these terms, lines of distinction between them, and myriad details related to actual implementation are, of course, highly contestable. On this foundation, we may now more comprehensively assess external governance mechanisms based on formal institutions and third-party enforcement.

Advantages and Disadvantages of External Governance

Sections 9.4 and 9.5 discussed the substantial advantages and disadvantages of self-governance, contrasting the cognitive, informational, and motivational benefits of utilizing local social capital against the problems of insularity and inequity. Section 10.1 pointed to the chief advantage of larger-scale macro-level institutional systems that mix formal institutions with third-party enforcement: they underlie growth and development. The present section has noted benefits of formal institutions concerning predictability and economies of design, but it has also noted problems of legitimacy when laws conflict with pertinent social norms and problems of third-party enforcement. Combining and extending these ideas, we now assess relative advantages and disadvantages of external governance as an element of institutional systems that span distinct communities.

The key benefits of external governance stem from its potential to harness trans-community social choreography to address self-governance failure. Summarizing prior arguments, we find that self-governance is subject to four key types of group failure:

(i) Insufficient willingness or ability to resolve local CAPs: owing to lack of knowledge, political will, or resources, groups may fail to establish mechanisms that address first- and second-order CAPs among their own members.

(ii) Fragility: community governance mechanisms may falter under external shock.

(iii) Internal inequities: unequal distributions of power often generate distributional inequities and potential for exploitation of disadvantaged members or subgroups.

(iv) Problems of insularity: groups may fail to achieve gains from exchange with other groups, fail to address or even consider CAPs that affect such groups (or larger society), or engage in conflict with other groups.

Regarding all four problems, larger-scale governance systems exhibit some distinct advantages. First, because they draw upon many communities, they likely have access to more resources than local units. These include obvious items such as money and personnel, along with information that spans communities or that arises from intercommunity interaction. Recall that dispersed knowledge arises from the division of labor. Larger-scale governing bodies often have greater incentives to invest in acquiring somewhat unique trans-community information than do more localized bodies. With respect to problems (i) and (ii), large-scale governance units may draw upon their resources to subsidize or assist local units. External assistance may be particularly useful for resolving second-order CAPs. For example, the Federal Reserve Board provides regional FED officials with information related to monitoring local banks.

Second, because they rely on broader and more dispersed institutional foundations of power, external governance systems are often less subject to manipulation by local interests or power holders than are local systems. Large landholders, for example, may exert far greater influence over the design of community social rules than they do over national legislation. Similarly, the mining industry may influence the Montana Legislature more than it does the US Congress.[30] Resistance to local manipulation may not only help redress certain local CAPs (problem (i)), it may also redress local inequities (problem (iii)). For example, following years of activity by the civil rights movement, Congress passed the 1965 Voting Rights Act. The Act required southern states to abandon voter registration procedures that excluded blacks; it also provided credible enforcement mechanisms.[31] Indeed, prior to passage of and enforcement of civil rights and voting rights legislation in 1964 and 1965, the Ku Klux Klan burned African American churches and homes in the South, while local authorities looked the other way (Branch 1988, 1998).

Third, large-scale systems have an ability to institute trans-community auxiliary transactions that can assist with problems (i) and (ii), balance local inequities (problem (iii)), and mitigate problems of insularity ((iv)). For example, by passing the 1965 Voting Rights Act, Congress created an arena for an auxiliary transaction (federal enforcement). Likewise, knowing that the Supreme Court, as an auxiliary transaction arena, can adjudicate disputes among the states, relatively few serious disputes arise.

More generally, large institutional systems have the potential to resolve at least some of the CAPs embedded within problems (i)–(iv) by extending core institutional influences across communities. Mixtures of formal and working rules indicate *ADICO* prescriptions (see Section 8.1) that define relevant categories of agents and behavior (knowledge partitions). Such rules designate positions from which third-party enforcers perform auxiliary transactions, and also designate relevant third parties, often organizations. Furthermore, these rules specify functions and incentives for enforcers at different levels of governance. For example, the FBI investigates domestic terrorism, such as the 1995 bombing of the Alfred P. Murrah Federal Building in Oklahoma City. State police enforce highway laws; local police enforce shoplifting; county courts adjudicate local property disputes; et cetera. Such arrangements enhance predictability; they create shared mental models that point to cause-and-effect relationships between core and auxiliary transactions. This large-scale choreography reduces the likelihood of severe coordination failure among communities (Heiner 1983).

External governance systems may thus motivate trans-community cooperation that would otherwise be difficult or impossible. Between 1781 and 1789, the 13 United States were loosely organized under the Articles of Confederation. Lacking the power to tax, the new nation faced extreme difficulties motivating its constituent states to contribute to national public goods, such as national defense and interstate transportation. There was no national court system for resolving disputes among the states (Morison 1994). Resolving national CAPs required more extensive mechanisms. Adoption of the US Constitution in 1789, a formal political institution par excellence, established the role of the federal government as a third-party enforcer, coordinator, and provider of national public goods.[32]

Recall from Chapter 4 that resolution of second-order CAPs requires exercising power. When institutional systems designate auxiliary transactions via collective-choice or constitutional rules that assign political, economic, and social positions, they deploy power—often efficiently. For example, the Environmental Protection Agency exercises power1 by specifying fines for excessive pollution—an auxiliary transaction that influences core market transactions. Similarly, by passing the 1965 Voting Rights Act, Congress altered the "rules of the game" for conducting elections in the South (and the entire United States). In so doing, it created a new auxiliary transaction—federal enforcement of voting rights—an exercise of power2. When implemented, this act (along with many other factors) helped erode blatant racial prejudices among whites—an example of power3.

Unfortunately, power can lead to abuse. More generally, as levels of trans-community authority increase, say, from towns to counties to states to nations, society faces successively greater principal-agent problems related to enforcement. Third-party enforcers (as individuals or organizations) are agents who possess material and social interests that may not align either with those of the parties over whom they exercise enforcement powers or with interests of society at large. Designated third-party positions may facilitate exercises of authority that exploit others or enhance enforcers' own wealth, or their power. Such enforcers may even strive to maintain institutional arrangements that are—from society's point of view—ineffective, dysfunctional, or obsolete.[33] For example, hoping to prolong his own power, Libyan dictator Colonel Muammar el-Qaddafi, in 2011, used his authority to marshal armed suppression of an initially peaceful civilian uprising.

Perhaps more ominously, formal institutions can grant certain actors power to alter existing institutions or design new ones with their own ends in mind. North (1990) notes that formal rules "are created to serve the interests of those with bargaining power to devise new rules" (16). Individuals and organizations that occupy institutionally designated rulemaking positions may exercise their power so as to exclude or marginalize potential challengers. Consequently, path-dependent, dysfunctional systems may emerge at either local or trans-community levels.

Thus the emergence of functional systems that mix formal institutions with third-party enforcement is far from automatic and, when established, such systems may not endure. Historical transitions from personal exchange to impersonal exchange faced considerable difficulties addressing novel circumstances and so, where successful, took on many different institutional forms (North 2005, 116–22). The Mediterranean community responsibility system lasted for 300 years, but eventually rising numbers of traders, competition, and heterogeneity (of products and traders) increased enforcement costs (by both lowering costs of misrepresentation and increasing costs of verification). These developments compromised the viability of contracts and the political support for the system (Greif 2006a, 2006b). By exacerbating second-order CAPs, the system's own success ultimately created self-undermining dynamics.

Because social norms influence concepts of legitimacy via their effects on cognition and preference, functional trans-community institutional systems require difficult-to-attain compatibility between formal institutions and slowly evolving social norms (North 2005, 119). Successful institutional functioning also requires similar compatibility between various levels of third- and second-party enforcers, all of whom possess their own agendas. To achieve functionality, both of these levels of governance—and the interactions between them—must simultaneously incorporate informal and formal social mechanisms that motivate both third- and second-party enforcers (or coordinators) to execute their functions without excessive abuse of their power (ideally without any abuse).

Nonetheless, each level of governance has its own comparative advantages that emerge from its ability to develop understandings and information within its own domain, as well as to coordinate and enforce—that is, institute auxiliary transactions—over its own scale of operation. We now address interactions among these various levels by developing the concept of polycentric governance.

10.3. COMBINING SECOND- AND THIRD-PARTY ENFORCEMENT: POLYCENTRIC GOVERNANCE

Drawing together and extending themes from previous sections, we argue that second-party governance—at any level of aggregation—should focus on addressing localized CAPs. In contrast, higher-level, trans-community, third-party governance should focus on CAPs that individual communities lack the resources or political will to address, including internal inequities; CAPs of trans-community interaction, including external impacts of one community's activity on another; and CAPs that affect larger social and physical environments.

The related concepts of polycentric governance (Ostrom, Tiebout, and Warren 1961) and public economies (Ostrom and Ostrom 1977; Ostrom 1998b) address interactions among governance units. *Polycentric governance* involves interdependent authority relations among formally independent centers of decision making at various levels of aggregation—ranging from neighborhood associations to municipalities, national governments, and international agencies. This concept may also apply to private-sector governance of workgroups, departments, corporations, and so forth.[34] Component members of a single polycentric system interact via competition, cooperation, or conflict; they also use common dispute-resolution mechanisms, such as local and regional courts. For example, in a metropolitan area, say, greater Los Angeles, different governments or agencies may compete over tax revenue, budget allocations, constituents, employees, and other resources. They may also enact cooperative agreements. In the 1950s, Los Angeles County contracted with nearby cities, including Lakewood, to provide or assist with certain public services, such as policing (Ostrom, Tiebout, and Warren 1961). At the same time, conflict among governance units can arise from competition over resources, problems with agreements, external impacts of one agency's actions on another, and so forth. To adjudicate disputes, such units may resort to courts, or less formal arbitration systems whose jurisdiction spans individual community boundaries, or they may jointly create third-party adjudicators. Within a polycentric system, no single agency has a monopoly on enforcement, coordination, or the provision of public goods.[35]

Public economies address important quasi-market, quasi-hierarchical interactions among components of polycentric governance systems related to resolving CAPs. They arrange for the provision, production, and management of various collective goods. For example, the European Union and member governments have jointly negotiated arrangements to provide for a common currency, the euro.[36] Decisions to provide collective goods typically involve forms of collective input, rather than market transactions. But arranging for such provision involves negotiating contractual agreements among constituent organizations, often with provisions for contingent renewal. Hence public economy mechanisms often lie somewhere between market and hierarchy.

Within public economies, *collective-consumption units* are governmental or nongovernmental organizations that arrange for (solve CAPs related to) the provision of collective goods—without necessarily producing them. They also establish limits on the use of common-pool resources.[37] For example, when governments hire private contractors to build roads, they act as collective-consumption units that provide a public good, but contractors produce it. Governments then regulate its use.[38] Collective-consumption units operate at different scales with different purposes. Examples include nonprofit organizations, government agencies, local governments, national governments, and international agencies. Within such units, the production of public services often involves some degree of participation from citizens. Students, for example, co-produce their own education by studying. Likewise, citizens help produce public safety by reporting crime, obeying traffic laws, locking up valuables, and so forth. Citizen co-production can reinforce arrangements for providing public goods via multiple reciprocal relationships that utilize and enhance local social capital.

The role of citizen co-production strengthens our previous claim that the viability of third-party enforcement—and that of attendant formal institutions—depends on localized conventions and social norms or, more generally, social capital at various levels of aggregation. Third-party enforcers need to attain sufficient legitimacy if they hope to achieve citizen cooperation in critical activities like sharing information. Police in Springfield, Massachusetts, for example, have received valuable assistance from neighborhoods in combating gangs (Goode 2012). Citizen loyalty to communities or identification with them can help to legitimate third-party intervention, provided that external enforcement activities exhibit general compatibility with locally pertinent norms. Citizen participation may also help discipline third-party enforcers toward bona fide enforcement and away from abuse of their power. Polycentricism is thus an outcome of multiple attempts to resolve first- and second-order CAPs that affect different communities at different levels of aggregation.

Nested Systems of Second and Third Parties

Having established the concepts of polycentric governance and public economies, we now address various levels of second- and third-party enforcement within such systems. Broadly speaking, polycentric governance involves nested systems of rule structures and associated agencies or organizations.[39] Consider a localized system of governance, such as a town or suburban community. We may say it operates at a system level v; it addresses level-v CAPs utilizing localized, level-v information and social capital, including governance structures and accompanying shared mental models. At community level v, enforcement mechanisms rely on second parties: a town enforces its own rules. Nevertheless, among subcomponents of v, such as individual citizens or local businesses, enforcement involves third parties, such as town police. Adjacent communities also operate at level v, utilizing somewhat different localized information and social capital to address different sets of level-v CAPs among their own subcomponents.

Various communities at level v, typically within the same region, interact as elements of a larger polycentric governance system: they compete over resources, engage in various

cooperative agreements or contracts, and face conflicts of interest that, at least in principle, can be adjudicated via common dispute-resolution mechanisms. Furthermore, such
communities function within larger physical and social environments that span community boundaries. Across such larger environments, coordination and enforcement—when
operational—emerge from sets of agreements, rules, associated understandings, and organizations at system level $v + 1$. We thus write the function $l_{v+1}(l_v)$ to signify the relationship between the two system levels: rules and organizations at system level $v + 1$ resolve
second-order CAPs of coordination and enforcement, along with first-order free-riding
CAPs that develop among subcomponents that operate at level v. Moreover, for a level-v
system, we could write an analogous relationship with its subcomponents as $l_v(l_{v-1})$. Likewise, we could extend successively larger or smaller systems and subsystems by adding to
or subtracting from any given system-level number.

Generally speaking, each system at a given level v has the best localized information about
its internal interactions and local environment. Normally, it has a comparative advantage
in constructing rules for resolving CAPs among its own subunits, according to the principles detailed in Chapter 9, subject to the same "dark side" limitations. Nevertheless, each
level-v unit, by itself, typically lacks the requisite cognition, information, and motivation
for even addressing (much less resolving) larger-order CAPs at levels $v + 1$ and higher—
indicating a potential role for higher-level rules and coordination. We may use Heiner's reliability condition (equation (6.5)) to explain the need for such higher-level rules. A system
at level v lacks both reliable information about and experience with social interactions and
environmental phenomenon at level $v + 1$. Accordingly, evolutionary pressure will tend to
exclude its consideration of technically feasible strategies that operate at level $v + 1$. Even
though some could be useful, level-v agencies do not know when or how to employ them.[40]

Addressing these larger problems thus requires coordination at a higher level, where
broader knowledge and experience (should it exist) could, at least in principle, facilitate
trans-community strategies or coordination and enforcement mechanisms that could pass
a pertinent reliability condition.[41] For example, local councils in the London metropolitan
area can, by themselves, do very little to arrange public transportation among communities. The Greater London Authority, by contrast, can engage in a broad set of strategies
associated with building, operating, and maintaining bus and underground (subway) transportation systems. Effectively, and perhaps counterintuitively, a level-$(v + 1)$ governing system can possess greater flexibility for addressing systemwide problems than its individual,
level-v, components (Heiner 1983).

Two final points deserve mention. First, as stated previously, the distinction between
second and third parties depends on the level of analysis. Moreover, the higher the level of
a system of governance ($v + 1 > v$), the more likely it will apply third-party enforcement to
lower levels. Enforcers at level $v + 2$ may act as third parties for actors at both levels $v + 1$ and
v. Second, the low levels of a hierarchy may be able to function with relatively informal institutions, but higher levels typically require the specified and recorded collective-decision
processes that characterize formal institutions. Neighborhood organizations and councils
may function on the basis of reciprocal relationships, social norms, and informal social
rules, but even town governments use formalized procedures for establishing ordinances

and regulations. Similarly, within firms, corporate policies typically emerge from formal collective-choice procedures, whereas small workgroups rely on informal mechanisms of coordination and enforcement.

10.4. CONCLUSION

The complex nexus of exchange that underlies contemporary economic development relies upon dense institutional systems that combine informal and formal institutions—in conjunction with multiple layers of second- and third-party enforcement. Political-economic governance is fundamentally polycentric.

We conclude with two simple principles on how to achieve more or less functional relationships in such nested hierarchical systems: First, formal institutions (at whatever level of governance) need to achieve (or reflect) some degree of compatibility with pertinent informal institutions—social norms in particular. Otherwise, formal prescriptions, notably those of laws and regulations, may fail to achieve intended outcomes—due to incompatibility with operating social equilibria. Second, each level in a polycentric system ideally should generate rules and utilize coordination and enforcement mechanisms in areas where it has a comparative advantage. The details of local interaction ought to be left to local, self-organized, and relatively informal governance mechanisms that can utilize and develop local social capital. But coordination among such level-v local units, and interactions with their shared (non-ergodic) social or physical environments, should be addressed at a higher governance level (typically $v + 1$). Such higher-level governance should, nevertheless, reflect or embody the activities of a rough coalition of v-level entities that institutes its own set of level-$(v + 1)$ coordination and enforcement mechanisms (i.e., third-party mechanisms from the viewpoint of level-v operators). Typically such mechanisms rely on somewhat more formal mixtures of institutions than those operating at lower governance levels. Analogous extensions up or down the system-level hierarchy follow. Generally speaking, we expect a higher-level system to have greater knowledge of and flexibility for addressing problems that span its constituents, because (at least in principle) it can gather information and experience concerning their interrelations and shared environment, and may also have some motivation for doing so. Likewise, we expect lower-level systems to possess far greater knowledge and flexibility for addressing localized problems with local social capital.

These principles are easily stated, but CAPs accompany every element and interaction. Concerning the first principle, noteworthy difficulties arise when laws of the larger society conflict with locally pertinent norms—as the 1957 Civil Rights Act did in the South, or as Prohibition did for the entire United States between 1920 and 1933. Concerning the second principle, a particular difficulty surrounds efforts by level-$(v + 1)$ units to redress perceived group failures at level v, notably inequities. Whereas—following a great deal of social protest initiated by the civil rights movement—the 1965 Voting Rights Act proved successful in confronting voting inequities in the South, the states of Arizona, Utah, and Texas still face difficulties enforcing laws against polygamy in specific small communities (Johnson 2008). Moreover, level-$(v + 1)$ perceptions of level-v failure may not be accurate or may serve the interests of level-$(v + 1)$ power holders. Additionally, pertinent norms may conflict. Indeed, the inevitable conflicts echo Dasgupta's core problem of rural political economy (see Section 9.6). Rephrasing slightly, this problem concerns how to merge third-party enforcement based on formal and informal institutions with mechanisms of second-party enforcement and governance based on localized social capital.

Finally, there is no guarantee that even viable institutional systems, at any level of governance, are either efficient or equitable (North 1990; Bowles 2004). Those who benefit from extant systems frequently can exercise power to diminish participation of potential opponents (e.g., by altering rules). Opponents typically have significantly less access to key sources of power: relevant institutional positions, per-capita access to resources, and ability to resolve (far more substantial) organizational CAPs. Chapter 12 will return to CAPs related to both sets of problems: policymaking and reforming institutions. First, Chapter 11 addresses underlying networks.

EXERCISES

10.1. Auxiliary transactions (some leeway on answers)
  a. Draw a general diagram that shows a core transaction and an auxiliary transaction. Indicate positions for enforcers and label each as either a third or a second party as appropriate. As relevant, indicate where organizations may fit in and where institutions may fit in. Briefly explain your diagram's logic.
  b. Adjust your diagram to show relationships among the Maghribi traders.
  c. Adjust your diagram to represent the Mediterranean community responsibility system.

10.2. Show that the pollution law discussed in connection with Figure 10.1 does not, by itself, alter the payoffs in the described game.

10.3. In the game in Figure 10.1 and the accompanying description, show that if $\alpha \geq 1 - \delta p$, neither player unilaterally violates the law.

10.4. Design a model of triadic power (see Chapter 4) that represents interactions between parties to an exchange and relevant second- and third-party enforcers. Be creative.

10.5. Draw a version of your answer to Exercise 10.1a that fits polycentric governance, and explain its basic logic.

10.6. Relate Section 10.3's discussion of level-v and level-$(v + 1)$ systems of governance to Heiner's reliability condition (equation (6.5)). Incorporate appropriate terms into the basic functions in (6.5) and explain your equation.

11 SOCIAL NETWORKS AND
COLLECTIVE ACTION

> There is a recent surge in economic research that is keenly striving to understand phenomena as *embedded in the underlying social structure*, i.e., integrated in the network of connections that define how agents interact and communicate.
>
> Fernando Vega-Redondo (2007)

In both Arruba and Boratonia, farmers interact regularly with some of their neighbors or associates, less with others, and not at all with still others. They exchange information, favors, and commodities. Some transactions, such as exchanges of personal information, are reserved only for friends or close associates. Other exchanges, such as comments on the weather and its impact on crops, may involve acquaintances or even strangers. Ideas concerning farming techniques, ways to organize work, or how to market produce may pass from one farmer to another or across groups. One person's ideas may affect another's actions. The extent of such influence depends on the degree to which specific farmers are connected to others. The chair of the local grain exchange has greater impact on community decisions, such as access to irrigation canals, than less connected farmers. Local connections can also help farmers uncover information from distant sources. Jack Smith, who lives on the west side of Arruba, may want to hear about radish irrigation techniques used by Sue Jones, who he believes lives on the east end of Boratonia. Knowing only her name, Jack asks his neighbor Jed Price, who has traveled to Boratonia, to help locate Sue through connections Jed made while traveling.

About three years ago, Phil and Ester (from the community of Sellville, just north of the center of Boratonia) began using drip hoses—a way to reduce evaporation. Three neighbors observed, and a week later adopted the technique. They talked at the local store. Two weeks after that, all of Sellville had adopted the technique. On their travels, Sellville farmers mentioned the new hoses to people they met. Within three weeks, virtually all farmers in Boratonia had ordered drip hoses. By then, of course, many Arruba farmers had heard as well. A week later, most of them had ordered the new hoses. Local connections had rapidly spread news of the new technique across the two communities.

Many readers of this book have heard of the small-world phenomenon of networks. A reasonably well known example concerns the actor Kevin Bacon. Suppose we list all actors who have appeared in a movie with Mr. Bacon, then consider all actors who have acted in a movie with someone who had acted with him, and then list how many acted with one of them, and so forth. We may call each level in this process a *degree of separation*. An actor who appeared in a movie with Kevin Bacon has one degree of separation from him.

Someone who did not actually act with him but appeared in a movie with someone who did has two degrees of separation, and so forth. How many degrees of separation would we need to encompass the vast majority of the movie acting community? In just three such steps—three degrees of separation—we can account for over 80%; with four degrees of separation, over 98%.[1]

Think of networks you belong to: family, friends, colleagues, classmates, acquaintances, or people with whom you share information. These are all types of *social networks*: configurations of relationships or communication pathways that somehow connect people. Transportation systems are also networks; there are networks of roads, railways, airline routes, even pedestrian walkways, sometimes with linkages between different transportation modes, as in driving to an airport. Electric power flows across vast networks of lines and terminals. These are physical networks. The World Wide Web is an information network. Accordingly, network analysis involves multiple disciplines. Biochemists may explore linkages among polymers or between polymers and monomers; DNA is a network. Biologists investigate links in food chains and links within predator-prey relationships. Computer scientists study networks on the Internet or wiring networks within hardware and code networks within software. Social scientists study multiple networks of social, political, and economic interaction—as this chapter's opening example suggests.

Networks have three core characteristics: structure; actions taken within a given structure; and evolutionary processes of formation, growth, and decay. *Network structure* reflects various configurations of linkages among different units and groupings. We may conceptualize network structure at both a micro level (local configurations) and a macro level (overarching characteristics). Activity flows across network connections. Networks serve as conduits for exchange, communication, influence, transportation, and so forth. Finally, networks continuously evolve: they add and drop connections, altering their structures.

Economic, political, and social exchanges operate within the context of social networks. Chapters 6–10 have established the importance of social context. Networks literally add dimension to context. For example, we may regard organizations as networks in which links serve as conduits for flows of information and influence. A CEO occupies a specific position within a dense web of corporate connections. Similarly, markets rely on, arise from, and sometimes embody networks of exchange among various buyers and sellers—producers and suppliers, distributors and consumers, borrowers and lenders, and so forth.

Networks thus influence economic, social, and political outcomes; the structure of social networks permits, conditions, or precludes interactions in multiple contexts. For example, Granovetter (1973) finds that a large proportion of job searches rely extensively on "weak" social ties—ties with interactions that occur once a year or less. Calvó-Armengol and Jackson (2004) find that network structures influence relations between social connections and types of employment. For the unemployed, networks influence the impact of unemployment duration on future employment via links of referral or reference (Montgomery 1991). Networks affect transmissions of new information or technique. When the antibiotic tetracycline was first introduced, it diffused most rapidly among doctors who were most integrated into the medical community, via social ties of friendship or advising relationships (Coleman, Katz, and Menzel 1966). In this regard, DeMarzo, Vayanos, and Zwiebel (2003) find that agents with influence in social networks have greater impact on the diffusion of ideas than do other agents. Similarly, Morris (2000) finds that social cohesiveness affects rates of diffusion.[2] Networks can even influence physical characteristics; after studying networks of more than 12,000 people over a period of 32 years, Christakis and Fowler (2007) report that a person's probability of weight gain is strongly associated with weight gain among friends. On a grander scale, social movements build around networks. Chwe (2000) finds that agents coordinate with their close connections, but (echoing Granovetter) he notes that intermediate-strength connections facilitate organization.

More comprehensively, social networks provide the "grid" upon or through which social, economic, and political exchanges occur. Networks are the foundation of social capital (Dasgupta 2011). They foster the trusting relationships that underlie exchange and the resolution of CAPs. For example, Gulati, Nohria, and Zaheer (2000) report that nonmarket relationships between various types of buyers and sellers support trade by stabilizing interactions during uncertain times. Stability, in turn, facilitates informal insurance mechanisms, allowing for flexibility in trade relationships. Likewise, Granovetter (1985) asserts that economic exchange is embedded within social networks. Coleman (1988) argues that network cohesiveness fosters enforcement of social norms and, more generally, creation of social capital and trust. Greif's (2006a) historical account of Mediterranean trade among the Maghribi (see Section 10.1) points to the importance of social networks as foundations of institutional systems that facilitate exchange relationships. On the other hand, network architecture may create CAPs. For example, CAPs of traffic congestion are fundamentally network problems.

We may regard institutions and institutional systems as networks: complex conduits of cognition, information, and motivation. In network relationships, the positions of individuals—the precise configurations of their connections to others within organizations or exchange relationships—condition their influence on opinions, ideas, and policies. Well-connected CEOs may dominate corporate policymaking; network positions confer power. Agents may also use network connections, and related notions of social identity, to locate information and create new relationships. Moreover, network architecture affects rates of diffusion of ideas or practices, sometimes generating punctuated equilibria—and then later, disturbances that undermine them. Network analysis thus informs our understandings of the potential for and the complexity of political, social, and economic exchange, as well as attendant CAPs.

This chapter's discussion offers a necessarily limited picture of a complex, evolving area of theory.[3] Section 11.1 introduces basic network concepts. Section 11.2 addresses the impact of micro-level network structure on the ability of agents to exert influence; network position can be a source of power. Section 11.3 addresses the searchability property of social networks; agents use local knowledge of network attributes based on social identity categories to locate distant information on individuals, groups, or ideas. Section 11.4 discusses *information cascades* across networks—sequences of rapid adoption of ideas or practices associated with such phenomena as fads, financial contagion, and revolution. Section 11.5 concludes.

11.1. ELEMENTARY NETWORK THEORY

In order to understand the impact of network structure, transmission, and evolution on exchange and collective action, we first address basic network theory.[4]

Basic Network Concepts

A *social network* embodies a set of relationships or exchanges among various groupings of individuals, specifying precisely who interacts with whom. Network interactions may be specific, as in transfers of financial information among banks, or quite general, as in friendship or acquaintance. Social networks tend to have the following features (Watts 2003):

(i) Many small densely interconnected groups that overlap in the sense of sharing one or more members.

(ii) Dynamism: networks grow, shrink, and alter configurations.

(iii) Patterns of new linkage that tend to follow patterns of prior connection: whom you interact with tomorrow usually has some relation to prior interactions.

(iv) Some potential for entirely new connections via individual choice or external circumstances. A student's new friends at college may not know her high-school friends.

To proceed, we establish a basic network vocabulary and properties.

Mathematically, a *network* (Γ) is a set of *nodes* (N) where set N consists of n nodes $\{i = 1, 2, \ldots, n\}$. *Nodes* are points or vertices that are usually connected to one or more other nodes by segments or *links*. We may use a set (or matrix) g to depict the presence or absence of links between all nodes within a network. For any pair of nodes i and j within network Γ, if node i is linked to j, we write $g_{ij} = 1$; if i is not linked to j, $g_{ij} = 0$. Thus g is the set of all such relationships between all possible pairings of nodes in Γ, and equation $\Gamma = (N, g)$ describes the network.[5]

In the social sciences, we may think of nodes as agents—either individuals or organizations—or possibly entities used by agents that connect them, such as web pages or highways. Links signify any type of relationship among agents—such as friendship, family connections, or work relations—that facilitates economic, political, social, or informational exchanges. Sometimes we may regard transactions themselves as links. Relevant transactions include buying or selling, exchange of political favors (e.g., vote trading), social exchanges (e.g., approval or disapproval), various forms of communication (e.g., phone calls or e-mail), and so on. Links may be either *undirected*, indicating two-way flows, such as exchanges among friends, or *directed*, going from one node to another, as an instruction from a manager to an employee.[6] Any two nodes can have undirected links, in-only links, out-only links, or no links. A single node with no links is *isolated*. Broadly speaking, we may examine network structure either from a micro level that focuses on describing linkage properties among small sets of nodes or from a macro level that summarizes average network properties.

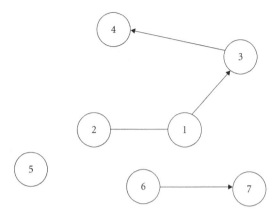

Figure 11.1   A basic network

Figure 11.1 illustrates a simple network. Nodes are circles. An undirected link connects nodes 1 and 2, while directed links connect node 1 to node 3, 3 to 4, and 6 to 7. Node 5 is isolated.

Basic Network Characteristics

To explain characteristics of networks, we follow Jackson (2008) by defining the following additional terms:

- The *degree* of a node i ($d_i(g)$) specifies the number of links attached to it. If node i is linked to nodes j and k but not to node l, then $g_{ij} = 1$, $g_{ik} = 1$, and $g_{il} = 0$. Thus $d_i(g) = 2$: node i is of degree 2 (assuming no other links).

- For directed networks, we distinguish between the *in-degree*—the number of incoming links (written as $g_{ji} = 1$ for all relevant j with whom i has incoming links), and the *out-degree*—the number of outgoing links (where $g_{ij} = 1$ for all relevant j with whom i has outgoing links). Thus, in Figure 11.1, $g_{34} = 1$ means that node 3 has an outgoing link to 4 and that 4 has an incoming link from 3; $g_{31} = 0$ means that 3 has no outgoing link to 1 and that 1 has no incoming link from 3; and $g_{13} = 1$ means that 1 has an outgoing link to 3 and that 3 has in incoming link from 1.

- The *neighborhood* of node i (N^i) is the set of nodes to which i is directly linked. For example, if node i is of degree 2, linked to nodes j and k, the neighborhood $N^i = \{j, k\}$. In Figure 11.1, nodes 2 and 3 are in the neighborhood of node 1. The *second-degree neighborhood* of i (N^i_2) also includes all direct links to each node j that is directly linked to i. (The term neighborhood without modification means first-degree neighborhood.)

- The *degree distribution* $\rho(\kappa)$ of network Γ describes the relative frequencies of nodes with different degrees. For all possible degrees $\kappa = 0, 1, \ldots, n-1$, $\rho(\kappa)$ specifies the fraction of nodes that are of degree κ. It shows, for all possible κ, the probability that any given node is of degree κ.

- A *path* is a sequence of links between two nodes that goes through distinct nodes without repetition.[7] We may draw a path from node 2 to nodes 1, 3, and 4, and another path from node 1 to nodes 3 and 4—but not in the opposite direction due to the directed links.
- A *geodesic* is the shortest path between two nodes.
- The *diameter* of a network Γ is its largest geodesic.

Networks have structures, and structure influences the flow of information, transactions, and exchanges within them. For example, in a sophomore high-school class, there are different groups of friends of different sizes and compositions. Some students belong to more than one group; others do not. Some students have many friends; others do not. Some friends of particular students know each other; others do not. To analyze network *structure*—that is, patterns of connection within networks—we define and discuss a few additional terms. A set of nodes is *connected* if all of its nodes can be reached by a path (of any length) from all other nodes. Many networks are not connected. We now define the *components* of a network Γ as the largest connected subsets of nodes within the network. For example, the network in Figure 11.1 has three components: nodes 1–4, node 5, and nodes 6 and 7, but not nodes 1–3.[8] A *fully connected* network has only one component: the entire network. The *size* of a component is the number of nodes within it. We define $\phi(s)$ as the fraction of components in a network of a specific size (s). In Figure 11.1, $\phi(4) = \phi(2) = \phi(1) = 1/3$ and $\phi(3) = 0$: one-third of the components are of respective sizes 4, 2, and 1; no components are of size 3.

Clustering

Another important structural feature of networks is clustering. Some network groupings are clustered in the sense that nodes with links to a specific node are also linked to each other. How many of your friends know each other? Some networks of friends are tightly clustered cliques. We can measure clustering at three levels: for an individual node, for a component, and for the entire network. The basic unit of clustering is a triplet. (Recall Basu's model of triadic power.) Consider a triplet of nodes i, j, and k, where i is a neighbor of both j and k. We say that these three nodes are *clustered* if and only if j and k are also linked. Now consider a node i that is connected to three other nodes: c, d, and e. For cluster analysis, we consider all possible triplets in which i could be linked to two other nodes; for this case, we have triplets $\{i, c, d\}$, $\{i, c, e\}$, and $\{i, d, e\}$. Node i's *individual clustering coefficient* specifies the portion of all pairs of nodes that are both directly linked to node i and linked to each other. We write

(11.1)
$$Cl_i(g) = \frac{\sum_{j,k} g_{ij} g_{ik} g_{jk}}{\sum_{j,k} g_{ij} g_{ik}} \quad \text{for all nodes } k \neq j \text{ that are linked to } i.$$

Note that symbols j and k represent all possible pairs of nodes among the nodes connected to node i. Here symbols j and k represent nodes c, d, and/or e in all possible pairs.

The numerator of (11.1) shows the total number of connections between all possible pairings of any two nodes j and k that are linked to node i. Recall that $g = 1$ if the nodes are connected and 0 otherwise. Thus, if nodes j and k are connected to i but are not connected to each other, then $g_{jk} = 0$ and product $g_{ij}g_{ik}g_{jk} = 0$. In the numerator of (11.1), if c is connected to both d and e but d and e are not themselves connected, $\sum_{j,k} g_{ij}g_{ik}g_{jk} = 2$. The denominator of (11.1) shows the total number of pairings of nodes linked to i ({cd, cd, de}). Thus $Cl_i(g) = 2/3$.[9] Calculations for higher-degree nodes follow the same principles. Individual clustering, then, measures the connectedness among nodes that are all linked to a specific node i. Members of social cliques, for example, characteristically have high individual clustering coefficients. More generally, if $Cl_i(g) > Cl_j(g)$, agent i has more closely connected contacts, such as friends or work associates, than j.

We consider one macro-level measure of clustering for a connected network (or component).[10] *Average* clustering takes the mean of $Cl_i(g)$ over the network (or component):

$$(11.2) \qquad Cl^{Av}(g) = \sum_{i=1}^{n} \frac{Cl_i(g)}{n},$$

where n is the number of nodes in the connected network (or component). Alternatively, we may count up all cases in a network (or component) where any node i is linked to any pair of other nodes j and k, and then calculate the proportion of all such nodes j and k that are themselves linked.

We may now use the concept of clustering to explain Granovetter's (1973) finding that weak links facilitate job search. For Granovetter, the strength of a tie between agents i and j within some group of agents (S) depends on their frequency of interaction, which, in turn, is influenced by the proportion of S who also interact with (are tied to) both i and j (1973, 1362). Thus clustering affects the strength of ties; as a rule, the tighter the clustering, the stronger the ties within a group. Information exchanges in groups with strong ties, however, tend to be redundant: j may have already told i what k said. Weak ties, on the other hand, can transmit information across disparate social groupings that have access to quite different sources of information.

The concept of bridges offers another way to consider relations between clustering and weak ties. A *bridge* is a link that establishes the only path in a network between two nodes (Granovetter 1973, 1364); its removal would leave no path between them. Removal of a bridge would create two separate components among the nodes on either side of it. Bridges are weak ties that link otherwise unconnected social groupings. In Figure 11.2, nodes 1–6 are tightly clustered and nodes 7–10 are less so. The link between nodes 3 and 9 is a bridge.[11] That weak tie may allow otherwise unavailable information to flow between these groups. More generally, a *local bridge of degree r* is the shortest path of length r between two nodes. For example, if we added a link from node 6 to node 10, the link between 3 and 9 would still be a local bridge between most nodes. Now if the quality of information deteriorates as the number of links it crosses increases, local bridges—typically weak ties—offer the most efficient routes of information transfer within networks. Not surprisingly, then, Granovetter (1973) finds weak ties—often bridges or local bridges—important for job search.

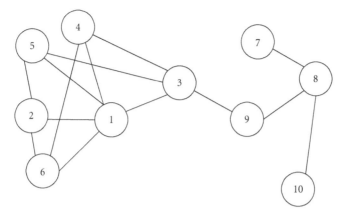

Figure 11.2   Network clusters and bridge

Centrality and Cohesiveness

The concepts of centrality and cohesiveness in a network follow from clustering. In social networks, some agents or groups of agents are more "connected" (in the colloquial sense) than others. They may have more influence or better access to information. To investigate this micro-level structural attribute of networks, we consider four measures. The first, individual clustering, appeared in equation (11.1); as stated, it describes the extent of connectedness among the nodes that are linked to a single node i. Second, we may broaden the idea of strong links to larger subsets by using the concept of cohesiveness within a particular grouping. Consider a single node i that belongs to some subset or group M within network Γ. We show the fraction of all of i's own connections that are within group M as

$$(11.3) \qquad H^i(M) = \frac{\sum_{j \neq i} g_{ij} \mid j \in M}{d_i(g)}.$$

The numerator of (11.3) shows the total number of links that i has to members of M, and the denominator shows i's degree (its total number of links). For example, suppose that Mary is an accountant who lives in a small town. Mary's $H^i(M)$ could represent the portion of her social contacts who are also accountants. Now, the *cohesiveness* of group M is the minimum $H^i(M)$ for all nodes i in group M:[12]

$$(11.4) \qquad H(M) = \min_{i \in M} H^i(M).$$

Suppose that 60% of Mary's acquaintances are accountants but only 10% of Bob's are, and no other accountant has a lower proportion than Bob. The cohesiveness $H(M)$ for such accountants would be 0.1. Bob's tendency to socialize with non-accountants has lowered the group's cohesiveness. Network groupings with high levels of cohesiveness tend to have strong internal ties and tend to be relatively closed to outside influences. The $H(M)$ for a small religious cult, for example, may be quite high.

A third measure, *decay centrality* (or closeness centrality), captures how transmission quality deteriorates over distances between nodes (on shortest paths). Nodes with lower degrees of separation are likely to experience more reliable transmission. We define the *decay centrality* of node i as

$$(11.5) \qquad\qquad Dc_i = \sum_{j \neq i} \delta^{l(i,j)},$$

where exponent $l(i, j)$ is the number of links on the shortest path between node i and j (set to infinity if the nodes are not linked) and δ ($0 < \delta < 1$) is the rate of transmission decay across links.[13] Decay centrality relates to our prior discussion of weak ties: weak ties (local bridges) offer efficient transmission because they are subject to less decay than possibly longer paths consisting of stronger ties.

Finally, key players in social networks often bring together (link) other participants. Accordingly, our fourth and most comprehensive measure, *betweenness centrality*, estimates the importance of a specific node i in connecting two other nodes j and k. Define $v(j, k)$ as the number of geodesics (shortest paths) between any two nodes j and k, and define $v^i(j, k)$ as the total number of such geodesics on which node i lies. We measure the *betweenness* of node i as the portion of shortest paths between all relevant other nodes j and k that include i:

$$(11.6) \qquad\qquad b^i = \sum_{j \neq k} \frac{v^i(j,k)}{v(j,k)}.$$

Consider two nodes i and j. If $b^i > b^j$, then node i is more central because it lies on more short paths between other pairs of nodes than j does. For example, in a trade network, a "middle man" i is likely to have a high b^i relative to that of a typical firm or customer, since most feasible paths from producer k to consumer j go through i.[14] Section 11.2 will assert that betweenness centrality affects the diffusion of information across networks and illustrates how strategic network positions can become sources of power.

Important Network Types and Characteristics

Because they evolve, we may classify networks by how they are formed. Broadly speaking, there are two extremes: networks may form in a spontaneous, essentially random fashion, or they could be completely structured, so that all new links have a fixed relationship to existing links.[15] Networks with small-world properties, notably social networks, emerge from both random and structured processes.

A *random network* forms by arbitrarily assigning links to a fixed number of initially unlinked nodes for a specific time period or until the network has reached a specified average degree. Links appear completely independently of each other. The degree distribution

$\rho(\kappa)$ becomes a Poisson distribution, indicating that the proportion of nodes of a specified degree κ declines rapidly as κ increases. The portion of nodes of degree 30 is much smaller than that of degree 6. Random networks, however, do not adequately represent social networks. Social networks have far greater proportions of high-degree nodes and notably more clustering than random generation processes could induce. Furthermore, random networks tend to lack local structure (Vega-Redondo 2007). Nevertheless, randomness remains part of social network formation.

Many social networks, by contrast, exhibit small-world properties. Recall our discussion of actors linked to Kevin Bacon. We now define a *small-world network* as a network with a large number of nodes, relatively high localized clustering, and yet a small diameter (the largest geodesic has a small number of links; Watts 2003). Ownership patterns of German firms in the 1990s offer an example. The network is large and connections among firms are sparse in the sense that most firms have a few connections, yet degrees of separation are low: "Thus, despite the overall low density of ties, the members of a network are linked with each other across clusters through a relatively small number of intermediaries" (Kogut and Walker 2001, 318). As we will see in Section 11.3, small-world networks are "searchable" in the sense that agents belonging to a grouping in one area of a network can uncover information from distant regions. Granovetter's (1973) discussion of the importance of weak ties in job search also suggests this property.

We illustrate small-world network formation with an artificial network that combines random and structured properties. Consider a large set of 1,000 nodes that are equally spaced along a circle, where every node is linked only to its two immediate neighbors.[16] Now assign a few (say, 10) links that extend from 10 randomly chosen nodes, located somewhere on the circle, to 10 other randomly chosen nodes. These links dramatically reduce network diameter (Watts and Strogatz 1998). The new links are local bridges; they create shortcuts across distant sections of the network. Figure 11.3 illustrates a similar network with 10 nodes and two random links.

Another important kind of network—a *scale-free* network—is formed by combining random growth with preferential attachment. New nodes are linked randomly to existing

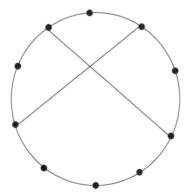

Figure 11.3   A small-world network

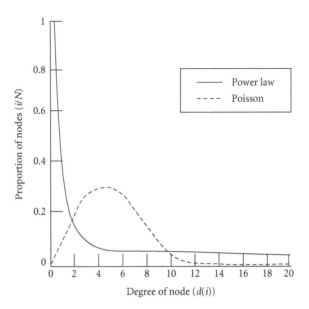

Figure 11.4 Power-law and Poisson distributions

nodes, but the probability of linking to an existing node increases in the number of links that node already has: *preferential attachment*. For example, if node *a* has twice as many links as node *b*, then a new node is twice as likely to connect to node *a* as it is to *b*. Thus, high-degree nodes tend to accumulate more future links than low-degree nodes. Furthermore, the degree distribution for scale-free networks reflects a power-law distribution (a type of "fat-tailed" distribution).[17] The proportion of very high-degree nodes, although low, is still much higher than that of a Poisson distribution (see Figure 11.4). Correspondingly, the degree of clustering is also much higher. Scale-free networks offer significantly closer approximations of social networks than do random networks.

Scale-free networks generate *hubs*—a few nodes with unusually high centrality. The presence of hubs creates small-world properties. An analogy with airline hubs fits perfectly: hub airports (e.g., O'Hare in Chicago) are network hubs with flight routes as links. One can usually fly from any large or medium-sized city to another in two flights. In social networks, the presence of hubs reflects the tendency of preferential attachment processes to create "rich-get-richer" phenomena whereby nodes formed early on typically accrue more links at higher rates than do other nodes. For example, Ijiri and Simon (1964) propose that businesses grow more or less randomly, but the probability of attaining a given rate of growth is proportional to prior growth (preferential attachment).

Large dispersed networks, such as the Web, tend to have scale-free properties. Websites for celebrities have exceedingly high degrees, while most others do not. Scale-free network models, however, have one important problem as representations of social networks: their formation process fails to reflect limitations on forming connections, such as connection costs that ultimately constrain the scale of social association. Thus hybrid models that mix scale-free and random network properties characterize many social networks (Jackson 2008). Social networks tend to exhibit the fat-tail, high-clustering, and small-world properties of scale-free networks, though often not as dramatically as technology-based networks like the Web. Surveying many network configurations across disciplines, Vega-Redondo (2007) finds the following core elements: clustering; small numbers of average links; and power-law distributions among dispersed networks (e.g., the Web) but not among more closely linked networks (e.g., circles of friends). On this foundation, we now turn to the flow of influence across networks.

11.2. INFLUENCE, DIFFUSION, AND SOCIAL LEARNING IN NETWORKS

Prior chapters have emphasized the importance of institutions, information, beliefs, and power in resolving CAPs—especially second-order CAPs—and thus the importance of these factors as foundations for complex exchange. This section focuses on a specific type of power that we call influence (defined below), relating it to transmission of information in networks. As an introduction, we present Basu's (2000) game-theoretic "man of influence" model. This model implicitly assumes a network structure that underlies relevant exchanges. By modeling the network, we can illustrate the source of influence. We proceed with a simple model of influence (the DeGroot model), which allows us to define leadership. We then apply such influence first to our network version of Basu's model and then to a network model of the Florentine oligarchy circa 1500.

Define a *person of influence* (P) as a person who "can get others to do him favors; that is he can get things done out of turn" (Basu 2000, 160); correspondingly, influence sways opinion. Suppose P occupies a position in some bureaucracy from which bureaucrats issue various licenses or permissions, favorable assignments, desirable appointments, and the like. We use the term *license* for all of these arrangements. Bureaucrats may operate in either the public or the private sector (e.g., as officials at prestigious private academies). Now define *asking a favor* as requesting a license of type z. If institutional practices (working rules and norms) allow enough leeway, bureaucrats can trade favors among themselves and with their constituents.[18] Person P facilitates such exchanges. Parties who seek favors ask P. For example, if a developer hopes to obtain a building permit—say, for a new office complex near a residential area—she may be able to persuade P to accelerate the process. P then persuades relevant bureaucrats to expedite review processes. In the model, compliance with P's requests is a best response for bureaucrats, indicating a social equilibrium based upon shared beliefs about P.[19] Basu is careful to note that his model describes an equilibrium, but (as for most Nash equilibria) does not explain how it comes about.

To proceed with the model, assume that there are $n \geq 3$ bureaucrats in n agencies and a single person of influence P. We number the bureaucrats $j = 1, 2, \ldots, n$. Each bureaucrat j can issue k_j licenses of type j. Assume that bureaucrats are not officially permitted to trade licenses as favors, but will do so under the right circumstances. Yet, they are not so corrupt as to accept bribes. Furthermore, bureaucrats experience guilt disutility (ψ) for each license they grant as favor. Each bureaucrat j, however, could use license $j + 1$ for personal benefit for a utility gain of β. For example, a bureaucrat in the traffic department may hope to secure a permit for his wife's business. In this sense, each bureaucrat is also a consumer. We assume that $3\psi > \beta > 2\psi$, so that no agent wants to exchange more than two licenses as favors.

The bureaucrats and P all hold the following two conjectures concerning their exchanges:

(i) P can and will do a favor for any bureaucrat j, so long as j does what P asks.

(ii) P conjectures that each j will give a maximum of two licenses to P or to whomever P designates.

If these beliefs are commonly held, a social equilibrium exists whereby each agent j asks P to deliver her a license of type $j + 1$. P then asks each $j + 1$ agent to give one license to each j, so that every bureaucrat j attains her desired license via exchanges coordinated by P.[20] Moreover, members of a size m subset of agents $j \in M$ have access to licenses that P wants; P requests a second license from each of them for personal use. Based upon conjectures (i) and (ii), all bureaucrats in M expect to receive positive utility $\beta - 2\psi$, all remaining bureaucrats expect $\beta - \psi$, and P expects utility $m\beta$. Thus, by focusing beliefs and actions on the role of P, these two conjectures jointly act as a social choreographer that designates a correlated equilibrium.

Relating this model to networks, P occupies the central position in a simple circular network with bureaucrats on the outside and P in the center; Figure 11.5 illustrates. Requests for licenses are directed links from P to all bureaucrats around the circle. Counterclockwise directed links between all adjacent nodes on the circle represent license transfers from each $j + 1$ to the corresponding j agent. Directed links from agents $j \in M$ to P (here agents $j - 1$ and $j - 3$) represent transfers of second licenses for P's own use. Note that all of these links reflect adherence to conjectures (i) and (ii). If any agent stops believing either conjecture, the rupture of one link causes the entire chain to collapse, and P's role evaporates. If, however, each agent's belief is conditioned by those of others, any change in conjectures (i) or

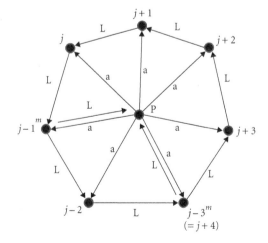

Figure 11.5   Person-of-influence network

N O T E : a = ask for license; L = give license; P = person of influence; m signifies a member of set M.

(ii) requires attaining a critical mass of disbelief: another CAP, reflecting another punctuated equilibrium.[21]

With this introduction, we now focus on networks as conduits of information, influence, and belief. Network structure affects information flow because the specific positions of agents (nodes) indicate the nature of their linkages with others. The DeGroot (1974) model offers a quite general illustration of how influence can affect information transmission across networks, though it does so by attaching different weights to specific agents' opinions, rather than by designating a specific role for network structure.[22] We address the role of structure subsequently.

Consider a network of three boundedly rational agents who influence each other's beliefs by transmitting information or opinions. Given their current knowledge of the world, agents possess a set of subjective priors concerning the likelihood of specific future events. For example, each agent may assign a probability to the prospect that a certain candidate will become the next president of the United States, that the quality of a certain product is good, or that a statement from a particular individual is true. For a particular type of outcome (candidate x gets elected), we may represent agents' priors as a vector of subjective probabilities in period $t = 0$: $\rho(0) = \{\rho_1(0), \rho_2(0), \rho_3(0)\}$. In subsequent periods, agents update their beliefs after hearing about others' beliefs. More precisely, in period 0, each agent receives a signal about x's election prospects with a unique error. Understanding the possibility of error, agents discuss their opinions. In period 1, following their discussion, each agent updates her own beliefs, placing different weights on the reports of other agents and on her own priors. These weights, in turn, reflect each agent's influence.

Thus, in period 1, we have

$$(11.7) \qquad \rho_i(1) = \sum_{j=1,2,3} \lambda_{ij}\rho_j(0) \text{ for each } i.$$

Note that j includes i. Each $\lambda_{ij} \in [0, 1]$ specifies the influence of agent j's prior on agent i's update. Using matrix notation, we write a 3×3 influence matrix X consisting of weights λ_{ij} along with a 3×1 column vector of priors $\rho(0)$. Updated beliefs $\rho(1)$ is the product $X \times \rho(0)$:

$$(11.8) \qquad X\rho(0) = \begin{pmatrix} \lambda_{11} & \lambda_{12} & \lambda_{13} \\ \lambda_{21} & \lambda_{22} & \lambda_{23} \\ \lambda_{31} & \lambda_{32} & \lambda_{33} \end{pmatrix} \begin{pmatrix} \rho_1(0) \\ \rho_2(0) \\ \rho_3(0) \end{pmatrix} = \begin{pmatrix} \rho_1(1) \\ \rho_2(1) \\ \rho_3(1) \end{pmatrix} = \rho(1).$$

In the matrix, the row indicators (the first listed subscripts) denote the weighted influences of the three opinions on each individual (influence received by that individual); these influences sum to 1 ($\sum_{j=1}^{3} \lambda_{ij} = 1$). Furthermore, column sums ($\lambda_j = \sum_{i=1}^{3} \lambda_{ij}$) denote the total influence that a single agent j exerts on all three agents; total influences typically differ by agent. Here column 1 shows the summed influence of agent 1's opinions, and so forth.

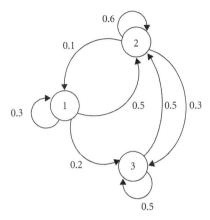

Figure 11.6   DeGroot influence network

SOURCE: M. O. Jackson (2008), *Social and Economic Networks*, Princeton, NJ: Princeton University Press. Reprinted with permission.
NOTE: Decimals are influence weights.

More generally, assuming influence weights remain constant, we may write an equation that represents updated beliefs for any time period t:

$$\rho(t) = X\rho(t-1) = X^t\rho(0). \tag{11.9}$$

To illustrate, suppose that, in initial period $t = 0$, agents 1, 2, and 3 respectively assign probabilities 20%, 40%, and 60% to the prospect of candidate x winning. Assume the influence weights shown in matrix X below. For period 1, then, we have

$$X\rho(0) = \begin{pmatrix} 0.3 & 0.5 & 0.2 \\ 0.1 & 0.6 & 0.3 \\ 0 & 0.5 & 0.5 \end{pmatrix} \begin{pmatrix} 0.2 \\ 0.4 \\ 0.6 \end{pmatrix} = \begin{pmatrix} 0.38 \\ 0.44 \\ 0.50 \end{pmatrix} = \rho(1). \tag{11.10}$$

Note that the influence weights (λ_j, the column sums) for the three agents are $\lambda_1 = 0.4$, $\lambda_2 = 1.6$, and $\lambda_3 = 1.0$. Agent 2 exerts the most influence. Accordingly, $\rho(1)$ shows that opinions of agents 1 and 3 move closer to agent 2's priors. In subsequent periods, opinions would move still closer. Figure 11.6 illustrates the relevant directed network. Arrows show directions of influence and decimals show weights λ_{ij}. From this simple model, we may define a *leader* as an agent who exerts more influence on updated opinions than other agents. Agent 2 is an opinion leader.[23]

Convergence and Insularity

The DeGroot model captures important properties of opinion convergence. As we saw in matrix equation (11.10), the differences in opinions among agents 1, 2, and 3 narrowed after one period. Over a sufficient number of periods, opinions would converge on a single position closer to agent 2's subjective prior than to those of either agent 1 or 3. More generally, we may define a *closed group* (M_c) as a subset of network nodes such that no node within M_c receives any transmissions from any node outside of it. Thus, for any $i \in M_c$ and $j \notin M_c$, $\lambda_{ij} = 0$. Jackson (2008) shows that, in any connected closed group within a directed network where opinion transmission follows the DeGroot model, opinions will converge to consensus over a sufficient period of time.

Although this model is highly artificial, applying it to multiple groups generates an important statement: within-group convergence can be a source of group failure, including between-group tension. Suppose there are several nearly closed groups that possess many strong internal ties and a few weak ties—such as infrequent economic exchanges—that link these groups to others in a network. Opinions within such tightly knit groups tend to converge. The emergent dominant opinions held by the various groups will likely differ, particularly if groups have leaders or persons of influence who, at some earlier time, held different priors. Internal convergence within groups can thus represent a type of insularity. Furthermore, divergent group opinions, particularly if reinforced by social norms, can be a source of conflict—another possible group failure. If so, CAPs may inhibit creating coordination or credible third-party enforcement that spans such groups.

Network Structure, Influence, and Power

Recall that Chapters 4 and 10 identified political, social, and economic positions as potential sources of power. The DeGroot model assigns influence weights that can signify leadership potential, but it does so without reference to network structure. Models of network structure, on the other hand, allow us to link network position with influence, as in Figure 11.5's person-of-influence model. That model, however, lacks a time dimension. A more interesting type of model combines influence, structure, and time. In this regard, we can use network structure to generate the weights for an influence matrix X. To give a simple illustration, we reinterpret Figure 11.5 so that P transfers information rather than licenses: P collects information from each agent $j + 1$, and passes it to agent j. Applying such transmission to equations (11.8) and (11.10), and adjusting the total number of participants, we find $\lambda_{iP} = 1$ for all i (including P) and $\lambda_{ij} = 0$ for all $j \neq P$: P controls all information.[24]

More generally, suppose that agent j's aggregate influence ($\lambda_j = \sum_{i=1}^{3} \lambda_{ij}$) depends on his network position. Assume an agent's betweenness, as represented in equation (11.6), determines his influence. Since j influences i, we substitute j for i in (11.6) to find j's betweenness:

$$(11.11) \qquad \lambda_j = b^j = \sum_{i \neq k} \frac{v^j(i,k)}{v(i,k)}.$$

For simplicity, assume that any agent j's influence is equally distributed among his neighbors. Thus, for each node i that is linked to j, g_{ij}, we have $\lambda_{ij} = \lambda_j / d_j(g)$. For instance, if node j is of degree 10, and if j's betweenness (from (11.11)) is 0.5, then j exerts influence amount 0.05 on each of his 10 neighbors.

We now illustrate betweenness influence using a more complicated network based on historical research. Here we use a family marriage network among oligarchs to illustrate

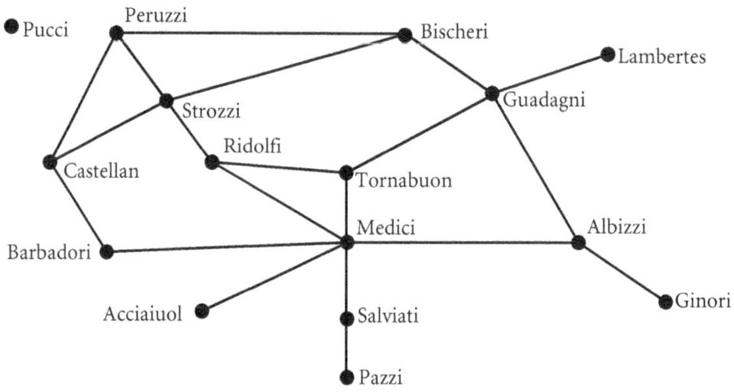

Figure 11.7   Florentine oligarchy circa 1500
s o u r c e : M. O. Jackson (2008), *Social and Economic Networks*, Princeton, NJ: Princeton University Press. Reprinted with permission.

how network position can confer power. Figure 11.7 replicates the drawing of a fifteenth-century interfamily marriage network in Florence.[25] With some arithmetic, we find that betweenness for the Medici family node = 0.522: they lie on just over half of all the shortest paths between any two other nodes. The next highest betweenness measure, 0.255, is for the Guadagni family. The Strozzi family, which might appear quite central, has a betweenness measure of only 0.103.

Now suppose that betweenness measures from Figure 11.7 determine each family's *political influence*—that is, their ability to affect political opinions in subsequent periods. Suppose that Figure 11.7 shows all of the families of the Florentine oligarchy circa 1500. Suppose further that the council presidency is contested. In period $t = 0$, each family enters a council meeting holding an initial opinion concerning their preferred candidate. At the meeting, all families report their initial opinion and then update their opinion on the basis of what they hear. We may use the model of equation (11.8) adjusted to include 17 participants, along with each family's influence weight (λ_j) as shown by their betweenness from (11.11). Suppose there are two candidates, Alfonso and Bochario. The Medici, Bischeri, and Tornabuon families initially support Bochario; all others support Alfonso. Yet Bochario wins the election held in period $t = 1$.[26]

As a micro-structural measure of a node's position in a network, a node's betweenness can represent the power that arises from an agent's political, economic, or social position in a network: network positions confer power. We can now relate this argument to our discussion in Chapters 7–10 as follows: institutional rules designate positions and establish behavioral prescriptions; organizations contain internal networks; networks span organizations; and networks transfer information and influence. Institutional systems incorporate mutually understood rules that structure cognition, information, and motivation; multiple overlapping networks facilitate transmission of these influences across organizations, communities, and individuals.

11.3. AFFILIATION, IDENTITY, AND SEARCHABLE NETWORKS

As we have seen, social networks have structures that generate small-world properties. This section investigates how group affiliation and social identities influence the formation and properties of social networks. It makes five key assertions. First, within networks, affiliation groups tend to form around categories of social identity. Second, affiliation groups tend to overlap in the sense of individuals belonging to multiple categories; such overlap creates shortcuts that, in turn, generate small-world properties. Third, individuals use affiliation categories (elements of their mental models) not only to conceptualize distinctions among groups but also to assess the social distances between or among individuals or groups. Fourth, individuals use local information and their conceptions of group affiliation to search networks in order to locate distant nodes. Fifth, the searchability properties of social networks reflect their importance as efficient conduits of information and influence that can facilitate multiple exchanges and also help to resolve CAPs.

On the basis of Watts, Dodds, and Newman (2002) and Watts (2004), we develop a model of a searchable network, with small-world properties, that utilizes group affiliations based upon social identity categories—in addition to traditional network links among individuals. More precisely, we construct a *bipartite* network—one with two distinct types of nodes and links: first, an actual network (like those already discussed) consisting of individuals linked in various groupings; and second, a perceived structure of affiliation categories related to social identities.[27] Naturally, the two representations interact. In the actual network, links among individuals tend to coalesce around various affiliation groups. A *group* is "any collection of individuals with which some well-defined set of characteristics is associated" (Watts, Dodds, and Newman 2002, 1303). We say that two agents (nodes) are *affiliated* if they belong to the same group. Groups usually have multiple internal links, indicating strong ties. Individuals simultaneously belong to several different groups (e.g., friends, occupation, family). Consequently, groups overlap—usually on the basis of weak ties that often serve as network shortcuts.

Group affiliations both coalesce around and help to define *social identities*, or "sets of characteristics attributed to them [individuals] by themselves and others by virtue of their association with, and participation in, social groups" (Watts, Dodds, and Newman 2002, 1303).[28] Moreover, an individual's choice concerning possible links often reflects affiliation *homophily*: a preference for associating with others with whom one shares at least one dimension of social identity.[29] Children tend to play with others their same age. Adult friendships often reflect affiliation similarities such as social class, occupation, ethnicity, or religion. Thus homophily affiliation based on social identities influences processes of network formation.

Upon this actual network, we layer a conceptual structure of affiliation categories associated with various kinds of social identity (e.g., occupation), each of which is arranged hierarchically into subcategories (health professionals, nurses, psychiatric nurses, etc.). These conceptual affiliation hierarchies provide the foundations for perceived measures of social distance. Agents use these measures to navigate vast social networks. More precisely, boundedly rational agents use their understandings of various hierarchically structured affiliation categories (elements of mental models) as knowledge partitions (epistemic devices) for ordering their perceptions of individuals and groups in terms of social distance. For example, people may classify and characterize groups on the basis of residence, religion, occupation, nationality, age, and so forth. By arranging each basic category into hierarchical subcategories, agents generate various perceptions of *social distance*— degrees of similarity or difference—between themselves and others, or among others. Agents then use such conceptions of social distance to search social networks.

With this background, we now develop a bipartite model of social affiliation based largely upon Watts, Dodds, and Newman (2002). This model exhibits four small-world properties: large size, high average clustering coefficients, low average diameter ($\bar{d}$), and searchability. The core premise of the model is that, at any point in time, individuals are endowed with two attributes: social identities and links to others.[30] We proceed first with the perceptual side of the bipartite model, relating perceived affiliation categories to measures of social distance. These perceived measures of social distance, however, do not depend on the length of actual network paths among individuals. Instead, they depend on conceptualized patterns of hierarchical classification within each type of affiliation.[31] Next, we construct a social network among individuals by using our measures of social distance to influence the probability of forming new links between specific nodes. We then apply the model to examine how agents can locate short paths across vast networks.

Turning to details, we start by constructing affiliation hierarchies and associated distance metrics. Assume that individuals establish their own hierarchical categorization of each relevant social dimension: one for location, one for occupation, one for ethnicity, and so forth. Each affiliation hierarchy begins with the entire known and relevant "world" at the top and proceeds to partition this general category into increasingly specific subcategories, ending at a bottom level consisting of specific affiliation groups. Such bottom-layer groups, called *cliques*, are of "manageable" size (no more than 100 members; Watts, Dodds, and Newman 2002). Cliques might be groups of friends, workmates, relatives, and the like. We assume full connectivity within cliques. For example, a conceptual hierarchy for an organization would include a top node representing the entire organization, followed by successive partitions into divisions, departments, sections, and then workgroups as the bottom-level cliques. Alternatively, one could geographically partition the United States into East and West, then Northeast and Southeast, Northwest and Southwest, and so forth, all the way down to neighborhoods or blocks. Figure 11.8 illustrates a simple, three-tier example.

In mathematical terms, an affiliation hierarchy contains K distinct levels and a specific branching coefficient (b), specifying the number of branches per point of distinction. In Figure 11.8, $K = 3$ and $b = 2$. For a given social dimension (e.g., occupation), we may represent the position of each clique by a vector of K entries, where each entry denotes the relevant branch at each level.[32] With $b = 2$ (as in Figure 11.8), we use the digits 0 and 1 to denote (respectively) a left-hand branch and a right-hand branch. For example, we may represent clique D with the row vector (011). On this basis, individuals use distinct affiliation hierarchies as they conceptualize each social category (occupation, etc.), and such conceptions may differ across individuals. One person may imagine 80 occupational dis-

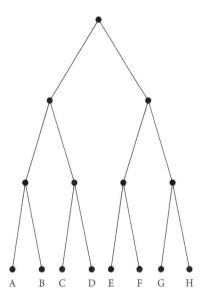

Figure 11.8   An affiliation hierarchy

tinctions and 12 geographic distinctions, while another might envision only 40 for occupation but 60 for location.

Finally, each agent belongs to several bottom-level cliques (or teams) in different social categories (age, occupation, ethnicity, etc.). An individual's specific collection of such
cliques constitutes her *social identity*.[33] We now use the concept of affiliation hierarchies to
define *social distance* as the number of steps needed to go from one person's clique to another's (counting membership in the same clique as one step). Thus, in Figure 11.8, if Ann
and Bob are both members of team A, their social distance is 1. Leaving Ann in A, if Bob is
in D, their social distance is 4, and if Bob is in H, their social distance is 6.

Using this framework, we proceed to develop actual social network ties among individuals. We call all individuals who interact (have links) *acquaintances*. Due to homophily, social
identity affiliations establish the primary basis for creating links. Consequently, as networks
evolve, homophily provides the basis for preferential attachment: the probability of establishing links between specific individuals decreases in their social distance (or increases in
their similarity) along relevant social dimensions. Note further that closeness in any one
affiliation category is sufficient for establishing acquaintance. Moreover, probabilities of association are greater in categories with smaller distances. For example, workmates who live
miles apart are more likely to associate on the basis of work than on the basis of residence.

To construct the network, each node (agent) is randomly assigned to an initial set of
cliques, one for each pertinent social category.[34] With this foundation, we assemble the network as follows:

1. Choose a node *i* at random.

2. Select a social distance (*x*) for a link to *i*, using a formula that generates lower probabilities of selection for greater social distances (or higher probabilities for lesser
   distances).[35]

3. Among the nodes that are social distance x from node i, randomly select one (node j) and connect these two nodes (unless they are already connected).

4. Repeat these steps successively for new nodes to produce a network with average density (average number of acquaintances) $\bar{d}$.

Having established a network, we now turn to its search properties.

Because overlapping social identity affiliations facilitate transmitting information across large social distances, they underlie both the small-world and searchability properties of social networks. To illustrate, assume that each agent knows her position within her own set of social categories (work team, residence, etc.) and at least some positions of her network neighbors. Agents remain ignorant of the rest of the network beyond vague ideas of further extension. Now consider the question of contacting a distant agent about whom one knows little. Suppose an agent (node) i wants to locate agent k to whom i is not connected; but i knows one or more of k's social categories (e.g., occupation, residence). Agent i contacts her neighbor (j) who appears to be closely linked to k along some social dimension. Agent i asks j to contact one or more of his neighbors using similar selection criteria in hopes of finding k. As an example, Watts (2003) offers a story in which he hopes to locate a Chinese peasant for whom he knows only name and province of residence. He imagines starting by asking a Chinese colleague to contact relevant people that she knows, perhaps someone from that province.[36]

In conducting these searches, agents use their understandings of various hierarchically ordered social categories (as in Figure 11.8) to identify routes that appear to have the shortest social distance for the relevant part of the search. Watts and his Chinese colleague are linked by work; she and the peasant are linked by country of origin. Watts (2003, 150–51) observes: "Social distance, in other words, emphasizes similarities over differences, and herein lies the resolution to the small-world paradox." Thus chosen agent j may be close to searcher i on one social dimension but closer to target k on another.[37] The simultaneous closeness of i to j on one dimension (work) and j and k on another (country of origin) enables agents to employ local network information to initiate searches across apparently large social distances. Here the overlap of affiliation categories generates shortcuts. Indeed, the presence of multiple conceptual social categories renders social networks searchable and simultaneously endows them with the small diameters characteristic of small-world networks. Hence information may travel across large social networks in relatively few steps.

Along these lines, Peter Killworth and Russell Bernard performed a "reverse" small-world experiment (1978/79).[38] They presented subjects with a list of possible search targets, and asked the subjects whom, among their acquaintances, they would first contact to reach each target. Subjects were then asked to explain their choices. The study's findings fit the model's predictions: most subjects reported that they would contact acquaintances on the basis of two or three characteristics (e.g., occupation, residence) from which they expected the most similarity between acquaintance and target.[39] Thus individuals utilize perceived hierarchical social identity affiliations to search portions of vast networks about which they know virtually nothing.

Overall, searchability is a generic property of social networks (Watts 2003, 156). Because individuals possess overlapping affiliations, certain links generate shortcuts across different social dimensions; thus social networks possess small-world properties.[40] Boundedly rational agents who know little about distant realms of networks use cognitive classifications of identity-based group affiliation as elements of their mental models; these knowledge partitions serve as epistemic devices for searching huge social networks. Naturally, information transmission accompanies search. In other words, the affiliation categories associated with social networks not only lend them small-world properties, via shortcuts, but also demonstrate how networks can become efficient conduits of information.

11.4. EPIDEMICS, SOCIAL INFLUENCE, AND INFORMATION CASCADES

Arguably, the single event of Mohammad Bouazizi's self-immolation on December 17, 2010, set off the Tunisian revolution ending with the resignation of President Zine El Abidine Ben Ali, 28 days later. The collapse of Lehman Brothers on September 15, 2008, initiated panic in US and global financial markets. Prior to their arrival in New York on February 7, 1964, the British rock band the Beatles was little known in the United States, but within weeks US teenagers—like those in Britain—had succumbed to Beatlemania (Gould 2007).

An *information cascade* occurs when "individuals in a population exhibit herd-like behavior because they are making decisions based the actions of other individuals rather than relying on their own information" (Watts 2002, 5766). Cascades may involve fashion, technological innovation, new ideology, or any new idea or practice that catches on rapidly across populations.

Using network theory, we make three assertions concerning information cascades. First, the incidence of cascades depends critically on the details of social network structure and on precisely where, within such structures, new ideas or innovations originate. Although quality surely matters, ideas that arise in many sections of networks go nowhere, whereas similar ideas originating in specific network locations can occasionally spread rapidly. Second, as the examples in the preceding paragraph suggest, the occurrence of information cascades is extremely difficult to predict. Third, information cascades inform our understanding of punctuated social equilibria. More precisely, the standing of certain ideas and practices within social networks can be simultaneously robust and fragile: robust because prevalent ideas or practices may persist, resisting multiple external shocks for extended periods; yet fragile because they may occasionally succumb to apparently small disturbances (Watts 2002).

We open our examination of the spread of social influence with a discussion of epidemics and proceed to the transmission of social influence.

Preliminaries: Epidemics and Networks

The spread of disease obviously represents an important CAP for society that may have implications on the ability to conduct exchange, as the plague in medieval Europe did. Network structure can affect both the extent of the problem and its potential resolution. The SIR model of contagious infection (Kermack and McKendrick 1927) offers context.[41]

Consider a specific strain of virus, such as the Hong Kong flu, that spreads via direct contact, and for which many agents develop immunity after being infected. Assume homogeneous mixing among agents (in effect no network). We may characterize social interaction by a single mixing coefficient (μ). There are three types of agents: susceptible, infected, and recovered (immune). At time period $t = 0$, one agent in the fixed population (N) is infected. Let $s(t)$, $i(t)$, and $r(t)$ designate the proportions of N that, at time $t \geq 0$, are (respectively) susceptible, infected, and recovered. Note that $s(t) + i(t) + r(t) = 1$. Each infected agent transmits the virus to others at mixing rate μ per period t. During each period, a fraction σ of infected agents recover. Note that only susceptible agents can become infected.

The following equations describe the time path of the three types of agents:

(11.12) $$ds/dt = -\mu s(t)i(t);$$

(11.13) $$dr/dt = \sigma i(t);$$

(11.14) $$di/dt = \mu s(t)i(t) - \sigma i(t).$$

Equation (11.12) states that the pool of susceptible agents declines steadily as more become infected (and thus are no longer susceptible). Mathematically, (11.12) follows from the mixing coefficient μ and the definitions of $s(t)$ and $i(t)$. Equation (11.13) states that the rate of recovery equals the per-period recovery fraction (σ) multiplied by the portion infected. In (11.14), the rate of infection equals negative the time trend of susceptibility (hence a positive entry) minus the rate of recovery. This relation follows from the requirement that proportions $s(t)$, $i(t)$, and $r(t)$ must always sum to 1; therefore, the three time trends must sum to 0.[42] Note that the SIR model's dynamics and outcomes depend entirely on the relative sizes of its two parameters—the mixing coefficient μ and the recovery fraction σ—irrespective of any network properties. For example, if $\mu < \sigma$, the disease will eventually die out. Policy implications are simple and general: to slow the spread of disease, reduce mixing and increase the recovery fraction via treatment.[43]

In society, however, individuals mix at different rates; hence network structure affects rates of contagion. For example, the initial spread of AIDS in the United States was greatly accelerated by the multiple sexual links of a particular individual who happened to be a Canadian flight attendant (Shilts 1987). In network terminology, flights were shortcuts between otherwise distant social groups that facilitated rapid spread of infection across a vast social network.

One can readily apply the SIR logic to networks. As before, contact spreads infection, but now network structure influences the amount and probability of contact for specific agents (nodes). Assume that some initial small proportion m of population size N in network Γ are infected. Each agent's mixing coefficient μ_i depends on how many neighbors it has (i.e., the degree of the node), so that $\mu_i = \mu_i(d_i)$. The rate of disease transmission now depends on the location of infected agents in the network, the distribution of degrees, and other structural characteristics such as clustering and betweenness. For example, because the Canadian flight attendant operated as a network hub with an extraordinarily high d_i, HIV spread rapidly. Moreover, factors like average network degree, the tendency of high-degree nodes to link to each other (associativity), and the near-certain presence (and location) of shortcuts across the network can influence rates of transmission (Watts 2004). Thus knowledge of network structure can reduce the costs of resolving CAPs associated with disease transmission. Public health officials might, for example, focus initial immunization or prevention efforts on identifiable network shortcuts.

Social Influence and Information Cascades

We now develop two models of social transmission that can apply to the spread or adoption of ideas or behaviors across groups. Here aggregated effects of individual decisions can significantly influence collective outcomes. These models differ from epidemic models in three critical respects:

(i) Agents possess memory: they base decisions on the cumulative impact of observed actions or on information received from others. The number of remembered observations affects subsequent probabilities of adoption of specific ideas or practices. By contrast, in epidemic models, like the SIR model, the probability of infection from a single contact is independent of prior contacts.

(ii) Large-scale transmission occurs only if a critical mass of infected agents can first be attained. By contrast, in epidemic models certain parameter values guarantee that a single infection will spread (or not spread) across a population.

(iii) For models that incorporate network properties, social influence tends to spread more widely across sparsely connected networks. By contrast, in epidemic models, dense connectivity accelerates the spread of disease.

With this background, we now develop two social influence models. Both can represent the rapid transmission and adoption of ideas or practices across populations—that is, information cascades. Our first model illustrates the transmission of imitative behavior independent of social network properties. Following Bikhchandani, Hirshleifer, and Welch (1992), we model transmission based upon observation of successive actions among substantively rational agents. Like the SIR model, this model generates a potential for contagious transmission that depends only on group parameters. Second, we develop a more complete model (based on Watts 2002) of informational cascades among linked, boundedly rational agents. Both models address binary decisions concerning whether or not to adopt a new idea. Both models can apply to decisions ranging from fads or technical innovation to participation in social movements or revolution. By comparing these two models, we illustrate the importance of network structure and its relationship to CAPs.

The Bikhchandani, Hirshleifer, and Welch (1992) model makes no reference to network structure, but implicitly uses a simple linear network. Before moving, agents privately observe an initial signal indicating whether the value (V) of an action or object is high (H) or low (L). If V actually is H, the signal specifies H with probability $\rho_i > 1/2$. But if V actually is L, the signal incorrectly specifies H with probability $1 - \rho_i$. The substantively rational agents do not know the actual V, but they do know their own ρ_i. For simplicity, assume equal observational probabilities across all agents: $\rho_i = \rho$. Moving in sequence, agents then choose be-

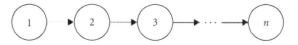

Figure 11.9   Model of imitative behavior transmission (after Bikhchandani, Hirshleifer, and Welch 1992)

tween A—adopt a new idea or practice—and N—do not adopt. They base their decisions on inferences drawn from their initial signals and from perfectly observed prior actions of others, which serve as additional signals. We may regard this process as a simple directional linear network in which agents (nodes) are arranged sequentially by number $1, 2, 3, \ldots, n$, where the numbers denote each node's position in the decision sequence. Each pair of agents is connected by a single directional link from a lower to a higher number. There is no information decay ($\delta = 1$). Figure 11.9 illustrates.

This model generates information cascades as follows. Agent 1 chooses A or N on the basis of her private signal (respectively, H or L). If agent 1 chooses A, agent 2 infers that 1 received signal H. If agent 1 chooses N, agent 2 infers that 1 received L. Assume agent 1 chooses A. If agent 2 receives signal H, he adopts, but if agent 2 receives L, he adopts only with probability 1/2. Converse arguments apply if agent 1 chooses N. If agent 3 observes sequence AA, she infers signal sequence HH and adopts regardless of her own signal. Likewise, if agent 3 observes sequence NN, she infers signals LL and so chooses N. It is straightforward to see that, under quite general conditions, an information cascade arising from sequences of identical observed actions can lead to action conformity AAA . . . or NNN . . . . It is also possible to have incorrect information cascades: AAA . . . when the actual value is L or NNN . . . when the actual value is H. Although the probability of incorrect cascades decreases as the accuracy of private signals (ρ) increases, incorrect cascades still occur with relatively high values of ρ (Bikhchandani, Hirshleifer, and Welch 1992, 998). The authors proceed to show that such imitative patterns can be fragile in the sense that small disturbances may reverse the direction of cascades from AAA to NNN or vice versa—particularly when ρ is close to 1/2.[44] Information cascades may thus constitute fragile punctuated equilibria.

A more complete conception of social networks facilitates a more sophisticated representation of information cascades. We know that boundedly rational agents face limited, costly, and asymmetrically distributed information with limited and costly cognition, generating a competence-difficulty (CD) gap. Consequently, they utilize their observations of neighbors' behavior (likely conditioned by patterns of reciprocity and pertinent social norms) to inform and frame their understandings of decisions they face. We have seen that network structure critically influences the extent and character of such interactions. In social networks, the influence of one person (Ann) on a second (Bob) often depends on how many other people Bob listens to.

Our second social influence model, based on Watts (2002), specifically addresses transmission of information, actions, or decisions among neighbors and across network structures. Because people pay attention to the opinions and practices of friends, acquaintances, and colleagues, their ideas, beliefs, and practices reflect social interactions. Network structure influences the prevalence of such interaction: some nodes are much more connected than others. Degrees of connectedness thus influence various rates and directions of imitation.

This model offers three hypotheses. The first replicates prior results, but the second and third point to the influence of network structure:

1. Prevalent ideas and practices are punctuated equilibria: only a tiny portion of all shocks (new ideas) created or received by a network can generate cascades that are large enough to notably shift outcomes.

2. Relatively small exogenous shocks (innovations) can occasionally trigger information cascades that dramatically alter agents' ideas or practices in sizeable regions of relevant networks. Whether they do so or not depends on relationships between the network structure—especially its micro-level attributes—and the precise network location of the initial shock.

3. Shocks that tip the balance need not be larger than shocks that fail to do so; hence, before they occur, disruptive shocks are extremely difficult to distinguish from non-disruptive ones. Predicting cascades is, at best, extremely difficult.

Thus certain informational equilibria in social networks are both robust and fragile: robust because they tend to resist nearly all shocks; yet fragile because a small shock that happens to impact a specific location within a network—a location with particularly conducive structural characteristics—can initiate a cascade of change.

As in the model of Bikhchandani, Hirshleifer, and Welch (1992), agents make a binary decision: whether to adopt or reject a new idea (or technique). Here, however, agents (nodes) respond to observed adoption by one or more network neighbors.[45] Consider the introduction of a new idea, a new way of thinking, a new technology, or a new social practice. Assume that network Γ consists of N nodes (agents) who possess no prior bias for or against new ideas and no resource constraints. A randomly designated agent or team (j) within Γ, whom we call an *innovator*, develops a new idea, technique, or practice (x). In evolutionary terms, x is a mutation.

We define agent i's *adoption threshold* (τ_{ai}) as the minimum proportion of adopting neighbors needed for i to adopt idea x:

$$(11.15) \qquad \tau_{ai} \equiv v_{ai}^{\min}/d_i,$$

where $\tau_{ai} \in [0, 1]$; $v_{ai}^{\min}$ denotes the minimum number of required adopters among i's neighbors; and, as before, d_i is i's degree. For example, if threshold $\tau_{ai} = 0.30$ and degree $d_i = 10$, then at least three neighbors must adopt x before i will do so $(v_{ai}^{\min} = 3)$. Adoption by i depends on whether the actual ratio of adopting neighbors to degree exceeds τ_{ai}. More precisely, the probability that agent i will adopt idea x is

$$(11.16) \qquad \rho_{ai}(x) = \begin{cases} 1 \text{ if } v_{ai}(x,h_x)/d_i \geq \tau_{ai}, \\ 0 \text{ otherwise.} \end{cases}$$

Here $v_{ai}(x, h_x)$ specifies the actual (not minimum) number of adopting neighbors as a function of idea x, specifically its innate appeal, and also its history of prior adoption h_x. Again, crossing threshold τ_{ai} depends on both $v_{ai}(x, h_x)$ and d_i. In particular, the higher d_i—that is, the more neighbors i has—the greater the number of adopting neighbors v_{ai} needed to cross a given threshold τ_{ai}. For example, if $\tau_{ai} = 0.20$, then adoption by one neighbor induces imitation for $d_i = 5$, but not for $d_i = 10$. In the latter case, two must adopt before i follows. Note further that equation (11.16) allows for three kinds of heterogeneity:

(i) Different agents may have different degrees ($d_i \neq d_j$); some have more neighbors.

(ii) Different agents may have different adoption thresholds for the same idea ($\tau_{ai1} \neq \tau_{aj1}$); Ann may be less (or more) subject to social influence than Bob.

(iii) The same agent may have different thresholds for different phenomena ($\tau_{ai1} \neq \tau_{ai2}$); Bob might quickly follow music fads but hesitate to follow clothing fads.[46]

Now define an *early adopter* as an agent who need only observe one adopting neighbor before following. For early adopters,

$$(11.17) \qquad\qquad \tau_{ai} \equiv v_{ai}/d_i < 1/d_i.$$

Equation (11.17) states that an early adopter must have a sufficiently low imitation threshold—specifically, a τ_{ai} less than the inverse of its degree. Thus low-degree nodes can be early adopters even if their adoption thresholds are relatively high, whereas high-degree nodes require quite low thresholds for early adoption. For any threshold $\tau_{ai} \in [1/2, 1)$, only nodes with $d_i = 1$ are early adopters; for any $\tau_{ai} \in [1/3, 1/2)$, only nodes with $d_i \leq 2$ are early adopters; for any $\tau_{ai} \in [1/4, 1/3)$, only nodes with $d_i \leq 3$ are early adopters, and so forth. Thus a given threshold determines the maximum degree for early adoption.[47] With respect to susceptibility to information cascades, we may now distinguish two basic types of nodes: early adopters and *stable nodes* (all other nodes). High-degree nodes tend to be stable because their actual thresholds τ_{ai} usually exceed the maximum level that (11.17) stipulates for early adoption.

For example, suppose that, in the professional network of eye surgeons in Des Moines, Iowa, Ann and Bob are colleagues; they are linked. Assume that Ann has 10 network neighbors (including Bob) and that Bob has five (including Ann). Furthermore, assume that both have the same adoption threshold: $\tau_{aAnn} = \tau_{aBob} = 0.19$. Now suppose that colleague Sue adopts new technique x. From (11.17), we see that Bob is an early adopter, but Ann is stable. Nevertheless, adoption by Bob raises Ann's v_{ai} enough to cross threshold τ_{aAnn}, so she now adopts technique x. If their colleague Phil has a threshold of 0.30, he will adopt only after Ann does. One can now see that the right configuration of adoption, neighbors, degrees, and thresholds could allow technique x to spread across a large portion of a network, in which case we call x a *globally cascading* idea or practice.

The transmission propensities of specific ideas or practices thus depend on relationships between average degrees within network groupings and the adoption thresholds of specific nodes. These propensities encounter two distinct constraints on cascade formation that each operate in distinct areas of networks. On one hand, sparsely connected regions of networks (i.e., those with an average degree close to 1) are relatively susceptible to localized transmission of new ideas. With a low $\bar{d}$ for the region, the portion of early adopters is likely to be high. Even so, since degree distributions are normally heterogeneous, such regions are likely to exhibit low connectedness, implying a relatively high number of small, separate components. Because ideas cannot escape from isolated components, fads and innovations that do arise usually remain isolated in small subsections of the overall network. Thus, in sparsely connected regions of networks, ease of imitation is not the chief constraint on information cascades; lack of connection is (Watts 2002).[48]

On the other hand, relatively connected regions are significantly less susceptible to rapid transmission of new ideas. With high $\bar{d}$ (between 3 and 14), such regions possess relatively few early adopters and many stable nodes (Watts 2002). Encountering few early adopters, most new ideas die out with little transmission. Hence network connectedness is not the principal constraint on global cascades; rather, the relative stability of preponderant high-degree nodes restrains adoption of new ideas.[49] Cascades seldom occur, but when they do, they may spread rapidly across large areas, becoming global cascades.

Noting that networks likely have both sparsely and more densely connected regions, we arrive at the following scenario for a global information cascade. By chance, an innovation shock x occurs within a small and sparsely connected network subsection (Γ_a) where $\bar{d}_a \approx 1$. Many nodes meet equation (11.17)'s early-adopter condition. Innovator j generates new idea x. At least one of j's neighbors (k) is an early adopter, and so follows. One or more of k's neighbors have low enough degrees and thresholds to also adopt. This process continues within a localized grouping (within Γ_a) that is connected to at least one other cluster by a local bridge.[50] The node on the other side (l) happens to be an early adopter. If some of l's neighbors and their neighbors meet equation (11.17)'s threshold, idea x spreads across the second cluster. This cluster may be larger and have several local bridges to other clusters, increasing the probability of early adoption in still other clusters. Sooner or later, x reaches more highly connected regions with a history of adoption. With the right τ_{ai}, v_{ai}, and d_i for its h_x, idea x can now spread rapidly and become a global cascade.

Taken as a whole, this social influence model offers two additional implications. First, although the quality of an innovation affects its innate appeal—suggesting relatively low adoption thresholds for high-quality ideas—network structure critically influences the propensity for given ideas to spread.[51] Second (as implied by hypothesis 2), with the right configuration of degrees and thresholds in relevant sections of networks, small shocks can lead to information cascades. Thus the size of a shock is not a good predictor of the likelihood of a cascade (hypothesis 3; Watts 2002). For example, few (if any) observers would have predicted that the self-immolation of a single individual, Mohammad Bouazizi, would initiate a cascading series of protests that ended in the resignation of Tunisian president Zine El Abidine Ben Ali, only 28 days later. An avalanche offers an analogy: in the rare circumstances when temperature, snow density, and other conditions are just right, a clump of snow falling off a tree on the edge of a cliff can cause an avalanche.

Overall, information cascades can present enormous CAPs, or they can represent sudden resolution of CAPs—or both, depending upon one's perspective. Those hoping to prevent unlikely harmful events not only face significant technical and organizational difficulties, they must also address the impact of both uncertain timing and doubtful occurrence on the motivation of others to act. It is hard to motivate people to take costly steps to prevent something that might happen sometime this year or next, in five years, or perhaps not at all. Moreover, those who benefit from the state of affairs in a possibly fragile system may resist not only change but even the concept that significant deterioration is possible (the reigning equilibria in their mental models resist such notions). The relatively small number of policymakers who, in 2006, anticipated the vulnerability of the financial system to severe crisis faced precisely this set of problems. On the other hand, the occasional appearance of harmful cascades may induce some agents (e.g., citizens or policymakers) to take costly preventative steps to avoid quite unlikely scenarios, consuming resources that could be deployed elsewhere.

Sometimes, information cascades can reflect extraordinarily rapid resolution of apparently intractable CAPs. For example, the swiftness of the 2011 revolution in Tunisia and the similarly rapid collapse of communism in Eastern Europe during the fall of 1989 both constituted sudden resolutions of enormous CAPs for regime opponents. Even so, the rapid pace of revolution generates another set of CAPs related to creating new institutions in a short period of time on the basis of insufficient experience with a novel state of the world.

Fortunately for social scientists, most human events do not mimic the near unpredictability of information cascades. During stable periods, institutional systems typically generate far more predictability by utilizing the social choreography of conventions, social norms, social rules, formal institutions, and established organizations; indeed, as transmitters of signals and influence, social networks play a critical role in maintaining such stability.

11.5. CONCLUSION

Social networks are ubiquitous in human interaction. They are so pervasive that they can be difficult to analyze or even notice. Families are networks; firms are networks; political parties, social clubs, and religious organizations are networks; markets are networks; communities and political systems are networks; the list goes on and on. Social network theory offers a set of tools that facilitates analysis of structures and processes of communication and related transmissions of information and influence—in particular, economic, political, and social exchanges. Our brief treatment has offered a sketch of some basic components, structural elements, and properties of social networks. It has outlined random, structured, and scale-free approaches to network formation. Social networks tend to reflect mixtures of structured and random processes, usually with some form of preferential attachment. Social networks thus exhibit attributes of scale-free networks—especially the small-world properties of large numbers of nodes, high localized clustering, and small average diameters.

The models developed in Sections 11.2–11.4 (a small sample of network models) illustrate the versatile potential of network analysis. Section 11.2's discussion demonstrated how network positions affect the ability of agents—via influence weights associated with their betweenness— to use transmissions of information or opinion to alter the beliefs of others. Well-positioned agents (Basu's "man of influence" or the Medici) may thus exercise power by exerting disproportionate impact on other agents' ideas or beliefs (power3). Network analysis thus complements the assertion, made in Chapters 4 and 10, that institutionally designated positions within organizations are sources of power. We find confirmation of the intuitive notion that connectedness confers power; network centrality is a source of influence.

As we saw in Section 11.3, social identity affiliations critically affect the development, utilization, and properties of social networks. Because identity affiliations engender preferential attachment based on homophily, they influence the structure and development of social networks. Because individuals possess multiple overlapping identity-based affiliations, the ensuing links among various categories of identity affiliation create (or delineate) network shortcuts (local bridges). These bridges, in turn, generate the small-world properties characteristic of social networks. Moreover, as already suggested in Chapter 8, identity classifications shape cognition: they are types of (or elements within) mental models. Accordingly, network-based identity affiliations provide conceptual foundations for perceptions of social distance. Moreover, the overlapping nature of identity affiliations (and their attendant shortcuts) provides a basis for searching distant regions of social networks. Thus social networks can facilitate the transfer of information and other forms of exchange across vast social distances.

Section 11.4 discussed a particular form of information transmission: information cascades. Information cascades reflect the combined influences of uncertainty, reciprocal behavior, and norm-induced tendencies for imitation among agents who receive information from (or observe actions of) network neighbors. Cascades then reflect both the limits and power of information processing among boundedly rational agents. More fundamentally, information cascades embody and signify both the robustness and fragility of ideas, practices, mental models, organizations, institutions, and institutional systems—as evidenced by a simultaneous ability to resist multiple shocks and yet also succumb to extraordinarily well-positioned, and often haphazard, small shocks.

Networks thus offer additional perspective on exchange relationships and on the sources, nature, and potential resolution of CAPs. Network formation may itself be a CAP. Agents who occupy strategic network positions may hinder resolution of CAPs, particularly ones associated with reform. Conversely, network positions may coordinate resolution. Indeed, the identity affiliation-based searchability properties of networks facilitate information flows and other exchanges that permit large-scale social coordination. In this regard (as discussed in Chapter 8), identity categories and responses reflect the influence of social norms; and networks themselves are a key component of social capital. As elements of social capital, networks facilitate (and engender) institutional social choreography via their ability to transmit information and influence in the form of behavioral prescriptions and auxiliary transactions that emerge from informal and formal institutions—and associated organizations. Simultaneously, by both designating and shaping the social, political, and economic positions of agents (including organizations) within their intricate terrain, social networks operate as fundamental components of institutional systems. As such they constitute foundations of complex economic, political, and social exchange. Social networks thus create, exacerbate, and help resolve myriad CAPs of social, political, and economic interaction.

Finally, the potential for networks to occasionally generate largely unpredictable information cascades presents affected parties a particularly challenging type of CAP. The uncertain timing and occurrence of information cascades renders their prevention difficult for those who hope to avoid them and, similarly, renders functional exploitation of their occurrence difficult for potential beneficiaries. These latter problems relate to our next topic. We will see in Chapter 12 that policymaking processes exhibit the properties of punctuated equilibria: they usually operate during periods of relative stability, during which institutional/network social choreography generates relatively predictable and slowly adjusting patterns. Yet occasional and largely unpredictable shocks can induce periods of rapid change—periods of dissolution, revolution, or rapid reform—that may be interpreted as information cascades. We now turn to policy.

EXERCISES

11.1. Use equation (11.1) to calculate the individual clustering coefficient for node i if node c is connected only to node d (not to e) and d and e are also not connected.

11.2. Calculate average clustering coefficients for both sections of Figure 11.2 and for the entire network.

11.3. In the model of Figure 11.5, relate the influence of person P to power3 (from Chapter 4). Develop a model representing the CAP that P's opponents would face in undermining her influence.

11.4. Rewrite equations (11.8) and (11.10) to illustrate an influence network consisting of P (from Figure 11.5) and five bureaucrats.

11.5. Demonstrate the outcome of the Florentine election referred to in the discussion of Figure 11.7.

11.6. Using Figure 11.9's depiction of the model proposed by Bikhchandani, Hirshleifer, and Welch (1992), show that, if ρ is 0.55, an incorrect information cascade (NNN . . .) could arise. Do the same for $\rho = 0.75$.

11.7. Concerning adoption thresholds:

   a. If $d_i = 6$ and $\tau_{ai} = 1/3$, what is the minimum number of required adopters for i to be an early adopter? Interpret your answer in a sentence (or two).

   b. Repeat part a for $d_i = 15$ and $\tau_{ai} = 1/2$.

   c. Relate your answers in parts a and b to Watts' observation that information cascades originate only in network areas where the average degree is no more than 14 (see notes 47 and 49).

IV POLICY, GROWTH, AND DEVELOPMENT

12 POLICY AND POLITICAL ECONOMY

> The one who adapts his policy to the times prospers, and likewise that the one whose policy clashes with the demands of the times does not.
>
> Niccolò Machiavelli (1640/1969)

In principle, the communities of Arruba and Boratonia could ameliorate their internal or mutual CAPs pertaining to water use by instituting various policies. Suppose that the governing bodies of both communities have just signed an agreement to limit use. Each might then adopt and implement new policies aimed at resolving internal CAPs that could interfere with honoring the agreement. They could, for example, impose a tax on use or subsidize limited use. Alternatively, they might create a water permit market by issuing or auctioning a set number of use permits. Farmers who conserve could then profit by selling permits to high-volume users, who would need to pay for their excess.[1] To create new policies, either community would have to start from existing arrangements, relationships, and understandings. Specific ideas may or may not reach the attention of policymakers. Groups that normally make community policy may resist input from others. Internal opposition, along with coordination or enforcement problems, may inhibit or preclude adoption of any of these policies, impede implementation, or otherwise compromise their effectiveness; yet without any policies, their agreement would likely remain only words on paper—leaving their water-use CAPs unresolved.

Problems of collective action, both first- and second-order, underlie the rationale for the existence of policy, but they also accompany processes of creating and implementing policy, and so constrain policymaking. Absent first-order CAPs that arise from variations on free-riding, policy prescription would be simple, at least in principle: implement universal laissez-faire policies. If pursuit of individual self-interest always generated social optima, as a naïve reading of Adam Smith might suggest, then unfettered markets would perfectly execute necessary coordination and discipline for optimal exchange among self-interested individuals. The invisible hand would effectively wave away attendant problems related to exploitation, rent seeking, poor quality, pollution, and so on. Furthermore, even in the presence of first-order CAPs, an absence of second-order CAPs—implying zero transaction costs of coordination and enforcement—would still permit "Coasian" bargaining to resolve first-order CAPs. Again, a basic laissez-faire policy would logically follow. Serious analysis of the contingency of collective action, however, undermines such a simplistic, indeed utopian, prescription. On the other hand, a designed policy remedy to either first- or second-order CAPs may not be effective or even possible. The CAPs that accompany policymaking processes limit the range of adoptable and implementable policies, sometimes severely. Thus we encounter complex relationships between self-interested activity, group outcomes, and a constrained potential for policy to either facilitate or impede resolution of first- or second-order CAPs. This chapter will outline these complexities.

To proceed, we define policy, beginning with public policy. According to Thomas Dye, "Public policy is whatever governments choose to do or not to do" (2008, 1). With a bit more refinement, Charles Cochran and Eloise Malone state: "Public policy consists of political decisions for implementing programs to achieve societal goals" (1995). Note the common thread of government choice or decision. Stressing the political side of policymaking, Deborah Stone asserts, "The strategies we call policy instruments are all ways of exerting power, of getting people to do what they otherwise might not do" (2002, 260). Stone's term "strategies" invokes game-theoretic interpretation. Thus policy is not a one-dimensional constrained-optimum decision made in isolation by some unified body of policymakers. Rather, it is a contingent plan that must consider anticipated actions and reactions of multiple parties. Policy remains a decision, but not any decision; it is a *strategic decision*, one that specifies a set of contingent actions and responses—or lack thereof. Moreover, policy involves exerting power. Combining these insights, we arrive at our working definition of *policy*:

> Policy constitutes one or more strategic decisions made by public or private governing bodies that are intended to influence actions of specific agents or groups via some implicit or explicit exercise of power—or possibly a strategic decision to ignore actions of others. In either case, policy carries an intention of achieving some set of social goals envisioned by relevant policy makers.

In short, policies are social mechanisms designed to achieve social goals. Policies are a form of collective voice. Policies may be either public or private.

All previous chapters in this text inform our discussion of policy. The first- and second-order CAPs described in Chapters 2 and 3 provide reasons for both the existence of policy and the simultaneous presence of multiple impediments to (or constraints on) creating, reforming, implementing, or dismantling policy. Chapter 4's concepts of power shed light on the nature and operation of policy, including its creation, reform, and implementation. The concepts of reciprocity and social preference, developed in Chapters 5 and 6, point to possible motivations of relevant individuals, such as policymakers, advocates, opponents, and the general public. Likewise, Chapter 6's concepts of individual and shared mental models demonstrate the importance of cognitive frameworks at both individual and group levels—with important implications on the cognitive role of institutions (as shared mental models). On this foundation, Chapter 7's conception of institutions, organizations, and institutional systems identifies sources and instruments of policymaking as well as relevant contexts and targets. In terms of Chapter 8, policymaking is an exercise in deliberate social choreography, within which informal and formal institutions both establish and constitute fundamental cognitive, informational, and motivational contexts that, in turn, shape policymaking and affect its implementation. The idea of self-governance from Chapter 9 illustrates how self-organization can generate policies in the form of social rules that address localized CAPs. Chapter 10's systems of formal and informal rules with third- and second-party enforcers are both platforms for and targets of policymaking. Policymaking operates in contexts of polycentric governance and focuses on maintaining or adjusting such systems, their operations, and multiple behavioral patterns within them. Finally, policy is made in and applied across networks; it feeds off of, responds to, and alters the network dynamics detailed in Chapter 11.

The core arguments of this chapter build upon these prior concepts with five basic arguments. First, we relate policy to institutions, noting causality in both directions. On one hand, existing institutions both permit and constrain policymaking. They provide the ground rules for creating, modifying, and implementing policy; they influence policymakers' motivations, shape the information to which they respond, and affect their cognitive processes (mental models). On the other hand, over time, established and implemented sets of policy rules become institutionalized; they evolve into institutions (or components therein). Indeed, policy formulation offers the critical method for deliberate design, creation, modification, or abolition of relatively formal institutions (rules). Second, the ability of policy to influence the behavior of agents—inducing them to take actions they would otherwise avoid or to refrain from actions they would otherwise undertake—constitutes an exercise of power. Power relations both permit and constrain policymaking. Third, the existence of both first- and second-order CAPs provides the raison d'être for policy. Policy can generate mechanisms of coordination and enforcement that may either facilitate or impede resolution of pre-existing CAPs. Fourth, turning this last relation on its head, policymaking processes themselves involve complex combinations of CAPs. Collective-action problems pervade the process of moving issues to policy agendas; they influence and constrain the design, adoption, and implementation of new policy; and they accompany the alteration, abandonment, or reversal of existing policy. Fifth—largely on account of CAPs that arise from the limited information-processing capacities of boundedly rational agents—policymaking processes tend to generate punctuated equilibria. Stable policy regimes persist for relatively long time periods until interrupted by short bursts of rapid change (policy emergence) that dismantle, significantly reform, or replace them.

Organizationally, this chapter follows each of these four linkages.[2] Section 12.1 addresses the first two links. It relates policy to institutions, finding causality in both directions: institutions frame policymaking; and adopted policies can create, alter, or destroy institutions. As background, this section summarizes the Institutional Analysis and Development (IAD) framework of the Workshop in Political Theory and Policy Analysis at Indiana University (hereafter, IU Workshop).[3] The section proceeds to contend that the ability of policy to influence behavior and alter institutions reflects its potential for exercising power. Section 12.2 expands upon a core assertion of this text: CAPs offer the key rationale for the existence of policy. Policymaking addresses CAPs by utilizing collective decision making to create social mechanisms for resolution—though not always successfully. Reversing perspectives, Section 12.3 asserts that both first- and second-order CAPs reside within and accompany all stages of policymaking. Collective-action problems limit the kinds of ideas even considered on policy agendas, the feasible adoption (or enactment) of considered policy ideas, and the implementation of adopted ideas. This section asserts further that successful policy implementation—to the degree that it occurs—creates punctuated equilibria that characterize the sequencing of policymaking processes. Section 12.4 concludes.

12.1. POLICY, INSTITUTIONS, AND POWER

Policymaking operates within, and acts upon, existing institutional contexts. Institutions establish the basic social parameters within which policymaking operates, as they simultaneously shape the motivation, available information, and cognition of policymakers. Yet policy is also the chief strategic instrument that individuals and organizations use to create, alter, or dismantle institutions. Consequently, policy and power are fundamentally linked. Implemented (and understood) policies alter behavior directly, indicating exercises of power1; and when policy changes institutions, it changes the rules of the game or alters preferences and beliefs—exercises of power2 and power3. This section addresses these issues—along with pertinent background on the nature of policy rules within the IAD framework—as foundations for both policy analysis and subsequent arguments concerning policymaking and CAPs. Ultimately, the ability of policy to institutionalize positions from which agents may exercise various powers underlies much of its potential to resolve CAPs; yet institutionalization also fosters CAPs that complicate policy reform.

Institutional contexts both permit and constrain policymaking. Contexts affect the motivation of relevant parties directly via incentives, and indirectly by influencing their preferences, information, and cognition—in particular their conceptions of problems and potential solutions. Some policymakers are paid; others expect future rewards; still others hope to defray costs to themselves or to parties they care about. Existing institutional systems determine or influence such incentives. Internalized social norms, moreover, affect conceptions of identity and associated motivations. President Lyndon B. Johnson's policy on the Vietnam War, for example, was partly motivated by his intense desire to avoid being the first US president to lose a war (Halberstam 1972). Furthermore, much of the information that Johnson received on the war's conduct passed through chains of military command, following established institutional procedures. On a somewhat broader scale, the substantial differences between European and US social welfare policy reflect impacts of distinct formal institutional configurations, along with different social norms concerning equality and the role of government, different information, and different conceptions of citizenship and nationhood.

From the opposite perspective, policies create, shape, and alter institutions, especially formal institutions. Policies take the form of rules that prescribe actions that are meant to be taken (or avoided) in certain contexts or circumstances. New policies alter pre-existing rules or create new ones. Indeed, reform of previously established institutions constitutes a major purpose of policymaking. Over time, moreover, successfully enacted and implemented policies—ones that end up being generally understood and enforced—become formal and social rules: they become types or elements of institutions. As such, they influence subsequent cognition, information, and motivation of government agents, interest groups, and the public. Paul Pierson (1993) refers to such influence as "policy feedback."

Policy-instituted formal rules often serve as foundations or reference points for various, less formal working rules. An operating unemployment insurance policy, for example, prescribes conditional actions that amount to rules of the game for both potential recipients and administrators. It specifies things like conditions under which terminated employees are eligible to receive benefits, how they should search for work, and various enforcement procedures. Officials in relevant agencies interpret such formal regulations, supplementing them with their own informal working rules, which may address borderline conditions and circumstances that policymakers had simply not anticipated. Thus policy-induced prescriptions usually combine both formal and informal elements. Informal rules, naturally, are less subject to deliberate design and depend critically on complex processes of policy implementation that interact directly with pre-existing social norms. To more fully understand both how institutions frame policymaking and how new policies alter institutions, we discuss the IAD framework developed by scholars at the IU Workshop.[4]

The Institutional Analysis and Development Framework

The IAD framework offers a comprehensive conceptual structure for analyzing institutions, policy, and behavior.[5] It identifies "major types of structural variables present to some extent in all institutional arrangements, but whose values differ from one type of institutional arrangement to another" (Ostrom 2007, 27). The foundational concept of this framework is the action situation. An *action situation* is any social setting in which two or more individuals or organizations engage in any form of transaction, including exchange, production, conflict, group decisions, problem solving, and so forth. The IAD framework delineates relationships among nested levels of action situations, associated rules, and external variables.[6]

An action situation has seven key elements (clusters of related variables), all of which relate to game theory:

  (i) The set of participants or players: individuals or organizations.

 (ii) The positions of participants: CEO, member, employee, and so on. From a game-theoretic perspective, positions designate categories of players that are differentiated by the timing of moves, available actions, potential impacts, and access to information and other resources.

(iii) The set of allowable actions, with associated functions (or processes) that map combinations of actions to outcomes. In an extensive-form game, such mappings appear as sequences of successive branches (action choices) on a game tree that end at specific terminal nodes.

 (iv) The possible outcomes that follow from specific combinations or sequences of actions. An outcome might be a successful trade or the election of a candidate. Possible outcomes influence, but do not determine, payoffs.[7]

  (v) The amount of "control each participant has over choice" (Ostrom 2007, 29). Individuals control some choices; but others, such as voting, depend on group interactions. Game-theoretically, a pre-game can represent a collective decision that affects possible actions (enhancing or limiting an agent's control) at one or more nodes in a subsequent game.

(vi) The information available to various participants concerning external factors and elements of their action situation (i.e., all other items in this list). Relevant game-theoretic concepts include information sets, subjective priors, and assumptions about common knowledge.

(vii) The costs and benefits that accompany various combinations of actions and outcomes. Net benefits offer incentives for specific actions. These net benefits (as interpreted via agents' utility functions), along with various impacts of external factors (moves by nature), jointly affect the payoffs associated with possible game outcomes.

Readers may note the similarity between these seven elements of an action situation and the rules of a classical game. Figure 12.1 depicts an action situation. Items (i)–(vii) appear in capital letters, along with arrows illustrating links among them. The left-hand side of the diagram shows the assignment of both participants and (possible) actions to positions. Within these contexts, agents make strategic decisions in response to information, degrees of control, and anticipated costs and benefits. Multiple strategic decisions then combine with external influences to produce outcomes.

Action situations operate within biophysical and social contexts summarized by the exogenous variables (or quasi-parameters) shown at the top of Figure 12.1. For example, the susceptibility of specific interactions to biophysical impacts depends on the type of interaction. Agricultural productivity reacts to rain, insects, and fungi, whereas contract negotiations in air-conditioned buildings usually do not. Likewise, the physical attributes of goods and resources can affect resolution of CAPs. Land lends itself to excludability far

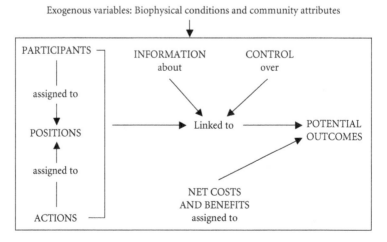

Figure 12.1   Elements of an action situation

SOURCE: Elinor Ostrom (2005, Fig. 2.1), *Understanding Institutional Diversity*, Princeton, NJ: Princeton University Press. Reprinted with permission.
NOTE: I added some of my own labels.

more easily than do fisheries or the atmosphere. Similarly, rates of biological reproduction influence the sustainability of harvested resources like fisheries. Even the relative mobility of harvested species (e.g., corn versus salmon) can influence the difficulty of establishing various property rights over the physical spaces in which they grow.

At a deeper level, exogenous social variables—notably institutions and community attributes, such as population heterogeneity and predominant beliefs—establish the basic parameters within which action situations operate. These exogenous factors influence participants' motivation, information, and cognition, and simultaneously affect pertinent types of interaction among various participants. Depending on the question and level of analysis, institutions and community attributes may act either as exogenous variables per se or as quasi-parameters. For quasi-parameters, specific action outcomes may, over time, alter associated values or paths of development (see Section 7.1).

This framework allows for a great deal of modeling flexibility. We can model agents' preferences as either material or social. We can model their cognition and decision processes as either substantively rational maximization or as boundedly rational adaptive learning via mental models. As in all modeling exercises, the benefits of alternative approaches depend on the analytical questions at hand. For most of this chapter, we use boundedly rational agents with social and material preferences. For specific questions, however, substantive rationality offers a more efficient approach.

We may now organize action situations into a nested hierarchy according to the type (or level) of rules they generate. Chapter 9 distinguished between operational rules, collective-choice rules, and constitutional rules. Each type of rule constitutes a fundamental element of the institutional context for a corresponding type of action situation; Figure 12.2 illustrates.[8] The vertical structure of the diagram depicts a four-level hierarchy of action situations, showing the most immediate (or direct) at the top, with successively less direct and more foundational (or "deeper") levels underneath. Note that external variables—representing biophysical and community attributes—influence interactions at all four levels. At the top, operational situations represent circumstances and action spaces for on-the-spot economic and social exchanges or applications of power—all of which directly influence outcome variables in the social and physical world. Operational action situations, however, reside in contexts shaped by operational rules that, in turn, arise from (are negotiated within) underlying collective-choice situations or arenas. For example, collective-choice decisions among Nepali farmers designate operational rules regarding farmer access to irrigation canals that, in turn, affect their daily water use (Lam 1998).[9]

Collective-choice situations operate in institutional contexts shaped by collective-choice rules that, in turn, emerge from underlying constitutional-choice situations or arenas. The US Constitution, a product of the constitutional arena of the 1787 Federal Convention in Philadelphia, specifies that each state shall have two senators (Article I, Section 3). This collective-choice rule frames operations in the collective-choice arena of the US Congress. Finally, constitutional rules are themselves outcomes of multiple complex interactions within more amorphous (and even deeper level) metaconstitutional situations—environments that establish the context for constitutional-choice arenas. Constitutional rulemaking responds to influences from community attributes, such as past history, social norms,

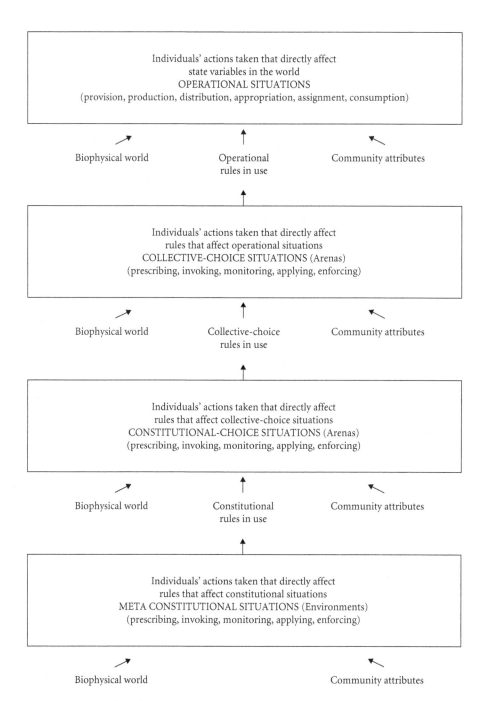

Figure 12.2 Hierarchy of action situations

SOURCE: Elinor Ostrom (2007, Fig. 2.2), "Institutional Rational Choice: An Assessment of the Institutional Analysis and Development Framework," in Paul A. Sabatier (Ed.), *Theories of the Policy Process*, 2nd ed., Cambridge, MA: Westview. Reprinted with permission.

NOTE: I added some of my own labels.

demographic characteristics, elements of culture, and legacies of pre-existing and contemporary institutions. For example, the procedures and understandings that structured interactions at the 1787 Federal Convention emerged from myriad influences within the metaconstitutional environment of the 13 colonies that became states. Such influences included events of the American Revolution; the experience of the new nation under the Articles of Confederation; the new states' social capital, including their social norms, uses of British common law, and other institutional legacies of Britain; the experience and knowledge available to leaders like James Madison and Alexander Hamilton, and so forth.[10]

Both constitutional- and collective-choice situations generate policy decisions, but with different impacts. Constitutional decisions directly affect subsequent collective decision making, but exert only indirect influence on daily operations. The policy decision of the 1787 Federal Convention that allocated two senators to each state has shaped interactions within the US Congress for over two centuries; yet its impact on the daily conduct of local businesses is, at most, indirect. Policy decisions made in collective-choice arenas, on the other hand, shape operational rules that exercise more immediate influence on behavior. For example, a state legislature (a collective-choice arena) might pass a cigarette tax (an operational rule) with the intent of influencing purchases (activity in an operational situation).

The vast majority of policymaking occurs within collective-choice situations. Indeed, a more complicated diagram would specify nested levels of collective-choice arenas in which lower levels establish (perhaps quasi-constitutional) rules that guide rulemaking procedures for higher-level arenas closer to operations. For example, the collective-choice arena of the US Congress designates certain regulatory powers to various federal agencies. Those agencies operate as collective-choice arenas for producing operational rules, such as Food and Drug Administration regulations requiring posted nutritional content on packaged foods.

Finally, note that formally designated constitutional- or collective-choice arenas create formal rules that we associate with formal institutions. Likewise, informally designated collective-choice situations create social rules. Broadly speaking, policymaking involves designing (and negotiating) formal rules that interact with informally created social rules and pre-existing social norms. Local self-governance typically involves a higher proportion of informal policymaking than does larger-scale governance. The interdependency of governance levels (polycentricism) thus applies to policymaking.

To more fully address the intended effects of policymaking—the social goals that accompany attempts to alter social mechanisms—we offer a second classification system for rules—one focused on policy intent. This rule typography is horizontal in the sense that it can apply to each of the three vertical rule classifications: constitutional, collective-choice, and operational rules. Recall from Chapter 8 the *ADICO* syntax of institutional statements. We may use the aim statements (*I*-statements in the syntax) to classify groups of rules by their intended purpose, independent of their vertical level (Ostrom and Crawford 2005). Intention-based rule classification can then inform policy analysis, because the aims of rules correspond to core objectives of the policymakers who design them.

There are seven aim-related categories of rules, each of which corresponds to an element or cluster of variables in the generic action situation of Figure 12.1: position rules, boundary rules, choice rules, aggregation rules, information rules, payoff rules, and scope rules.[11]

Position rules designate social, economic, or political positions that can be filled by various participants. They establish platforms that permit relevant agents to take specific actions in various situations. Sometimes these rules stipulate desired numbers of occupants for positions, such as one CEO or two senators per state.[12] Other designated positions include member, owner, committee chair, manager, employee, senator, and so on.

Boundary rules affect entry into and exit from specific positions. They can address eligibility and selection criteria, including such factors as personal attributes, acquired characteristics, and possession of resources. They may also regulate movement within hierarchies. Examples include corporate promotion policies and eligibility criteria for US citizenship. Boundary rules also regulate conditions under which individuals are required to, permitted to, or not allowed to leave certain positions. Prisoners are not allowed to leave jail before they have served their time. Employees, on the other hand, usually can quit at will (the key distinction between capitalism and slavery), though sometimes not until terms of a contract have been fulfilled. Term limits require that certain office holders (e.g., some governors) exit their positions after one or two terms in office.

Choice or authority rules assign sets of actions, rights, duties, and liberties to occupants of specific positions. They affect the power that accompanies specific positions and the distribution of power among them. For example, legislatures have authority to enact specific kinds of laws, and governors have authority to veto. Citizens under the age of 18 do not have the right to vote. For policy purposes, agenda-setting rules are an important type of choice rule. Agenda rules may limit the number or types of items considered on agendas or grant discretion to various positions, such as committee chairs. Choice rules often specify the contexts in which certain authorities pertain. For example, particular managers may supervise some jobs but not others.[13]

Aggregation rules designate procedures for summing the inputs from various participants into decisions related to subsequent actions. These rules affect how much weight or influence each participant carries in making such decisions. Collective-choice rules necessarily involve some kind of aggregation rule. Such rules may designate symmetric input, as in equal individual votes with decisions determined by majority, plurality, or consensus. Alternatively, inputs may be asymmetric, as in unilateral decisions (by CEOs or experts), oligarchic votes (by the elders, an unelected board, or a politburo), committee approval prior to consideration by a larger body (the committee system in the US Congress), or weighted individual votes (votes per share for stockholders).[14] Certain position holders, such as committee chairs, may not be allowed to vote.[15] Some aggregation rules address cases of no agreement, as in: "maintain the status quo" or "refer to an external authority."

Information rules affect communications related to specific actions conducted by or among parties who hold specific positions. These rules specify whether certain transmissions of information among individuals, within organizations, or between organizations are required, permitted, or forbidden.[16] They may also prescribe information content, quality, frequency, or accuracy. Sales reports, for example, should include the number and type of items sold, must be documented with receipts, should be filed weekly, and must refer directly to revenue data. Ultimately, these rules shape information feedback pertaining to social or physical environments, current or previous actions of specific parties, outcomes of actions, and so forth.

Information rules are particularly important to policy and institutional analysis for three related reasons. First, because they affect the information feedback that accompanies institutions and institutional systems, they shape the adaptability and sustainability of various institutional or organizational arrangements—in particular, whether such arrangements are ultimately self-reinforcing or self-undermining.[17] Second, because communication flows are the foundation of networks, information rules critically affect network creation, development, and functioning. Transmission of sales reports, for example, can create a network. Third, because information about an agent's past behavior underlies common perceptions of that agent's trustworthiness, information rules affect the formation and utilization of social capital.

Payoff rules "affect the benefits and costs that will be assigned to particular combinations of actions and outcomes" (Ostrom 2007, 38). They establish incentives for specific position holders related to specific possible actions. While payoff rules are clearly important components of economic institutions, they can also prescribe political and social rewards or sanctions. For example, these rules may stipulate pay frequency (as in monthly paychecks) and conditions (piecework), or contractual contingencies (provisions for cost overruns).[18] Alternatively, they may designate social recognition (e.g., titles) as rewards for time spent building networks. Payoff rules may also specify material sanctions, such as fines or time in jail. On account of their distributional implications, positions that allow designated parties to influence policies on payoff rules may be highly sought after or contested.

Scope rules focus on observable outcome variables, such as pollution levels, rather than specific actions. More precisely, they can establish performance targets or ranges for specific outcomes without necessarily specifying how those targets should be reached. The cap-and-trade system for reducing sulfur dioxide (SO_2) emissions, initiated by the 1990 Clean Air Act, offers an example. The Environmental Protection Agency (EPA) has allocated participating utilities permits to emit SO_2 at their power plants according to a precise formula.[19] Utilities are required to limit SO_2 output to levels stipulated by permits they hold, but utilities are allowed to trade permits among each other; and they exert considerable discretion over how to actually reduce emissions.[20] Scope rules offer important policy instruments because they often appear more legitimate, and so may generate less opposition, than rules that attempt to regulate specific activities. On the other hand, outcome targets (e.g., quality of education) are often difficult to measure and subject to policy controversy.

Each of these seven rule categories indicates (and also reflects) possible aims or social goals for policy decisions. These rules, however, do not work as independent influences on behavior; rather, they participate in generating joint configurations of influence within complex environments. The actual effect of a single rule depends on interactions with other rules and external variables; thus impacts are not limited to primary aims. For example, the American Medical Association has established boundary rules concerning qualifications of physicians. Because boundary rules affect market supply, they—along with position, information, choice, aggregation, payoff, and possibly scope rules, and (of course) external market conditions—affect the salaries actually received by both physicians and other medical professionals.[21] Thus the design component of policymaking involves crafting combinations of the seven rule types—while also striving to anticipate partially understood interactions among specific rules, along with potentially less well understood external influences. Both the power and the limits of policymaking depend critically on how these factors jointly affect the social goals of policy.

This classification scheme, then, offers a useful tool for policy analysis. Consider a relatively simple common-pool resource (CPR) problem, such as overgrazing on an easily divisible and excludable plot of land. Some would say that resolution merely involves assigning property rights. As discussed in Chapter 9, however, property rights are complicated. They include specifications related to access (position and boundary rules), withdrawal (choice, aggregation, payoff rules, and information rules), management (position, choice, aggregation, and information rules), exclusion (position, boundary, and possibly choice and information rules), and alienation (position and choice rules). Scope rules may play a role as well. Thus even defining relatively transparent property rights requires complicated mixtures of at least six of the seven horizontal types of rules. (See this chapter's appendix for a game illustration.) Crafting such rule architecture thus requires a series of policy decisions at some level (or levels) of governance.[22]

Policy analysis related to rule design should then consider at least the following:

- which rule types are needed to achieve intended social goals;
- how to combine needed types;
- within each type, which specific prescriptions appear most promising;
- possible motivations of relevant individuals and organizations, including enforcers;
- anticipated effects of interactions among different rules and different rule types, including relevant capacities and constraints; and
- anticipated interactions with external variables.

Feasible policymaking must address all of these issues within the context of the institutional systems in which they operate. For example, will designated enforcers find it in their interest to enforce? Will they abuse their power? Along these lines, Agrawal and Chhatre (2007) find that external involvement in local governance of forest resources in the Indian Himachal Pradesh has reduced forest sustainability.

Returning to vertical rule classifications, policies reflect combinations of all seven horizontal types of rules—all of which are designed and negotiated within one or more of Figure 12.2's lower three action situations. All seven horizontal rule types can be components of the constitutional, collective-choice, and operational rules that actually emerge from metaconstitutional, constitutional-choice, and collective-choice situations. In this hierarchy, rules designed at one level (e.g., collective-choice situations) affect interactions at the next-higher level (e.g., operational situations). Thus the policies that accompany the governance of entities like CPRs mix the seven horizontal rule types at different vertical levels. Indeed, policy analysts may use this perspective to interpret Ostrom's (1990, 2005) list of the design features of successfully self-organized CPR management (reported in Section 9.4).[23] On a broader scale, political and economic institutions involve complex combinations of all seven horizontal and three vertical rule categories that emerge from relevant action situations—typically as outcomes of policy decisions.[24]

New policies, however, only become institutionalized (i.e., achieve the status of institutions) when the shared mental models of relevant participants generally converge in a manner that suggests (or better yet implies) expected adherence to policy prescriptions. If successfully institutionalized, policy decisions tend to accrue path dependency via feedback effects on cognition, information, and motivation. In particular, policy-induced formal institutions that acquire sets of complementary, less formal working rules—along with compatible social norms—can become self-enforcing, and even self-reinforcing, punctuated equilibria. For example, reflecting a policy decision of its authors, the US Constitution established the enduring practice that the Senate must approve the president's nominees for positions on the Supreme Court. This institution has gained such force that violation is practically inconceivable. The ability of policy to effect enduring institutional change leads to our next topic.

Power and Policymaking

Because policymaking involves strategic decision making with intent to alter behavior, it constitutes an exercise of power. Furthermore, policy establishes sources of power; it creates positions (such as seats in legislatures, managerial posts, judgeships) from which designated parties exercise power. In many cases, policy may ratify, formalize, and extend tentative behavioral patterns that emerge from informal resolution of CAPs and/or informal decision-making arrangements. Successful revolutionaries, for example, typically enact many policies in efforts to institutionalize their possibly fragile hold on power. Various other politically successful organizations or coalitions may do the same, albeit less dramatically, with hopes of instituting policy agendas.[25]

To examine relationships between power and policy, we merge three conceptual frameworks. More specifically, we apply Chapter 4's discussion of the three faces of power and Stone's (2002) five realms of policy influence to Figure 12.2's vertical hierarchy of rules and action situations. Chapter 4's discussion of the three faces of power (based on Lukes 1974) provides a broad conceptual foundation. Recall that power1 directly influences behavior; power2 alters rules of the game, including expectations of other players; and power3 alters preferences and beliefs of targeted actual or potential opponents. On a somewhat different track, Stone (2002, Part IV) focuses on policy influence. More precisely, she discusses five realms of policy influence:

(i) Inducements: understood rewards or punishments assigned to specific actions.

(ii) Mandates: required or prohibited actions, with understood sanctions.[26]

(iii) Rights: permissions to take specific actions, backed by government power.

(iv) Powers: strategies that affect who makes certain decisions.

(v) Persuasion: use of argumentation to alter opinions and conceptions.

These realms of influence are not categories of rules. Instead, they delineate principal domains of impact that arise from combinations of policy rules.

As we have seen, Figure 12.2's four-level hierarchy of action situations illustrates the basic contexts within which policymaking operates. As such, each action situation represents a type of context that conditions how exercises of power influence both behavior and rule-making (i.e., policymaking). For example, in collective-choice situations, uses of power can affect the crafting of operational rules that, in turn, affect behavior—including subsequent exercises of power—in operational situations. Exercises of power in constitutional-choice arenas have similar impact on collective-choice rules and situations.

We now associate successful policy, as it emerges from any of the action situations, with all three faces of power and all five realms of influence. Mutually understood and previously enacted policies can—as operational, collective-choice, or constitutional-choice rules—specify inducements or mandates (realms (i) and (ii)) that affect behavior in their designated action situations—exercising power1. Established operational rules facilitate such exercises of power1 in operational situations, while collective-choice rules do the same for collective-choice situations. For example, the monetary disincentive specified by a cigarette tax is intended to reduce smoking, and life imprisonment is meant to deter murder. Both policies, once enacted, constitute transparent exercises of power1 in their relevant operational situations. Similarly, by using established procedures to assemble votes, majority coalitions can exercise power1 in collective-choice or constitutional-choice arenas.[27]

At a somewhat deeper level, policies that establish constitutional- and collective-choice rules designate positions with various rights (realm (iii)) and powers (realm (iv)) in collective-choice and operational situations, respectively. These positions are sources of both power1 and power2. For example, the Sixteenth Amendment to the US Constitution states that "The Congress shall have power to lay and collect taxes on incomes, from whatever source derived without apportionment among the several States, and without regard to any census or enumeration." Congressional legislation, in turn, has authorized the Internal Revenue Service to exercise powers associated with collecting taxes.

The ability of policy to create, alter, or destroy institutions attests to its most profound relationship to power. Agents who successfully create and implement policies exercise power2 and often power3. Policies enacted in collective-choice arenas alter operational rules, changing the rules of the game in operational situations. Likewise, successful changes in collective-choice rules, via policymaking in deeper-level collective-choice or constitutional-choice arenas, alter the rules of the game in higher-level collective-choice arenas. These policy changes typically involve assignment or modification of rights and powers (realms (iii) and (iv)) in a manner that can affect inducements and mandates (realms (i) and (ii)).[28] For example, the 1990 Clean Air Act, an outcome of policy decisions made in the collective-choice arena of the US Congress, assigned new powers to the EPA. On that basis, the EPA—itself a less deep collective-choice arena—instituted the operational rules associated with the cap-and-trade system on SO_2 emissions.[29] The new policy demonstrated exercises of power2 by both the Congress and the EPA. More dramatically, as a key policy achievement of the civil rights movement and its allies, the 1965 Voting Rights Act changed the rules of the game concerning racially based access to the franchise in the southern United States, undermining a cornerstone of the Jim Crow segregation system that had endured in that region from the 1880s until 1965.

Finally, policy enactment and implementation can influence beliefs and mental models in ways that indicate exercises of power3. Policy changes in collective-choice and constitutional-choice situations involve Stone's fifth realm of policy influence: persuasion.[30] Recall from Chapter 4, however, that, in order to count as an exercise of power3, persuasion must involve a deliberate attempt to manipulate preferences and beliefs of actual or potential opponents. For example, at least from the point of view of the plaintiffs, we may regard the Supreme Court's 1954 *Brown v. Board of Education* decision (which mandated desegregation of public schools) as an exercise of power3, because it contributed to altering beliefs and values that surrounded the policy debates on civil rights and race. Historian David Halberstam writes: "The *Brown v. Board of Education* decision not only legally ended segregation [in schools], it deprived segregationist practices their moral legitimacy as well" (1993, 423). The 1964 Civil Rights Act and 1965 Voting Rights Act had even greater impacts.

Indeed, these two acts offer a striking example of the use of policy to institutionalize elements of an agenda that had emerged from largely successful resolution of substantial CAPs associated with opposing segregation in the South. The civil rights movement initiated and coordinated large-scale opposition to segregation under extraordinarily dangerous conditions. In so doing, it helped to create a political environment in which the core policy ideas behind these acts could actually reach serious policy agendas—and then become law by action of the US Congress, over fierce opposition.[31] Unlike the impotent 1957 Civil Rights Act, which technically guaranteed voting rights for African Americans everywhere in the United States, these two later acts were successfully implemented and so became institutionalized. The combined influence of the civil rights movement, the 1954 *Brown v. Board of Education* decision, the 1964 Civil Rights Act, and the 1965 Voting Rights Act, not only changed the applicable rules of numerous political and economic games, it shifted preferences and beliefs regarding race relations. For example, staunch segregationist and former Alabama governor George Wallace, who in 1963 personally stood at the door of the University of Alabama in order to block the entrance of two black students, began in 1979 to apologize for his prior positions (Raines 1998).[32] That an astute politician like Wallace wanted or felt obligated to apologize is itself an indication of the degree to which beliefs, values, and power had shifted. Thus the power of policy to effect substantive change by reorienting or reconstructing institutions can, on occasion, be enormous. Indeed, this ability of policy to harness the social choreography of institutions lies at the foundation of its ability to, within limits, address CAPs—our next topic.

12.2. POLICY AS A POTENTIAL REMEDY TO CAPS

Collective-action problems can motivate members of affected groups to construct social mechanisms that they believe will modify individual behavior—so as to align it more closely with group interests, or perhaps interests of certain members. Indeed, the core thesis of this book is that such mechanisms are a necessary, though often flawed, prerequisite for development. To the extent that social mechanisms for resolving CAPs are deliberately crafted human artifacts, they embody policies; they make and apply policy statements. In other words, when the pursuit of individual interest leads to outcomes that appear undesirable, groups, subgroups, or individuals may attempt to create various mechanisms of governance, rules, prescriptive statements, and/or decisions, all with the intent of altering the behavior of various parties so as to mitigate perceived problems. Thus actual or perceived CAPs motivate policy formation. This section examines these issues.

Broadly speaking, the social goals of policy amount to addressing myriad first- and second-order CAPs that arise from either market or group failure. Recall Olson's contention that small groups can utilize selective, largely social, incentives for aligning individual and group interests. Whenever such mechanisms emerge from deliberate decisions and design (however informal), they constitute internal policy for such groups.[33] Chapter 8's discussion of relatively informal irrigation-use rules enacted by communities of Nepali farmers offers an example. Larger groups, however, tend to rely on more formally designated policy with more explicit enforcement. At either level, policy decisions frame the design (or crafting) of such mechanisms and their accompanying prescriptive statements. Likewise, a collective decision not to address a CAP also constitutes a policy. In either case, CAPs offer the core motivation for the existence of policy.

For economists, the most transparent rationale for economic policy concerns addressing CAPs of traditional market failures that accompany the provision of public goods, use of common resources, and any form of externality (Weimer and Vining 1992). For example, the 1990 Clean Air Act's cap-and-trade system for sulfur dioxide (SO_2) responded to numerous health and environmental problems attributable to SO_2 emissions. This policy effectively internalized SO_2 externalities by defining and enforcing new property rights over emission permits and creating a market for trading them. Often, economic policy prescribes mechanisms for defining, enforcing, and regulating transfer of property rights. To conceptualize the relevant issues, this text has defined public goods broadly to include creating institutions and generating trust, along with more traditional items like regulating the money supply. Definitions of externalities and common resources are similarly broad; the latter may include overuse of entities ranging from an office copying machine to public parks, highways, fisheries, oceans, or the global atmosphere. Economic policy, then, addresses multiple CAPs associated with conducting economic exchanges, establishing markets, defining and enforcing property rights, and mediating broadly defined market failures.

Closely related first-order CAPs also arise from group failure or both group and market failure.[34] For example, overuse of the Colorado River involves mixes of private and government activities at various levels, including the following: watering lawns, recreation, agriculture, and industrial production; local, state, and federal regulation; US-Mexican relations; and various pricing mechanisms.[35] Likewise, to the extent that the 2007–2010 financial crisis reflected a prior hesitancy of the Federal Reserve and other agencies to involve themselves in regulating investment banks, the crisis represented both a market failure and a policy failure. Many difficult policy issues involve group failure, ranging from local community interactions to local, regional, national, and international governance.

Recall Chapter 10's four types of self-governance failure that external governance could, in principle, address: insufficient willingness or ability to resolve local CAPs; vulnerability of governance mechanisms to external shocks; internal inequities related to power and resources; and problems of insularity, including an unwillingness to address CAPs that affect other groups. Any of these group failures may call for policy remedy at combined or higher governance levels. We now add three additional types of group failure that often motivate policy response:

(i)   Problematic relationships between groups (often an outcome of insularity). Groups that typically experience low transaction costs to collective action (to self-organization) can pass costs of resolving CAPs on to other groups (McGinnis 2011b). Groups may also attempt to use their governance mechanisms against rivals; military conquest offers an all-too-frequent example. Transnational policy can attempt to remedy such problems. For example, in the 1990s the UN provided Somalia with valuable food aid, but by 2012 international efforts to end their civil war had generated (at best) mixed results (Global Security 2012).

(ii) Failure of previously adopted policy; dysfunctional policy creates CAPs. In 1933, the disastrous Eighteenth Amendment to the US Constitution—Prohibition—was repealed.

(iii) Failure of institutions to adapt to internal or external change creates CAPs related to the sustainability of institutional systems. The reform program of former Soviet general secretary Mikhail Gorbachev failed to adequately address the Soviet system's inability to achieve levels of growth attained by Western countries.

We may illustrate general principles of policy redress for either market or group failure with a simple prisoners' dilemma (PD) game. Consider the two-player game in Figure 12.3.[36] Assume that $H > C > D > L$ for both players. If r (reward for cooperating) and p (punishment for defection) are 0, the game has a PD structure, representing a first-order CAP. In principle, policy decisions could address such CAPs by designating target levels of contribution to a public good (C_A and C_B). Additional policy could then address second-order CAPs of enforcing commitments to contribute by assigning selective rewards for cooperation and/or punishments for defection—along with designated enforcers (not shown).[37] Government taxes on cigarettes and subsidies on home ownership (via mortgage tax deductions) illustrate this kind of policy. When effective, such policy simultaneously addresses both first- and second-order CAPs.

Analysis from Chapters 2 and 3, however, suggests limitations. Necessary conditions for success include sufficient rewards and/or penalties along with adequately informed and motivated enforcers who can observe contribution and defection with sufficiently high probabilities. Lack of resources, information, or motivation among enforcers may prevent policy from achieving its intended objectives.

		Player B	
		C	D
Player A	C	$C_A + r, C_B + r$	$L_A + r, H_B - p$
	D	$H_A - p, L_B + r$	$D_A - p, D_B - p$

Figure 12.3   PD with third-party enforcement

Not surprisingly, then, we find that a great deal of policy is also motivated by second-order CAPs that arise from efforts to remedy first-order CAPs of market or group failure. Second-party enforcers at one governance level may lack the resources to design and implement effective enforcement. Neighborhood organizations often endeavor to reduce crime, but lack the resources and authority to apprehend offenders. More generally, potential policy resolutions to first-order CAPs may fail for lack of credible enforcement. The UN Kyoto Protocol, a treaty signed by 84 nations in 1999, mandated that 37 industrialized countries reduce average carbon dioxide emissions over the 2008–2012 period by 5% compared to their average 1990 emissions (UNFCC 2011). As of 2005 and 2010, greenhouse gas emissions levels in most Kyoto signatory countries—other than transition economies—had exceeded the Kyoto limits, although accounting for the impacts of land-use changes on net carbon emissions generated more optimistic assessment of compliance in 2010 (Betsill 2011; UNFCC 2012). In either case, a failure to generate country compliance with agreed Kyoto Protocol targets represents a second-order CAP of group failure. Subsequent annual UNFCC conferences, such as the Doha 2012 UN Climate Change Conference, reflect attempts to reformulate negotiated climate policy.[38]

Collective-action problems that emerge from relationships between potential second- and third-party enforcers tend to generate three types of policy response. First, policy may institute or activate mechanisms of third-party coordination and/or enforcement. In so doing, various policies designate the positions from which third-party enforcers or coordinators operate, along with their responsibilities and limitations. For example, the state of Iowa has a policy that the state police enforce speed limits on interstate highways but may not search vehicles without cause.

Second, external policies directly affect second-party enforcement within self-organized groups by shaping the environments in which they operate, along with incentives, information, and understandings. Recall Chapter 9's discussion of second-party enforcement among Turkish fishers regarding use of their common resource. If Turkish national policy had, in fact, prohibited cooperatives, the local enforcement mechanism would have failed because defectors could have credibly threatened to report second-party enforcers to external authorities (Ostrom 1990). On a broader scale, government definition and enforcement of property rights facilitates negotiating agreements and exchanges among private businesses and consumers. Major goals of such policy include assisting second-party enforcers in resolving internal second-order CAPs and coordinating enforcement activities across different second parties. For example, state policy prohibiting assault may help managers enforce work rules by effectively ruling out extreme forms of defection.

Third, policy may attempt to shape relationships between second- and third-party enforcers. Recall from Chapter 3 that information asymmetries typically render third-party mechanisms, such as the court system, incapable of fully enforcing contracts.[39] Involved second parties, such as managers and workers, must therefore create somewhat complementary internal enforcement mechanisms. Hence another social goal of policy is to shape such interactions within institutional systems. For example, the 1935 National Labor Relations Act specifies arbitration mechanisms for company-union bargaining, but leaves the details of such bargaining to the involved parties.

When policy mechanisms effectively orchestrate third- and second-party enforcement and coordination, they lower transaction costs. Many second-order—and, by extension, first-order—CAPs associated with complex economic, political, and social exchange may indeed be resolved. In this sense, policy underlies development. As stressed in Chapter 10, however, interactions between second- and third-party enforcers—and the accompanying relations between formal and informal institutions, especially social norms—influence actual adherence to rules, and thereby condition the feasibility and effectiveness of policy. In particular, these relationships affect the degree to which designated policies are actually implemented. Indeed, implementation presents policymakers with another set of CAPs that often constrain or preclude policy effectiveness. First, however, we consider how the various stages of policymaking are themselves CAPs and how such CAPs affect the feasibility of adopting specific policy prescriptions.

12.3. THE POLICYMAKING PROCESS AS A SET OF INTERRELATED CAPS

Reversing Section 12.2's perspective, we now examine sets of interrelated CAPs that accompany policymaking processes. While Sections 12.1 and 12.2 have demonstrated the potential power of policymaking, this section addresses constraints on feasible policy. Broadly speaking, CAPs of policymaking restrict its potential in three related manners: (i) they limit the kinds of policy ideas that receive sufficient consideration to reach actual policy agendas; (ii) among ideas considered, they limit enactment; and (iii) among those enacted, they compromise effective implementation. Note that while this section emphasizes policy process, use of backwards induction regarding policy enactment or implementation informs the analysis of policy feasibility. Because policy shapes formal institutions and institutions shape the cognition, information, and motivation of both policymakers and intended targets, a comprehensive analysis of policy design and policy impacts should consider policymaking processes as they operate within the context of relevant institutional systems. A failure to understand policy process can lead analysts to propose theoretically efficient but ultimately unattainable policy ideas.

In principle, policy may attempt either to maintain existing behavioral patterns (policy-induced or not) or to implement change—incrementally, boldly, or somewhere in between. While maintenance also involves CAPs, we focus on incremental modification and substantive change—reform.[40] We begin with background on basic CAPs, players, and stages of policymaking. We proceed to discuss punctuated policy equilibria—meaning configurations of interaction whereby stable periods of policymaking, which are dominated by specialized policy subsystems, face occasional disruption by spurts of substantive reform that accompany the emergence of distinct new policies. New and differently configured periods of stability often follow. We next summarize game-theoretic representations and conclude with a discussion of policy implementation.

Background Concepts

Reform-oriented policymaking involves CAPs that originate from two fundamental and related sources: path-dependent, pre-existing institutional systems; and the inevitable presence of multiple concerned parties. Because new policies must originate from extant institutional systems, reform emerges from the cognition, information, and motivation that flow from pre-existing informal and formal institutions, interacting with related organizations and interests.[41] Furthermore, because successfully implemented policies typically evolve into institutions, established policies develop difficult-to-dislodge punctuated equilibria. Potential resistance to change, orchestrated by those who benefit from the status quo, reinforces the accompanying path dependence of established policies.

All of these processes involve multiple parties whose interests may differ. Key participants affect policymaking in various manners:

- Policy officials—such as legislative, executive, and judicial actors, or private-sector managers and employee representatives—enact and implement policy.

- Interest groups, consisting of organizations and coalitions, may seek to either change or maintain existing policy.

- Political parties frame issues and put pressure on policy officials, notably through their ability to influence elections.

- Research organizations (universities and think tanks) provide information and conceptual frameworks to officials and interest groups; their interpretations of complex issues shape policy debates.

- Citizens seek to influence interest groups, political parties, and policy officials.

- The media transmit information to all of the above participants and, more fundamentally, frame issues using images, stories, and symbols.

- *Policy entrepreneurs* are agents from any of the above categories who invest resources, such as time, money, and reputation, into promoting specific policies (Kingdon 2003).[42]

Parties who seek reform (often policy entrepreneurs and allies) face multiple CAPs. From the point of view of those who expect to benefit, policy-induced reform usually amounts to a public good. Furthermore, because reform creates externalities, some gain at others' expense. Potential conflicts and power relationships thus compound policy CAPs. Policy processes typically involve first-order CAPs related to negotiating agreements on the content of specific proposals, along with the allocation of costs and benefits that accompany policy design, promotion, and the inevitable presence of opposition. Ensuing second-order CAPs concern enforcing any such agreements, and also coordinating complicated arrays of activity meant to influence opinion, create pressure, and oppose challenges.

We examine these CAPs within three basic stages of policymaking processes:

(i) *Policy emergence:* how specific issues and proposals generate enough interest to reach policy *agendas*—that is, how particular issues gain sufficient attention to reach discussion agendas. And then how specific proposals become one of a few considered alternatives for addressing such issues (decision agendas).

(ii) *Policy enactment:* process of selecting among short lists of alternatives when adopting new policy provisions, or when modifying (or repealing) existing policies.

    (iii) *Policy implementation:* how relevant agents apply or carry out specific enacted policies or policy provisions.

Each stage offers its own set of CAPs. We begin with emergence and enactment before addressing implementation.

Policy Subsystems and Punctuated Equilibria

To represent stages (i) and (ii), we merge three approaches: the punctuated-equilibrium policy theory of Frank Baumgartner and Bryan Jones (1993); the advocacy coalition framework of Paul Sabatier and Christopher Weible (2007); and the multiple-streams concept of policy emergence from John W. Kingdon (2003). The Baumgartner and Jones punctuated equilibrium framework can encompass the other two approaches. These two authors assert that long periods of policy stability arise from the ability of policy subsystems (intermediate-level institutional systems) to enact and implement clusters of related policies while, simultaneously, limiting outside input. External events or sufficient opposition, however, occasionally spawn periods of rapid change in policy substance or process. Within this overall pattern, Sabatier and Weible's advocacy coalition framework addresses the incremental change that characterizes policy enactment during periods of stasis, while Kingdon's concept of policy emergence addresses the disruption of prior stasis that engenders rapid and substantive reform.

    According to Baumgartner and Jones (1993), interactions among different approaches to information processing, operating at different levels of analysis, generate the punctuated-equilibrium property of policy processes. Individuals and organizations process information differently. Given their limited cognitive capacities, boundedly rational individuals necessarily engage in *serial information processing*: they consider only one (or perhaps a few) issue(s) at a time. By contrast, organizations or coalitions utilize *parallel information processing*: they consider several issues simultaneously, by assigning specific areas to specialized subgroups. Policymaking processes employ both methods at three levels of aggregation: individual or micro-level serial processing; subsystem or intermediate-level parallel processing; and aggregate or macro-level serial processing.[43] Interactions among agents at these three levels create punctuated policy equilibria. Herein intermediate-level processing generates stable and incremental policy enactment, whereas correlated shifts of attention at the micro and macro levels lead to occasional bursts of reform—policy emergence.

    At the *micro level*, individual serial processing of policy information responds to the images and frameworks that emerge during policy debates. Because boundedly rational individuals absorb information selectively, they focus on the most salient (or pressing) information. They economize on cognition costs by using heuristics that highlight specific, familiar areas and by utilizing their mental models to frame conceptions of social categories and causal relationships. Accordingly, the strategic use of images, stories, and symbols within policy debates can affect micro-level information processing by either enhancing or diminishing the salience of specific problems or potential remedies.[44] When effective, such representations can simultaneously capture the serial attention of multiple individuals. Images, symbols, and stories thus act as correlating events that can focus (choreograph) perceptions and expectations across multiple individuals. For example, stories or photographs of spectacular crimes may enhance the salience of proposals to stiffen penalties and, likewise, diminish the appeal of rehabilitation. Sufficiently correlated individual responses to such stories, images, symbols, and/or events may then engender information cascades of changing opinion. For example, media images of the 1979 Three Mile Island nuclear accident contributed to shifting public opinion against construction of new nuclear plants (Baumgartner and Jones 1993, 79–82).

Intermediate-level policymaking involves two related dynamics. First, the use of parallel information processing by groups of specialists solves enormous coordination CAPs posed by the limitations of individual serial processing and the (necessarily accompanying) balkanization of knowledge. Second, relatively exclusive policy subsystems dominate policy processes in a manner that fosters relatively long-term policy stasis. We now elaborate.

Parallel information processing involves an intellectual division of labor whereby multiple groupings of policy specialists simultaneously address issue areas that correspond to their expertise. Issue areas have topical, social, and/or geographic boundaries. Some specialists may consider crime in Des Moines, Iowa; others may investigate how gender affects access to education in sub-Saharan Africa. Policy specialists attain expertise in various fashions, including researching, debating, organizing, and lobbying. They occupy institutionally designated positions in both public- and private-sector organizations: legislatures, bureaucracies, corporations, think tanks, nonprofits, and so on. Interactions within and among such specialized groups create, follow, and reinforce sets of policy procedures and outcomes that characterize policy subsystems.

Policy subsystems are interactive aggregations of specialists or experts that dominate policymaking in specific areas.[45] They tend to operate either as quasi-monopolies consisting of one advocacy coalition or as relatively stable negotiated relationships among a few advocacy coalitions (True, Jones, and Baumgartner 2007). An *advocacy coalition* is a grouping or network of individuals and organizations who share core beliefs and/or material interests and who coordinate activity in pursuit of specific policy objectives (Sabatier 1988; Sabatier and Weible 2007).[46] For example, after the 1947 passage of the Federal Insecticide, Fungicide, and Rodenticide Act, a subsystem (triangle) consisting of chemical manufacturers, farm interests, and the US Department of Agriculture managed pesticide policy until the early 1960s (Baumgartner and Jones 1993).

As the name suggests, *policy subsystems* are intermediate-level institutional systems in which participating organizations utilize mutually understood and accepted configurations of procedures in order to formulate policy. By limiting external input, policy subsystems generate negative-feedback dynamics that reinforce existing policy outcomes: intermediate-level stability. More specifically, they operate as follows:

- Policy subsystems use their own collective-choice rules to both designate positions with specific responsibilities and assign them to key policymakers. They create and allocate sources of power.

- On such institutional foundations, policy subsystems influence cognitive, informational, and motivational input to designated policymakers.

- By controlling or influencing releases of information and images to the media and to the public at large, policy subsystems shape opinion and thereby influence policy-making environments.[47]

Policy subsystems thus establish key boundaries on policymaking within their target areas via the activity of one or a few advocacy coalitions. They resolve manageable internal CAPs of designing and negotiating incremental policy changes. More significantly, they contain or prevent external disruption by designing rules that limit outside input and by effectively buying off actual or potential challengers with incremental changes—including negotiated or announced compromises or benefits. Policy subsystems may also employ symbolic gestures to placate potential opponents, particularly unorganized ones. "The most intensive dissemination of symbols commonly attends the enactment of legislation which is most meaningless in its effects on resource allocation" (Edelman 1964). Likewise, strategic information release can foster favorable images. For example, in the 1950s, images of "atoms for peace" reinforced the stability of that era's nuclear policy subsystem, which consisted of the Atomic Energy Commission, the Joint Committee on Atomic Energy, scientists, and industry officials (Baumgartner and Jones 1993). By orchestrating such (self-enforcing) activities, policy subsystems constitute a type of structurally induced equilibrium (Shepsle 1979), with path-dependent qualities.

Finally, lack of public attention to the often technical policy areas managed by subsystems lends support to their continued operation, reinforcing their stabilizing negative-feedback influence on policymaking (Baumgartner and Jones 1993; True, Jones, and Baumgartner 2007). The pesticide subsystem dominated its highly technical policy area between 1947 and the early 1960s, with little external input and little public complaint. Thus parallel-processing, intermediate-level policy subsystems (consisting of one or a few advocacy coalitions) create and sustain the enduring phase of punctuated equilibrium policy processes; for significant time periods they constitute self-enforcing, and even self-reinforcing, mid-level institutional systems—systems that enact and maintain prevailing policies within their areas of specialization.

Macro-level information processing addresses regional, national, or transnational policy issues by spanning multiple policy subsystems. Decisions at this level often establish general policy frameworks that intermediate-level systems then manage. For example, the 1990 Clean Air Act assigned specific duties to the EPA. Like their micro-level counterparts, macro processors—such as chief executives, leaders of legislative bodies, and such bodies taken as a whole—process information serially. In this regard, note that even though legislatures use committee structures for parallel processing of multiple issues, as a whole they can only enact important legislation one or a few issues at a time. For example, during the summer of 2009, the US Congress as a body focused attention on health care reform. Indeed, intermediate-level processing shields macro-level operators from a barrage of potential issues.

Like micro-level attention, macro-level attention responds to issue salience; it responds to particularly noticeable or memorable events, images, symbols, and stories. Furthermore, because macro attention is a scarce resource, various interests and coalitions compete for it.

Macro-level attention may react to dramatic events (e.g., 9/11), publicized intermediate-level failures (the response to Hurricane Katrina), and/or efforts of new participants and oppositional groups to call attention to specific issues (True, Jones, and Baumgartner 2007). Once attained, macro attention often prompts intervention into intermediate-level subsystem processing. Given the power relations conferred by institutional structures, such intervention can alter or disrupt intermediate-level policy regimes. Macro-level operators may, for example, invoke increased oversight, convene public hearings on subsystem practices, or reallocate subsystem duties to external agencies. Substantive reform usually engages some form of macro intervention.

Overall, the ability of intermediate-level subsystem processing to limit input generates stability (via negative feedback), whereas the susceptibility of both micro- and macro-level processing to large shifts in the salience of problems or solutions (via positive feedback) creates some potential for substantive reform.[48] Even during stable periods, oppositional advocacy coalitions, which often operate or emerge on the edges of policy subsystems, attempt to alter policy or replace existing subsystems. For example, starting in the 1960s, the early environmental movement challenged the pesticide policy subsystem. Short periods of punctuated change can then emerge when sufficiently noticeable outsider activity and/ or external events focus macro-level attention and intervention on problems that appear to be either produced or ignored by existing intermediate-level subsystems. To induce reform, opposition coalitions actively seek such attention. They endeavor to create or utilize alternative forums or arenas (venues) for venting complaints and enacting contrary policy (Baumgartner and Jones 1993; True, Jones, and Baumgartner 2007). They may ask for Congressional hearings; they may file lawsuits; they may ask state or local authorities to oppose federal decisions, or vice versa.[49] Alternatively, opposition coalitions may seek to replace macro-level policymakers with their own allies.

Orchestrating the necessary coordination and attention naturally presents significant CAPs for potential reformers. Successful resolution of these CAPs may undermine key elements of pre-existing policies and/or policy subsystems, initiating somewhat chaotic periods of policy emergence. To address such policy emergence, we turn to Kingdon's multiple-streams framework (2003).

Multiple Streams, Policy Emergence, and Punctuated Change

Policy emergence connotes the rapid ascension of a previously unconsidered (or underconsidered) policy idea to the attention of decision makers who occupy positions from which they could enact it. Successful emergence typically disrupts previously established policy equilibria; policy emergence creates dynamic instability. For reform proponents, achieving the requisite partial unraveling of established intermediate-level institutional patterns both involves and creates a unique set of CAPs. Policy emergence requires disrupting elements of prior social choreography. Consequently, participants find themselves operating farther outside of their pertinent problem-complexity boundary—thus with a greater CD gap—than in more stable times. Accordingly, policy emergence theory augments our concepts of individual serial information processing and organizational parallel processing with the following assumptions:[50]

- Varying pressures, complex environments, and time constraints force policymakers to operate under conditions of *ambiguity*: "a state of having many ways of thinking about the same circumstances or phenomena" (Feldman 1989, 5; cited in Zahariadis 2007). Under such pressure, either policymakers find that their mental models fail to produce clear cause-and-effect relationships, or they find themselves torn between competing mental models.

- The time constraints of complex decision making generate *problematic preferences*: in order to meet deadlines, policymakers must often make decisions without having worked out their own preferences over several incompletely understood alternatives (Zahariadis 2007).[51]

- Agents have unclear understandings of relevant *organizational technology*: they lack coherent conceptions of the processes by which organizations transform largely informational inputs into decision outputs. Such lack of clarity can arise from unclear jurisdictional boundaries among governance agencies and accompanying "turf" disputes.

- Finally, participation in policy-relevant endeavors is *fluid*: agents move into and out of relevant agencies and organizations, thus adding and subtracting information, perceptions, and understandings. Organizational knowledge changes.

As a consequence, collective decision making reacts to shaping or manipulation of understandings by images, salient appeals, and the framing of information. Outcomes depend on who pays attention to what and when (Zahariadis 2007, 68). In efforts to move their issues to policy agendas, policy entrepreneurs strategically use information, symbols, and images—hoping to thereby influence conceptions of problems and solutions. Symbols and images can, for example, offer compelling interpretations of largely internalized social norms.[52] A picture of a militiaman with rifle and tricorne hat may promote a perspective on what it means to be patriotic. Stories of decline featuring various heroes and villains may heighten the salience of specific problems and solutions in manners that shape policy debates. Metaphors ("spaceship earth") and synecdoche (the "welfare queen" as representative of problems with public assistance) can likewise shift attention (Stone 2002). Especially during periods of emergence, policy processing operates in such unclear and shifting cognitive contexts.

Kingdon's three-streams framework illustrates policy emergence. It identifies fundamental conditions that allow policy ideas or proposals to escape from the morass of public and private issues to reach the substantive attention of policymakers—that is, to reach a substantive policy *agenda*.[53] Policy emergence requires the simultaneous presence of favorable conditions within at least two of three relatively independent policy processing "streams": the problem stream, the policy stream, and the political stream. Such convergence creates *windows of opportunity*: short periods when policy entrepreneurs can advance particular issues or proposals to policy agendas (Kingdon 2003). Each stream possesses its own dynamics.

The *problem stream* represents the flow of perceptions—held by the public at large, the media, various interests, and policymakers—concerning the immediacy and seriousness of various undesirable situations that policy could possibly affect.[54] Dynamics in the problem stream reflect mixtures of information, perception, and circumstance that emerge from three related potential influences: feedback from existing policy, salient problem indicators, and focusing events. For example, feedback on the effectiveness of prior transportation regulation generated a "storm of criticism" that contributed to deregulation of railroads during the Carter administration (Kingdon 2003, 102). Analogously, in 1985, British scientists published a salient problem indicator: using satellite data, they found that atmospheric ozone levels over Antarctica had declined by 30%. Subsequent research identified chlorofluorocarbons (CFCs; used in coolants) as the principal cause. Two years later, 27 countries signed the Montreal Protocol, committing each to reducing CFC use 50% by 1999 (Rowlands 1995).[55] Focusing events—occurrences that catapult issues or problems to public, media, or official attention—can have more spontaneous impact. For example, the 1989 *Exxon Valdez* oil spill focused public and media attention on potential environmental hazards from oil tankers. Congress subsequently passed legislation requiring double hulls on oil tankers. Focusing events, in particular, can generate coordinated shifts in the attention of serial-processing individuals.

The *policy stream* filters the flow of ideas within and among policy communities; it generates relatively short lists of proposals they hope to place on policy agendas. *Policy communities* are groups of specialists, operating either inside or outside of policy subsystems, who focus on specific policy areas such as health care, education, or the environment. Specialists may work for government agencies, think tanks, the media, industry, or other interested parties. Within the policy stream, interactions among groups of specialists serve to select specific policy ideas for advancement. Policy selection involves three basic criteria: (i) technical feasibility or prospects for reasonable implementation; (ii) normative acceptability to specialists, various constituencies, and relevant policymakers; and (iii) ability to meet perceived budget and public-acceptability constraints. For example, during the US debate on health care reform in 2009, the idea of a single-payer health care system did not emerge as a serious proposal because it appeared contrary to the values of many policymakers and specialists concerning the proper role of government, and because it appeared to involve too much federal spending at a time of large and salient deficits. Thus, within the policy stream, ideas matter. Ideas that survive applicable selection criteria can emerge from policy communities as short-list proposals.

The third stream, the *political stream*, responds to the institutional positions, negotiations, and actions or reactions of various interests or constituencies—and especially to power relationships among them. Kingdon (2003) identifies national mood, activities of organized groups, and turnover in government personnel as key political-stream variables. Concerning mood, politicians may compete to present proposals that appear to fit public consensus opinions; when opinions diverge, they may compete to offer "balanced" solutions (Zahariadis 2007). Similarly, successfully organized groups, like the National Rifle Association, can attract sufficient political attention to move issues to substantive policy agendas. Likewise, government turnover—shifts in the personnel who occupy rulemaking positions—affects the prospects of policy ideas. When the Reagan administration took office in January 1981, prospects for enhanced environmental regulation dimmed while those for tax cutting improved.

Both the policy and political streams exhibit critical-mass, bandwagon effects. In the policy stream, information cascades of acceptability or rejection can emerge from tendencies of specialists to influence each other's opinions via transmission of information and understandings.[56] The political stream, by contrast, exhibits more prominent power dynamics. Bargaining complicates processes of garnering support, and manipulating cultural symbols can enhance support and fend off opposition. Once bandwagon effects gain momentum, parties often join in, hoping to influence the outcome and perhaps attain a share of any emergent pie. Pieces of legislation that barely survive procedural votes can end up passing with substantive majorities.

Overall, reform proponents who hope to propel their policy ideas onto substantive agendas face a series of CAPs within each of Kingdon's three streams; they face, additional CAPs related to merging two or more streams, and even more CAPs associated with exploiting temporary windows of opportunity. Many such CAPs emerge from the public-good properties of enacting new policy: high required initial investment (fixed cost), often distributed among many parties, with subsequent uncertain and largely non-exclusive (though seldom equally shared) benefits. With respect to the problem stream, proponents need to generate a critical mass of attention (an information cascade) within the media, interest groups, think tanks, the public, and, of course, policymakers. Coordination problems, sometimes exacerbated by issues of equity, compound inherent public-good CAPs. In the policy stream, success requires assembling a critical mass of specialists within relevant policy communities who favor particular approaches or proposals. In the political stream, proponents need to attract a critical mass of coalition partners, garner sufficient support from strategically located interests, and avoid or neutralize opposition from coalitions of potential adversaries. Reformers must attain enough overall support to influence—or, better yet, designate—key decision makers. Naturally, complications of negotiation, compounded by second-order coordination and enforcement CAPs, can arise among supporters, between supporters and opponents, with various other interests, and among relevant decision makers.

Reformers may face still larger CAPs as they try to merge streams, manipulate one stream when another is favorable, or take advantage of windows of opportunity created by external processes. In terms of information processing, such windows present opportunities to either gain the attention of current macro-level policymakers or replace them with already attentive allies. At the macro level, scarce, serial attention responds to opportunities for action, biases of players, positions of key players, and the number of competing issues (Zahariadis 2007, 75).[57] Windows allow policy entrepreneurs to gain such attention by influencing any of these factors and by enhancing the salience of their own issues so as to diminish the immediacy of potentially competing issues. In so doing, they may manipulate the problematic preferences of serial-processing macro-level policymakers, who (at least during periods of emergence) operate under conditions of ambiguity in environments with unclear organizational technologies.

As they strive to correlate attention across multiple audiences, policy entrepreneurs often frame issues with appeals to internalized social norms. They appeal to corresponding identities of the public, important constituents, and/or relevant policymakers. For example, prior to enactment of the National Health Service Act of 1946 and other key welfare legislation, the influential Beveridge Report—issued in 1942—appealed to British ideals of universal security from poverty (Lowe 2005, 13–17). In fact, during the Second World War, the report was air-dropped into German-occupied territories "as an expression of the ideals for which the Allies were fighting" (14). Beveridge had quite an impact.[58]

Among the streams, the political and problem streams are most important for seizing or creating macro-level attention (Kingdon 2003).[59] Accordingly, rapid periods of change often emerge from two interacting sources: (1) policy entrepreneurs and their allies in reform coalitions gather a critical mass of attention and political support; and/or (2) these parties are able to exploit externally induced (sometimes accidental) focusing events that substantially alter perceptions of problems, existing policies, or the functioning of subsystems. Such changes can disrupt the self-reinforcing negative-feedback mechanisms within previously stable subsystems. Instead, positive-feedback dynamics emerge: challenges to existing policy generate growing support for change with steadily increasing salience. As calls for change gather momentum across the public, various interests, and policymakers, macro-level attention can shift: first, toward the now prominent problems and reform solutions, and then toward intervention into the previously stable operations of extant policy subsystems. If so, policy emergence—a cascade for change—has arrived.

Sometimes attaining a critical mass of support itself constitutes a focusing event. For example, one could interpret the presence of large protests in Cairo's Tahrir Square and in other Egyptian cities on January 25, 2011, both as a salient indicator that regime opponents had achieved a critical mass of support, and as a focusing event that ignited the subsequent change in regime. President Hosni Mubarak, in power since 1981, resigned on February 11, 2011. Likewise, an external or apparently random focusing event may energize opposition enough to create a critical mass. The self-immolation of Mohammad Bouazizi on December 17, 2010, sparked the revolution that ousted Tunisian president Zine El Abidine Ben Ali on January 14, 2011.[60] Most punctuated policy change, however, does not involve revolution.

Baumgartner and Jones (1993) distinguish two types of policy emergence. Successful waves of enthusiasm tend to foster the creation of new subsystems, whereas waves of criticism tend to alter or dismantle them.[61] For example, following steadily increasing pressure from environmentalist groups, changes in public attitudes, and a number of salient media images—such as photographs and stories of the fire on the Cuyahoga River in Cleveland, Ohio, on June 22, 1969—the Nixon administration, with the approval of Congress, established the Environmental Protection Agency (EPA) on December 2, 1970.[62] This macro-level intervention fundamentally altered environmental policymaking. It created a critical new player (the EPA) with designated power to generate a new set of rules. Yet the same environmental movement also created pressure for dismantling: waves of criticism of the Atomic Energy Commission led to its replacement, in 1974, by the Nuclear Regulatory Commission, shifting the focus of nuclear policy from promotion toward regulation.

To sum up arguments in this section, policy processes and outcomes exhibit properties of punctuated equilibria. During stable periods, policy subsystems—intermediate-level institutional systems that rely on one or a few advocacy coalitions—dominate policymaking.

By engaging in parallel information processing, they both limit external input and resolve society-wide CAPs of coordinating information feedback. Consequently, policy enactment involves only incremental change, significantly limiting the range of politically feasible policymaking. Potential reformers face substantial CAPs if they hope to achieve substantive change.

To break these political constraints—so as to dismantle existing subsystems, create new subsystems, or both—reformist policy entrepreneurs and coalition allies need to somehow orchestrate policy emergence. They must resolve public-good, enforcement, and critical-mass coordination CAPs that reside within each of Kingdon's three streams, along with additional CAPs related to merging streams and effectively seizing opportunities to exploit short-lived windows of opportunity. When they do so successfully, reformers either create enough attention among macro-level policymakers to initiate substantive intervention into intermediate-level processing, or they accomplish the same by replacing macro officials with allies (as in Tunisia). In either case, macro-level intervention can disrupt previously existing policy subsystems and thereby initiate rapid (punctuated) policy change: policy emergence. Finally, successful periods of reform often create institutional legacies; they initiate or alter institutional systems, usually in the form of policy subsystems, in a manner that sets the stage for a subsequent period of stasis with limited incremental change: a new policy equilibrium.

Notes on Game-Theoretic Modeling of Policy CAPs

Game theory facilitates modeling policy-related CAPs. Analysts may use all of the previously discussed CGT, EGT, or IEGT games to represent components of this section's punctuated-equilibrium policy framework—and thereby illustrate processes, outcomes, and attendant tradeoffs. Any of these formulations can help identify both the potential of and limits to feasible policy in periods of stasis or emergence.

During periods of policy stasis, established policy subsystems generate relatively stable social equilibria that reflect established rules of the game for most policy encounters. Behaviors and expectations then follow relatively predictable channels that limit numbers of players and available strategies. Competence-difficulty gaps may be small enough to foster exercises of substantive rationality. Classic game-theoretic models can then illustrate CAPs, policy decisions, and outcomes. For example, the simple PD game of Figure 12.3 could represent resolved or unresolved CAPs. Specific policies might specify levels of r and/or p that could generate stable cooperative social equilibria—or fail to do so—with regard to various public-good, externality, or CPR problems. One could augment this model with social preference payoffs, imperfect observation, or repeated interaction. Alternatively, adverse selection or principal-agent models can represent second-order CAPs arising from incomplete information among policymakers or coalition partners, or between policymakers and the public. Games of battle could model a need for cooperation in the face of some disagreement among coalition partners. Nash bargaining games, as in Figure 4.1, could represent possible outcomes of negotiations among partners within established policy subsystems or between adversaries. Multi-player assurance games could represent stable policy (or pre-policy) equilibria that involve either full or zero participation in some desirable or undesirable activity. Games of chicken, with either two or many players, could represent internal conflicts that might render a subsystem vulnerable to external disturbance.[63] Multi-player chicken could also represent nonoptimal mixed-participation equilibria. In any of these cases, EGT and IEGT models can inform prospects of survival for specific policies, coalitions, or policy regimes.

With respect to policy emergence, CGT multi-player games of assurance with network externalities can represent CAPs of attaining a critical mass of support within either the problem stream or the policy stream. Here one agent's belief in (or action supporting) reform confers positive externalities on other potential reformers. Applying this argument to Figure 12.4, functions $C(n)$ and $D(n)$ can respectively denote levels of pro- and anti-reform sentiment, with each depending on the number of reform supporters (n). If reformers can achieve a critical mass of support—an amount above level n^* (the internal Nash equilibrium), a positive-feedback mechanism generates continuously increasing support, leading to a pro-reform equilibrium at $n = N$. Alternatively, two-player chicken could represent competition for macro-level attention between two reformist entrepreneurs who have different proposals: their struggle for attention could lead to rejection of both proposals.[64] Extending the analysis, EGT or IEGT games can represent the survival prospects of policy ideas within either stream. Relevant fitness payoffs can represent the success potential for new (mutant) policy ideas or practices vis-à-vis old ones. Ultimately successful ideas or regimes exhibit evolutionary stability.[65]

Within the political stream, Chapter 4's models can represent negotiation and power relations. For given sets of rules, the Nash bargaining model may illustrate internal coalition bargaining over proposals, positions, or allocations of costs and benefits. Well-positioned parties often have less need for agreement, reflecting better fallback positions and greater access to sources of power, which, in turn, imply greater bargaining power (power1) and greater chances for success or dominance. At a deeper level, Section 4.3's models of strategic moves can represent efforts by entrepreneurs or coalitions to bias policy decisions or processes in their favor (power2), possibly initiating policy emergence. One party may

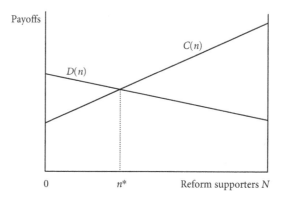

Figure 12.4   Multi-player policy assurance

seize a first move to bar an opponent access to a decision arena or delete its items from a policy agenda. Issuing threats or promises may accomplish similar goals. Basu's (2000) landlord-laborer-merchant game (Section 4.4) can illustrate triadic exchanges that enhance the ability of strategically located entrepreneurs or coalitions to utilize credible threats. At a still deeper level, Section 4.5's sketch of a diffused dictatorship model could illustrate successful use of cultural symbols, images, stories, or appeals to social norms to discredit potential opponents and diminish their desire to challenge (power3). Finally, if proponents can manipulate identity concepts, the models in Section 8.5 (including a variant of Figure 8.9) could apply.[66]

Such game-theoretic approaches to policy processes and outcomes related to enactment and emergence can inform policy analysis. Ultimately, however, policies are not effective unless they are successfully implemented.

Policy Implementation and Related CAPs

The discussion in Section 12.2 has asserted that accepted and implemented policies gradually become institutions. But complex processes of implementation determine the degree to which enacted policies really achieve such institutionalization. For example, we might contrast the fully institutionalized practice of the US Senate ratifying or denying the president's Supreme Court appointments with the relatively nonbinding and inconsistently applied laws against underage drinking in the United States. Successful policy implementation normally depends on cooperation of multiple participants with diverse interests. Thus attaining realization of policy goals presents proponents and enactors of policy with yet another set of CAPs concerning how to actually put their policies into effect.[67] Such implementation CAPs limit feasible policy, sometimes severely.

The literature offers several approaches to implementation. A top-down approach (Van Horn and Van Meter 1976) assumes that well-informed policy designers enact policy in a single authoritative document—a clear regulation or statute—which specifies unambiguous policy goals. A known chain of command transmits specified goals and relevant strategies through various levels of implementation.[68] A bottom-up approach, on the other hand, assumes that multiple sources of policy direction, along with conflicts among policymakers, generate ambiguous goals for enacted policies. Energy policy, for example, arises from many statutes and regulations that lead to differing interpretations among competing interests. Furthermore, "street-level" policy implementers, such as teachers, social service workers, and police, develop and negotiate actual working policies (Elmore 1979; Lipsky 1980).

These contrasting approaches can be merged (Giandomenico and Wildavsky 1984; Elmore 1985; Sabatier 1986). Enacted policy establishes general, though possibly ambiguous, objectives—usually with some indication of envisioned contingencies. More precisely, stated policy designates the relevant action arenas, a list of key positions, roles for such positions, possible or appropriate policy tools, and available resources.[69] Most importantly, policy statements—such as pieces of legislation—conceptualize the problems that specific policies are meant to address, along with a general approach to solving them (Giandomenico and Wildavsky 1984). Such statements establish shared conceptual frameworks (shared mental models) that encompass basic objectives and obstacles—and thus help to coordinate policy implementation.[70] Policy statements, however, cannot anticipate all contingencies or possible constraints that ultimately affect implementation.[71] Moreover, stated goals are always somewhat ambiguous or vague, "because that is how we can agree to proceed without having to agree on exactly what to do" (Giandomenico and Wildavsky 1984, 144).[72]

Implementation, then, is an evolutionary process of discovery that continuously influences policy realization. The various officials who apply policies always act with some discretion. They may interpret, select among, or alter possibly ambiguous objectives in response to newly discovered constraints or resources.[73] For example, the British National Health Service Act of 1946 specified that "The services so provided shall be free of charge, except where provision of this act expressly provides for the making and recovery of charges" (Giandomenico and Wildavsky 146). During its first two years of operation, however, costs of the National Health Service exceeded estimates by 40%. Consequently, in 1951 and 1952, Parliament added provisions to charge patients for prescriptions and ophthalmic and dental services (Lowe 2005, 186–89). Thus implementation of Britain's national health policy encountered unexpected constraints that led to adjusting its terms.

From the point of view of policymakers, the uncertainties of implementation often present CAPs. Implementation typically involves principal-agent problems whereby policy designers or enactors, or even society at large, act as principals and various designated public or private officials and employees serve as agents. As with other principal-agent problems, informal and formal institutions mediate agents' beliefs, strategy selection, interactions, and ensuing outcomes. Particularly difficult implementation CAPs arise when stated policy goals conflict with social norms held by involved, well-positioned parties. Such parties may include officials or employees assigned to implementation, second-party enforcers from relevant groups or communities, and parties whose activities tend to generate the first- or second-order CAPs that the stated policy is intended to redress.

As discussed in Chapter 10, conflicts between laws or regulations and prevalent social norms can render the former ineffective, particularly if third-party enforcement depends upon complementary second-party enforcement and/or information gathered from affected groups or communities. Recall that consumers or citizens co-produce certain public goods by cooperating with officials and providing information. Effective implementation may thus require willing co-production. Recall further that material incentives can sometimes crowd out reciprocity or other prosocial behaviors that are motivated by social preferences and normative values. Policies that rely on only material rewards or sanctions may thus backfire (Bowles 2012). Overall, effective implementation frequently requires that policy goals be perceived as generally legitimate by implementers, affected groups, and/or the public at large.

More generally, the greater the opposition arising from affected groups, the greater the necessary commitment of policy implementers. Between 1957 and 1965, the dedication of federal officials to enforcing civil rights legislation shifted dramatically. Thus, even though powerful southern politicians, like Strom Thurmond and George Wallace, adamantly opposed the 1964 Civil Rights Act and the 1965 Voting Rights Act, both acts were successfully implemented with credible enforcement provisions. This implementation was possible, however, because the civil rights movement had effectively altered perceptions concerning the legitimacy and importance of equal civil and voting rights for African Americans—and the corresponding illegitimacy, indeed immorality, of the institutions of segregation—to important policymakers, large segments of the US public, and the media. By the time these laws had passed Congress, racial social norms had already begun to shift. Enormous CAPs of the enactment and implementation of reform had been largely resolved: the punctuated equilibrium that had supported the Jim Crow institutional system of southern segregation had collapsed. Effective implementation can be powerful.

Nevertheless, because successful implementation is often problematic, examining the associated CAPs informs policy analysis of both the power and limitations of various policy mechanisms for remedying the CAPs they are intended to address.

12.4. CONCLUSION: COLLECTIVE ACTION, POLICY ANALYSIS, AND ENDOGENOUS GOVERNANCE

Policymaking involves conceptualizing, designing, negotiating, and implementing complex strategic decisions—made at some level of governance—that are intended to influence behavior via exercises of power. Collective-action problems both explain the existence of policy and shape policymaking processes. Existing institutional systems provide the motivational, informational, and cognitive context in which policymaking operates. Social norms affect participants' endogenous preferences and identity concepts. Extant formal institutions establish key positions and roles from which policymakers operate. Institutions thus establish parameters that limit policy conception, enactment, and implementation. Yet policies also create, alter, and dismantle institutions and institutional systems. Policymaking itself involves crafting formal rules and their expression in the form of working rules. When effectively implemented, policy rules become institutionalized: they evolve into institutions or components of institutions that shape cognition, information, and motivation. Indeed, the ability to alter institutions is a cherished goal of reform, though one that faces immense difficulty arising from the multiple CAPs that accompany policymaking.

The Institutional Analysis and Development framework of the Indiana University Workshop in Political Theory and Policy Analysis offers conceptual tools for institutional and policy analysis. In this framework, an action situation provides a general structure for conceptualizing influences of position, motivation, possible actions, information, incentives, and external factors on policy interactions and outcomes. A nested vertical hierarchy of action situations represents interactions within, relationships among, and influences on different levels of rulemaking—constitutional, collective-choice, or operational. Similarly, horizontal categorization of rules by their social goals (aims)—where categories reflect targeted structural elements of action situations—facilitates analyzing tradeoffs among alternative mechanisms for achieving policy objectives.

The ubiquitous presence of CAPs within and among groups, communities, and nations provides the key rationale for policymaking—its raison d'être. Policies attempt to address traditional market failures and/or group failures within communities or at various levels of governance. Regarding second-order CAPs, policies strive to shape relations within and between third- and second-party enforcers—a key problem of political economy whose resolution influences prospects for exchange and development.

With respect to CAPs of policymaking, the punctuated-equilibrium policy theory of Baumgartner and Jones (1993) offers an encompassing analytical framework. Policy formulation depends on levels of information processing by boundedly rational agents who occupy specific positions in relevant processes. An overall pattern of enduring periods of policy stasis, which are periodically interrupted by short periods of rapid change, emerges from the limitations of serial information processing experienced by micro- and macro-level agents—combined with the parallel processing of specialized intermediate-level agents and coalitions within issue- and area-specific policy subsystems. As intermediate-level institutional systems, policy subsystems operate under the dominant influence of one or a few advocacy coalitions. Policy subsystems then create path-dependent motivational, informational, and cognitive patterns that foster stability. Associated negative-feedback dynamics arise from (often deliberate) limitations on external policy input, use of incremental change to buy off potential opponents, and inclinations of system beneficiaries (who often hold important positions) to oppose substantive change. Achieving reform, therefore, presents considerable CAPs.

The occasional occurrence of bursts of rapid change (or emergence) also reflects information-processing capacities. Policy emergence operates at both micro and macro levels, with destabilizing positive feedback. Reformist policy entrepreneurs must take advantage of short-lived windows of opportunity that arise when favorable conditions exist in the problem, policy, and political streams. To promote emergence, entrepreneurs create or utilize focusing events, salient indicators, publicity, and/or symbols—often with appeals to norms and identity concepts—in order to focus or manipulate the serial attention, and the sometimes ambiguous preferences, of micro-level public citizens and macro-level top policymakers. If the latter intervene sufficiently into intermediate-level subsystems, or are themselves replaced by reformers, substantive policy change occurs.

Likewise, CAPs of policy implementation indicate that merely enacting policy does not guarantee success. Attendant principal-agent problems emerge from two main sources: the inability of proponents or enactors (principals) to fully specify contingencies, and the potential motivational conflicts between enactors and implementers—agents who necessarily exercise some discretion over working policies, and who often possess their own incentives, values, and understandings. Additional complications may arise from any of the following: multiple conflicting and ambiguous policy statements; conflicts between third- and second-party enforcers; and potential conflict between formally stated policies, informal social rules, social norms, and concepts of identity. Even so, enacted policy statements often coordinate or influence action by establishing access to resources and by framing understandings of problems, policy goals, and available measures. Thus, to enhance prospects for success, policy proponents should endeavor to anticipate implementation CAPs as they design the combinations of rules that normally constitute policy. All of these factors demonstrate that policymaking is fundamentally an experimental, learning process.

Policy analysts may thus benefit from understanding action situations in which policymaking operates, pertinent rule classifications, and the workings of punctuated-equilibrium policy stasis, emergence, and policy implementation—each with its associated CAPs. Analysts may also benefit from taking seriously the notion that systems of governance emerge endogenously from social, economic, and political processes that respond to CAPs. Regarding policy advice, Basu (2000, 166) states the following:

> If prices are very high, few economists would say that producers should lower the price. If, seeing high unemployment in an economy, a person—for instance a politician— advises entrepreneurs to employ more laborers, or consumers to demand more goods, this typically causes economists to share a laugh. . . . The same economists then go on to advise government to take steps to lower prices or curtail unemployment or expand the fiscal deficit or curtail the fiscal deficit, forgetting that the individuals in government are also, like the consumers and producers, agents with their own agenda.

Thus it is foolish for policy analysts to expect policymakers to follow even wise advice that conflicts with their own interests. Still, policy advice can play a role—as evidenced by the existence of a rather large industry devoted to this purpose. Moreover, policy analysis can assist the necessarily limited serial information processing of boundedly rational policymakers and their associates. Policy analysts can offer interpretations and models (cognitive frameworks); they can provide scarce, costly information; they can appeal to internalized social norms such as service to the public, community, or nation; and they can appeal to concepts of identity such as the idea of a dedicated public servant.[74]

Finally, since development requires establishing reliable processes of complex exchange that entail resolution of multiple CAPs, and since all deliberate crafting of institutions and procedures constitutes policymaking, it follows that development requires policy. Policymaking underlies development because policymaking can facilitate resolution of CAPs. Chapter 13 offers a more detailed discussion of how CAPs influence the prospects for development.

EXERCISES

12.1. Suppose four communities that operate at system level v (see Section 10.3) have formed a coalition that establishes $(v + 1)$-level coordination and enforcement. Use the IAD framework to describe relationships between second- and third-party enforcers in such a system.

12.2. Section 9.4 listed Ostrom's (1990, 2005) design features of successful CPR management. Relate these items to the seven types of horizontal rule classifications.

12.3. Relate the decisions and outcomes addressed in Exercise 12.2 to Figure 12.2's vertical hierarchy of action situations.

12.4. Write a paragraph or short essay explaining which horizontal and vertical types of rules are most applicable to political and economic institutions.

12.5. Suppose that advocacy coalitions A and B have distinct policy proposals that they hope to advance to a policy agenda. Unless they collaborate, however, the prospects for success are dim.

    a. Draw a two-player game of battle that illustrates this situation. Assign payoffs, explain them, and discuss the game's implications.

b. Draw a Nash cooperative bargaining model (see Figure 4.1) that could represent negotiations between coalitions A and B over their preferred proposals. Explain key terms (fallback positions, etc.) and possible outcomes.

c. For each game in parts a and b above, think of two strategic moves that coalition A might use to advance its prospects.

12.6. Suppose that coalition A has contracted with coalition B to lobby for its goals, but B has some policy preferences of its own. Draw and explain a version of Figure 3.6 that could apply to this situation.

12.7. Repeat Exercise 12.5 (alter the story as needed) for a game of chicken.

12.8. (Creative) Write fitness functions (see Sections 6.5 and 8.3) for policy ideas for advocacy coalitions A and B. Assume that A's ideas are predominant. Explain your functions, and specify the conditions that would lead to evolutionary stability.

12.9. Develop a triadic bargaining model (see Section 4.4) that illustrates policy contestation within the political stream.

12.10. (Creative) Model a process of policy emergence in the political stream. Begin with a model similar to the multi-player assurance game in Figure 12.4; then add the complication of bargaining among parties with distinct interests.

12.11. Create a version of Figure 8.9 (and its related equations) that illustrates manipulation of identity within the political stream during a period of policy emergence.

APPENDIX TO CHAPTER 12

To illustrate the complexity of even simple, transparent property rights, we construct two versions of a game of "snatch" (Ostrom 2005, 34–37; Ostrom and Crawford 2005, 210–14). The first version (see Figure 12A.1) involves no policy. Player 1 decides whether or not to make an offer. For example, for two adjacent sheep farmers, an offer might be "I will give you two rams for one ewe." Player 2 then chooses exchange (accept the offer), snatch (one or more sheep), or refuse the offer. The second version (see Figure 12A.2) incorporates policy rules that create minimal property rights, and adds a move immediately after a snatch, in which player 1 chooses between reporting player 2 to a judge, or not reporting. Here we assume that the judge automatically punishes (hence the judge does not move).

For the game in Figure 12A.1, we set all seven types of horizontal rules (see Section 12.1) to "default" conditions that could fit a pure, common-law system. These defaults are as follows:[1]

(i) Position: one position (exchange participant).

(ii) Boundary: anyone can hold the position.

(iii) Choice: all players can take any physically possible action.

(iv) Aggregation: players act independently, and physical conditions determine how actions aggregate to affect outcomes.

(v) Information: each player can communicate anything via any available channel to anyone.

(vi) Payoff: any player may retain any outcome (and its associated payoff) that they can physically defend.

(vii) Scope: each player may affect any state of the world in any physically possible manner.

The simultaneous presence of all seven defaults indicates a Hobbesian state of nature (Ostrom and Crawford 2005, 211).

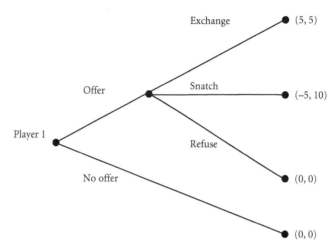

Figure 12A.1   Game of snatch

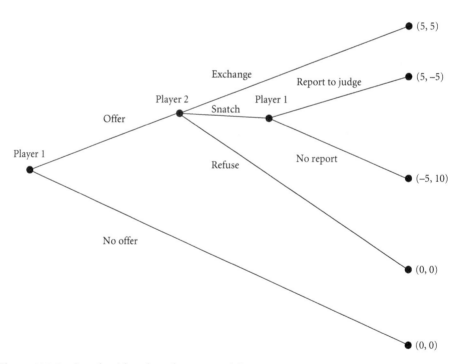

Figure 12A.2   Snatch with enforced property rights

Given these rules, player 1 anticipates a snatch and so makes no offer. Accordingly, the Nash equilibrium outcome in Figure 12A.1 is (No offer). Because exchange cannot occur without an offer, this outcome is inefficient. Indeed, on a broad scale, such an outcome would preclude development—a significant CAP. An important type of policy remedy involves defining and enforcing property rights. Establishing minimal property rights, in turn, requires a legal system that both defines and assigns rights to ownership and then enforces such rights with sanctions for violation.

A minimal institutional system that enforces property rights over easily divisible and excludable domains (such as land), with regard to easily observed entities and actions (such as trading sheep), still requires specification of at least position, boundary, choice, and aggregation rules. Hence Figure 12A.2's version of snatch incorporates the following minimal rules:[2]

- Position rule: There are two positions: exchange participant and judge.
- Boundary rules:
  (1) All participants are permitted to exchange, and anyone barring their entry may face sanction. Note the importance of the enforcement provision: interested parties might attempt to bar access to potential competitors.
  (2) Members of the community select the judge on the basis of merit and integrity; if not, the other rules do not take effect.
- Choice rules:
  (1) All participants are permitted to offer exchanges of goods they own for goods owned by others. Those who interfere with exchange may be punished.
  (2) Any participant whose goods are snatched may report to a judge.[3] Anyone who interferes with reporting may face sanction.
  (3) The judge must decide whether reports are accurate.
  (4) If the judge discovers a (now illegal) snatch, the judge must sanction the snatcher, or else the judge will be sanctioned.
- Aggregation rule: Before any exchange occurs, all parties must agree or else the exchange will not occur.

We can now combine these rules with default conditions on the remaining three rules to illustrate resolution of this relatively simple CAP. In Figure 12A.2 (which assumes that the judge accepts the report as accurate and sanctions the snatcher), the Nash equilibrium outcome is (Offer, Exchange). We find resolution of the CAP associated with a clearly delineated exchange.

This example illustrates that—even for the transparent exchange of excludable commodities—establishing the foundations of property rights involves a combination of specific rule types—at least the four shown above, possibly with multiple provisions for each type. Additional rules could fill in more details. Position and choice rules could specify who sanctions the judge; an aggregation rule could prescribe how a group might select the judge;

a payoff rule could stipulate precise levels of sanction.[4] Moreover, from the point of view of exchange participants, judges are third-party enforcers who need compensation, possibly financed through taxation—another set of rules. Also, selection of judges is a political process. Thus the creation of even minimal economic institutions of property rights for simple transparent exchanges involves policymaking with political dimensions and implications: again, political economy.

KNOWLEDGE, COLLECTIVE ACTION, INSTITUTIONS, LOCATION, AND GROWTH

> The increasing returns story of poverty traps says that poverty is a problem of coordination.
>
> William Easterly (2002)

Over time, Arruba has prospered considerably. It is part of a growing regional economy that has diversified into manufacturing, service, and information sectors. With 2% annual growth of per-capita income, average residents earn nearly 4.5 times the income of their great-grandparents, 75 years ago. At that time, Boratonia was the more prosperous community, with 20% higher average income. Boratonia, however, remains primarily agricultural and has not grown appreciably. Over the same 75 years, its average income grew just over 40%. Arruba's average income is now more than 2.5 times higher.

Scholars have identified two basic causes of this stark contrast in long-term growth. One concerns the generation and use of knowledge; the other concerns institutions and governance. Arruba's regional economy has attracted skilled workers. There are universities, research centers, and knowledge-intensive industries. People exchange ideas across intricate networks ranging from friends and schoolmates to formal work connections. Each set of new ideas establishes foundations for future advances. People realize that if they invest time and effort into acquiring skills and knowledge, they can live better in the long run. Boratonia, on the other hand, tends not to produce new knowledge. Agriculture dominates production; there are few universities and no knowledge-intensive industries. Farming techniques have improved somewhat on account of imported machinery, but external competition holds prices down, limiting increases in income. With few local opportunities to employ knowledge productively, most residents do not extensively pursue education; those who do often leave for Arruba or elsewhere.

The second difference between the two communities is institutional. Boratonia is located in a country governed by a corrupt oligarchy with a strikingly unequal distribution of wealth. When oligarchs notice successful individuals who are not part of their clique, they fear competition and find ways to make life difficult for them. Authorities may discover some new illegal activity and assess fines or require a license. To make matters worse, these interventions seem random. Residents thus have little incentive to acquire skills or innovate. Worse yet, prevailing norms discourage girls from attaining much education. By contrast, Arruba is located in a country with relatively accessible democratic political institutions and broadly accessible property rights, with substantial public funding for infrastructure, research, accessible health care, and universally available education. Many residents find their efforts to acquire new knowledge or develop new production techniques at least potentially rewarding.

Economic development requires resolving CAPs. Prior chapters have detailed how complex exchange depends on extensive institutional social choreography. Credible commitment and coordination emerge from intricate institutional systems that rely on the combined influence of informal and formal institutions, with second- and third-party enforcers linked in polycentric configurations. This chapter focuses specifically on relationships between exchange, CAPs, institutions, distribution, and long-term economic growth. It identifies three basic influences on such relations: the unique properties of knowledge, unequal distributions of power, and the configuration of institutions. Regarding the first influence, the nonrival properties of knowledge engender skill and knowledge complementarities that create increasing returns to the clustering of knowledge. These complementarities—combined with the cognitive limits of boundedly rational agents, who then encounter CAPs of coordination—foster an uneven geographic distribution of productive skills, marked by the notable presence of innovation clusters and pockets of stagnation—growth centers and poverty traps. This disparity constitutes both a source and a manifestation of substantial distributional inequity between regions with different knowledge potentials—another source of CAPs.

Regarding the second and third influences, growth processes operate within contexts of economic institutions that interact with political institutions within institutional systems. Because powerful parties can alter the distribution of output, the development of reliable economic institutions requires resolution of second-order CAPs that emerge from unequal distributions of power. These CAPs involve creating credible social commitments that power holders will refrain from using their advantage to seize gains from others' efforts. Such credibility emerges from appropriately configured political institutions. Therefore, the distribution of power and the material interests of power holders jointly condition economic growth: distribution and growth are inseparable, as are economics and politics.

Long-term growth relies on adequately resolving second-order CAPs that interfere with negotiating and implementing credible commitments. In recent history, two basic types of institutional systems have demonstrated a capacity to resolve such CAPs: limited dictatorships and democracies. Dictatorship may more readily facilitate large-scale political coordination. Democracies, however, possess advantages of more inclusive political and economic institutions and (for the most part) greater long-term sustainability. Even so, knowledge-based clustering, unequal access to resources, and unequal distributions of power foster CAPs related to limiting the extent of distributional inequality, as well as derivative CAPs of sustaining inclusive democratic institutions.

Our discussion proceeds as follows. Section 13.1 briefly reviews key findings of macroeconomic theories of growth that relate long-term increases in average living standards to advances in technological knowledge. Section 13.2 asserts that the nonrival properties of knowledge and skill complementarities generate an uneven clustering (or agglomeration) of innovation centers and poverty traps. Ultimately, such agglomeration reflects two contrasting dynamics: (i) self-reinforcing cycles of innovation that arise from concentrations of knowledge; and (ii) recurrent cycles of stagnation that emerge from pervasive CAPs of coordination, arising within environments that offer individuals minimal incentives to invest effort in accumulating knowledge. Section 13.3 addresses power, institutions, and growth. It discusses relationships of political and economic institutions to CAPs of commitment, the implications of such CAPs on both growth and distribution, and potential resolution via either democratic inclusion or the selective enforcement mechanisms of limited dictatorships. Ultimately, those who prefer the democratic path to development must confront CAPs of establishing relatively accessible political institutions founded upon relatively dispersed political power. Moreover, because access to resources is a source of power, the long-term sustainability of growth-enhancing democratic political institutions requires resolution of additional CAPs related to the sometimes self-reinforcing tendency of market-based economic institutions to distribute income and wealth unevenly. Section 13.4 concludes.

13.1. STANDARDS OF LIVING AND TECHNICAL KNOWLEDGE

Knowledge underlies the ability of economies to increase average standards of living. There are two relevant categories: the knowledge embodied in human beings as a reflection of prior learning, and knowledge that is generally available to members of society who have both access to it and the cognitive capacity to absorb it. Economists refer to the first type as *human capital*, meaning the knowledge and skills that individuals accumulate via education and training. The second type is *social knowledge*. Social knowledge is nonrival: once developed, basic ideas (such as the theory of relativity) can be absorbed simultaneously by anyone with access and ability. One person's use of $e = mc^2$ does not diminish the ability of others to use it. These two types of knowledge are intricately linked: because possessing human capital allows one to absorb and incorporate social knowledge, an individual's accumulated human capital, to a large degree, reflects her previously absorbed social knowledge.

With respect to economic growth, the most important form of social knowledge is technology. *Technology* "is society's pool of knowledge regarding the industrial arts" (Mansfield 1971, 9)—that is, knowledge concerning processes of production.[1] Production processes are both physical and social. The general term *technology* thus includes *technical knowledge* related to physical production relationships, along with *organizational knowledge* related to structuring and motivating the social interactions that accompany human labor as an input in the processes of production. Some readers may find productive knowledge, even just its technical component, to be a surprising definition of technology. One might associate technology with computers, nuclear power plants, or the space shuttle. But consider the following: A computer made last week, like one made in 1981, is a hunk of metal and plastic; yet the new computer can perform tasks that were not even imagined in 1981. Advances in knowledge regarding how to assemble silicon chips, other components, and software have made the difference; that is technical change. Often economists think of technical knowledge as designs or blueprints, whereas organizational knowledge is embodied in institutions or, more broadly, social capital.[2] Note that technical knowledge typically advances faster than organizational knowledge, so that most technological change reflects advances in technical knowledge.

The two growth models most commonly used in intermediate macroeconomics texts are Robert Solow's (1956) neoclassical growth model and Paul Romer's (1990) endogenous growth model. Both models identify technological advance—or, more generally, accumulation of knowledge—as the most important proximate cause of long-run economic growth. Both models use growth in output per capita as the key measure of growth—an indicator of growth in average standards of living. The Solow model makes two key assumptions: (i) there are two factors of production, labor (L) and capital (K); and (ii) there are constant returns to combined factors, implying diminishing marginal returns to each. The underlying Cobb-Douglas production function shows:

$$(13.1) \qquad\qquad Y = AK^{\alpha}L^{(1-\alpha)},$$

where A represents total factor productivity (TFP)—that is, output per combined unit of capital and labor (K and L), a proxy for technology; α is an exponent that specifies the relative contributions of K and L ($0 < \alpha < 1$). Converting to output per worker, we write $y = Y/L$. Dividing (13.1) through by L and defining k as the capital/labor ratio K/L, we have $y = Ak^{\alpha}$. To solve the model, we need to find the steady-state (unchanging) levels of k and y, given A. The steady-state value of k (k^*) occurs when the rate of depreciation in the capital stock (adjusted for population growth) equals the rate of investment, a function of savings per worker. Because y depends on k, k^* determines steady-state level of output per capita (y^*).[3]

For our purposes, the Solow model generates three results. First, in the absence of technological advance (when $\Delta A/A = 0$), the steady-state outcome (k^*, y^*) signifies a long-run, zero-growth equilibrium. Second, if we add an exogenous rate of technical change—say, 2% per year—then k^* and y^* both grow at that rate. Thus technological advance is the source of long-term increases in living standards. Third, given equal access to technology, long-run rates of growth across countries should converge to the same level: $\Delta A/A$.[4]

Mankiw, Romer, and Weil (1992) modify the Solow model to include human capital as a third factor of production. Here the level of human capital per worker (h) affects the long-run rate of growth of y, though technical change has greater impact since it augments both steady-state levels h^* and k^*. In either version of the Solow model, the source of technological change remains unexplained. Lucas (1988) introduces a more nuanced approach to knowledge. He models human capital with constant (as opposed to diminishing) returns and then adds externalities that enhance the productivity of both K and L. Lucas can then explain persistently different growth rates among nations on the basis of different average levels of human capital.

Romer's (1990) endogenous growth model takes another step by making technological change a function of both human capital and pre-existing knowledge. Romer separates the rival component of knowledge (human capital) from its nonrival, social component (technology) and then links them. Nonrivalry means that the costs of producing knowledge need only be borne once. Once created, the design for a new good (such as a hybrid automobile) could, in principle, be used simultaneously by an unlimited number of capable producers.[5]

By contrast, if a firm wants a second factory staffed by capable workers, it must build the factory, hire new workers, and train them. Thus, when firms combine nonrival technological knowledge with the three factors—capital, labor, and human capital—the resulting production function exhibits increasing, rather than constant, returns to scale.

Here is a simple illustration. Let X represent combined inputs of capital, labor, and human capital. As in the Mankiw, Romer, and Weil model, these rival inputs jointly exhibit constant returns to scale. In this framework, technological knowledge A is nonrival. Now fix A but multiply X by $\lambda > 1$. With constant returns to X, output increases by a factor of λ, thus:

$$(13.2) \qquad F(A, \lambda X) = \lambda F(A, X).$$

If $\lambda = 2$, (13.2) shows that doubling all rival inputs in X doubles output. But, if we also multiply A by λ, output must increase proportionally more than λ. That is,

$$(13.3) \qquad F(\lambda A, \lambda X) > \lambda F(A, X).$$

Thus, once we add nonrival knowledge, our production function shows increasing returns: doubling all inputs, including knowledge, more than doubles output. Incorporating this dynamic into a growth model, Romer (like Solow) finds that output per worker grows at the rate of technological advance, but here such advance is endogenous. More specifically, the amount of technological knowledge in the current period (A_t) depends on current human capital devoted to research and development (R&D; H_{At}) and pre-existing knowledge (A_{t-1}) so that $A_t = F(H_{At}, A_{t-1})$.[6] We may now represent the rate of technological advance as

$$(13.4) \qquad dA/dt = \phi H_A A,$$

where dA/dt is the rate of growth of A. Equation (13.4) states that the rate of technical advance equals parameter ϕ multiplied by the product of R&D-related human capital and the existing stock of technological knowledge.

This equation makes two interesting statements: First, the rate of technical advance depends on the allocation of human capital to R&D—as opposed to other activities, such as the daily operations of advertising or warfare. Second, because technical advance also depends on the level of existing knowledge, nonrival knowledge tends to build upon itself. New knowledge uses and complements existing knowledge. Before developing the theory of relativity, Einstein had thoroughly absorbed Newtonian physics. Contemporary students discuss ideas that were unknown or poorly understood 50 years ago.

This complementarity between new and prior knowledge affects localized incentives to devote effort to acquiring knowledge and skills, and thereby influences the growth dynamics within specific regions—leading toward either growth or stagnation. The ensuing location-based developmental inequality is thus, in part, an intrinsic characteristic of interactions between knowledge and economic exchange. Such interactions, moreover, take place within institutional systems, with attendant power relationships that influence agents' cognition, information, and motivation regarding actions such as devoting effort to one's acquisition of knowledge. These relationships both shape prospects for growth and bind growth to distribution. The next two sections develop these statements more fully.

13.2. NONRIVAL KNOWLEDGE, INCREASING RETURNS, AND POVERTY TRAPS

Interactions between human capital and nonrival knowledge shape the development of market exchange. These interactions not only establish foundations for technological advance, they also foster an extraordinarily uneven geographic distribution of production, strikingly unequal standards of living, and similarly unequal rates of growth. Overall, such relations contribute to the simultaneous existence of enduring poverty traps in certain locations and centers of innovation in others.[7] Here are some historical examples.

Prior to 1980, Bangladesh had no textile industry of significance. In April 1980, Desh Garments Ltd. began producing shirts in a joint venture with Daewoo, a South Korean textile firm. In 1979, these firms had signed an agreement stipulating that Daewoo would train 130 Desh workers in Korea and that Desh would pay Daewoo royalties on its sales. In 1981, Desh cancelled the agreement and began production on its own. Its production grew from 80,000 shirts in 1980 to 2.3 million in 1987. Meanwhile, 115 of the 130 Korean-trained workers quit Desh and started new textile firms of their own, diversifying into other types of clothing. Subsequently, Bangladeshis set up operations in Europe. By the early 2000s, ex-Desh workers had generated $2 billion in garment sales (Easterly 2002, 146–48). Their South Korean training had initiated a strikingly rapid spread of technical and organizational know-how.[8]

Two thousand years earlier, the rural French hamlet of Bardou and nearby iron mines were linked to the rest of the Roman Empire by a network of sturdy roads (the remains of which have lasted to present times as hiking trails). The iron, however, was not processed in Bardou, but shipped to one or more nearby cities (possibly Nimes or Lugdunum, now Lyons) for processing. During the fourth century, the hamlet, roads, and mines were abandoned. Starting in the sixteenth century, Bardou was resettled by squatters as an impoverished rural hamlet. Bardou retained its small size until 1870, when people began leaving. By about 1940, only three families remained (Jacobs 1985, 32–33). Paris, by contrast, has grown steadily since medieval times.

The distribution of city size—few very large cities, more medium cities, and many small towns—follows a striking empirical regularity called the rank-size rule or Zipf's law (Zipf 1949; see also Krugman 1995; Gabaix 1999; Ioannides and Overman 2003). Mathematically, at any point in time, the size distribution follows a power-law equation:

$$(13.5) \qquad\qquad N_j = k / R_j^b,$$

where N is the population of city j, R is its size rank (e.g., 1 for Tokyo in Japan), b is an exponent close to 1, and k is a parameter (Krugman 1995, 43). Figure 13.1 illustrates. Note that we should not expect the traditional economic influences associated with comparative advantage (e.g., closeness to water and various resources) to have any such regularity; nor would such a distribution arise from purely random processes. Interestingly, Axtell (2001)

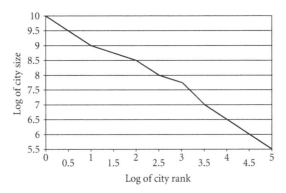

Figure 13.1   Zipf's law and city size (approximate)

finds a Zipf distribution for firm size in the United States, where size may reflect either revenue or number of employees.[9] Recall from Chapter 11 that social networks often have power-law properties.

In Section 13.1, we saw that, because nonrival technical knowledge complements existing knowledge, it generates increasing returns in production. The Bangladesh textile story illustrates another property of nonrival knowledge: it leaks or "spills over," flowing rapidly among interested parties. Because knowledge is difficult to contain, it is a partially excludable good (Romer 1990).[10] People talk; they share ideas; they observe and pay attention to ideas that may help them. Consequently, originators of ideas rarely capture all of their benefits. Although Daewoo profited from its short-lived contract with Desh, it received only a tiny portion of the wealth created by the knowledge it had transferred to 130 Bangladeshi textile workers.

Extending logic from Section 13.1, we now posit three complementary explanations for intrinsic economic tendencies toward geographic disparities in living standards and growth rates. First, as prior reasoning in this text should make clear, knowledge cannot spread everywhere simultaneously in equally utilizable form. Cognitively limited agents can take in only so much knowledge, though adaptive learning (acquisition of human capital) improves one's capacity. Thus localized groups of individuals who lack relevant human capital have limited ability to absorb specific types of knowledge—arguably as Bangladesh did regarding textile production prior to its interactions with Daewoo. Furthermore, spillover requires connection. Knowledge spreads through various networks of agents who are able to absorb it. When 130 Desh workers trained in South Korea, they enhanced their human capital for textile production and, simultaneously, created a network that transmitted nonrival textile knowledge from South Korea to Bangladesh. Thus the realization of increasing returns to knowledge in specific locations requires some form of knowledge transmission (via networks) along with sufficient human capital for absorption.

Second, like social knowledge, related skills are themselves complementary. Easterly (2002) offers the following dramatic example. On January 28, 1986, the space shuttle *Challenger* exploded shortly after takeoff because of a faulty O-ring. The extraordinarily complex assembly of the *Challenger* involved the efforts of thousands. One or perhaps a few small mishaps transformed a potentially enormous success into a tragic failure. More generally, in any kind of team production (virtually all production), the value created by one person's labor depends on the skills of co-workers. Within specific teams, the human capital of one individual tends to complement that of co-workers. We thus expect localized increasing social returns (private returns plus externalities) to follow from investments in complementary skills. Furthermore, relatively highly skilled workers who understand skill complementarities attempt to match—that is, work and associate with—others with similarly high skill (Lucas 1988; Easterly 2002, 155–56). For example, the most highly skilled lawyers tend to locate in the same areas, such as New York City. Moreover, to minimize costly mistakes, employers tend to assign high-value production to highly skilled groups of workers.[11]

Third, group membership dynamics create and reinforce localized knowledge and skill complementarities. Individual decisions to invest in knowledge acquisition respond to role-model and peer effects that follow from "an intrinsic desire to behave like certain others," dependencies of individual payoffs on group actions, and information transmission (Durlauf 2006, 147). Thus we expect localized norms—especially norms of reciprocity—and the structure of local social networks to affect such motivation in complementary fashions. Norms of reciprocity can generate network externalities (as illustrated by multi-player assurance games, such as Figure 12.4) from knowledge investments. Likewise, network centrality (see Figure 11.5's person of influence) can represent the power of role models.[12]

These knowledge, skill, and group membership complementarities suggest that the highest returns to skilled labor should accrue in areas where it is most abundant, such as Tokyo, New York, and London, rather than in areas where it is scarce, such as rural Kentucky, Bolivia, and Ethiopia.[13] The ensuing clustering of skills and knowledge implies an uneven distribution of production and innovation. Innovation centers reap the benefits of concentrated skills and knowledge-based increasing returns, whereas no-growth areas lack the critical mass needed to generate such returns.

We represent these arguments more formally with a localized version of equation (13.4). For a given industry or knowledge sector j,

$$(13.6) \qquad dA_j/dt = \phi H_{Aj} A_L(\Gamma_L).$$

The growth rate of knowledge in sector j equals the product of parameter ϕ, the human capital devoted to R&D in sector j (H_{Aj}), and available existing knowledge in the relevant location (A_L)—itself a function of the locally available network (Γ_L). As a rule, sector knowledge A_j is a subset of available local knowledge A_L, which, in turn, is a subset of all social knowledge A.

We may interpret knowledge sector j in a variety of fashions: it could be an industry, a field of research, a geographic location, or any combination of these elements. In each case, the growth of j's knowledge depends on available human capital and existing local knowledge. Although local knowledge has a geographic element, locally available networks (e.g., industry connections) can extend available knowledge beyond geographic boundaries, and local networks usually do not include all possible connections within a given locality. For example, Seattle-based researchers for Boeing likely have more links to Chicago (corporate headquarters) than to most other Seattle firms. Nonetheless, groups within different localities have access to different networks. Thus equation (13.6) implies that inherent properties of knowledge (i.e., nonrivalry, complementarity, and network transmission) generate sector-, field-, industry-, and location-specific agglomerations. Given increasing returns to knowledge investment, we expect similar agglomerations of innovation and growth.[14]

With one addition, we can explain the simultaneous presence of dispersed clusters of innovation along with poverty traps. We now apply traditional economic logic to knowledge acquisition: individuals invest time and effort into acquiring new knowledge (or building human capital) when such investment appears likely to offer sufficient rewards. Combining the logic of group and skill complementarities with that of equation (13.6), an individual's return on effort devoted to the acquisition of knowledge (r_{hi}) depends on her present human capital (h_i), the average human capital of locally available co-workers (H_L), pertinent reciprocity norms (Ψ_{RL}), the existing stock of locally available knowledge (A_L), and the knowledge infrastructure K_H (e.g., presence of schools). In terms of material payoffs, agents expect their efforts devoted to knowledge acquisition to yield sufficient rewards if

$$(13.7) \qquad\qquad r_{hi}(h_i, H_L, \Psi_{RL}, A_L(\Gamma_L), K_H) > r_L,$$

where r_L is the locally applicable discount rate.

Equation (13.7) makes several interesting statements: First and most directly, individuals will not invest in knowledge acquisition unless their perceived return r_{hi} is sufficiently high. This notion alone can explain a great deal of apparently irrational behavior, such as the failure of individuals in many localities to invest in human capital acquisition that could pay off—were they located elsewhere. Second, returns depend on one's own prior investment (h_i); typically, one cannot go to law school without first obtaining a college degree. Note further that the other variables in (13.7) condition the effects of h_i on returns r_{hi}.[15] For example, norms or role-model effects may influence how agents interpret relationships between their existing human capital and their anticipated returns to additional human capital investment.

Third, the skill complementarities implied by H_L and the group membership effects implied by Ψ_{RL} jointly indicate that an individual's return to knowledge investment depends on the investment behavior of potential work colleagues and local role models. Thus decisions to invest in human capital resemble a multi-player game of assurance among local workers or potential entrepreneurs.[16] An adjusted version of Figure 12.4 can illustrate. In this context, we define $C(n)$ as the payoff to investing in human capital, n as the number (or proportion) of local potential colleagues who have invested (or whom one expects to do so concurrently); and we define $D(n)$ as the payoff to other activities—such as leisure, housework, or immediate market work. The model generates two Nash equilibria: a poverty trap with no human capital investment and an innovation cycle with full investment. A critical-mass tipping point n^* marks the dividing line between the positive-feedback dynamics that engender virtuous circles of innovation above n^* and poverty traps below it. Escaping a poverty trap equilibrium (where $n = 0$) requires coordinating simultaneous investment by at least n^* agents. Note that the slopes of both curves, and hence the position of n^*, depend on A_L, which, in turn, depends on prior investments in human capital and on the locally accessible network (Γ_L; as in equation (13.6)).

This model can also illustrate an applicable "brain drain" phenomenon. Well-connected individuals normally have greater access to knowledge and hence more inclination to invest in acquisition; they may hope to relocate if locally available colleagues appear unpromising. Relatively skilled and connected workers in undeveloped areas may then move to higher-skill areas in order to reap benefits of association. Such migration reinforces the already present (and already implied) path dependence of decisions to invest in human capital— exacerbating coordination CAPs in underdeveloped areas. For all of these reasons, both innovation centers and poverty traps can emerge as (punctuated) social equilibria.[17]

On this basis, we offer a rough explanation for the uneven Zipf distribution of city sizes. Because the geographic distribution of access to resources can explain only a fraction of the extreme locational unevenness of production, increasing returns to various scales of production must be involved (Krugman 1995). Geographic clustering of cities reflects a positive-feedback process whereby firms locate in areas with knowledge-based production and market potential. Consequently, city clusters attract relatively skilled populations, who, in turn, increase production and market potential.[18] Using terminology from Chapter 11, such movement constitutes network growth via preferential attachment, whereby new connections tend to follow productive existing ones. Cities are knowledge centers built around groupings of skills created by complementarities and matching; they are large clusters (or sometimes hubs) in knowledge-transmission networks. Zipf's law is a type of power-law distribution; scale-free networks demonstrate power-law properties; social networks exhibit scale-free properties; and cities both embody and reflect social networks based on the productive potential of nonrival knowledge and social complementarities.

Thus areas with historical legacies that have generated high knowledge and skill concentrations tend to innovate and grow via self-reinforcing feedback linked to high returns on knowledge investments. Likewise, areas with historically low knowledge concentrations tend to fall into poverty traps because returns to knowledge investments fail to exceed local discounting thresholds. Although dynamic cities create virtuous cycles of innovation, uneven geographic clustering of production and skills operates within cities as well.[19] Localized feedback effects emerge from the same basic influences and complementarities. We thus observe substantial developmental inequities across neighborhoods of any large city (New York, Tokyo, Rio de Janeiro), in addition to analogous differences in developmental outcomes between larger regions, such as Silicon Valley and rural Kentucky, or Japan and Zimbabwe. The emergent path dependency generates relatively enduring (punctuated) social equilibria. In 1840, rural Kentucky was poor compared to New York. It remains so today. Poverty traps at any level of aggregation thus reflect problems of coordination that emerge from inherent properties of knowledge and exchange within social groups.

13.3. SOCIAL CONFLICT, INSTITUTIONS, COLLECTIVE ACTION, AND LONG-RUN GROWTH

Medium- to long-term economic growth requires that multiple parties who invest effort and material resources into developing human capital, physical capital, and various types of productive and organizational technologies can—prior to investing—receive credible assurance of sufficient returns (or likely returns) to render their efforts worthwhile. Section 13.2 described impediments to such assurance arising from location-based coordination CAPs that accompany nonrival knowledge and exchange. Interactions between power and institutions impose additional barriers. Indeed, creating broad assurance of sufficient return from investments requires resolving CAPs of creating credible commitments to enforce certain rights over such returns. It requires limiting the ability of powerful agents to seize the benefits from other parties' efforts and investments. Figure 5.7's holdup game offers a simple illustration. At a macro governance level, either democracies or limited dictatorships can, in principle, create serviceable credible commitment. Either resolution, however, faces issues of sustainability and distributional equity that tend to create additional CAPs. This section begins with a general discussion of commitment problems and potential democratic resolution, before addressing possible resolution by limited dictatorships, and then turning to issues of sustainability.

Acemoglu, Johnson, and Robinson (AJR; 2004a) argue that growth and distribution are linked because economic institutions drive long-run growth and political institutions shape the formation of economic institutions.[20] More precisely, AJR make four key assertions. First, economic institutions are the fundamental source of long-run growth because they structure incentives to invest in physical capital, human capital, and development of technology. Economic institutions that facilitate public-good provision, address other first-order CAPs, and define and enforce *widely accessible property rights*—rights that allow relatively equal opportunities to invest—tend to foster growth. Such institutions allow multiple parties the potential to reap returns from their investments. Note, however, that property rights themselves need not be accessible. Dictators may define and enforce exclusive property rights for their families and supporters.

Second, because economic institutions affect the distribution of output and income, conflicts of interest arise among various groups and individuals concerning the design of economic institutions. AJR call this proposition the social conflict theory of institutions.[21] Parties that possess political power tend to dominate such conflicts; thus economic institutions emerge as outcomes of distributional conflicts that are mediated by differential political power.[22] Political power takes two basic forms: de facto power and de jure power. Immediately operative (on-the-spot) or *de facto* power arises from the relative access of individuals and groups to resources (the distribution of resources) and from the ability of groups to resolve CAPs of organization. De facto power—especially that which accompanies the resolution of organizational CAPs—tends to be relatively short-lived, that is, unless it can be institutionalized, in which case it becomes de jure power. *De jure* power emerges from positions designated by relatively enduring formal political institutions.

We may then envision a hierarchy of political-economic institutions whereby political institutions establish de jure power (by designating positions) that, in turn, influences the formation and modification of economic institutions, which then shape economic outcomes. Figure 13.2 illustrates. The three basic sources of power occupy the left-hand side of the diagram. (Note the similarity to Chapter 4's sources of power.) In initial period *t*, political institutions generate de jure political power. At the same time, the distribution of resources and the ability of concerned parties to resolve organizational CAPs jointly create

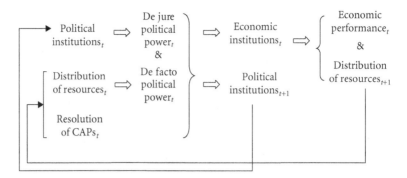

Figure 13.2   Political and economic institutions

SOURCE: D. Acemoglu, S. Johnson, and J. A. Robinson (2004), "Institutions as the Fundamental Cause of Long-Run Growth," Working Paper 10481, National Bureau of Economic Research, Cambridge, MA. Reprinted with permission.

de facto power. Both types of power affect the nature of economic institutions in period t as well as political institutions in the next period, $t + 1$. Period-t economic institutions, in turn, affect not only economic performance during period t, but also the distribution of resources in period $t + 1$. Finally, both $(t + 1)$-variables feed back into their respective t-variables for the subsequent period, and thereby establish that period's sources of de jure and de facto power. And so the process continues.

This representation accords with Chapter 7's discussion of quasi-parameters (based on Greif 2006a). Elaborating on the historical example from Section 7.1, the political institutions of the British monarchy established economic institutions that facilitated a significant expansion of the British Atlantic trade, beginning in the sixteenth century.[23] Trade, in turn, fostered accumulation of wealth among Atlantic merchants, increasing their share of resources—a quasi-parameter. Over time, merchants (and landholders with whom they allied) attained sufficient resources, and resolved organizational CAPs, allowing them to challenge the monarchy during the English Civil War of 1642–1651 and the Glorious Revolution of 1688. Once these groups had gained de facto power, they used it to alter political institutions so as to restrain the king's influence. They augmented the powers of Parliament, shifting the distribution of de jure power in their favor—preserving their hold on power. Subsequently, Parliament altered economic institutions. In 1694, for example, Parliament established the Bank of England, creating a reliable source of credit for merchants, with subsequent feedback effects on their wealth (access to resources).[24]

By itself, however, the logic of Figure 13.2 does not address the question posed by what AJR call the political Coase theorem. Given potential inefficiencies that could arise from various distributions of political power, they ask: "But why do the groups with conflicting interests not agree on the set of economic institutions that maximize aggregate growth (the size of the aggregate pie) and then use their political power simply to determine the distribution of the gains?" (Acemoglu, Johnson, and Robinson 2004a, 3). The authors answer with their third assertion: parties with political power cannot credibly commit to abstain from using it to seize portions of shared future gains. In other words, the standard game-theoretic problem of issuing credible promises applies directly to institutional formation. Equivalently, establishing credible agreements to share future gains constitutes a second-order CAP in which those who possess the means of enforcement (power) cannot credibly commit to use it against their own interests. AJR further assert that regime opponents face a related commitment problem. In this regard, suppose that parties who lack political power offer the following bargain: if you hand us political power, we promise to treat you well and give you a share of economic gains. This reverse-perspective commitment problem speaks to the difficulty of dislodging dictators in the face of revolts that appear likely to succeed. Revolutionaries, who are often motivated by reciprocal anger over past injustices, usually cannot credibly promise to abstain from prosecuting dictators and seizing their assets, much less awarding them future economic gains.[25]

Fourth, AJR assert that problems of credible commitment link the formation of economic institutions to the distribution of political power. Because those who possess power care about their distributional shares, because distributional shares are a direct outcome of economic institutions, and because economic institutions affect long-run growth, distribution and growth are inseparable. The political and economic sides of macro political-economy are likewise inseparable.[26]

Several of the examples noted by AJR illustrate their arguments. They attribute differences in the nineteenth-century banking systems in the United States and Mexico to their respective colonial legacies. Early seventeenth-century British colonists in North America entered a sparsely populated area with few obviously exportable resources. In order to retain settler allegiance, the British state and colonizing companies granted colonists access to land, along with relatively democratic political institutions. Moreover, high mobility, combined with the availability of sparsely settled land, generated a relatively equal distribution of economic resources, leading to a relatively equal distribution of de facto power among colonists, at least in the North.[27] By contrast, Spanish colonists in Mexico encountered a large indigenous population and readily exploitable silver mines. In order to control the indigenous population and extract silver, the Spanish created a centralized colonial administration.[28]

Colonial institutions created legacies in both countries. The United States established limitations on executive and other forms of de jure political power via constitutionally mandated checks on executive and legislative power, with independent judicial review. Mexico, however, retained its colonial inheritance of centralized political power. Subsequently, in the United States, relatively powerful groups of farmers and merchants demanded broad access to credit. They gradually forced the states to allow competitive banking. By contrast, in Mexico, the powerful central government profited from granting limited monopoly rights to a handful of banks. By 1910, the United States had 25,000 banks, and Mexico had 42, with two of them controlling 60% of the market.[29]

Similarly, in both Britain and Holland, constraints on the power of their monarchies allowed merchant representatives in their respective Parliaments to enact relatively accessible commercial property rights, with accompanying financial markets. By contrast, the relatively unrestricted Portuguese and Spanish monarchies instituted monopolies over colonial trade in order to maximize the flow of gold and silver into state coffers. The Spanish government even prohibited its Latin American colonies from importing non-Spanish goods; it also limited exporting to specific ports. For example, before the mid-eighteenth century, Argentinian exports had to be carried over the Andes Mountains to Lima, Peru, before shipment overseas. Needless to say, these economic institutions were not efficient.

To conclude, AJR propose the following quite general democratic prescription for growth-inducing institutional construction: Establish broadly accessible foundations of political power rooted in democratic formal political institutions. Such institutions should prescribe mechanisms that distribute or separate governing powers (executive, legislative, judicial) across multiple types of agents and, via elections, render legislative and the top executive positions accessible and accountable to multiple parties. The subsequent dispersion of political power should create incentives for those sharing power to provide key public goods and establish broadly accessible property rights with credible enforcement. By offering a broad array of citizens the potential to profit from investment activity, such economic institutions should secure a foundation for economic growth. North and Weingast (1989) argue that essentially this formula created foundations for the long-term economic growth of Britain that led to the first Industrial Revolution.[30]

Although AJR's framework implies that this democratic political route fosters long-term growth through its ability to provide public goods and establish credible enforcement, their approach does not necessarily stipulate that democratic political institutions are the only means of creating needed credibility. Indeed, Prezworski, Alvarez, and Cheibub (2000) find impressive growth rates in many dictatorships. To complicate matters further, Acemoglu and Robinson (2008) argue that elites can capture democratic processes by using their (often substantial) de facto power. We proceed with these issues in order.

Armando Razo (2008) directly addresses the question of credible commitment and growth under dictatorship. Using the historical example of the 1876–1911 regime of Porfirio Díaz in Mexico, Razo defines a *limited dictatorship* as one in which several powerful parties constrain the ability of a dictator to unilaterally enact policy. Limited dictators can establish credible commitments to enforce selective, rather than universal, property rights by making commitments to specific well-placed asset holders. Asset holders, in turn, privately arrange with other officials for third-party enforcement that limits the ability of the dictator to renege, thus rendering his selective commitments credible. A sufficient number of these arrangements can offer foundations for growth.[31]

More precisely, Razo argues that limited dictatorships have the following characteristics:

- Dictators care about their own income and maintaining power.

- Because of restrictions on general access to legislative and executive positions and the lack of an independent judiciary, dictators exert greater discretion over policymaking than do executives in democracies.

- The presence of high levels of executive discretion and the simultaneous absence of an independent judiciary mean that promises to uphold universal property rights are not credible.

- Asset holders (potential investors) care about profits and their own property rights, but they do not care about enforcement of others' rights. In fact, limited enforcement creates benefits by excluding competition.[32]

- Dictators have supporters to whom they owe favors, and such supporters have some influence over government operations. If these supporters are organized and share a mutually understood stake in preserving their privilege, informal arrangements between the dictator and such supporters can limit his discretion.[33]

- Formal institutions play an important but hidden role: they establish durable positions from which key actors operate, even though such actors may not operate as officially prescribed. For example, police commissioners, military officers, or bureaucrats may take bribes; their formal position establishes a context (a set of action arenas) in which bribery can be effective.

Given these conditions, selective property rights enforcement operates as follows. Dictators offer selected private asset holders *policy contracts*: promises to enforce and respect their property rights in return for a tax or payment. By themselves, such promises are not credible: with no independent judiciary, one cannot expect public organizations, such as courts, to sanction a dictator for violating promises. Instead, investors privately arrange for enforcement from powerful public officials (such as military officers) and occasionally private parties (bank presidents) who occupy positions from which they could punish the dictator for reneging on selective promises. Investors offer these parties some portion of their rent in return for promises to sanction the dictator should he violate his commitments.

Figure 13.3 illustrates the commitment problem for a single policy contract with a single party and a single enforcer.[34] The dictator (D) moves first, offering a policy contract or not. The asset holder (A) decides whether to invest or not. The dictator then decides whether to honor or renege on the contract. If he reneges, the enforcer (E) decides whether or not to punish. The following terms represent the associated payoffs: R is the return on A's investment; t is the tax rate; b is the bribery rate (or enforcement fee) paid to E; C_D is the cost to D of issuing a contract (e.g., salaries of relevant officials); p is punishment; v is A's fallback position (earnings with no investment); and c_p is the cost to E of punishing D. Razo defines an *enforcement condition*, under which E will choose to punish the dictator if called upon, as $R > R^* \equiv c_p/b$. A *commitment condition* shows the amount of punishment needed to induce the dictator to honor his commitment: $p \geq p^* \equiv (1 - t)R$. If both of these conditions are met and if $C_D/R \leq t \leq (1 - b) - v/R$, then a subgame perfect equilibrium exists where D honors, A invests, E would willingly punish, and D chooses $t = (1 - b) - v/R$.[35]

This game illustrates that a private policy contract could be credible; yet in actual dictatorships, the supply of enforcers with enough power to unilaterally punish the dictator is small or nonexistent. Thus asset holders and enforcers can both do better by creating informal overlapping private enforcement networks. In this scenario, single asset holders contract with multiple enforcers, some of whom protect more than one policy contract. The intuition behind this arrangement is straightforward: all enforcers share rents with

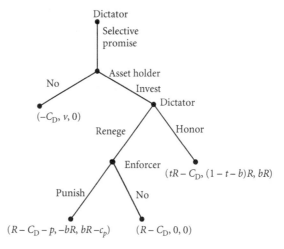

Figure 13.3   Private protection game

SOURCE: Armando Razo (2008), *Social Foundations of Limited Dictatorship: Networks and Private Protection during Mexico's Early Industrialization*, Stanford, CA: Stanford University Press.

investors and thus have a stake in holding the dictator off. If the dictator reneges on a single promise within a network, other arrangements may suffer, giving many enforcers an incentive to punish the dictator.[36] Credible enforcement of the dictator's selective commitments thus relies on overlapping protection networks—networks that emerge from private rent-sharing agreements between selected asset holders and powerful officials. Such networks create a mutual interest among powerful participants in maintaining conditions for growth, thereby creating foundations for long-term growth.

The Díaz dictatorship illustrates these principles. Díaz took power in 1876 following a long period of economic stagnation. At that time, the executive branch of the Mexican government was relatively weak. To increase his own power and to generate conditions for growth, Díaz and his supporters arranged the following triad of political and economic exchanges:

(i) Powerful officials in the Congress and elsewhere ceded discretion in economic policymaking to Díaz. By doing so, they created assurance that his regime would endure.

(ii) Díaz offered protection to selected asset holders, establishing barriers to entry in their industries that generated substantial rents.[37] Because he enjoyed policy discretion, asset holders could expect reasonable longevity for such agreements.

(iii) Asset holders shared their rents with specific powerful public and military officials, many of whom sat on their boards. Shared rents gave officials an incentive to ensure that Díaz did not renege on his private arrangements.

Even though these arrangements were informally negotiated and implemented, formal political institutions provided necessary context and foundations for the expected longevity of such relationships: these institutions established the positions from which key officials operated, allowing them to undertake their dual roles as public officials and private enforcers.

Thus the Díaz dictatorship blurred the lines between economic and political actors. About one-fifth of public officials had business experience before taking office, and high-level officials typically held both government and business positions. Furthermore, many participating public officials also had military connections. Depending on the year, between 25% and 50% had prior experience as military officers; many state governors were also generals. Díaz himself was a general who derived support from his success against the French in the 1860s (Razo 2008, Chaps. 4 and 5). Military support both protected Díaz from challenges and reinforced limits on his discretion: military officials with private agreements could punish Díaz for reneging on private commitments. The limited dictatorship thus rested on foundations of network connections among government office holders, business, and the military. In Sabatier's terms, the limited dictatorship comprised a macro-level policy system in the form of an iron triangle built upon these three elements.

These arrangements took the form of overlapping networks, with two types of overlap: private and public. First, shared board memberships served as interconnecting links (or short bridges) among corporations. Bankers, for example, often sat on the boards of key manufacturing firms, and vice versa. A second network involved protection arrangements with public officials. Here officials were nodes and shared board positions created similarly overlapping connections among them.[38] Figure 13.4 (Figure 6.5 in Razo 2008) shows a network among officials with more than 10 shared board memberships. As in other social networks, some links are much more connected than others. The most connected official, Mexico City mayor Fernando Pimentel y Fagoaga, was a member of Mexico's monetary commission, a major banker, and a senator from a prominent family whose lineage traced back to New Spain (colonial Mexico).[39]

The networks of the Díaz regime thus signified "a critical mass of central players with dense connections who had the ability and incentives to curtail predation [by Díaz]" (Razo 2008, 144). The Díaz limited dictatorship fostered economic growth in Mexico for its duration by offering credible promises to protect selective property rights of well-placed asset holders.[40] Prior to Díaz's ascension to power in 1876, the Mexican economy had stagnated. By 1911, when he was forced into exile by revolution, Mexico had undergone early industrialization.

On a broader scale, and again following Razo (2008), we briefly turn to underlying principles. Dictatorships need to meet three conditions in order to operate as institutional systems capable of generating relatively enduring, growth-inducing social equilibria—that is, to function as successful limited dictatorships:

(i)   an economic environment capable of producing significant rents for a substantial but limited set of asset holders;

(ii) a distribution of political power within which coordinated activity among regime beneficiaries has the potential to create credible threats of punishing the dictator; and

(iii) overlapping social networks in the private and public sectors that generate mutual interest in preserving economic rents obtained from selective property right

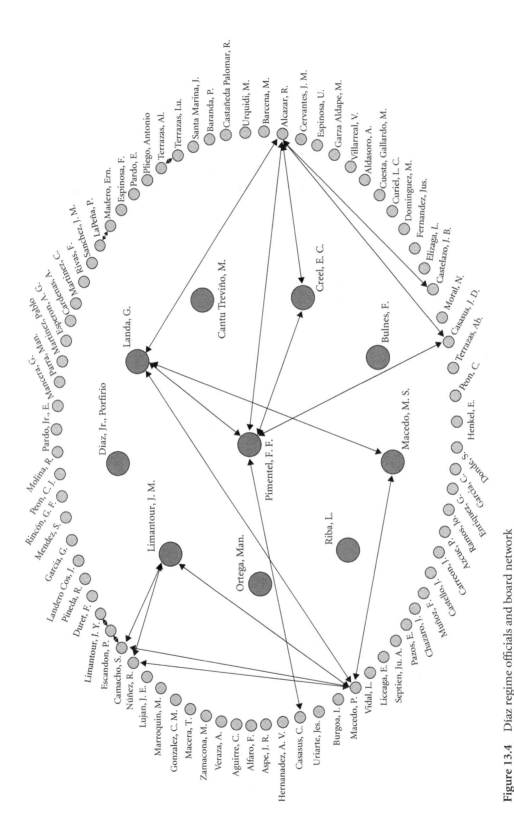

Figure 13.4 Díaz regime officials and board network

SOURCE: Armando Razo (2008), *Social Foundations of Limited Dictatorship: Networks and Private Protection during Mexico's Early Industrialization*, Stanford, CA: Stanford University Press. Reprinted with permission from Stanford University Press.

enforcement, with shared understandings of such mutual interests, and avenues for coordination.

We draw three general conclusions. First, the conditions for successful limited dictatorships are restrictive; we do not observe many limited dictatorships because most dictatorships lack at least one of these conditions.[41] Second, as the Mexican Revolution illustrates, political-economic sustainability is a problem for limited dictatorships. Selective rights enforcement not only generates general discontent among the excluded masses, it also tends to create simmering divisions among elites. In June 1910, Francisco Madero (son of a wealthy hacienda family with links to the regime) ran against Díaz on an Anti-Reelectionist Party ticket; he and 5,000 supporters were jailed (Skidmore and Smith 2005). In October, Madero declared himself provisional president and issued a call to arms to overthrow Díaz. Discontented business leaders (notably, Commander Pascual Orozco), industrial workers, army deserters, peasants (led by Emiliano Zapata)—together with ranchers and bandits (led by Pancho Villa)—answered the call in November. In May 1911, Díaz was exiled to Europe (Wolf 1969; Meyer, Sherman, and Deeds 2007). In terms of prior concepts, we may regard strife among elites and rising distributional inequity as quasi-parameters whose values slowly grew under the Díaz regime. Accumulation of a critical mass of discontent generated conditions amenable to revolt, and its success punctured the dictatorship's social equilibrium.

Third, limited dictatorships create problematic political legacies related to the persistence of at least some of their selective enforcement and exclusion mechanisms. Even after the Mexican Revolution, the social networks of the Díaz era—along with many accompanying inequities—remained largely intact.[42] Thus, as Greif (2006a) argues, institutional systems can generate legacies that extend beyond their lifetimes, indicating yet another variant of path dependency.

For a final perspective on institutions and commitment, we discuss a potential constraint on the ability of democratic institutions to generate social equity. Acemoglu and Robinson (2008, 2012) argue that, even with formal democratic political institutions, elites can "capture" democratic regimes so as to alter political and economic institutions in their favor. Specifically, elites have significant access to de facto power stemming from their access to resources and advantages of relatively homogeneous small-group organization. Unorganized majorities, by contrast, face significant organizational CAPs, with far fewer per-capita resources. Elites may use their de facto power to bias economic and political institutions and outcomes in their favor.

The post–Civil War South offers an example of elite capture. The Civil War ushered in dramatic changes in formal political and economic institutions. The Thirteenth Amendment to the US Constitution abolished slavery; the Fourteenth Amendment stated that all persons born in the United States are citizens with full rights under the law; and the Fifteenth Amendment declared that the right to vote "shall not be denied or abridged by the United States or by any State on account or race, color, or previous condition of servitude." It also gave Congress the power to enforce its provisions.[43] Yet, as Acemoglu and Robinson note (2008, 269), "the South largely maintained its pre–Civil War agricultural system based on large plantations, low-wage uneducated labor, and labor repression, and it remained relatively poor until the middle of the twentieth century." Elite use of de facto power intervened to uphold this system despite substantive change in the highest-level political institution, the US Constitution. Specifically, debt peonage replaced slavery in agriculture; various private and public policies limited labor mobility; blacks were disenfranchised; and intimidation, violence, and lynching suppressed resistance and removed sympathetic officials. Between 1870 and 1890, exercises of de facto power—largely based on plantation ownership and the vigilante terrorism of the Ku Klux Klan—altered state and local political institutions, generating complementary and durable de jure power: the political and economic institutions of the Jim Crow system of legal segregation.[44] Democracy had thus been captured and remained so until the civil rights era, which punctured the pre-existing social equilibrium, and presaged a new one.

13.4. CONCLUSION

Achieving sustained long-term and moderately equitable economic growth requires resolution of multiple CAPs that simultaneously involve the properties of nonrival knowledge and the configuration (or characteristics) of political and economic institutions. As indicated by macroeconomic growth models, advances in technical and organizational knowledge provide the proximate cause of long-term growth in average standards of living. The properties of knowledge, therefore, fundamentally influence growth dynamics. Because knowledge is nonrival, new knowledge complements existing knowledge, and knowledge is only partially exclusive. Yet, despite its nonrivalry, knowledge is not universally accessible; it flows through networks, within which access depends on connections. Unfortunately, certain localities or sectors may lack necessary (or potentially beneficial) linkages. Moreover, boundedly rational humans can absorb only so much knowledge, and the ability to absorb knowledge depends on already attained human capital. Hence skill complementarities arise in team production—inducing highly skilled workers to seek each other out, and highly productive employers pursue them. Localized peer and role-model effects—often responding to norms of reciprocity—create additional skill and knowledge complementarities. Thus areas and sectors that possess substantial pre-existing knowledge tend to provide strong incentives for investing in new knowledge, whereas areas and sectors with only sparse knowledge offer few such incentives. Consequently, we find unevenly distributed clusters, or agglomerations, of knowledge and skill. Moreover, high-knowledge clusters create growth-inducing innovation centers, whereas low-knowledge clusters create few innovations and so become poverty traps. In sum, the properties of nonrival knowledge tend to generate location- and sector-based distributional inequities that point to coordination CAPs for less developed areas and equity-related CAPs for society at large.

Institutions condition all of these interactions. Although technological knowledge may be the proximate cause of growth, investments in research, human capital, and physical capital occur within institutional settings that shape the motivation, information, and cognition of potential investors. Economic institutions resolve important second- and first-order CAPs by defining and enforcing multiple property rights and by creating prescriptions meant to address market failure related to broadly defined public goods, externalities, and common-pool resources. In so doing, economic institutions influence incentives to learn, provide effort, and invest—simultaneously affecting the distribution of output.

Because agents who occupy positions of power care about their distributional shares and can use their power to shape institutional construction, they attempt to design economic institutions with their distributional interests in mind. The enduring political power conferred by de jure political institutions—with input from exercises of more short-lived de facto power—thus frames the construction or modification of economic institutions. These relationships create a commitment problem—a type of second-order CAP—with respect to establishing reliable economic institutions. What prevents power holders from seizing gains created by the efforts or investments of others? Anyone who expects their own gain to be seized will not invest. Ultimately, this commitment problem links growth to distribution: long-term economic growth occurs only when parties with political power find it in their interest to construct or allow institutions that limit their ability to seize economic gains produced by others. Growth and distribution are thus interdependent (they coevolve), and power relationships may create substantial CAPs related to both.[45]

Generally speaking, there are two ways to resolve the commitment problem at a macro level: the democratic method and the limited-dictatorship method. The democratic method involves establishing formalized limits on the political power available to specific agents (executives, in particular), by separating legislative from executive power, establishing elections for legislative and top executive positions, and by creating an independent judiciary. Elections establish relatively accessible entry (compared with known alternatives) into important political positions and also offer some degree of public accountability. This partial dispersion of power limits the ability of key political actors to offer selective property rights, and accessibility generates competition. As a consequence, power holders may find it in their interest to support reasonably inclusive economic institutions that foster provision of public goods, along with broadly defined and broadly accessible property rights.

By contrast, when political power is concentrated, two basic outcomes are possible: full dictatorships, which do not foster growth; and limited dictatorships, which may foster growth. Under full dictatorship, the commitment problem is simply not resolved and the economy enters a vicious cycle of repression and no growth. Nevertheless, the dictator is content with power and a large distributional share (North Korea comes to mind). In the case of a successful limited dictatorship, credibility arises from networks of privately arranged enforcement that possess the capacity to punish a dictator for reneging on private commitments to honor selective property rights. Because selective enforcement offers specific asset holders incentives to invest, the economy as a whole can grow for a relatively long, though not indefinite, period; but the distribution of output is likely to be highly inequitable. The limited dictatorship of Porfirio Díaz in Mexico, reigning between 1876 and 1911, offers an example.

Combining ideas from Sections 13.1–13.3, we should expect the locational implications of nonrival knowledge to interact with economic and political institutions. Democracies and limited dictatorships both contain clusters of growth, along with poverty traps. Still, we expect greater disparity between high- and low-growth sectors and localities, in limited dictatorships. Only high-growth sectors earn large enough rents to warrant selectively enforced property rights. Individuals who are stuck in poverty traps not only confront an absence of incentives to invest in knowledge (as explained in Section 13.2), they also have no reason to expect adequate or fair enforcement of their property rights.

We close this chapter by discussing five complications. First, the sustainability of limited dictatorships as foundations for growth is debatable. Second, their exclusive nature can have lasting impact on political institutions in the form of persistent political inequities that can impede longer-term growth, as in Mexico's Díaz legacy. Third, the benefits of economic growth induced by limited dictatorships accumulate with structured inequality that concentrates benefits on those who possess selective policy contracts. Such growth does not either reflect or accompany broad economic development, much less political or social development.

Fourth, in democracies, unequal access to resources—a consequence of unequal distribution of income and wealth—engenders inequitable access to de facto power that can subsequently lead to the capture of democratic institutions by elites. Such capture may generate inefficiencies, create its own distributional inequities—including institutionally induced poverty traps—and complicate efforts to reduce various unequal distributional outcomes that follow from the clustering of knowledge centers. Moreover, as discussed in Chapters 3 and 4, positional inequities that operate within exchange processes (e.g., owner-employee; landlord-tenant) allow for exercises of power based on triadic relationships in market exchange. Again, outcomes need not be either efficient or equitable.[46] On a broader scale, powerful agents may create public or private policy subsystems that sustain or enhance extant economic and political inequities. The disadvantaged, on the other hand, may face the substantial CAPs of initiating reform (as discussed in Chapter 12). Over time, sustained increases in economic inequality may signify a changing quasi-parameter that could move a democratic system in the direction of limited dictatorship. Elite capture may generate pockets of selectively enforced property rights or, more colloquially, privilege.

Fifth, there is no inherent reason for property rights to be broadly accessible; indeed, universal property rights are themselves a public good. We should not expect asset holders to prefer broad access to property rights, given that they may benefit from limits on potential competition. Thus establishing economic institutions that prescribe widely accessible (rather than selective) property rights—in addition to facilitating the provision of other public goods—presents a complex series of CAPs associated with institutional construction and modification. Those interested in the democratic route to growth must address multiple complicated CAPs related to achieving a broad distribution of de facto and de jure power that, in turn, creates incentives for powerful actors to establish accessible, accountable, and sustainable political institutions. These institutions can, in turn, serve as foundations for credible and accessible economic institutions. Unfortunately, nonrival knowledge tends to create distributional inequities. Unequal access to resources then generates corresponding inequities in the distribution of de facto power—a quasi-parameter that, over time, creates formally based and informally reinforced power asymmetries. Such asymmetries can then facilitate elite capture of democratic institutions. Creating sustainable and moderately equitable democratic institutions thus requires recurrent resolution of additional CAPs associated with tempering distributional inequities.

EXERCISES

13.1. For the Solow model of equation (13.1) and accompanying text, let $s = 0.2$, $d = 0.12$, and $n = 0.03$, $\alpha = 0.75$, and $\Delta A / A = 0$.

    a. Solve for k^* and y^*.

    b. Suppose that $\Delta A / A = 0.02$. Country A operates with values specified in your answer to part a. Country B has a savings rate of 0.3. Prove that the two countries converge to the same long-run rates of growth for y and k of 0.02.

13.2. Use numbers to contrast the constant returns outcome from equation (13.2) with the increasing returns from (13.3). Discuss the implications on relationships between knowledge, location, and growth.

13.3. Create a game of assurance to show interactions between two workers with complementary skills.

13.4. Apply the identity model of Figure 8.9 to the statements about membership dynamics found on page 334.

13.5. Develop a version of Figure 11.5 that illustrates a role-model phenomenon related to human capital investment.

13.6. Construct a model that illustrates a localized brain drain phenomenon as a multiplayer assurance game (like that in Figure 12.4). Show the relevant functions, and explain the outcomes.

13.7. (Advanced) Develop an IEGT model of brain drain based upon a two-player assurance game (like that in Exercise 13.3) as a stage game. Incorporate social payoffs that reflect conformity, as well as material payoffs that reflect returns to complementary skills.

13.8. Demonstrate the listed conditions for a subgame perfect equilibrium that apply to Figure 13.3. Indicate conditions for the existence of other possible subgame perfect equilibria for this game, and explain your reasoning.

14 CONCLUSION

Successful exchange, and indeed development, requires some ability to resolve fundamental collective-action problems. Such problems (CAPs) arise from any conflict between the unfettered pursuit of individual goals—typically self-interest—and the perceived well-being of at least a portion of some group, such as a club, community, firm, region, or nation. Because CAPs represent the archetypal social dilemma of strategic interaction among purposeful agents, their relationship with exchange has served as the unifying principle of this book. Collective-action problems reveal the core logic behind multiple market and group failures—failures that accompany (broadly defined) common-pool resources, externalities, and public goods, including problems of establishing commitment and trust. Moreover, resolution of CAPs—especially problems of orchestrating sufficient coordination, enforcement, and trust for reliable commitment—underlies successful social, political, and economic exchange within markets and groups. Thus CAPs lie at the foundations of political economy. Their resolution facilitates and, in fact, permits, economic, political, and social development.

In addressing these themes, this text pursues two parallel lines of reasoning: one methodological, and one thematic. Methodologically, we incorporate the versatile techniques of game-theoretic modeling to illustrate the strategic interactions that permeate political economy. Strategic interactions—that is, engagements in which one agent's activity affects outcomes for others—provide foundations for social scientific analysis. Game-theoretic agents may signify individuals, organizations, or groups, ranging from small social groups to firms, political parties, religious organizations, communities, and nations. Game-theoretic modeling allows analysts to systematically specify how various mixtures of incentives, motivations, information, and understandings influence agents' actions (their strategic choices)—and, ultimately, how combinations of such actions generate or affect the possible outcomes of myriad strategic engagements. Furthermore, these models can represent the impact of specific social, political, economic, or physical contexts on such interactions and their outcomes. In particular, the rules of a game may indicate how physical and social contexts (or environments) condition strategic interactions by specifying who interacts with whom, the positions relevant agents occupy, what they can or cannot do, when they can act, and what they know. In this regard, the rules of a game may characterize the conditioning influences of informal and formal institutions. Moreover, game-theoretic models possess the versatility to represent such interactions at levels ranging from minimalist micro exchanges of favors between two individuals up to macro-level transactions between unified nations or vast populations.

Our discussion incorporates several approaches to game theory. Most of our models reflect strategic interactions operating within given (already established) contexts involving two or many players. Here we rely primarily on classical game-theoretic (CGT) models, where substantively rational agents possess the cognitive ability to offer best responses, with or without complete information. We supplement traditional materially based models with findings of behavioral game theory concerning social preference. Classical game-theoretic models can then portray innumerable interactions and outcomes of exchanges, along with associated first- and second-order CAPs. In so doing, these models can account for the following elements: material and social incentives (or preferences); complete or incomplete information; exercises of power; impacts of norms; conceptions of identity; and broader institutional contexts. Alternatively, to represent dynamic learning processes among boundedly rational agents, we use evolutionary game theory (EGT), a modeling framework in which agents inherit strategies from past learning. In EGT games, interactions among agents generate average fitness payoffs that affect the reproductive potential of their strategies—via social transmission. Selective transmission (of relatively successful practices) can then represent social learning related to strategic approaches, preference orientations, or the development of norms and other institutions. Finally, we use epistemic game theory to model boundedly rational agents' (necessarily limited) individual and shared understandings. Epistemic game theory can illustrate the core influences of informal and formal institutions on strategic behavior via signals (prescriptions) that correlate understandings and behavior: social choreography.

Game-theoretic models, like any other technique of analysis, cannot represent all such interactions at once. Consequently, we employ many different models (or variations of models) in order to present alternative perspectives and levels of analysis targeted to specific questions. Moreover, we complement game theory in two basic fashions. First, we use social network analysis to show how structures of connection among agents affect transmissions of influence and information. Network analysis informs our discussion of relations between institutions, position, power, information flows, the nature of punctuated equilibria, and the ability of institutional systems to affect growth. Second, we supplement both game theory and network analysis with more general theoretical statements and a brief summary of the institutional analysis and development framework (of the Indiana University Workshop in Political Theory and Policy Analysis). These broader approaches allow us to sketch principles of interaction that are too complicated to model. Nevertheless, because they complement more formal analysis, we use these broad approaches to establish conceptual foundations for much of our modeling. All in all, our varied conceptual methods both follow and elucidate theoretical precepts related to collective action and exchange: the themes of this book.

Two basic types of collective-action problems can impede the exchanges that underlie development. First-order CAPs arise from multiple opportunities for free-riding associated with providing (broadly defined) public goods, reducing production of negative externalities, increasing production of positive externalities, and/or limiting use of common-pool resources. These basic first-order CAPs both emerge from and compromise the viability of economic, political, and social exchanges—and sometimes prevent their occurrence altogether. Nevertheless, in principle, members of small groups could recognize their common interests and negotiate agreements to resolve first-order CAPs. But orchestrating the coordination, enforcement, and trust needed for credible agreements on first-order CAPs presents second-order CAPs.

Second-order CAPs usually reflect information asymmetries and create substantial transaction costs. In this regard, adverse selection models can portray coordination problems that accompany defining the actual or de facto property rights (or qualities) to be exchanged before a transaction is conducted. Similarly, principal-agent models reflect information asymmetries regarding the degree to which the post-contractual (or post-agreement) actions of agents live up to their associated commitments. Between them, these models yield five key results. First, adverse selection can lead to inefficient exchange or complete market failure—that is, no exchange. Transaction costs may thus preclude development. Second, principal-agent models of moral hazard problems imply that parties to exchanges must, themselves, construct costly internal enforcement mechanisms—a process that generates inefficiencies and potential barriers to exchange. Third, internal enforcement leads to non-clearing markets—notably, labor and capital markets. Fourth, nonclearing markets allow certain parties within exchange processes to exercise power over other parties. Fifth, the complexities of resolving both first- and second-order CAPs imply that attention to material payoffs alone cannot explain many instances of observed resolution. Hence relationships between agents' motivations and the various social contexts wherein they interact merit investigation.

Power relationships condition the social contexts for processes related to both exchange and CAPs. We posit three related sources of power: access to resources, ability to resolve organizational CAPs, and institutionally designated positions. Power itself exhibits three faces or dimensions. First, for given mutually understood rules and contexts, parties exercise power by mustering support or by applying force (power1). Second, agents can manipulate rules, expectations, and/or external opinions so as to limit the ability of potential opponents to enter arenas or operate effectively within them; they can mobilize bias by using strategic moves (power2). Third, agents may endeavor to manipulate the beliefs of potential opponents in efforts to reduce or eliminate their willingness to resist—often by appealing to values or cultural symbols (power3). Exercises of power may sometimes move successively up these three levels—in the process gaining momentum and steadily becoming more difficult to dislodge. Furthermore, power2 and power3 interact with social preferences and institutions.

The concept of social preference, reciprocity in particular, begins to address the question of how small groups may actually resolve difficult CAPs. Intrinsic reciprocity—a desire to reward kind and punish unkind behavior—can explain why agents willingly reward cooperative behavior or punish uncooperative behavior, even at a cost to themselves. Such willingness may resolve both second- and first-order CAPs by facilitating reliable exchanges among groups of familiar agents. Moreover, reciprocity responds to strategic context—in particular the nature of the strategic choices (e.g., degrees of discretion) available to specific parties. Reciprocity may also interact with other forms of social preference, such as inequality aversion or a concern for social welfare. Explaining larger-scale resolution of CAPs, however, requires deeper investigation into motivation, information, and cognition, as well as the potential for institutions to influence these factors.

Theories of rationality address relationships between understandings and motivation. Substantive rationality—goal-oriented behavior in which agents have the cognitive ability to choose best responses—underlies CGT representations of interactions based upon material and/or social preferences. Substantive rationality operates in reasonably well-understood institutional contexts. The concept of bounded rationality—goal-oriented behavior in the face of limits and costs to cognition—takes us farther. It allows for a more comprehensive representation of the various effects of social context, especially institutions, on the motivation, information, and cognition of agents. Boundedly rational agents address frequently encountered conditions of fundamental uncertainty (reflecting a competence-difficulty gap) by employing heuristics. More broadly, they develop mental models: conceptual frameworks that incorporate heuristics, classification systems, patterns, and cause-effect relationships to produce conclusions or judgments. The development of heuristics and mental models, moreover, follows an evolutionary logic. Hence evolutionary game-theoretic models can portray the associated learning processes. Because the reevaluative learning that alters mental models requires substantial cognitive effort, mental models operate as punctuated equilibria. Furthermore, some mental models—notably ideologies and institutions—are shared; they are common cognitive frameworks that affect understandings of multiple agents. Accordingly, the evolutionary and punctuated-equilibrium logic of mental models applies to institutions as well—on a grander scale.

An institution is a set of jointly self-enforcing and mutually understood conventions, social norms, social rules, formal rules, and beliefs that prescribe behavioral regularities in particular social contexts. Institutions not only motivate certain behaviors via the social and material incentives embedded in conventions, norms, and rules, they also influence the types of information received by (or available to) agents. More fundamentally, norms (as informal institutions) can shape the development of preference orientations, and all institutions shape agents' understandings of various causal relationships and social categories that pertain to the contexts in which they operate. As such, institutions facilitate some degree of predictability in otherwise non-ergodic environments. Within institutional contexts, organizations behave as agents that interact strategically with other agents (usually other organizations). Organizations often provide enforcement and, through their actions, alter institutions (sometimes unintentionally). Institutional systems then incorporate both institutions and organizations into large-scale mechanisms of social choreography. Agents who become dissatisfied with elements of institutional systems (or sometimes systems as a whole) may engage in exercises of either exit or voice. Loyalty, a type of social preference, tends to reinforce voice.

Informal institutions—conventions, norms, and social rules—resolve CAPs that extend beyond small reciprocal groups. Conventions, such as schedules, offer prescriptions that motivate self-enforcing coordination among strangers in relevant contexts. Social norms facilitate resolution to much broader ranges of CAPs. Norms convey shared, ethically based, agent- and context-specific behavioral prescriptions among groups of adherents. Normative prescriptions (typically) motivate various degrees of observance via both internalization and anticipated (though largely spontaneous) social sanctioning. Conformity or solidarity effects may follow. Norms of reciprocity—a nearly universal type of norm—extend reciprocal enforcement mechanisms across, and sometimes even between or among various, large groups. Deeply internalized rationality-limiting norms are so well established that followers do not even consider violation. While such norms may facilitate resolving certain internal CAPs among adherents, they can seriously impede effective interaction with groups that subscribe to different norms. More generally, all internalized norms influence ethical and cognitive elements of agents' identity concepts: people tend to identify with normative prescriptions that they believe in. In all of these cases, the ethical characteristics of norms convey particularly compelling influences on motivation and cognition. Finally, social rules prescribe context-specific behaviors, along with informally designated enforcers and predictable sanctions.

Relatively informal institutions—and, more generally, the shared understandings and trust that accompany localized social capital—facilitate governance among self-organized groups. Such groups must negotiate reasonably legitimate agreements for resolving first-order CAPs. They also need to establish credible mechanisms for internal (second-party) coordination and enforcement. Broadly speaking, self-governance offers profound advantages and disadvantages. Its many advantages arise from its ability to incorporate localized and timely information about both social and physical environments into the crafting of rules, procedures, and accompanying incentives. Participation in designing and negotiating rules, moreover, strengthens agents' cognition regarding both their environment and techniques of cooperation; exercising voice within groups is an art. The disadvantages of self-governance stem from its potential to create, maintain, or increase internal inequities, along with inherent tendencies toward group insularity with respect to possible external impacts of their own activity and to the perspectives and problems of outsiders, other groups, or society at large. Any of these factors may lead to social conflict.

Formal institutions and third-party enforcement can (depending on conditions) mitigate certain problems of group insularity, but these mechanisms may also undermine or otherwise conflict with local social capital and second-party enforcement. In particular, laws function well if they more or less complement relevant social norms, or, more generally, if they are compatible with prevailing social equilibria. If not, laws may not generate adherence; they may remain only words on paper. Likewise, third-party enforcement works best when it complements second-party enforcement. More fundamentally, complex exchange cannot operate without formal institutions and third-party enforcement—second-order CAPs would interfere. Establishing complex exchange requires developing institutional systems that merge relatively compatible formal and informal institutions with corresponding mixes of third- and second-party enforcement—at multiple levels. Effective governance is thus polycentric: it combines different levels of authority and different mechanisms for providing collective goods, coordination, and enforcement—all operating across interrelated domains. Compatibility among such institutional and organizational levels, moreover, tends to foster adaptation to changes in non-ergodic environments, creating potential for sustainability. Once successfully established, governance arrangements operate as punctuated social equilibria.

All of these activities function within social networks. Network positions, many of which are institutionally assigned, affect the ability of agents to transmit information and exert influence: they are sources of power. Social networks tend to form around identity-based social affiliation categories, a type of preferential attachment. Consequently, social norms can influence network development by shaping conceptions of identity. Moreover, agents can utilize their own hierarchical conceptions of delineations within affiliation categories—such as those for occupation—to locate information from (or search) distant network regions. Overlaps among such affiliations (e.g., occupation and residence) generate network shortcuts. Shortcuts, in turn, facilitate searching social networks and simultaneously generate their small-world properties. Furthermore, the imitative behavior of boundedly rational agents within networks—often prompted by patterns of reciprocity and conformity effects of social norms—creates a potential for information cascades: rapid, herdlike sequences of successive adaptation of ideas or practices. Information cascades point to both the robustness and the fragility of punctuated social equilibria that accompany shared ideas, informal and formal institutions, patterns of organizational behavior, and encompassing institutional systems. Such configurations are robust because they can withstand multiple shocks; yet they are fragile because apparently minor shocks may dislodge them. During the stable phases of punctuated social equilibria, established network structures help to foster relatively predictable social environments for boundedly rational agents. But information cascades signify disruptions that typically emerge with little or no warning.

Policy and policymaking reflect all of the previously discussed interactions. Policies attempt to address CAPs—the chief rationale for policy—and CAPs limit the nature and scope of feasible policy. Institutions establish the contexts within which policymaking operates, as they concurrently shape the motivation, information, and cognition of policymakers. At the same time, policies emerge from deliberate attempts to craft and implement context-specific behavioral prescriptions (rules of operation) or, more generally, from attempts to create, alter, or abolish institutions. As such, policymaking involves exercises of power, reflecting expressions of voice. Moreover, policymaking processes establish punctuated equilibria. During the stable phase of such equilibria, policy subsystems (i.e., policy-relevant institutional systems consisting of coalitions of specialists) tend to dominate policymaking in their areas of expertise—by excluding others and offering incremental concessions to opponents. Reformers thus face organizational and even cognitive CAPs associated with generating impetus for substantive change. Dramatic reform arises from periods of policy emergence—types of information cascades that tend to follow disruptive external events and/or successful efforts of opposition coalitions to force large shifts in attention among top policymakers and the population at large. Without successful implementation, however, enacted policies fail to achieve intended objectives. Functional policy implementation requires that intended targets and enforcers of policy find it worthwhile to follow its prescriptions. Ensuing CAPs reflect a general need for accordance among formal policy prescriptions, derived working rules, and relevant social norms—with similar compatibility between third- and second-party enforcers. Fruitful policy analysis needs to consider such interactions; and, again, functional governance tends to be polycentric.

Problems of governance link long-term growth to distribution. For given institutional arrangements, the most important proximate source of long-term growth is the development of nonrival technological knowledge. Nonrival knowledge generates increasing returns, and (as a type of good) knowledge is, at most, only partially excludable. Access to knowledge, however, depends on agents' cognitive abilities—partially embodied in their accumulated human capital—and their network connections. Because the human capital of different agents is complementary in production processes, skilled workers tend to match with each other. Peer and role-model effects—often induced by social norms and patterns of reciprocity—reinforce such complementarities. These patterns, along with increasing returns and network connections, lead to an uneven locational and sectoral clustering (agglomeration) of knowledge, human capital, production, and, ultimately, prosperity. The associated clustering of innovation centers and poverty traps creates substantial, path-dependent distributional inequities.

Institutional configurations exert potentially greater influence. Ultimately, development requires resolution of CAPs that accompany the negotiation, design, and implementation of credible constraints on the ability of powerful agents to seize the gains from others' investments in knowledge and production. Failure to do so leads to institutionally based poverty traps. Democracies and limited dictatorships, however, have the capacity to resolve these CAPs in a manner that achieves moderately long-term growth—if not equitable development. Democracies can foster growing economies by creating relatively inclusive political institutions that distribute de jure power across multiple participants, and simultaneously limit the power of specific position holders (such as chief executives). These arrangements tend to offer relevant power holders incentives to create and maintain broadly accessible economic institutions. For their part, limited dictatorships can enforce selective (not universal) property rights via networks of (selected) asset holders and third-party enforcers who, jointly, have the capacity to credibly threaten a dictator for violating his commitments. Nevertheless, long-term viability remains unclear, and inequities abound.

Even for democracies, inequities that arise from either the inherent properties of knowledge—with its tendencies to generate unequal agglomerations—or particular institutional configurations (e.g., policy subsystems) can lead to the capture of democratic institutions by interests that derive considerable de facto power from asymmetrically distributed wealth. Over time, such capture may foster the enactment of selective property rights: institutionalized privilege, signifying a move in the direction of limited dictatorship (or crony capitalism). Thus additional CAPs involving relationships between distributional equity, the accessibility and longevity of democratic institutions, and the foundations of growth that fosters broadly based development necessarily follow.

We conclude that collective-action problems matter for political economy not only because they reflect social dilemmas that arise from interactions of political power with market exchange, but more fundamentally, because market exchange and other forms of economic, political, and social development depend on prior resolution of multiple first-order CAPs of market and group failure and associated second-order CAPs of coordination and enforcement.

NOTES

1. These rules operate in the context of enforcement provided by Madison city police; vendors do not, for example, arrest or prosecute thieves. The vendors' association negotiates with city and state authorities on use of the Capitol grounds. While some regulations about animals may originate in state law, the 75% and 60-days rules are probably homemade.

CHAPTER 1

1. Discussions of related developments appear in Colander, Holt, and Rosser (2005), Colander (2006), Becker (2007), and Ferguson (2011).

2. Classical game theory assumes mutual understanding of interdependence, but evolutionary game theory need not do so.

3. Evolutionary game theory was initially developed by biologists (e.g., Smith 1989). For an insightful and more recent text, see Gintis (2009a).

4. Strategies (not individuals) are the *dramatis personae* of evolutionary game theory (Bowles 2004, 60).

5. Agent-based models (Epstein 2006; Miller and Page 2007) can represent complex evolutionary processes.

6. On behavioral game theory, see Camerer (2003); on epistemic game theory, see Gintis (2009b).

7. Nobel Prize awards to John Nash, Reinhard Selton, John Harsanyi, Thomas Schelling, Robert Aumann, Leonid Hurwicz, Eric Maskin, and Roger Myerson indicate the transformative implications of game theory.

8. For an economic perspective on social network theory, see Jackson (2008). More intuitive discussions appear in Barabási (2003) and Watts (2003).

9. The assumption of perfect information may be inconsistent with rational self-interest: Why rule out potential gains from concealing information?

10. For a discussion of moral hazard, see Milgrom and Roberts (1992).

11. See Hurwicz (1972, 2008), Maskin (1999, 2008), Dasgupta, Hammond, and Maskin (1979), and Myerson (1982, 2008). This literature also discusses the efficiency of alternative social mechanisms.

12. In efficiency wage models, principal-agent problems of labor exchange generate involuntary unemployment (Shapiro and Stiglitz 1984; Bowles 1985; Akerlof and Yellen 1990). Stiglitz (1987) also considers markets other than labor.

13. North (1990, Chap. 4) mentions a similar problem. Williamson's (1985) holdup problem also implies a potential for contested exchange.

14. Rodrik (2007) discusses the developmental significance of information-related market failure.

15. On behavioral economics, see Camerer, Loewenstein, and Rabin (2004).

16. In this regard, Bowles (2004) distinguishes between other-regarding preferences and process-regarding preferences.

17. See also Akerlof (1982) and Fehr and Gächter (1998).

18. Sociological approaches include Blau (1964) and Molm (1997). Economic approaches include Holländer (1990), Kandel and Lazear (1992), Barron and Gjerde (1997), Gächter and Fehr (1999), and Fehr and Fischbacher (2000).

19. On morale, see Akerlof and Yellen (1990), Bewley (1999), Howitt (2002), and Akerlof and Kranton (2005).

20. See Fehr, Kirchsteiger, and Riedl (1993), Fehr and Falk (1999), Fehr and Gächter (2002), and Bowles and Polanía-Reyes (2012).

21. Bowles (1998a) reviews the endogenous preference literature.

22. Schelling (1978) and Bowles (1998a) address how path dependence emerges from interdependent preferences.

23. Dixit, Skeath, and Reiley (2009) allow for reciprocity or altruism in payoffs.

24. Prospect theory addresses cognitive responses to uncertainty and changing environments; overviews appear in Kahneman (2003) and Rabin (2003).

25. Heiner (1983) illustrates the evolutionary logic of heuristics. As in biological evolution, selection need not generate any form of social optimum (North 1990).

26. Organizations are actors (players) whereas institutions are rules; Chapter 7 elaborates.

27. On the economics of social norms, see, for example, Akerlof (1982), Fehr and Gächter (2000), López-Pérez (2006, 2008), and Dequech (2009).

28. See, for example, E. Ostrom (2005, 2011) and McGinnis (2011a).

CHAPTER 2

1. This outcome could reflect either short-sighted pursuit of gain or long-term pursuit with a high discount rate.

2. In Chapter 8, the term "social norm" will basically signify what Hume means by "convention."

3. Even for Smith, the division of labor creates repetitive work that diminishes intelligence—a CAP. Smith advocated public provision of education for all socioeconomic classes.

4. Coase (1992) stresses theoretical implications of the Coase theorem: because Pigou assumed zero transaction costs (via pure competition), his analysis of externalities is

flawed; it fails to address relationships between transaction costs and legal assignment of rights.

5. Following Ostrom, we later relate second-order CAPs to institutional design.

6. Converting such divergent values (when observable) to a common metric is far more problematic and contestable than counting fish.

7. A *normal-form* (or *strategic-form*) two-player game is a matrix that shows strategies for both players and their payoffs for all possible combinations of strategies. This form typically represents *simultaneous games*—games in which either the players move at the same time, or the player who moves second cannot observe the first player's move before choosing its move.

8. More precisely, a Nash equilibrium is a list of strategies, one for each player, such that no player can do better by unilaterally changing strategies as long as all others stick to the list (Dixit, Skeath, and Reiley 2009, 93).

9. For a PD game, H signifies "high" payoff (to a single defector) and L signifies "low" payoff (to a single cooperator), while C and D, respectively, signify payoffs if both choose C or both choose D.

10. Much of the logic (and some of the notation) used in this discussion appeared in Dixit, Skeath, and Reiley (2009, Chap. 12). The externality function is new.

11. The discussion of water use that accompanies Figure 2.2 indicates a PDI game in which $b(2) = b(1) = 9$, $c(2) = 5$, and $c(1) = 10$. Yet if $b(2) = 7$ and $b(1) = 6$, the game becomes PDII.

12. Exercise 2.1 asks the reader to construct an extensive-form representation of chicken and explain the first-mover advantage.

13. For a formal discussion of returns to scale and variants of two-player collective-action games, see Heckathorn (1996).

14. Two high-school students drive toward each other with the options of driving straight or swerving. Swerving diminishes one's status, but if both drive straight, they crash.

15. Chicken IV could show negative externalities and twin social optima at (C, D) and (D, C).

16. Exercise 2.2 asks the reader to generate a sequential game of battle that illustrates a first-mover advantage.

17. See, for example, Binmore (1992, 180–91). Our Figure 4.1 illustrates the Nash bargaining model and Chapter 4's discussion relates it to exercises of power.

18. Because distributional conflict may hinder bargaining, a linear accounting of transaction costs may understate its difficulties; in fact, the probability of breakdown may increase exponentially in the number of disputed issues.

19. Similar r and p terms could also resolve CAPs related to chicken and battle.

20. N-player battle is more complex and will not be addressed in this book.

21. Chapter 3 will address this latter point.

22. This equation, with modified notation, is taken from Fehr and Schmidt (1999, 836–37).

23. Exercise 2.3 asks the reader to prove this assertion.

24. If the marginal participant contributes, then the number contributing becomes $n+1$.

25. In this model, provision and production are synonyms. We ignore consumption externalities.

26. These distinctions parallel Schelling's strict versus looser CPR-related problems (1978, 112–13).

27. If salmon fishing imposed negative externalities on cod fishers, then $D(n)$ would have a negative slope.

28. *N*-player chicken reflects *negative feedback*, whereby movement in one direction engenders a response in the opposite direction.

29. With discrete payoffs, some would do slightly better than others.

30. I borrow the $T(n)$ notation and the general function (but not its specifics) from Dixit, Skeath, and Reiley (2009, Chap. 12).

31. Sustainable management is unlikely if the agent acquired the resource for short-term financial speculation.

32. Exercises 2.6 and 2.7 address social optima in CPR games.

33. Dixit and Skeath (2004) use this example.

34. Exercise 2.8 asks the reader to draw the graph.

35. Multi-player assurance generates *positive feedback*, whereby movement in one direction encourages more of the same.

36. Complementary knowledge exists when one person's knowledge increases the productivity of another's.

37. Development economist Nicholas Stern (2006) calls climate change "the greatest and widest-ranging market failure ever seen."

38. What is more, involved firms, organizations, and agencies may themselves constitute rough coalitions of groups or individuals.

CHAPTER 3

1. Ostrom (1990) defines second-order CAPs as problems of institutional construction. Chapters 7–10 in this text similarly link institutions to second-order CAPs.

2. "Neither Coase nor many of the subsequent studies of transaction costs have attempted to define precisely what it is about transactions that is so costly" (North 1990, 28).

3. Attributes include things like the taste or juiciness of an orange.

4. Technically, the NYSE provides a *club good*: membership makes it exclusive, and for members it is nonrival.

5. Exercise 3.1 asks for a diagram.

6. Coase's (1960) two-player examples of negotiated resolutions implicitly assume either full enforcement by the courts (at no cost to the bargaining parties) or that such parties can costlessly and fully implement their agreements.

7. Note that $\gamma(N - n) = g_i$ (from (3.2)). Whenever $np_{ji} > c_i - \alpha$, potential defectors contribute; hence the impact of β from (3.2) is incorporated into α and c in (3.3).

8. Exercise 3.2 asks the reader for proof.

9. In this case, setting punishment $p = 0$, Figure 3.3 is equivalent to Figure 2.3 for $b(1) = \alpha c$, $b(1) - c(1) = (\alpha - 1)c$, and $b(2) - c(2) = (2\alpha - 1)c$; with $\gamma > 0$, no player will administer punishment.

10. Exercises 3.3–3.5 relate to items 1, 2, and 6.

11. Exercise 3.6 asks the reader to draw this game.

12. Exercise 3.7 asks for proof. An alternate test considers whether defecting forever would pay. Dixit, Skeath, and Reiley (2009, 399–409) offer a clear explanation of repeated PD games.

13. Exercise 3.8 asks for proof.

14. Exercise 3.9 asks the reader to design a more forgiving contingent strategy.

15. "By opportunism I mean self-interest seeking with guile" (Williamson 1985, 47). Guile implies strategic manipulation of information.

16. Likewise, the young and healthy may not purchase private medical insurance or the most reliable borrowers may not ask for loans. Alternate specifications can set q^e to permit some sales.

17. Dixit, Skeath, and Reiley (2009, Chap. 14) present intuitive signaling and screening models; they also review mechanism design.

18. Principals and agents can also appear in adverse selection problems.

19. While driving home on a day of drafting this chapter, I serendipitously overheard a National Public Radio interview conducted over someone's work phone. Jokingly, the reporter asked, "May I tell your boss?" The interviewee replied, "Please don't."

20. Reports of inefficient effort would typically amount to hearsay in court; perhaps fortunately, few laws prohibit actions like reading e-mail on the job.

21. We focus on effort, but similar logic applies to sharing information.

22. Even if contracts could specify all contingencies, the transaction costs of writing them out would preclude exchange for all but the simplest labor processes.

23. This model is derived from Bowles (1985); see also Bowles and Gintis (1992) and Bowles (2004). Similar models appear in Shapiro and Stiglitz (1984) and Bulow and Summers (1986).

24. See Bowles (1985, 21).

25. Here w is an input into the production of e, and the worker's body is a fixed factor with limited physical and mental capacity; hence diminishing returns.

26. In technical terms: the tangency shows a first-order condition for maximization, and diminishing returns to effort indicate fulfillment of the relevant second-order condition.

27. One could represent this outcome as the point on a resolution frontier that most favors the employer.

28. In an imperfect competition framework, the natural rate (or non-accelerating inflation rate of unemployment, NAIRU) can include involuntary unemployment (Carlin and Soskice 1990). Efficiency wage models provide a microfoundation for Keynesian unemployment (Summers 1988).

29. Monitoring and wages are substitute inputs into the production of effort (Bowles 1985).

30. See Dickens and Katz (1987).

31. See Exercise 3.11.

32. Credit screening with contingent renewal can also address adverse selection (risky clients). If credit histories are public knowledge, contingent renewal for a single agent may involve two or more principals.

33. "An equilibrium is a situation in which some motion or activity or adjustment or response has died away, leaving something stationary, at rest, 'in balance'" (Schelling 1978, 25).

34. See Dixit and Skeath (2004, 272–77) for a numerical version. If project success were perfectly correlated with managerial effort, owners could deduce (observe) effort from success: the P-A problem would vanish.

35. On a grander scale, social mechanisms may address both reporting problems of adverse selection and commitment problems of moral hazard (Myerson 2008).

CHAPTER 4

1. Cited in Bowles (2004).

2. Dahl (1957, 202–3) states: "A has power over B to the extent that he can get B to do something that B would not otherwise do." This definition allows nonstrategic effects (impact of bread purchase on an unknown farmer) and nonpower forms of influence (non-self-interested persuasion) and therefore is too broad (Bowles and Gintis 2008, Vol. 6, 566).

3. That is, in encounters that lend themselves to such models. Outcomes of power exchanges need not be Pareto optimal, hence operational bargaining frontiers may be internal (rather than Pareto frontiers).

4. Chapter 13 elaborates on the macro side of this argument.

5. The prior conceptual approach echoes the story of a drunk looking for his keys under a streetlight. A passing officer asks: "Where did you lose your keys?" The drunk points: "Over there." "Then why are you looking here?" "Because this is where the light is."

6. Chapters 5 and 6 introduce broader rationality concepts that allow for social preference and limited cognition.

7. Here the term "conventional" signifies the Walrasian approach or approximate translations thereof in many undergraduate texts.

8. Applying this logic to labor markets—where some argue that capital exerts power over labor—Paul Samuelson states: "in a perfectly competitive market it really does not matter who hires whom; so have labor hire capital" (1957, 894). Cited in Bowles (2004).

9. If $d_i = x_i$ for all i, the contract zone collapses to a single point: nothing to gain or lose.

10. Our use of "instruments of power" should not be confused with Lindblom's (1957) concept of instrumental power.

11. Communicating possible sanctions, as in threats, falls under type (i).

12. These distinctions are regions of a spectrum, not fully distinct categories. Boulding (1989) offers a somewhat different typology for three faces of power.

13. *Negative feedback* implies that an action generates a reaction that works against it. As in Adam Smith, self-interested opponents undermine exercises of power but not enough to eliminate political power.

14. Schattschneider (1960) develops the concept of mobilizing bias as a critique of pluralism. Bacharach and Baratz (1962) use this idea as the foundation of their second face of power.

15. In ongoing war, invasion likely constitutes an exercise of power1, whereas in international negotiations over the use of resources, invasion could indicate power2.

16. Evidence of power2 includes observable grievances related to observable nondecisions (Gaventa 1980, 15).

17. Miliband's (1969, 180–82) concept of "engineering of consent" is similar to power3.

18. It is easy to imagine examples of (iv) in contemporary politics.

19. If society at large is the source of bias, it is not clear who exercises power or how they do so. Digeser (1992) refers to such undirected power as the "fourth face" of power—a concept that this book does not develop.

20. The concepts of power1 and power2 both associate interest with preferences. For power3, "wants may themselves be a product of a system which works against their interests"; here Lukes (1974, 38) relates peoples' wants to what they would prefer if they had a choice. Because demands and grievances are usually not observable, identifying power3 empirically is difficult. Gaventa (1980) makes a contribution by observing changes in both the behavior and preferences of coal miners over time.

21. "In the first-dimensional approach . . . power may be understood primarily by looking at who prevails in bargaining over the resolution of key issues" (Gaventa 1980, 13–14).

22. In Section 4.2, manipulations of fallback positions are strategic moves.

23. Nash assumed equal bargaining strengths ($\alpha = \beta = 1/2$); here α and β are independent variables.

24. Exercise 4.1 asks the reader to design a two-stage game.

25. In the football example, the scalper's ticket price of $25 is x_{n-1} and the fan's value of watching the last quarter (also $25) is x_n; both keep $25 of a $50 value.

26. Exercise 4.2 presents an odd number of periods.

27. Exercise 4.3 asks for proof.

28. A comprehensive game may include both. The college slang associated with the term "pre-game"—drinking before a social event—actually fits the concept of a strategic move quite well.

29. For Schelling, "A strategic move is one that influences the other person's choice, in a manner favorable to one's self, by affecting the other person's expectations on how one's self will behave" (1960, 160).

30. An SPE is Nash in every subgame.

31. A statement made without a commitment of resources, would not alter expectations.

32. Even so, success is not guaranteed.

33. This outcome indicates an SPE of the altered game. In some cases, a *perfect Bayesian equilibrium* (Nash at every information set with expectations based on appropriate conditional probabilities) may be required.

34. Exercise 4.6 asks for an example.

35. *Strategic uncertainty* means uncertainty concerning either prior or contemporaneous moves of other players.

36. Exercise 4.7 offers an example.

37. Parties typically use threats for deterrence (prevention of an undesired action) and promises for compliance (attainment of a desired action).

38. Elster (1989a) notes some ambiguity concerning the definition of a fallback position. In cases where failed negotiation indicates termination of a relationship, the fallback indicates each party's best outside option. In cases where failure to agree does not end their relationship, fallbacks indicate relevant internal alternatives, such as a strike.

39. Basu's example: A may offer B a bribe to buy a vote. From one angle, A exerts power over B, but if B had previously signaled a reluctance to vote as A wishes, B may have induced A to pay, in which case, B exerts power over A. One might even regard the exchange of money for a vote as a voluntary market transaction.

40. Exercise 4.8 asks for proof.

41. The firm enjoys a *strategic asymmetry* arising from its ability to pre-commit (Bowles 2004, 249).

42. In the labor market, the supply side is the long side. In other markets, such as capital markets, the demand side is the long side.

43. Harsanyi (1962, 68) refers to enforcement rents as "the cost of A's power over B" (cited in Bowles and Gintis 1992, 340–41).

44. The effort model outcome is both technically and Pareto inefficient (Bowles and Gintis 1992).

45. One could ask why the bankers' models were systematically wrong—a CAP in its own right (Ferguson 2010).

46. Chapter 11's discussion of Basu's "man of influence" model presents a network example.

47. A full modeling of power3 would make an excellent exercise for a graduate course.

48. Mice in the children's story "belling the cat" face a similar CAP: all would benefit from placing a bell on the cat, but none wants to take the risk. Dixit and Nalebuff (1991) use this example.

49. If absolutely nobody has deliberately influenced such beliefs, then conditioned power is not "power" as defined here, though it would fit Digeser's (1992) concept of the fourth face of power.

50. Exercise 4.9 asks the reader to model this game. Chapter 8 uses the term "socially enforced convention" for a similar condition.

51. A series of challenges to the senator made by US Army lawyer Joseph Nye Welch (characterized by his famous remark broadcast on national TV, "have you no sense of decency, sir, at long last?") contributed decisively to the infamous senator's "dethroning" (Oshinsky 1983). Welch instigated the realization that McCarthy could, in fact, be challenged. Chapter 11 discusses the large shifts in ideas known as information cascades.

52. Akerlof's (1976) discussion of Robert Moses suggests a similar combination of power2 and power3.

CHAPTER 5

1. Reciprocal relationships are a key component of social capital. Chapter 8 will elaborate.

2. The association of self-interest with rationality adds an implicit normative dimension to seemingly positive analysis.

3. These preferences are also exogenous to economic processes.

4. Fehr and Fischbacher call the traditional approach the "extreme self-interest assumption" (2002, C1).

5. On the failings of standard rational actor models, see North (1990, Chap. 3).

6. Conditional cooperators initially cooperate if they expect others to do so and continue to cooperate if others reciprocate. Willing punishers sacrifice material gain to punish defectors.

7. Chapter 6 considers reciprocity as a type of social preference.

8. Gintis (2000) and Bowles (2004) use the term "strong reciprocity" for essentially the same concept. For Ostrom (2000a) a reciprocal player is a conditional cooperator who also willingly punishes or rewards.

9. Different concepts of legitimacy can reflect adherence to different social norms; Chapter 8 will elaborate.

10. See Sobel (2005) for a review of relevant theoretical and experimental literature.

11. Both terms appear in Bowles (2004).

12. Equation (5.1) is a simplified version of an equation in Falk and Fischbacher (2006). Technically, a_j includes i's expectation of j's choice of strategy within an entire strategy set, as well as what i thinks j expects i to do.

13. An alternative form of equation (5.1) could replace $\Delta(\pi_j + \phi_j)$ with a term indicating i's response.

14. In (5.1), the terms β and ψ signify that the product $\kappa\Delta(\pi_j + \phi_j)$ is respectively greater than or less than 0. We assume that the same value β follows strategy combinations (C, C) or (D, D) and that the same ψ follows (C, D) or (D, C). We relax this assumption in Section 5.3.

15. More generally, β and ψ are respective functions of n and $(N-n)$. For simplicity, we assume that $\beta(n) = n\beta$ and that (the function) $\psi(N-1-n) = (N-1-n)\psi$ for all $N \leq N^s$; we also drop q_i from equation (2.2).

16. Equation 5.3 is derived by comparing i's payoffs to C and D following j's move of D.

17. López-Pérez (2009) makes an analogous "law of demand" argument for following social norms.

18. Exercise 5.2 asks for proof of these two points and adds random assignment of the first mover.

19. Figure 5.2 resembles Camerer and Thaler's (2003) simplified version of Rabin's (1993) model.

20. The "framing" (descriptions or introductions) of problems can influence resolution by signaling intentions.

21. If only one player trusts the other, (C, D) follows.

22. Note that $\rho((2\alpha - 1)c + \beta) + (1 - \rho)\beta = \rho(2\alpha - 1)c + \beta$.

23. Exercise 5.4 asks the reader to modify Figure 5.3 to include reciprocal reward.

24. More generally, we could write a cost of punishment function $c_p(p)$; here we assume that $c_p(p) = c_p p$.

25. Equation (5.7) presents an alternative specification of $c_p p$.

26. More generally, if the r-type observes the e-type's move and if punishment is the final move, it makes no difference who moves first or whether the first two moves are simultaneous.

27. Costs rise with the number of communications, and members of large groups exhibit less familiarity than members of small ones.

28. Technically, the larger are β and ψ, the larger is the "basin of attraction" for a $(C, n = N - 1)$ equilibrium.

29. Economists and sociologists approach social exchange somewhat differently. Economists focus on relations to incentives and scarcity, typically with formal modeling, whereas sociologists focus on relations to social standing. Economic works include Holländer (1990), Kandel and Lazear (1992), Barron and Gjerde (1997), Gächter and Fehr (1999), and Fehr and Fischbacher (2002). Sociological works include Blau (1964) and Molm (1997).

30. "Since the social distance among people is likely to be smaller the more often they interact with each other, the repeatedness of interactions is positively correlated with the importance of approval incentives" (Gächter and Fehr 1999, 344). Reciprocal behavior responds to social proximity. Chapter 6 will address endogenous preferences.

31. The first assumption fits the idea that cooperating is a social norm. Chapter 8 extends this logic. Exercise 5.5 asks for a version of equation (5.7) with rewards for cooperators.

32. This value is found by taking the derivative of (5.7) with respect to p and setting it equal to 0.

33. Rewards to cooperators would reinforce this effect by raising the endpoint on the $C(n + 1)$ function.

34. Evolutionary game theory can address multi-player games of more than one type. See Chapter 6.

35. Exercise 5.6 asks the reader to develop parallel models.

36. Fehr and Falk (1999) find experimental evidence of reciprocity in employment relationships. Fehr, Gächter, and Kirchsteiger (1996) report that reciprocal employment relationships influence wage differentials. Fehr, Kirchsteiger, and Riedl (1993) report the emergence of non-market-clearing wages in fair-wage experiments.

37. The fair-wage model offers a Pareto improvement: both parties are somewhat better off.

38. Principal-agent problems and holdup problems are partially overlapping sets.

39. Complete contracting is impossible either because the investments are too complex or because actions, such as managerial effort, cannot be fully specified and observed (Grossman and Hart 1986).

40. Bénabou and Tirole (2006) model these problems. Bowles and Polanía-Reyes (2012) review the relevant literature and develop several models.

41. The core idea of this example appears in Sobel (2005).

42. Exercise 5.8 asks for a variant in which each player believes the other has good intentions.

CHAPTER 6

1. We augment Simon's notion of substantive rationality by including social preference. Our treatment is consistent with the game-theoretic use of nonmaterial payoffs (e.g., Dixit, Skeath, and Reiley 2009).

2. We alter notation slightly. Bolton and Ockenfels (2000) present a similar model.

3. When $\gamma_i = 0.5$, i is indifferent between giving up a dollar to reduce advantageous inequality and keeping the dollar.

4. Exercise 6.1 asks the reader for a graph.

5. A desire for aggregate efficiency is arguably a form of social preference to which many economists adhere. Smith (1759/1976) argues that humans are often inclined to sympathize with others—meaning to identify with their emotions. In our terminology, this is a form of social preference.

6. Camerer (2003) reviews the extensive experimental literature on these games.

7. Cox (2004) also finds experimental evidence of the importance of context in reciprocity.

8. According to these authors, "a decision-maker can more easily enforce his or her preferred actions against opposition by secretly constraining the set of available actions or by pretending that certain actions are not available" (Falk, Fehr, and Fischbacher 2003, 25).

9. For simplicity, we combine equation (5.1)'s $\pi_i(s) + \phi_i(s)$ into $\pi_i(s)$ and do the same for π_j. We also drop the t-term in $\kappa_j(a_j, t)$ and replace a_j with s^*.

10. Exercise 6.2 asks for a π_D equation that fits the Charness-Rabin concept of social welfare.

11. Hayek (1945) asserts that markets coordinate dispersed information.

12. The permanent-income hypothesis argues that consumers base current consumption decisions on rational calculations of expected permanent (rather than temporary) income (Friedman 1957).

13. Conlisk's (1996) discussion of asset bubbles pre-dated the 2007–2010 financial crisis.

14. This behavior violates monotonicity of preferences.

15. Samuelson (1969) argues that an "ergodic hypothesis" is necessary for scientific economics.

16. See Knight (1921). Keynes (1936/1964, Chap. 12) uses the same concept of uncertainty. North (2005) discusses a non-ergodic economy.

17. Basu (2000) differs and offers examples of internally inconsistent preferences. Gintis (2009b) does not use the term "bounded rationality," but he does state that his approach is consistent with that taken by Simon and Kahneman.

18. Kahneman notes that S1 shares these characteristics with immediate perception.

19. Selten (1978, 1990) posits three categories of thought: routine, imagination, and reasoning. Imagination—that is, forward-looking visualization of prospects or possibilities—could occupy the middle of the S1–S2 spectrum. For an insightful discussion of imagination in economics, see Bronk (2009).

20. Traditional theory presupposes reference-independent preferences that depend only on outcomes. Tracing the origins of utility theory back to Bernoulli (1738), Kahneman labels this utility concept "Bernoulli's error" (2003, 1455).

21. "Indeed, the incorrect assumption that initial endowments do not matter is the basis of Coase's theorem and of its multiple applications" (Kahneman 2003, 1457, citing Kahneman, Knetsch, and Thaler 1990). Thaler's (1980) experiments indicate an endowment effect whereby people would sell a mug they own for twice the price they would pay to get it.

22. Agents who use an "affect" heuristic base their judgments on initial like or dislike (Kahneman 2003).

23. This dynamic is analogous to cost minimization in economics.

24. Cognitive effort follows a traditional law of increasing costs.

25. Heiner (1983) uses a variation on this argument to assert that predictable behavior is possible only in the presence of rules that limit strategic options.

26. Exercise 6.3 asks for proof. Note that the problem-complexity boundary occurs at the value of environmental complexity (ξ) for which $e_{cs}(\xi) = e_{csL}$.

27. Arthur (1992) discusses experimental results, reported by Feldman (1962), in which subjects find patterns in purely random sequences of numbers and then formulate hypotheses concerning future sequences. Pattern-based reasoning fosters generalization and analogy, both of which underlie understandings and theories (North 2005).

28. Analogously, biologists discuss the "power" of natural selection: the rate at which selective adaptation to environmental change alters mean population characteristics over time. There is concern over whether the power of selection is sufficient to foster adequate adaptation—rather than extinction—of some species to rapid environmental change (Hendry 2005).

29. Unlike pure Bayesian expectations, sufficient observation of problems or inconsistencies can lead to complete reevaluation (Kahneman 2003). Mental models are analogous to Kuhn's (1970) scientific paradigms.

30. "There is a continuum of theories that agents can hold and act upon without ever encountering events which lead them to change their theories" (Hahn 1987, 324; cited in North 2005, 62).

31. Jehiel and Newman (2012) develop a game-theoretic model of social learning with incomplete information; their model implies that coordinative social mechanisms within firms (or other organizations) follow a temporal cycle, alternating between greater and lesser degrees of incentive compatibility. The cycle arises because observable mistakes or incentive-incompatible outcomes convey information that is unavailable under full incentive compatibility.

32. Chapter 8 discusses group insularity.

33. Chapter 7 defines institutions more precisely and distinguishes between institutions and organizations.

34. We cannot even list all possible strategies for a two-player game of chess, much less "solve" the game.

35. This is Simon's "satisficing" function (the goal is to do satisfactorily). A more general value function could be inserted into the model. Bounded rationality does not require satisficing.

36. For an insightful argument on how technical change increases uncertainty, see Bronk (2009).

37. Heiner relates $1 - \rho_r$ and ρ_w to Type I and Type II errors in statistical estimations (1983, 565, note 17).

38. An agent that knows ρ_g, $\rho_r(v)$, and $\rho_w(v)$ faces risk, not uncertainty as in a classical substantive rationality model. See Exercise 6.4.

39. Thus, unlike Bayesian maximization, the reliability criterion discards some possibly useful actions. "Intrinsic in behavioral rules is the ignoring of or lack of alertness to potential information" (Heiner 1983, 572).

40. "Uncertainty generates rules which are adapted only to likely or recurrent situations" (Heiner 1983, 567).

41. Consumers have difficulty forming preferences over items or activities for which they lack relevant experience (Heiner 1983, 567–69). For example, insurance contracts typically address contingencies that we hope never to experience.

42. Darwinian biological selection also does not imply optimality (Dawkins 2008).

43. In biology, relevant entities subject to reliability conditions could be molecular or physiological subsystems within organisms, individual organisms, species, or environments (Heiner 1983, 569).

44. Selection pressure is not reducible to a single maximizable scalar.

45. See Smith (1989). For an insightful recent text, see Gintis (2009a).

46. In biological terms, such inheritance constitutes a social phenotype.

47. This distinction is roughly analogous to that between pure strategy and mixed strategy NE in CGT. Other, more complicated EGT equilibrium concepts, such as stochastic stability, are also possible (Young 1996).

48. As in biological evolution, selection need not generate any form of social optimum (Gould and Lewontin 1979; Crespi 2000). Evolutionary game theory can represent endogenous preference formation (Bowles 1998a), the evolution of conventions and social norms (Young 1996; Basu 2000), and ultimately institutional formation (North 2005). Berninghaus, Güth, and Kliemt (2003) address evolutionary approaches to a range of cognitive ability, extending from full substantive rationality to "zero-intelligence," full evolutionary programming of decisions.

49. Exercise 6.5 asks the reader to draw the relevant diagrams for equations (6.6) and (6.7).

50. Equations (6.8)–(6.10) appear in Dixit, Skeath, and Reiley (2009) but with slightly different notation.

51. If m is not "small" (say, over 5%), then we need to use more complicated replicator equations to represent evolutionary outcomes and dynamics. See Gintis (2009a, Chaps. 11–13).

52. Exercise 6.6.b asks the reader to show these results.

53. Exercise 6.8 asks the reader to show an ESS from equation (6.10) satisfies (6.5).

54. Real-world bargaining heuristics are probably more nuanced than strategy *B*, but even so parties typically do not benefit from even considering myriad contingencies with which they have little experience (those that do not satisfy (6.5)).

55. Exercise 6.10 asks the reader to show that X and Y are each an ESS and to graph the model.

56. A more general model could let ε_x and ε_y represent mistakes in executing X and Y. In addition, a new, mistakenly introduced mutant strategy Z could enter with probability ε_z.

57. Exercise 6.11 asks the reader to explain the terms in equation (6.14).

58. Chapter 5 took such a disposition as exogenous.

59. "Nature can thus mislead her agents, in that preferences and fitnesses can diverge, but cannot mislead herself, in that high fitness wins the day" (Samuelson 2001, 226–27).

60. There is an extensive literature on the evolutionary origins of reciprocal behavior. See, for example, Trivers (1971, 2006), Hamilton (1964), Axelrod and Hamilton (1981),

Gintis (2000), Bowles and Gintis (2004a), and Berninghaus, Korth, and Napel (2007). Güth and Napel (2006) use IEGT arguments to explain the origins of inequality aversion.

61. In terms of equation (5.7), $u_p = (\psi_c - p) - p^2/\psi$. This simplified model assumes that, in (5.7)'s terms, $\beta_d = \psi_d = 0$. The dashed line between the j nodes on the second move indicates an *information set*, meaning that j has not observed i's move; effectively, this is a simultaneous game shown in extensive form.

62. Güth and Yaari (1992) derive this conclusion after considering all possible combinations of positive and negative values for u_p among two matched players along with mixed strategies.

63. For related arguments, see Axelrod (1984), Binmore (1994), Sethi and Somanathan (2001), Fehr and Henrich (2003), Bowles (2004), Boyd et al. (2005), and Trivers (2006) .

CHAPTER 7

1. This assertion presupposes Gaussian probability distributions of errors, negative-feedback processes, and no substantive interaction effects. The strong rational expectations hypothesis (Snowdon, Vane, and Wynarczyk 1994, 188–93) offers an example.

2. Acemoglu (2003) describes this idea as "the political Coase theorem."

3. North wrote this critique in 1990. Many contemporary neoclassical economists address informational CAPs. Rodrik (2007), for example, argues that informational market failures affect economic development and institutional evolution.

4. North's concept of institutions as "rules of the game" implies common knowledge.

5. Dequech (2009) also regards institutions as shared conceptual frameworks.

6. For Greif, rules alone (even when mutually understood) fail to explain the motivation for adherence.

7. The concept of a common understanding of a game's rules "captures the cognitive and informational roles of social rules" (Greif 2006a, 138).

8. Institutions are complicated social equilibria, and not everyone subscribes to prescribed behaviors. A social equilibrium is not a fully stable entity; it is an evolving and generally self-enforcing pattern of behavior and belief; social equilibria are simultaneously both targets for and attractors of multiple levels of individual and group activity.

9. Associated probabilities, however, are not necessarily well understood or Gaussian (see Chapter 6).

10. Hurwicz (2008) asserts that social mechanisms (institutions) establish game forms.

11. Chapter 12 elaborates on (i); Chapter 10 elaborates on (iii).

12. Analytical focus on influence 1a economizes on the cognitive costs to analysts and readers.

13. Exercise 7.3 asks the reader to explain.

14. Recall that a *focal point* is a single equilibrium among those for a multi-equilibrium game on which players' expectations converge. Epistemic game theory addresses the more general concept of correlated equilibria (Gintis 2009b). Chapter 8 summarizes this approach.

15. Bowles (2004) discusses this two-way causality between institutions and preferences.

16. Chapter 10 elaborates.

17. Conversely, some argue that—given the pervasiveness of informational and other transaction cost constraints—economic institutions create efficient outcomes (Coase 1937; Williamson 1985; Grossman and Hart 1986).

18. Knight (1992) and Bowles (2004) develop this point.

19. A basic supply/demand model offers an example of negative feedback: excess demand tends to increase the market price and so reduce the quantity demanded.

20. New institutions often complement old ones by extending earlier parameters of enforcement or benefits to coordination (Greif 2006a).

21. Hirschman notes that economists often overlook exit's ability to motivate improvement within firms—a key benefit of competition.

22. See Sections 3.3 and 4.4 for more on costs of exit and power.

23. A third option is to accept the status quo.

24. Exercise 7.6 asks the reader to develop an equation for the exit-voice tradeoff.

25. The severe initiation function in Hirschman's diagram is not relevant to this argument.

26. Once Joseph Stalin had gained power in the Soviet Union, he began executing Communist Party loyalists—including Lenin's close associate Leon Trotsky, whom Stalin's agents tracked down in Mexico. Anticipating this possibility, Trotsky had exited the Soviet Union, but apparently not his relationship with Stalin.

27. Exercise 7.8 asks the reader to use equation (6.5) for evaluating forms of voice.

CHAPTER 8

1. While driving on the wrong side of the road would likely invoke informal or formal sanction, risk of accident is enough to deter driving on the wrong side; hence coordination is the main enforcement mechanism.

2. Internalized norms may also serve as focal points (Dal Bó 2007).

3. The RLN concept is consistent with Heiner (1983): "Intrinsic to behavioral rules is the ignoring or lack of alertness to potential information, the reaction to which would direct behavior into more complex deviations from such rules" (572).

4. Note we interpret the abbreviation RLN to connote either a singular or a plural form. In subsequent pages, we will do the same for abbreviations for coordinating conventions and other types of norms.

5. A permission deontic indicates that others should not interfere with a permitted action (often a right). If citizens have the right to vote, nobody should interfere with their voting.

6. Bowles defines social norms as "ethical prescriptions governing actions toward others" (2004, 97). For Fehr and Gächter (2000), a social norm is a behavioral regularity among some population that is both expected and socially enforced. We combine these two conceptions.

7. Similarly: "We may follow a practice or a tradition not because we like it, or even think it defensible, but merely because we think that most other people like it" (Thaler and Sunstein 2009, 59).

8. Figure 8.1 is not a development path for informal institutions. Both initial position and movement (or its absence) may reflect factors other than longevity.

9. The ethical-content distinction between *CC* and TSN may also be a spectrum.

10. This lack of an explanation for development (or origins) is one of the difficulties in teaching the Nash equilibrium concept.

11. North (2005) stresses the importance of convergence of beliefs for socially beneficial outcomes.

12. Expectations converge from "the intrinsic magnetism of particular outcomes, especially those that enjoy prominence, uniqueness, simplicity, precedent, or some rationale that makes them qualitatively differentiable from the continuum of possible alternatives" (Schelling 1960, 70).

13. Observations of γ need not be independent; this is how correlated strategies differ from mixed strategies (Aumann 1987).

14. A correlated equilibrium is a broader concept than a Nash equilibrium; the former does not require that agents know (accurately expect) others' strategies (Aumann 1987). Any rationalizable set of strategies could be a correlated equilibrium (Gintis 2009b). For an intuitive discussion of rationalizability, see Dixit, Skeath, and Reiley (2009, 157–62).

15. Exercise 8.2 asks the reader to demonstrate this game outcome. This game appears in Gintis (2009b, 41–44). He offers another case where neither player knows the other's γ and both use Bayesian probabilities for best responses to γ.

16. Knowledge partitions are similar to information sets in extensive-form games. Note that a cell in a knowledge partition need not be the same as a cell in a normal-form game.

17. Gintis' (2009b) knowledge structure also includes a knowledge operator that specifies the conditions under which specific events are known.

18. For Gintis, norms interpret events and motivate certain responses; they indicate correlated equilibria. Formal institutions share choreographic functions. Chapter 10 elaborates.

19. Bowles (2004) develops this point.

20. Dequech's (2009) concept of a strong decision-theoretic norm is similar to our notion of a *CC*, noting the cognitive (or epistemic) content.

21. Some conventions (e.g., course schedules) can arise from formal decision processes, blurring the distinction between formal and informal institutions.

22. Various local prohibitions on inside smoking have also become norms. Chapter 10 will argue that complementarity between norms and laws makes the latter easier to enforce.

23. Imprecise definitions of "reasonable" and "contribute" may lead to disputes and exercises of power2 and power3.

24. An information set in an extensive-form game is "a collection of decision nodes satisfying: (i) the player has the move at every node in the information set, and (ii) when the play of the game reaches a node in the information set, the player with the move does not know which node in the information set has (or has not) been reached" (Gibbons 1992, 119).

25. Shame arises from a disjuncture between how we act and who we expect ourselves to be; perceived disjuncture increases in the number of adherents (López-Pérez 2010).

26. As with Chapter 5's r-types, ψ can motivate reciprocal punishment.

27. The H and L payoffs of Figure 2.2 are normalized to 1 and 0, respectively.

28. In Elster's (1989b) terminology, internalization strength can reflect the intensity of a norm's "grip on the mind."

29. In a multi-player version, assurance becomes path dependent; see Exercise 8.5.

30. We do not attempt to model the ensuing evolution of norms.

31. Mengel (2008) models interactions in which the degree of integration between groups of differing types determines the probabilities of mixed encounters and prospects for cooperation.

32. Figures 8.4, 8.5a, and 8.5b are the stage games for this indirect evolutionary model.

33. See Chapter 6 for a discussion of ESS. If players make errors with some probability, evolutionary outcomes are punctuated equilibria, with greater stability for e-types (see Exercise 8.6).

34. Exercise 8.8 asks the reader to demonstrate this point.

35. A more sophisticated model could include three types of players (see Exercise 8.9).

36. Starting with a low ρ (say, below 0.25), ρ could cross the 0.5 threshold by accident over a long time period; e-types are asymptotically ESS when ρ is low, and strictly ESS when ρ exceeds 0.5.

37. Mengel (2008) finds that if agents belong to distinct interacting groups, norms with intermediate levels of internalization can increase cooperation.

38. Here the c-types resemble Ostrom's (2000a) conditional cooperators.

39. We assume a sufficiently large N so that we ignore the difference between n and $n+1$.

40. In a more complicated model, c is a function of the number contributing. If taking the subway is C and driving is D, the equation $c = c(n)$ with $c' > 0$, could reflect crowding of subways.

41. Parameters c and ς affect the basins of attraction associated with the full-cooperation and full-defection NE.

42. Exercise 8.10 asks the reader to demonstrate these outcomes; Exercise 8.11 asks advanced readers for an IEGT model.

43. Recall from Chapter 5 that r-types engage in strategic positive reciprocity.

44. Exercise 8.12 asks the reader to rewrite equation (8.2) as $C(n)$ and $D(n)$ functions for r-types.

45. For discussion of reciprocal enforcement of social norms, see Carpenter, Matthews, and Ong'ong'a (2004) and López-Pérez (2009).

46. Exercise 8.13 asks advanced readers to develop one or more three-player IEGT models.

47. Reciprocity norms can be ancillary to other, more specific norms (see Chapter 10 on ancillary laws). Exercise 8.14 asks advanced readers to model adherence to Ψ_R.

48. Strategies (i) and (ii) apply A- and C-statements; strategy (iii) mixes I- and D-statements.

49. Note the resemblance of the statement in equation (8.11) to Section 6.5's concept of an evolutionary neutral strategy.

50. Exercise 8.15 asks the reader for proof.

51. Perhaps everyone "knows" that Swedes do not cut in line whereas some Americans do.

52. Exercise 8.16 asks the reader to explain four other cell entries.

53. For an economic discussion, see Bowles (2004). For biological examples, see Wilson (1975) and Wilson and Dugatkin (1997).

54. Jenkins (1996) asserts that society imposes identity categories (e.g., male or female) on individuals, but individuals influence their identity by choosing groups with which to associate. We use the broader term "social category" to include both imposed and chosen groupings. For an insightful review of approaches to identity, see Frank (2011).

55. Identities can serve as quasi-parameters: roughly fixed in the short run but nonetheless slowly evolving.

56. Identity is a source (or motivator) of social preference.

57. Padavic (1991) describes this experience.

58. Exercise 8.17 asks the reader to demonstrate the relations in these four cases.

59. Sen does not refer to identity, but he notes an example where one person takes offense at another's reading *Lady Chatterley's Lover.*

60. Cited in Akerlof and Kranton (2010, 102). On a lighter note, Nelson (1993, 5) reports that, when asked about her father during a job interview, the popular song "Papa Was a Rolling Stone" went through her head (she notes that, actually, her father was a dentist).

61. Street-level drug dealers ("foot soldiers") earn about $200 per month (Levitt and Venkatesh 2000) but face far greater risks than low-paid formal-sector workers, such as fast food workers.

62. Members of minority groups who try to blend in may be held to higher cultural standards than members of dominant groups.

63. Chapter 13 asserts that individual investments in human capital respond to average local investments. Exercise 8.18 asks advanced readers to develop a model of social exclusion.

64. For discussion of how employee participation affects productivity, see Levine (1995).

65. Prendergast's (1999) review reports mixed results on the benefits of incentive pay. For a critique of sole reliance on the use of explicit material incentives in policy, see Bowles (1998b).

66. Akerlof and Kranton (2010, Chap. 5) provide a variety of instructive examples.

67. Akerlof and Kranton (2010) note, however, that excessive unit loyalty may create tendencies to cover up members' mistakes.

CHAPTER 9

1. Experiments show that groups that lack internal communication tend to overuse CPRs more than a Nash equilibrium would indicate (though the NE already indicates some overuse). See, for example, Ostrom, Walker, and Gardner (1992).

2. Ostrom (1990) and Ostrom, Gardner, and Walker (1994). Platteau and Seki (2001) and Poteete, Janssen, and Ostrom (2010) review many studies.

3. See Graeff (2009).

4. The related concept of clubs (Buchanan 1965) addresses voluntary associations that provide public goods exclusively to designated club members. See also Sandler (2002).

5. According to Dasgupta (2011, 2), "if the idea of social capital is to serve a useful purpose in economics, it should be interpreted as interpersonal networks where members develop and maintain trust in one another to keep their promises by the device of 'mutual enforcement' of agreements."

6. Chapter 11 addresses social networks.

7. Note the similarity to Chapter 3's moral hazard: moral hazard signifies lack of trust.

8. Dasgupta (2000, 331) distinguishes between having trust and having confidence in others. The latter assesses ability to undertake actions. We might lack confidence in the police if they lack sufficient training, but we would distrust corrupt police regardless of their training.

9. Here we follow Dasgupta (2011) and Ostrom and Ahn (2009) and diverge somewhat from Putnam (1993).

10. This statement is consistent with Dasgupta (2000), though he does not use the production analogy.

11. Organization-specific social capital for firms or agencies includes, for example, internal incentives (salaries) and personnel policies. Organizational loyalty can offset incentives to defect (Stiglitz 2000), as when loyal employees do not leave for higher-paying jobs.

12. "To create social capital in a self-conscious manner, individuals must spend time and energy working with each other to craft institutions—that is, sets of rules that will be used to allocate the benefits derived from an organized activity and to assign responsibility for paying costs" (Ostrom 2000b, 178).

13. Significant social dynamics also accompany human capital development (learning). But human capital can be regarded as an individual attribute.

14. Mike McGinnis suggested the third-order CAP idea to me. My former research assistant, Catherine Scott, gave me the student organization example.

15. Similarly, investment in human capital is a deliberate act, but skills may also emerge more or less spontaneously from unplanned social interactions.

16. See Apesteguia and Maier-Rigaud (2006) on distinctions between public-good and CPR problems.

17. Exercise 9.1 asks the reader to show that resource use at the NE is not socially optimal. Equation (9.1)'s model appears in Ostrom, Gardner, and Walker (1994).

18. See Lipset (1963) on the role of legitimacy in politics.

19. Ostrom (2000b) cites Schelling (1960) and Elster (1979) on signaling pre-commitment. Exercise 9.2 asks creative readers to design a signaling model of pre-commitment. See Dixit and Skeath (2004, Chap. 9) for an intuitive signaling model.

20. Exercise 9.3 asks the reader to justify these statements concerning cost and benefit rules.

21. Upstream users may also have less incentive to contribute to maintenance. With respect to use, the upstreamers face an internal multi-player PD game: no individual has an incentive to limit use (Lam 1998).

22. Distributional conflicts typically possess normative dimensions that are reflected in the rhetoric of adversaries.

23. Dependency influences bargaining power (Bacharach and Lawler 1981). A prior strategic move by team A to establish its upstream advantage would indicate exercise of power2.

24. Exercise 9.4 asks the reader to demonstrate the relationships shown in Table 9.1.

25. Exercise 9.6 asks the reader to describe three possible enforcement mechanisms for an irrigation agreement and to model one of them.

26. For reviews, see Camerer (2003), Ostrom, Gardner, and Walker (1994), and Poteete, Janssen, and Ostrom (2010).

27. The model uses an "asymmetric, forward-looking, non-binary approach" (Isaac, Walker, and Williams 1994, 23). Here short-term anticipations are learning experiments rather than CGT deductions.

28. This model could also reflect the nondistributional aspects of a CPR problem by defining "contribution" as limiting one's use of the resource.

29. This success criterion is consistent with Simon's (1955) model as described in Section 6.4.

30. Contributions c_j may differ among players.

31. By contrast, for CPR problems, resource value does not increase with group size. The Nash equilibrium level of use increases in group size, but the socially optimal level of use does not—indicating a tendency toward greater overuse as group size increases (Ostrom, Gardner, and Walker 1994).

32. Exercise 9.7 asks the reader to demonstrate that C^* increases in N.

33. The definitions of "medium" and "large" depend on the pertinent problem and its context.

34. Exercise 9.8 asks advanced readers to augment equation (9.5) so as to address sanctioning.

35. Huck and Rey-Biel (2006) use conformity dynamics to model the emergence of team leadership.

36. Bowles (1985) labels the Coasian conception of the firm "neo-Hobbesian."

37. Employees usually can quit firms at a cost. Citizen exit from government becomes more difficult as we move from local to regional to national levels. Firms, however, can often exit government via relocation or outsourcing.

38. Carpenter et al. (2009) state that their model can apply to large teams.

39. Exercise 9.9 asks the reader to show that equation (9.6) is a variant of equation (2.2).

40. We assume a group large enough that the distinction (made in Chapters 2 and 5) between N and $N-1$ is irrelevant.

41. Contracts for punishments would be incomplete for reasons indicated in Chapter 3.

42. For technical completeness: $c_{pi}(0) = c'_{pi}(0) = c''_{pi}(0) = 0$: the cost of zero punishment along with its first and second derivatives is zero. Also, $c'''_{pi}(p_{ij}) \geq 0$ for $p_{ij} > 0$ (Carpenter et al. 2009, 3).

43. The product λb_j here is similar to κ in equation (5.2).

44. Exercise 9.10 asks the reader to prove this point. Exercise 9.11 asks the reader to show that equation (9.8) is a variant of equation (5.2).

45. Exercise 9.12 asks advanced readers to construct an indirect evolutionary model that indicates why reciprocity norm Ψ_R could be successful.

46. Huck and Kosfeld (2007) design an evolutionary model of norm enforcement via self-organized neighborhood watch arrangements.

47. Coase (1960) implicitly assumes this dichotomy between full and no property rights. Demsetz (1967) discusses communal property rights, but assumes prohibitive transaction costs to establishing rights 1–4, and so effectively equates communal property rights with nonownership.

48. Schlager and Ostrom (1999) and Poteete, Janssen, and Ostrom (2010) review multiple studies. These authors cite Brunckhorst (2000), Paavola and Adger (2005), Trawick (2003), and Degnbol and McCay (2007) as studies that use these property rights typologies based upon extensive, worldwide surveys.

49. Poteete, Janssen, and Ostrom (2010, 228–31) provide a more detailed list.

50. See Ostrom, Gardner, and Walker (1994) on the importance of face-to-face communication and for a review of related experimental work.

51. Exercising voice is an art (Hirschman 1970).

52. Generating trust indicates emotional coordination (Section 5.2).

53. Moe (1990, 1991) discusses similar effects in more general terms. Similarly, Acemoglu, Johnson, and Robinson (2004a) note the importance of broad participation in the design of political institutions.

54. Poteete, Janssen, and Ostrom (2010, 100–101) present this list in detail and relate it to many other studies.

55. Keohane (1984) discusses cooperation among advanced developed countries.

56. See also McGinnis (2005). A human inclination toward self-organization may be automatic, but success is not.

57. Platteau and Seki (2001) note that a single hierarchical firm could address risk pooling but then the boat owners would become employees. Without residual claimancy (see Section 9.3), they would lack incentives to carefully manage the resource, monitor each other, and share information. In such cases, management becomes an external enforcement agency.

58. Problems arise either if high-performing members attach too little value to being best or if low performance generates too much stigma (Platteau and Seki 2001).

59. Bloch, Genicot, and Ray (2007, 66) define the *degree of fragility* of a norm as the probability that its enforcement constraints will fail in relevant states of the environment.

60. Communal projects of the Kofyar in Nigeria disproportionately benefit large land owners. Likewise, "in India, access to the commons is often restricted to the privileged (for example, caste Hindus), who are also among the bigger land owners" (Dasgupta 2000, 358).

61. Note the similarity to conditioned power (see Section 4.5). Sen (1999) makes similar arguments concerning localized restrictions on the rights of women and others.

62. For discussion of the importance of social cohesion in development, see Easterly (2006).

63. Air pollution provides an example.

64. Factors like residential location and ascriptive S1 cognitive processes (see Section 6.3) can account for such groupings. Bowles and Gintis (2004b) define *parochialism* as a property of social networks whereby members identify themselves on the basis of religious faith, ethnicity, or loyalty. On international resource conflict, see Klare (2002).

65. Residents of Scandinavian social democracies have expressed fears that immigration will undermine cooperative social norms (Lindbeck 1995).

CHAPTER 10

1. See Gelt (1997) on problems with US-Mexican Colorado River treaties.

2. Recall from Chapter 3 that the distinction between second and third parties depends on context. For a local medical practice, the American Medical Association is a third-party enforcer; for the profession as a whole, it is a second-party enforcer.

3. The rulemaking hierarchy for informal rules is often less precise.

4. A paraphrase of Harold Lasswell's (1936) famous title: *Politics: Who Gets What, When, and How.*

5. Political rules "broadly define the hierarchical structure of the polity, its basic decision structure, and the explicit characteristics of agenda control" (North 1990, 47).

6. Chapter 12 lists a more detailed set of rule categories related to rule intent from Ostrom and Crawford (2005).

7. On group failure and the analogy with market failure, see McGinnis (2011b). Chapter 12 will relate group failure to policy.

8. Section 10.3 elaborates on this concept, citing Ostrom, Tiebout, and Warren (1961).

9. "Groups regard a political system as legitimate or illegitimate according to the way in which its values fit with theirs" (Lipset 1963, 64).

10. North states: "The growth of knowledge is dependent on complementary institutions, which will facilitate and encourage such growth and there is nothing automatic about such development" (2005, 99).

11. These types of exchange relationships are regions of a spectrum rather than distinct categories.

12. Human tendencies toward social cooperation arise from the evolutionary processes over millennia (Boyd and Richerson 1985). Boyd and Richerson (1992) model the evolution of reciprocal behavior.

13. Among the Maghribi, forced exit offered a harsh punishment, and the threat of forced exit indicated a form of community voice.

14. Exercise 10.1 asks the reader to diagram auxiliary transactions for the Mediterranean CRS and Maghribi traders.

15. Before the industrial revolution, nearly all people lived at close to subsistence levels; increases in agricultural productivity facilitated larger populations (Fogel 2004). The economic theories of Adam Smith, Thomas Malthus, and Karl Marx all reflect this historical legacy.

16. Recall Chapter 6's example that a two-player, two-strategy game has four possible outcomes; a three-player, three-strategy game has 27 (3^3) outcomes; and so forth.

17. In terms of epistemic game theory, agents' knowledge partitions are too imprecise to distinguish between conditions for good and bad use.

18. Adam Smith recognized this problem: "In the progress of the division of labour, the employment of the far greater part of those who live by labour . . . comes to be confined to a few very simple operations. . . . The man whose whole life is spent in performing a few simple operations . . . has no occasion to exert his understanding or to exercise his invention in finding out expedients for removing difficulties which never occur" (1776/1976, Vol. II, 385).

19. The labels "third" and "second" party depend on the level of analysis in nested hierarchies, ranging from local to macro levels. Higher levels exert third-party influence over lower levels, as states do over municipalities.

20. Laws are outcomes of precisely specified collective-choice rules that are conditioned by anterior collective-choice and constitutional rules.

21. Any cost of administering punishment less than δx would suffice.

22. Though rarely used in stable systems, material retaliation against enforcers is often feasible. Even in stable systems, social retaliation is not uncommon.

23. Exercise 10.2 asks the reader to demonstrate.

24. Exercise 10.3 asks the reader to show this relationship.

25. Basu calls this assertion the "core theorem of law and economics" (2000, 117).

26. Social rules possess some of the same advantages.

27. Mechanism design theory (e.g., Maskin 2008) evaluates (formal) institutions as social mechanisms whose design reflects specific social goals. Chapter 12 will regard formal rules as outcomes of policy decisions.

28. Lynching operates on informal institutional foundations.

29. Gutiérrez, Hilborn, and Defeo (2011) report on benefits of community governance of 130 fisheries.

30. Some of the enthusiasm for "states' rights" in the US accords with material self-interest.

31. By 1965, the civil rights movement had shifted social norms and political expectations enough so that the 1965 Voting Rights Act (unlike the 1957 Civil Rights Act) was actually enforced: it became an institution.

32. The Preamble of the US Constitution states: "We the People of the United States, in Order to form a more perfect Union, establish Justice, insure domestic Tranquility, provide for the common defense, promote the general Welfare, and secure the Blessings of Liberty to ourselves and our Posterity, do ordain and establish this Constitution for the United States of America." Although the Founders lacked contemporary vocabulary, elements on this list are fundamental national public goods that suggest potential for many more specific public goods.

33. The title of Hurwicz's (2008) paper: "But Who Will Guard the Guardians?"

34. Polycentric governance may transcend geographical boundaries. The American Medical Association enforces regulations across multiple localities. McGinnis (2011b), citing Hooghe and Marks (2001, 2003), distinguishes between type I (geographically based) and type II (transaction-based) polycentric governance.

35. Andersson and Ostrom (2008) investigate worldwide polycentric systems of resource management. Ostrom (2010) reviews empirical studies on water districts and law enforcement.

36. Events of 2011–2012 suggest that CAPs related to provision of the euro have not been fully resolved.

37. Recall that public services, once established, often exhibit the properties of common-pool resources.

38. Collective consumption units may arrange for provision in five basic manners: own production, contracting with a private firm, contracting with a different government

agency, establishing standards for various producers and allowing consumers to choose among them, and issuing vouchers to consumers (Ostrom and Ostrom 1977).

39. Our approach to nested systems uses Heiner's concept of hierarchical structure (1983, 583–86).

40. Exercise 10.6 asks the reader to relate this argument concerning the use of strategies at level v to Heiner's reliability condition.

41. "Consequently, the only way more sophisticated behavior could arise from such subsystems is for a number of them to evolve into the subcomponents of a still larger system" (Heiner 1983, 583).

CHAPTER 11

1. These percentages were calculated using Table 3.1 in Watts (2003, 94).

2. Most of these examples and citations appear in Vega-Redondo's (2007) comprehensive review.

3. For a nontechnical introduction to network theory, see Barabási (2003) and Watts (2003). For a more formal treatment, see Jackson (2008). For complexity in large networks, see Vega-Redondo (2007).

4. Definitions and most notation used in the following two subsections are borrowed from Jackson (2008) and/or Vega-Redondo (2007).

5. This equation specifies the graph of a network.

6. In a *directed network*, the number of links $g_{ij} \neq g_{ji}$.

7. A *walk* is a sequence of links between nodes that may "visit" nodes more than once.

8. Nodes 1–3, though connected, are not a component because they are only a part of the larger connected subset 1–4.

9. Here $g_{ij} = g_{ik} = 1$ for nodes c, d, and e, since all are connected to i, but $g_{jk} = 1$ for both $\{c, d\}$ and $\{c, e\}$ and $g_{jk} = 0$ for $\{d, e\}$. Hence the sum of products $g_{ij}g_{ik}g_{jk}$ for all possible combinations of j and k (that is, $\{cd, ce, de\}$) $= 1 + 1 + 0 = 2$. Exercise 11.1 considers a variation of this configuration.

10. For a related macro-level measure of overall clustering, see Jackson (2008).

11. Exercise 11.2 asks the reader to calculate average clustering coefficients for each section and for the entire network.

12. See Vega-Redondo (2007).

13. Note the similarity to a discount factor (same symbol).

14. The betweenness centrality of a network sums b^i over all nodes; see Vega-Redondo (2007, 35–36).

15. This distinction resembles that in sociology between structure and agency (Watts 2003). Free agency generates networks without regard to structure.

16. Technically, this is a one-dimensional lattice network (Vega-Redondo 2007).

17. A power-law distribution for degrees: $p(\kappa) = m^\gamma \kappa^{-\gamma-1}$, where m is the rate of node formation and γ is the power distribution parameter (Jackson 2008, 132).

18. This model applies where "bureaucratic norms are sluggish" (Basu 2000, 160).

19. For Basu, compliance is a perfect Bayesian equilibrium.

20. For agent n, we consider agent $j = 0$ to be $j + 1$.

21. Note the similarity between P's influence and Chapter 4's discussion of conditioned power (see also Basu 2000, Chap. 6). Exercise 11.3 asks the reader to model a CAP that P's opponents would face in undermining her influence.

22. The present discussion of the DeGroot model closely follows that in Jackson (2008, Chap. 8).

23. Here we depart slightly from Jackson, who defines a leader more narrowly as an agent for whom $\lambda_{ii} = 1$ (so that others have no impact on the leader's updates).

24. Exercise 11.4 asks the reader to rewrite equations (11.8) and (11.10) to reflect the influence network of P and five bureaucrats.

25. Figure 11.7 is borrowed from Figure 1.1 in Jackson (2008, 4), which is based on data from Padgett and Ansell (1993).

26. Exercise 11.5 asks the reader to show this outcome. The election story is fictional, but the Medici were powerful.

27. Wasserman and Faust (1994) developed the concept of a bipartite network.

28. Social identity here focuses on group affiliation; Chapter 8's individual identity adds other components as well.

29. There is some debate over the degree to which homophily depends on choice as opposed to limited opportunities arising from location, organizations, rules, and the like (Kossinets and Watts 2009).

30. Both voluntary and involuntary group affiliations can reflect and contribute to social identity.

31. Affiliation becomes "the substrate on which the actual network of social ties is enacted" (Watts 2003, 118).

32. One can characterize an affiliation hierarchy using only parameters K and b (Watts, Dodds, and Newman 2002). A more complicated model could assign different branching coefficients to each point.

33. Categories represent social structure based upon identities (Watts, Dodds, and Newman 2002). We assume that social categories and ensuing hierarchies are independent. Technically, an agent's social identity is her position in an H-dimensional coordinate vector, where H is the number of relevant hierarchies.

34. Watts, Dodds, and Newman (2002) assume that affiliation decisions are sufficiently complicated that randomness is a reasonable approximation.

35. More precisely: choose link distance x with $\rho(x) = \gamma \exp[-\alpha x]$; γ is a normalizing constant; parameter α denotes the importance of homophily in link formation (Watts, Dodds, and Newman 2002, 1303; I have modified notation slightly).

36. In Milgram (1967), randomly chosen residents of Omaha and Boston were asked to use social connections to locate a Boston stockbroker. Each resident was asked to mail a document to the one person they knew, on a first-name basis, who they thought had the best chance of sending the document to the stockbroker; the recipients were then asked to do the same. Among the 20% of letters that reached the Boston broker, the mean number of intermediaries was 5.2. See also Travers and Milgram (1969).

37. Agents i and j can be close on dimension h_1 while j and k are close on dimension h_2. Social distance violates triangle inequality and hence is not a true metric of distance.

38. This experiment reverses the procedure used in Milgram (1967). See note 36.

39. Interestingly, Watts, Dodds, and Newman (2002) predict that most efficient searches use two or three social dimensions.

40. By contrast, neither computer networks nor electric power networks are searchable by their own (nonhuman) nodes.

41. In this model, the letters S, I, and R stand (respectively) for the number of susceptible, infected, and recovered individuals.

42. An intuitive explanation of these equations (using slightly different notation), along with illustrations and exercises, appears at https://www.math.duke.edu/education/ccp/materials/diffcalc/sir/sir1.html.

43. A more complicated model could add immunization.

44. Exercise 11.6 asks for an illustration.

45. An agent's choice in this model represents a type of binary decision with externalities (see Schelling 1973).

46. Watts (2002) uses a random network (Poisson distribution of degrees), but equations (11.15) and (11.16) could also be applied to scale-free or other degree distributions.

47. More generally, agent i's *critical upper degree* (d_{ci}) is the maximum degree for which agent i becomes an early adopter. If $\tau_{ai} = 1/3$, $d_{ci} = 3$; if $\tau_{ai} = 1/4$, $d_{ci} = 4$; and so on (Watts 2003). Exercise 11.7 offers examples.

48. If $\bar{d} < 1$, network and epidemic dynamics are the same (Watts 2002).

49. If $\bar{d} > 14$, stability precludes cascades (Watts 2002).

50. The literature refers to such a cluster as a "percolating" cluster (Vega-Redondo 2007; Jackson 2008).

51. Einstein's equation $e = mc^2$ is an idea with tremendous appeal. If someone else had arrived at the same idea 20 years earlier or if Einstein had lived in Russia instead of Switzerland, it might have gone nowhere.

CHAPTER 12

1. Readers may recognize this final example as a description of a cap-and-trade system.

2. Discussion of policy in this text is necessarily limited. For an intuitive introduction, see Birkland (2011).

3. See Ostrom (2005, 2011); McGinnis (2011a).

4. This section could have appeared in Chapter 10, but it applies more directly to the present discussion. Exercise 12.1 asks the reader to relate the IAD framework to Section 10.3's discussion of governance levels.

5. For a summary, see Ostrom (2007); for more detail, see Ostrom (2005).

6. This concept fits with Greif's (2006a) assertion that transactions are the basic unit of institutional analysis. An action situation is the context within which specific transactions occur.

7. The net payoff from winning an election, for example, can depend on salary earned, opposition encountered once in office, and utility valuations of all such factors.

8. Figure 12.2 is taken, with a few wording changes, from Ostrom (2007, 45).

9. For collective-choice and constitutional-choice interactions, we use "arena" as a synonym for "situation." For metaconstitutional interactions, we use "environment" as a synonym for "situation."

10. Private constitutional rules, such as corporate bylaws, also reflect historical legacies.

11. See Ostrom and Crawford (2005, 193–210) and Ostrom (2007, 36–39). An earlier list appears in Ostrom, Gardner, and Walker (1994).

12. In game-theoretic terms, positions are sets of nodes in a game to which certain actions will be assigned; positions may also indicate categories of players (e.g., first mover).

13. Interpreted game theoretically, authority rules and physical laws determine the shape of game trees in extensive-form games.

14. Levin and Nalebuff (1995) list 13 methods for ranking votes. In terms of game theory, aggregation rules specify how combinations of strategies are transformed into intermediate or final outcomes (Ostrom, Gardner, and Walker 1994).

15. Karotkin and Paroush (1994) discuss six types of asymmetric aggregation rules among four-member groups.

16. In game-theoretic terms, information rules affect information sets in extensive-form games, subjective priors and conditional probabilities in Bayesian and epistemic games, and knowledge partitions in epistemic games.

17. Pierson (1993) emphasizes the information feedback properties of policy.

18. Payoff rules can arise from different aggregation procedures: contracts emerge from negotiations, whereas pay schedules typically arise from managerial or committee decisions.

19. The EPA "allocated each affected unit . . . a specified number of [SO_2] allowances related to its share of heat input during the baseline period" (Stavins 1998, 70).

20. Cap-and-trade systems also involve position rules, boundary rules, aggregation rules, and payoff rules.

21. Choice and scope rules are residuals: any rule that is not one of the other five types is either a choice rule, if it focuses on action, or a scope rule, if it focuses on outcome (Ostrom and Crawford 2005, 209–10).

22. Part of the appeal of libertarian economics arises from its implication that society can avoid or minimize politics in the economy: market exit mechanisms reduce the need for the politics of voice. Since property rights are complex rules, however, politics is inescapable, and attempts to ignore it can lead to serious policy error.

23. Exercises 12.2 and 12.3 ask readers to relate Ostrom's CPR list to horizontal and vertical rule classifications. Ostrom (2005, Chap. 8) elaborates on rule types and self-governance of CPRs.

24. Exercise 12.4 asks the reader to apply rule types to political and economic institutions.

25. Chapter 13's distinction between de facto and de jure power relates to institutionalization of policy.

26. Stone actually uses the term "rules" rather than "mandates," but our use of "rules" applies to inducements, rights, and powers as well. "Mandate" is more precise and accords with Stone's argument.

27. Because the rules of the game are understood, these policies are not strategic moves.

28. Such changes (in collective-choice rules) involve complex combinations of the seven horizontal rule types.

29. On sulfur dioxide provisions of the 1990 Clean Air Act, see Stavins (1998); for a general discussion, see Hubbell et al. (2010).

30. Campbell (2012) reviews literature on the feedback impacts of implemented policy on political systems, via its influence on public beliefs.

31. Branch's (1988, 1998) detailed history of the civil rights movement discusses this legislation. See also Patterson (1996).

32. Wallace's 1963 inauguration speech was written by Ku Klux Klan member Asa Carter (Raines 1998).

33. Using similar reasoning, Basu (2000) asserts that government is endogenous.

34. Firms are groups, but some forms of group failure do not involve markets.

35. Gelt (1997) addresses these issues.

36. Figure 12.3 is a copy of Figure 2.7.

37. Analogously, Hardin (1968) suggests selective government-mandated incentives to align individual and group interests.

38. For details, see http://unfccc.int/meetings/doha_nov_2012/meeting/6815.php.

39. Ironically, both Hardin and Coase assume effective third-party enforcement. Hardin resolves CPR problems via enforceable government mandates. For Coase, the judicial system can fully enforce negotiated contracts that fully specify relevant contingencies. Neither author appreciates the complexity of second- and third-party interactions and relationships between formal and informal institutions.

40. Here reform can be good or bad: the Nazis reformed the policy structure of Weimer Germany.

41. Dawkins (2008) asserts that evolutionary modification resembles redesigning an airplane engine on the basis of its existing configuration—while the plane is already in flight. This analogy fits reform based on institutionally shaped patterns of cognition.

42. Entrepreneurs' motivations may be material (income), value-driven (fairness), or solution-driven (as in seeking to apply "pet" solutions). Supply-side advocates may seek problems that suggest tax cuts; environmentalists may seek problems that suggest environmental regulation.

43. Sabatier and Weible (2007) use the term "meso" for intermediate.

44. "A symbol is anything that stands for something else. Its meaning depends on how people interpret it, use it, or respond to it" (Stone 2002, 137).

45. Policy subsystems operate at overlapping levels. A local housing agency might be part of housing and land-use subsystems at state and federal levels (Sabatier and Weible 2007, 193).

46. Sabatier and Weible model a two-coalition subsystem mediated by policy brokers. "The vast majority of policymaking occurs within policy subsystems and involves negotiations among specialists" (2007, 193). Mills (1956) describes an "iron triangle" (policy monopoly) of top-level military, industry, and US government officials.

47. For a review, see Campbell (2012).

48. Recall that with negative feedback, a disruption induces motion in the opposite direction, whereas with positive feedback, disruption induces continued motion in the same direction.

49. The 1969 banning of the insecticide DDT marked the end of the pesticide subsystem (Baumgartner and Jones 1993, 97).

50. Kingdon (2003) draws upon the garbage can model of "organized anarchies" (Cohen, March, and Olsen 1972); he critiques Lindblom's (1959) incrementalist approach.

51. Drucker (1985) notes that the supply of time is completely inelastic.

52. "Political manipulation aims primarily to provide meaning, clarification, and identity" (Zahariadis 2007, 69). Within firms, employers and workers interpret established workplace customs to their own advantage (Doeringer and Piore 1971).

53. Birkland (2011, 169–76) discusses levels of agendas. Kingdon (2003, 1) quotes Victor Hugo: "Greater than the tread of mighty armies is an idea whose time has come."

54. The problem stream affects perceptions of conditions—situations that humans cannot alter—as opposed to problems—situations that humans can affect.

55. American scientists failed to notice the decline because they had programmed their computers to discard observations outside of an expected range, and a value of 30% exceeded their expectations (Rowlands 1995, 55). In our terminology, their mental models precluded considering such observations until British data induced re-evaluative learning.

56. The network principles of Section 11.4's information cascades apply to transmissions within the policy and political streams.

57. Zahariadis cites March and Romelaer (1976) on an attention function that responds to these variables.

58. Beveridge did not anticipate such a large impact; in the context of the war, his appeal to British ideals fell on receptive ears.

59. "Waves of popular enthusiasm surrounding a given issue provide the circumstances for policymakers to create new institutions to support their programs" (Baumgartner and Jones 1993, 83).

60. Many other conditions (high unemployment, rapidly rising food prices) cultivated public susceptibility to such an apparently random dramatic event.

61. Baumgartner and Jones (1993) identify the waves of enthusiasm with Downs (1972) and waves of criticism with Schattschneider (1960).

62. *Time* magazine (8/1/1969): "Some River! Chocolate-brown, oily, bubbling with subsurface gases, it oozes rather than flows. 'Anyone who falls into the Cuyahoga does not drown,' Cleveland's citizens joke grimly. 'He decays.' . . . The Federal Water Pollution Control Administration dryly notes: 'The lower Cuyahoga has no visible signs of life, not even low forms such as leeches and sludge worms that usually thrive on wastes.' It is also—literally—a fire hazard." See also http://www.ohiohistorycentral.org/entry.php?rec=1642.

63. Exercises 12.5–12.7 ask for CGT examples.

64. An "all pay" auction may also apply: many policy entrepreneurs invest, but only one wins the tournament and gains access to a policy agenda. Anticipation of potential loss may complicate associated CAPs.

65. Exercise 12.8 asks for an example.

66. Exercises 12.9–12.11 ask for examples of models in this paragraph.

67. This discussion touches on a large literature. For an overview, see Birkland (2011, Chap. 9). Bowles (1998b) asserts that over-reliance on explicit material incentives may undermine policy intent—a type of implementation problem.

68. This approach assumes that designers understand the motivations and capacities of policy implementers who share similar values and policy goals.

69. This list resembles Section 12.1's types of rules.

70. The conceptual frameworks established by policy statements constitute a key source of policy feedback (Pierson 1993).

71. Note the parallel to Chapter 3's incomplete private-sector contracts.

72. Some ambiguity of purpose, expressed via symbols such as the American flag, allows proponents of specific policies (e.g., liberals or conservatives) to attract support from diverse constituencies (Stone 2002, 157–62).

73. "Policies are continuously transformed by implementation actions that simultaneously alter resources and objectives" (Giandomenico and Wildavsky 1984, 145).

74. Bartlett (1973) discusses the role of information as a source of power. Le Grand (2003) discusses the motives of policymakers invoking the images of both knight and knave.

APPENDIX TO CHAPTER 12

1. This list is a close paraphrase of the list that appears in Ostrom and Crawford (2005, Table 7.2, 211).

2. Most of the following points are a close paraphrase of Ostrom and Crawford (2005, Table 7.3, 212). Rule (3) does not appear in Ostrom and Crawford's Table 7.3, but is consistent with their argument.

3. This rule could double as an information rule.

4. Likewise, an expanded version of Figure 12A.2 could specify the judge's actions and possible sanctions to the judge for not acting. An extended version could specify a party for sanctioning the judge, along with its possible actions.

CHAPTER 13

1. Romer (1990, S72) defines technological change as "improvement in the instructions for mixing together raw materials."

2. Institutional procedures, as a component of social capital, can reflect accumulated organizational knowledge, whereas human capital reflects accumulated individual knowledge.

3. At k^*, $sy^* = (n + d)k$, where s is savings per unit output (S/Y), n is the rate of population growth, and d is the rate of capital depreciation. We assume that output per worker and output per capita grow at the same rate.

4. For more detail, see an intermediate macroeconomics text such as Dornbusch, Fischer, and Startz (2011) or Mankiw (2010).

5. For Romer (1990, S75), "nonrival goods can be accumulated without bound on a per capita basis." Costs of duplication are "trivial compared to the cost of creating the design in the first place." For an intuitive discussion of Romer's model, see Jones (2010).

6. Arrow (1962) asserts that technical change "can be ascribed to experience" (156).

7. For an overview on approaches to poverty traps, see Bowles, Durlauf, and Hoff (2006).

8. The knowledge transmitted to Desh also addressed how to navigate trade restrictions, how to acquire credit, and how to attain government support (Easterly 2002, 148–50).

9. Recall that power-law distributions characterize scale-free networks. The Zipf distribution also describes patterns of Internet traffic, word usage, immune system response, and percolation processes (Axtell 2001, 1818).

10. Copyrights and patent laws are institutional mechanisms that attempt to prevent knowledge spillover by establishing excludability over specific types of knowledge.

11. Naturally, other factors, such as institutionally structured incentives, influence such decisions.

12. Exercises 13.3–13.5 address topics in this paragraph.

13. Diminishing returns analysis predicts the opposite. In the United States, where climate and mechanization favor agriculture, only 2% work in agriculture. In arid, mountainous Ethiopia, where the tsetse fly kills cattle, 57% of the labor force does so. Skill complementarities draw labor away from agriculture in the United States and toward agriculture in Ethiopia: "Comparative advantage in agriculture and manufactures is itself manufactured" (Easterly 2002, 161).

14. Breschi and Lissoni (2001) criticize the knowledge spillover literature for failing to account adequately for pools of skilled workers and transaction relationships conducted across networks. We address these factors.

15. The magnitude and sign of derivative dr_{hi}/dh_i depend on the other variables.

16. "Local" can be defined geographically, by industry, by occupation, etc.

17. Exercises 13.6 and 13.7 ask for models.

18. Krugman notes that local clustering produces three externalities, initially noticed by Marshall (1890/1979): large markets with increasing returns create efficient production of intermediate goods; "thick" labor markets with multiple skills; and information sharing. Costs of congestion work against these advantages—otherwise, we would expect to observe one huge megalopolis (Krugman 1995).

19. Scale-free networks imply that similar patterns exist at different scales of operation.

20. A less formal version of this argument with many historical examples appears in Acemoglu and Robinson (2012).

21. Knight (1992) also employs a social conflict theory of institutions.

22. Existing institutions reflect the distribution of bargaining power at the time they were constructed (North 1990).

23. Acemoglu, Johnson, and Robinson (2005) discuss effects of the Atlantic trade on growth. For a more comprehensive treatment, see Brenner (1993).

24. The Navigation Acts of 1651 and 1660 offer other examples (Acemoglu, Johnson, and Robinson 2005).

25. Former Chilean dictator Augusto Pinochet largely circumvented this problem via his 1978 amnesty law and his positions as commander-in-chief of the Chilean army and senator-for-life. When he ceded power in 1990 under domestic and international pressure, he thought he was immune from prosecution. (Pinochet's regime killed at least 3,200 and tortured another 28,000 (Rother 2006).) But, while traveling in England in 1998, he was nearly extradited to Spain to face charges for the deaths of Spanish citizens in Chile. (Intervention by former British prime minister Margaret Thatcher saved him.) In 2004, court challenges by human rights advocates led to charges in Chile, but Pinochet died before the process finished.

26. Contracting problems generate a similar inseparability of political and economic processes at the micro level (see Chapter 3).

27. Acemoglu, Johnson, and Robinson cite Morgan (1975) and Keyssar (2000) on these points.

28. Acemoglu, Johnson, and Robinson (2004a) cite Engerman and Sokoloff (1997) and Acemoglu, Johnson, and Robinson (2004b) on these points.

29. Acemoglu, Johnson, and Robinson (2004a) cite Haber (2002) on these points; the figures are from page 24 of Haber.

30. Rights were restricted to male wealth holders: broad access for that time.

31. Razo asserts that the concept of a limited dictatorship suggests institutional foundations for Olson's stationary banditry (1993, 2000), but he also notes that Olson uses universal property rights, an idea Razo finds incompatible with dictatorship.

32. Universal (or widely accessible) property rights are a public good.

33. Citing Linz (2000), Razo refers to this arrangement as limited pluralism.

34. This game (with slightly different notation) appears as Figure 2.2 in Razo (2008, 37).

35. Exercise 13.8 asks for demonstration of these conditions and for other possible SPE.

36. See Razo (2008, Chap. 2) for a more formal statement of these arguments.

37. As Razo reports, "key players in each of these industries received market power in response to their political influence and direct economic benefits that they could provide to the Díaz government" (2008, 87). Table 6.2 (143) presents the relevant data.

38. A network of 103 public officials on corporate boards had an average density of about 8%; this figure "represents a fairly large number of connections given all the possibilities" (Razo 2008, 144).

39. Razo uses three measures of network centrality: a node's degree; its individual betweenness (see equation (11.4)); and its eigenvalue (or Bonacich centrality), which also incorporates the centrality of a node's connections (2008, 142–55).

40. Banks occupied most central nodes in the Díaz network, with links to manufacturing, transportation, and mining; governors typically sat on their boards. Officials' family links provided additional stakes in the economic system (Razo 2008, Chap. 6).

41. Razo argues that dictatorships in sub-Saharan Africa lack all three conditions (2008, Chap. 7).

42. Razo cites Haber, Razo, and Maurer (2003) on the network legacies of the Díaz regime. Along similar lines, Kirkpatrick (2012) reports a failure to uproot Mubarak's network of influence after Egypt's revolution.

43. Interestingly, the Fourteenth Amendment also specifies that no one who had previously "engaged in insurrection or rebellion" against the United States (i.e., anyone who supported the Confederacy) shall "hold any office, civil or military." (Congress, however, may waive this restriction with a two-thirds vote in both houses.)

44. For historical accounts, see Wright (1986), Foner (1988), and Ransom and Sutch (2001).

45. For a policy discussion that addresses both growth and distribution, see Baily, Burtless, and Litan (1993).

46. For an evolutionary collective-action perspective on institutional poverty traps, see Bowles (2006).

REFERENCES

Acemoglu, Daron (2003), "Why Not a Political Coase Theorem?" Working Paper 9377, National Bureau of Economic Research, Cambridge, MA.

Acemoglu, Daron, Simon Johnson, and James A. Robinson (2004a), "Institutions as the Fundamental Cause of Long-Run Growth," Working Paper 10481, National Bureau of Economic Research, Cambridge, MA.

———— (2004b), *Institutional Roots of Prosperity*, The 2004 Lionel Robbins Lectures, unpublished manuscript.

———— (2005), "The Rise of Europe: Atlantic Trade, Institutional Change and Economic Growth," *American Economic Review* 98(1), 546–79.

Acemoglu, Daron, and James A. Robinson (2008), "Persistence of Power Elites and Institutions," *American Economic Review* 98(1), 267–93.

———— (2012), *Why Nations Fail*, New York: Crown.

Agrawal, Arun, and Ashwini Chhatre (2007), "State Involvement and Forest Co-Governance: Evidence from the Indian Himalayas," *Studies in Comparative International Development* 42(1–2), 67–86.

Akerlof, George A. (1970), "The Market for Lemons: Quality Uncertainty and the Market Mechanism," *Quarterly Journal of Economics* 84(2), 488–500.

———— (1976), "The Economics of Caste and of the Rat Race and Other Woeful Tales," *Quarterly Journal of Economics* 90(4), 599–617.

———— (1982), "Labor Contracts as Partial Gift Exchange," *Quarterly Journal of Economics* 97(4), 543–69.

Akerlof, George A., and Rachel E. Kranton (2000), "Economics and Identity," *Quarterly Journal of Economics* 115(3), 715–52.

———— (2005), "Identity and the Economics of Organizations," *Journal of Economic Perspectives* 19(1), 9–32.

———— (2010), *Identity Economics: How Our Identities Shape Our Work, Wages, and Well-Being*, Princeton, NJ: Princeton University Press.

Akerlof, George A., and Janet Yellen (1990), "The Fair Wage-Effort Hypothesis and Unemployment," *Quarterly Journal of Economics* 105(2), 255–83.

Alchian, Armen A., and Harold Demsetz (1972), "Production, Information, and Economic Organization," *American Economic Review* 62(5), 777–95.

Andersson, Krister P., and Elinor Ostrom (2008), "Analyzing Decentralized Resource Regimes from a Polycentric Perspective," *Policy Sciences* 41(1), 71–93.

Apesteguia, Jose, and Frank P. Maier-Rigaud (2006), "The Role of Rivalry: Public Goods versus Common-Pool Resources," *Journal of Conflict Resolution* 50(5), 646–63.

Arrow, Kenneth J. (1962), "The Economic Implications of Learning by Doing," *Review of Economic Studies* 29(3), 155–73.

Arthur, W. Brian (1992), "On Learning and Adaptation in the Economy," Working Paper 92-070038, Santa Fe Institute, Santa Fe, NM.

——— (1994), "Inductive Reasoning and Bounded Rationality," *American Economic Review* 84(2), 406–11.

Aumann, Robert J. (1987), "Correlated Equilibrium as an Expression of Bayesian Rationality," *Econometrica* 55(1), 1–18.

Axelrod, Robert (1984), *The Evolution of Cooperation*, New York: Basic Books.

Axelrod, Robert, and William D. Hamilton (1981), "The Evolution of Cooperation," *Science* 211, 1390–96.

Axtell, Robert L. (2001), "Zipf Distribution of U.S. Firm Sizes," *Science* 293, 1818–20.

Bacharach, Peter, and Morton Baratz (1962), "The Two Faces of Power," *American Political Science Review* 56(4), 947–52.

——— (1970), *Power and Poverty: Theory and Practice*, Oxford: Oxford University Press.

Bacharach, Samuel B., and Edward J. Lawler (1981), *Bargaining: Power, Tactics and Outcomes*, San Francisco: Jossey-Bass.

Baily, Martin, Gary Burtless, and Robert Litan (1993), *Growth with Equity: Economic Policymaking for the Next Century*, Washington, DC: Brookings Institution.

Baldwin, James (1961/1991), *Nobody Knows My Name*, London: Penguin.

Barabási, Albert-László (2003), *Linked: How Everything Is Connected to Everything Else and What It Means for Business, Science, and Everyday Life*, New York: Plume.

Barron, John M., and Kathy P. Gjerde (1997), "Peer Pressure in an Agency Relationship," *Journal of Labor Economics* 15(2), 235–54.

Bartlett, Richard (1973), *Economic Foundations of Political Power*, New York: Free Press.

Basu, Kaushik (2000), *Prelude to Political Economy: A Study of the Social and Political Foundations of Economics*, Oxford: Oxford University Press.

Baumgartner, Frank R., and Bryan D. Jones (1993), *Agendas and Instability in American Politics*, Chicago: University of Chicago Press.

Becker, William E. (2007), "Quit Lying and Address the Controversies: There Are No Dogmata, Laws, Rules or Standards in the Science of Economics," *American Economist* 51(1), 3–14.

Bénabou, Roland, and Jean Tirole (2006), "Incentives and Prosocial Behavior," *American Economic Review* 96(5), 1652–78.

Berninghaus, Siegfried, Werner Güth, and Hartmut Kliemt (2003), "From Teleology to Evolution," *Journal of Evolutionary Economics* 13(4), 385–410.

Berninghaus, Siegfried, Christian Korth, and Stefan Napel (2007), "Reciprocity—An Indirect Evolutionary Analysis," *Journal of Evolutionary Economics* 17(5), 579–603.

Bernoulli, Daniel (1738/1954), "Exposition of a New Theory on the Measurement of Risk," *Econometrica* 22(1), 22–36.

Betsill, Michele (2011), "International Climate Change Policy: Toward the Multilevel Governance of Global Warming," in Regina S. Axelrod, Stacy D. VanDeveer, and David Leonard Downie (Eds.), *The Global Environment*, Washington, DC: CQ Press.

Bewley, Truman F. (1999), *Why Wages Don't Fall during a Recession*, Cambridge, MA: Harvard University Press.

Bikhchandani, Sushil, David Hirshleifer, and Ivo Welch (1992), "A Theory of Fads, Fashion, Custom, and Cultural Change as Informational Cascades," *Journal of Political Economy* 100(5), 992–1026.

Binmore, Kenneth (1992), *Fun and Games: A Text on Game Theory*, Lexington, MA: Heath.

——— (1994), *Game Theory and the Social Contract*, vol. 1: *Playing Fair*, Boston: MIT Press.

Birkland, Thomas (2011), *An Introduction to the Policy Process: Theories, Concepts and Models of Public Policymaking*, 3rd ed., Armonk, NY: M.E. Sharpe.

Blau, Peter M. (1964), *Exchange and Power in Social Life*, New York: Wiley.

Bloch, Francis, Garance Genicot, and Debraj Ray (2007), "Reciprocity in Groups and the Limits to Social Capital," *American Economic Review Papers and Proceedings* 97(2), 65–69.

Bolton, Gary E., and Axel Ockenfels (2000), "ERC: A Theory of Equity, Reciprocity and Competition," *American Economic Review* 90(1), 166–93.

Boulding, Kenneth (1989), *Three Faces of Power*, London: Sage.

Bowles, Samuel (1985), "The Production Process in a Competitive Economy: Walrasian, Neo-Hobbesian, and Marxian Models," *American Economic Review* 75(5), 16–36.

——— (1998a), "Endogenous Preferences: The Cultural Consequences of Markets and Other Economic Institutions," *Journal of Economic Literature* 36(1), 75–91.

——— (1998b), "Policies Designed for Self-Interested Citizens May Undermine 'The Moral Sentiments': Evidence from Economic Experiments," *Science* 320, 1605–9.

——— (2004), *Microeconomics: Behavior, Institutions, and Evolution*, Princeton, NJ: Princeton University Press.

——— (2006), "Institutional Poverty Traps," in Samuel Bowles, Steven N. Durlauf, and Karla Hoff (Eds.), *Poverty Traps*, New York: Russell Sage Foundation, 116–38.

——— (2012), *Machiavelli's Mistake: Why Good Laws Are No Substitute for Good Citizens*, New Haven, CT: Yale University Press.

Bowles, Samuel, Steven N. Durlauf, and Karla Hoff (Eds.) (2006), *Poverty Traps*, New York: Russell Sage Foundation.

Bowles, Samuel, and Herbert Gintis (1992), "Power and Wealth in a Competitive Capitalist Economy," *Philosophy and Public Affairs* 21(4), 324–53.

——— (2002), "Social Capital and Community Governance," *Economic Journal* 112(483), F419–F436.

——— (2004a), "The Evolution of Strong Reciprocity: Cooperation in Heterogeneous Populations," *Theoretical Population Biology* 65(1), 17–28.

——— (2004b), "Persistent Parochialism: Trust and Exclusion in Ethnic Networks," *Journal of Economic Behavior and Organization* 55(1), 1–23.

———— (2008), "Power," in Steven N. Durlauf and Lawrence E. Blume (Eds.), *The New Palgrave Dictionary of Economics*, 2nd ed., New York: Palgrave Macmillan.

Bowles, Samuel, and Sandra Polanía-Reyes (2012), "Economic Incentives and Social Preferences: Substitutes or Complements?" *Journal of Economic Literature* 50(2), 1–57.

Boyd, Robert, Herbert Gintis, Samuel Bowles, and Peter J. Richerson (2005), "The Evolution of Altruistic Punishment," in Herbert Gintis, Samuel Bowles, Robert Boyd, and Ernst Fehr (Eds.), *Moral Sentiments and Material Interests: The Foundations of Cooperation in Economic Life*, Cambridge, MA: MIT Press, 215–28.

Boyd, Robert, and Peter J. Richerson (1985), *Culture and the Evolutionary Process*, Chicago: University of Chicago Press.

———— (1992), "How Microevolutionary Processes Give Rise to History," in Matthew H. Nitecki and Doris V. Nitecki (Eds.), *History and Evolution*, Albany: State University of New York Press, 179–209.

Branch, Taylor (1988), *Parting the Waters: America in the King Years 1954–63*, New York: Simon & Schuster.

———— (1998), *Pillar of Fire: America in the King Years 1963–65*, New York: Touchstone.

Brenner, Robert (1993), *Merchants and Revolution: Commerical Change, Political Conflict, and London's Overseas Traders, 1550–1653*, Princeton, NJ: Princeton University Press.

Breschi, Stefano, and Francesco Lissoni (2001), "Knowledge Spillovers and Local Innovation Systems: A Critical Survey," *Industrial and Corporate Change* 10(4), 975–1005.

Bronk, Richard (2009), *The Romantic Economist: Imagination in Economics*, Cambridge: Cambridge University Press.

Brunckhorst, David J. (2000), *Bioregional Planning: Resource Management beyond the New Millennium*, Amsterdam: Harwood Academic.

Buchanan, James M. (1965), "An Economic Theory of Clubs," *Economica* 32(125), 1–14.

Bulow, Jeremy I., and Lawrence H. Summers (1986), "A Theory of Dual Labor Markets with Applications to Industrial Policy, Discrimination and Keynesian Unemployment," *Journal of Labor Economics* 4(3), 376–414.

Burke, Mary A., and H. Peyton Young (2009), "Social Norms," in Alberto Bisin, Jess Benhabib, and Matthew Jackson (Eds.), *The Handbook of Social Economics*, Amsterdam: North-Holland, 311–38.

Calvó-Armengol, Antoni, and Matthew O. Jackson (2004), "The Effects of Social Networks on Employment and Inequality," *American Economic Review* 94(3), 426–54.

Camerer, Colin F. (2003), *Behavioral Game Theory: Experiments in Strategic Interaction*, Princeton, NJ: Princeton University Press.

Camerer, Colin F., George Loewenstein, and Matthew Rabin (2004), *Advances in Behavioral Economics*, Princeton, NJ: Princeton University Press.

Camerer, Colin F., and Richard H. Thaler (2003), "In Honor of Matthew Rabin: Winner of the John Bates Clark Award," *Journal of Economic Perspectives* 17(3), 159–76.

Campbell, Andrea L. (2012), "Policy Makes Politics," *Annual Review of Political Science* 15, 331–51.

Campbell, Carl M., III, and Kunal S. Kamlani (1997), "The Reasons for Wage Rigidity: Evidence from a Survey of Firms," *Quarterly Journal of Economics* 112(3), 759–89.

Carlin, Wendy, and David Soskice (1990), *Macroeconomics and the Wage Bargain*, Oxford: Oxford University Press.

Carpenter, Jeffrey P., Samuel Bowles, Herbert Gintis, and Sung-Ha Hwang (2009), "Strong Reciprocity and Team Production: Theory and Evidence," *Journal of Economic and Behavior and Organization*, 71(2), 221–32.

Carpenter, Jeffrey P., Peter H. Matthews, and Okomboli Ong'ong'a (2004), "Why Punish? Social Reciprocity and the Enforcement of Prosocial Norms," *Journal of Evolutionary Economics* 14(4), 407–29.

Charness, Gary, and Matthew Rabin (2002), "Understanding Social Preferences with Simple Tests," *Quarterly Journal of Economics* 117(3), 817–69.

Christakis, Nicholas A., and James H. Fowler (2007), "The Spread of Obesity in a Large Social Network over 32 Years," *New England Journal of Medicine* 357(4), 370–79.

Chwe, Michael Suk-Young (2000), "Communication and Coordination in Social Networks," *Review of Economic Studies* 67(1), 1–16.

Coase, Ronald (1937), "The Nature of the Firm," *Economica* 4(16), 386–405.

——— (1960), "The Problem of Social Cost," *Journal of Law and Economics* 3, 1–44.

——— (1992), "The Institutional Structure of Production," *American Economic Review* 82(4), 713–19.

Cochran, Charles L., and Eloise F. Malone (1995), *Public Policy: Perspectives and Choices*, New York: McGraw-Hill.

Cohen, Michael D., James G. March, and Johan P. Olsen (1972), "A Garbage Can Model of Organizational Choice," *Administrative Science Quarterly* 17(1), 1–25.

Colander, David (2006), *The Stories Economists Tell: Essays on the Art of Teaching Economics*, Boston: McGraw-Hill.

Colander, David, Richard P. F. Holt, and J. Barkley Rosser (Eds.) (2005), *The Changing Face of Economics: Interviews with Cutting Edge Economists*, Ann Arbor: University of Michigan Press.

Coleman, James S. (1988), "Social Capital in the Creation of Human Capital," *American Journal of Sociology* 94(Suppl.), S95–S120.

Coleman, James S., Elihu Katz, and Herbert Menzel (1966), *Medical Innovation: A Diffusion Study*, New York: Bobbs-Merrill.

Conlisk, John (1996), "Why Bounded Rationality?" *Journal of Economic Literature* 34(2), 669–700.

Cox, James C. (2004), "How to Identify Trust and Reciprocity," *Games and Economic Behavior* 46(2), 260–81.

Crawford, Sue, and Elinor Ostrom (2005), "A Grammar of Institutions," in Elinor Ostrom, *Understanding Institutional Diversity*, Princeton, NJ: Princeton University Press, 137–74.

Crespi, Bernard J. (2000), "The Evolution of Maladaptation," *Heredity* 84(6), 623–29.

Cyert, Richard M., and James G. March (1963), *A Behavioral Theory of the Firm*, Englewood Cliffs, NJ: Prentice Hall.

Dahl, Robert (1957), "The Concept of Power," *Behavioral Science* 2(3), 201–15.

——— (1961), *Who Governs? Democracy and Power in an American City*, New Haven, CT: Yale University Press.

Dal Bó, Pedro (2007), "Social Norms, Cooperation and Inequality," *Economic Theory* 30(1), 89–105.

Dasgupta, Partha (2000), "Economic Progress and the Idea of Social Capital," in Partha Dasgupta and Ismail Serageldin (Eds.), *Social Capital: A Multifaceted Perspective*, Washington, DC: World Bank, 325–424.

——— (2011), "A Matter of Trust: Social Capital and Economic Development," in Justin Y. Lin and Boris Pleskovic (Eds.), *Annual World Bank Conference on Development Economics, Global 2010: Lessons from East Asia and the Global Financial Crisis*, New York: World Bank, 119–56.

Dasgupta, Partha, Peter Hammond, and Eric Maskin (1979), "The Implementation of Social Choice Rules: Some General Results on Incentive Compatibility," *Review of Economic Studies* 46(2), 185–216.

Davidson, Paul (1991), "Is Probability Theory Relevant for Uncertainty? A Post-Keynesian Perspective," *Journal of Economic Perspectives* 5(1), 129–43.

Dawkins, Richard (2006), *The Selfish Gene*, 30th Anniversary Edition, Oxford: Oxford University Press.

——— (2008), *The Extended Phenotype: The Long Reach of the Gene*, rev. ed., New York: Oxford University Press.

Degnbol, Poul, and Bonnie J. McCay (2007), "Unintended and Perverse Consequences of Ignoring Linkages in Fisheries Systems," *ICES Journal of Marine Science* 64(4), 793–97.

DeGroot, Morris H. (1974), "Reaching a Consensus," *Journal of the American Statistical Association* 69(345), 118–21.

DeMarzo, Peter M., Dimitri Vayanos, and Jeffrey Zwiebel (2003), "Persuasion Bias, Social Influence, and Unidimensional Opinions," *Quarterly Journal of Economics* 118(3), 909–67.

Demsetz, Harold (1967), "Toward a Theory of Property Rights," *American Economic Review Papers and Proceedings* 50(2), 347–59.

Denzau, Arthur T., and Douglass C. North (1994), "Shared Mental Models: Ideologies and Institutions," *Kyklos* 47(1), 3–31.

Dequech, David (2009), "Institutions, Social Norms, and Decision-Theoretic Norms," *Journal of Economic Behavior and Organization* 72(1), 70–78.

Diamond, Jared (1997), *Guns, Germs and Steel: The Fates of Human Societies*, New York: Norton.

Dickens, William T., and Lawrence F. Katz (1987), "Inter-Industry Wage Differences and Industry Characteristics," in Kevin Lang and Jonathan S. Leonard (Eds.), *Unemployment and the Structure of Labor Markets*, New York: Blackwell, 48–89.

Diers, Jim (2004), *Neighbor Power: Building Community the Seattle Way*, Seattle: University of Washington Press.

Digeser, Peter (1992), "The Fourth Face of Power," *Journal of Politics* 54(4), 977–1007.

Dixit, Avinash K., and Barry J. Nalebuff (1991), *Thinking Strategically*, New York: Norton.

Dixit, Avinash K., and Susan Skeath (2004), *Games of Strategy*, 2nd ed., New York: Norton.

Dixit, Avinash K., Susan Skeath, and David H. Reiley Jr. (2009), *Games of Strategy*, 3rd ed., New York: Norton.

Doeringer, Peter, and Michael Piore (1971), *Internal Labor Markets and Manpower Analysis*, Lexington, MA: Heath.

Dornbusch, Rudiger, Stanley Fischer, and Richard Startz (2011), *Macroeconomics*, 11th ed., New York: McGraw-Hill.

Downs, Anthony (1972), "Up and Down with Ecology: 'The Issue Attention Cycle,'" *Public Interest* 28, 38–50.

Drucker, Peter F. (1985), *The Effective Executive*, New York: Harper & Row.

Dunn, Richard S. (1970), *The Age of Religious Wars 1559–1689*, New York: Norton.

Dur, Robert, and Hein Roelfsema (2010), "Social Exchange and Common Agency in Organizations," *Journal of Socio-Economics* 39(1), 55–63.

Durlauf, Steven N. (2006), "Groups, Social Influence, and Inequality," in Samuel Bowles, Steven N. Durlauf, and Karla Hoff (Eds.), *Poverty Traps*, New York: Russell Sage Foundation, 141–75.

Dye, Thomas R. (2008), *Understanding Public Policy*, Upper Saddle River, NJ: Pearson/Prentice Hall.

Easterly, William R. (2002), *The Elusive Quest for Growth*, Cambridge, MA: MIT Press.

——— (2006), "Social Cohesion, Institutions and Growth," Working Paper 94, Center for Global Development, Washington, DC.

Edelman, Murray (1964), *The Symbolic Uses of Politics*, Urbana: University of Illinois Press.

Edlin, Aaron S., and Stefan Reichelstein (1996), "Holdups, Standard Breach Remedies, and Optimal Investment," *American Economic Review* 86(3), 478–501.

Elmore, Richard (1979), "Backward Mapping: Implementation Research and Policy Decisions," *Political Science Quarterly* 94(4), 601–16.

——— (1985), "Forward and Backward Mapping," in Kenneth Hanf and Theo A. J. Toonen (Eds.), *Policy Implementation in the Federal and Unitary Systems*, Dordrecht: Martinus Nijhoff, 33–70.

Elster, Jon (1979), *Ulysses and the Sirens: Studies in Rationality and Irrationality*, Cambridge: Cambridge University Press.

——— (1989a), *The Cement of Society*, New York: Cambridge University Press.

——— (1989b), "Social Norms and Economic Theory," *Journal of Economic Perspectives* 3(4), 99–117.

Engerman, Stanley L., and Kenneth L. Sokoloff (1997), "Factor Endowments, Institutions, and Differential Growth Paths among New World Economies," in Stephen Haber (Ed.), *How Latin America Fell Behind*, Stanford, CA: Stanford University Press, 260–306.

Epstein, Joshua M. (2006), *Generative Social Science: Studies in Agent-Based Computational Modeling*, Princeton, NJ: Princeton University Press.

Erlanger, Steven (2012), "Euro Debt Crisis Is Political Test for Block," *New York Times*, February 6, http://www.nytimes.com/2010/02/06/world/europe/06europe.html.

Falk, Armin, Ernst Fehr, and Urs Fischbacher (2003), "On the Nature of Fair Behavior," *Economic Inquiry* 41(1), 20–26.

Falk, Armin, and Urs Fischbacher (2006), "A Theory of Reciprocity," *Games and Economic Behavior* 54(2), 293–315.

Fehr, Ernst, and Armin Falk (1999), "Wage Rigidity in a Competitive Incomplete Contract Market," *Journal of Political Economy* 107(1), 106–34.

Fehr, Ernst, and Urs Fischbacher (2002), "Why Social Preferences Matter—The Impact of Non-Selfish Motives on Competition, Cooperation and Incentives," *Economic Journal* 112(478), C1–C33.

Fehr, Ernst, and Simon Gächter (1998), "Reciprocity and Economics: The Economic Implications of *Homo Reciprocans*," *European Economic Review* 42(3–5), 845–59.

——— (2000), "Fairness and Retaliation: The Economics of Reciprocity," *Journal of Economic Perspectives* 14(3), 159–81.

——— (2002), "Altruistic Punishment in Humans," *Nature* 415, 137–40.

Fehr, Ernst, Simon Gächter, and Georg Kirchsteiger (1996), "Reciprocal Fairness and Noncompensating Wage Differentials," *Journal of Institutional and Theoretical Economics* 152(4), 608–40.

——— (1997), "Reciprocity as a Contract Enforcement Device: Experimental Evidence," *Econometrica* 65(4), 833–60.

Fehr, Ernst, and Joseph Henrich (2003), "Is Strong Reciprocity a Maladaptation? On the Evolutionary Foundations of Human Altruism," Working Paper 859, Center for Economic Studies, Munich.

Fehr, Ernst, Georg Kirchsteiger, and Arno Riedl (1993), "Does Fairness Prevent Market Clearing? An Experimental Investigation," *Quarterly Journal of Economics* 108(2), 437–59.

Fehr, Ernst, Alexander Klein, and Klaus M. Schmidt (2007), "Fairness and Contract Design," *Econometrica* 75(1), 121–54.

Fehr, Ernst, and Klaus M. Schmidt (1999), "A Theory of Fairness, Competition, and Cooperation," *Quarterly Journal of Economics* 114(3), 817–68.

Feldman, Julian (1962), "Computer Simulation of Cognitive Processes," in Harold Borko (Ed.), *Computer Applications in the Behavioral Sciences*, Englewood Cliffs, NJ: Prentice Hall, 336–59.

Feldman, Martha S. (1989), *Order without Design: Information Production and Policy Making*, Stanford, CA: Stanford University Press.

Ferguson, William D. (2005), "Fair Wages, Worker Motivation, and Implicit Bargaining Power in Segmented Labor Markets," *Journal of Institutional and Theoretical Economics* 161(1), 126–54.

——— (2010), "The Financial Crisis as a Collective-Action Problem," Working paper, Department of Economics, Grinnell College, Grinnell, IA.

——— (2011), "Curriculum for the Twenty-First Century: Recent Advances in Economic Theory and Undergraduate Economics," *Journal of Economic Education* 42(1), 31–50.

Fogel, Robert W. (2004), *The Escape from Hunger and Premature Death, 1700–2100: Europe, America, and the Third World*, Cambridge: Cambridge University Press.

Foner, Eric (1988), *Reconstruction: America's Unfinished Revolution, 1863–1867*, New York: HarperCollins.

Frank, Aaron B. (2011), "Identity Theory and Agent-Based Modeling," Working paper, Center for Social Complexity, George Mason University, Fairfax, VA.

Friedman, Milton (1957), *A Theory of Consumption*, Princeton, NJ: Princeton University Press.

Fudenberg, Drew, and Eric Maskin (1986), "The Folk Theorem in Repeated Games with Discounting or with Incomplete Information," *Econometrica* 54(3), 533–54.

Gabaix, Xavier (1999), "Zipf's Law for Cities: An Explanation," *Quarterly Journal of Economics* 114(3), 739–67.

Gächter, Simon (2007), "Conditional Cooperation: Behavioral Regularities from the Lab and the Field and Their Policy Implications," in Bruno S. Frey and Alois Stutzer (Eds.), *Economics and Psychology: A Promising New Cross-Disciplinary Field*, Cambridge, MA: MIT Press, 19–50.

Gächter, Simon, and Ernst Fehr (1999), "Collective Action as a Social Exchange," *Journal of Economic Behavior and Organization* 39(4), 341–69.

Galbraith, John K. (1983), *The Anatomy of Power*, Boston: Houghton-Mifflin.

Gaventa, John (1980), *Power and Powerlessness: Quiescence and Rebellion in an Appalachian Valley*, Urbana: University of Illinois Press.

Gelt, Joe (1997), *Sharing Colorado River Water: History, Public Policy, and the Colorado River Compact*, Tucson: Water Resources Research Center, University of Arizona.

Giandomenico, Majone, and Aaron Wildavsky (1984), "Implementation as Evolution," in Jeffrey L. Pressman and Aaron Wildavsky (Eds.), *Implementation*, 3rd ed., Berkeley: University of California Press.

Gibbons, Robert (1992), *Game Theory for Applied Economists*, Princeton, NJ: Princeton University Press.

Gintis, Herbert (2000), "Strong Reciprocity and Human Sociality," *Journal of Theoretical Biology* 206(2), 169–79.

——— (2009a), *Game Theory Evolving: A Problem-Centered Introduction to Strategic Interaction*, 2nd ed., Princeton, NJ: Princeton University Press.

——— (2009b), *The Bounds of Reason*, Princeton, NJ: Princeton University Press.

Global Security (2012), "Somalia Civil War," http://www.globalsecurity.org/military/world/war/somalia.htm.

Goode, Erica (2012), "With Green Beret Tactics, Combating Gang Warfare," *New York Times*, April 30.

Gould, Jonathan (2007), *Can't Buy Me Love: The Beatles, Britain and America*, New York: Harmony.

Gould, Stephen J., and Niles Eldredge (1977), "Punctuated Equilibria: The Tempo and Mode of Evolution Reconsidered," *Paleobiology* 3(2), 115–51.

Gould, Stephen J., and Richard C. Lewontin (1979), "The Spandrels of San Marco and the Panglossian Paradigm: A Critique of the Adaptationist Programme," *Proceedings of the Royal Society of London* 205, 581–98.

Graeff, Peter (2009), "Social Capital: The Dark Side," in Gert T. Svendsen and Gunnar L. H. Svendsen (Eds.), *Handbook of Social Capital: The Troika of Sociology, Political Science and Economics*, Northampton, MA: Elgar, 143–61.

Granovetter, Mark (1973), "The Strength of Weak Ties," *American Journal of Sociology* 78(6), 1360–80.

——— (1985), "Economic Action and Social Structure: The Problem of Embeddedness," *American Journal of Sociology* 91(3), 481–510.

Greif, Avner (2006a), *Institutions and the Path to the Modern Economy: Lessons from Medieval Trade*, Cambridge: Cambridge University Press.

——— (2006b), "History Lessons: The Birth of Impersonal Exchange: The Community Responsibility System and Impartial Justice," *Journal of Economic Perspectives* 20(2), 221–36.

Grossman, Sanford J., and Oliver D. Hart (1986), "The Costs and Benefits of Ownership: A Theory of Vertical and Lateral Integration," *Journal of Political Economy* 94(4), 691–719.

Grossman, Sanford J., and Elhanan Helpman (1991), *Innovation and Growth in the Global Economy*, Cambridge, MA: MIT Press.

Gulati, Ranjay, Nitin Nohria, and Akbar Zaheer (2000), "Strategic Networks," *Strategic Management Journal* 21(3), 203–15.

Güth, Werner (1995), "An Evolutionary Approach to Explaining Cooperative Behavior by Reciprocal Incentives," *International Journal of Game Theory* 24(4), 323–44.

Güth, Werner, and Stefan Napel (2006), "Inequality Aversion in a Variety of Games: An Indirect Evolutionary Analysis," *Economic Journal* 116(514), 1037–56.

Güth, Werner, and Menahem Yaari (1992), "Explaining Reciprocal Behavior in Simple Strategic Games: An Evolutionary Approach," in Ulrich Witt (Ed.), *Explaining Process and Change: Approaches to Evolutionary Economics*, Ann Arbor: University of Michigan Press, 23–34.

Gutiérrez, Nicolás L., Ray Hilborn, and Omar Defeo (2011), "Leadership, Social Capital and Incentives Promote Successful Fisheries," *Nature* 470, 386–89.

Haber, Stephen (2002), "Political Institutions and Banking Systems: Lessons from the Economic Histories of Mexico and the United States," Working paper, Department of Political Science, Stanford University, Stanford, CA.

Haber, Stephen, Armando Razo, and Noel Maurer (2003), *The Politics of Property Rights: Political Instability, Credible Commitments, and Economic Growth in Mexico (1876–1929)*, Cambridge: Cambridge University Press.

Hahn, Frank (1987), "Information, Dynamics, and Equilibrium," *Scottish Journal of Political Economy* 102(5), 912–50.

Halberstam, David (1972), *The Best and the Brightest*, New York: Random House.

——— (1993), *The Fifties*, New York: Villard.

Halliday, David, Robert Resnick, and Jearl Walker (2008), *Fundamentals of Physics*, 8th ed., New York: Wiley.

Hamilton, William D. (1964), "The Genetical Evolution of Social Behavior," *Journal of Theoretical Biology* 7(1), 1–52.

Hardin, Garrett (1968), "The Tragedy of the Commons," *Science* 162, 1243–48.

Harsanyi, John (1962), "Measurement of Social Power, Opportunity Costs, and the Theory of Two-Person Bargaining Games," *Behavioral Science* 7(1), 67–81.

Havel, Vaclav (1986), "The Power of the Powerless," in Jan Vladislav (Ed.), *Living in Truth*, London: Faber & Faber.

Hayek, Friedrich A. (1945), "The Use of Knowledge in Society," *American Economic Review* 35(4), 519–30.

Heckathorn, Douglas D. (1996), "The Dynamics and Dilemmas of Collective Action," *American Journal of Sociology* 61(2), 250 –77.

Heiner, Ronald A. (1983), "The Origin of Predictable Behavior," *American Economic Review* 73(4), 560 –95.

Helderman, Rosalind S., and Anita Kumar (2011), "Partisan Sparks Likely over Virginia's Proposed Redistricting Plan," *Washington Post*, April 11, http://www.washingtonpost .com /local /politics /partisan-sparks-likely-over-virginias-proposed-redistricting -plans/2011/04/11/AFTQ47MD_story.html.

Hendry, Andrew P. (2005), "The Power of Natural Selection," *Nature* 403, 694 –95.

Hirschman, Albert O. (1970), *Exit Voice and Loyalty*, Cambridge, MA: Harvard University Press.

Holländer, Heinz (1990). "A Social Exchange Approach to Voluntary Contribution," *American Economic Review* 80(5), 1157 – 67.

Homans, George C. (1953), "Status among Clerical Workers," *Human Organization* 12(5), 5 –10.

——— (1954), "The Cash Posters," *American Sociological Review* 19(5), 724 –33.

Hooghe, Leisbet, and Gary Marks (2001), *Multi-Level Governance and European Integration*, Lanham, MD: Rowman & Littlefield.

——— (2003), "Unraveling the Central State, but How? Types of Multi-Level Governance," *American Political Science Review* 97(2), 233 – 43.

Howitt, Peter (2002), "Looking Inside the Labor Market: A Review Article," *Journal of Economic Literature* 40(1), 125 –38.

Hubbell, Brian J., Richard V. Crume, Dale M. Evarts, and Jeff M. Cohen (2010), "Regulation and Progress under the 1990 Clean Air Act Amendments," *Review of Environmental Economics and Policy* 4(1), 122 –38.

Huck, Steffen, and Michael Kosfeld (2007), "The Dynamics of Neighbourhood Watch and Norm Enforcement," *Economic Journal* 117(516), 270 – 86.

Huck, Steffen, and Pedro Rey-Biel (2006), "Endogenous Leadership in Teams," *Journal of Institutional and Theoretical Economics* 162(2), 253 – 61.

Hume, David (1739/1978). *A Treatise of Human Nature*, Oxford: Clarendon.

Hurwicz, Leonid (1972), "On Informationally Decentralized Systems," in C. B. McGuire and Roy Radner (Eds.), *Decision and Organization*, Amsterdam: North-Holland, 297–336.

——— (2008), "But Who Will Guard the Guardians?" *American Economic Review* 98(3), 577 – 84.

Ijiri, Yuji, and Herbert Simon (1964), "Business Firm Growth and Size," *American Economic Review* 54(2), part 1, 77 – 89.

Ioannides, Yannis M., and Henry G. Overman (2003), "Zipf's Law for Cities: An Empirical Examination," *Regional Science and Urban Economics* 33(2), 127 –37.

Isaac, R. Mark, and James M. Walker (1988), "Group Size and Effects in Public Goods Provision: The Voluntary Contribution Mechanism," *Quarterly Journal of Economics* 103(1), 179 –200.

Isaac, R. Mark, James M. Walker, and Arlington W. Williams (1994), "Group Size and the Voluntary Provision of Public Goods," *Journal of Public Economics* 54(1), 1 –36.

Jackson, Matthew O. (2008), *Social and Economic Networks*, Princeton, NJ: Princeton University Press.

Jacobs, Jane (1985), *Cities and the Wealth of Nations: Principles of Economic Life*, New York: Vintage.

Jehiel, Philippe, and Andrew F. Newman (2012), "Loopholes, Social Learning, and the Evolution of Contract Form," Unpublished manuscript, Department of Economics, University College, London.

Jenkins, Richard (1996), *Social Identity (Key Ideas)*, New York: Routledge.

Johnson, Kirk (2008), "Texas Polygamy Raid May Pose Risk," *New York Times*, April 12.

Jones, Charles I. (2010), *Macroeconomics, Economic Crisis Update*, New York: Norton.

Kahneman, Daniel (2003), "Maps of Bounded Rationality: Psychology for Behavioral Economics," *American Economic Review* 93(5), 1449–75.

Kahneman, Daniel, Jack L. Knetsch, and Richard H. Thaler (1990), "Experimental Tests of the Endowment Effect and the Coase Theorem," *Journal of Political Economy* 96(8), 1325–48.

Kahneman, Daniel, and Amos Tversky (1979), "Prospect Theory: An Analysis of Decisions under Risk," *Econometrica* 47(2), 263–91.

Kandel, Eugene, and Edward P. Lazear (1992), "Peer Pressure and Partnerships," *Journal of Political Economy* 100(4), 801–17.

Karotkin, Drora, and Jacob Paroush (1994), "Variability of Decisional Ability and the Essential Order of Decision Rules," *Journal of Economic Behavior and Organization* 23(3), 343–54.

Keohane, Robert O. (1984), *After Hegemony: Cooperation and Discord in the World Political Economy*, Princeton, NJ: Princeton University Press.

Kermack, W. O., and A. G. McKendrick (1927), "A Contribution to the Mathematical Theory of Epidemics," *Proceedings of the Royal Society of London, Series A* 115, 700–721.

Keynes, John M. (1936/1964), *The General Theory of Employment, Interest and Money*, New York: Harcourt Brace.

Keyssar, Alexander (2000), *The Right to Vote: The Contested History of Democracy in the United States*, New York: Basic Books.

Killworth, Peter D., and H. Russell Bernard (1978/79), "The Reversal Small-World Experiment," *Social Networks* 1(2), 159–92.

Kingdon, John W. (2003), *Agendas, Alternatives, and Public Policies*, 2nd ed., New York: Longman.

Kirkpatrick, David D. (2012), "Revolt Leaders Cite Failure to Uproot Old Order in Egypt," *New York Times*, June 14.

Klare, Michael T. (2002), *Resource Wars: The New Landscape of Global Conflict*, New York: Holt.

Knight, Frank (1921), *Risk, Uncertainty, and Profit*, New York: Houghton-Mifflin.

Knight, Jack (1992), *Institutions and Social Conflict*, Cambridge: Cambridge University Press.

Kogut, Bruce, and Gordon Walker (2001), "The Small World of Germany and the Durability of National Networks," *American Sociological Review* 66(3), 317–35.

Kossinets, Gueorgi, and Duncan J. Watts (2009), "Origins of Homophily in an Evolving Social Network," *American Journal of Sociology* 115(2), 405–50.

Krugman, Paul R. (1995), *Development, Geography, and Economic Theory*, Cambridge, MA: MIT Press.

Kuhn, Thomas (1970), *The Structure of Scientific Revolutions*, 2nd ed., Chicago: University of Chicago Press.

Laitos, Robert (1986), "Rapid Appraisal of Nepal Irrigation Systems," Water Management Synthesis Report 43, Colorado State University, Fort Collins.

Lam, Wai Fung (1998), *Governing Irrigation Systems in Nepal: Institutions, Infrastructure, and Collective Action*, Oakland, CA: ICS Press.

Lasswell, Harold (1936), *Politics: Who Gets What, When, and How*, New York: McGraw-Hill.

Le Grand, Julian (2003), *Motivation, Agency, and Public Policy: Of Knights & Knaves, Pawns & Queens*, Oxford: Oxford University Press.

Lerner, Abba (1972), "The Economics and Politics of Consumer Sovereignty," *American Economic Review* 62(2), 258–66.

Levin, Jonathan, and Barry Nalebuff (1995), "An Introduction to Vote-Counting Schemes," *Journal of Economic Perspectives* 9(1), 3–26.

Levine, David (1995), *Reinventing the Workplace: How Business and Employees Can Both Win*, Washington, DC: Brookings Institution.

Levitt, Steven D., and Sudhir Alladi Venkatesh (2000), "An Economic Analysis of a Drug-Selling Gang's Finances," *Quarterly Journal of Economics* 115(3), 755–89.

Lindbeck, Assar (1995), "Welfare State Disincentives with Endogenous Habits and Norms," *Scandinavian Journal of Economics* 97(4), 477–94.

Lindblom, Charles (1957), *Politics and Markets*, New York: Basic Books.

——— (1959), "The Science of Muddling Through," *Public Administration Review* 19(2), 79–88.

Linz, Juan J. (2000), *Totalitarian and Authoritarian Regimes*, Boulder, CO: Rienner.

Lipset, Seymour Martin (1963), *Political Man: The Social Bases of Politics*, Garden City, NY: Anchor.

Lipsky, David (2003), *Absolutely American: Four Years at West Point*, Boston: Houghton-Mifflin.

Lipsky, Michael (1980), *Street Level Bureaucracy: Dilemmas of the Individual in Public Services*, New York: Russell Sage.

López-Pérez, Raúl (2006), "Introducing Social Norms in Game Theory," in Alessandro Innocenti and Patrizia Sbriglia (Eds.), *Games, Rationality and Behaviour: Essays on Behavioural Game Theory and Experiments*, London: Palgrave Macmillan, 26–46.

——— (2008), "Aversion to Norm Breaking: A Model," *Games and Economic Behavior* 64(1), 237–67.

——— (2009), "Followers and Leaders: Reciprocity, Social Norms and Group Behavior," *Journal of Socio-Economics* 38(4), 557–67.

——— (2010), "Guilt and Shame: An Axiomatic Analysis," *Theory and Decision* 69(4), 569–86.

Lowe, Rodney (2005), *The Welfare State in Britain since 1945*, New York: Palgrave Macmillan.

Lucas, Robert (1988), "On the Mechanics of Economic Development," *Journal of Monetary Economics* 22, 3–42.

Lukes, Steven (1974), *Power: A Radical View*, New York: Palgrave Macmillan.

Machiavelli, Niccolò (1640/1969), *The Prince*, Menston, UK: Scolar Press.

Mankiw, N. Gregory (2010), *Macroeconomics*, 7th ed., New York: Worth.

Mankiw, N. Gregory, David Romer, and David N. Weil (1992), "A Contribution to the Empirics of Economic Growth," *Quarterly Journal of Economics*, 107(2), 221–40.

Mansfield, Edwin (1971), *Technological Change: An Introduction to a Vital Area of Modern Economics*, New York: Norton.

March, James G., and Pierre J. Romelaer (1976), "Position and Presence in the Drift of Decision," in James G. March and Johan P. Olsen (Eds.), *Ambiguity and Choice in Organizations*, Bergen, Norway: Universitetforlaget, 251–76.

Marshall, Alfred (1890/1979), *Principles of Economics*, London: Macmillan.

Maskin, Eric (1999), "Nash Equilibrium and Welfare Optimality," *Review of Economic Studies* 66(1), 23–38.

——— (2008), "Mechanism Design: How to Implement Social Goals," *American Economic Review* 98(3), 567–76.

McGinnis, Michael (2005), "Beyond Individualism and Spontaneity: Comments on Peter Boettke and Christopher Coyne," *Journal of Economic Behavior and Organization* 57(2), 167–72.

——— (2011a), "An Introduction to IAD and the Language of the Ostrom Workshop: A Simple Guide to a Complex Framework," *Policy Studies Journal* 39(1), 169–83.

——— (2011b), "Costs and Challenges of Polycentric Governance," Mimeo, Workshop in Political Theory and Policy Analysis, University of Indiana, Bloomington.

McKean, Margaret (1992), "Success on the Commons: A Comparative Examination of Institutions for Common Property Resource Management," *Journal of Theoretical Politics* 4(2), 256–68.

Mengel, Friederike (2008), "Matching Structure and the Cultural Transmission of Social Norms," *Journal of Economic Behavior and Organization* 67(3–4), 608–23.

Meyer, Michael C., William L. Sherman, and Susan M. Deeds (2007), *The Course of Mexican History*, 8th ed., Oxford: Oxford University Press.

Milgram, Stanley (1967), "The Small World Phenomenon," *Psychology Today* 2, 60–67.

Milgrom, Paul, and John Roberts (1992), *Economics, Organization and Management*, Englewood Cliffs, NJ: Prentice Hall.

Miliband, Ralph (1969), *The State in Capitalist Society: An Analysis of the Western Systems of Power*, London: Weidenfeld & Nicolson.

Miller, John H., and Scott E. Page (2007), *Complex Adaptive Systems*, Princeton, NJ: Princeton University Press.

Mills, C. Wright (1956), *The Power Elite*, Oxford: Oxford University Press.

Moe, Terry (1990), "Political Institutions: The Neglected Side of the Story," *Journal of Law, Economics, and Organization* 6(Special Issue), 213–53.

——— (1991), "Politics and the Theory of Organization," *Journal of Law, Economics, and Organization* 7(Special Issue), 106–29.

Molm, Linda D. (1997), *Coercive Power in Social Exchange*, Cambridge: Cambridge University Press.

Montgomery, James D. (1991), "Social Networks and Labor Market Outcomes," *American Economic Review* 81(5), 1408–18.

Morgan, Edmund S. (1975), *American Slavery, American Freedom: The Ordeal of Colonial Virginia*, New York: Norton.

Morison, Samuel Eliot (1994), *The Oxford History of the American People*, Vol. 1, London: Penguin.

Morris, Stephen (2000), "Contagion," *Review of Economic Studies* 67(1), 57–78.

Mustard, David B. (2001), "Racial, Ethnic, and Gender Disparities in Sentencing: Evidence from the U.S. Federal Courts," *Journal of Law and Economics* 44(1), 285–314.

Myerson, Roger B. (1982), "Optimal Coordination Mechanisms in Generalized Principal-Agent Problems," *Journal of Mathematical Economics* 10(1), 67–81.

———— (2008), "Perspectives on Mechanism Design in Economic Theory," *American Economic Review* 98(3), 586–603.

Nannestad, Peter (2004), "Immigration as a Challenge to the Danish Welfare State?" *European Journal of Political Economy* 20(3), 755–67.

Nelson, Jill (1993), *Volunteer Slavery: My Authentic Negro Experience*, Chicago: Noble Press.

North, Douglass C. (1990), *Institutions, Institutional Change and Economic Performance*, Cambridge: Cambridge University Press.

———— (2005), *Understanding the Process of Economic Change*, Princeton, NJ: Princeton University Press.

North, Douglass C., and Barry R. Weingast (1989), "Constitutions and Commitment: The Evolution of Institutional Governing Public Choice in Seventeenth-Century England," *Journal of Economic History* 49(4), 803–32.

Nowell-Smith, Patrick H. (1954), *Ethics*, London: Penguin.

Olson, Mancur (1971), *The Logic of Collective Action*, Cambridge, MA: Harvard University Press.

———— (1982), *The Rise and Decline of Nations: Economic Growth, Stagflation, and Social Rigidities*, New Haven, CT: Yale University Press.

———— (1993), "Dictatorships, Democracy and Development," *American Political Science Review* 87(3), 567–76.

———— (2000), *Power and Prosperity: Outgrowing Communist and Capitalist Dictatorships*, New York: Basic Books.

Oshinsky, David M. (1983), *A Conspiracy So Immense: The World of Joe McCarthy*, New York: Free Press.

Ostrom, Elinor (1990), *Governing the Commons: The Evolution of Institutions for Collective Action*, Cambridge: Cambridge University Press.

———— (1992), *Crafting Institutions for Self-Governing Irrigation Systems*, San Francisco: ICS Press.

———— (1998a), "A Behavioral Approach to the Rational Choice Theory of Collective Action," *American Political Science Review* 92(1), 1–22.

———— (1998b), "The Comparative Study of Public Economics," *American Economist* 42(1), 3–17.

———— (2000a), "Collective Action and the Evolution of Social Norms," *Journal of Economic Perspectives* 14(3), 137–58.

——— (2000b), "Social Capital: A Fad or a Fundamental Concept?" in Partha Dasgupta and Ismail Serageldin (Eds.), *Social Capital: A Multifaceted Perspective*, Washington, DC: World Bank, 172–214.

——— (2005), *Understanding Institutional Diversity*, Princeton, NJ: Princeton University Press.

——— (2007), "Institutional Rational Choice: An Assessment of the Institutional Analysis and Development Framework," in Paul A. Sabatier (Ed.), *Theories of the Policy Process*, 2nd ed., Cambridge, MA: Westview, 21–64.

——— (2010), "Beyond Markets and States: Polycentric Governance of Complex Economic Systems," *American Economic Review* 100(3), 641–72.

——— (2011), "Background on the Institutional Analysis and Development Framework," *Policy Studies Journal* 39(1), 7–27.

Ostrom, Elinor, and T. K. Ahn (2009), "The Meaning of Social Capital and Its Link to Collective Action," in Gert T. Svendsen and Gunnar L. H. Svendsen (Eds.), *Handbook of Social Capital: The Troika of Sociology, Political Science and Economics*, Northampton, MA: Elgar, 17–35.

Ostrom, Elinor, and Sue Crawford (2005), "Classifying Rules," in Elinor Ostrom, *Understanding Institutional Diversity*, Princeton, NJ: Princeton University Press, 186–215.

Ostrom, Elinor, and Roy Gardner (1993), "Coping with Asymmetries in the Commons: Self-Governing Irrigation Systems Can Work," *Journal of Economic Perspectives* 7(4), 93–112.

Ostrom, Elinor, Roy Gardner, and James Walker (1994), *Rules, Games, and Common-Pool Resources*, Ann Arbor: University of Michigan Press.

Ostrom, Elinor, James Walker, and Roy Gardner (1992), "Covenants with and without a Sword: Self-Governance Is Possible," *American Political Science Review* 86(2), 404–17.

Ostrom, Vincent (1980), "Artisanship and Artifact," *Public Administration Review* 40(4), 309–17.

Ostrom, Vincent, and Elinor Ostrom (1977), "Public Goods and Public Choices," in Emanuel S. Savas (Ed.), *Delivering Public Services: Toward Improved Performance*, Boulder, CO: Westview, 7–49.

Ostrom, Vincent, Charles M. Tiebout, and Robert Warren (1961), "The Organization of Government in Metropolitan Areas: A Theoretical Inquiry," *American Political Science Review* 55(4), 831–42.

Paavola, Jouni, and W. Neil Adger (2005), "Institutional Ecological Economics," *Ecological Economics* 53(3), 353–68.

Padavic, Irene (1991), "The Re-creation of Gender in a Male Workplace," *Symbolic Interaction* 14(3), 270–94.

Padgett, John F., and Christopher F. Ansell (1993), "Robust Action and the Rise of the Medici 1400–1434," *American Journal of Sociology* 98(6), 1259–1319.

Patterson, James T. (1996), *Grand Expectations: The United States, 1945–1974*, New York: Oxford University Press.

Pencavel, John (1992), "The Behavior of Worker Cooperatives: The Plywood Companies of the Pacific Northwest" (with Ben Craig), *American Economic Review* 82(5), 1083–1105.

Penrose, Edith (1959), *The Theory of the Growth of the Firm*, New York: Wiley.

Pierson, Paul (1993), "When Effect Becomes Cause: Policy Feedback and Political Change," *World Politics* 45(4), 595–628.

Platteau, Jean-Philippe, and Erika Seki (2001), "Community Arrangements to Overcome Market Failure: Pooling Groups in Japanese Fisheries," in Masahiko Aoki and Yujiro Hayami (Eds.), *Communities and Markets in Economic Development*, Oxford: Oxford University Press, 344–402.

Polsby, Nelson W. (1963), *Community Power and Political Theory*, New Haven, CT: Yale University Press.

Posner, Eric (1997), "Social Norms and the Law: An Economic Approach," *American Economic Review* 87(2), 365–69.

Poteete, Amy, Marco Janssen, and Elinor Ostrom (2010), *Working Together: Collective Action, the Commons, and Multiple Methods in Practice*, Princeton, NJ: Princeton University Press.

Prendergast, Canice (1999), "The Provision of Incentives in Firms," *Journal of Economic Literature* 37(1), 7–63.

Prezworski, Adam, Michael H. Alvarez, and Jose Antonio Cheibub (2000), *Democracy and Development: Political Institutions and Material Well-Being in the World, 1950–1999*, Cambridge: Cambridge University Press.

Putnam, Robert D. (1993), *Making Democracy Work: Civic Traditions in Modern Italy*, Princeton, NJ: Princeton University Press.

Rabin, Matthew (1993), "Incorporating Fairness into Game Theory and Economics," *American Economic Review* 83(5), 1281–1302.

———— (2003), "The Nobel Memorial Prize for Daniel Kahneman," *Scandinavian Journal of Economics* 105(2), 157–80.

Raines, Howell (1998), "George Wallace, Segregation Symbol, Dies at 79," *New York Times*, September 14.

Ransom, Roger L., and Richard Sutch (2001), *One Kind of Freedom: The Economic Consequences of Emancipation*, 2nd ed., Cambridge: Cambridge University Press.

Razo, Armando (2008), *Social Foundations of Limited Dictatorship: Networks and Private Protection during Mexico's Early Industrialization*, Stanford, CA: Stanford University Press.

Rodrik, Dani (2007), *One Economics, Many Recipes: Globalization, Institutions, and Economic Growth*, Princeton, NJ: Princeton University Press.

Romer, Paul (1990), "Endogenous Technological Change," *Journal of Political Economy* 98(5), S71–S102.

Rother, Larry (2006), "Chile's Leader Attacks Amnesty Law," *New York Times*, December 24.

Rowlands, Ian H. (1995), *The Politics of Global Atmospheric Change*, New York: Manchester University Press.

Rubenstein, Ariel (1986), "Perfect Equilibrium in a Bargaining Model," *Econometrica* 50(1), 97–109.

Rutherford, Malcolm (1994), *Institutions in Economics: The Old and New Institutionalism*, Cambridge: Cambridge University Press.

Sabatier, Paul A. (1986), "Top-Down and Bottom-Up Approaches in Implementation Research: A Critical Analysis and Suggested Synthesis," *Journal of Public Policy* 6(1), 21–48.

——— (1988), "An Advocacy Coalition Model of Policy Change," *Policy Sciences* 21(2–3), 129–68.

Sabatier, Paul A., and Christopher M. Weible (2007), "The Advocacy Coalition Framework: Innovations and Clarifications," in Paul A. Sabatier (Ed.), *Theories of the Policy Process*, 2nd ed., Cambridge, MA: Westview, 189–220.

Sampson, Robert J., Stephen W. Raudenbush, and Felton Earls (1997), "Neighborhoods and Violent Crime: A Multilevel Study of Collective Efficacy," *Science* 277, 918–24.

Samuelson, Larry (2001), "Introduction to the Evolution of Preferences," *Journal of Economic Theory* 97(2), 225–30.

Samuelson, Paul (1957), "Wages and Interest: A Modern Dissection of Marxian Economics," *American Economic Review* 47(6), 884–921.

——— (1969), "Classical and Neoclassical Theory," in Robert Clower (Ed.), *Monetary Theory*, London: Penguin.

Sandler, Todd (2002), *Collective Action: Theory and Applications*, Ann Arbor: University of Michigan Press.

Schattschneider, Elmer E. (1960), *The Semisovereign People*, New York: Holt, Rinehart & Winston.

Schelling, Thomas C. (1960), *The Strategy of Conflict*, Cambridge, MA: Harvard University Press.

——— (1973), "Hockey Helmets, Concealed Weapons, and Daylight Saving: A Study of Binary Choices with Externalities," *Journal of Conflict Resolution* 17(3), 381–428.

——— (1978), *Micromotives and Macrobehavior*, New York: Norton.

Schlager, Edella, and Elinor Ostrom (1992), "Property-Rights Regimes and Natural Resources: A Conceptual Analysis," *Land Economics* 68(3), 249–69.

——— (1999), "Property Rights Regimes and Coastal Fisheries: An Empirical Analysis," in Mike McGinnis (Ed.), *Polycentric Governance and Development: Readings from the Workshop on Political Theory and Policy Analysis*, Ann Arbor: University of Michigan Press, 84–113.

Schuman, Howard, and Stanley Presser (1981), *Questions and Answers in Attitude Surveys*, San Diego: Academic.

Selten, Reinhard (1978), "The Chain Store Paradox," *Theory and Decision* 9(2), 127–59.

——— (1990), "Bounded Rationality," *Journal of Institutional and Theoretical Economics* 146(4), 649–58.

Sen, Amartya K. (1970), "The Impossibility of a Paretian Liberal," *Journal of Political Economy* 78(1), 152–57.

——— (1999), *Development as Freedom*, New York: Random House.

Sethi, Rajiv, and E. Somanathan (2001), "Preference Evolution and Reciprocity," *Journal of Economic Theory* 97(2), 273–97.

Shapiro, Carl, and Joseph E. Stiglitz (1984), "Equilibrium Unemployment as a Worker Discipline Device," *American Economic Review* 75(3), 433–44.

Shepsle, Kenneth (1979), "Institutional Arrangements and Equilibrium in Multidimensional Voting Models," *American Journal of Political Science* 23(1), 27–59.

Shilts, Randy (1987), *And the Band Played On: Politics, People, and the AIDS Epidemic*, New York: St. Martin's.

Simon, Herbert (1955), "A Behavioral Model of Rational Choice," *Quarterly Journal of Economics* 69(1), 99–118.

——— (1987), "Rationality in Psychology and Economics," in Robin M. Hogarth and Melvin W. Reder (Eds.), *Rational Choice: The Contrast between Economics and Psychology*, Chicago: University of Chicago Press, 25–40.

Skidmore, Thomas E., and Peter H. Smith (2005), *Modern Latin America*, 6th ed., Oxford: Oxford University Press.

Smith, Adam (1759/1976), *The Theory of Moral Sentiments* (D. D. Raphael and A. L. Macfie, Eds.), Oxford: Clarendon.

——— (1776/1976), *An Inquiry into the Nature and Causes of the Wealth of Nations*, Oxford: Clarendon.

Smith, Maynard (1989), *Evolutionary Genetics*, Oxford: Oxford University Press.

Snowdon, Brian, Howard Vane, and Peter Wynarczyk (1994), *A Modern Guide to Macroeconomics*, Brookfield, VT: Elgar.

Sobel, Joel (2005), "Interdependent Preferences and Reciprocity," *Journal of Economic Literature* 43(2), 392–436.

Solow, Robert (1956), "A Contribution to the Theory of Economic Growth," *Quarterly Journal of Economics* 70(1), 65–94.

Stavins, Robert S. (1998), "What We Can Learn from the Grand Policy Experiment: Lessons from SO2 Allowance Trading," *Journal of Economic Perspectives* 12(3), 69–88.

Stern, Nicholas (2006), "The Stern Review: The Economics of Climate Change, Executive Summary," http://www.hm-treasury.gov.uk/d/Executive_Summary.pdf.

Stigler, George (1989), "Two Notes on the Coase Theorem," *Yale Law Journal* 9, 631–33.

Stiglitz, Joseph E. (1987), "The Causes and Consequences of the Dependence of Quality on Price," *Journal of Economic Literature* 25(1), 1–48.

——— (2000), "Formal and Informal Institutions," in Partha Dasgupta and Ismail Serageldin (Eds.), *Social Capital: A Multifaceted Perspective*, Washington, DC: World Bank, 59–70.

——— (2002), "Information and the Change in the Paradigm in Economics," *American Economic Review* 92(3), 460–501.

Stone, Deborah (2002), *Policy Paradox: The Art of Political Decision Making*, rev. ed., New York: Norton.

Strayer, Joseph R. (1970), *Medieval Origins of the Modern State*, Princeton, NJ: Princeton University Press.

Summers, Lawrence H. (1988), "Relative Wages, Efficiency Wages and Keynesian Unemployment," *American Economic Review* 78(2), 383–88.

Thaler, Richard H. (1980), "Toward a Positive Theory of Consumer Choice," *Journal of Economic Behavior and Organization* 1(1), 39–60.

Thaler, Richard H., and Cass R. Sunstein (2009), *Nudge: Improving Decisions about Health, Wealth, and Happiness*, New York: Penguin.

Travers, Jeffrey, and Stanley Milgram (1969), "An Experimental Study of the Small-World Problem," *Sociometry* 32(4), 425–33.

Trawick, Paul (2003), "Against the Privatization of Water: An Indigenous Model for Improving Existing Laws and Successfully Governing the Commons," *World Development* 31(6), 977–96.

Trivers, Robert L. (1971), "The Evolution of Reciprocal Altruism," *Quarterly Review of Biology* 46(1), 35–57.

——— (2006), "Reciprocal Altruism Thirty Years Later," in Peter M. Kappeler and Carel P. van Schaik (Eds.), *Cooperation in Primates and Humans: Mechanisms and Evolution*, Berlin: Springer-Verlag, 67–84.

True, James L., Bryan D. Jones, and Frank R. Baumgartner (2007), "Punctuated-Equilibrium Theory," in Paul A. Sabatier (Ed.), *Theories of the Policy Process*, 2nd ed., Cambridge, MA: Westview, 155–87.

Tversky, Amos, and Daniel Kahneman (1992), "Advances in Prospect Theory: Cumulative Representation of Uncertainty," *Journal of Risk and Uncertainty* 5(4), 297–323.

UNFCC (United Nations Framework Convention on Climate Change) (2011), "Kyoto Protocol," http://unfccc.int/kyoto_protocol/items/2830.php.

——— (2012), "Fact Sheet: The Kyoto Protocol," http://unfccc.int/files/press/backgrounders/application/pdf/fact_sheet_the_kyoto_protocol.pdf.

United Nations (2010), "Security Council Imposes Additional Sanctions on Iran, Voting 12 in Favor to 2 Against, with 1 Abstention," http://www.un.org/News/Press/docs/2010/sc9948.doc.htm.

US Bureau of Labor Statistics (2011), "Table 11: Employed Persons by Detailed Occupation, Sex, Race, and Hispanic or Latino Ethnicity," http://www.bls.gov/cps/cpsa2011.pdf.

Van Horn, Carl E., and Donald S. Van Meter (1976), "The Implementation of Intergovernmental Policy," in Charles O. Jones and Robert D. Thomas (Eds.), *Public Policy Making in a Federal System*, Beverly Hills, CA: Sage.

Vega-Redondo, Fernando (2007), *Complex Social Networks*, Cambridge: Cambridge University Press.

Wasserman, Stanley, and Katherine Faust (1994), *Social Network Analysis*, Cambridge: Cambridge University Press.

Watts, Duncan J. (2002), "A Simple Model of Global Cascades on Random Networks," *Proceedings of the Natural Academy of Sciences* 99(9), 5766–71.

——— (2003), *Six Degrees: The Science of a Connected Age*, New York: Norton.

——— (2004), "The 'New' Science of Networks," *Annual Review of Sociology* 30, 243–70.

Watts, Duncan J., Peter S. Dodds, and M. E. J. Newman (2002), "Identity and Search in Social Networks," *Science* 296, 1302–5.

Watts, Duncan J., and Steven H. Strogatz (1998), "Collective Dynamics of 'Small-World' Networks," *Nature* 393, 440–42.

Weimer, David L., and Aidan R. Vining (1992), *Policy Analysis: Concepts and Practice*, 2nd ed., Englewood Cliffs, NJ: Prentice Hall.

Williamson, Oliver E. (1975), *Markets and Hierarchies: Analysis and Antitrust Implications*, New York: Free Press.

——— (1985), *The Economic Institutions of Capitalism*, New York: Free Press.

——— (2000), "The New Institutional Economics: Taking Stock, Looking Ahead," *Journal of Economic Literature* 38(3), 595–613.

——— (2010), "Transaction Cost Economics: The Natural Progression," *American Economic Review* 100(3), 673–90.

Wilson, David S., and Lee A. Dugatkin (1997), "Group Selection and Associative Interactions," *American Naturalist* 149(2), 336–51.

Wilson, Edward O. (1975), *Sociobiology: The New Synthesis*, Cambridge, MA: Harvard University Press.

Wilson, William J. (1996), *When Work Disappears: The World of the New Urban Poor*, New York: Vintage.

Wolf, Eric R. (1969), *Peasant Wars of the Twentieth Century*, New York: Harper & Row.

Wright, Gavin (1986), *Old South, New South*, New York: Basic Books.

Young, H. Peyton (1996), *Individual Strategy and Social Structure: An Evolutionary Theory of Institutions*, Princeton, NJ: Princeton University Press.

——— (2007), "Social Norms," Discussion Paper 307, Department of Economics, Oxford University.

——— (2009), "Innovation Diffusion in Heterogeneous Populations: Contagion, Social Influence, and Social Learning," *American Economic Review* 99(5), 1899–1924.

Zahariadis, Nikolaos (2007), "The Multiple Streams Framework: Structure, Limitations, Prospects," in Paul A. Sabatier (Ed.), *Theories of the Policy Process*, 2nd ed., Cambridge, MA: Westview, 65–92.

Zipf, George K. (1949), *Human Behavior and the Principle of Least Effort*, Cambridge, MA: Addison-Wesley.

INDEX

Page numbers for definitions are in boldface; italic page numbers indicate material in tables or figures.

multi-player games, 34–35; based on conditional cooperators (c-types), 184–85; based
on reciprocal players (r-types), 99–100;
chicken, 36–39; and negative externalities,
36; and network externalities, 39–40; and
policy assurance, *316*; provision of public
goods as, 35–36, 96, *98*, 102–3; reciprocity and social exchange in, 99–104. *See also*
evolutionary game theory; indirect evolutionary game theory
multiple-streams framework. *See* three-streams
framework; policy emergence
mutants/mutations, 132, 137, 138–39, 188,
279, 316, 369n56. *See also* evolutionary game
theory
mutual monitoring, 26. *See also* second-party
enforcement; team production
mutual understandings, 205, 210, 215, 220. *See
also* epistemic game theory; shared mental
models

Nalebuff, Barry, 364n48
Napel, Stefan, 369–70n60
Nash cooperative bargaining model, 33, 68–69,
73–78, 82–83
Nash equilibrium, **28**, **171**, 359n8
National Health Service Act (1946, UK), 314,
318
National Labor Relations Act (1935, US), 304
National Rifle Association (NRA), 312
nation-states, 238
natural selection, 136
"Nature of the Firm, The" (Coase), 13
negative externalities, 5, 23, 29, 31–32, 34,
36–39, 228, 352
negative feedback, **360n28**
negative-feedback mechanisms (processes or
dynamics), 78, **158**, 308, 314, 362n13; influence on policy, 309, 310, 314, 320
neighborhood (of a network node), **258**; first
degree, 258; second degree, 258
neighborhood organizations, 220, 251, 304
Nelson, Jill, 195, 374n60
neoclassical economic theory, 92–93. *See also*
conventional economic theory; price theory
neoclassical growth model (Solow), 15, 330–31

Nepali farmers: advantages of community
governance for, 222–23; collective-choice decisions among, 293; first-order CAPs among,
209–10; internal and external enforcements
for, 244–45; self-organization of, 201; and
social capital, 212; and social rules, 153, 205
nested hierarchies, 223
nested (property) rights, 221
nested systems (of enforcement), 250–52
network externalities, **39**, 39–40, 41, 47, 111;
and knowledge acquisition, 334; and policy
emergence, 316
networks, **204**; basic, *258*, 258–59; betweenness
centrality of, 262; biological, 255; centrality
and cohesiveness of, 261–62; clustering of,
259–61; connected, 259; decay centrality
of, 262; degree distribution of, 258; degree
of separation of, 254–55; directed, 380n6;
fully connected, 259; linear, *278*; physical,
255; random, 262, 263–65; scale-free, *263*,
263–64; structure of, 255; types of, *263*,
263–65, *264*. *See also* node; social networks
network structure, **255**. *See also* networks
network walk, 380n7
Newman, M. E. J., 271–72
node (of a network), **257**, 257–58, *258*; in-
degree of, 258; isolated, 257; neighborhood
of, 258; out-degree of, 258; stable, 280
Nohria, Nitin, 256
nonclearing markets, 10, 17, 60, 352; and enforcement or power, 63, 68; labor, 57, 84. *See
also* effort model; moral hazard; principal-
agent (P-A) problems
non-ergodic environments/processes, **12**,
12–13, 124–26, 158–60
nonmaterial reciprocal punishment, 11. *See also*
reciprocity; social preference
nonrival knowledge, 15, 19, 328, 329; Bangladeshi
textile example of, 332–33; and endogenous
growth, 330–32; and increasing returns,
332–36; interactions with institutions, 346–48
nontransparent consumer goods/services, *62*
normal-form game, 28, 81; two-player, 359n7.
See also individual game matrices
normatively indeterminate, **65**
norms. *See* social norms

and, 139–41; and information cascades, 267; and Jim Crow system, 319; local institutional systems as, 228; and network externalities, 39–40; networks and, 256; path dependence and, 34–35, 39–41, 110, 128, 158–60, 198; policy subsystems and, 307–10; and policy theory, 14–15; and reciprocity, 103; reevaluative learning and, 128, 130; and social norms, 185, 189. *See also* path dependence; positive-feedback mechanisms

punishment: as instrument of power, 69–71; material, 93, 95, 101–2, 187; reciprocal, 98–99, *99, 143*; social, 93, 95, 101–2, 187. *See also* enforcement; reward; sanctions

punishment stage (of a two-stage game), 241

pure altruism, 118

pure competition, 6–7, 67–68

purely altruistic players, **118**

pure social exchange, **102**. *See also* social exchange

pure spite, 118

Putnam, Robert, 203, 205

Qaddafi, Muammar el-, 248

quasi-parameter, 158, **159**, 293, 338. *See also* auxiliary transaction

Rabin, Matthew, 119, 122

race relations, 44, 195, 300, 319

"race to the bottom" phenomenon, 51

random network, **262**, 263–65

rank-size rule, 332–33

rational actor, **92, 115**, 150. *See also* agents; bounded rationality; substantive rationality

rational egoists (e-types), **91, 93**; and conditional cooperators (c-types), 184–85; free-riding by, 182–84; with inequality-averse players, 118; motivation for, 93; and principled agents (p-types), 182–84, *183*; and provision of public goods, 177–80, *179, 180, 181*; and reciprocal actors (r-types), 185–86; and reciprocity, 94–98, 103, 109, 119; and social punishment, 102–3, 185–86. *See also* agents

rationality, **125**; minimalist conception of, 125; nature of, 11–12; and rational actors, 92, 150; and rational choice theory, 114–15; and ra-

tional maximization, 123; and RLN, 167–71, *170, 171, 188*, 188–90, *190*; and social preference, 119–22; theory of, 114. *See also* agents; bounded rationality; rational egoists; substantive rationality

rationality-limiting norm (RLN), **167**, 167–71, *170, 171*, 188–90, *190*; sari wearing as an example, 167, 169–70, 188–89. *See also* Basu; social norms

Ray, Debraj, 226

Razo, Armando, 340–45, *342, 344*, 388n31, 388n33, 388nn37–39

reciprocal actors (r-types), **93**; vs. inequality-averse agents, 118; and intrinsic reciprocity, 94–99; motivation for, 93; and multi-player reciprocity, 99–100; and reciprocal conflict, 108–9, *109*; resentment of shirking by, 217–18; and social punishment, 102; and two-player reciprocity, 103. *See also* agents

reciprocal preference. *See* reciprocity

reciprocal punishment, 98–99, *99, 143*

reciprocity, **11**; and altruism, 94; applications and extensions of, 104–9, *107, 109*; and conflict, 108–9, *109*; context-dependent, 119–22; and gift-exchange mechanisms, 105; intrinsic, 90–94; loyalty and, 161; and punishment, 98–99, *143*, 187, 215; and social enforcement of TSN, 185–86; as social norm, 186–88. *See also* intrinsic reciprocity; reciprocal actors

reevaluative learning, **128**, 135, 159. *See also* mental models

reference agents, **116**, 116–17

reference dependence (as a heuristic), **126**. *See also* cognition; heuristics

Reiley, David, Jr., 77

relationship-specific investment, **106**, 106–8. *See also* holdup problem

reliability condition (Heiner), 131, **133**, 133–35, 139, 163, 239, 251, 369n43

reliability ratio, **133**

reliable action, **133**

reporting game, 47–48, *48*

reputation: community, 225; establishing, 80; and indirect reciprocity, 94; as motivation, 24; and prosocial behavior, 212; and shirking, 218–19

union bargaining: and level of solidarity, 76; and Nash cooperative bargaining model, 82; National Labor Relations Act (1935, US), 304; as upward vertical voice, 161

United Nations: Copenhagen Climate Change Conference, 40; Kyoto Protocol, 304; Montreal Protocol, 312; Security Council sanctions, 78–79, 81

United States: Articles of Confederation, 247, 295; and British common law, 160, 295; Constitution (*see* Constitution); Federal Convention (1787), 293–95; legacy of colonialism in, 339; and North Korea, 81, *82*; Senate, 317. *See also* Congress

unit labor costs, **104**, 104–5

unkind/unfair intentions, 95. *See also* reciprocity

upward vertical voice, 161

US-Canadian fishing disputes, 228

Van Horn, Carl, 317

Van Meter, Donald, 317

variable threat bargaining, 82

Vayanos, Dimitri, 255–56

Vega-Redondo, Fernando, 254, 265

vertical exercise of voice, 161

vertical rule classification, 295, 298–99

vicarious problem solving, 114

Vietnam War, 290

vigilante "justice," 244

Villa, Pancho, 345

virtuous social feedback (of reciprocity), 212

viruses, 276

voice, 160–63, **161**, *162*, and community governance, 220, 223; and policymaking, 288, 355

voting, 71–72, 161, 241, 247

Voting Rights Act (1965, US), 72, 247, 300–301, 318–19

Walker, James, 212–15

Wallace, George, 301, 318

wars, 108–9

Watts, Duncan, 271–72, 278–79

weak links and job searches, 260

Wealth of Nations (Smith), 24

Weible, Christopher, 307, 384n46

Weil, David, 330–31

Welch, Ivo, 277–80

Welch, Joseph Nye, 364n51

West Point military academy, 191

widely accessible property rights, **337**

Wildavsky, Aaron, 318, 386n73

Williams, Arlington, 212–15

Williamson, Oliver, 13, 216

Wilson, William Julius, 196

windows of opportunity (in policy emergence), **311**

withdrawal rights, **221**, 298. *See also* property rights

workers: boundedly rational, 132–33; demonstrating trust in, 108; eliciting quality effort from, 56–59, 84, 104–5, 196–97; exit by, 160; and holdup problem, 107; morale of, 104–6

working rules (or rules in use), **233**

Workshop in Political Theory and Policy Analysis, 14–15, 26, 224–25, 291, 319. *See also* Institutional Analysis and Development (IAD) framework; IU Workshop

World Wide Web, 255

Yaari, Menahem, 142, 370n62

Young, Peyton, 166–67

Zaheer, Akbar, 256

Zapata, Emiliano, 345

zero-contribution thesis, **25**, 34–35, 40; and second-order CAPs, 47, 53, 63

zero-contribution equilibrium (or outcome), 100, 204

Zipf's law, 332–33, 336

Zwiebel, Jeffrey, 255–56

Zwingli, Huldrych, 196